W9-ACL-286

DATE DUE

JUN 0 3 2010			
JUN 0 7 2010			

Demco, Inc. 38-293

Game
Programming
Gems

Game Programming Gems

Edited by Mark A. DeLoura

CHARLES RIVER MEDIA

Boston, Massachusetts

Cover Design: Tyler Creative
Cover Image: Mark Peasley

CHARLES RIVER MEDIA
25 Thomson Place
Boston, MA 02210
617-757-7900
617-757-7969 (FAX)
crm.info@thomson.com
www.charlesriver.com

This book is printed on acid-free paper.

Mark DeLoura. *Game Programming Gems.*

ISBN-13: 978-1-58450-049-0
ISBN-10: 1-58450-049-2

Library of Congress Cataloging-in-Publication Data

Game programming gems / edited by Mark DeLoura.
    p. cm.
  Includes bibliographical references and index.
  ISBN-13: 978-1-58450-049-0 (hardcover with cd-rom : alk. paper)
  ISBN-10: 1-58450-049-2 (hardcover with cd-rom : alk. paper)
  1. Computer games--Programming. I. DeLoura, Mark A.
  QA76.76.C672G3597 2000
  794.8'1526--dc22   2007000166

Printed in the United States of America
07 9 8 7 6

Contents

SECTION 1 PROGRAMMING TECHNIQUES 1

1.0 **The Magic of Data-Driven Design** 3
Idea #1: The Basics 3
Idea #2: The Bare Minimum 3
Idea #3: Hard-Code Nothing 4
Idea #4: Script Your Control Flow 4
Idea #5: When Good Scripts Go Bad 5
Idea #6: Avoiding Duplicate Data Syndrome 6
Idea #7: Make the Tool That Makes the Data 7
Conclusion 7

1.1 **Object-Oriented Programming and Design Techniques** 8
Coding Style 9
Class Design 11
Class Hierarchy Design 12
Design Patterns 12
Summary 19
References 19

1.2 **Fast Math Using Template Metaprogramming** 20
Fibonacci Numbers 20
Factorial 22
Trigonometry 23
Compilers in the Real World 24
Trigonometry Revisited 24
Templates and Standard C++ 25
Matrices 25
Summary 30
Listing 1.2.1 31
Listing 1.2.2 32
Listing 1.2.3 32

    Listing 1.2.4 33

    Listing 1.2.5 34

    References 35

1.3   **An Automatic Singleton Utility** **36**

    Definition 36

    Advantages 36

    The Problem 37

    Traditional Solution 37

    A Better Way 38

    An Even Better Way 38

    References 40

1.4   **Using the STL in Game Programming** **41**

    STL Types and Terminology 41

    STL Concepts 42

    Vectors 43

    Lists 46

    Deques 48

    Maps 50

    Stacks, Queues, and Priority Queues 53

    Summary 54

    References 55

1.5   **A Generic Function-Binding Interface** **56**

    Requirements 56

    Platform Concerns 57

    Attempt #1 57

    Attempt #2 58

    Half of the Solution 60

    Calling Conventions 61

    Calling the Function 63

    Completing the Solution 64

    Conclusion 66

    References 67

1.6   **A Generic Handle-Based Resource Manager** **68**

    The Method 69

    The Handle Class 70

    The HandleMgr Class 71

    Sample Usage 72

    Notes 73

    Listing 1.6.1 73

    Listing 1.6.2 75

    Listing 1.6.3 77

    References 79

1.7   **Resource and Memory Management** **80**
The Resource Class 80
The Resource Manager Class 83
How Handles Work 86
Possible Extensions and Modifications 87
Conclusion 87

1.8   **Fast Data Load Trick** **88**
Preprocess Your Data 88
Save Your Data 89
Load Your Data the Simple Way 90
Load Your Data More Safely 90

1.9   **Frame-Based Memory Allocation** **92**
The Challenges of Conventional Memory Allocation 92
Introduction to Frame-Based Memory 92
Allocating and Releasing Memory 95
Example 98
Conclusion 99

1.10 **Simple, Fast Bit Arrays** **101**
Overview 101
Array of Bits 101
Other Arrays 102
Application 103
References 103

1.11 **A Network Protocol for Online Games** **104**
Definitions 104
Packet Tampering 105
Packet Replay 105
Additional Techniques 107
Reverse Engineering 107
Implementation 108
References 108

1.12 **Squeezing More Out of Assert** **109**
The Basics of Assert 109
Assert Trick #1: Embed More Information 110
Assert Trick #2: Embed Even More Information 111
Assert Trick #3: Make It Less Awkward 111
Assert Trick #4: Write Your Own 111
Assert Trick #5: This One Is Priceless 112
Assert Trick #6: Only If You're Totally Hard-Core 113
Assert Trick #7: Make It Easier—Copy and Paste 113
References 114

1.13   Stats: Real-Time Statistics and In-Game Debugging **115**

Why: A Need-Driven Technology 115
How: An Evolutionary Process 116
What: A C++ Class-based System 117
Where: Applicability 119
Summary 119

1.14   Real-Time In-Game Profiling **120**

Getting Down to Specifics 120
What Will the Profiler Tell You? 121
Adding Profiler Calls 123
Profiler Implementation 123
Details on ProfileBegin 124
Details on ProfileEnd 125
Details on Processing the Profiling Data 125
Further Enhancements 125
Putting It All Together 126
Listing 1.14.1: ProfileBegin 126
Listing 1.14.2: ProfileEnd 127
Listing 1.14.3: ProfileDumpOutputToBuffer 128
Listing 1.14.4: StoreProfileInHistory and GetProfileFromHistory 129
References 130

SECTION 2   MATHEMATICS **131**

2.0   Predictable Random Numbers **133**

Predictable Random Numbers 133
Alternative Algorithms 135
Algorithms for Infinite Universes 136
Conclusion and Future Developments 139
References 140

2.1   Interpolation Methods **141**

Frame-Rate-Dependent Ease-Out Using Floating-Point Math 141
Frame-Rate-Dependent Ease-Out Using Integer Math 142
Frame-Rate-Independent Linear Interpolation 144
Frame-Rate-Independent Ease-In and Ease-Out 144
Danger Zone 146
Listing 2.1.1: CEaseOutDivideInterpolation Definition 147
Listing 2.1.2: CEaseOutShiftInterpolation Definition 147
Listing 2.1.3: CLinearInterpolation Definition 148
Listing 2.1.4: CEaseInOutInterpolation Definition 149

2.2   Integrating the Equations of Rigid Body Motion **150**

Kinematics: Translation and Rotation 150

Dynamics: Forces and Torques 154
Special Properties of Rigid Bodies 155
Integrating the Equations of Motion 158
References 159

2.3   Polynomial Approximations to Trigonometric Functions **161**
Polynomials 162
Domain and Range 163
Even and Odd Polynomials 166
Taylor Series 167
Truncated Taylor Series 171
Lagrange Series 172
Dealing with Discontinuities 175
Conclusion 176

2.4   Using Implicit Euler Integration for Numerical Stability **177**
Integrating Initial Value Problems and Stability 177
The Explicit Euler Method 178
The Implicit Euler Method 179
Inaccuracy 181
Finding Implicit Solutions 181
Conclusion 181
References 181

2.5   Wavelets: Theory and Compression **182**
The Principle 182
An Example 184
Applications 184
References 186

2.6   Interactive Simulation of Water Surfaces **187**
The Wave Equation in Two Dimensions 187
Boundary Conditions: Islands and Shorelines 190
Implementation Issues 190
Interacting with the Surface 191
Rendering 193
References 194

2.7   Quaternions for Game Programming **195**
Treat Quaternions as Matrix Replacements 195
Why Not Just Use Euler Angles? 196
What Do X, Y, Z, and W Represent? 196
From What Math Is This Derived? 197
How Do Quaternions Represent Rotations? 198
References 199

2.8   Matrix-Quaternion Conversions **200**

Quaternion Rotations 200
Quaternion-to-Matrix Conversion 200
Matrix-to-Quaternion Conversion 202
References 204

2.9   Interpolating Quaternions **205**

Quaternion Calculus 205
Quaternion Interpolation 206
Sample Code 208
Derivation 2.9.1: Deriving Slerp 209
Derivation 2.9.2: Deriving the Power Form of Slerp 210
Derivation 2.9.3: Deriving Spline Interpolation 211

2.10   The Shortest Arc Quaternion **214**

Motivation 214
Numerical Instability 214
Derivation of Stable Formula 215
Remaining Instability Condition 216
Source Code 217
Virtual TrackBall 217
References 218

SECTION 3   ARTIFICIAL INTELLIGENCE **219**

**3.0   Designing a General Robust
          AI Engine** **221**

Event-Driven vs. Polling Objects 221
The Message Concept 222
State Machines 223
An Event-Driven State Machine Using Messages 223
Confession Time 225
Another Small Confession 226
State Machine Building Blocks 227
State Machine Message Routing 227
Sending Messages 229
Sending Delayed Messages 229
Deleting a Game Object 230
Enhancement: Defining the Scope of a Message 231
Enhancement: Logging All Message Activity and State Transitions 232
Enhancement: Swapping State Machines 233
Enhancement: Multiple State Machines 233
Enhancement: A Queue of State Machines 233
Scripting Behavior Outside the Code 234
Conclusion 234

Listing 3.0.1: Message Router 235
Listing 3.0.2: Functions to Deal with Delayed Messages 236
References 236

3.1   A Finite-State Machine Class **237**
The FSMclass and FSMstate 239
Defining the FSMstate 239
Defining the FSMclass 240
Creating States for the FSM 242
Using the FSM 243
Listing 3.1.1 243
Listing 3.1.2 244
Listing 3.1.3 245
Listing 3.1.4 245
Listing 3.1.5 246
Listing 3.1.6 246
Listing 3.1.7 246
Listing 3.1.8 247
Listing 3.1.9 247
References 248

3.2   Game Trees **249**
The Negamax Variation on the Minimax Algorithm 250
Alpha-Beta Pruning 251
Move-Ordering Methods 252
Refinements on Alpha-Beta 253
References 253

3.3   The Basics of A* for Path Planning **254**
The Problem 254
An Overview of the Solution 254
Listing 3.3.1: The A* Algorithm 255
Properties of A* 256
Applying A* to Game-Path Planning 256
Weaknesses of A* 261
Further Work 262
References 262

3.4   A* Aesthetic Optimizations **264**
Straight Paths 264
Straight Paths in a Polygonal Search Space 265
Smooth Paths 265
A Pre-Computed Catmull-Rom Formula 267
Improving the Directness of Hierarchical Paths 268
Hierarchical Pathfinding on Open Fields 269
Eliminating Pauses During Hierarchical Searches 270
Maximizing Responsiveness 270

       Conclusion 271
       References 271

3.5   **A* Speed Optimizations** **272**
       Search Space Optimization 272
       Algorithmic Optimization 276
       Conclusion 282
       Listing 3.5.1: Node Object 283
       Listing 3.5.2: Priority Queue Object 283
       Listing 3.5.3: STL Comparison Function 283
       Listing 3.5.4: Four Open List Operations 283
       Listing 3.5.5: A* Implemented with a Master Node List and a Priority Queue Open
          List 285
       References 287

3.6   **Simplified 3D Movement and Pathfinding Using Navigation Meshes 288**
       In a Nutshell 288
       Construction 290
       Roll the Dice and Move Your Mice 290
       Getting There Is Half the Fun 293
       It Works, But It Ain't Pretty 296
       Conclusion 297
       Listing 3.6.1: Intersecting a 2D Line with a Cell of the Navigation Mesh 297
       Listing 3.6.2: Resolving Motion on a Navigation Mesh 298
       Listing 3.6.3: Building a Navigation Path on the Mesh Using A* 300
       References 304

3.7   **Flocking: A Simple Technique for Simulating Group Behavior** **305**
       Implementation 307
       The Code 309
       Limitations and Potential Improvements 312
       Listing 3.7.1: The CFlock Class Definition 312
       Listing 3.7.2: The CBoid Class Definition 314
       Resources and Acknowledgments 317

3.8   **Fuzzy Logic for Video Games** **319**
       How Fuzzy Logic Works 319
       Fuzzy Logic Operations 321
       I Brake for Fuzzy Control 322
       Other Applications of Fuzzy Logic 328
       Conclusion 328
       Resources 329

3.9   **A Neural-Net Primer** **330**
       Biological Analogs 330
       Applications to Games 331
       Neural Nets 101 332

Pure Logic, Mr. Spock 338
Classification and "Image" Recognition 341
The Ebb of Hebbian 345
Playing the Hopfield 346
Conclusion 350

SECTION 4 POLYGONAL TECHNIQUES **351**

4.0   Optimizing Vertex Submission for OpenGL **353**
Immediate Mode 353
Interleaved Data 354
Strided and Streamed Data 355
Compiled Vertex Arrays 356
Eliminating Data Copy—Vendor Extensions 357
Data Format 358
General Recommendations 359
Conclusions 359
References 360

4.1   Tweaking a Vertex's Projected Depth Value **361**
Examining the Projection Matrix 361
Tweaking the Depth Value 362
Choosing an Appropriate Epsilon 363
Implementation 364
Source Code 364

4.2   The Vector Camera **366**
Introduction to the Vector Camera 367
Local Space Optimization 368
Conclusion 370

4.3   Camera Control Techniques **371**
A Basic First-Person Camera 371
Scripted Camera 373
Camera Tricks 377

4.4   A Fast Cylinder-Frustum Intersection Test **380**
The View Frustum 381
Calculating Effective Radii 382
The Algorithm 382
Implementation 385
Listing 4.4.1 385

4.5   3D Collision Detection **390**
Overview of the Algorithms 390
Bounding Sphere Collision Detection 390

  Triangle-to-Triangle Collision Detection 393
  Listing 4.5.1 397
  Listing 4.5.2 398
  Listing 4.5.3 400

4.6 **Multi-Resolution Maps for Interaction Detection** **403**
  Using a Grid 403
  Problems with Varying Object Size 403
  Multi-Resolution Maps 405
  Source Code 406

4.7 **Computing the Distance into a Sector** **412**
  The Problem 412
  Description of the Algorithm 414
  Applications 415

4.8 **Object Occlusion Culling** **421**
  Frustum Culling 422
  Occlusion Culling 423
  Summary 425
  Listing 4.8.1: Field of View Culling Code 425
  Listing 4.8.2: Occlusion Culling Code 429

4.9 **Never Let 'Em See You Pop— Issues in Geometric Level of
  Detail Selection** **432**
  LOD Selection 433
  Magnification Factor 434
  Hysteresis Thresholding 435
  Implementation 435
  Other Issues 437

4.10 **Octree Construction** **439**
  Octree Overview 439
  Octree Data 440
  Building the Tree 440
  Polygon Overlap 442
  Neighbors 442
  Applications 443
  Conclusion 443
  References 443

4.11 **Loose Octrees** **444**
  Quadtrees 444
  Bounding Volumes 445
  Partitioning Objects 446
  Making It Loose 448
  Comparison 451
  Conclusion 453

4.12   View-Independent Progressive Meshing **454**

Progressive Mesh Overview 455
Variations on the Theme 455
Edge Choice Functions 458
Difficult Edges 458
Implementation 459
Source Code 463
References 463

4.13   Interpolated 3D Keyframe Animation **465**

Linear Interpolation 465
Interpolating Vertices and Normals 467
Hermite Spline Interpolation 467
Spline Interpolating Vertices 469
Why Hermite Splines? 470
Summary 470
References 470

4.14   A Fast and Simple Skinning Technique **471**

Why Low-Polygon Count? 471
The Method 471
Summary 472
Listing 4.14.1 472
Listing 4.14.2 475
References 475

**4.15   Filling the Gaps— Advanced Animation Using Stitching and
          Skinning** **476**

Stitching 477
Skinning 480
Advanced Topics 483
References 483

4.16   Real-Time Realistic Terrain Generation **484**

Landscaping 484
Buildings 490
Naming Algorithms 493
References 498

4.17   Fractal Terrain Generation—Fault Formation **499**

Fault Formation 499
Decreasing dHeight 500
Generating Random Lines 500
Erosion 501
Sample Code 502
References 502

4.18   Fractal Terrain Generation—Midpoint Displacement **503**

Midpoint Displacement in One Dimension 503
Midpoint Displacement in Two Dimensions—Diamond Square 505
Diamond Square in Height Fields 507

4.19   Fractal Terrain Generation—Particle Deposition **508**

MBE Models 508
Particle Deposition 508
Inverting the Caldera 509
Sample Code 511
References 511

SECTION 5   PIXEL EFFECTS **513**

5.0   2D Lens Flare **515**

Approach 515
Implementation 517
Source Code 518

5.1   Using 3D Hardware for 2D Sprite Effects **519**

Going 3D 519
Setting Up the 3D Scene 519
Setting Up the Texture 520
Drawing the 3D Sprite 520
Adding Effects 522
Conclusion 523

5.2   Motif-Based Static Lighting **524**

Conventional Static Lighting 524
Motif-Based Static Lighting 528
Conclusion 534

5.3   Simulated Real-Time Lighting Using Vertex Color Interpolation . . . **535**

Lighting Method 535
Artwork Creation 536
Interpolated Lighting 537
Conclusion 538
Listing 5.3.1: Example Code 539

5.4   Attenuation Maps **543**

Explanation 543
Comparing Attenuation Maps and Light Maps 547
CSG Effects 547
Range-Based Fog 548
Other Shapes 548
Conclusion 548

5.5 Advanced Texturing Using Texture Coordinate Generation **549**

Simple Texture Coordinate Animation 549
Texture Projection 550
Reflection Mapping 553
References 554

5.6 Hardware Bump Mapping **555**

How Do I Apply a Bump Map to an Object? 555
Choosing a Space for the Normals 556
Another Approach: Using Tangent Space Bump Mapping 557
A Solution: Texture Space Bump Mapping 559
Texture Space Issues 561
Conclusion 561
References 561

5.7 Ground-Plane Shadows **562**

Shadow Math 562
Implementation 565
Extensions 566

5.8 Real-Time Shadows on Complex Objects **567**

Introduction 567
The Light Source, Blocker Object, and Receiver Object 567
The Objectives of This Article 569
Creating the Shadow Map 570
Projecting the Shadow Map on a Receiver Object 577
Rendering the Receiver Objects 578
Extensions and Enhancements to the Basic Algorithm 579
References 580

**5.9 Improving Environment-Mapped Reflection Using Glossy
Prefiltering and the Fresnel Term** **581**

The First Incorrect Assumption 582
The Second Incorrect Assumption 584
Conclusion 584
Acknowledgments 585
References 585

5.10 Convincing-Looking Glass for Games **586**

Introduction 586
Transparent Objects 586
Rasterizer, Frame Buffer, Z-Buffer, and Pixel Blending 586
Opaque Objects vs. Transparent Objects 587
Drawing Opaque Objects 588
Drawing Transparent Objects 588
Reflections 592
Colored Glass 592

Putting It All Together 593
Implementation 593
References 593

5.11   Refraction Mapping for Liquids in Containers **594**
Introduction 594
Refraction Term 594
Reflection Term 597
Fresnel Term 597
Rendering with Hardware 597
Future Extensions to This Technique 598
Conclusion 599
References 599

APPENDIX 6.0   THE MATRIX UTILITY LIBRARY **601**
Specification 601
Source Code 602
Acknowledgments 602

APPENDIX 6.1   THE TEXT UTILITY LIBRARY **603**
Specification 603
Source Code 603

APPENDIX 6.2   ABOUT THE CD-ROM **604**

INDEX **605**

Foreword

Mark A. DeLoura

Welcome to *Game Programming Gems*! I'm proud to deliver this volume into your hands. Within this book, you will find the combined wisdom of over 40 very talented game developers. These developers have worked together to create a book of game programming tips that will give you a *POWER UP*! If you implement the techniques that they have developed during their long hours in the trenches, your enemies will act smarter, your hero will skewer goblins more smoothly, and your 3D environments will have gamers scared to turn their lights off at night.

As a lead engineer at Nintendo, I talk with a lot of game developers. Whether they're asking me a question about our latest game console hardware or about a complicated game algorithm, one thing has become clear to me: we are all about questions. As game developers, we are often called upon to do tasks we have *no* idea how to perform. Heck, that's half the fun of being a game programmer! But when that happens, where do you turn? Do you go to your bookshelf; do you go to the Web? Perhaps you have an archive of magazines you search through. For game development, there really is no *one* definitive source. But wouldn't it be great if there was a place you knew you should always go to first? That's what we set out to create with this book.

Game development is a broad field that incorporates many of the same computer graphics techniques *and* other complicated algorithms from fields as diverse as Artificial Intelligence and Interactive Music. But when I asked game programmers, "What kind of book do you really wish you had on your shelf?" the overwhelming reply was to create a book full of knowledge from expert programmers, but specific to game programming. This would be a book full of techniques learned from long hours of programming, which could help both the expert *and* the novice.

The articles in this book address a broad slice of the technical problems you may face as a game programmer. There are a great number of very focused techniques, and quite a few sections that are more general. The intent is that no matter what programming level you're at, by reading this book you will gain a new level of expertise. For example, in the articles that are more general, we establish an overview of a technique, and then move on to more detailed discussions of how to use it. Great examples of this are the articles on quaternions, and the series of articles on the A* path-planning algorithm.

About Standards

One of the challenges we faced in creating this book was how to present technical material in an environment that pushes technology at such a rapid pace. The obvious answer was to settle on established standards. So, all of the articles in this book use either C or C++ for programming, OpenGL for the graphics language, and will run on Windows and Linux. One constant in our industry is that the platforms we work on will continue to evolve—we hope that by using the most portable languages possible, and targeting the most popular operating systems, the information in this book will continue to be useful a decade from now. (Okay, actually several excellent articles are very tightly bound to Windows and Visual C++, but they are so good we let the platform-independence thing slide!)

Standards are very important to our industry. As new technologies are gobbled up by big corporations in their quest to out-patent each other, it becomes very clear how important it is for us to share our knowledge among ourselves instead. Why? Well, some of the best games I've played lately are from small game development houses— if they have to worry about patent infringement and licensing fees, it's much more likely that some real "gems" will never be created! We can support each other and encourage better games by avoiding software patents, sharing the information we learn with our community, and using third-party standards.

Technologies that are not owned by any one particular company—for example, the C++ programming language—can become tools for our use instead of items in some company's power-grab maneuvers. With game development schedules getting longer and longer, the last thing we all need to worry about is whether we're going to have to port our game to some competitor's operating system or libraries. UGH. Who needs that kind of stress? We've got enough to do!

A common analogy that you may have heard is that the motion picture industry didn't really take off until some standards were set for a common film size and technique. This reference of course is being made by someone who is promoting standards for the game industry. But okay, let's face it, I'm only going to use a standard if it benefits me. If there's some standard library and I can't look at the code, or it's written poorly and runs slow, why the heck would I use it? This is why the idea of open source is so key to our community. The best possible way to learn a technique is to read the source code. Standards are great, but basically useless unless we can look at the source and feel comfortable that they're not going to hinder our game's performance.

GLUT (the OpenGL Utility Toolkit) is a great example of how software can really serve people and become a standard just by being great. Mark Kilgard's toolkit has gained wide popularity. Due to it being so completely open source (basically public domain), the software has been tuned and tweaked to the point where you'd be stupid *not* to use it if you're doing a simple cross-platform application. Today, GLUT is a platform-independent toolkit that is very robust, and very useful. Source code in this book uses GLUT to enable execution on multiple platforms, and if it weren't out there, quite frankly it would have been a big pain for us to do this ourselves.

Okay, that's enough soapboxing. I hope that after reading this book, you are inspired to write up your own excellent techniques and submit them to *Game Developer* magazine (www.gdmag.com), Gamasutra (www.gamasutra.com), or present them at the Game Developer's Conference (www.gdconf.com). Everyone wins when you spread your expertise among the community: you win by gaining prestige and connections to others, and those who learn from you get the benefit of your wisdom!

The Power of Story

There's something about the power of a good story that really affects people. People remember the best book they've read, the best movie they've seen, and they relate to these things as if they are a part of who they are. And in some sense, they are. A good story contains messages, subtle or blatant, that people grasp onto and incorporate into their lives.

We all love to lose ourselves in a good story, and games are the best stories. In a game, you're no longer just the observer—you're the main character! The messages we convey have even more impact in this setting. It's important for us to be responsible for what we create in our games. In the environment of blame created in the void left behind by yet another school shooting, our development community stands out as a very likely target. Other story-telling mediums (books, television, movies) have firm regulations and rigid categorization, in an attempt to protect the public from consuming "negative" messages. It is extremely important that we are clear in our intentions behind the games we create, and intelligently express this in order to avoid the kind of cultural censorship these other mediums have adopted. As the game development community grows larger and more prominent, this is a challenge we are certain to face.

It is truly an exciting time to be a part of our industry. We're on the cusp of really breaking into the mainstream. The day when you'll be able to download the latest Miyamoto to your deck instead of watching today's pay-per-view event on it is close at hand. What will our world be like in five years, or ten? I can't wait to find out.

Acknowledgments

Creating a book like this is certainly not a task for one person. In fact, I probably would have jumped off a bridge if I'd had to do this alone. Fortunately, many talented people assisted in the production of this book. Of course it's impossible for me to thank them all here (this is beginning to sound like an Oscar speech or something...), but let me try anyway. BIG thank you's to the *authors*, first and foremost. Without their years of experience, and their dedication and hard work on their articles, this volume could not exist! Similarly, a big thank you to the publisher Charles River Media, and especially Jenifer Niles and Dave Pallai. They gave me a big boost when I first brought this idea to them, and were an unending source of enthusiasm and wisdom. There were a number of game developers who did not write for this book but were actively involved: Jeff Lander, Chris Hecker, Chris Taylor, Mark Haigh-Hutchinson, Richard Nelson, Stephen White, Mark Kilgard, and Elaine Hutchison all provided a great deal of assistance. Dante Treglia and Steve Rabin each wrote several articles, and they were excellent sounding boards for me when I needed to sort something out for the book. There are many people who didn't have a direct impact on the book, but impacted me personally: Andrew Glassner for the *Graphics Gems* series, Adrienne McEntee and Blyth Benshoof for moral support, Sonja for companionship (meow), Jim Merrick at Nintendo for clearing the legal red tape that allowed me to create this book, and my parents and friends for keeping me sane. Also, thanks to Jennifer Pahlka, Alan Yu, Alex Dunne, and Brad Kane of the CMP Game Media Group for the excellent job they do encouraging communication in our industry.

I hope you enjoy the book !

—Mark A. DeLoura

About the Cover Image

Mark Peasley

This scene is from the title *Dungeon Siege* by Gas Powered Games, to be released in 2001. *Dungeon Siege* is an action fantasy role-playing game that combines elements of a role-playing game (RPG) with a real-time strategy (RTS) game. It is an immersive 3D world with a free-floating, user-controlled camera. This scene is from the Northern region of the world. Generic tile sets for a region are created and textured in 3D Studio Max, then exported and constructed via an inhouse editor. Character animations are done using a single skin mesh over a skeletal bone system. The animation system detects the type of weapon the character has, and then alters the stance and attack methods accordingly. An advanced particle system allows for special effects such as snow, rain, fire, and magic. Being roasted by the Dragon is optional . . .

Author Index

Ahmad, Anis, a3ahmad@undergrad.math.uwaterloo.ca

Bilas, Scott, Gas Powered Games, scottb@aa.net, http://www.aa.net/~scottb

Boer, James, Lithtech, Inc., jimb@lith.com

DeLoura, Mark A., Nintendo of America Inc., madsax@satori.org,
    http://www.satori.org/madsax

Dietrich, Sim, NVIDIA Corporation, sim.dietrich@nvidia.com

Dybsand, Eric, Glacier Edge Technology, edybs@ix.netcom.com

Edwards, Eddie, Naughty Dog, Inc., eddie@naughtydog.com

Freitas, Jorge, Electronic Arts Canada, Inc., jorgef@ea.com

Ginsburg, Dan, ATI Research, Inc., ginsburg@alum.wpi.edu

Gomez, Miguel, Lithtech, Inc., miguel@lith.com

Hagland, Torgeir, Shiny Entertainment, torgeir.hagland@powertech.no

Isensee, Pete, Emerald City, PKIsensee@msn.com, http://www.tantalon.com

Kaiser, Kevin, velderon@warp3000.com

King, Yossarian, Electronic Arts Canada, Inc., yking@ea.com

Kirmse, Andrew, LucasArts Entertainment Company, akirmse@lucasarts.com

LaMothe, André, Xtreme Games LLC, ceo@xgames3d.com

Le Chevalier, Loïc, Infogrames, llechevalier@fr.infogrames.com

Lecky-Thompson, Guy W., LeckyT@GameBox.net

Lengyel, Eric, lengyel@C4Engine.com

Marselas, Herbert, Ensemble Studios, hmarselas@ensemblestudios.com

McCuskey, Mason, Spin Studios, mason@spin-studios.com, http://www.spin-studios.com/

Melax, Stan, Bioware Corp., melax@cs.ualberta.ca, http://www.cs.ualberta.ca/~melax

Mitchell, Jason L., ATI Research, Inc., JasonM@ati.com

Nagy, Gabor, Sony Computer Entertainment America, Gabor_Nagy@Playstation.sony.com, http://www.equinox3d.com

Olsen, John, Microsoft, Inc., infix@xmission.com.

Paull, David, Tanzanite Software, cosmodog@tanzanite.to, http://www.tanzanite.to

Peasley, Mark, Gas Powered Games, mpeasley@gaspowered.com, http://www.pixelman.com/

Rabin, Steve, Nintendo of America Inc., stevera@noa.nintendo.com

Ranck, Steven, Midway Home Entertainment, sranck@home.com, http://www.members.home.net/sranck

Round, Tim, timround@hotmail.com

Shankel, Jason, Maxis, shankel@pobox.com

Snook, Greg, Mighty Studios, greg@mightystudios.com

Stout, Bryan, bstout@mindspring.com

Svarovsky, Jan, Mucky Foot Productions, jan@svarovsky.freeserve.co.uk, http://www.svarovsky.freeserve.co.uk/

Treglia, Dante II, Nintendo of America Inc., danttr01@noa.nintendo.com

Ulrich, Thatcher, Slingshot Game Technology, Inc., tu@tulrich.com, http://www.tulrich.com

Vlachos, Alex, ATI Research, Inc., avlachos@ati.com

Woodcock, Steven, Raytheon Technical Services Company, ferretman@gameai.com, http://www.gameai.com/

Woodland, Ryan, Nintendo Technology Development, ryanwo01@noa.nintendo.com

PROGRAMMING TECHNIQUES

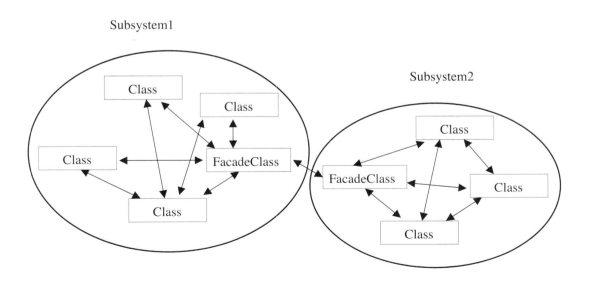

1.0

The Magic of Data-Driven Design

Steve Rabin

Games are made up of two things: *logic* and *data*. This is a powerful distinction. Separate, they are useless, but together, they make your game come alive. The logic defines the core rules and algorithms of the game engine, while the data provides the details of content and behavior. The magic happens when logic and data are decoupled from each other and allowed to blossom independently.

Obviously, game data should be loaded from files, not embedded inside the code base. The genius comes from knowing how far to run with this concept. This article gives seven ideas that will revolutionize the way you make your games, or at least confirm your suspicions.

Idea #1: The Basics

Create a system that can parse text files on demand (not just at startup). This is essential to putting data-driven design to work. Every game needs a clean way to read in general-purpose data. The game should eventually be read in binary files, but the ability to read in text files during development is crucial. Text files are dead simple for editing and making changes. Without altering a single line of code, your whole team, including testers and game designers, can try out new things and experiment with different variations. Thus, something that is trivial to implement can quickly become an indispensable tool.

Idea #2: The Bare Minimum

Don't hard-code constants. Put constants in text files so that they can be easily changed without recompiling code. For example, basic functionality such as camera behavior should be exposed completely. If this is done properly, the game designer, the producer, and the kid down the street will all be able to alter the behavior of the camera with nothing more than Notepad. Game designers and producers are often at the mercy of programmers. By exposing algorithm constants, non-programmers can tune and play with the values to get the exact behavior they desire—without bothering a single programmer.

Idea #3: Hard-Code Nothing

Assume that anything can change, and probably will. If the game calls for a split screen, don't hard-code it! Write your game to support any number of viewports, each with its own camera logic. It isn't even any more work if it's designed right. Through the magic of text files, you could define whether the game is single-screen, split-screen, or quad-screen. The files would also define all the starting camera values, such as position, direction, field of view, and tilt. The best part is that your game designers have direct access to all elements within the text files.

When core design decisions are flexible, the game is allowed to evolve to its full potential. In fact, the process of abstracting a game to its core helps tremendously in the design. Instead of designing to a single purpose, you can design each component to its general functionality. In effect, designing flexibly forces you to recognize what you should really be building instead of the limited behavior outlined in the design document.

For example, if the game calls for only four types of weapons, you could program a perfectly good system that encompasses all of them. However, if you abstract away the functionality of each weapon, using data to define its behavior, you'll allow for the possibility of countless weapons that have very distinct personalities. All it takes is a few changes in a text file in order to experiment with new ideas and game-play dynamics. This mindset allows the game to evolve and ultimately become a much better game.

Did You Believe Me When I Said "Nothing"?

The truth is that games need to be tuned, and great games evolve dramatically from the original vision. Your game should be able to deal with changing rules, characters, races, weapons, levels, control schemes, and objects. Without this flexibility, change is costly, and every change involves a programmer—which is simply a waste of resources. If change is difficult, it promotes far fewer improvements to the original design. The game will simply not live up to its full potential.

Idea #4: Script Your Control Flow

A *script* is simply a way to define behavior outside of the code. Scripts are great for defining sequential steps that need to occur in a game or game events that need to be triggered. For example, an in-game cut-scene should be scripted. Simple cause-and-effect logic should also be scripted, such as the completion conditions of a quest or environment triggers. These are all great examples of the data-driven philosophy at work.

When designing a scripting language, branching instructions require some thought. There are two ways to branch. The first is to keep variables inside the scripting language and compare them using mathematical operators such as equals (=) or less than (<). The second is to directly call evaluation functions that compare variables that exist solely inside the code, such as `IsLifeBelowPercentage(50)`. You could always use a mix of these techniques, but keeping your scripts simple will pay off. A game designer will have a much easier time dealing with evaluation functions than declaring variables, updating them, and then comparing them. It also will be easier to debug.

Unfortunately, scripts require a scripting language. This means that you need to create an entirely new syntax for defining your behavior. A scripting language also involves creating a script parser and possibly a compiler to convert the script to a binary file for faster execution. The other choice is to use an existing language such as Java, but that requires a large amount of peripheral support as well. In order not to sink too much time into this, it pays off to design a simple system. Overall, the tendency is to make the scripting language too powerful. The next idea explains some pitfalls of a complicated scripting language.

Idea #5: When Good Scripts Go Bad

Using scripts to data-drive behavior is a natural consequence of the data-driven methodology. However, you need to practice good common sense. The key is remembering the core philosophy: Separate logic and data. Complicated logic goes in the code; data stays outside.

The problem arises when the desire to data-drive the game goes too far. At some point, you'll be tempted to put complicated logic inside scripts. When a script starts holding state information and needs to branch, it becomes a *finite state machine*. When the number of states increases, the innocent scriptwriter (some poor game designer) has the job of programming. If the scripting becomes sufficiently complex, the job reverts to the programmer who must program in a fictional language that's severely limiting. Scripts are supposed to make people's jobs easier, not more difficult.

Why is it so important to keep complicated logic inside the code? It's simply a matter of functionality and debugging. Since scripts are not directly in the code, they need to duplicate many of the concepts that exist in programming languages. The natural tendency is to expose more and more functionality until it rivals a real language. The more complicated scripts become, the more debugging information is needed to figure out why the scripts are failing. This additional information results in more and more effort devoted to monitoring every aspect of the script as it runs.

As you probably guessed, non-trivial logic in scripts can get very involved. Months of work can be wasted writing script parsers, compilers, and debuggers. It's as though programmers didn't realize they had a perfectly good compiler already in front of them.

The Fuzzy Line

There is no doubt that the line between code and scripts is fuzzy. Generally, it's a bad idea to put artificial intelligence (AI) behavior in scripts, whereas it's generally a good idea to have a scripted trigger system for making the world interactive. The rule should be: If the logic is too complicated, it belongs in the code. Scripting languages need to be kept simple, so they don't consume your game (and all of your programming resources).

However, some games are designed to let players write their own AI. Most commonly, these games are first-person shooters that allow the creation of bots. When this is the goal, it's inevitable that the scripting language will resemble a real programming language. An example of this situation is Quake C. Since bot creation was a requirement of the design, resources and energy had to be put into making the scripting language as useful as C. A scripting language of this magnitude is a huge commitment and shouldn't be taken lightly.

Above all, remember that you don't want your game designers or scriptwriters programming the game. Sometimes programmers are trying to shirk responsibility when they create scripting languages. It's all too easy to lure game designers into programming the game. Ideally, programmers should be boiling down the problem and exposing the essential controls in order to manipulate the logic. That's why programmers get paid the big bucks!

Idea #6: Avoiding Duplicate Data Syndrome

It's standard programming practice to never duplicate code. If you need the same behavior (for example, a common function) in two different spots, it needs to exist in only one place. This idea can be applied to data by using references to global chunks of data. Furthermore, by taking a reference to a chunk of data and modifying some of its values, you end up with a concept very close to inheritance.

Inheritance is a great idea that should be applied to your data. Imagine that your game has goblins that live inside dungeons. In any particular dungeon, your data defines where each goblin stands, along with its properties. The right way to encapsulate this data is to have a global definition of a goblin. Each dungeon's data simply has a reference to that global definition for every instance of a goblin. In order to make each goblin unique, the reference can be accompanied by a list of properties to override. This technique allows every goblin to be different while eliminating duplicate data.

This idea can be taken to multiple levels by allowing each chunk of data to have a reference. Using this technique, you can have a global definition of a goblin along with another global definition of a fast goblin that inherits from the basic goblin. Then inside each dungeon definition, regular goblins or fast goblins can be instanced trivially. Figure 1.0.1 shows this inheritance concept using referencing and overriding of values.

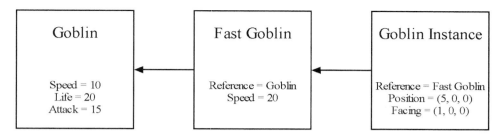

FIGURE 1.0.1. Data inheritance.

Idea #7: Make the Tool That Makes the Data

With any large game, text files eventually become unruly and hard to work with. The real solution is to make a tool that writes the text files. Call this tool a game editor, a level editor, or a script editor, but you'll speed up the game development process by building the right tools. Having a tool doesn't change the data-driven methodology; it merely makes it more robust and efficient. The time you save always makes the extra tool development time worth it.

Conclusion

It's easy to buy into the data-driven methodology, but it's harder to visualize the dramatic results. When everything is data driven, amazing possibilities unfold.

An example of this rule is the game Total Annihilation. The designer, Chris Taylor, pushed data-driven design to the limit. Total Annihilation was an RTS that featured two distinct races, the Arm and the Core. Although the entire game was centered on these two factions, they were never hard-coded into the game. Theoretically, data could have been added to the game to support three races, even after the game shipped. Although this possibility was never exploited, Total Annihilation took full advantage of its flexibility. Since all units were completely defined by data, new units were released on a weekly basis over the game's Web site. In fact, many people created their own units with functionality that shocked even the game's developers.

The data-driven design helped Total Annihilation maintain a committed following in a crowded genre. Since Total Annihilation, other games, such as The Sims, have employed the same idea by providing new data content over their Web sites. Without developers' serious commitment to the data-driven philosophy, this unprecedented expandability wouldn't be possible.

1.1

Object-Oriented Programming and Design Techniques

James Boer

It is easy to understand the popularity of C++ among game programming professionals. While not straying too far from the highly portable and efficient roots of C, it also offers the design benefits of an object-oriented language. Inherent in this power, though, is the requirement that C++ code be properly designed and implemented. Although the object-oriented programming (OOP) paradigm was created to enhance program design, portability, and maintainability, the brutal fact of the matter is that poorly designed C++ programs can be worse than poorly written C programs.

Many books and articles give good advice on general object-oriented design practices; very few teach those practices with game programmers specifically in mind. Game programmers are a slightly different breed than the typical application programmer. Because their work is always expected to be cutting edge, pushing both human and hardware constraints to the limit, game developers tend to be much more willing to bend or even break traditional programming design rules. Unfortunately, this tendency often has the negative side effect of creating unmaintainable code due to a poor understanding or implementation of basic OOP principles.

As games grow more and more complex, companies are looking to reuse more and more code to mitigate ever-increasing development costs. Engine licensing is becoming more prominent as companies focus on content and game play and will undoubtedly grow into a major and separate support industry in the near future. This sort of development work requires much more stability and long-term planning than was previously known in the game development world. No longer is it acceptable to completely scrap your previous code with each new game.

This article obviously can't even begin to cover all that a game programmer needs to know. Instead, it identifies key areas in which a game programmer, and a company, can take steps to improve the quality and consistency of production code, which will in turn lead to both more robust and more reusable libraries and game engines. We also point you toward resources that much more thoroughly cover the topics discussed.

Coding Style

Programming style can often degrade into a religious argument. I'm not going to enter the debacle of where curly braces should be placed, but it is important for a company to adopt a style, and for everyone in that company to use it.

A company, not to mention an individual, should strive for consistency in class, function, and variable naming conventions as well. Many companies have adopted a simplified Hungarian notation scheme. The Hungarian notation was invented by Dr. Charles Simonyi, chief software architect of Microsoft, years ago in order to help standardize variable naming conventions. Some argue that such a naming convention is unnecessary in a type-safe language such as C++ and creates more work when changing data types (since it requires changing the variable prefix), but others appreciate the ease and speed with which data types are visually identified.

The basic premise of Hungarian notation is to preface the variable name with an identifier describing the type of data the variable represents. For instance, an integer variable named `SomeVariable` would instead be named `iSomeVariable`. In addition to variable types, pointers can be represented. A pointer to some class `Foo` might be called `pFooObj`. Prefixes can also be combined to provide more information than a single prefix can provide. For instance, a pointer to an integer would be represented by the prefix `pi`, or a pointer to a pointer would be represented as `pp`.

Other types of scope information are often used in front of the type prefix. Member variables are labeled with `m_`, so an integer member variable might be labeled `m_iSomeVar`. Global variables (tsk, you shouldn't even really be using these) are represented as `g_`, and some variations represent static variables as `s_`, although this isn't seen as often. Although the formal Hungarian notation can be somewhat complex, many companies have adopted a simplified version of it. Table 1.1.1 presents an example of a common variation on formal Hungarian notation. You can find other descriptions in books such as [Petzold96], or you can find Simonyi's original paper on the World Wide Web in various locations.

The most commonly used notational types are listed in the table. Objects are generally not given any prefix, with the exception of a few common classes such as those representing 3D vectors and points. Your company might adopt conventions for representing other commonly used utility classes as well. Note that most of the descriptive tags are quite logical and would not require you to look them up in a table.

The exact syntax you adopt is not as important as the relative consistency of everyone who conforms to it. If all company code looks similar, it will be easier for programmers to work on code that they might not have written.

One word of caution: Don't over-engineer a coding specification. A page or two should really be all that's required to describe the company style. If programmers have to look up how a variable should be named, they'll be far less likely to use the standard. I hesitate to recommend strictly adhering to Simonyi's original system. It's far too complex for day-to-day operations, and since readability is now more important

Table 1.1.1 An Example of Hungarian Notation

Type	Description
I	Integer
F	Float
D	Double (float)
L	Long (integer)
C	Character
B	Boolean
Dw	Double word
W	Word
by *or* byte	Byte
Sz	C-style (null-terminated) string

Common Extensions	Description
Str	C++ string object
H	Handle (user-defined type)
V	Vector (user-defined class)
Pt	Point (user-defined class)
Rgb	RGB triplet (user-defined struct or type)

Modifier	Description
P	Pointer to
R	Reference to
U	Unsigned
a *or* ary	Array of

Scope	Description
m_	Member variable
g_	Global variable
s_	Static variable

than type safety, there's no reason to create hard-to-read code when a simplified version will work just as well.

Class names should also be designed for ease of maintenance and readability. A convention that has gained some popularity among Windows programmers is the use of class prefixes to indicate general design intent. Classes beginning with the letter *C* are designated as *Concrete classes*, or classes with a specific use and implementation. Classes beginning with the letter *I* are *Interface classes,* or classes intended to be used as design templates. These classes are not used directly by applications; instead, they allow other classes to be derived from them.

In addition to or instead of these class prefixes, it can also be helpful to prefix classes by functionality. For instance, all classes dealing with a user interface (UI) system can be prefaced with *UI*. This is especially helpful in programming environments and tools that sort classes in a project alphabetically.

Class Design

C++ classes offer an unlimited amount of design flexibility, which can be both a good and a bad thing. There are no naming requirements, other than for your constructor and your destructor. However, you might want to self-impose a standardized class naming convention. Here is a simple example:

```
class Sample
{
public:
    Sample()      { Clear(); }
    ~Sample()     { Destroy(); }

    void Clear();

    bool Create();
    void Update();
    void Destroy();
};
```

The first thing you'll notice about this class is the trivial constructor. Implementing classes this way is a good idea for a number of reasons. To start with, the C++ constructor has no return value. Therefore, it's simply not a good idea to do anything that might fail. So instead, we simply call Clear(), a function that clears out all the internal member variables. The benefit of clearing variables in a separate function is that it allows you to clear the class variables at any time. You'll see why this is especially important later.

At times, you won't want to "activate" a class the moment it is created. This often happens for wrapper classes that are themselves members of another class. Lastly, there is an efficiency issue. Divorcing the object's actual creation point from the constructor allows you to dynamically create an object once but repeatedly call the Create() and Destroy() members to reuse the same object's memory. Dynamically allocating memory is expensive, so when possible, it's best to avoid doing so. As mentioned, the Create() and Destroy() members do the work of actually creating and destroying whatever it is the object represents. The Create() function has a simple bool value for indicating success or failure. This value is both intuitive and easy to implement. Another popular choice of return type is standardized error code types (usually signed integers). Bools are easy to use but require additional error-querying mechanisms if return codes are not provided. Exception handling, although theoretically superior to simple return values, tends to be both expensive in run-time performance and easy for programmers to overlook. In addition, exception handling is not self-documenting, as error codes or return values are in header files.

There is also an important caveat for the `Destroy()` function. Since we want both the convenience of automatic cleanup and the flexibility of "destroy and recreate on demand," we need to make sure that the `Destroy()` function can be called multiple times safely or without the `Create()` function having been called. Be sure to call the `Clear()` function at the end of your destroy function in order to reset all the object variables back to their initial states.

Game programming often means programming a real-time system instead of the more common event-based programming model found in most commercial applications. We might want to recognize this difference in our class designs. The last portion of the class is the `Update()` function. This is the "step" function, or the function that gets called once every frame. It's a big help to agree on a common name for this function. Depending on the class, you might or might not want to implement the `Update()` function with a bool return value to allow for checking of run-time errors in the step function.

Class Hierarchy Design

Knowing how to make the most of class reuse through inheritance is a key factor in object-oriented programming. Although a complete discussion of relationships between objects and how to implement them is beyond the scope of this article, there is a single design rule that is of such importance that it bears brief mention.

There are two primary methods of extending classes to work with each other: inheritance and layering. *Inheritance,* of course, is deriving one class from another. *Layering* is when one object is contained as a member of another object. Layering is also known by such terms as *composition, containment,* and *embedding.*

The simple rule is this: If an object has an *is-a* relationship to another object, use public inheritance. If a *has-a* relationship describes the objects best, then use layering. What exactly do the terms *is-a* and *has-a* mean? Pretty much exactly what they sound like. If we use them in a sentence, the meaning becomes clearer:

Class Corvette *is-a* type of class Car.
Class Corvette *has-a* type class Radio.

When deciding how to relate classes to each other, it's often helpful to actually speak the two relationships out loud. More often than not, the correct answer simply sounds correct.

Design Patterns

When creating a solution to a common programming problem, most developers unconsciously refer to a similar problem that they have solved previously and then extrapolate the new solution from the old. Design patterns are about formalizing these general software solutions to give a common frame of reference when discussing everyday engineering tasks. A number of design patterns are described more thoroughly in other books, but here we discuss patterns most commonly used by and relevant to game developers.

The Singleton Pattern

The *singleton pattern* is used when a single global object must be accessed across a wide number of classes and/or modules. Simply creating a non-local static object works, but there are many problems inherent with that practice, not the least of which is determining when the object will actually be created, compared with other objects with the same global scope requirements. The singleton pattern solves this problem by forcing access through a class, which stores a static object internally. Here's what a basic implementation might look like:

```
class Singleton1
{
public:
    Singleton1& Instance()
    {
        static Singleton Obj;
        return Obj;
    }
private:
    Singleton1();
};
```

This simple code solves the problem quite elegantly. However, if you want to derive new classes from this one, you'll be hard pressed to come up with as elegant an extension. By changing the design and requiring more specific intervention during object creation and deletion, though, we can expand on the basic singleton concept and allow extensibility to our original class:

```
class SingletonBase
{
public:
    SingletonBase()
    { cout << "SingletonBase created!" << endl; }
    virtual ~SingletonBase()
    { cout << "SingletonBase destroyed!" << endl; }
    virtual void Access()
    { cout << "SingletonBase accessed!" << endl; }
    static SingletonBase* GetObj()
    { return m_pObj; }
    static void SetObj(SingletonBase* pObj)
    { m_pObj = pObj; }
protected:
    static SingletonBase* m_pObj;
};
```

```
SingletonBase* SingletonBase::m_pObj;

inline SingletonBase* Base()
{
    assert(SingletonBase::GetObj());
    return SingletonBase::GetObj();
}

// Create a derived singleton-type class
class SingletonDerived : public SingletonBase
{
public:
    SingletonDerived()
    { cout << "SingletonDerived created!" << endl; }
    virtual ~SingletonDerived()
    { cout << "SingletonDerived destroyed" << endl; }
    virtual void Access()
    { cout << "SingletonDerived accessed!" << endl; }
protected:
};

inline SingletonDerived* Derived()
{
    assert(SingletonDerived::GetObj());
    return (SingletonDerived*)SingletonDerived::GetObj();
}

// Using the code...
// The complex singleton requires more work to use, but is
// more flexible. It also allows more control over object
// creation, which is sometimes desirable.
SingletonDerived::SetObj(new SingletonDerived);

// Notice that the functionality has been overridden by the new
// class, even though accessing it through the original method.
Base()->Access();
Derived()->Access();

// This variation on a singleton unfortunately requires both
// explicit creation and deletion.
delete SingletonDerived::GetObj();
```

This modified form of the singleton class is not quite as simple in the construction and destruction phases, but the global access, which is the primary point of the singleton, remains as accessible as ever. Furthermore, with the addition of inline accessor functions, the code becomes quite easy to read from the user's perspective.

Singleton patterns are often used in situations in which you traditionally might think of using a global object or pointer to reference a single instance of a class. An example might be a manager-type class, where only a single instance (thus, the name of the pattern) is required. Classes that manage an application's sound, a user interface, graphics, or even the game or application itself are all likely candidates to become singleton-type classes.

So, why go to all this bother instead of simply creating a global object or pointer? There are a few great reasons. First, if you were planning on creating global objects, accessing an object through a single function is easier than having to extern a global object in all your files. In addition, you gain the benefit of controlling exactly when your object is initialized. Second, if you're using a pointer instead of an object, you gain C++ control over every access of the object, meaning that you gain benefits of access control, in turn meaning that you can do things such as monitor every time the class is accessed. Finally, if you create your singleton with derived classes in mind using the techniques described, you can extend your base class while maintaining compatibility with the existing base class. Let's examine how this might work.

In order to make the most of this sort of extensibility, you can imagine a scenario such as the following: Library A utilizes a singleton class, as described previously. Library B must use Library A in order to function, so it is dependent on those classes and includes their header files. Application C makes use of both Libraries A and B but requires changes to be made to Library A for some game-specific items. Instead of having to create a new version of the library (and lose any improvements made to the original library by, say, a concurrent project), Application C can simply derive a new class (Class D) from Library A. If, as part of our singleton convention, we require that the application is responsible for allocating the object, we can substitute derived Class D for Class A. By creating a new accessor function with a new name that returns a pointer to Class D instead of Class A, we can access all of D's new functions. However, Class B will continue to use the old accessor function that returns a pointer to A and so will expect the old functions to function similarly to the way they did before. Note that virtual functions' behavior can be overridden, but you must ensure that the new functionality is compatible with the old to preserve backward compatibility.

In this way, the singleton pattern allows you to create a primitive library versioning scheme. You can see how a simple technique can evolve into a powerful mechanism for code organization and reuse. You can find in this book another variation of the singleton pattern in the article "An Automatic Singleton Utility," by Scott Bilas. In this article he describes an elegant method of using templates and public inheritance to automate the creation of singleton classes.

Façade Pattern

The singleton segues nicely into the next pattern we'll investigate: the *façade pattern*. This pattern is generally used as what is often referred to as a *manager class*. This is a class that provides a single interface to a large collection of related classes, usually some sort of subsystem. These classes are often designed as singletons because it usually makes sense to have only one manager object per type of subsystem. For example, you need only a single object to manage access to your audio or graphical user interface subsystems.

A façade or manager is necessary in order to keep interdependencies between classes, otherwise known as *coupling*, to a minimum. One can imagine in a theoretical

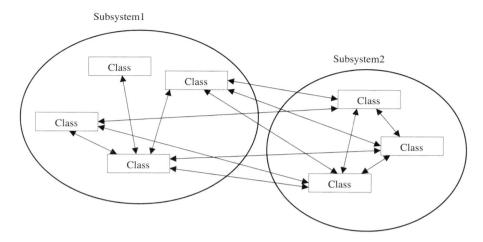

FIGURE 1.1.1 An example of bad coupling.

worst-case scenario that every class in a project "knows" about and requires explicit access to every other class, as illustrated in Figure 1.1.1. The maximum number of interdependencies between classes can be described as $(n-1)^2$, where n is the number of classes in a project.

The problem with this sort of interdependency comes when an entire subsystem needs to be heavily modified or even replaced. Object-oriented programming protects against implementation changes within single classes, but a new paradigm is needed for protection against more sweeping changes. The façade pattern solves the same sort of problem that object-oriented programming protects against, but on a much larger scale.

The general rule of thumb when implementing façade classes is this: Whenever possible, avoid exposing internal subsystem classes to outside systems. This is not always possible to do entirely, but with some clever coding and function wrapping, you can reduce the exposure of these classes a great deal, as illustrated in Figure 1.1.2. Every class you hide means that there is less work to be done the next time that subsystem has to be reimplemented.

State Pattern

Almost every game programmer has had to deal with the problem of keeping track of constantly shifting game states in real time. States usually start out as simple enumerations, and behavior is implemented based on switching between states in a `switch` `...` `case` structure. Problems can develop, however, when the number of states starts growing larger and functionality must be shared in a greater number of these states. A cut-and-paste nightmare can quickly ensue, wherein the programmer tries to find all the states that share code and make sure that any changes to one state occur in all of them.

Subsystem1

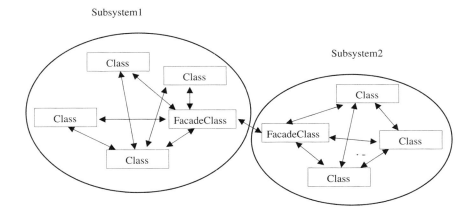

FIGURE 1.1.2. Using façade classes to reduce interdependencies.

A more elegant object-oriented solution is to simply use objects to represent logical states. The advantages of using objects are that states are better encapsulated, states can logically share code in their base classes, and new states can easily be derived from existing ones using inheritance. These advantages reduce the typical problem of having to cut and paste code between discrete states, as shown in Figure 1.1.3.

Although the pattern does not specify how state transitions are to be made, it can often make sense to leave the transitions of classes to a central manager. In this manner, inter-object dependencies can be avoided, leaving only the manager to worry about having to know all the different state objects. Better yet, the states can simply be enumerated and created through the use of a factory object, which is explained in the next section.

The state pattern does not necessarily have to be used only to represent discrete game states. It can also be used in AI systems or even to represent different types of game modes within a single game. By representing each game mode as a different object, for example, you gain the flexibility of allowing new behavior to be added after

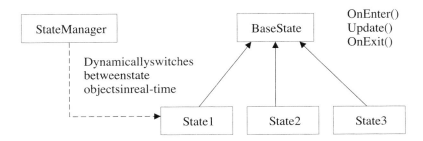

FIGURE 1.1.3. Using the state pattern.

the initial release through the use of dynamic link libraries (DLLs) or other means of adding an object to existing code dynamically.

Factory Pattern

The *factory pattern* deals with organization in the creation of objects. A form of the pattern is defined as a method for allowing abstract interface classes to specify when to create concrete, derived implementation classes. This method is often required in application frameworks and other similar class hierarchies. However, game programmers often deal with a specific subset of the factory pattern—namely, the use of factory objects with enumerated object creation located in a central class, usually via a single-member function.

In English, this means that a single object is responsible for creating a wide variety of other objects, usually related by a common base class. This class often takes the form of a class with a single method that accepts some sort of class ID and returns an allocated object. The advantages of clustering object allocation into a single location are especially noteworthy for game developers:

- Dynamic memory allocation is expensive, so you want to carefully monitor allocations. Allocating all objects in a central area makes it easier to monitor these allocations.
- Often, common initialization or creation methods must be called for all objects within a class hierarchy. If all object allocation is put into a central area, it becomes easy to perform any common operations (such as inserting them into a resource manager)on all objects.
- A factory allows extensibility by allowing new objects to be derived from the existing factory. By passing in a new class ID (which can easily be obtained from data instead of code), you can provide run-time extensibility of new classes without changing the existing base code.

The final point stresses extensibility as a benefit of using the factory pattern. For this reason, creating simple functions or static classes should be avoided, since you cannot derive new classes from them:

```
BaseClass* ClassFactory::CreateObject(int id)
{
    BaseClass* pClass = 0;
    switch(id)
    {
    case 1:
        pClass = new Class1;
        break;
    case 2:
        pClass = new Class2;
        break;
    case 3:
        pClass = new Class3;
        break;
```

```
    default:
        assert(!"Error! Invalid class ID passed to factory!");
    };

    // perhaps perform some common initialization is needed
    pClass->Init();

    return pClass;
}
```

You can see that there is technically nothing sophisticated about a factory creation method. However, centralizing these object allocations provides a powerful organization and extensibility mechanism.

Factory patterns are used whenever large numbers of different objects within an object hierarchy must be dynamically created at run time. This can include AI objects, resources such as textures or sounds, or even more abstract objects such as game states (as in the previous discussion).

Summary

Developing good object-oriented techniques is not an end in itself. It should pervade every aspect of your code, which will save you time and trouble in the long run. Well-written object code is more flexible, more maintainable, and more extensible than procedural code. Game programmers have not adopted a complex new language and coding paradigm for their personal entertainment; there is a method to their madness.

There are several references listed at the end of this article. Do yourself a favor and immediately pick them up if you don't yet own them. They are indispensable tools in learning the finer points of both object-oriented programming and C++ language usage in general.

References

[Gamma94] Gamma, et. al., *Design Patterns,* Addison-Wesley Longman, Inc., 1994.

[Meyers98] Meyers, Scott, *Effective C++,* second edition, Addison-Wesley Longman, Inc., 1998.

[Meyers96] Meyers, Scott, *More Effective C++,* Addison-Wesley Longman, Inc., 1996.

[Petzold96] Petzold, Charles, *Programming Windows 95,* Microsoft Press, Inc., 1996.

1.2

Fast Math Using Template Metaprogramming

Pete Isensee

When programmers think of C++ templates, they usually think of things like the STL, generic containers, and type-safe macros. Most programmers are unaware that templates can act as virtual compilers, creating tremendously optimized code in terms of both speed and size. This unforeseen quality of templates was first noticed by Erwin Unruh in 1994. He presented the C++ Standards committee with a template program that didn't compile but instead coerced the compiler into generating a list of prime numbers in its error messages [Veldhuizen99].

This discovery led a number of language experts to focus on the use of templates as precompilers. Todd Veldhuizen and David Vandevoorde greatly expanded on this capability, showing that virtually any algorithm could be templatized, provided the input parameters to the algorithm were known at compile time [Veldhuizen95]. Given a good compiler, intermediate code can be completely optimized away, resulting in extraordinary efficiency.

The best way to see this in action is to consider a simple example.

Fibonacci Numbers

The Fibonacci sequence looks like this: 0, 1, 1, 2, 3, 5, 8, 13, ... The general equation for the sequence is *Fib(n) = Fib(n-1) + Fib(n-2)*. A typical function to recursively generate Fibonacci numbers is as follows:

```
unsigned RecursiveFib( unsigned n )
{
   if( n <= 1 )
      return n;
   return RecursiveFib( n-1 ) + RecursiveFib( n-2 );
}
```

Believe it or not, this simple function runs in *exponential* time. It's highly inefficient and should never be used in production code. The function is simply a stepping-off point for generating a templatized version:

```
template< unsigned N > struct Fib
{
   enum
   {
      // Recursive definition
      Val = Fib< N-1 >::Val + Fib< N-2 >::Val
   };
};

// Specialization for base cases
// (termination conditions)
template <> struct Fib< 0 > { enum { Val = 0 }; };
template <> struct Fib< 1 > { enum { Val = 1 }; };

// Make the template appear like a function
#define FibT( n ) Fib< n >::Val
```

An example "call" to the template via the #define:

```
std::cout << FibT( 4 ); // Fib< 4 >::Val
```

Some important things to note about the templatized version are as follows:

- The template function is not really a function at all—it's an enumerated integer called Val, recursively determined *at compile time*. The notation Val = Fib<N-1>::Val + Fib<N-2>::Val is uncommon but valid C++ syntax.
- Fib is defined as a struct to simplify the notation. Struct data is public by default, which is exactly what we want. Similar notation is used for all the following code listings.
- The template parameter N is used to specify the function input. This is an uncommon but perfectly acceptable use of template parameters. For example, std::bitset<N> uses the numeric value N as its template parameter to define the number of bits represented. This numeric parameter must be known at compile time. Calling FibT(i) when i is a non-const variable will generate a compiler error.
- To terminate the recursion, you must handle the base case properly. For Fibonacci numbers, the base case is when N is zero or one. With templates, the way to handle base cases is with template specialization. The notation template<> indicates a specialization. When N is zero or one, Val = N.

Now consider how a compiler might evaluate FibT(4):

```
= Fib<4>::Val
= Fib<3>::Val + Fib<2>::Val
= Fib<2>::Val + Fib<1>::Val + Fib<1>::Val + Fib<0>::Val
= Fib<1>::Val + Fib<0>::Val + 1 + 1 + 0
= 1 + 0 + 1 + 1 + 0
= 3
```

Since all inputs are known at compile time, a compiler can reduce `FibT(N)` to a constant. In other words, the compiler can produce *exactly the same* code as though you had written:

```
std::cout << 3; // Fib(4)
```

This is an amazing tool to have in your C++ tool kit. It's not every day you can go from *exponential run time* to *constant run time*. With template metaprogramming, the price you pay is additional compile time instead of additional execution time. For games, execution time is usually more critical than compile time, so this technique is very appealing.

Factorial

Here's another example of turning a standard function into a templatized version. First, the standard C++ version for reference:

```
unsigned RecursiveFact( unsigned n )
{
    return ((n <= 1) ? 1 : (n * RecursiveFact(n - 1)));
}
```

And the template metaprogram version:

```
// Templatized factorial(n)
template< unsigned N > struct Fact
{
    enum { Val = N * Fact< N - 1 >::Val };
};

// Specialization for base case
template <> struct Fact< 1 >
{
    enum { Val = 1 };
};

// Make the template appear like a function
#define FactT( n ) Fact< n >::Val
```

As in the Fibonacci example, the compiler can reduce a "call" such as `FactT(4)` to the constant 24. We've gone from linear run time to constant run time. That's a powerful argument for using metaprogramming. There are two drawbacks: a compile-time penalty, which is typically insignificant, and a code readability penalty, which can usually be hidden by a well-defined macro such as `FactT(n)`.

Let's step back for a moment. Template metaprogramming is compelling and undeniably efficient, but not many games require a Fibonacci sequence or factorial number generation. Even if they did, it's not likely that the code will know the required input parameters at compile time. Is this just a neat C++ party trick, or is this something that's actually useful?

Trigonometry

Time for a more complicated example. Let's take on the sine function. Many games use sine tables or a similar method for fast trig calculations. What if we could make the compiler read something like $x = sine(1.234)$ and generate a single move instruction? Template metaprogramming to the rescue!

Generating standard trig functions involves using a series expansion. For sines, the expansion looks like this:

$$sine(x) = x - (x^3 / 3!) + (x^5 / 5!) - (x^7 / 7!) + (x^9 / 9!) - \ldots$$

where x is in radians, $0 <= x < 2\pi$. To compute the terms efficiently, we can rewrite the expansion:

$$sine(x) = x * term(0)$$

where *term(n)* is computed recursively as:

$$term(n) = 1 - x^2 / (2n + 2) / (2n + 3) * term(n+1)$$

You can write this expansion without templates as follows:

```
double Sine( double fRad )
{
   const int iMaxTerms = 10;
   return fRad * SineSeries( fRad, 0, iMaxTerms );
}

double SineSeries( double fRad, int i, int iMaxTerms )
{
   if( i > iMaxTerms )
      return 1.0;

   return 1.0 - ( fRad * fRad / (2.0 * i + 2.0) / (2.0 * i + 3.0)
                  * SineSeries( fRad, i + 1, iMaxTerms ) );
}
```

Increasing iMaxTerms improves accuracy at the expense of run-time speed. It's not difficult to convert this to a templatized version. The solution is presented in Listing 1.2.1. The solution uses two template objects: Sine<R> computes $R * term(0)$ and Series<R,I> computes *term(I)* recursively out to the number of terms specified by MaxTerms. With the template metaprogramming version:

```
double x = SineT( 1.234 );
```

the compiler can theoretically generate the same code as though we had written:

```
double x = 0.94381820937463368;
```

The actual value of *sin(1.234)* is 0.94381820937463370..., so the template version, which evaluates 10 terms, is accurate to approximately 15 decimal places! Without much effort, we have a solution in which we can get sines for free (i.e., constant time) by using the compiler as the workhorse. We don't have to compute a table at run time or embed a table in our executable, because the compiler can generate the table entries we need (and *only* the ones we need) at compile time.

Compilers in the Real World

There's potentially a big problem with template metaprogramming. Many compilers available today (circa 2000) can't reduce the recursion and mathematics involved with complex template-based algorithms. In the sine example, evaluating the series expansion to 10 terms requires the compiler to reduce approximately 20 floating-point multiplications, 50 integer multiplications, 20 FP divides, 10 FP subtractions, and 10 recursive calls down to one or two move instructions. *Could* a compiler do that? Of course. *Should* a compiler do that? Probably, given ample resources (RAM and time). *Will* a compiler do that? It depends.

I tested the preceding examples using Microsoft Visual C++ 6.0. VC6 did a splendid job with the Fib and factorial templates, producing single move instructions for each. It had more difficulty on the sine template, generating code that is inferior even to the C run-time sin() function! By default, VC6 was able to unroll the recursion to only eight levels, and it hardly optimized the arithmetic at all. Using the VC6-specific `#pragmas inline_depth(255) and inline_recursion(on)` allowed VC6 to unroll the recursion completely and optimize away all the math, so fortunately, good results are still possible.

The moral of the story is that all optimizations are guilty until proven innocent. Examine the code produced by the compiler, and evaluate the performance before and after templates are introduced as an optimization. You might need to tweak some compiler flags to get the results you want. In the future, expect compiler writers to focus more heavily on template optimization and template metaprogramming itself. In the meantime, program softly and carry a big profiler.

Trigonometry Revisited

Given that C++ compiler technology is still immature when it comes to dealing with templates, is there anything we can do to improve our chances of the compiler doing the right thing? Listing 1.2.2 shows another attempt at the sine function. The recursion has been removed and the series expansion is inline out to 10 terms. We're down to 12 multiplications, 21 divides, and 10 subtractions. We've also eliminated the template specialization since it's no longer needed.

The resulting function is a bit easier to handle, from both a readability standpoint as well as a compiler standpoint. Indeed, VC6 has an easier time with this version. The special #pragmas are no longer required for the compiler to generate a constant.

At this point can we clearly see the benefits and drawbacks of the technique. Template metaprogramming can generate massive speed improvements—sometimes, but not always.

Templates and Standard C++

Not many compilers are completely compliant with the C++ standard, especially when it comes to templates. Templates are so flexible and powerful, compiler writers have a tough job getting them right. In no place is this more apparent than Visual C++, which was slow to adopt templates in the first place and slower still to conform to the standard. For example, VC6 does not support partial specialization, making the specialized versions for many of the template functions more complicated and less generic than they need to be.

Much more important, however, is the support or non-support of floating-point template parameters. The sine template functions in Listing 1.2.1 and Listing 1.2.2 use a floating-point template parameter for the incoming radian value. However, according to the C++ standard, "a non-type template-parameter shall not be declared to have floating point … type." In other words, on a conforming compiler,

```
template< double R > struct Sine // compiler error
```

gives an error message. The solution is to use a reference parameter instead:

```
template< double& R > struct Sine // OK
```

Interestingly and unfortunately, Visual C++ 6.0 *supports* floating-point types as template parameters but does *not* support references as parameters. It has things completely backward! To use the sine template code on conforming compilers, change `double R` to `double& R`.

Matrices

Where template metaprogramming really comes into its own is the handling of matrix operations. Three-dimensional games heavily use matrices. Templatizing key functions can generate noticeable speed improvements. In the following section, we use templates to improve initializing, transposing, and multiplying matrices.

Identity Matrices

The *identity matrix* contains elements whose values are zero, with the exception of the diagonal, which contains ones. We begin with a typical implementation. Note the embedded for loops:

```
matrix33& matrix33::identity()
{
    for (unsigned c = 0; c < 3; c++)
        for (unsigned r = 0; r < 3; r++)
            col[ c ][ r ] = ( c == r ) ? 1.0 : 0.0;
    return *this;
}
```

The template metaprogram version is shown in Listing 1.2.3. The parameters for the template version include the matrix Mtx, the size of the matrix N (a square matrix is assumed), the current row R and column C. At every iteration, we evaluate the next element of the matrix.

The key thing to notice is the method by which we loop over the columns and rows. At each step in the algorithm, we know I, which simply goes from 0 to N squared. Given I, we can compute the current row by taking I modulus N. For example, if N is 3, the row sequence would be: 0, 1, 2, 0, 1, 2, 0, 1, 2, 0. The current column is I divided by N mod N. If N is 3, the column sequence would be 0, 0, 0, 1, 1, 1, 2, 2, 2, 0. The template specialization terminates the algorithm when I reaches N squared. Now we can replace the original version with:

```
matrix33& matrix33::identity()
{
    IdentityMtxT( matrix33, *this, 3 );
    return *this;
}
```

The compiler can expand the new version to:

```
matrix33& matrix33::identity()
{
    col[ 0 ][ 0 ] = 1.0;
    col[ 0 ][ 1 ] = 0.0;
    // ...
    col[ 2 ][ 1 ] = 0.0;
    col[ 2 ][ 2 ] = 1.0;
    return *this;
}
```

In other words, the compiler can *completely unroll the loop*. Of course, we could have unrolled the loop ourselves, but the template version is a general solution. It will work for square matrices of *any* size (provided you include the specialization). For example, the code for 4×4 matrices would look like:

```
matrix44& matrix44::identity()
```

```
{
    IdentityMtxT( matrix44, *this, 4 );
    return *this;
}
```

Matrix Initialization

We can create templatized initialization code by using the same technique we used in generating the identity matrix. In fact, the only line that needs to change in Listing 1.2.3 is the line that determines each matrix element value:

```
mtx[ C ][ R ] = ( C == R ) ? 1.0 : 0.0; // identity matrix
```

which is replaced by:

```
mtx[ C ][ R ] = 0.0; // zero matrix
```

or more generally by:

```
mtx[ C ][ R ] = static_cast< F >( Init ); // init matrix
```

where F is the type of value stored in each element and Init is a numeric template parameter that defaults to zero. The general solution allows you to easily initialize matrix elements to any constant value.

Matrix Transposition

Transposing a matrix flips the matrix using the diagonal as the axis:

```
matrix33& matrix33::transpose()
{
    for (unsigned c = 0; c < 3; c++)
        for (unsigned r = c + 1; r < 3; r++)
            std::swap( col[ c ][ r ], col[ r ][ c ] );
    return *this;
}
```

This algorithm cries out for optimization because it does so little actual work. For a 3×3 matrix, there are only three swaps. For a 4×4 matrix, there are only six. Listing 1.2.4 shows the template implementation. We can now replace the original with:

```
matrix33& matrix33::transpose()
{
    TransMtxT( matrix33, *this, 3 );
    return *this;
}
```

which the compiler will expand to:

```
matrix33& matrix33::transpose()
```

```
    {
        std::swap( col[0][1], col[1][0] );
        std::swap( col[0][2], col[2][0] );
        std::swap( col[1][2], col[2][1] );
        return *this;
    }
```

The embedded for loops are optimized away, leaving only the swaps themselves. Swap itself is an inline function, so we're down to only nine move instructions. Doesn't get much better than that.

Matrix Multiplication

For our final look at metaprogramming, we templatize *matrix multiplication*. A typical non-templatized implementation looks like this:

```
    matrix33& matrix33::operator *= (const matrix33& m)
    {
        matrix33 t;
        for (unsigned r = 0; r < 3; r++)
        {
            for (unsigned c = 0; c < 3; c++)
            {
                t[c][r] = 0.0;
                for (unsigned k = 0; k < 3; k++)
                    t[c][r] += col[k][r] * m[c][k];
            }
        }
        *this = t;
        return *this;
    }
```

The corresponding template metaprogram version is shown in Listing 1.2.5. Matrix multiplication has an inner loop that becomes the additional template parameter K. Unlike the identity or transposition algorithms, which expand to N squared iterations, multiplication expands to N *cubed* iterations (note that the specializations take "N cubed" as a parameter). Now we can replace the original version with:

```
    matrix33& matrix33::operator *= (const matrix33& m)
    {
        matrix33 t;
        ZeroMtxT( matrix33, t, 3 );
        MultMtxT( matrix33, t, *this, m, 3 );
        *this = t;
        return *this;
    }
```

We initialize the resulting matrix to be empty (zeroed) so that the += operator in the MultMtxImpl template will work properly. The compiler can expand the new multiplication operator to something like this:

```
matrix33& matrix33::operator *= (const matrix33& m)
{
   matrix33 t;

   // ZeroMtxT
   t[0][0] = 0.0;
   // ...
   t[2][2] = 0.0;

   // MultMtxT
   t[0][0] += col[0][0] * m[0][0];
   t[0][0] += col[1][0] * m[0][1];
   // ...
   t[3][3] += col[2][0] * m[0][2];
   t[3][3] += col[3][0] * m[0][3];

   *this = t;
   return *this;
}
```

The multiplication template is a general solution for any square matrix. The code for any arbitrary $N \times N$ matrix would be:

```
matrixNN& matrixNN::operator *= (const matrixNN& m)
{
   matrixNN t;
   ZeroMtxT( matrixNN, t, N );
   MultMtxT( matrixNN, t, *this, m, N );
   *this = t;
   return *this;
}
```

Actual Matrix Performance

How efficient are the templatized matrix operations? The general-purpose answer is that your mileage will vary depending on the quality of the compiler and the compiler options you choose.

I tested the matrix operations using VC6 with full optimizations, optimizing for speed, using the inline option "any suitable" and the #pragmas `inline_depth(255)` and `inline_recursion(on)`. I benchmarked each operation 100 million times, with the results shown in Table 1.2.1. All times are in milliseconds. The Unrolled column indicates whether or not the compiler was able to unroll the recursion.

To see relative performance, I graphed these results to show how much faster the templatized versions operated compared with the non-templatized versions (see Figure 1.2.1).

With the exception of multiplying 4×4 matrices, the templatized versions were all considerably faster. Not surprisingly, the matrix transposition operations showed the best improvements. In the cases of the simpler algorithms, the compiler was able to completely unroll the template recursion. However, for multiplying 4×4 matrices

Table 1.2.1 Matrix Operation Test Results

Operation	Non-Templatized (in Milliseconds)	Templatized (in Milliseconds)	Unrolled
matrix33::zero	33,992	29,330	Completely
matrix44::zero	36,063	30,292	Completely
matrix33::identity	45,827	29,526	Completely
matrix44::identity	46,845	29,905	Completely
matrix33::transpose	35,338	29,955	Completely
matrix44::transpose	90,638	30,245	Partially
matrix33::op *=	62,904	50,352	Partially
matrix44::op *=	326,890	792,901	Partially

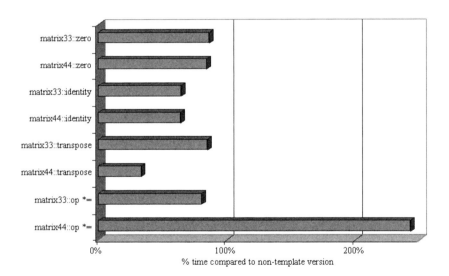

FIGURE 1.2.1. Relative performance of template functions.

(4^3 operations), the compiler only partially unrolled the recursion, and the overhead of the recursive function calls far outweighed any inlining improvements, so the resulting function was much slower than the original. These results simply show the importance of profiling your "optimizations."

Summary

Templates can be a highly effective way of generating algorithms directly in the instruction stream. The ability to reduce and unroll code in a generic way can be a very powerful programming technique. The notation for template metaprogramming is unusual at first, but it's not much more difficult than examining standard recursive calls. Macros can be used to hide the notation from the calling code.

The metaprogramming technique can be extended to a wide variety of functions, including square-root calculations, greatest common divisors, matrix inversions—even sorting. Any algorithm for which at least some of the input parameters are known at compile time can benefit from template metaprogramming.

Current compilers are still limited in dealing with templates, especially recursive templates. Compiler template error messages can range from cryptic to undecipherable. As with any optimization, there is often a time and space tradeoff. In many cases, template metaprogramming can generate the best of both worlds: very small and fast code. In other cases, unrolled code can be much larger than the original version, reducing or even eliminating the speed advantage. Nevertheless, expect to see template metaprogramming play a significant role in C++ libraries and games of the future.

Listing 1.2.1

```cpp
// Series expansion for sin( R ).
// For conforming compilers, change double R to double& R
template< double R > struct Sine
{
    enum { MaxTerms = 10 }; // increase for accuracy
    static inline double sin()
    {
        return R * Series< R, 0, MaxTerms >::val();
    }
};

template< double R, int I, int MaxTerms >
struct Series
{
    enum
    {
        // Continue is true until we've evaluated M terms
        Continue = I + 1 != MaxTerms,
        NxtI = ( I + 1 ) * Continue,
        NxtMaxTerms = MaxTerms * Continue
    };

    // Recursive definition called once per term
    static inline double val()
    {
        return 1 - R * R / (2.0 * I + 2.0) /
               (2.0 * I + 3.0) * Series< R * Continue, NxtI,
                                         NxtMaxTerms >::val();
    }
};

// Specialization to terminate the loop
```

```
template <> struct Series< 0.0, 0, 0 >
{
    static inline double val() { return 1.0; }
};

// Make the template appear like a function
#define SineT( r ) Sine< r >::sin()
```

Listing 1.2.2

```
// Series expansion for sin( R ).
// For conforming compilers, change double R to double& R
template < double R > struct Sine
{
    // All values known at compile time.
    // A decent compiler should be able to reduce
    // to a single constant.
    static inline double sin()
    {
        double Rsqr = R * R;
        return R * ( 1.0 - Rsqr / 2.0  / 3.0
                   * ( 1.0 - Rsqr / 4.0  / 5.0
                   * ( 1.0 - Rsqr / 6.0  / 7.0
                   * ( 1.0 - Rsqr / 8.0  / 9.0
                   * ( 1.0 - Rsqr / 10.0 / 11.0
                   * ( 1.0 - Rsqr / 12.0 / 13.0
                   * ( 1.0 - Rsqr / 14.0 / 15.0
                   * ( 1.0 - Rsqr / 16.0 / 17.0
                   * ( 1.0 - Rsqr / 18.0 / 19.0
                   * ( 1.0 - Rsqr / 20.0 / 21.0
                   ) ) ) ) ) ) ) ) ) );
    }
};

// Make the template appear like a function
#define SineT( r ) Sine< r >::sin()
```

Listing 1.2.3

```
// Templatized identity matrix; N is matrix size
template< class Mtx, unsigned N > struct IdMtx
{
    static inline void eval( Mtx& mtx )
    {
        IdMtxImpl< Mtx, N, 0, 0, 0 >::eval( mtx );
    }
};

// Assigns each element of the matrix
template< class Mtx, unsigned N, unsigned C, unsigned R,
          unsigned I >
struct IdMtxImpl
{
```

```
    enum
    {
       NxtI = I + 1,            // Counter
       NxtR = NxtI % N,         // Row (inner loop)
       NxtC = NxtI / N % N      // Column (outer loop)
    };
    static inline void eval( Mtx& mtx )
    {
       mtx[ C ][ R ] = ( C == R ) ? 1.0 : 0.0;
       IdMtxImpl< Mtx, N, NxtC, NxtR, NxtI >::eval( mtx );
    }
};

// Specialize for 3x3 and 4x4 matrix
template<> struct IdMtxImpl< matrix33, 3, 0, 0, 3*3 >
{
    static inline void eval( matrix33& ) {}
};
template<> struct IdMtxImpl< matrix44, 4, 0, 0, 4*4 >
{
    static inline void eval( matrix44& ) {}
};

// Make the template appear like a function
#define IdentityMtxT( MtxType, Mtx, N ) \
        IdMtx< MtxType, N >::eval( Mtx )
```

Listing 1.2.4

```
// Templatized transpose; N is matrix size
template< class Mtx, unsigned N > struct TransMtx
{
    static inline void eval( Mtx& mtx )
    {
       TransMtxImpl< Mtx, N, 0, 1, 0 >::eval( mtx );
    }
};

template< class Mtx, unsigned N, unsigned C, unsigned R,
          unsigned I >
struct TransMtxImpl
{
    enum
    {
       NxtI = I + 1,
       NxtC = NxtI / N % N,
       NxtR = ( NxtI % N ) + NxtC + 1
    };
    static inline void eval( Mtx& mtx )
    {
       if( R < N )
          std::swap( mtx[ C ][ R ], mtx[ R ][ C ] );
       TransMtxImpl< Mtx, N, NxtC, NxtR, NxtI >::eval( mtx );
    }
```

```
};

// Specialize for 3x3 and 4x4 matrix
template<> struct TransMtxImpl< matrix33, 3, 0, 1, 3*3 >
{
    static inline void eval( matrix33& ) {}
};
template<> struct TransMtxImpl< matrix44, 4, 0, 1, 4*4 >
{
    static inline void eval( matrix44& ) {}
};

// Make the template appear like a function
#define TransMtxT( MtxType, Mtx, N ) \
        TransMtx< MtxType, N >::eval( Mtx )
```

Listing 1.2.5

```
// Templatized multiplication; N is matrix size
template< class Mtx, unsigned N > struct MultMtx
{
    static inline void eval( Mtx& r, const Mtx& a, const Mtx& b )
    {
        MultMtxImpl< Mtx, N, 0, 0, 0, 0 >::eval( r, a, b );
    }
};

template< class Mtx, unsigned N, unsigned C, unsigned R,
          unsigned K, unsigned I >
struct MultMtxImpl
{
    enum
    {
        NxtI = I + 1,           // Counter
        NxtK = NxtI % N,        // Internal loop
        NxtC = NxtI / N % N,    // Column
        NxtR = NxtI / N / N % N // Row
    };
    static inline void eval( Mtx& r, const Mtx& a, const Mtx& b )
    {
        r[ C ][ R ] += a[ K ][ R ] * b[ C ][ K ];
        MultMtxImpl< Mtx,N,NxtC,NxtR,NxtK,NxtI >::eval( r,a,b );
    }
};

// Specialize for 3x3 and 4x4 matrix
template<> struct MultMtxImpl< matrix33, 3, 0, 0, 0, 3*3*3 >
{
    static inline void eval( matrix33&, const matrix33&,
                             const matrix33& ) {}
};
template<> struct MultMtxImpl< matrix44, 4, 0, 0, 0, 4*4*4 >
{
    static inline void eval( matrix44&, const matrix44&,
```

```
                                      const matrix44& ) {}
};

// Make the template appear like a function
#define MultMtxT( MtxType, r, a, b, N )         \
        MultMtx< MtxType, N >::eval( r, a, b )
```

References

[Veldhuizen99] Veldhuizen, Todd, "Techniques for Scientific C++." Available www.extreme.indiana.edu/~tveldhui/papers/techniques/, August 1999.

[Veldhuizen98] Veldhuizen, Todd, et al., "Blitz++ Numerical Class Library." Available www.oonumerics.org/blitz/,August 1998.

[Veldhuizen96] Veldhuizen, Todd, and Kumaraswamy Ponnambalam, "Linear Algebra with C++ Template Metaprograms," *Dr. Dobb's Journal*, August 1996.

[Veldhuizen95] Veldhuizen, Todd, "Using C++ Template Metaprograms," *C++ Report,* May 1995.

[Pescio97] Pescio, Carlo, "Binary Constants Using Template Metaprogramming," *C/C++ Users Journal*, February 1997.

[Karmesin99] Karmesin, Steve, et al., "PETE, Portable Extension Template Engine," Available www.acl.lanl.gov/pete/, February 1999.

1.3

An Automatic Singleton Utility

Scott Bilas

This article presents an easy and safe method to provide access to a C++ class singleton while retaining control over when it is instantiated and destroyed.

Definition

A *singleton* is an object that has only one instance in a system at any time. Some common examples of singletons in games are managers for texture maps, files, or the user interface. Each is a subsystem that's generally assumed to be available once the game has started and will stay in existence until the game shuts down.

Some of these subsystems can be implemented using global functions and static variables. An example would be a memory manager's `malloc()` and `free()` functions. These types of subsystems are not singletons in that they don't have their functionality encapsulated into a class and can't be represented using a single instance of that class. There's no reason a memory manager such as this couldn't be converted into a class and used as a singleton, but this practice isn't common.

An example of a singleton is a *texture map manager*. It could be called `TextureMgr` and have methods such as `GetTexture()` and `UseTexture()`. Its purpose would be to find texture maps in the file store, convert them to system graphics objects, make them available to the rasterizer(s), and own them until they are no longer needed, at which point it deletes them. Only one instance of `TextureMgr` will be needed in the system, so this class would naturally be used as a singleton.

Advantages

What's the point of singletons? First, they provide conceptual clarity because labels are very important. Calling a class a singleton and following a naming convention (such as `-Mgr`, `-Api`, `Global-`, etc.) relates important details about how we intend that class to be used.

Singletons also provide notational convenience. Every object in a C++ system must be owned by something. The ownership pattern of these objects depends on the game, but it often resembles a multilevel hierarchy, in which each higher level owns a set of child objects, each of which in turn can own child objects. Each object publishes a set of functions to access its children. For example, to get at the `TextureMgr` instance, you might need to call a sequence of functions such as `GetApp()->GetServices()->GetGui()->GetTextureMgr()`, where each function returns a pointer to the requested child object. This system is inconvenient and not exactly efficient, considering the multiple dereferences. Singletons can solve this problem because they are treated as global objects.

The Problem

Well, then why not just use global objects? They are certainly convenient; the `TextureMgr` object could be accessed through a `g_TextureMgr` object reference that has been declared with external linkage at global scope (or within a namespace) or perhaps through a function that returns a reference to that object instead. However, the construction and destruction order of global objects is implementation dependent and generally impossible to predict in a portable manner.

There are workarounds to all these problems, but what we really want is a way to have the convenience advantage of treating a singleton like a global object, without the inconvenience of losing control over when and where it gets constructed and destroyed.

Traditional Solution

The textbook solution to managing a singleton usually looks something like this:

```
TextureMgr& GetTextureMgr( void )
{
    static T s_Singleton;
    return ( s_Singleton );
}
```

There are many variations that use templates and macros for notational convenience, but the effect is still the same. This solution allows a singleton to only be instantiated on demand—the first time this function is called. It's convenient to use, but it leaves its destruction up to the compiler and requires that it be done only at application shutdown time. We need more control than that. Order of destruction is very important in a game in that some subsystems must be shut down and destroyed before others. Furthermore, what if we want to shut down only part of the game while it's still running? Doing so is impossible with this solution.

A Better Way

All we're really after is the ability to track a singleton, and for that what we need is a pointer to it. What if we were to do something like this:

```
class TextureMgr
{
    static TextureMgr* ms_Singleton;

public:
    TextureMgr( void )  {  ms_Singleton = this;  /*...*/  }
    ~TextureMgr( void )  {  ms_Singleton = 0;     /*...*/  }

    // ...

    TextureMgr& GetSingleton( void )  {  return ( *ms_Singleton );  }
};
```

Add a few assertions for safety purposes, and this solution would work! We can now construct and destroy a TextureMgr wherever we like, and accessing the singleton is as simple as calling TextureMgr::GetSingleton(). However, this solution is still a little inconvenient, given that the same code (to track the singleton pointer) needs to be added to every singleton class.

An Even Better Way

A more generic solution is to use templates to automatically define the singleton pointer and do the work of setting it, querying it, and clearing it. It can also check (through assert()) to make sure that we aren't accidentally instantiating more than one. Best of all, we can get all this functionality for free just by deriving from this simple little class:

```
#include <cassert>

template <typename T> class Singleton
{
    static T* ms_Singleton;

public:
    Singleton( void )
    {
        assert( !ms_Singleton );
        int offset = (int)(T*)1 - (int)(Singleton <T>*)(T*)1;
        ms_Singleton = (T*)((int)this + offset);
    }
    ~Singleton( void )
        {  assert( ms_Singleton );  ms_Singleton = 0;  }
    static T& GetSingleton( void )
        {  assert( ms_Singleton );  return ( *ms_Singleton );  }
    static T* GetSingletonPtr( void )
```

```
                { return ( ms_Singleton );  }
    };

    template <typename T> T* Singleton <T>::ms_Singleton = 0;
```

To convert any class into a singleton, you only need to do these three easy steps:

1. Publicly derive your class `MyClass` from `Singleton <MyClass>`.
2. Make sure that you're constructing an instance of `MyClass` somewhere in the system before using it. How you instantiate it doesn't matter. You can let the compiler worry about it by making it a global or local static, or you can worry about it yourself via `new` and `delete` through an owner class. Regardless of how and when you construct the instance, it will get tracked and could be used as a singleton through a common interface by the rest of the system.
3. Call `MyClass::GetSingleton()` to use the object from anywhere in the system. If you're lazy like me, you can `#define g_MyClass` to be `MyClass::GetSingleton()` and treat it exactly like a global object for notational convenience.

Here is a sample usage of the class:

```
class TextureMgr : public Singleton <TextureMgr>
{
public:
    Texture* GetTexture( const char* name );
    // ...
};

#define g_TextureMgr TextureMgr::GetSingleton()

void SomeFunction( void )
{
    Texture* stone1 = TextureMgr::GetSingleton().GetTexture( "stone1" );
    Texture* wood6 = g_TextureMgr.GetTexture( "wood6" );
    // ...
}
```

The `Singleton` class's only purpose in life is to automatically register and unregister any instance of its derived (`MyClass`) type as it is constructed and destroyed. We're deriving `MyClass` from `Singleton <MyClass>` purely to inherit this convenient functionality. This doesn't affect the size of the class in any way; it only adds some automatic function calls.

So how does this work? All the important work is done in the `Singleton` constructor, where it figures out the relative address of the derived instance and stores the result in the singleton pointer (`ms_Singleton`). Note that the derived class could be deriving from more than just the `Singleton`, in which case "this" from `MyClass` might be different from the `Singleton` "this." The solution is to take a nonexistent object sitting at address `0x1` in memory, cast it to both types, and see the difference. This difference will effectively be the distance between `Singleton <MyClass>` and its derived type `MyClass`, which it can use to calculate the singleton pointer.

References

Meyers, Scott, *More Effective C++*, Addison-Wesley Publishing Co., 1995.

1.4

Using the STL in Game Programming

James Boer

In 1997, C++ was officially standardized, ending a nine-year process that not only defined the official language specifications but also gave C++ programmers a massive new set of tools in the form of the standard C++ library. A large portion of this library is the *Standard Template Library,* or *STL.* The STL is a collection of container (collections of data) classes, ranging from vectors to balanced binary trees. In addition to the basic containers, the STL provides a massive assortment of algorithms that can operate on those basic containers.

A common concern is whether using STL will slow down your code. The truth of the matter is that the STL was designed with speed as a foremost priority. For instance, vectors do no bounds checking, and iterators are never validated before attempting to access a container. The net result is that, for example, STL vectors can produce code with performance equivalent to that of a simple dynamically allocated array. Other containers fare just as well when put under the performance microscope. The STL was designed for high-efficiency C++ applications. Don't lose sleep about using them extensively in your code.

STL Types and Terminology

The STL is a large and somewhat complex portion of the Standard C++ library. Using the STL effectively requires the understanding of the basic components and how they work together.

Containers

STL containers represent the classic data abstractions and organization schemes such as vectors, lists, queues, and maps. However, we should make a few distinctions between certain types of containers and how they are implemented.

The STL containers' vector, list, and deque (pronounced "deck") are implicit data types that both describe an abstract data type and imply a specific method of implementation. A *vector* is, of course, a dynamically resizable array. The *list* is implemented as a double-linked list. A *deque,* or double-ended queue, is implemented in a manner that allows amortized constant time insertion or deletion of elements at either end of a randomly accessible array-type structure. Deques are also known as *sequence containers* because they store ordered sets of data, meaning that the order in which you insert the data affects the order in which they are stored.

Containers such as stack, queue, and priority_queue are slightly higher-level abstractions. They describe a container's behavior but allow for different types of underlying implementations. For example, a queue might be implemented using a vector, list, or deque internally. These are known as *container adapters*. Container adapters, because they rely on sequence containers as their underlying data, also fall into that category as well.

Other containers, such as a map, set, multimap, or multiset, are all implemented internally as red-black trees (balanced binary trees) but offer different container behaviors. These are also known as *associative containers* because the data inserted into them is ordered based on a certain sorting criteria.

Iterators

Iterators can be thought of as pointers to elements in the containers, and indeed the STL even uses pointer notation for traversal and access to container data. For instance, the ++ operator moves the iterator to the next element in a container, much the way a pointer to an element in an array can be incremented. In addition, like pointers, the actual data can be accessed by dereferencing the iterator using the * operator.

Algorithms

Unlike what you might expect, *algorithms* designed to operate on STL classes do not come in the form of member functions of the container classes. Instead, they exist in the form of stand-alone functions that operate on iterators. Why did the designers of STL choose this seemingly anti-OOP design paradigm?

By separating the data from the algorithms, the designers dramatically reduced the number of combinations of specialized algorithms. Since each container has similar types of iterators, each algorithm had to be written only once instead of once for each container. The downside is that there are sometimes less than obvious side effects or suboptimal solutions. In most cases, however, specialized member functions are all you need to perform most basic operations on your containers.

STL Concepts

A few basic concepts are important to working with the STL. First, it is important to understand the methods used to determine ranges when working with a container. Two methods common to all containers begin() and end(), return the full range of the container. As you can see in Figure 1.4.1, `begin()` returns the first element in the container, but `end()` returns the position *beyond the last valid element.*

There are several advantages to organizing the ranges in this manner. First, special-case coding for empty lists is eliminated. Second, iterating through containers has a simple ending criteria: continue as long as `end()` is not reached. The disadvantages of this system are that it is somewhat less intuitive, and reverse iteration requires special members and iterators.

It obviously becomes important to remember not to dereference an iterator that is pointing at `end()`. Such behavior is undefined.

When you use functions specifying a range, functions in STL usually take as parameters two iterators, one specifying the beginning element and one specifying the end element. To pair effectively with `begin()` and `end()`, these functions assume an inclusion of the first element specified and exclusion of the last element specified. Mathematically, the following notation usually designates this sort of range:

range [begin...end)

There is another aspect of the STL design of which you should be aware. STL containers pass information by value, not by reference. This means that when dealing with small data types, it is acceptable to allow the container to make a copy of the data. With larger data structures or classes, it becomes advantageous to pass in pointers to these objects or structs. Otherwise, every insertion or access results in a copy constructor being called.

Vectors

STL *vectors* are essentially resizable arrays. Note that although the formal C++ standard does not specify what underlying data structures are to be used for containers, the performance and interface requirements leave little ambiguity as to how they will be implemented in practice. Thus, all versions of STL will likely be very similar, with only minor variations in implementation details.

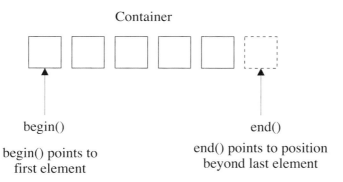

FIGURE 1.4.1. `end()` points after the last valid element.

Vectors behave almost identically to standard C arrays, with one major exception: they are dynamically resizable. However, it is important to understand the nature of this resizing.

Vectors are implemented as arrays that periodically need to reallocate memory and transfer data to a new array. This means two things for developers. First, a vector can allocate more memory than it currently needs, due to the requirement that it might be expected to grow at any time. Second, adding an element to the end of a vector is described as *constant time*—it is important to remember that this means *amortized constant time*. In other words, some grow functions can require a substantial amount of resources as they allocate new memory, copy the existing array into this new block, and delete the old memory, but they do not require these extra resources every time. Depending on implementation, a vector can allocate twice its current allocated memory when it runs out of buffer space.

It is also critical that you understand when a vector reallocates memory, since doing so invalidates any iterators currently pointing to elements in the vector. Let's examine the functions to help more precisely manage a vector's internal memory, after viewing the code:

```
#include <vector>
#include <iostream>

using namespace std;

// Typedef the container and iterator names for better
// readability
typedef vector<int> IntVector;
typedef IntVector::iterator IntVectItor;

void main()
{
    // Create a vector object of integers
    IntVector c;
    // Reserve room for 10 integers
    c.reserve(10);

    // Fill the vector with 3 different elements
    c.push_back(3);
    c.push_back(99);
    c.push_back(42);

    // Now loop and print out all the element values
    for(IntVectItor itor = c.begin(); itor != c.end(); ++itor)
        cout << "element value = " << (*itor) << endl;

    // Since the elements have been created, we can access or
    // replace them just like a normal array.
    c[0] = 12;
    c[1] = 32;
```

```
        c[2] = 999;
        for(int i = 0; i < c.size(); i++)
            cout << "element value = " << c[i] << endl;
    }
```

This example shows most of the basic principles you need to know to start using STL containers. Notice at the top of the listing the inclusion of the appropriate header files for this program. In addition, note the usage of namespace std. Like all portions of the C++ library, the STL is part of the std namespace and so requires you to declare such in your program.

Next, we see typedefs for the type of container and iterator we want to use in the program. This is a very common practice; it not only makes the code easier to read, but it becomes easier to change the underlying data structure, if desired. (We'll see how easy that is next.)

The next section of code creates the vector container object v and proceeds to call a vector-only function that reserves 10 integers' worth of memory. The code proceeds to push_back() 3 integers onto the back of the vector. Since we have preallocated well over this amount of memory, no additional memory allocation is required.

There are a few routines that you might find helpful when you want to closely monitor and control the allocation of your vector's memory. As shown, you can reserve a buffer in the vector by calling reserve() and passing a size parameter. This value can be retrieved by calling capacity(). If capacity()==reserve() and another element is inserted into the array, a memory allocation will take place and all current iterators will be invalidated. In order to determine the maximum amount of memory that can be allocated for a single vector, use the max_size() function.

The push_front(), push_back(), pop_front(), and pop_back() functions are common to all basic ordered containers (vector, list, and deque). These functions obviously add and remove elements from the front and back of the container. Due to the implementation of a vector, you want to avoid push_front() or pop_front() on these types of containers, if possible, due to the $O(n)$ performance, but they are available for use if you absolutely need them.

The final portion of sample code demonstrates one of the most commonly used components of STL usage: the iteration loop. We use a for loop with an iterator determining the current position. The initial position is set to begin(), and the iterator increments with the prefix ++ operator until the iterator equals end(), at which point the exit condition of the loop is satisfied. Every container with an accessible iterator can be looped through in this manner.

Since the iterator is the only item keeping track of the current position in the vector, we must use it to extract any information we want. We can see that in keeping with the notion of a pointer, we simply dereference the iterator to access the data.

After the standard iteration loop, we see an example of a vector in use like a typical array. It is important to note that array subscripting cannot be used to insert elements into a list—only to access existing elements.

Lists

The STL *list* is perhaps the most widely used of the basic STL structures. It is implemented as a doubly linked list, so any insertion and deletion of elements is done in true constant time. The tradeoff for this capability is the loss of random access that the vector and deque allow.

One beauty of using STL containers is the consistent naming conventions and methods used throughout the library. Once you learn the basics of manipulating one type of container, you essentially know how to use them all.

Using a list is even simpler than using a vector. The push_front() and push_back() functions work exactly as you would expect. Iterating through the list also works exactly as we saw in the vector example. In this code, we see many of the same techniques used in the vector class:

```
#include <list>
#include <iostream>

using namespace std;

class Foo
{
public:
    Foo(int i)              { m_iData = i; }
    void SetData(int i)     { m_iData = i; }
    int GetData()           { return m_iData; }
private:
    int m_iData;
};

// Typedef the container and iterator names for better
// readability
typedef list<Foo*> FooList;
typedef FooList::iterator FooListItor;

void main()
{
    // Create a list container of integers
    FooList c;

    // Fill the list with 3 different elements
    c.push_back(new Foo(1));
    c.push_back(new Foo(2));
    c.push_back(new Foo(3));

    // Iterator through the list
    for(FooListItor itor = c.begin(); itor != c.end();)
    {
        if((*itor)->GetData() == 2)
            // demonstrates proper method of removing an
            // element from the middle of the list.
        {
            delete (*itor);
```

```
                        itor = c.erase(itor);
                    }
                    else
                        ++itor;
                }

                // Make sure to delete all the objects, since the list
                // destructor will not do this automatically for you
                for(FooListItor itor2 = c.begin(); itor2 != c.end();
                    ++itor2)
                    delete (*itor2);
            }
```

We see in this example the same basic type of container manipulation, but we have added the wrinkle of using user-defined objects instead of built-in data types. This is a much more common usage scenario, so we examine how it differs in practice from inserting data by value.

STL containers do not operate on the data you pass into them. Rather, they make copies of the data they receive and distribute. In order to negate the cost of copying large data structures in memory, you'll want to pass pointers to larger, dynamically allocated objects. Naturally, our objects are ridiculously small for example purposes, but they could conceivably be large enough to seriously affect performance if we copied a large number of them.

There are a few things to remember when working with pointers to dynamically allocated structs or objects. First, and perhaps most obviously, is that you are responsible for freeing any allocated memory when you are finished with the objects. Since the container has no idea what type of data might be used, there is no way for the container to automatically deallocate memory for you.

Second, and perhaps less obvious, is that many operations appear to fail because they are operating directly on the object or struct pointers instead of on the objects or structs themselves. Take the list's sort() function, for example. It operates by using the < operator to determine value and sort accordingly. Even if a proper operator is designed for class Foo, the list still sorts on the actual value of the pointer, not by the value of the data in the object.

It therefore becomes necessary to design your own compare operator that dereferences the pointers before comparing them. See the sample code in the article "Resource and Memory Management," by James Boer, to see how this comparison can easily be done.

The third "gotcha" is appropriate to all pointer manipulation routines but also bears mentioning in the context of STL. When copying containers, remember that only the pointers are being copied, not the objects. If you create duplicate pointers, it could become extremely difficult to know which objects to delete. There are only two solutions to this problem: Use smart pointers with your objects or avoid STL routines and algorithms that copy elements from container to container.

You should also be wary of removing an element from a list while iterating through the list. Since removing an element to which you are currently pointing invalidates the iterator, you must be sure to make proper use of the erase() function's return value, which retrieves the next valid position in the container. By assigning this return value to the old iterator, we essentially skip ahead of the invalidated position. However, this leaves us with another problem. Since we've already incremented the iterator to the next position, we run into trouble when the for loop tries to increment it again at the end of the loop. To solve this problem, we remove the increment operator from the body of the for loop and place it conditionally inside the loop itself, incrementing only when an element is not erased.

It is often preferable to use algorithms to erase elements from a container instead of iterating through them manually. Algorithms such as remove_if() perform the same operation safely and efficiently. Unfortunately, a complete listing and description of the provided algorithms (and how to create your own) could fill up an entire book, so I recommend the resources listed at the end of this article for further study.

Deques

Deques, or double-ended queues, are designed for situations in which inserting and removing elements from either end of the container must be performed, but inserting and removing elements from the middle of the container is not required (or doesn't have to occur often). Like vectors, deques can perform insertions and removals at the front and back of the container in amortized constant time, and inserting or deleting elements from the middle is somewhat slow. Deques also allow random access, but because of the slightly more complex nature of the internal data of a deque, which is arranged in a linked series of memory blocks, random access is not quite as efficient as with vectors. Unlike vectors, though, there is no mechanism in place for determining exactly when additional memory allocations will take place.

```
#include <deque>
#include <iostream>

using namespace std;

// Typedef the container and iterator names for better
// readability
typedef deque<int> IntDeque;
typedef IntDeque::reverse_iterator IntDequeRItor;

void main()
{
    // Create a deque container of integers
    IntDeque c;

    // Fill the deque with 3 different elements
    c.push_front(3);
    c.push_front(2);
```

```
c.push_front(1);
c.push_back(3);
c.push_back(2);
c.push_back(1);

// Cycle BACKWARD through the list - special iterators and

// notation is necessary to do this.
for(IntDequeRItor ritor = c.rbegin(); ritor != c.rend();
    ++ritor)
    cout << "Value = " << (*ritor) << endl;

// remove the first and last elements
c.pop_front();
c.pop_back();

// Accessing elements directly - if needed remember to
// check to see the deque is not empty. Accessing non-
// existent elements will lead to undefined behavior;
// probably an access violation
if(!c.empty())
{
    cout << "Front = " << c.front() << endl;
    cout << "Back = " << c.back() << endl;
}
}
```

We see in the preceding listing the familiar code of STL usage, but with a few new twists this time. First, let's introduce the reverse iterator. You might notice that all our iterations up to this point have been in the positive direction. Although bidirectional iterators do exist, it often is much simpler to create a dedicated *reverse iterator* and utilize it as you use the standard iterator.

The reason we need a reverse iterator is that because of the bounding conditions of a container (illustrated in Figure 1.4.1), we can't simply iterate backward and expect to be able to check for the same exit conditions (itor != begin()). This would leave the first element in a container out of the iteration loop. Instead, we utilize a reverse iterator combined with the rbegin() and rend() functions. These functions work exactly like their forward-looking cousins, but rbegin() actually accesses the last element, whereas rend() points to a position in front of the first valid entry. This exactly mirrors the forward versions of these functions. Because the reverse iterator travels backward when the increment operator is applied, you can use the exact same syntax for looping through all elements in a container.

In this example, we also introduce the opposites of push_front() and push_back(), pop_front() and pop_back(). These functions simply remove an element from the front or back of a container, respectively. Note that the value of the element is not returned. You must use two more functions we introduce in this example to access the front or back elements: front() and back(). These functions return the value of the front or back element in the container. In the example, we check to ensure that the container is not empty using the empty() function before trying to access these elements. Accessing elements in an empty list results in "undefined behavior," which you can expect to probably result in some sort of access violation; `pop_front()` and `pop_back()`simply are "no-ops" when performed on an empty container.

Maps

STL *maps* are perhaps the most complex (relatively speaking) of the basic containers to use and perhaps the most versatile. Here we examine maps instead of the other tree-based structures: sets, multisets, and multimaps. Learning the fundamentals of maps allows you to easily use the other container types, so we leave that research up to you.

The map is essentially a value-pairing container. Two arbitrary types of data are paired as a key/value structure and inserted into the container. Looking up the value via the key then can occur in `0(log n)` time. Although not quite as efficient as a hash table, the difference is often negligible and has the advantage of sorting the data during insertion. This process allows iteration of completely sorted data, which is a beneficial consequence of the method of storage (a balanced binary tree, otherwise known as a *red-black tree*).

```cpp
#pragma warning(disable:4786)
#include <map>
#include <iostream>
#include <string>
#include <algorithm>

using namespace std;

// This function object allows us to compare map containers
template <class F, class S>
class value_equals
{
private:
    S second;
public:
    value_equals(const S& s) : second(s)
    {}
    bool operator() (pair<const F, S> elem)
    { return elem.second == second; }
};


// Typedef the container and iterator names for better
// readability
typedef map<int, string> isMap;
typedef isMap::value_type isValType;
typedef isMap::iterator isMapItor;

void main()
{
    isMap c;
```

```
// Insert key / value pairs
c.insert(isValType(100, "One Hundred"));
c.insert(isValType(3, "Three"));
c.insert(isValType(150, "One Hundred Fifty"));
c.insert(isValType(99, "Ninety Nine"));

// display all the keys and values
for(isMapItor itor = c.begin(); itor != c.end(); ++itor)
    cout << "Key = " << (*itor).first << ", Value = "
    << (*itor).second << endl;

// You can also access the map like an associative array
cout << "Key 3 displays value " << c[3].c_str() << endl;

// Or insert like this as well
c[123] = "One Hundred Twenty Three";

// Find and remove a specific element based on the key
isMapItor pos = c.find(123);
if(pos != c.end())
    // erasing an element invalidates any iterators
    // pointing to it.  Calling pos++ now would result in
    // undefined behavior.
    c.erase(pos);

// Find and remove an element based on the value
pos = find_if(c.begin(), c.end(), value_equals
    <int, string>("Ninety Nine"));
if(pos != c.end())
    c.erase(pos);

// If you must remove elements while iterating through
// the list...
for(isMapItor itr = c.begin(); itr != c.end(); )
{
    if(itr->second == "Three")
        c.erase(itr++);
    else
        ++itr;
}
}
```

We're introduced to a new intermediate data type in this example, the *value_type*, which represents the key/data pair representing every element in the container. For convenience, we've typedef'ed this type along with the other usual types.

Inserting combined key/data values uses the insert() function like any other container, with the only difference being that you must insert type map::value_type. The map sorts every entry as it is inserted, so at any given time the container is always sorted by keys. We can see this as we iterate through the map and display all the keys and their associated values.

Accessing keys and data through iterators means an additional structure to navigate through. Dereferencing the iterator returns the value_type structure, which has two data members: first and second. Accessing first gives you the key value; accessing second gives you the data value.

In addition to access through iterators, maps also provide random access via their key values. The map acts like an associative (or sparse) array. Elements can be accessed or inserted using the index() operator. Caution must be used when using this operator, however. If you attempt to access an element with an index that does not yet exist, the element is created with a default constructor and is inserted into the map. This might not be the intended behavior and so is something to watch out for.

Moving, on, we see a simple method of finding an element based on the key using the find() function. Since the keys are sorted, this function performs in O(log n) time.

If we want to find an element based on the value, we must do a bit more work. At best, this work will be performed in linear time, since the data is sorted on the key rather than the value. The solution to this problem gives us our first look at generic STL algorithms. We use the find_if() algorithm for this particular problem. The function requires three parameters: an iterator telling where to begin, an iterator telling when to stop, and a function telling when the algorithm should return a true value. The iterators are self-explanatory, but the function object, or *functor*, requires some further elaboration.

In STL, classes with overloaded function operators (did you even know you could do that?) are used in place of functions. This replacement enables both encapsulated and type-safe solutions to generic programming problems. The function object provided in this example simply compares the second value in a value_pair and returns the result. Initializing the object with the result we want to search against provides a clean and completely encapsulated solution. Note that for most solutions, STL provides ready-to-use function objects that you can simply plug into your code. See a comprehensive STL book for a listing of different algorithms and function objects available to use.

The previous paragraph describes the preferred method of searching for values in a container, but if you must iterate through and remove elements manually in a map, we also show you the proper way to do that. Removing elements while iterating through a map poses a special problem because for speed reasons, the designers of STL neglected to have the erase() function return the value of the next valid position, as other containers do. Unfortunately, because of this failure, we cannot use the simple method of removing elements, as shown in our second code snippet. Instead, we have to resort to a bit of trickery to make sure we don't invalidate our iterator.

In this example, instead of incrementing the iterator inside the for loop, we do it inside the body in a conditional manner. Notice that when an element must be erased, we post-increment the iterator when passing it as the parameter to erase(), but if an element doesn't need to be erased, we perform the standard pre-increment operator instead. Because of the order in which the operations occur, this method allows safe iteration without having to resort to using temporary iterators. Unfortunately, the necessity of this sort of coding creates far more possibility of buggy code than if the designers had just sacrificed a bit of speed in the `erase()` function. With any luck, the standards committee will consider revising this function in the future to avoid these types of kludgy workarounds.

This might be a good time to answer a question you might want to ask, namely, "Why do you always use the pre-increment operator in your iteration loop?"

The answer is efficiency. The post-increment operator must return a copy of its old value, so it might require the use of a temporary object. The two solutions work the same way, but unless there's a specific reason to use the post-increment (or post-decrement) operator, as in the previous example, you should prefer the pre-increment and pre-decrement operators.

Stacks, Queues, and Priority Queues

We lump together stacks, queues, and priority queues because using them is simple enough that they require little additional explanation. These containers are really examples of *container adapters* because they are implemented as restricted interfaces on top of existing containers.

Stacks

The STL *stack* class provides three primary members—`push()`, `pop()`, and `top()`—for adding and removing elements from the container. These member functions respectively push an element on the stack, pop it off the stack, or retrieve the top element. To check the current state of the stack, `size()` and `empty()` are provided.

The stack is implemented as a deque by default, but it allows you to change the implementation in the constructor.

```
// Implements a stack with deque as the underlying
// container type.
stack<int> c;

// Implements a stack with a vector as the underlying
// container type.
stack<int, vector<int> > c;
```

Note that using a vector might not be as poor a choice as it seems, because `push()`, `pop()`, and `top()` actually map to `push_back()`, `pop_back()`, and `back()`. Any container that supports these functions can be used as the underlying implementation for the stack class. Notice that in the second line of code in the preceding example, we make sure to put a space between the two greater-than operators. Otherwise, they would be incorrectly parsed as a single stream operator, `>>`.

It is important to also know that the stack class, like many STL containers, prefers speed to safety. Thus, the class assumes that when you call `pop()` or `top()`, a valid element actually exists. It is therefore important to always remember to use size() or empty() to verify that a stack is not empty before performing these operations on it. Queues and priority queues work in the same manner, so the same warnings apply to these containers as well.

Queues

The *queue* class works much like the stack class except that elements are pushed onto the back and popped off the front. The following members are defined for the queue class for element manipulation: push(), pop(), front(), back(). back() refers to the location in which elements are inserted, and front() refers to the location from which elements are removed.

Like the stack class, the queue also defines size() and empty() to manage the size. As with the stack class, you can specify a container other than the default deque to be used as the underlying implementation. Unlike stack, a vector used with a deque makes a poor choice due to the bad performance when inserting elements at the front of a vector. However, a list might make sense in some situations.

Priority Queue

The *priority queue* works identically to a queue but differs in one important respect: all inserted elements are immediately sorted in descending order based on a comparison using the < (less-than) operator. Because of the sorting functionality, an additional third parameter is offered in the constructor, allowing you to override the default < operator with your own function. This ability could come in especially handy if you are inserting pointers to objects instead of passing in the objects by value. Avoiding sorting the queue based on the value of the pointers requires writing a functor class that calls the < operator after first dereferencing the pointers. There is an example of this functor in the article "Resource and Memory Management," with code sample provided.

Summary

The STL is a powerful new tool available for C++ programmers. By understanding both its strengths and its limitations, you can make the most of the features now available without compromising the speed or integrity of your code.

Entire books have been written explaining how to use the STL. It is therefore obviously impossible to think that this article could do justice to the broad functionality that exists in this library. If you want to fully utilize the power of STL, there is no substitute for a good reference book. Several excellent tutorials and references are listed in the following References section.

References

[Nicolai99] Josuttis, Nicolai M., *The C++ Standard Library: A Tutorial and Reference,* Addison Wesley Longman, Inc., 1999.

[Stroustrup97] Stroustrup, Bjarne, *The C++ Programming Language,* third edition, Addison Wesley Longman, Inc., 1997.

[Breymann98] Breymann, Ulrich, *Designing Components with the C++ STL,* Addison Wesley Longman, Inc., 1998.

1.5

A Generic Function-Binding Interface

Scott Bilas

Scripting engines and network messaging have an important requirement in common: They must be able to interface with the game's functionality in a type-safe, efficient, and convenient way. This article provides a method for exporting functions and then binding to them dynamically at run time. It does so without sacrificing run time speed or convenience.

Requirements

The basic requirement for our scripting engine is that we can call a function and possibly pass it parameters. For this task, we need to know the function's name, its location in memory, and the parameters it takes. The types for these parameters must be types that we support directly in the scripting engine as part of the language. Let's assume we support `bool`, `float`, `int`, `string`, and `void`.

The basic requirement for our network remote procedure calls (RPCs) is that we can call a function on a remote machine and possibly pass it parameters. Given that our machines will probably be running the code at different memory addresses, we can't pass function pointers over the network and must instead convert them into a token that both sides recognize. For this token, we use a serial ID that can be converted back and forth to an actual function pointer very quickly. In addition, we need to know how to recognize strings and memory pointers in the parameters so that the data they point to can be packed at the end of the RPC chunk for handoff to the network transport.

For convenience, we should be able to simply call an RPC-capable function without having to do any explicit parameter packing from the caller's code. If the call is meant for another machine, the called function should automatically send its parameters and serial ID to the network transport, then return immediately. If meant for local execution, it would just directly execute the code. The dispatcher on the remote machine would look up functions based on the serial ID and then call them directly after resolving to a function pointer.

Platform Concerns

This is a good place to point out that the sample code provided with this article is very specific to a particular platform: Visual C++ 6.0 running on an x86 version of Win32. In particular:

1. There's a little bit of assembly code in here that is obviously x86 specific.
2. The name mangling and unmangling and how calling conventions work is specific to Visual C++ 6.0.
3. I use the specific way that Win32 image (DLL/EXE) exports work.

At the very least, the concepts if not the implementation are still portable to other platforms. All the x86 assembly code can be converted to any other instruction set, although you need knowledge of the calling conventions of that platform for it to work. Dynamic link libraries (DLLs) are hardly unique to Win32; all this article needs is a table that maps exported function names to memory addresses. Finally, you should be able to figure out how other compilers (especially open source compilers such as GCC) mangle and unmangle names.

Attempt #1

Let's get back to the task at hand. We are trying to find a way to export game functionality in a generic way so that it can be called from scripts or passed over the network as RPCs. Here is a really simple solution:

```
void Foo( void );
void Bar( void );
// ...

enum eFunction
{
    FUNCTION_FOO,
    FUNCTION_BAR,
    // ...
};

struct Function
{
    typedef void (*Proc)( void );

    const char* m_Name;
    Proc        m_Proc;
    eFunction   m_Function;
};

Function g_Functions[] =
{
    {  "Foo", Foo, FUNCTION_FOO,  },
    {  "Bar", Bar, FUNCTION_BAR,  },
```

```
        // ...
    };
```

The eFunction enumeration provides a serialized list of unique IDs for all available functions. The Function structure maps a text name onto a function pointer and unique ID. Finally, the g_Functions array is the set of all published functions in the system. Our example function exports are, of course, Foo and Bar.

Our imaginary scripting engine can search through the g_Functions array when it's compiling a script to resolve function calls by name and then call the procedure directly once it is found. Hopefully, this lookup would be done through an index for speed. Our imaginary network-messaging system could convert function calls into their eFunction IDs and use those IDs to resolve the RPC on the other machine. It's easy and simple.

This solution would work fairly well but suffers from a critical drawback: all functions must be the same—they must all take no parameters and return void. We could change the Function::Proc type so that the functions could at least return a value and take some parameters. However, this is not an acceptable solution, because it's highly unlikely that all published functions will have identical signatures. Besides that, it's a very inconvenient limitation, considering the large and varied function sets required of modern games.

One way to work around this problem is to cast parameters back and forth from their real types to the common types required by Function::Proc. We could, for example, have each function pass two or three unsigned integers and pack our real parameters into them. This is a common and efficient technique used by application programming interfaces (APIs) for callbacks such as window procedures. However, it's unsafe and can't be supported very well by a general-purpose scripting language. It would also be impossible to figure out which of the generic parameters are pointers, a flaw that makes passing the parameters over the network for RPCs very difficult. Hacks are on the horizon. Let's try something else.

Attempt #2

A common partial fix to the problems of Attempt #1 is to provide a package class that stores the parameters in an internal buffer and provides add and extract methods to serialize data in and out of the object:

```
    struct Parameters
    {
        std::vector <unsigned char> m_Data;

        bool       ExtractBool  ( void );
        int        ExtractInt   ( void );
        float      ExtractFloat ( void );
        const char* ExtractString( void );
```

```
            void AddBool  ( bool );
            void AddInt   ( int );
            void AddFloat ( float );
            void AddString( const char* );
        };

        void Foo( Parameters& params )
        {
            int   param1 = params.ExtractInt  ();
            float param2 = params.ExtractFloat();
            // use param1, param2...
        }

        void Bar( Parameters& params );
        // ...

        enum eFunction
        {
            FUNCTION_FOO,
            FUNCTION_BAR,
        };

        struct Function
        {
            typedef void (*Proc)( Parameters& );

            std::string m_Name;
            Proc        m_Proc;
            eFunction   m_Function;
        };

        Function g_Functions[] =
        {
            {  "Foo", Foo, FUNCTION_FOO,  },
            {  "Bar", Bar, FUNCTION_BAR,  },
            // ...
        };
```

Now we can pass generic parameters to any function—a big improvement! This method, however, has its own set of drawbacks, some of which it shares with the first attempt.

First, this solution is inherently nontype-safe and dangerous because of its add/extract functions. The C++ compiler cannot check the types at compile time because it doesn't know what's supposed to go into a Parameters object; by its very definition, it can hold anything. The best we can do is provide some basic run-time checking by storing a type each time an Add method is called and then checking those types from the called function each time an Extract method is called. This isn't very efficient and can be error-prone. Furthermore, any time the function parameters change, every call to that function must be searched for and updated to match. The compiler can't detect changes like this, and the manual search-and-replace function is another error-prone process. Missing one changed call by accident could introduce latent and difficult-to-find bugs.

Calling functions in this way is also tedious and inefficient. The add/extract process adds a lot of memory copying and verification overhead. It also has serious engineering time overhead. A simple function can no longer be added to an export list; it must now change its function signature and have a prologue that converts a `Parameters` object into local variables. Likewise, callers must construct the `Parameters` object to begin with, although this requirement can be made a little easier through some clever template work. Still, there must be a better way.

Half of the Solution

Let's start at the end and work back to the beginning for the solution. What we're really looking for here is a function specification table that gives us everything we need to know about how to call a particular function in a completely generic way. We need to be able to set up the stack with a chunk of memory (i.e., push the parameters), jump directly to the function for the call, and then retrieve the return value to pass back to the original caller. For this task, we need to know the function's name, location in memory, return type, parameter types, and calling convention:

```
// function specification
struct Function
{
    // simple variable spec
    enum eVarType
    {
        VAR_VOID, VAR_BOOL, VAR_INT, VAR_FLOAT, VAR_STRING,
    };

    // possible calling conventions
    enum eCallType
    {
        CALL_CDECL, CALL_FASTCALL, CALL_STDCALL, CALL_THISCALL,
    };

    typedef std::vector <eVarType> ParamVec;

    std::string  m_Name;
    void*        m_Proc;
    unsigned int m_SerialID;
    eVarType     m_ReturnType;
    ParamVec     m_ParamTypes;
    eCallType    m_CallType;
};

typedef std::vector <Function> FunctionVec;

// the global set of specifications for exported functions
FunctionVec g_Functions;
```

Assume for the moment that we have a way to fill g_Functions with specifications for all our exported functions (I'll explain how to do that a little later). Now, how can we use this information to actually call functions? First we must know how our platform's various calling conventions work.

Calling Conventions

You can check your compiler's documentation to see how its calling conventions work. On Visual C++ for x86 Win32, all function calls have certain things in common:

1. The stack grows downward, and all parameters are pushed from right to left. In effect, parameters go from left to right on the stack for increasing memory addresses.

2. The stack pointer (esp) always points to the lowest memory address of the stack, which unfortunately has the name of "top." It must be dword (4-byte) aligned, so each parameter pushed must be likewise aligned to a dword. The push instruction decrements esp first, then stores the data. The pop instruction loads data first, then increments esp.

3. Parameters passed by value are pushed on the stack in their entirety. Doubles (8-byte) and user-defined types are just copied onto the stack. The memory addresses contained by references and pointers are directly pushed onto the stack.

4. Simple non-float return values such as integers and pointers are stored in the eax register. Eight-byte structures are returned in edx and eax as a pair. Floats and doubles are returned through the FPU in ST0. Return values for user-defined types have their addresses pushed onto the stack last, but they will also be returned in eax.

Here are the two calling conventions that we'll be supporting:

- __cdecl. The caller cleans up the stack, meaning that it is responsible for popping its own arguments off the stack after the call completes. This convention is required for variable argument functions because the called function doesn't necessarily have the information it needs to pop the correct number of arguments. This is the default calling convention for static and global functions in C and C++.

- __stdcall. The called function cleans up the stack. This is the standard convention used for Win32 API calls, probably because it is more efficient in terms of client code size.

Support for the other three calling conventions (__fastcall and the two thiscall variants) is beyond the scope of this article, but it could be worth looking into and supporting, depending on the application.

Now we have enough information to do generic function calls with these two conventions. We also need a function to retrieve a floating-point value from the FPUs STO register (as is convention) to be stored in a generic return value. Here are some functions that do the dirty work:

```
DWORD Call_cdecl( const void* args, size_t sz, DWORD func )
{
    DWORD rc;                   // here's our return value...
    __asm
    {
        mov    ecx, sz         // get size of buffer
        mov    esi, args       // get buffer
        sub    esp, ecx        // allocate stack space
        mov    edi, esp        // start of destination stack frame
        shr    ecx, 2          // make it dwords
        rep    movsd           // copy params to real stack
        call   [func]          // call the function
        mov    rc, eax         // save the return value
        add    esp, sz         // restore the stack pointer
    }
    return ( rc );
}

DWORD Call_stdcall( const void* args, size_t sz, DWORD func )
{
    DWORD rc;                   // here's our return value...
    __asm
    {
        mov    ecx, sz         // get size of buffer
        mov    esi, args       // get buffer
        sub    esp, ecx        // allocate stack space
        mov    edi, esp        // start of destination stack frame
        shr    ecx, 2          // make it dwords
        rep    movsd           // copy it
        call   [func]          // call the function
        mov    rc, eax         // save the return value
    }
    return ( rc );
}

__declspec ( naked ) DWORD GetSTO( void )
{
    DWORD f;                    // temp var
    __asm
    {
        fstp dword ptr [f]      // pop STO into f
        mov eax, dword ptr [f]  // copy into eax
        ret                     // done
    }
}
```

Now, given a function's address and some parameters stored in a memory buffer, we can call a function in an almost completely generic way.

Calling the Function

Before making the actual call, our client subsystem (scripting engine, network RPCs, etc.) needs to do a little preliminary work. First it looks up the instance of the `Function` structure within `g_Functions` that corresponds to the function it will be calling. For the scripting engine, we want to verify that the function's specification matches up with what we're expecting: Check and convert any parameters if necessary, or give an error if it's a mismatch. This procedure could be expensive and should be done during the script compilation phase, and not in real time.

Looking up the `Function` instance for network RPCs is a little more complicated. A good way to set this up is to intercept the call from within the function that is destined to be called over the network. Look in `g_Functions` for the `Function` instance with the highest `m_Proc` value that is less than the current instruction pointer (`eip`) to figure out which function is currently being called. Here is an example:

```
__declspec ( naked ) DWORD GetEIP( void )
{
    __asm
    {
        mov eax, dword ptr [esp]
        ret
    }
}

// sample RPC'able function
void NetFoo( bool send, int i )
{
    // FindFunction() should look in g_Functions for highest 'm_Proc'
    // less than 'ip' and return it
    static const Function* sFunction = FindFunction( GetEIP() );
    if ( send )
    {
        // RouteFunction() should pack up the parameters and send the
        // request over the network.
        RouteFunction( sFunction, (BYTE*)&send + 4 );
        return;
    }

    // ... normal execution of NetFoo
    printf( "i = %d\n", i );
}
```

The next step is to construct the parameter buffer to pass to the function. For a scripting engine based on a virtual machine, this is easy; all our parameters are already on a dword-aligned virtual stack. We can simply take the address of the start of the parameters and pass it along. For network RPCs, it will be a little more difficult. We can't pass pointers generically over the network, but we can make a special case for strings, so analyze the `m_ParamTypes` for `VAR_STRING` types and append the contents of the string to the end of the buffer that gets sent to the network transport. On the receiving end, resolve the pointers to point to the appended data, and then use the start of the chunk as the beginning of the parameter buffer.

Now that we have the Function instance and our parameter buffer, we call either Call_cdecl() or Call_stdcall(), depending on m_CallType, passing in the parameter buffer and m_Proc. Then we can either use the return value or call GetST0() to get it if m_ReturnType is a float or double. That's all there is to calling a function generically!

Completing the Solution

Until now we've been assuming that the g_Functions array has already been set up. Let's go back and fill in this hole now. There are several ways to fill out the g_Functions array. Perhaps the easiest to implement but least safe to use is to apply macros or a function to set it up:

```
float Foo( int, const char* );
int Bar( void );

void SetupFunctionExports( void )
{
    {
        Function function;

        function.m_Name       = "Foo";
        function.m_Proc       = Foo;
        function.m_SerialID   = g_Functions.size();
        function.m_ReturnType = Function.eVarType::VAR_FLOAT;
        function.m_ParamTypes . push_back( Function.eVarType::VAR_INT );
        function.m_ParamTypes . push_back( Function.eVarType::VAR_STRING );
        function.m_CallType   = Function.eCallType::CALL_CDECL;

        g_Functions.push_back( function );
    }


    {
        Function function;

        function.m_Name       = "Bar";
        function.m_Proc       = Bar;
        function.m_SerialID   = g_Functions.size();
        function.m_ReturnType = Function.eVarType::VAR_INT;
        function.m_CallType   = Function.eCallType::CALL_CDECL;

        g_Functions.push_back( function );
    }
}
```

This example is illustrative but not exactly optimal. It could be improved with some helper functions and macros to make it easier to add new functions to the table. However, it will always be unsafe and inconvenient. Adding a new function to the table means that someone has to write some code that specifies its types, name, and calling convention. Changing a function (adding a parameter, for example) without updating the table could introduce some nasty and hard-to-debug problems. It is a lot of work to keep the function specifications in sync with the actual function prototypes.

We need a way to build this table automatically and safely eliminate these problems. Fortunately, the C++ compiler already has all the information we need. While parsing the function's prototype, the compiler builds an internal representation of the function—its return type, parameters, calling convention, and so on—exactly what is required to construct a function specification! Unfortunately, we don't have access to this information from within the code, and besides, all that information gets thrown away when the linker constructs the final EXE. We could probably find a way to use the PDB (debug symbols database) to query for what we need, but we can't ship debug symbols with the game. Besides, we wouldn't have an easy way to tell which functions are for export and which aren't.

Combining the export table functionality of a Win32 image file with the C++ language's name-mangling facility gives us the information we require. If we tag a function for export using the `__declspec( dllexport )` keywords, that function's name and address will appear in the EXE (or DLL) export table. In addition, because this is a C++ application, those names will be mangled to support type safety and overloaded name resolution. Mangled names are encoded with all the information we require, so all we need is to decode the names into a form we can understand and then use that to build the `Function` entry to add to `g_Functions`.

The name-mangling format is completely implementation specific and undocumented, and it even changes from release to release of Visual C++, so attempting to reverse-engineer it is probably not a good idea. It's also unnecessary; Microsoft exported a name-unmangling function called `UnDecorateSymbolName()` from both ImageHlp.dll and DbgHelp.dll that does exactly this. So if we were to take our `Foo()` function from the last sample and DLL-export it, the entry `?Foo@@YAMHPBD@Z` would appear in the EXE's export table. If we unmangle the name, here's what we get back: `float __cdecl Foo(int,char const *)`. Now this is something we can easily parse and convert to a `Function` entry for addition to our `g_Functions` table.

So now our procedure for building `g_Functions` is:

1. Iterate over all entries in the EXE's export table, and retrieve each function's address and mangled name.
2. Unmangle each name to get a function prototype in text form.
3. Parse the function prototype to retrieve name, type, and calling convention information.
4. Store the results in a new entry within `g_Functions`. Repeat for each export.

Iterating over the exports to get the function addresses and mangled names requires knowledge of the binary format of Win32 Portable Executable (PE) format files. A specification for this format is available from the Microsoft Developer Network

Library (http://msdn.microsoft.com). Search for the ".edata" section within the library entry for the Microsoft Portable Executable and Common Object File Format Specification to find the structure of a Win32 export table.

There's one final little detail. The entries in the export table point to a jump table, which in turn points to the actual functions. This detail isn't important if all you're interested in is binding to functions and calling them generically. However, if you need to be able to do a reverse lookup and convert eip from within the called function to find its Function instance (required for RPCs, as described earlier), you need to get the actual address of the function for comparison, not the address of the entry in the jump table. This is easy enough: Dereference the address given by the DLL export entry to find the jump table entry. The first byte will be 0xE9 (jmp), followed by a 4-byte offset to the actual entry point of your function. Take the address given by the DLL export entry, add 5 for the full jmp instruction, add the 4-byte offset, and this will be the address of the entry point of your function. This address can then be used for reverse lookup to find the Function instance from within g_Functions.

Conclusion

We now have everything we need to call functions in a completely generic way. In order to publish a function in the system and allow other subsystems such as scripting and network RPCs to bind to it, we simply tag it with __declspec(dllexport) (this verbose tag is best wrapped in a macro to reduce clutter). At run time, the function-binding publisher iterates over the Win32 export table and extracts name, type, and calling convention information from each entry. Other subsystems can look up functions by memory address, name, or serial ID and call them generically using Call_cdecl() or Call_stdcall().

This seems like quite a bit more work to implement than necessary, and for smaller projects with small export sets, it probably is. Larger projects, on the other hand, will probably be changing constantly. The good news is that, once the basic work is done, adding new functions to the system is as simple as tagging them for export, and they'll immediately be available. This process more than pays for itself and is a powerful ability to give any engineer on your team. When combined with a general-purpose scripting engine, the process can be turned into a useful debugging tool as well as serving the content-specific needs for which it was originally written.

In the interests of space and simplicity, we have left out many of this article's features. The generic function-binding concept can be taken much further in a variety of ways. It can easily be enhanced to include support for pointers and references, variable argument functions, and passing more than just strings over a network. User-defined types could be supported for RPC packaging through a serialization interface that can be detected and called directly when post-processing RPC parameter buffers for outbound network buffers. In addition, support for calling class member functions is a very useful tool and can be easily added. Finally, one feature that might or might not be necessary is a tool that will post-process an EXE, stripping off the exports table and converting it into a native data format for direct import into g_Functions. This tool could be necessary either for security reasons (to prevent cheating, perhaps) or to make it unnecessary to ship DbgHelp.dll with the game.

References

Microsoft Developer Network Library, http://msdn.microsoft.com.

1.6

A Generic Handle-Based Resource Manager

Scott Bilas

All computer applications are databases. They spend most of their time juggling data resources—creating, destroying, caching, modifying, querying, saving, and restoring objects of various types. Games typically contain multiple types of databases, each of which is generally hard-coded for each different case, to keep things speedy. Some examples of game databases are file systems, texture managers, font managers, and game actor managers. On top of those, there is a wide variety of domain-specific databases that completely depend on the game's genre and content.

A resource database that's built into all C++ games is the *basic object memory manager*. A programmer calls new to construct a new object and passes its pointer around so that other objects can pass it messages. When the object is no longer needed, somebody deletes it, and its resources are returned to the system. This method works very well in general, but it breaks down when we have to worry about shared resources. This is where we need a more specialized database.

Let's use a font object for our example. At minimum, the font consists of a bitmap and a set of specifications, such as the X, Y (or U, V) locations of its character cells, so the graphics system can render it to the screen. Such an object is fairly heavy duty in terms of memory usage and creation time. Different systems in the game, such as the development console and a text control within the GUI, want to use font objects, but we can't have each system creating its own local copy of the font object. Obviously, that would be slow and consume a lot of memory. To solve this problem, we need to come up with a way to share font objects. Our solution is called the FontMgr and features methods that get pointers to fonts, loading them on the fly and caching them until they are no longer needed. The FontMgr is made available from a global location (possibly as a singleton; see the article "An Automatic Singleton Utility") and is responsible for all the font objects in the system.

What we're really talking about here is a specialized database. The FontMgr is responsible for juggling font resources and, now that it's considered an API, suddenly takes on additional responsibilities as the central clearinghouse for fonts. What if someone tells the FontMgr to delete a font to free up resources, but some systems in the game still have pointers to it? How do we guarantee safety of the system without sacrificing performance? Will we be copy-pasting this code again (with slight tweaks) when it comes time to build the MousePointerMgr? This article presents a simple, safe, generic, and efficient way to manage controlled resource objects.

The Method

The job of a resource manager is to create resources on demand, hand them out to anyone who asks, and then eventually delete them. Handing out those resources as simple pointers is certainly easy and convenient, but it's not a very safe way to do it. Pointers can "dangle"; one part of the system can tell the resource manager to delete a resource, which then immediately invalidates all other outstanding pointers. There's no good way to prevent the dangling pointer problem from happening, and the only way we would find out that someone was attempting to dereference a deleted object is when the game crashes. The problem is that, with pointers, there's no way to know how many references are outstanding, given that clients can copy the pointers as many times as they like without telling the manager about it.

Another problem is that the underlying data organization can't change with pointers. Any reallocation of buffers immediately invalidates all outstanding pointers. This becomes especially important when you are saving the game to disk. Pointers can't be saved to disk, because the next time the game is loaded, system memory will probably be configured differently or you could even be on a completely different machine. The pointers must be converted into a form that can be restored, which will probably be an offset or a unique identifier of some sort. Working around this problem isn't exactly trivial and can require a lot of work to support in client code.

So it's plainly not a good idea for a safe and flexible resource manager to be handing out pointers. Rather than using pointers or attempting to write some kind of super-intelligent, overly complicated "smart pointer," we can add one layer of abstraction and use handles instead, putting the burden on the manager class. Handles are an ancient programming concept that APIs have been using with great success for decades. An example of a handle is the HANDLE type returned by the CreateFile() call in Win32's file system. A file handle, representing an open file system object, is created through the CreateFile() call, passed to other functions such as ReadFile() and SetFilePointer() for manipulation, and then finally closed off with CloseHandle(). Attempting to call those functions with an invalid or closed handle does not cause a crash; instead, it returns an error code. This method is efficient, safe, and easy to understand.

Handles almost always fit into a single CPU register for efficient storage in collections and passing as parameters to functions. They can be easily checked for validity and provide a level of indirection that allows the underlying data organization to change without invalidating any outstanding handles. This has significant advantages over passing around pointers. Handles can also be easily saved to disk, because the data structures they refer to can be reconstructed in the same order on a game restore. This facility allows the handles to be stored directly, with no conversions necessary, because they are already natively in unique identifier form.

The Handle Class

A fast and safe way to represent handles is to use an unsigned integer composed of two bitfield components (this class appears in Listing 1.6.1). The first component (m_Index) is a unique identifier for fast dereferencing into the handle manager's database. The handle manager can use this number however it likes, but perhaps the most efficient use is as a simple index into an std::vector. The second component (m_Magic) is a "magic number" that can be used to validate the handle. Upon dereferencing, the handle manager can check to make sure that the magic number component of the handle matches up with its corresponding entry in the database.

The Handle class is very simple and really doesn't do much except manage the magic number. Upon calling Init(), the handle is given the next magic number, which automatically increments and wraps around, if necessary. Note that the magic number is not intended to be a GUID. Its purpose is to serve as a very simple and fast validity check, and it relies on the high improbability of a condition arising where one object happens to have the same index and magic number (via wrapping) as another. The magic number of zero is reserved for the "null handle" where the handle's data is zero. The default Handle constructor sets itself to null, a state that returns true on an IsNull() query. This is convenient to use for an error condition; a function that creates an object and returns a handle to it can simply return a null handle to indicate that an error occurred.

In most ways, the Handle class acts as a read-only unsigned integer. It's not intended to be modified after being created, although it can safely be assigned back to null to reset it. Notice that Handle is a parameterized class, taking a TAG type to fully define it. The template parameter TAG doesn't do anything except differentiate among types of handles; an object of type TAG is never used anywhere in the system. The motivation here is type safety. With Handle not parameterized, a handle meant for one type of resource could be passed to a function expecting a handle to a different type of resource, without a complaint from the compiler. So to keep things safe, we create a new handle type, taking any unique symbol and using it for the parameter. The TAG type can really be anything so long as it is unique across Handle types, but it's convenient to define an empty struct and use that in the typedef for a handle, like this texture handle example:

```
struct tagTexture  {  };
typedef Handle <tagTexture> HTexture;
```

Now we need a handle manager that is responsible for acquiring, dereferencing, and releasing objects (via handles) for a higher-level owner.

The HandleMgr Class

The `HandleMgr` *class* is a parameterized type composed of three main elements: a data store, a magic number store, and a free list (this class appears in Listing 1.6.2). The data store is simply a vector (or any other randomly accessible collection) of objects of type `DATA`. The `DATA` type, the first type parameter for `HandleMgr`, should be a very simple class that contains context information about the resource that it controls. For example, in a `HandleMgr` that manages files, the `DATA` type would probably have only the file handle and the name of the file:

```
struct FileEntry
{
    std::string m_FileName;
    HANDLE      m_FileHandle;  // OS file handle
};

struct tagFile  {  };
typedef Handle <tagFile> HFile;
typedef HandleMgr <FileEntry, HFile> FileHandleMgr;
```

This simple handle manager maintains a set of context objects that correspond to all the open files that it knows about. The `FileHandleMgr` class will probably not be used directly by clients but will instead be owned by another class (call it `FileMgr`) that handles the abstraction and knows about the problem domain (that is, what `DATA` is supposed to represent). This class might look something like this:

```
class FileMgr
{
    FileHandleMgr m_Mgr;

public:
    HFile OpenFile ( const char* name );
    bool  ReadFile ( HFile file, void* out, size_t bytes );
    bool  CloseFile( HFile file );

    // ...
};
```

Upon calling any of these methods, `FileMgr` asks its `m_Mgr` to dereference the handle to get at the actual `FileEntry` object. After verifying that the dereference succeeded (it will fail on an invalid handle), it then performs the operation.

For our `HandleMgr` class, each handle references exactly one element within the object store, plus its corresponding element in the magic number store. Dereferencing the handles to get at the actual `FileEntry` object is as simple as using the `m_Index` component of the handle as an index into the object store (a very fast operation).

When dereferencing the handle, the code also checks the `m_Magic` component against the same index in the magic number store to make sure the handle is valid. As handles are freed and reacquired, corresponding entries in the magic number store are updated with the new handle magic numbers. This process nearly guarantees that "dangling" handles on released objects won't refer to unexpected objects when the slots are filled by a later handle acquisition but instead simply fail to work and return an error code. Obviously, the magic number store always has the same number of elements as the object store.

As objects are released, the handle manager adds the indices of the slots they occupy to the free list. This saves it the trouble of needing to search through the object store to find an open slot, which results in a tasty O(n) complexity for new handle acquisition. It's important to note that the DATA type is not your typical C++ class. It shouldn't have constructors and destructors that do anything important, such as acquire and release local resources. Objects contained within the object store are constructed, destroyed, and copied as the vector class sees fit. Note that the std::string used in the sample FileEntry is "simple" enough for our needs; it's reference-counted, which minimizes the impact of its constructors and destructors and makes it nearly free for vector to copy.

When asked to acquire an object from the store, we'll likely end up reusing an object that has already been constructed but is no longer in use, as indicated by its entry in the free list. This object needs its members reinitialized before it can be used, because it won't have had the constructor call to set it up. When an object is freed from the store, it is not destroyed; instead, it has its index added to the free list and as such needs its resources manually freed. These minor limitations arise from the fact that we're embedding our DATA type directly in vector, rather than using pointers and creating and destroying the objects with new and delete for each handle acquisition and release. The major advantage here is speed, in that the objects don't have to be completely brought up and shut down each time. To make things more convenient, the initialize/shutdown code can be moved into member functions for easy callback by the HandleMgr owner.

The amount of handle validation necessary could depend on the application and could even be chosen through an additional template parameter for HandleMgr. For example, the test for an invalid handle might be found unnecessary and could be removed (although the debug assertion should always remain). For a more robust system in which error handling is important, the code could, upon detecting an invalid handle, set an error condition and then abort the function call.

Sample Usage

Listing 1.6.3 provides a sample texture manager class. This class allows clients to ask the manager for textures by name and constructs them on demand. It automatically unloads the textures on deletion and provides a set of query functions to use the textures. The textures are indexed by name for speedy lookup to make sure that the same texture is not added to the store twice. It would be a simple exercise to add reference counting to this example to make it safer, replacing `DeleteTexture()` with `Release-Texture()`.

For another (larger) sample of file handle usage, see the sample code for my GDC 2000 talk, *It's Still Loading? Designing an Efficient File System,* available online at www.aa.net/~scottb/gdc/.

Notes

The `HandleMgr` class is very simple and is meant to illustrate some basic concepts, but it can be expanded in a number of ways, either with the existing `HandleMgr` or separate classes:

- Create a `HandleMgr` that works better with larger DATA objects, holding them indirectly through pointers. It should also allow hiding of the data structure to clients.
- Add automatic reference counting as standard functionality, rather than leaving it the responsibility of the owner of the `HandleMgr`.
- Add support for constant-time iteration over the potentially sparse object store by embedding a linked list within its elements. Use STL-style iterator naming and operation for consistency.
- Many databases, such as a font manager or texture manager, likely require indexes to access objects by name to retrieve handles. Build this requirement in as a standard feature or as a separate (derivative) class.
- The `HandleMgr` system is especially effective when combined with the singleton pattern (see the article "An Automatic Singleton Utility" elsewhere in this book). Many of a game's databases are naturally singletons.
- Take the singleton pattern a little further and make the TAG type of `Handle` actually be the type that it corresponds to within the `HandleMgr`. Then the `Handle` could have an `operator ->` that dereferences itself into a TAG by directly accessing the singleton that manages it.
- Save-game functionality should be fairly easy to add, but it is necessarily specific to your game's architecture. The handles can be saved out directly; just make sure that the `HandleMgr` stores the indexes for its objects along with the object data, and on restore, all handles will remain valid.

Listing 1.6.1

```cpp
#include <cassert>

template <typename TAG>
class Handle
{
    union
    {
```

```
        enum
        {
            // sizes to use for bit fields
            MAX_BITS_INDEX = 16,
            MAX_BITS_MAGIC = 16,

            // sizes to compare against for asserting dereferences
            MAX_INDEX = ( 1 << MAX_BITS_INDEX) - 1,
            MAX_MAGIC = ( 1 << MAX_BITS_MAGIC) - 1,
        };

        struct
        {
            unsigned m_Index : MAX_BITS_INDEX;  // index into resource
                                                   array
            unsigned m_Magic : MAX_BITS_MAGIC;  // magic number to check
        };
        unsigned int m_Handle;
    };

public:

// Lifetime.

    Handle( void ) : m_Handle( 0 )  {  }

    void Init( unsigned int index );

// Query.

    unsigned int GetIndex ( void ) const {  return (  m_Index  );  }
    unsigned int GetMagic ( void ) const {  return (  m_Magic  );  }
    unsigned int GetHandle( void ) const {  return (  m_Handle );  }
    bool         IsNull   ( void ) const {  return ( !m_Handle );  }

    operator unsigned int ( void ) const {  return (  m_Handle );  }
};

template <typename TAG>
void Handle <TAG> :: Init( unsigned int index )
{
    assert( IsNull() );              // don't allow reassignment
    assert( index <= MAX_INDEX );   // verify range

    static unsigned int s_AutoMagic = 0;
    if ( ++s_AutoMagic > MAX_MAGIC )
    {
        s_AutoMagic = 1;     // 0 is used for "null handle"
    }

    m_Index = index;
    m_Magic = s_AutoMagic;
}

template <typename TAG>
```

```cpp
inline bool operator != ( Handle <TAG> l, Handle <TAG> r )
    {  return ( l.GetHandle() != r.GetHandle() );  }

template <typename TAG>
inline bool operator == ( Handle <TAG> l, Handle <TAG> r )
    {  return ( l.GetHandle() == r.GetHandle() );  }
```

Listing 1.6.2

```cpp
#include <vector>
#include <cassert>

template <typename DATA, typename HANDLE>
class HandleMgr
{
private:
    // private types
    typedef std::vector <DATA>         UserVec;
    typedef std::vector <unsigned int> MagicVec;
    typedef std::vector <unsigned int> FreeVec;

    // private data
    UserVec  m_UserData;     // data we're going to get to
    MagicVec m_MagicNumbers; // corresponding magic numbers
    FreeVec  m_FreeSlots;    // keeps track of free slots in the db

public:

// Lifetime.

    HandleMgr( void )  {  }
    ~HandleMgr( void )  {  }

// Handle methods.

    // acquisition
    DATA* Acquire( HANDLE& handle );
    void  Release( HANDLE  handle );

    // dereferencing
    DATA*       Dereference( HANDLE handle );
    const DATA* Dereference( HANDLE handle ) const;

    // other query
    unsigned int GetUsedHandleCount( void ) const
        {  return ( m_MagicNumbers.size() - m_FreeSlots.size() );  }
    bool HasUsedHandles( void ) const
        {  return ( !!GetUsedHandleCount() );  }
};

template <typename DATA, typename HANDLE>
DATA* HandleMgr <DATA, HANDLE> :: Acquire( HANDLE& handle )
{
    // if free list is empty, add a new one otherwise use first one found
```

```
    unsigned int index;
    if ( m_FreeSlots.empty() )
    {
        index = m_MagicNumbers.size();
        handle.Init( index );
        m_UserData.push_back( DATA() );
        m_MagicNumbers.push_back( handle.GetMagic() );
    }
    else
    {
        index = m_FreeSlots.back();
        handle.Init( index );
        m_FreeSlots.pop_back();
        m_MagicNumbers[ index ] = handle.GetMagic();
    }
    return ( m_UserData.begin() + index );
}

template <typename DATA, typename HANDLE>
void HandleMgr <DATA, HANDLE> :: Release( HANDLE handle )
{
    // which one?
    unsigned int index = handle.GetIndex();

    // make sure it's valid
    assert( index < m_UserData.size() );
    assert( m_MagicNumbers[ index ] == handle.GetMagic() );

    // ok remove it - tag as unused and add to free list
    m_MagicNumbers[ index ] = 0;
    m_FreeSlots.push_back( index );
}

template <typename DATA, typename HANDLE>
inline DATA* HandleMgr <DATA, HANDLE>
:: Dereference( HANDLE handle )
{
    if ( handle.IsNull() )  return ( 0 );

    // check handle validity - $ this check can be removed for speed
    // if you can assume all handle references are always valid.
    unsigned int index = handle.GetIndex();
    if (    ( index >= m_UserData.size() )
         || ( m_MagicNumbers[ index ] != handle.GetMagic() ) )
    {
        // no good! invalid handle == client programming error
        assert( 0 );
        return ( 0 );
    }

    return ( m_UserData.begin() + index );
}

template <typename DATA, typename HANDLE>
```

```
inline const DATA* HandleMgr <DATA, HANDLE>
:: Dereference( HANDLE handle ) const
{
    // this lazy cast is ok - non-const version does not modify anything
    typedef HandleMgr <DATA, HANDLE> ThisType;
    return ( const_cast <ThisType*> ( this )->Dereference( handle ) );
}
```

Listing 1.6.3

```
#include <vector>
#include <map>
#include <cassert>

// ... [ platform-specific surface handle type here ]
typedef LPDIRECTDRAWSURFACE7 OsHandle;

struct tagTexture  {  };
typedef Handle <tagTexture> HTexture;

class TextureMgr
{

// Texture object data and db.

    struct Texture
    {
        typedef std::vector <OsHandle> HandleVec;

        std::string  m_Name;        // for reconstruction
        unsigned int m_Width;       // mip 0 width
        unsigned int m_Height;      // mip 1 width
        HandleVec    m_Handles;     // handles to mip surfaces

        OsHandle GetOsHandle( unsigned int mip ) const
        {
            assert( mip < m_Handles.size() );
            return ( m_Handles[ mip ] );
        }

        bool Load  ( const std::string& name );
        void Unload( void );
    };

    typedef HandleMgr <Texture, HTexture> HTextureMgr;

// Index by name into db.

    // case-insensitive string comparison predicate
    struct istring_less
    {
        bool operator () ( const std::string& l, const std::string& r )
            const
            {  return ( ::stricmp( l.c_str(), r.c_str() ) < 0 );  }
```

```
    };

    typedef std::map <std::string, HTexture, istring_less > NameIndex;
    typedef std::pair <NameIndex::iterator, bool> NameIndexInsertRc;

// Private data.

    HTextureMgr m_Textures;
    NameIndex   m_NameIndex;

public:

// Lifetime.

    TextureMgr( void )  {  /* ... */  }
    ~TextureMgr( void );

// Texture management.

    HTexture GetTexture   ( const char* name );
    void     DeleteTexture( HTexture htex );

// Texture query.

    const std::string& GetName( HTexture htex ) const
        {  return ( m_Textures.Dereference( htex )->m_Name );  }
    int GetWidth( HTexture htex ) const
        {  return ( m_Textures.Dereference( htex )->m_Width );  }
    int GetHeight( HTexture htex ) const
        {  return ( m_Textures.Dereference( htex )->m_Height );  }
    OsHandle GetTexture( HTexture htex, unsigned int mip = O ) const
        {  return ( m_Textures.Dereference( htex )->GetOsHandle( mip ) );
}
};

TextureMgr :: ~TextureMgr( void )
{
    // release all our remaining textures before we go
    NameIndex::iterator i, begin = m_NameIndex.begin(), end =
        m_NameIndex.end();
    for ( i = begin ; i != end ; ++i )
    {
        m_Textures.Dereference( i->second )->Unload();
    }
}

HTexture TextureMgr :: GetTexture( const char* name )
{
    // insert/find
    NameIndexInsertRc rc =
        m_NameIndex.insert( std::make_pair( name, HTexture() ) );
    if ( rc.second )
    {
        // this is a new insertion
        Texture* tex = m_Textures.Acquire( rc.first->second );
```

```
            if ( !tex->Load( rc.first->first ) )
            {
                DeleteTexture( rc.first->second );
                rc.first->second = HTexture();
            }
        }
        return ( rc.first->second );
    }

    void TextureMgr :: DeleteTexture( HTexture htex )
    {
        Texture* tex = m_Textures.Dereference( htex );
        if ( tex != 0 )
        {
            // delete from index
            m_NameIndex.erase( m_NameIndex.find( tex->m_Name ) );

            // delete from db
            tex->Unload();
            m_Textures.Release( htex );
        }
    }

    bool TextureMgr::Texture :: Load( const std::string& name )
    {
        m_Name = name;
        // ... [ load texture from file system, return false on failure ]
        return ( true /* or false on error */ );
    }

    void TextureMgr::Texture :: Unload( void )
    {
        m_Name.erase();
        // ... [ free up mip surfaces ]
        m_Handles.clear();
    }
```

References

[Bilas00] Bilas, Scott, GDC 2000 Talk, *It's Still Loading? Designing an Efficient File System,* available online at www.aa.net/~scottb/gdc/.

Meyers, Scott, *More Effective C++*, Addison-Wesley Longman, Inc. , 1995.

Resource and Memory Management

James Boer

Computer and video games, more than any other type of software, often require handling vast amounts of media resources such as graphics, sound effects, music, video, models, animation, and other types of memory-hogging data. Dealing with this large amount of data while maintaining a relatively reasonable memory footprint is not a trivial task. In this article we examine the workings of a simple resource manager and discuss how it might be both used and extended in real-world applications.

First, let's clearly define our problem and how we expect to solve it. Within a given time in which it is not acceptable to display a loading screen or break the action, we expect to use more data in our game than we can hold in memory at one time. It is also assumed that we have a medium from which we can dynamically load our data while the game is playing. On console systems, this would most likely be a CD or DVD type of device, whereas on the PC it is probably the hard drive.

Our solution entails creating resource objects that are able to automatically load, discard, and reload their data based on usage patterns. We will also create a manager to coordinate the available resources and control access to the resource objects. This will be accomplished through the use of handles, which are essentially just unique identification numbers.

The Resource Class

To begin with, let's examine the base resource class:

```
class BaseResource
{
public:

    enum PriorityType
    {
        RES_LOW_PRIORITY = 0,
        RES_MED_PRIORITY,
        RES_HIGH_PRIORITY
    };
```

```
BaseResource()              {  Clear();  }
virtual ~BaseResource()     {  Destroy();  }

// Clears the class data
virtual void Clear();

// Create and destroy functions.  Note that the Create()
// function of the derived class does not have to exactly
// match the base class.  No assumptions are made regarding
// parameters.
virtual bool Create()       {  return false;  }
virtual void Destroy()      {}

// Dispose and recreate must be able to discard and then
// completely recreate the data contained in the class with
// no additional parameters
virtual bool Recreate() = 0;
virtual void Dispose() = 0;

// GetSize() must return the size of the data inside the
// class, and IsDisposed() lets the manager know if the
// data exists.
virtual size_t GetSize() = 0;
virtual bool IsDisposed() = 0;

// These functions set the parameters by which the sorting
// operator determines in what order resources are
// discarded
inline void SetPriority(PriorityType priority)
  {  m_Priority = priority;  }
inline PriorityType GetPriority()
  {  return m_Priority;  }

inline void SetReferenceCount(UINT nCount)
  {  m_nRefCount = nCount;  }
inline UINT GetReferenceCount()
  {  return m_nRefCount;  }
inline bool IsLocked()
  {  return (m_nRefCount > 0) ? true : false;  }

inline void SetLastAccess(time_t LastAccess)
  {  m_LastAccess = LastAccess;  }
inline time_t GetLastAccess()
  {  return m_LastAccess;  }

// The less-than operator defines how resources get
// sorted for discarding.
virtual bool operator < (BaseResource& container);

protected:
  PriorityType  m_Priority;
  UINT          m_nRefCount;
  time_t        m_LastAccess;

};
```

The `BaseResource` class acts as a template from which other resource container classes must be derived. Several member functions must be overridden by any base class and are critical to how the system works.

It is expected that the initial `Create()` function will load some amount of resource data from disk or even from another location in memory. It is critical for the class to retain the necessary data in order to repeat this operation as many times as necessary in the `Recreate()` function. This may mean, for example, storing the path and file information of a bitmap to be loaded. The application must override the `Dispose()` and `Recreate()` functions in order to allow the resource manager to swap the resource in and out of memory as it sees fit. Keep in mind that only the most significant portion of the resource (e.g., the bitmap data, the sound buffer, and the like) , not *all* the class data, must be swapped out.

`GetSize()` and `IsDisposed()` are two more functions that must be overridden properly for the system to work. `GetSize()` is fairly intuitive. The function should return the size of the data that can currently be swapped out. If the data has already been swapped out, the function should return a size of zero. Technically, you could calculate the actual size of the object by including all the other data members, but in all practicality, this method is really not worth the effort. `IsDisposed()` must return **true** if the data has been discarded and **false** if it has not. The class makes no assumptions about how you can determine this state. It is up to the derived class to provide any necessary data members to keep track of this state, if needed. Often simply checking to see if a pointer is **null** works instead of adding a data member.

A number of other data access functions provide access to the data members `m_Priority`, `m_nRefCount`, and `m_LastAccess`. The first, `m_Priority`, is an enumeration defining the general priority of a resource (high, medium, low). High-priority items tend to stay in memory longer, and low-priority items should be swapped out first. The function `m_nRefCount` indicates the number of times the resource has been locked. We examine this function a bit later. The `m_LastAccess` function is the time at which the resource was last accessed.

The less-than operator (<) is what determines the priority of sorting resources for discarding. The default function looks like this:

```
bool BaseResource::operator < (BaseResource& container)
{
    if(GetPriority() < container.GetPriority())
        return true;
    else if(GetPriority() > container.GetPriority())
        return false;
    else
    {
        if(m_LastAccess < container.GetLastAccess())
            return true;
        else if(m_LastAccess > container.GetLastAccess())
            return false;
        else
        {
```

```
                    if(GetSize() < container.GetSize())
                        return true;
                    else
                        return false;
                }
            }
        return false;
    }
```

You can see from this function that resources are sorted first by priority, then by access time, and last, by size. Although a rather primitive algorithm, it works surprisingly well for many situations. If you require a different or more sophisticated algorithm, you can either modify the base code or supply a new sorting operator in the derived class.

The Resource Manager Class

The other half of the managed resource problem is supplying a manager that can organize all the stored resources, provide access on demand, and handle the dynamic disposal and reallocation of resources to stay within a memory budget. Let's examine the ResManager class to see how it works:

```
class ResManager
{

public:

    ResManager()            {  Clear();  }
    virtual ~ResManager()   {  Destroy();  }

    void Clear();

    bool Create(UINT nMaxSize);
    void Destroy();

    // -----------------------------------------------------------
    // Resource map iteration

    // Access functions for cycling through each item.  Giving
    // direct access to the map or iterator causes a stack
    // pointer fault if you access the map across a dll
    // boundary, but it's safe through the wrappers.
    inline void GotoBegin()
        {  m_CurrentResource = m_ResourceMap.begin();  }
    inline BaseResource* GetCurrentResource()
        {  return (*m_CurrentResource).second;  }
    inline bool GotoNext()
        {  m_CurrentResource++;  return IsValid();  }
    inline bool IsValid()
        {  return (m_CurrentResource != m_ResourceMap.end())
        ? true : false;  }
```

```
// -----------------------------------------------------------
// General resource access

// Allows the resource manager to pre-reserve an amount of
// memory so an inserted resource does not exceed the
// maximum allowed memory
bool ReserveMemory(size_t nMem);

// If you pass in the address of a resource handle, the
// Resource Manager will provide a unique handle for you.
bool InsertResource(RHANDLE* rhUniqueID,
BaseResource* pResource);
bool InsertResource(RHANDLE rhUniqueID,
BaseResource* pResource);

// Removes an object completely from the manager.
bool RemoveResource(BaseResource* pResource);
bool RemoveResource(RHANDLE rhUniqueID);

// Destroys an object and deallocates it's memory
bool DestroyResource(BaseResource* pResource);
bool DestroyResource(RHANDLE rhUniqueID);

// Using GetResource tells the manager that you are about
// to access the object.  If the resource has been
// disposed, it will be recreated before it has been
// returned.
BaseResource* GetResource(RHANDLE rhUniqueID);

// Locking the resource ensures that the resource does not
// get managed by the Resource Manager.  You can use this
// to ensure that a surface does not get swapped out, for
// instance.  The resource contains a reference count
// to ensure that numerous locks can be safely made.
BaseResource* Lock(RHANDLE rhUniqueID);

// Unlocking the object lets the resource manager know
// that you no longer need exclusive access.  When all
// locks have been released (the reference count is 0), the
// object is considered safe for management again and can
// be swapped out at the manager's discretion.  The object
// can be referenced either by handle or by the object's
// pointer.
int Unlock(RHANDLE rhUniqueID);
int Unlock(BaseResource* pResource);

// Retrieve the stored handle based on a pointer to the
// resource.  Note that
// resource.  Note that it's assumed that there are no
// duplicate pointers, as it will return the first match
// found.
RHANDLE FindResourceHandle(BaseResource* pResource);
```

```
protected:

    // Internal functions
    inline void AddMemory(UINT nMem)
     {   m_nCurrentUsedMemory += nMem;   }
    inline void RemoveMemory(UINT nMem)
     {   m_nCurrentUsedMemory -= nMem;   }
    UINT GetNextResHandle()
     {   return —m_rhNextResHandle;   }

    // This must be called when you wish the manager to check
    // for discardable resources.  Resources will only be
    // swapped out if the maximum allowable limit has been
    // reached, and it will discard them from lowest
    // to highest priority, determined by the resource class's
    // < operator.  Function will fail if requested memory
    // cannot be freed.
    bool CheckForOverallocation();

protected:
    RHANDLE      m_rhNextResHandle;
    UINT             m_nCurrentUsedMemory;
    UINT             m_nMaximumMemory;
    ResMapItor      m_CurrentResource;
    ResMap       m_ResourceMap;
};
```

The heart of the resource manager is the data member m_ResourceMap. This is an STL map, which means that every unique resource handle (which is simply an unsigned int) is paired with a pointer to a resource object.

Handles can either be pre-assigned (perhaps hard-coded or read from script files) or dynamically assigned by the resource manager itself. Keep in mind that the current implementation is very primitive. It simply starts at the maximum value for handles and works down. Mixing these two methods works well if your user-defined ID values start relatively low. This method gives you several billion handle values before you run out of room. If you plan to use that many resources, you'll want to implement a more sophisticated handle distribution scheme.

Once the resource manager object has called the Create() function and passed in the target memory limit, the manager is ready to use. Simply call the InsertResource() function to insert resources into the manager. If you pass in the address of a handle instead of passing it by value, the function fills in the value for you. In the example program. we created a factory class that automatically allocates, creates, and then inserts the resource object into the manager.

It is important to understand one thing about the resource manager. When you specify the memory target, the InsertResource() function allows the memory target to be briefly exceeded by the amount of the current resource. The manager then swaps out resources until the currently used memory is lower than the threshold specified. Although this method may be acceptable if your resources are allocating out of a common memory pool or you are working in an environment with true virtual memory, it could create problems if you are working with fixed amounts of specialized memory, such as audio or texture memory.

Requesting the manager to reserve an amount of memory for the resource you are about to load can solve the problem. This function, called `ReserveMemory()`, takes a standard *size_type* parameter. The function returns **true** if it can free up the requested amount of memory. After this function successfully returns, you can then call `InsertResource()`. Most likely, the `ReserveMemory()` function would be called in the resource class's `Create()` function after loading some sort of resource header information, which would probably inform how much memory needs to be allocated to hold the entire resource. Once the memory is reserved by the resource manager, the `Create()` function can finish the data loading and insert the resource into the manager. In order to optimize this process, you might want to pre-load this information and store it in a globally accessible table.

How Handles Work

This system uses handles in order to prevent clients from directly manipulating objects, which allows the manager the freedom to swap out resources as it sees fit. In order to gain access to a resource, the client must call a member function and pass in the handle in order to get back a pointer to the resource. Here's how it looks:

```
SomeResource* pRes = (SomeResource*)resmgr.GetResource(hResHandle);
if(!pRes)
    return Error;

// the resource can now be safely used before any other calls are
// made to the manager
```

It is important to remember that the resource pointer must be considered valid only until another call to the resource manager is made. Accessing another resource could cause the resource manager to swap out the resource you were previously accessing. You will most likely want to put asserts in your resource class's code to ensure that their member functions are not called if the resource has been disposed.

If for any reason you do want to get and hold onto a pointer to a resource, there is a mechanism in place to do so: the `Lock()` function. Locking a resource increments the reference count on the object, which prevents the resource manager from disposing of the object until the resource has been unlocked with, of course, the function `Unlock()`. It is important to remember to eventually unlock objects you've locked, or the resource manager assumes that it is not allowed to dispose of the resource when the program closes, and memory leaks could ensue. Since the resource manager has every resource indexed, it properly disposes of all resources automatically when its destructor is called.

Possible Extensions and Modifications

The use of a resource manager is extremely beneficial in managing large amounts of resources effectively. Although there is a slight increase in difficulty when accessing resources, this difficulty is offset by the simplicity of automatic memory management.

If your application's entire data set is already indexed in the resource manager, a pre-caching system could be implemented by using existing functionality. To load a resource that has been determined a candidate for pre-caching, you should access the resource using the `GetResource()` function and raise the priority level. This method forces any swapped data in those resources to be reloaded and made ready for direct access as well as discourages further swapping because of the heightened priority. For a resource that is no longer needed, simply lower the priority level in the resource, and it is automatically discarded when more memory is needed for other data.

In addition to these enhancements, clients might want to build in more comprehensive reporting functions. A feedback loop could be created to report on resources that are being discarded more than average, and the priority could be adjusted to minimize these sorts of problems. By effectively setting priority levels, perhaps even dynamically, clients can dramatically improve the performance of the manager.

Other techniques you might want to try are featured in a related article in this book, "A Generic Handle-Based Resource Manager," by Scott Bilas. Rather than using the manager as a virtual memory system, this resource manager instead focuses on techniques such as using templates and more intelligent, type-safe handles.

Conclusion

As the amount of data content that modern games must manipulate grows, the techniques for dealing with such vast quantities of data must also evolve. Creating an effective and efficient resource manager can help streamline the development process by allowing programmers to worry less about memory constraints and memory leaks, at the same time providing a powerful tool for monitoring resource usage.

1.8

Fast Data Load Trick

John Olsen

One of the constant challenges with game programming is to make things fast. Whenever you leave someone staring at a screen waiting, you break the flow of information and risk losing that player. One critical element is the time it takes to load data files into memory. With larger and larger game levels, you end up with longer and longer load times. Here is a trick that can be used to reduce your load times.

Preprocess Your Data

One of the most important things you can do to your level data is to preprocess as much as you possibly can. This can be done either with a stand-alone utility program, such as a separate level editor used to edit your in-game data, or within the game itself during development by enabling custom data-packing code for development builds. I've used both methods, even on different portions of the same game, with good results.

For the ultimate in fast data load times, you need to preprocess your data into the final format it will take within the game. With a bit of planning, you can lay out your C++ classes or C structures in a way that makes them good candidates for high-speed loading. Any data to be saved must be a non-static member variable, and no pointers should be saved in the data file.

If you need pointers in your data, be sure to never use them before setting them up properly after loading, since the data saved out in the pointer member is almost certain to contain bad data when it is reloaded. Another possible option is to replace pointers with a handle or index number of some sort. See the article "A Generic Handle-Based Resource Manager," by Scott Bilas, for details.

Since C++ uses virtual function tables, you should make sure to not use any virtual functions in your class, or it will end up calling into seemingly random memory locations when you overwrite your table with stale data. If you want to play it really safe, you can experiment with making all your accessor functions static, guaranteeing they won't show up in your data.

Save Your Data

Once your data is all filled into structures, either in-game or in a stand-alone preprocessing tool, you can write that data out to disk. For C++, you can use your `this` pointer and `sizeof()` for the class. For C, just use the structure pointer and `sizeof()` for the structure. Be sure not to use `sizeof(this)` or you will get the size of the pointer rather than the size of the structure. This size is the size of the non-static member data for your class, along with any padding built into the class by the compiler.

Ideally, you have nested all your necessary data into one parent block holding all the others, so you can load everything in one large read. You have to break things up into multiple saves and loads if you are using anything but one continuous section of memory.

The following example code shows how this might be done in C++, with the game data class having member functions to perform the loading and saving. Please forgive the odd mixture of C++ classes with C file handling. If you're enough of a purist to be bothered by it, I'm sure it's easy for you to change to your preferred method:

```cpp
#include <stdio.h>

class GameData
{
public:
    bool Save(char *fileName);
    bool Load(char *fileName);
    bool BufferedLoad(char *fileName);
    // Add accessors to get to your game data.
private:
    // Only open one file at a time.
    static FILE *fileDescriptor;
    // Game data goes here.
    int data[1000]; // Replace this with your data format.
 };

bool GameData::Save(char *fileName)
{
    fileDescriptor = fopen(fileName, "wb");
    if(fileDescriptor)
    {
        fwrite(this, sizeof(GameData), 1, fileDescriptor);
        fclose(fileDescriptor);
        // Report success writing the file.
        return TRUE;
    }
    else
    {
        // Report an error writing the file.
        return FALSE;
    }
}
```

Load Your Data the Simple Way

Saving the data as described previously makes it really easy to get the data back into your application later when you load the desired level. Just read the data back into the game, into the same structure or class you wrote it from:

```
bool GameData::Load(char *fileName)
{
    // Open the file for reading.
    fileDescriptor = fopen(fileName, "rb");
    if(fileDescriptor)
    {
        fread(this, sizeof(GameData), 1, fileDescriptor);
        fclose(fileDescriptor);
        // Report success reading the file.
        return TRUE;
    }
    else
    {
        // Report an error reading the file.
        return FALSE;
    }
}
```

Load Your Data More Safely

There is at least one really important thing to watch out for on certain console gaming hardware. Some systems always read out to the end of the current sector on a disk. For example, the Sony PlayStation loads data from CD-ROM in multiples of 2,048 bytes. This means that if you read data directly into your structure, you stomp on whatever is in memory after that structure if it isn't some multiple of 2,048 bytes in length.

To avoid this memory stomp, you need to have a temporary buffer large enough to hold the data file padded out to a 2K boundary. Should you be reading several files, don't allocate and free a buffer each time. Instead, get the largest buffer size, allocate the buffer once, and reuse it for all reads. Free it after all the reads are completed. Only the simpler single-read method is shown here.

If you are using a system with very tight memory, you might have already mapped out your entire memory usage and avoided dynamic memory all together. In that case, you need to find a buffer somewhere in memory that is not in use at the time you need to read data files. Use that as your temporary buffer instead of using the dynamic memory allocation shown below:

```
// Check your hardware to see what size of blocks it reads.
// Put that value into this define.
#define READ_GRANULARITY 2048

bool GameData::BufferedLoad(char *fileName)
{
```

```
        // Make sure there is room in the read buffer.
        // This could be made smaller to match the
        // known read size by making it a multiple of the
        // READ_GRANULARITY, but this way is a bit faster.
        char *tempBuffer = new char[sizeof(GameData) + READ_GRANULARITY];
        if(!tempBuffer)
        {
            // Could not allocate the buffer.
            // Return an error code.
            return FALSE;
        }
        fileDescriptor = fopen(fileName, "rb");
        if(fileDescriptor)
        {
            fread(tempBuffer, sizeof(GameData), 1, fileDescriptor);
            fclose(fileDescriptor);
            memcpy(this, tempBuffer, sizeof(GameData));
            delete tempBuffer;
            // Report success reading the file.
            return TRUE;
        }
        else
        {
            delete tempBuffer;
            // Report an error reading the file.
            return FALSE;
        }
    }
```

Now you are well on your way to highly optimized level loads. By preprocessing your data, you save the CPU time used to convert data into a usable format, and you compress the amount of data to be read. The best optimizations are those win/win situations in which the result is both smaller and faster.

1.9

Frame-Based Memory Allocation

Steven Ranck

This article presents a simple and extremely fast memory allocation system that prevents memory from becoming fragmented between game levels. It can be used for a wide range of game modules during level-loading time. In addition, the system is extremely fast at both allocating and de-allocating memory and can be used on any type of platform, from console to PC to arcade.

The Challenges of Conventional Memory Allocation

One problem with standard memory allocation systems that include malloc() and new is that memory can become fragmented and result in deteriorated game performance and the possibility of insufficiently large memory blocks available. When an application requests a block of memory, sophisticated operating systems, such as UNIX and Microsoft Windows, employ advanced memory management systems that can logically rearrange physical chunks of memory to create the requested contiguous memory block. But this rearrangement comes at the cost of CPU cycles that the game could ordinarily have used. With game consoles, where the operating system is little more than a tiny set of slimmed-down library functions, there is no such sophisticated memory manager.

Introduction to Frame-Based Memory

A solution to these challenges of conventional memory allocation is *frame-based memory*. Frame-based memory eliminates memory fragmentation and is very fast. However, it is not useful as a general-purpose memory allocation system like malloc() and new. Frame-based memory is best suited for game and level initialization modules.

As shown in Figure 1.9.1, frame-based memory works like a stack. At initialization time, the game allocates a single memory block from the operating system, which

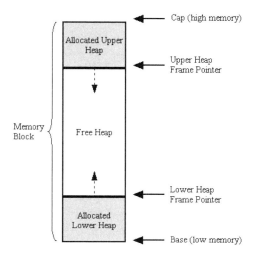

FIGURE 1.9.1. Frame-based memory representation.

will be used and managed by the frame memory system. This memory block is allocated only once throughout the lifetime of the game and is released back to the operating system just before the game terminates. In Figure 1.9.1, the entire block denoted by Memory Block is used by the frame memory system. From the memory block's pointer, we compute the Base and Cap memory pointers, optionally aligning them to a memory boundary that fits the specific system the application was designed to run on. The Base pointer points to the lowest aligned memory address in our Memory Block, and the Cap pointer points to the next higher-aligned memory address just outside the top of our Memory Block (as seen by the placement of the arrow in Figure 1.9.1). The Memory Block, the Base pointer, and the Cap pointer remain constant throughout the life of the game. Finally, the Lower Heap Frame and Upper Heap Frame pointers are set equal to the Base and Cap pointers, respectively. We'll see later how these two pointers change as allocations and de-allocations are made during the course of the game. The following code initializes the frame memory system:

```
typedef unsigned char u8;
typedef unsigned int uint;

#define ALIGNUP( nAddress, nBytes ) ( (((uint)nAddress) + \
(nBytes)-1) & (~((nBytes)-1)) )

static int _nByteAlignment;     // Memory alignment in bytes
static u8 *_pMemoryBlock;       // Value returned by malloc()
static u8 *_apBaseAndCap[2];    // [0]=Base pointer, [1]=Cap pointer
static u8 *_apFrame[2];         // [0]=Lower frame pointer, [1]=Upper
                                // frame pointer
```

```
// Must be called exactly once at game initialization time.
// nByteAlignment must be a power-of-2.
// Returns 0 if successful, or 1 if an error occurred.
int InitFrameMemorySystem( int nSizeInBytes, int nByteAlignment ) {
    // Make sure nSizeInBytes is a multiple of nByteAlignment:
    nSizeInBytes = ALIGNUP( nSizeInBytes, nByteAlignment );

    // First allocate our Memory Block:
    _pMemoryBlock = (u8 *)malloc( nSizeInBytes +
        nByteAlignment );
    if( _pMemoryBlock == 0 ) {
        // Not enough memory. Return error flag:
        return 1;
    }

    _nByteAlignment = nByteAlignment;

    // Set up Base pointer:
    _apBaseAndCap[0] = (u8 *)ALIGNUP( _pMemoryBlock,
        nByteAlignment );

    // Set up Cap pointer:
    _apBaseAndCap[1] = (u8 *)ALIGNUP( _pMemoryBlock +
        nSizeInBytes, nByteAlignment );

    // Finally, initialize the Lower and Upper frame pointers:
    _apFrame[0] = _apBaseAndCap[0];
    _apFrame[1] = _apBaseAndCap[1];

    // Successful!
    return 0;
}
```

To shut down the frame memory system:

```
void ShutdownFrameMemorySystem( void ) {
    free( _pMemoryBlock );
}
```

Exactly once during game initialization, a call is made to InitFrameMemory
System(), passing in the total number of bytes to be managed by the frame memory
system and the byte alignment. All allocations made through the frame memory
system maintain the byte alignment. Note that the ALIGNUP() macro requires that the
nBytes parameter be a power of 2.

At this point, the frame memory system is ready to use. It maintains two individual heaps: the Lower Heap allocates upward, and the Upper Heap allocates downward, as shown in Figure 1.9.1. It is completely up to the game how it wants to utilize
each heap. For example, the Upper Heap could be used to store 3D geometry data
and the Lower Heap used for sound data. In this example, independent allocations
made by the geometry and sound modules would not fragment memory, because the
two heaps are physically separated.

Allocating and Releasing Memory

Frame memory allocation works like a stack. A call is made to the system, requesting a chunk of memory from one of the two heaps. If the lower heap is specified, the Lower Heap Frame pointer is bumped up by the amount allocated, and its value prior to the modification is returned. The Lower Heap Frame pointer always points to the next available byte of memory. If, on the other hand, the upper heap is specified, the Upper Heap Frame pointer is bumped *down* by the amount allocated, and the new value is returned. This is because the Upper Heap Frame pointer always points to the last allocated byte of memory. If the two frame pointers cross each other, there isn't enough memory to satisfy the request. The following function performs the allocation:

```
// Returns a pointer to the base of the memory block,
// or returns 0 if there was insufficient memory.
// nHeapNum is the heap number: 0=lower, 1=upper.
void *AllocFrameMemory( int nBytes, int nHeapNum ) {
    u8 *pMem;

    // First, align the requested size:
    nBytes = ALIGNUP( nBytes, _nByteAlignment );

    // Check for available memory:
    if( _apFrame[0]+nBytes > _apFrame[1] ) {
        // Insufficient memory:
        return 0;
    }

    // Now perform the memory allocation:

    if( nHeapNum ) {
        // Allocating from upper heap, down:

        _apFrame[1] -= nBytes;
        pMem = _apFrame[1];

    } else {
        // Allocating from lower heap, up:

        pMem = _apFrame[0];
        _apFrame[0] += nBytes;
    }

    return (void *)pMem;
}
```

This function performs frame-based memory allocation very quickly. Since frame memory is allocated like a stack, it must be de-allocated the same way. This is where frames are introduced. A *frame* is a handle that the game retrieves from the memory system and is used to free memory. Memory can be freed only by using a frame. A frame acts as a bookmark within the pages of memory allocated by the system. When a frame is freed, all memory allocated since the frame was obtained is freed. Figure 1.9.2 demonstrates the use of a frame.

In Figure 1.9.2, (b) and (c) show two individual memory allocations being made via the `AllocFrameMemory()` function. In (d), the game obtains a frame from the memory system. The frame is simply a handle that the game will later use to free memory. In (e) and (f), the game allocates another two blocks of memory. In (g), the

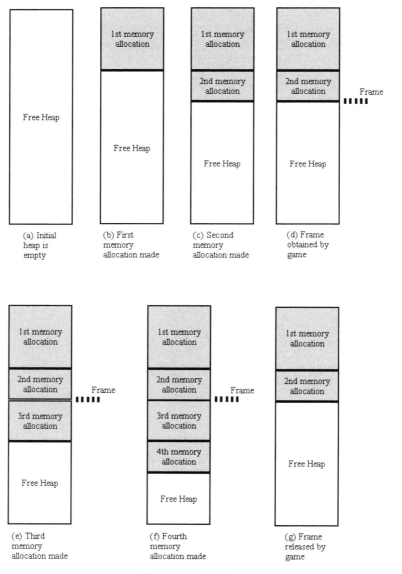

FIGURE 1.9.2. Memory allocation and release.

game wants to release all memory allocated since the frame was obtained. The following function obtains a frame for either the upper or lower heap:

```
typedef struct {
    u8 *pFrame;
    int nHeapNum;
} Frame_t;

// Returns a Frame handle which can be used to
// later release memory allocated henceforth.
// nHeapNum is the heap number: 0=lower, 1=upper.
Frame_t GetFrame( int nHeapNum ) {
    Frame_t Frame;

    Frame.pFrame = _apFrame[nHeapNum];
    Frame.nHeapNum = nHeapNum;

    return Frame;
}
```

To the memory system, a frame is a copy of the specified heap number and its current frame pointer. But to the game, it's simply a handle, Frame_t. To release memory, we implement the following function:

```
void ReleaseFrame( Frame_t Frame ) {
    _apFrame[Frame.nHeapNum] = Frame.pFrame;
}
```

The game calls ReleaseFrame() to release all memory allocated since the time that Frame was obtained by GetFrame(). There is no limit to the number of simultaneous frames the game can allocate, provided that the frames are released in the order opposite of that in which they were obtained. However, the memory system doesn't require that frames be released. For example, if Frame 1, Frame 2, and Frame 3 are obtained, it is valid to release Frame 3 and then Frame 1, provided that Frame 2 is never released.

Having two independent heaps has several advantages. Consider our previous example of the upper heap being used to store 3D geometry, and the lower heap being used to store sound data. Suppose that allocations between the two heaps were made as follows: 3D block allocated, sound block allocated, another 3D block allocated, another sound block allocated. When the 3D memory is freed (both blocks), unused memory holes are not created and fragmentation is prevented. The largest chunk of available memory is always equal to the total size of the free heap. Likewise, the largest chunk of available memory in the lower heap is always identical to the largest chunk of available memory in the upper heap.

Example

Consider the following application example:

```
#define _HEAPNUM 1 // Arbitrary. We'll use the upper heap (1).

extern int GetObjectSize( const char *pszObjectName );
extern int LoadFromDisk( const char *pszObjectName,
        void *pLoadAddress );

static void *_pObject1;  // Where our CopCar object will be loaded.
static void *_pObject2;  // Where our RobberCar object will be loaded.
// Loads the CopCar and RobberCar objects from disk into
// _HEAPNUM.
// Returns 0 if successful, or 1 if not successful.
int LoadCarObjects( void ) {
    Frame_t Frame;

    // Get a frame handle:
    Frame = GetFrame( _HEAPNUM );

    // Attempt to load the CopCar object:
    _pObject1 = LoadMyObject( "CopCar" );
    if( _pObject1 == 0 ) {
        // Object couldn't be loaded. Release memory:
        ReleaseFrame( Frame );
        return 1;
    }

    // Attempt to load the RobberCar object:
    _pObject2 = LoadMyObject( "RobberCar" );
    if( _pObject2 == 0 ) {
        // Object couldn't be loaded. Release memory:
        ReleaseFrame( Frame );
        return 1;
    }

    // Objects loaded ok. Keep the memory around:
    return 0;
}

// Allocates memory from _HEAPNUM and loads the specified object
// from disk into the allocated memory. Returns a pointer to the
// object if successful, or 0 if not successful.
void *LoadMyObject( const char *pszObjectName ) {
    int nObjectSize;
    void *pObject;

    nObjectSize = GetObjectSize( pszObjectName );
    if( nObjectSize == 0 ) {
        // Trouble getting object size:
        return 0;
    }
```

```
        pObject = AllocFrameMemory( nObjectSize, _HEAPNUM );
        if( pObject == 0 ) {
            // Insufficient memory:
            return 0;
        }

        if( LoadFromDisk( pszObjectName, pObject ) ) {
            // Trouble loading object from disk:
            return 0;
        }

        // Object loaded successfully:
        return pObject;
    }
```

In the preceding example, the function `LoadCarObjects()` gets a frame but releases it only if there was a problem while loading the objects. If both objects loaded without issue, the frame is not released and the function returns with the memory intact. It's possible that a higher-level function obtained its own frame encapsulating all object-loading functions in addition to `LoadCarObjects()`. When it comes time to free all object memory, the higher-level function simply calls `ReleaseFrame()` with the frame it had obtained.

Conclusion

Since frame-based memory works like a stack, it is imperative that frames are released in the order opposite of that in which they were obtained; otherwise, memory corruption can occur. Detecting violations of this condition is simple. Consider this replacement function for releasing a frame:

```
    void ReleaseFrame( Frame_t Frame ) {
        // Check validity if releasing in lower heap (0):
        assert( Frame.nHeapNum==1 ||
            (uint)Frame.pFrame<=(uint)_apFrame[0] );

        // Check validity if releasing in upper heap (1):
        assert( Frame.nHeapNum==0 ||
            (uint)Frame.pFrame>=(uint)_apFrame[1] );

        // Release frame:
        _apFrame[Frame.nHeapNum] = Frame.pFrame;
    }
```

This code detects attempts to release frames in the incorrect order in debug builds of the game. Further assertions could be added to detect additional validity problems with the parameters.

One final point worth noting is that for game platforms with multiple independent types of memory (main, sound, texture, geometry, and so forth), a frame-based memory system could easily be implemented for each memory type and then linked together to provide a master frame. Recall the preceding example. Suppose that Load-FromDisk() loaded geometry, textures, and sound for the specified model. The geometry is to be placed in system memory, the textures into texture memory, and sound into sound memory. In this case, there would be three independent frame memory systems linked together by a master frame:

```
typedef struct {
    Frame_t SysmemFrame;            // System memory Frame
    Frame_t TexmemFrame;            // Texture memory Frame
    Frame_t SoundmemFrame;          // Sound memory Frame
} MasterFrame_t;
```

1.10

Simple, Fast Bit Arrays

Andrew Kirmse

We love bitwise operations because they are fast and they pack data efficiently, but we hate them because they are error-prone and depend on the machine's word size. What we really want is an abstraction of bitwise operations that gives us all the benefits but hides the unpleasant details.

Overview

The three C++ classes in this article implement arrays of bits. The base class, `BitArray`, is a simple one-dimensional array of bits. Its subclass `BitArray2D` is a two-dimensional array of bits, and the `TwoBitArray` subclass is an array of integer elements whose values can range from 0 to 3. Each of the classes can be manipulated through English-language methods or, alternatively, through familiar operators. The classes feature clear syntax, portability, range checking, correct use of `const`, and high performance.

The C++ Standard Template Library (STL) includes a one-dimensional array of bits in the header bit set. Although feature-rich, many implementations are cryptic at best and difficult to extend or modify (for a sample implementation, see [SGI98]). Some STL implementations also depend on parts of the C++ standard such as member templates and namespaces that are missing from some compilers. The implementations in this article are straightforward and easy to integrate with existing code. They also provide additional features that are useful for game development.

Array of Bits

The base class `BitArray` acts just like a normal C++ array of bools, although you are of course free to interpret the bits as integers with values of 0 and 1. The bits are stored in a buffer of longs in an endian-independent manner. Syntactically, you can treat a `BitArray` as similar to a regular C++ array, with the added benefit of dynamic array bounds and additional operators. For example, you can do the following:

```
BitArray bits(num_bits), other_bits(num_bits);
bits.Clear();
```

```
bits[10] = true;
if ((bits & other_bits).AllBitsFalse()) {}
```

The class implements the standard bitwise operators &, |, ^, &=, |=, ^=, and ~. It does not implement shift operations.

In the interest of high performance, a BitArray is not initialized with any particular value when it is created. The **Clear**() method sets all bits to false. As a further optimization, small BitArrays that can fit inside a machine word do not allocate any additional memory. This makes the class useful for even small sets of flags. This syntax:

```
flags[FLAG_INDEX] = true;
```

is clearer than the traditional:

```
flags |= 1 << FLAG_INDEX;
```

BitArray and the other classes call **assert** when an array index is out of bounds. In real-time games, this is generally preferable to throwing an exception, as the STL does, due to the overhead associated with exceptions.

The array subscript operator in BitArray is implemented with a useful C++ pattern known as a *proxy class*. (See [Meyers95] for more information about proxy classes.) The proxy class BitProxy represents a single bit in the BitArray. In the expression:

```
a[10] = true;
```

we assign to the BitProxy *a[10]* using **operator=**, while in the expression:

```
bool val = a[10];
```

we merely read the value of a bit via the bool operator. The BitProxy class allows us to delay evaluation of the expression *a[10]* until we know the context in which it is used (reading or writing). This is a very handy trick that is also used in the other bit array classes.

Note that the BitProxy object must be returned by value, so it might incur the cost of instantiating and deleting a temporary object. In normal circumstances, where the bit value is immediately read or assigned to, the compiler is able to optimize away this temporary object.

Other Arrays

BitArray2D is a two-dimensional analog of BitArray. For the most part, it behaves just like any other two-dimensional array:

```
BitArray2D bits(10, 20);
bits[5][4] = true;
```

Note that the array subscript operator for `BitArray2D` returns an `ArrayProxy`, which is a proxy class representing a single row of the array. `ArrayProxy` itself has a subscript operator that returns a proxy for a particular bit in the array. These mechanics are necessary to allow the familiar C++ double-subscripting syntax.

`BitArray2D` intentionally does not treat its subscripted elements as one-dimensional `BitArrays`:

```
bits2d[5] = bit_array;     // illegal!
bits2d[5].FlipAllBits();   // illegal!
```

Although it's certainly possible to allow such operations, it would complicate the `ArrayProxy` class considerably, and these uses are comparatively rare.

`BitArray2D` is implemented as a single `BitArray` that contains as many bits as the two-dimensional array. Because `BitArray2D` does not have the same public interface as `BitArray`, it inherits from `BitArray` via `private`. Like `BitArray`, all of its functions are short and inlined.

The final class, `TwoBitArray`, provides an array of two-bit values. (Arrays with more bits per element are easy extensions to this class.) The implementation is an almost trivial use of a `BitArray` with twice as many elements as the `TwoBitArray`. Although extremely simple, this class is a convenient way to pack state information into a minimum of space.

Application

Even such traditional low-level C constructs as bit arrays can benefit from implementation in C++. The C++ code is easier to read and understand for a performance cost that is almost always negligible. For games, this means less time spent developing and debugging code that is necessary for many applications.

If you use these classes in major data structures in a game (e.g., state bits attached to each cell in a two-dimensional array of tiles), it might be useful to add operators to read and write the array to a stream. If you do, be careful to pay attention to endianness when dealing with the array's contents, if portability is important.

The sample code includes a test program that illustrates usage of these bit array classes.

References

[SGI98] SGI, "STL header bit set," available online at www.sgi.com/Technology/STL/bitset, 1998.

[Meyers95] Meyers, Scott, *More Effective C++*, Addison-Wesley Longman, Inc., 1995.

1.11

A Network Protocol for Online Games

Andrew Kirmse

Most encryption schemes assume that a trusted sender and a trusted recipient want to communicate over an untrusted channel. It seems absurd to suggest that the sender could deliberately try to fool the recipient, yet this is exactly the problem facing designers of online games. Some players cannot be trusted, and worse, they have complete access to the encryption algorithm and all communications via the client executable. Under such circumstances we cannot hope to provide completely secure communications, but we can make the attacker's job more trouble than it's worth. This article presents some practical techniques for building an application-level communications protocol for online games.

Definitions

Protocol design is most interesting in client/server games, where one or more untrusted clients communicate with a trusted central server. (Cheating is certainly also a problem in peer-to-peer games, but because no entity is trusted in such games, the situation is hopeless.) The consequences of cheating in a client/server game is high because the server, as the only trusted entity, maintains the game state and verifies all client commands. When the game state is persistent, a single successful cheat can destabilize a game involving thousands of players.

We consider protocol security features in a client/server system. The client and server communicate by sending packets over a network channel, which might be reliable (typically TCP) or unreliable (UDP). Although clients can also communicate directly with each other, perhaps for chat or voice, we assume that any data that need to be secured are sent only between a client and the server.

Each packet contains two parts: the *header*, containing administrative information, and the *payload*, containing the actual data we want to communicate. The goal of the network protocol is to deliver the sender's original payload to the recipient. Any modifications to the sender's sequence of payloads should be detected. We deal only with delivery of the payload, leaving the details of packet ordering and reliability to lower levels in the protocol stack.

Packet Tampering

Most protocol hackers are casual: they change bytes in a packet and see what happens. The first line of defense against such attacks is a simple checksum. A checksum is a short number produced by combining every byte of the packet. The sender computes the checksum of the packet and sends both the packet and the checksum to the recipient. The recipient takes the packet and recomputes its checksum; if the computed checksum doesn't match the checksum from the sender, the packet is corrupt and should be rejected. It's important to include the entire packet, including the header, in the checksum computation, so that the recipient can detect changes to the header as well as the payload.

A perfect checksum computation would produce a different value if any byte of the packet were changed to any other value. A perfect checksum would be too long to be useful, of course, but hash functions have the same design goal and make excellent checksums. Particularly useful are one-way hash functions, which scramble their input to the extent that reconstructing any part of the input from the hash value is impossible for practical purposes. The MD5 algorithm is well tested, publicly available, and fast enough for use in games. A public domain implementation is available online [Plumb93].

There are two weaknesses in this simple checksum mechanism. First, because the client executable contains the checksum computation code, an attacker can reverse engineer the checksum algorithm, and then compute valid checksums for any message. Second, an attacker can capture valid packets and resend them later, an attack known as *packet replay*.

Packet Replay

In a packet relay attack, a malicious user captures a packet from the client (typically using a packet sniffer), and then sends it multiple times. A common tactic is to use packet replay to perform commands faster than the game allows, even if there are timing checks in the client. For example, a client might use a timer to send a certain command to the server at most once per second, no matter how frequently the player issues the command. Using packet replay, a single user might issue the same command hundreds of times per second.

A system designer might try to stop this particular attack by putting a similar once-per-second timer check on the server as well. In the face of widely variable network latency, however, this defense is impractical. Although it detects most packet replay attacks, varying network delays can make packets bunch together by the time they reach the server, causing legal command sequences to be rejected. We certainly do not want our security scheme to mark law-abiding players as cheaters.

To guard against packet replay, each packet should contain some state information, so that even packets with identical payloads have different bit patterns. Something as simple as a number that increments with each sent packet would do, although that scheme is too easy for an attacker to figure out. A better answer is to use a state machine to produce successive identifying numbers for successive packets. A fast and reasonably complicated method is a linear congruential random number generator of the type typically found in system libraries. Such generators operate as follows:

```
State = (State + a) * b
```

where *a* and *b* are carefully chosen integers. (For a discussion of this generator, see [Knuth98].)

The sender and recipient each keep a linear congruential random number generator for their connections. When sending a packet, the sender produces a random number and adds it to the packet, simultaneously stepping its random number generator. The receiver checks the random number in the incoming packet against its generator; if the numbers don't match, the packet has been tampered with. If the numbers do match, the receiver steps its random number generator to prepare for the next packet.

There are two complications with this scheme. The first is how the sender and receiver initially synchronize their state machines. They could each start their state machines with the same fixed seed, but then the initial stream of packets would always have the same bit patterns and thus would be vulnerable to analysis. Instead, the server can initialize its state machine with randomly generated seed values and send these to the client in its first message.

The second complication is how to keep the state machines synchronized during communication. On a reliable connection, packets are never lost, so synchronization is guaranteed. When packets are dropped or reordered, however, the situation becomes more complicated. If a message is lost, the sender's state machine will have advanced one more step than the receiver's; subsequent packets will be rejected, even though they are legitimate. A simple solution is to rely on a true sequence number sent with each packet (most games include this number with messages anyway, to provide a reliable connection over an unreliable transport). Given a sequence number, the receiver can determine how many times to step its state machine to catch up to the current packet. If the application allows out-of-order delivery, the old state of the state machine will have to be stored for use when an out-of-order packet arrives later.

The **rand** function provided with most run-time libraries is inappropriate for use as a state machine because of its low precision (many implementations have only 15 bits) and its obvious choice as a source of random numbers. A fast, high-quality random number implementation is given in [Booth97].

Additional Techniques

Ideally, two packets with identical payloads should show as little correlation in their bit patterns as possible, to frustrate analysis of the payload. An easy way to remove all correlation between two sets of data is to combine them with a sequence of random bits, using the exclusive-or (XOR) operator. Assuming the previously described packet replay defense, the sender and receiver already have synchronized random number generators. Thus, the sender can generate a sequence of random numbers for each packet and XOR these into the packet payload; the receiver generates the same sequence of numbers and retrieves the original payload in the same way.

Even the fact that two packets have the same length can give an attacker a clue that the packets encode similar data. To further frustrate attacks, each packet can contain a variable amount of random "junk" data, meant only to vary the length of the packet. The length of the junk data is determined by yet another synchronized state machine. The sender checks its state machine to determine how much junk to generate and inserts that number of random bytes into an outgoing packet. The receiver simply ignores the junk data. Increasing the amount of junk data helps to further hide the payload but costs additional bandwidth. In typical applications in which bandwidth is limited, the average length of junk data should be made small compared to the average payload size.

Reverse Engineering

The hardest problem to address, and ultimately the downfall of any scheme to stop protocol tampering, is that the client contains the entire encryption algorithm and thus can always be reverse engineered. Some steps you can take to make reverse engineering harder are as follows:

- Remove all symbols and debugging information from any code released to the public.
- Don't isolate buffer encryption and decryption in their own functions; instead, combine these with some other network code. This is one area in which it can be worthwhile to trade maintainability for security.
- Compute "magic numbers" (such as initialization seeds) at run time instead of placing their values directly in the executable.
- Include a good encryption scheme in *every* version of the client, even early betas. If any client version lacks encryption, a user can record a stream of unencrypted packets from one client and then use knowledge of the packet payload to help break the encryption in a later version.
- Remember that your goal is to make cheating prohibitively expensive, not impossible.

Implementation

The implementation included with this article includes a C++ class `SecureTransport` that uses all the previously described techniques . A `SecureTransport` object encapsulates a two-way connection between a sender and a recipient. For each direction, the object maintains four linear congruential random number generators as protocol state machines. These are initialized to static values, with the understanding that the server would send random seeds in its first message to the client. The class uses the state machines as follows:

1. It XORs the length field at the start of the header. (This is unnecessary if the underlying protocol provides a packet length as in UDP.)
2. A message sequence number is used to prevent packet replay.
3. It determines the length of junk data in each packet.
4. It generates random bits to XOR the payload.

A separate random number generator is used to generate the actual junk data. During debugging, it is useful to set the junk data to a known constant value.

References

[Booth97] Booth, Rick, *Inner Loops,* Addison-Wesley Developers Press, 1997.

[Knuth98] Knuth, Donald, *The Art of Computer Programming, Volume 2: Seminumerical Algorithms,* third edition, Addison-Wesley Longman, Inc., 1998.

[Plumb93] Plumb, Colin, "md5.c,"available online at http://src.openresources.com/ debian/src/admin/HTML/S/rpm_2.4.12.orig%20rpm-2.4.12%20lib%20md5. c.html, 1993.

1.12

Squeezing More Out of Assert

Steve Rabin

Almost everybody uses assert, but not everybody is getting the most out of it. This article contains seven cool little tricks that can be used to squeeze more functionality out of assert. If you're already familiar with assert, skip down to "Assert Trick #1." Otherwise, read on ...

The Basics of Assert

Every programmer should religiously use the assert macro. The assert macro is a simple, painless way to double-check your assumptions, and it will save you every time. By giving the assert macro a condition to evaluate, you're asserting that this condition should be TRUE. If the condition evaluates to FALSE, assert brings up a dialog box telling you that a problem has occurred. You can then choose to ignore the assert and continue executing your code, abort the program, or break directly into the code where the assert failed.

The assert macro lets you program defensively. If you know a pointer should be NULL, you should assert that it is NULL. By making assert a habit in your code, you'll catch mistakes before they have a chance to bite you.

Vector normalization is an example of an important place to use asserts. In the following function, three assumptions must be met for the code to execute without wreaking havoc. The *src* and *dst* vector pointers must both be valid, and the length of the *src* vector must not be zero.

```
#include <assert.h>
void VectorNormalize( Vec* src, Vec* dst )
{
   float length;

   assert( src != 0 );   // Check that the src vector is not NULL
   assert( dst != 0 );   // Check that the dst vector is not NULL

   length = sqrt( (src->x*src->x) + (src->y*src->y) +
      (src->z*src->z) );
```

```
        assert( length != 0 );    // Check that the length is not zero
                                  // (to avoid dividing by zero)

        dst->x = src->x / length;
        dst->y = src->y / length;
        dst->z = src->z / length;
    }
```

Since the VectorNormalize function needs to be blazingly fast, we can't afford to waste time checking the assumptions in release builds. However, while the game is in development, we need to be aware of any problems that come up. That's where assert makes a lot of sense. The assert macro doesn't get compiled in release builds, so assumptions can be tested during development and automatically removed when compiled in release. This allows you to sprinkle asserts throughout your code without worrying about removing them before your game ships.

Since the assert macro is not compiled under release builds, it's incredibly important that you don't change the state of your program within the assert. As a rule, don't call functions or alter any variables inside it. The result would be behavior that differs between your debug and release versions, which could be disastrous.

Why not just put permanent error checking inside the VectorNormalize function? This function is so low level that it doesn't have a clue how to remedy any problems. Hopefully (cross your fingers), every piece of code that calls VectorNormalize checks for these assumptions because it can directly deal with problems. If a piece of code fails to check those assumptions, the assert will be triggered inside VectorNormalize, and a programmer can then know to fix the actual code that caused the error.

Assert Trick #1: Embed More Information

One of the drawbacks of the traditional assert macro is that it doesn't tell you much information. If assert(src != 0) fails, it brings up the string "*src != 0*" in the assert dialog box. Unfortunately, this doesn't give you much to go on. Unless you're running the game from your debugger, it's not very clear what the problem is. One technique is to embed more information inside your condition. Consider the following VectorNormalize function:

```
#include <assert.h>
void VectorNormalize( Vec* src, Vec* dst )
{
   float length;

   assert( src != 0 && "VectorNormalize: src vector pointer is NULL" );
   assert( dst != 0 && "VectorNormalize: dst vector pointer is NULL" );

   length = sqrt( (src->x*src->x) + (src->y*src->y) + (src->z*src->z) );

   assert( length != 0 && "VectorNormalize: src vector is zero length" );
```

```
    dst->x = src->x / length;
    dst->y = src->y / length;
    dst->z = src->z / length;
}
```

When the first assert fails in this code, the assert box displays the string `"src != 0 && "VectorNormalize: src vector pointer is NULL""`. Even if your testers are running the game, they can tell you the function name where the assert failed, along with the reason.

Assert Trick #2: Embed Even More Information

Sometimes programmers simply type `assert(0)` if the program execution reaches an ugly spot. You can pull the same trick of inserting a descriptive string simply by negating the string to make it false. For example:

```
    assert( !"VectorNormalize: The code should never get here" );
```

This line accomplishes the same thing as `assert(0)` while also giving you some great debugging information.

Assert Trick #3: Make It Less Awkward

The first two tricks can be combined in seconds by writing a simple macro. This macro takes two arguments, the first being the condition to evaluate and the second being the descriptive string. This mimics the first two tricks but makes it easier to type and read:

```
    #define Assert(a,b)    assert( a && b )
```

The following two lines use the new macro:

```
    assert( src != 0, "VectorNormalize: src vector pointer is NULL" );
    assert( 0, "VectorNormalize: The code should never get here" );
```

Assert Trick #4: Write Your Own

Eventually everyone should use an assert macro that's been truly customized. The idea is to write your own assert dialog box code so that you can have more control over adding features.

A very annoying problem of the standard C assert is that it breaks into the debugger in the file assert.c—not the line in your program where the assert appears. By writing your own assert macro, the debugger breaks directly to the assert line that you typed. This avoids the needless step of backtracking up the stack to get to the spot you're actually interested in. The following is an example of a custom assert macro:

```
#if defined( _DEBUG )
extern bool CustomAssertFunction( bool, char*, int, char* );

#define Assert( exp, description ) \
    if( CustomAssertFunction( (int)(exp), description, __LINE__,\
    __FILE__ ) ) \
    { _asm { int 3 } } //this will cause the debugger to break here

#else
#define Assert( exp, description )
#endif
```

The above macro calls `CustomAssertFunction`, which you have to write yourself. `CustomAssertFunction` should bring up a dialog box stating the assert information and allow the user to either continue or break. If the user chooses to break, `CustomAssertFunction` should return TRUE, and the debugger will break on the `Assert` line (that's what the `int 3` instruction does on the PC). Otherwise, the function should return FALSE, and the program will continue executing.

Assert Trick #5: This One Is Priceless

Once you have a custom assert macro, you can add an "Ignore Always" option to your assert dialog box. This is an amazing feature that lets you ignore an assert once and have it remember to never bother you again. It's particularly useful when an assert is failing every frame, but you still want to run your game without clicking through a million asserts. To implement this feature, each assert keeps track of whether it should be ignored and purposely suppresses itself if it should fail in the future.

Practically, the way to implement "Ignore Always" is to place a static boolean within the assert macro. This boolean then remembers whether the assert is to be ignored. Initially, the boolean is set to FALSE. When the code executes, it checks this boolean before it even evaluates the assert condition. If the boolean is FALSE, it calls the `CustomAssertFunction` with the pointer to the boolean as an argument. If the assert condition fails and the user selects "Ignore Always" in the assert dialog box, it then sets the boolean to TRUE. The following is the code for the macro:

```
#if defined( _DEBUG )
extern bool CustomAssertFunction( bool, char*, int, char*, bool* );

#define Assert( exp, description ) \
    { static bool ignoreAlways = false; \
      if( !ignoreAlways ) { \
          if( CustomAssertFunction( (int)(exp), description, \
                            __LINE__, __FILE__, &ignoreAlways ) ) ) \
          { _asm { int 3 } } \
      } \
    }
```

```
#else
#define Assert( exp, description )
#endif
```

Assert Trick #6: Only If You're Totally Hard-Core

There's a nagging problem with assert that shows up clearly in the VectorNormalize sample function. The problem is that the source of the error is not inside VectorNormalize. The true error is in the function that called VectorNormalize, which narrows it down to only several hundred routines! If this type of assert fails without the debugger running, the assert is virtually useless. Surprisingly, this is a common situation, since testers rarely run games from the debugger.

The simple solution is to provide stack information inside the assert dialog box! John Robbins, a writer for *Microsoft Systems Journal*, coined the name superassert to describe this implementation. In his column "BugSlayer," he worked out a Windows-specific example, complete with source, which can be used as a reference [Robbins99].

Assert Trick #7: Make It Easier—Copy and Paste

It's really cool when a simple trick makes work a lot easier. This trick falls into that category. If the assert provides tons of great debugging information such as the stack, why not make it really easy for testers to pass it along?

In the Windows environment, you can have a button on the assert dialog box that copies the information to the clipboard! With a few simple mouse clicks, anyone can easily copy and paste the assert into an e-mail or bug report. This simple, powerful idea will help your testers convey accurate, meaningful information back to programmers.

The following code copies an arbitrary string into the clipboard. You'll want to alter it slightly and put it inside your CustomAssertFunction.

```
if( OpenClipboard( NULL ) )
{
    HGLOBAL hMem;
    char szAssert[256];
    char *pMem;

    sprintf( szAssert, "Put assert info here" );
    hMem = GlobalAlloc( GHND|GMEM_DDESHARE, strlen( szAssert )+1 );

    if( hMem ) {
        pMem = (char*)GlobalLock( hMem );
        strcpy( pMem, szAssert );
        GlobalUnlock( hMem );
```

```
        EmptyClipboard();
        SetClipboardData( CF_TEXT, hMem );
    }

    CloseClipboard();
}
```

References

[McConnell93] McConnell, Steve, *Code Complete,* Microsoft Press, 1993.

[Robbins00] Robbins, John, Debugg*ing Applications,* Microsoft Press, 2000.

[Robbins99] Robbins, John, *Microsoft Systems Journal:* BugSlayer, available online at www.microsoft.com/msj/defaulttop.asp?page=/msj/0299/bugslayer/bugslayer0299top.htm (code available at www.microsoft.com/msj/0299/code/Feb99BugSlayer.zip), February 1999.

[Saltzman99] Saltzman, Marc. *Game Design: Secrets of the Sages*, Brady Publishing, 1999.

1.13

Stats: Real-Time Statistics and In-Game Debugging

John Olsen

Everyone spends more time debugging than they would really like to. This huge time sink has led to the development of a system I call *Stats,* a real-time debugging and data-editing system. This system can make life for you, the programmer, easier through simplified debugging and data tracking in a live system as it executes on the target platform. This technology has been used on commercial products for both PCs and consoles. The name is derived from the word *statistics* because the original inspiration for the idea was the display of numeric statistics from within a game solely for the purpose of debugging.

The tool set described here is fairly simple to implement, highly extensible, and highly applicable to many facets of game software design and testing. This means that it is easy for you to customize to your particular needs, which often vary from one project to the next.

Why: A Need-Driven Technology

Both PC and console systems have problems with debugging full-screen, real-time applications. On the PC, you must resort to network-based debugging, multiscreen systems, or the ability to pop between windowed and full-screen mode during the debugging session. Sometimes the debugging environment does not allow access to some or all of the data while the system is running, and hitting a breakpoint at the wrong point in a real-time loop can lock up your system. In the case of video game consoles (referred to simply as *consoles* hereafter), you have no keyboard, so something like a drop-down window for a command-line interface, such as is often used by first-person shooters, is pretty much out as a debugging tool. We are trying to fix the shortcomings of debugging environments, but it would also be nice to have a way to reduce the edit/compile/run loop a bit.

Every programmer who has worked with a real-time loop is sure to have war stories of the nasty bug that took forever to find. Sometimes the code runs differently when you single-step through it. Sometimes you need to debug a live network game to reproduce a problem, or better yet, debug both ends of a network game at once.

Consoles have the added difficulty of having a limited path back to mass storage, if the path exists at all. On some console development systems, it is possible to access the development PC file system to read and write files, but once you go to CD or cartridge, the data path back to the PC grows very restricted. About the only option left is to store data onto memory cards, then read the memory cards on a development system that has access to a PC file system.

Console game systems, and embedded systems in general, have some problems the PC crowd may not run into. The debuggers for console systems have been getting better over time, but there is still a great deal of room for improvement. Furthermore, not a lot of debugging can be done once you burn your game onto a CD.

At some point, almost every project has put a frame-rate counter on the screen or displayed some other sort of data from a live system. Other common items that are hard to get at with a debugger but are easy to track in a live system are the polygon count, culling efficiency, and general execution times based on the content of the viewport. It makes you want to build a system for displaying arbitrary lists of numbers. It certainly got under my skin, and eventually I did something about it.

The idea of an in-game display can be expanded to include editing of the data, which can help in a number of ways. First, debuggers don't typically let you read and write data files. Second, with an in-game editor, whether keyboard or controller based, you can edit the actual game data as you run the game. Third, the edited data can be loaded and saved on a PC or console development system.

How: An Evolutionary Process

The code included in this chapter evolved over the years from a simple displayed list of numbers that could not be edited to a list of text labels and read-only numbers, ultimately to the current version, which includes multiple pages of data that can be edited while the game is running. The text-based display is simply an overlay displayed on top of the game itself.

For many projects, it has worked out to be a lot easier to use an editable version of Stats rather than cheat codes. Stats can be used to toggle particular features on and off, and a set of related features can all be displayed together on a single page. With this setup, you can get to some really detailed data on system behavior while the system is still running.

Consoles, with their debugging drawbacks, can benefit particularly well from an additional method of debugging that does not rely on the tool set provided by the console manufacturer.

What: A C++ Class-based System

To start, the full code for each class and its member functions can be found on the book's accompanying CD-ROM. You might want to refer to it as you go through the following material.

A similar implementation of this Stats system took less than a week to design as a C++ class using a common Stat base class and derived types for each displayed data type. The system consists of a base Stat class, which is the container for everything, and separate pages, which each contain a number of entries.

There is a tradeoff with the way you end up printing Stats to the screen. If you put your printing code in the derived Stat class, it is less portable, but you can do interesting things such as having a Stat that is rendered as a bar graph. If you simply have the Stats fill in a string to be dumped to the display device, as in the provided sample, you have a highly portable implementation that can be used more easily for cross-platform development.

The base of the system is a class that holds a linked list of pages and some other information that needs to be global to the Stats system. An Initialize() function takes the place of the constructor because it is a fully static class that may not have an instance created, resulting in no call to a constructor. The base system has a Print() function that calls the Print() function for the current page.

The Windows-based sample code also has keyboard input processing, which takes an array of boolean key states as input. The array is built by tracking WM_KEYDOWN and WM_KEYUP messages from Windows in the event-processing loop of the program. On a console, you pass in an array containing the controller state. With each pass through the real-time loop, both the CheckInput() and Print() functions need to be called. Pages are added automatically by having their constructor call the base AddPage(), since it is simpler to not make the programmer remember to do it for each page he or she adds.

The initialization is needed simply to guarantee that the base isn't pointing at random data that would be interpreted as a page. It also sets up the limits for how many lines belong on a full screen.

Each page in the linked list owned by the base class contains zero or more entries. One of these pages is always the current page, whether it is displayed or hidden. Entries are added to pages using the common entry parent class. The constructors for entries automatically call the AddEntry() function, similarly to the way the page constructor calls AddPage().

Each page contains a linked list of entries. The entry constructor is used to set up the initial state of the Stat, including the page on which it appears, a text label, and the relative priority of the entry (which can be thought of as a line number). Derived types also have an initial value, should the derived type need to be initialized with a particular value. The virtual functions of the default class CStatEntry are to be overridden in each derived class so that the parent system can access each Stat type through a common interface.

Adding a new class is done by copying one of the classes derived from `CStatEntry` to a new class name, renaming it, and adding an appropriate variable to hold the value. Once that is done, you need to rewrite parts of the member functions to match the new data type.

The actual data stored in a Stat varies based on the Stat type and is included in the derived Stat classes. Each data type has its own `Print()` function to replace the base class virtual function. This function is very useful because the base class can then go through a list of generic Stat pointers and tell each to print without having to worry about what type it is. Navigation is also simplified by basing all Stats on a common parent class. Using the parent type as a generic Stat pointer helps keep things organized and under control. With multiple pages and each page having a current item to keep track of, it can get a bit confusing otherwise.

One typical use for Stats is converting fixed-point statistics to printable floating-point equivalent values. Stats can be a bit of a processor pig on large pages, but it can save a great deal of development time. The value 1.75 is easier to read than 56 and having to mentally divide by 32 to get the floating-point equivalent of a certain six-bit fixed-point number.

Adding Stats to an application requires three things:

1. Call `CStatBase::Initialize()` at startup.
2. Call `CStatBase::CheckInput()` each pass through the real-time loop to update the Stats keyboard state or the controller state on a console.
3. Call `CStatBase::Print()` after rendering the screen to display the Stats on top of your real-time image.

Implementation time for a new Stat type varies depending on complexity, but a simple numeric type can be added in under 10 minutes. A type using enumerations, vectors, matrices, or something more complex takes longer but is pretty straightforward as well.

A derived Stat type in the sample code called a `CStatIntPtr` deserves a little bit of extra explaining because of its slightly different interface and the interesting things you can do with it. The value stored in the Stat is a pointer to an integer. When it is printed, the value of the integer being pointed at is shown. This feature allows you to declare a Stat and have it automatically update the displayed value as it changes instead of having to set the value of the Stat in each frame. It also allows you to directly edit the value of the number being pointed to, one of the more powerful advantages of this system. You have direct access to a variable within your running code by adding just one line of debug code to declare an instance of a Stat.

Typical execution time for running a similarly designed implementation of Stats on a Sony PlayStation has been under 2 milliseconds per frame, with enough Stats being displayed to cover the entire screen. For reference, one frame at 30 frames per second takes 33.3ms, so Stats uses less than 6% of the processor when showing a full page of data. Since you obviously want to compile without Stats for your release build, this time is given back to the rest of the program when development nears completion. The percentage of processing time used on a PC title should be quite a bit smaller.

One word of warning on this implementation of Stats. It isn't designed to work with pages and entries appearing and vanishing. All page and entry instances should be declared static. It isn't too hard to change it over to allow for dynamic creation and deletion of Stats, but having static Stats has always been sufficient, so the extra effort was never put into it. You can change the classes to enforce this current behavior by building destructors into each function with an `assert` that halts the program when it discovers a Stat being destroyed due to its going out of scope.

Where: Applicability

One readily apparent use of Stats is for user interface prototyping, where you want to set up your screen flow without having real screens available yet. A typical menu can be set up in a few minutes, allowing you to bypass unfinished user interface code. You have much less to design, since the text-based interface is already implemented in Stats. Simply write your bypass Stats, and you are off and running again instead of waiting for someone else to finish some critical chunk of code.

You could incorporate Stats into a racing title for in-game editing of direction and path indicators. Stats can be set up to trigger loading, moving, and saving the direction markers while the game is running. It's also been used previously to edit AI capabilities and to load and save several kinds of data files, including the batch processing of script files into memory dumps of a class. (See the article "Fast Data Load Trick" for details.) It can also be used to trigger the export of frame calculation time based on world position to build charts that indicate high load areas.

Stats also give a convenient way to jump to arbitrary levels within a game. There are any number of things you might want to override or turn on and off while the game is running! Some examples are highlighting collisions, tweaking camera behavior, indicating player speed, setting environmental lighting, and so on. It greatly simplifies the life of the modeler if it is possible to edit the camera offsets and field of view in the application as well. Then those numbers can be easily plugged into modeling software once instead of looping through the build-test-build-test sequence a dozen times.

Summary

On the projects I have worked on in which we have used the Stats system, it has saved a great deal of time, not only for the software designers but also for art and level designers. Stats is an easy way to add a debug interface to an application, whether for PC or console. It's even pretty easy to retrofit Stats into an existing application, should you be halfway through development when you find that brick-wall bug that stops you in your tracks.

1.14

Real-Time In-Game Profiling

Steve Rabin

Profiling code is a routine step in most software development, but it's an even more crucial step in games. Since games are constantly pushing the envelope, they need to be frequently monitored for hot spots or stupid mistakes that can bog down the frame rate. When the frame rate turns south, the source of the problem could be anyone's guess until a real measurement is taken. Was it the AI code that was tweaked last night, or was it the collision detection code that was altered this morning? Or even worse, it could be an area of code that hasn't been touched for weeks that's now interacting badly with some new data. The only way to know is to profile it.

This article shows you how to add profiling code directly inside your game. Not only will you be able to quickly find the hot spots in your code, but in addition, anyone— other programmers, producers, designers, artists, and testers—can pop this information on screen. This information makes profiling an accessible tool that ultimately helps fine-tune your code and find bugs. For example, if the frame rate tanks every time a big fire-fight occurs, is it the complexity of the graphics or the collision logic that's responsible? When profiling is at your fingertips, a simple press of a button can tell you the answer.

Some people are adamant about not profiling their code until they're close to being finished with a module. "Why should I worry about speed when I'm still trying to make it work?" they reason. Although there is some truth to this thought, it's invaluable to be able to see how your code is actually performing. Many times I've profiled a module in the middle of development only to discover that the function I thought was being called all the time never got called or got called twice as much. Obviously, this is a tool that can help debugging at any point in development.

Getting Down to Specifics

This real-time profiler allows you to monitor any spot or segment of code you're interested in. It works by calling a function at the beginning and at the end of the area you want to profile. Each sample, consisting of a `ProfileBegin` and a `ProfileEnd`, is identified with a unique name that you choose. Using the supplied code, you wrap `ProfileBegin( "InsertSampleNameHere" )` and `ProfileEnd( "InsertSampleNameHere" )` around the code you want to look at. It's important to note that the string names need to match exactly (`asserts` catch any cases where they don't).

The Overhead of Profiling

Overall, the profiler takes a negligible amount of time to keep track of your samples, especially since you're going to watch only a handful of spots at a time. Unfortunately, displaying the results on screen probably hurts your frame rate a little, depending on how it is implemented and how much text is displayed. If your on-screen text is badly implemented (or not implemented at all), you could always represent it graphically on screen or let the data accumulate and dump it to a text file. Furthermore, as with any debugging code, you can always wrap it so that it doesn't compile when building a release version. However, until you get close to shipping, you definitely want to be able to activate the profiler in your optimized builds.

Since the monitoring does take some amount of time, don't monitor very small, simple snippets of code, especially if they are executed hundreds of times a frame. The monitoring takes more time than the code fragment and causes it to look worse than it really is. An example is monitoring a function such as VectorNormalize() that is called hundreds of times a frame. The profiler accurately tells you how many times it is called, but the timing information is useless. In this case, resort to using a professional profiler.

It's important to note that this real-time profiler shouldn't replace a traditional profiler. A real profiler can give you benefits that can't be duplicated using this technique. Rather, this real-time profiler should augment the profiling that you'd normally do. Think of this profiler as a quick-and-dirty way to find out useful information. When you're ready for very accurate measurements, switch to a professional profiler.

What Will the Profiler Tell You?

This profiler gives you the following information at the end of each frame. You'll most likely want to have this information printed to the screen or some other output device. This article won't help you render the on-screen text (refer to the article "The Text Utility Library," by Dante Treglia II, in this book), but it gives the following important data:

1. Unique name of the sample point
2. Average, minimum, and maximum percentages of frame time spent on that sample
3. Number of times the sample was called per frame
4. Relationship of this sample point to other sample points (parent/child)

The profiler tries to be smart about samples and keep track of parent/child relationships. For example, if you sample the main loop of your game and the graphics draw routine that's inside the main loop, the parent/child relationship is taken into consideration. The results shown in Table 1.14.1 are displayed.

Table 1.14.1 Sample Results I

```
 Ave | Min | Max | # | Profile Name
- - - - - - - - - - - - - - - - - - - - - - - - - - - - - - - - - - - - -
14.3 | 11.9 | 34.9 | 1 | Main Game Loop
85.7 | 65.1 | 88.1 | 1 |   Graphics Draw Routine
```

Here are some observations about the results shown in Table 1.14.1:

1. The Graphics Draw Routine accounts for 85.7% of the frame rate.
2. Everything other than the Graphics Draw Routine accounts for 14.3% of the frame rate.
3. The Graphics Draw Routine is called inside the Main Game Loop (noted by the indentation).
4. The Main Game Loop should take 100% of the frame time, but since the Graphics Draw Routine is being profiled inside of the Main Game Loop, it's subtracted.
5. The Main Game Loop spikes with 34.9%, whereas its average is a low 14.3%, indicating that some code within the Main Game Loop is periodically hogging the frame time. Perhaps it's the AI code or physics code; add more samples to the profiler to find out.
6. The Main Game Loop and the Graphics Draw Routine are both called once per frame (noted under the # column).

After adding more profiler samples to better identify the spiking problem, the results shown in Table 1.14.2 might result.

Table 1.14.2 Sample Results II

```
 Ave | Min | Max |  # | Profile Name
- - - - - - - - - - - - - - - - - - - - - - - - - - - - - - - - - - - - -
 2.4 | 1.8 | 2.8 |  1 | Main Game Loop
 2.2 | 1.9 | 2.3 |  1 |   Game Object Update
 7.6 | 6.5 | 27.4 | 32 |    AI Update
 1.1 | 0.8 | 1.3 |  1 |   Collision Detection
 1.0 | 0.9 | 1.1 |  1 |   Physics
85.7 | 65.1 | 88.1 |  1 |   Graphics Draw Routine
```

From the results shown in Table 1.14.2, we can see that there are 32 calls to the AI Update sample (probably 32 game objects that require AI). The AI Update is clearly the sample that's spiking, with 27.4% on some frames. There must be some code inside the AI Update that is periodically called. Perhaps the work that the code does can be spread over several frames so that the frame rate doesn't hiccup anymore. Continue to add profile samples until the exact segment of code is identified. Tracking down problems with the profiler is that easy.

Adding Profiler Calls

As mentioned earlier, you must wrap the code you want to profile with `ProfileBegin` and `ProfileEnd`. You should always wrap the main loop of your program and then call `ProfileDumpOutputToBuffer` as the last thing in your game loop. `ProfileDumpOutput-ToBuffer` formats the profile information into a text buffer so that you can display it to the screen somewhere inside the main loop. The following is an example of a properly wrapped game loop:

```
void main {
    //Initialization Code Here
    ProfileInit();   //You must call this before the main loop

    while( !ExitGame ) {
        ProfileBegin( "Main Loop" );

        ReadInput();
        UpdateGameLogic();

        ProfileBegin( "Graphics Draw Routine" );
        RenderScene();
        RenderProfileTextBuffer();     //Output profile text from last
                                       // frame
        ProfileEnd( "Graphics Draw Routine" );

        ProfileEnd( "Main Loop" );
        ProfileDumpOutputToBuffer();   //Buffer will be drawn next
                                       // frame
    }
}
```

Profiler Implementation

On a given frame, each profile sample needs the following information:

```
typedef struct {
    bool bValid;               //Whether this data is valid
    uint iProfileInstances;    //# of times ProfileBegin called
    int iOpenProfiles;         //# of times ProfileBegin w/o
ProfileEnd
    char szName[256];          //Name of sample
    float fStartTime;          //The current open profile start time
    float fAccumulator;        //All samples this frame added
together
    float fChildrenSampleTime; //Time taken by all children
    uint iNumParents;          //Number of profile parents
} ProfileSample;
```

Over many frames, we need to keep history information on samples taken. The following information will be stored over the long term:

```
typedef struct {
   bool bValid;          //Whether the data is valid
   char szName[256];     //Name of the sample
   float fAve;           //Average time per frame (percentage)
   float fMin;           //Minimum time per frame (percentage)
   float fMax;           //Maximum time per frame (percentage)
} ProfileSampleHistory;
```

For simplicity and speed, pre-allocate an array of `ProfileSample(s)` and `Profile-SampleHistory(s)`. Pre-allocating the data makes it so we don't take a hit on allocating and destroying memory every time a sample is taken. Before any samples are taken, call `ProfileInit` to initialize both arrays and record the start time.

Two functions are used for referring to time: `GetTime` and `GetElapsedTime`. `GetTime` should return system time in seconds (at the exact time it's called). `GetElapsedTime` should return the amount of time passed since the last frame (calculated by `1/current_frame_rate`).

```
#define NUM_PROFILE_SAMPLES 50
ProfileSample g_samples[NUM_PROFILE_SAMPLES];
ProfileSampleHistory g_history[NUM_PROFILE_SAMPLES];
float g_startProfile = 0.0f;
float g_endProfile = 0.0f;

void ProfileInit( void )
{
   uint i;

   for( i=0; i<NUM_PROFILE_SAMPLES; i++ ) {
      g_samples[i].bValid = false;
      g_history[i].bValid = false;
   }

   g_startProfile = GetTime();
}
```

Details on ProfileBegin

We're now ready to record a sample, so let's look at the function `ProfileBegin` in Listing 1.14.1. When this function is called, it first needs to check whether or not a sample by the same name exists. If it finds one, it means that this sample has been called before on this frame. In that case, we want to increment `iOpenProfiles`, increment `iProfileInstances`, and mark the `fStartTime`.

The variable `iOpenProfiles` is incremented by `ProfileBegin` and decremented by `ProfileEnd`. In effect, it keeps track of how many profile samples have begun and not ended. Note that this implementation does not deal properly with recursive calls (a sample begun more than once before being ended). For that reason, there is an `assert` that catches this condition.

The variable `iProfileInstances` is incremented by `ProfileBegin` in order to count how many times the sample has been called on a frame. As you might remember, this is one of the key pieces of information that is displayed in the output. If the sample has never been called this frame, the code finds a sample in the array that isn't being used and initializes it.

Details on ProfileEnd

Although `ProfileBegin` is fairly straightforward, the real work is done in `ProfileEnd`. This is the function that tallies the results and properly accounts for parent/child –relationships.

The first step in `ProfileEnd` is to find the sample in the array. Once the sample is found, the end time is recorded and the variable `iOpenProfiles` is decremented. Then the code loops through all samples, counting how many open samples currently exist (parents) and remembering the index of the most recently opened one (the immediate parent). The number of parents is then recorded in `iNumParents`. If there was a parent, the sample time is noted in the immediate parent's structure (to be subtracted from its sample time later).

Since this sample might be opened again on this frame, this sample time is saved in the `fAccumulator` so that another sample can use `fStartTime`. Listing 1.14.2 shows the `ProfileEnd` function.

Details on Processing the Profiling Data

All that's left is to process, format, and dump the data into a text buffer. This is done at the very end of the main game loop in the function `ProfileDumpOutputToBuffer`. Listing 1.14.3 shows this function. Note that two functions, `ClearTextBuffer` and `PutTextBuffer`, are used for outputting the text to the buffer. You have to supply these functions. `PutTextBuffer` puts the text string you give it into a vertically scrolling buffer so that each successive call inserts the new text string at the end of the last one. `ClearTextBuffer` simply clears the vertical scrolling buffer.

Two other functions, `StoreProfileInHistory` and `GetProfileFromHistory`, are also referenced. Both are outlined in Listing 1.14.4. These functions help keep track of the average, minimum, and maximum frame rate percentages for each sample. By calling `StoreProfileInHistory`, you are averaging the current measurement with every sample taken in the past. Then `GetProfileFromHistory` retrieves the new averages for you to display.

Further Enhancements

As you probably realized, this profiler is written completely in C (except for the C++ commenting style). By converting it to C++, it's possible to eliminate the need for the

ProfileEnd function. The trick is to exploit Class constructors and destructors. Carefully examine the following code, which profiles the for loop:

```
{
    ProfileInstance profile_instance( "Timing the For Loop" );

    for( int i=0; i<10000; i++ );
}
```

In the code, a ProfileInstance object is declared and initialized with a descriptive string. When its constructor is called, the string is recorded along with the system time. This information is then saved to global data structure much like the Profile-Begin function.

Since the object profile_instance is within the curly brackets, it is destroyed when program execution leaves that scope. Therefore, the destructor is called immediately after the for loop. The destructor records the system time and saves the information to the global data structure, exactly as the ProfileEnd function does.

Since the profiling line is now a little more awkward, we can streamline it by writing a simple macro:

```
#define Profile(a)        ProfileInstance profile_instance(a)
```

The profiling example with the macro looks like this:

```
{
    Profile( "Timing the For Loop" );

    for( int i=0; i<10000; i++ );
}
```

The beauty of this enhancement is that the profiling code now occupies a single line. Even better, it doesn't require a terminating statement containing a perfectly matching string. Profiling has never been so easy!

Putting It All Together

Amazingly enough, it doesn't take much to put together a fairly competent profiler. Simply realizing it is practical is the hardest part. On the CD that accompanies this book, you'll find the completely implemented profiler. In no time, this little profiler will become one of your most important debugging tools.

Listing 1.14.1: ProfileBegin

```
void ProfileBegin( char* name )
{
    uint i = 0;

    while( i < NUM_PROFILE_SAMPLES && g_samples[i].bValid == true ) {
```

```
        if( strcmp( g_samples[i].szName, name ) == 0 ) {
          //Found the sample
          g_samples[i].iOpenProfiles++;
          g_samples[i].iProfileInstances++;
          g_samples[i].fStartTime = OSGetTime();
          assert( g_samples[i].iOpenProfiles == 1 ); //max 1 open at once
          return;
        }
        i++;
    }

    if( i >= NUM_PROFILE_SAMPLES ) {
        assert( !"Exceeded Max Available Profile Samples" );
        return;
    }

    strcpy( g_samples[i].szName, name );
    g_samples[i].bValid = TRUE;
    g_samples[i].iOpenProfiles = 1;
    g_samples[i].iProfileInstances = 1;
    g_samples[i].fAccumulator = 0.0f;
    g_samples[i].fStartTime = GetTime();
    g_samples[i].fChildrenSampleTime = 0.0f;
}
```

Listing 1.14.2: ProfileEnd

```
void ProfileEnd( char* name )
{
    uint i = 0;
    uint numParents = 0;

    while( i < NUM_PROFILE_SAMPLES && g_samples[i].bValid == true )
    {
        if( strcmp( g_samples[i].szName, name ) == 0 )
        { //Found the sample
            uint inner = 0;
            int parent = -1;
            float fEndTime = GetTime();
            g_samples[i].iOpenProfiles--;

            //Count all parents and find the immediate parent
            while( g_samples[inner].bValid == true ) {
                if( g_samples[inner].iOpenProfiles > 0 )
                { //Found a parent (any open profiles are parents)
                    numParents++;
                    if( parent < 0 )
                    { //Replace invalid parent (index)
                        parent = inner;
                    }
                    else if( g_samples[inner].fStartTime >=
                             g_samples[parent].fStartTime )
                    { //Replace with more immediate parent
                        parent = inner;
```

```
            }
          }
          inner++;
        }

        //Remember the current number of parents of the sample
        g_samples[i].iNumParents = numParents;

        if( parent >= 0 )
        {  //Record this time in fChildrenSampleTime (add it in)
           g_samples[parent].fChildrenSampleTime += fEndTime −
              g_samples[i].fStartTime;
        }

        //Save sample time in accumulator
        g_samples[i].fAccumulator += fEndTime −
           g_samples[i].fStartTime;
        return;
      }
      i++;
    }
}
```

Listing 1.14.3: ProfileDumpOutputToBuffer

```
void ProfileDumpOutputToBuffer( void )
{
   uint i = 0;

   g_endProfile = GetTime();
   ClearTextBuffer();

   PutTextBuffer( "  Ave :   Min :   Max :   # : Profile Name\n" );
   PutTextBuffer( "------------------------------\n" );

   while( i < NUM_PROFILE_SAMPLES && g_samples[i].bValid == TRUE ) {
      uint indent = 0;
      float sampleTime, percentTime, aveTime, minTime, maxTime;
      char line[256], name[256], indentedName[256];
      char ave[16], min[16], max[16], num[16];

      if( g_samples[i].iOpenProfiles < 0 ) {
         assert( !"ProfileEnd() called without a ProfileBegin()" );
      }
      else if( g_samples[i].iOpenProfiles > 0 ) {
      assert( !"ProfileBegin() called without a ProfileEnd()" );
      }

      sampleTime = g_samples[i].fAccumulator −
         g_samples[i].fChildrenSampleTime;
      percentTime = ( sampleTime / (g_endProfile - g_startProfile ) )
         * 100.0f;

      aveTime = minTime = maxTime = percentTime;
```

```
            //Add new measurement into the history and get ave, min, and max
            StoreProfileInHistory( g_samples[i].szName, percentTime );
            GetProfileFromHistory( g_samples[i].szName, &aveTime,
                &minTime, &maxTime );

            //Format the data
            sprintf( ave, "%3.1f", aveTime );
            sprintf( min, "%3.1f", minTime );
            sprintf( max, "%3.1f", maxTime );
            sprintf( num, "%3d", g_samples[i].iProfileInstances );

            strcpy( indentedName, g_samples[i].szName );
            for( indent=0; indent<g_samples[i].iNumParents; indent++ ) {
                sprintf( name, "   %s", indentedName );
                strcpy( indentedName, name );
            }

            sprintf(line,"%5s : %5s : %5s : %3s : %s\n", ave, min, max,
                num, indentedName);
            PutTextBuffer( line );        //Send the line to text buffer
            i++;
        }

    {  //Reset samples for next frame
        unit i;
        for( i=0; i<NUM_PROFILE_SAMPLES; i++ ) {
            g_samples[i].bValid = FALSE;
        }
        g_startProfile = GetTime();
    }
}
```

Listing 1.14.4: StoreProfileInHistory and GetProfileFromHistory

```
void StoreProfileInHistory( char* name, f32 percent )
{
    uint i = 0;
    float oldRatio;
    float newRatio = 0.8f * GetElapsedTime();
    if( newRatio > 1.0f ) {
        newRatio = 1.0f;
    }
    oldRatio = 1.0f - newFraction;

    while( i < NUM_PROFILE_SAMPLES && g_history[i].bValid == TRUE ) {
        if( strcmp( g_history[i].szName, name ) == 0 )
        {  //Found the sample
            g_history[i].fAve = (g_history[i].fAve*oldRatio) +
                (percent*newRatio);
            if( percent < g_history[i].fMin ) {
                g_history[i].fMin = percent;
            }
```

```
        else {
            g_history[i].fMin = (g_history[i].fMin*oldRatio) +
                (percent*newRatio);
        }

        if( percent > g_history[i].fMax ) {
            g_history[i].fMax = percent;
        }
        else {
            g_history[i].fMax = (g_history[i].fMax*oldRatio) +
                (percent*newRatio);
        }
        return;
    }
    i++;
}

if( i < NUM_PROFILE_SAMPLES )
{  //Add to history
    strcpy( g_history[i].szName, name );
    g_history[i].bValid = TRUE;
    g_history[i].fAve = g_history[i].fMin = g_history[i].fMax =
        percent;
}
else {
    assert( !"Exceeded Max Available Profile Samples!" );
}
}

void GetProfileFromHistory( char* name, f32* ave, f32* min, f32* max )
{
    uint i = 0;
    while( i < NUM_PROFILE_SAMPLES && g_history[i].bValid == TRUE ) {
        if( strcmp( g_history[i].szName, name ) == 0 )
        {  //Found the sample
            *ave = g_history[i].fAve;
            *min = g_history[i].fMin;
            *max = g_history[i].fMax;
            return;
        }
        i++;
    }
    *ave = *min = *max = 0.0f;
}
```

References

[Abrash97] Abrash, Michael, *Michael Abrash's Graphics Programming Black Book*, The Coriolis Group, 1997.

[McConnell93] McConnell, Steve, *Code Complete*, Microsoft Press, 1993.

[Meyers95] Meyers, Scott, *More Effective C++*, Addison-Wesley Longman, Inc., 1996.

MATHEMATICS

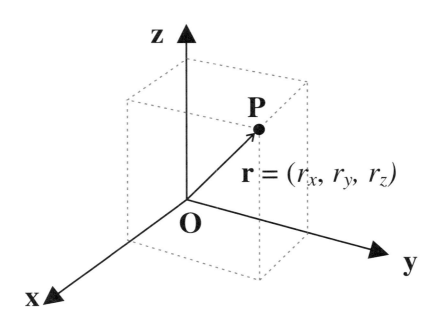

2.0

Predictable Random Numbers

Guy W. Lecky-Thompson

A large proportion of the success of a game in today's marketplace depends on a sufficiently detailed backdrop against which the game action can take place. Not only that, but the backdrop could also take an active role in the interaction between player and game. In search of this elusive mix, the traditional approach has been to simply hand-craft level data and store it in a relatively complex and space-consuming level file, to be replayed in real time.

Occasionally, however, the depth of some games falls below the expectations of the audience. This disappointment is caused by the fact that the game is sometimes simply not big enough; once the battles have been fought and the blood spilled, the player is left with something of an anticlimax.

Even with huge resources at their disposal, game designers often run out of the space needed to distribute a large and complex game, especially when the images used for rendering are photorealistic and the sound awesome, with thumping music and sampled explosions. These are important ingredients, but designers might often feel, rightly, that they are sacrificing something in return. This is especially evident in resource-limited environments such as we find in the handheld and console market.

One example of a huge and complex game is Elite. This game was originally written by David Braben and Ian Bell for the BBC Model B computer in 1980. It has since been ported to all home computer formats and is still as widely played now as in its heyday. The original game ran on a machine with 32KB of memory (16KB ROM and 16KB RAM), but it still boasted a depth of play that has yet to be matched: near-infinite planets, each with names and individual characteristics.

This article is a study of a technique that can be used to provide the depth of play that the audience deserves, even in limited-resource environments, such as that faced by the original Elite, without sacrificing any of the other vital ingredients that make up the perfect game.

Predictable Random Numbers

The underlying principle of this technique is that, to provide the illusion of infinity in a game universe, we need to satisfy two conditions of resolution. These we can term *macro-infinite* and *micro-infinite*. The first relates to the size of the universe in question, or the number of discrete entities. The second condition indicates the level of detail that each object supports. We shall see in the course of this article how both of these conditions can be achieved using the same underlying technique.

To avoid the storage of vast quantities of level data that will never satisfy the resolution requirements we have identified, we need to be able to generate the universe in real time, from the point of view of the player. Not only that, but this universe must also have the same appearance each time the game is restarted or played on a different platform or machine.

In order to simplify the issue slightly, we can assume that each object in the universe is expressed by its placement within the universe and a set of properties that indicate how it is to appear to the player. Each object can also interact with the player, which we discuss later in the article.

By way of example, let us consider as game universe a simplified model of our own. That is, we have a container object, the Galaxy, which contains a number of Stars. At game time, we would like to populate the Galaxy with Stars in a fashion that is both repeatable (it always "looks" the same from the player's perspective) and contains enough planets to provide a reasonable illusion of infinity.

To achieve this goal, we construct a series of Star objects and set the placement attributes of each one such that they exist at given points within the Galaxy. Consider that the placement attributes consist of an x and a y coordinate, and it is obvious that we need to generate values to place in these holders. This is where the predictable random number sequences are used; we can use a series of generated random numbers to provide us with coordinates for each of the Stars.

The simplest approach is provided by the ANSI C specifications and gives us the following two functions:

```
srand (seed)
rand()
```

Every time we need a sequence of numbers, we need a two-stage operation. The first seeds the generator with a given value, which is used to propagate the sequence. The same sequence is generated every time we seed with the same value. Thus the sequence is repeatable, but we do not need to store it anywhere, because it can be created on the fly. Thus we can generate a near-infinite galaxy entirely in game time, reducing our static storage requirements beyond measure.

The following is very simple pseudocode showing this concept in action for a given Galaxy of limited size. Assuming a possible grid of 100×100, we have 10,000 possible spaces into which we can place Stars. Notice that the seeding is performed once and once only per sequence of numbers; in the following case, we are seeding on galaxy number 1:

```
srand (1)
for galaxy_x = 1 to 100
```

```
for galaxy_y = 1 to 100
probability = rand() % 100
if probability > 70 then
        universe (galaxy_x,galaxy_y) = star
else
        universe (galaxy_x, galaxy_y) = no_star
```

Observant readers might have noticed a possible drawback: we still need to store the location of each Star somewhere, which requires about 10,000 bytes of space in real time. This size would never have fit inside a machine with 16KB of RAM. Even if it could, it is not scalable, even by a factor of 10.

Therefore, we should refine the technique a little. From the preceding example, we see that there is a 70% chance of a Star existing at a given point *x, y*. The number that determines this percentage is created from a seeded sequence based on the simple seed 1. Given that we would like a near-infinite population, it makes more sense to perform this calculation on an as-needed basis, as in the following code:

```
int StarAt (int nGalaxy, int nX, int nY)
{
    int x, y, nReturn;

    srand (nGalaxy);
    for (y = 0; y <= nY; y++)
    {
        for (x = 0; x < nX; x++)
        {
            nReturn = rand() % MAXIMUM_VALUE;
        }
    }
    return nReturn;
}
```

Alternative Algorithms

Many and varied chaotic and semi-chaotic algorithms give rise to the kind of behavior that we use here. This is not a mathematics paper, and some of the advanced algorithms that could be used require more processing power than is available, considering all the other operations that are being performed during game play, so we shall restrict ourselves to the discussion of a simple approach.

This approach can be represented by the following pseudocode:

```
Choose two large integers, Gen1 and Gen2, such that one
    is double the other
Choose a seed value that is between 1 and the smaller
    of the large integers
Choose a value Max that represents the highest number
    that is to be returned
```

```
For each iteration,
    Multiply Gen1 by the seed, and add Gen2
    The new seed is remainder of this value divided by Max
Return seed as the random value
```

This code works by first taking a repeatable sequence of numbers, which follow a pattern with a given starting point (a multiplication and addition) and then breaks the pattern by taking the remainder of a division. This result is then used to begin a new sequence with the same base equation. In this way, a fairly random sequence is built up. The source code for this sequence follows. This is taken from the Pseudorandom class, whose source code is provided on the accompanying CD.

```
PseudoRandomizer::PseudoRandomizer(unsigned long ulGen1,
                                   unsigned long ulSeed,
                                   unsigned long ulMax)
{
        this->ulGen1 = ulGen1;
        this->ulGen2 = ulGen1 * 2;
        this->ulSeed = ulSeed;
        this->ulMax  = ulMax;
}

unsigned long PseudoRandomizer::PseudoRandom()
{
        unsigned long ulNewSeed;

        ulNewSeed = (this->ulGen1 * this->ulSeed) + this->ulGen2;

        // Use modulo operator to ensure < ulMax
        ulNewSeed = ulNewSeed % this->ulMax;

        this->ulSeed = ulNewSeed;
        return this->ulSeed;
}
```

There is one final limitation. The largest number that can be generated using this system is 4,294,967,295. It follows from the previous algorithmic description that the sequence begins to repeat itself after the 4,294,967,295th iteration. This is a limitation of the data type used, a 32-bit unsigned integer. If greater numbers are required, it is necessary to move to a different representation.

Algorithms for Infinite Universes

So far, we have seen how we can decide on the existence of a game feature at a given location. We have satisfied half our brief: that of macro-infinite resolution. Now it is time to turn our attention to the use of pseudo-random numbers on the features and detail of the game objects: micro-infinite resolution.

In essence, micro-infinite resolution is all about zooming in on a point and seeing what we find there. To take our current example, we might say that each Star is orbited by zero or more Planets. These Planets orbit at a certain distance from the Star. They have other characteristics we examine later; specifying their location is enough for now.

In order to specify these items, we might choose to add an attribute to our Star class which gives the number of Planets, and calculate this. The following code extract shows how we can calculate an attribute of our Star class, the number of Planets:

```
/* Taken from header file */

class star {
private :
    ...
    int x_position, y_position;
    int number_of_planets;
    ...
public :
    ...
    void SetNumberOfPlanets();
    ...
};

/* Taken from implementation file */

void star::SetNumberOfPlanets() {
    pseudorandom->seed(this->x_position + (this->x_position
        * this->y_position));
    this->number_of_planets = pseudorandom->generate() % 20;
}
```

We have skipped into a slightly higher gear with this code, some of which bears explaining. First, we are seeding on a unique value for the Star, based on the position given by the *x* and *y* coordinate properties of the Star object. This means that for each Star, we can generate values that are seeded for that particular object. Thus we reduce the probability of having two identical Star objects in circulation.

A second point to note is that we have taken the modulo of the generated number in order to limit the number of planets that may orbit this Star. To introduce more realism (and hence, a larger micro-infinite resolution), this code could be adapted based on other attributes of the Star, such as size, intensity, or proximity.

Armed with this information, we can now consider how we might use a similar technique that will enable us to generate a distance value for a given planet. As noted, the important starting point is the seed that is used to determine the features of the object. Bearing in mind that the seed should be unique to each possible planet, we must somehow incorporate the position of the parent Star as well as that of the Planet. The following code extract shows a possible approach:

```
/* Taken from header file */
```

```
class planet {
private :
    ...
    int distance_from_star;
    ...
public :
    ...
    void SetDistanceFromStar(int planet_number,
         int star_x_position, int star_y_position);
    ...
};

/* Taken from implementation file */

void planet::SetDistanceFromStar  (int planet_number
                                   int star_x_position,
                                   int star_y_position) {

    pseudorandom->seed(planet_number + (star_x_position +
       (star_x_position * this->star_y_position)));
    this->distance_from_star = pseudorandom->generate() % 20;
}
```

So, we have effectively "zoomed in" from Universe to Star to Planet, as far as specifying positions is concerned. To complete the backdrop (and our discussion of micro-infinite resolution), we should start to add properties using more sequences of predictable random numbers.

The key to this next stage is the ability to isolate for a given object in the universe a set of attributes that describe the object. After we have done that, it is necessary to decide on the representation of these attributes, given that a constant stream of random numbers is available.

Each of these attributes may in itself be an object (as Planet is to Galaxy is to Universe), with properties of its own that can be set in a similar way, by seeding on a unique reference. For the next example, we shall assume that we require a map of the Planet object and that this map is represented by a simple grid into which we can place other objects. The whole code for the Universe, Galaxy, Planet, and Map objects is contained on the CD that accompanies this book. The pseudocode might look like this:

```
// Define the map size (side x side)
map->grid_side = pseudorandom->generate() % 100

// Place an object on the map for a given position x,y
pseudorandom->seed((map->grid_side * y) + x)
map->grid_square(x,y) = pseudorandom->generate() % 2
```

(The modulo value 2 could be taken to mean that 0 is water and 1 is land, for example.)

In the preceding examples, the seeding has been omitted. As can be seen from the supplied code examples, the seed is generated on an object-by-object basis at instantiation of the object. In fact, the supplied code also stores a number of attributes used to generate the seed, which have been omitted here for the sake of brevity.

It can be proven from watching the ANSI `srand` and `rand` functions working together that there is more to choosing the seed than first meets the eye. Earlier, we proposed:

```
srand (x_position + (x_dimension * y_position))
```

where the generator is seeded on the unique reference generated for the point (*x, y*) based on the dimension of the target container. However, repeated runs using `srand` and `rand` show that this method produces a result that is far from chaotic. (See the article "Real-Time Realistic Terrain Generation," which contains a figure showing a pattern that is a result of using this technique with the ANSI generator.)

The CD that accompanies this book contains the entire code for the Pseudorandom class, but the following algorithm, which can be used for seeding the generator properly using just the ANSI functions or used along with the Pseudorandom class itself, is worth repeating here:

```
srand (y_position)
x = x_position
while x > 0
    rand()
    x = x − 1
```

The next call to `rand` yields the required number, which can be considered the first in the ensuing sequence.

Conclusion and Future Developments

In this article, we have seen how we can use macro- and micro-infinite resolution techniques, propagated by sequences of pseudo-random numbers, seeded on a unique object reference. These techniques enable us to create near-infinite game universes within the constraints of a limited-resource environment, by run-time generation.

Developers may choose to use this information "as is" or enhance it further. For example, events can also be approached in the same way, seeded on the play history, or in real time. This technique would ensure that if a fire occurred at a tavern at a given point in time (possibly in connection with actions made by a player), we could predict when it would happen and thus ensure that it took place at the same time in each game session.

The key to successful use of predictable random numbers lies in the judicious use of the seed in parallel with the object properties and play state.

References

Lecky-Thompson, Guy W., "Algorithms for an Infinite Universe," *Gamasutra,* available online at www.gamasutra.com/features/19990917/infinite_01.htm, September 17, 1999; contains a detailed discussion of the effects that can be achieved using this technique.

2.1

Interpolation Methods

John Olsen

Have you ever wanted to have your program move something from one location to another gradually over time? There are dozens of ways to do that, with varying degrees of flexibility and varying CPU requirements. Four of these methods are discussed in this article, giving details on how each method behaves:

- Frame-rate-dependent ease-out using floating-point math
- Frame-rate-dependent ease-out using integer math
- Frame-rate-independent linear interpolation
- Frame-rate-independent ease-in and ease-out

All these methods share some common ground. You start at a specific point, you want to be at some other point, and you might or might not have a time limit in mind for how long it should take to get there. The source and destination could be any numeric value or combination of values. For instance, they could be a temperature, altitude, 3D position, a direction or velocity vector, or any number of things. The interpolation is meant simply to take you from one value to another along a smooth path of some sort.

Should you want to perform these interpolation methods on a vector, for instance, you apply the algorithm to each component of the vector separately.

Frame-Rate-Dependent Ease-Out Using Floating-Point Math

This method behaves in a frame-rate-dependent manner, so it behaves differently if called at 10 frames per second than it does at, for instance, 20 frames per second. This means that you want to use this method only if accuracy is not your prime concern.

The concept behind this method is that you want to compute a weighted average of the current value and the desired value, with a heavier weight on the current value. This can be done with Equation 2.1.1. The new x value equals x_o, the original value, multiplied by a weighting factor, added to the final destination x value. The sum is divided by the total weights to properly preserve the scale. The resulting x is used as x_o for the next pass through the equation.

$$x = (x_o * (weight - 1) + x_f) \,/\, weight \tag{2.1.1}$$

The weight must be a value greater than one to get the expected behavior from this equation. Higher weights make it take longer to reach the desired position. This generates a smooth curve, as shown in Figure 2.1.1, which shows how the value changes rapidly at first, then settles toward the destination value as it approaches, which is called *ease-out*.

The sample C++ class that can be used for floating-point ease-out interpolation is named `CEaseOutDivideInterpolation` and can be found in Listing 2.1.1. You call `Setup()` when you are beginning an interpolation, passing in your starting and ending values and a scale factor that controls how quickly the interpolation occurs. With each pass through your real-time loop, you call `Interpolate()` to do the work, then call `GetValue()` to retrieve the current interpolated value. Interpolate returns TRUE when the interpolated value is no longer changing, indicating you are as close as you are going to get to the target. With this floating-point code, it could take a very long time to reach a steady state.

Frame-Rate-Dependent Ease-Out Using Integer Math

This method is very CPU friendly because it uses no division. This method is more important on console systems or older hardware with limited floating-point support. It works fast but has some restrictions on flexibility, even compared with the previous method.

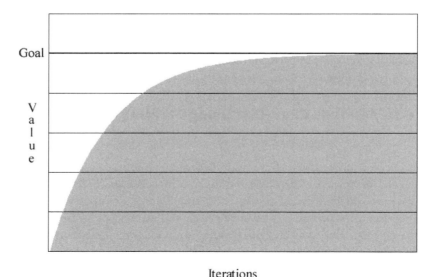

FIGURE 2.1.1. Floating-point ease-out.

The process of building a weighted average using integer math has some interesting side effects. The rate of change tends to stick at specific levels during the interpolation, and you are likely to never quite reach the destination point due to round-off errors. Equation 2.1.2 shows the modifications used. The values for $(2^n - 1)$ and n are things you want to hard code for speed, which gives a form similar to Equation 2.1.3, where ">>" represents a shift operator, as in the C language. The computations have some difficulties with round-off, as shown in Figure 2.1.2, which is much less smooth compared with Figure 2.1.1 and the floating-point method.

$$x = (x_o * (2^n - 1) + x_f) >> n \tag{2.1.2}$$

$$x = (x_o * 7 + x_f) >> 3 \tag{2.1.3}$$

Even with the less-than-smooth curve, this method is very useful for larger values. It tends to work well with fixed-point math, where some number of bits in your integer value is defined to be the fractional portion. For instance, a 32-bit number may be thought of as 20 bits for the integer portion and 12 bits for the fractional portion. To convert from the integer representation to the fixed-point representation in that case, you divide by 4,096. Increasing the scale in that way allows for much smoother behavior, resulting in a curve more similar to the one shown in Figure 2.1.1.

Listing 2.1.2 contains a sample C++ class called `CEaseOutShiftInterpolation` that can be used for integer-based ease-out interpolation. You call `Setup()` when you

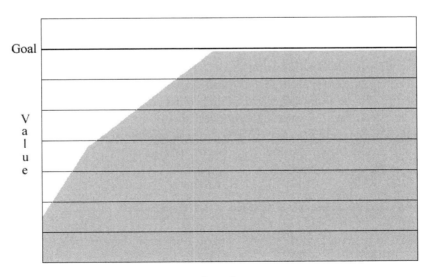

Iterations

FIGURE 2.1.2. Integer ease-out.

are beginning an interpolation, passing in your starting and ending values and a shift factor that controls how quickly the interpolation occurs. With each pass through your real-time loop, you call `Interpolate()` to do the work, then call `GetValue()` to retrieve the current interpolated value. `Interpolate()` returns TRUE when the interpolated value is no longer changing, indicating you are as close as you are going to get to the target. With the integer-based code, this will likely happen before you actually reach the desired target.

Frame-Rate-Independent Linear Interpolation

In the case of a linear interpolation, you want to compute an ideal velocity at the beginning of the move and simply apply that velocity each frame. This method gives a straight line when charted, as shown in Figure 2.1.3. A bit of entry-level physics shows how to get that velocity in Equation 2.1.4. If you are measuring x in feet and t in seconds, that gives you a velocity in feet per second.

$$v = (x_f - x_o) / t \tag{2.1.4}$$

Next you need to apply that velocity to each frame. To do this properly so that it is frame-rate independent, you need to know how long the frame took. Once you have that time per frame, you can calculate the change in position, using the already computed velocity, and add it to the original value, as shown in Equation 2.1.5. If you take a shortcut and calculate the velocity as distance per frame instead of distance per second, you lose the frame-rate-independent feature but can gain a little time by avoiding the multiply in Equation 2.1.5.

$$x = x_o + t_f * v \tag{2.1.5}$$

The sample C++ class that can be used for linear interpolation in Listing 2.1.3 is called `CLinearInterpolation`. You call `Setup()` when you are beginning an interpolation, passing in the starting and ending values and how long you want it to take to get there. With each pass through your real-time loop, you call `Interpolate()` with the length of time you want to process, then call `GetValue()` to retrieve the current interpolated value. Interpolate returns TRUE when the specified time has expired and you are at the desired target point.

Frame-Rate-Independent Ease-In and Ease-Out

Now we're getting to the point where a little more background in physics comes in handy. In order to produce a proper ease-in and ease-out, we need to begin with a zero velocity, speed up at a constant acceleration to some maximum velocity at the halfway point, then slow back down to be at a zero velocity as we arrive at the destination point. This process is shown in Figure 2.1.4.

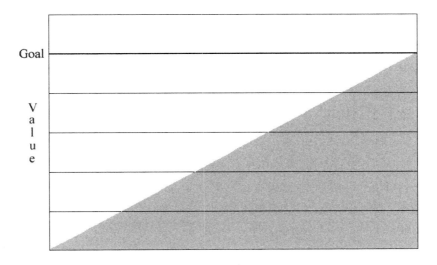

FIGURE 2.1.3. Linear interpolation.

The first step is to calculate the acceleration required. The acceleration is simply inverted for the second half of the trip. Any physics text should give you the necessary math, shown in Equation 2.1.6. We need to solve this equation for acceleration. We want to start at zero velocity, with x representing the average of the start and end points rather than the final destination, which gives Equation 2.1.7.

$$x = x_o + v_o t + \frac{1}{2} a t^2 \tag{2.1.6}$$

$$a = \frac{2(x - x_o)}{t^2} \tag{2.1.7}$$

Once the acceleration is known, you need to apply that acceleration to each frame. This method is similar to the way it was done in the linear interpolation in that you must take the time per frame into account. To start, the velocity is zero. At each frame, it is determined whether you are in the first or second half of the trip so you know whether to accelerate or decelerate. The velocity is incremented or decremented by some amount using Equation 2.1.8, then the velocity is applied to the position, as shown in Equation 2.1.5, the same as in the linear interpolation version but with a velocity that changes each frame. This velocity should be very near zero by the time you expect to be at the destination point, but it might not be an exact match due to round-off errors.

$$v = v_o + at \tag{2.1.8}$$

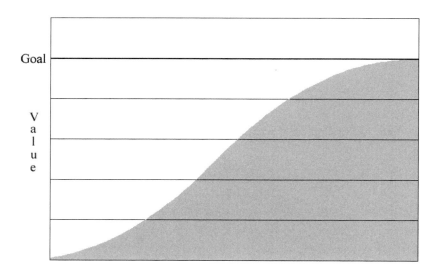

FIGURE 2.1.4. Ease-in and ease-out.

The final sample C++ class for this article is in Listing 2.1.4 and is one that can be used for ease-in and ease-out interpolation, named `CEaseInOutInterpolation`. The interface is identical to the linear interpolation class, which makes it convenient to swap one out for the other when testing. You call `Setup()` when you are beginning an interpolation, passing in the starting and ending values and how long you want it to take to get there. With each pass through your real-time loop, you call `Interpolate()` with the length of time you want to process, then call `GetValue()` to retrieve the current interpolated value.

Danger Zone

There are some things that you need to be very careful with as you apply interpolation in various portions of your software. Angles are problematic, since the naïve version of the algorithm would tell you that the angle halfway between an angle of 1°and 359° is 180°, when the proper answer might be 0°, depending on how you want the interpolation to behave. You need to be careful to assure that your numbers are in the proper ranges before interpolating angles, quaternions, or any values for which there are multiple ways to show the same value.

Furthermore, when referring to the sample code, you will likely want to take the ideas shown in the code and optimize them to meet your specific needs rather than use the code as it is.

Listing 2.1.1: CEaseOutDivideInterpolation Definition

```
class CEaseOutDivideInterpolation : CEaseOutShiftInterpolation
{
public:
    bool Setup(float from, float to, float divisor)
    {
        if(divisor <= 0)
        {
            return false;
        }
        _value = from;
        _target = to;
        _divisor = divisor;
        return true;
    }
    bool Interpolate() // Note: Not time dependent.
    {
        float oldValue = _value;
        if(_divisor > 0)
        {
            _value = (_value * (_divisor-1.0f) +
                    _target)/_divisor;
        }
        // Not likely to be true very often.
        return (_value == oldValue);
    }
    float GetValue()
    {
        return _value;
    }
private:
    float _value;
    float _target;
    float _divisor;
};
```

Listing 2.1.2: CEaseOutShiftInterpolation Definition

```
class CEaseOutShiftInterpolation
{
public:
    bool Setup(int from, int to, int shift)
    {
        if(shift <= 0)
        {
            return false;
        }
        _value = from;
        _target = to;
        _shift = shift;
```

```
            return true;
        }
        bool Interpolate() // Note: Not time dependent.
        {
            int oldValue = _value;
            if(_shift > 0)
            {
                _value = (_value * ((1 << _shift) - 1) +
                        _target) >> _shift;
            }
            // lots more likely to be true than with float version.
            return (_value == oldValue);
        }
        int GetValue()
        {
            return _value;
        }
    private:
        int _value;
        int _target;
        int _shift;
    };
```

Listing 2.1.3: CLinearInterpolation Definition

```
    class CLinearInterpolation
    {
    public:
        bool Setup(float from, float to, float time)
        {
            if(time < 0)
            {
                return false;
            }
            _remainingTime = time;
            _value = from;
            _step = (to-from)/time; // Calculate distance per second.
            return true;
        }
        // Return TRUE when the target has been reached or passed.
        bool Interpolate(float deltaTime)
        {
            _remainingTime -= deltaTime;
            _value += _step*deltaTime;
            return (_remainingTime <= 0);
        }
        float GetValue()
        {
            return _value;
        }
    private:
        float _value;
        float _step;
        float _remainingTime;
    };
```

Listing 2.1.4: CEaseInOutInterpolation Definition

```cpp
class CEaseInOutInterpolation
{
public:
    bool Setup(float from, float to, float time)
    {
        if(time <= 0)
        {
            return false;
        }
        _value = from;
        _target = to;
        _speed = 0.0f;
        // derived from x=x0 + v0*t + a*t*t/2
        _acceleration = (to-from)/(time*time/4);
        _remainingTime = _totalTime = time;
        return true;
    }
    bool Interpolate(float deltaTime)
    {
        _remainingTime -= deltaTime;
        if(_remainingTime < _totalTime/2)
        {
            // Deceleration
            _speed -= _acceleration * deltaTime;
        }
        else
        {
            // Acceleration
            _speed += _acceleration * deltaTime;
        }
        _value += _speed*deltaTime;
        return (_remainingTime <= 0);
    }
    float GetValue()
    {
        return _value;
    }
private:
    float _value;
    float _target;
    float _remainingTime;
    float _totalTime;
    float _speed;
    float _acceleration;
};
```

2.2

Integrating the Equations of Rigid Body Motion

Miguel Gomez

This article is intended as a tutorial on the theory and practice of simulating rigid body motion. The Newton-Euler equations of motion are derived, and some simple numerical integration methods are given. The reader is assumed to have taken college-level introductory courses in classical mechanics, linear algebra, calculus, vector analysis, and differential equation theory.

Kinematics: Translation and Rotation

In order to derive the differential equations that describe the motion of a rigid body, we need to lay some groundwork. First off, let's give ourselves a fixed coordinate frame with respect to which all our dynamic variables can be specified. By a *fixed coordinate frame*, we mean three linearly independent vectors (the basis) and a reference position (the origin) that is not translating or rotating (an inertial frame). Let's be easy on ourselves and use mutually orthogonal unit vectors for our basis (an *orthonormal basis*). We call this fixed frame the *world frame*, or *world space*. Any point in space can be specified with respect to this coordinate frame by three numbers, as shown in Figure 2.2.1.

An independent piece of matter the volume of which is negligible is called a *particle*. When the volume of a piece of matter becomes significant, it is called a *body*. The amount of matter in a particle or a body is its *mass*, and the amount of mass per unit volume is its *density*. In general, a body can have any shape and even deform over time. If the matter inside a body is distributed unevenly, it has *non-uniform density*. No matter how a body's mass is distributed, at any instant in time there is a point in space that is the *center of mass* of the body, $\mathbf{r}_{cm}$. The position of the center of mass is calculated with a weighted sum of every mass element, m_i, in the body:

$$\mathbf{r}_{cm} = \frac{\sum \mathbf{r}_i m_i}{\sum m_i} = \frac{\sum \mathbf{r}_i m_i}{M},$$

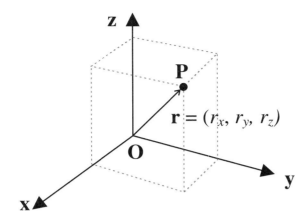

FIGURE 2.2.1. The vector **r** extends from the origin, **O**, to the point **P**.

When mass is continuously distributed throughout its volume, this sum becomes the integral:

$$\mathbf{r}_{cm} = \frac{\int \mathbf{r}\rho(r)dV}{\int \rho(r)dV} = \frac{\int \mathbf{r}\rho(r)dV}{M}.$$

In this case, each mass element is calculated by multiplying a volume element dV by a three-dimensional density function $\rho(\gamma)$:

$$m_i = \rho(\mathbf{r})dV.$$

It is helpful to associate a *local* coordinate frame with a body. For our purposes, the best choice for the origin is $\mathbf{r}_{cm}$, which we can take to mean the position of the body. Our orthonormal basis $\mathbf{R} = \{\mathbf{R}^0, \mathbf{R}^1, \mathbf{R}^2\}$ corresponds to the local X, Y and Z axes of the body (Figure 2.2.2).

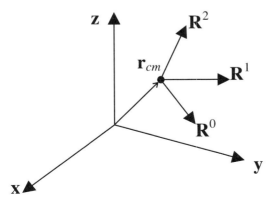

FIGURE 2.2.2. The vectors $\mathbf{R}^0$, $\mathbf{R}^1$, $\mathbf{R}^2$ define the x, y, and z axes of the local body frame.

It is also convenient to think of $\mathbf{R}^0$, $\mathbf{R}^1$, and $\mathbf{R}^2$ as the columns of a matrix $\mathbf{R}$, so that:

$$\mathbf{R} = \begin{bmatrix} R_x^0 & R_x^1 & R_x^2 \\ R_y^0 & R_y^1 & R_y^2 \\ R_z^0 & R_z^1 & R_z^2 \end{bmatrix}$$

This makes it easy to transform a vector from a body's local space to world space, and vice versa:

$\mathbf{v}_{world} = \mathbf{R}\mathbf{v}_{local}$ and $\mathbf{v}_{local} = \mathbf{R}^T \mathbf{v}_{world}$ (since $\mathbf{R}^T = \mathbf{R}^{-1}$ for an orthonormal basis)

Transforming a point is just as easy:

$\mathbf{r}_{world} = \mathbf{R}\mathbf{r}_{local} + \mathbf{r}_{cm}$ and $\mathbf{r}_{local} = \mathbf{R}^T (\mathbf{r}_{world} - \mathbf{r}_{cm})$

If at time t_1 a body's position is $\mathbf{r}_1$, and at time t_2 its position is $\mathbf{r}_2$ (Figure 2.2.3), then its *average velocity* between t_1 and t_2 was:

$$\mathbf{v}_{ave} = \frac{\mathbf{r}_2 - \mathbf{r}_1}{t_2 - t_1} = \frac{\Delta \mathbf{r}}{\Delta t}.$$

As we sample the trajectory at smaller and smaller time intervals, we approximate the *instantaneous velocity* of the particle, which is the true velocity of the particle at any time, t, and is equal to the derivative of its position with respect to time:

$$\mathbf{v} = \lim_{\Delta t \to 0} \frac{\Delta \mathbf{r}}{\Delta t} = \frac{d\mathbf{r}}{dt}.$$

Similarly, if its velocity changes from one instant to another, it is said to be accelerating, given by:

$$\mathbf{a} = \lim_{\Delta t \to 0} \frac{\Delta \mathbf{v}}{\Delta t} = \frac{d\mathbf{v}}{dt}.$$

In addition to translation, a body can undergo *rotation*. The amount of rotation the body experiences per unit time is called its *angular velocity* (also called *rotational velocity*), given by:

$$\lim_{\Delta t \to 0} \frac{\Delta \theta}{\Delta t} = \omega,$$

where $d\theta$ is a very small rotation (in radians) and ω is the angular velocity about the center of mass.

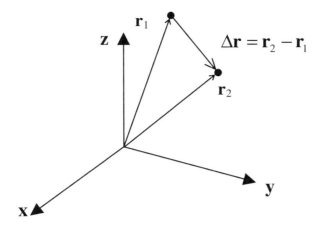

FIGURE 2.2.3. A body moves from $\mathbf{r}_1$ to $\mathbf{r}_2$ over a time $\Delta t = t_2 - t_1$.

Representing a finite rotation with a vector is kind of a cheat. Strictly speaking, finite rotations, no matter how small, cannot be considered vectors because they are not *commutative*. This means that if a body were rotated about the first axis by the first angle, then rotated about the second axis by the second angle, it would not *necessarily* achieve the same orientation as if the operations had been reversed. On the other hand, *infinitesimal* rotations (if you believe in them) are not order dependent, so they can be considered vectors. This is why angular velocity can be thought of as a vector [Chow95].

If a vector $\mathbf{r}$ is rotating at a constant angular velocity, then its time derivative with respect to the fixed world frame is:

$$\frac{d\mathbf{r}}{dt} = \frac{\partial \mathbf{r}}{\partial t} + \omega \times \mathbf{r}.$$

If the length of $\mathbf{r}$ is not changing, then the derivative simplifies to:

$$\frac{d\mathbf{r}}{dt} = \omega \times \mathbf{r}.$$

Using this relationship, the time derivative of $\mathbf{R}$ is:

$$\frac{d\mathbf{R}}{dt} = \omega^* \mathbf{R},$$

where the antisymmetric matrix:

$$\omega^* = \begin{bmatrix} 0 & -\omega_z & \omega_y \\ \omega_z & 0 & -\omega_x \\ -\omega_y & \omega_x & 0 \end{bmatrix}$$

takes the place of the cross product [Baraff97a].

Dynamics: Forces and Torques

Newton's first law of motion states that a body remains stationary or maintains a constant velocity unless acted on by an external *force*. This is also known as the law of conservation of *linear momentum*. The linear momentum vector, **p**, of a body is calculated by multiplying its velocity, **v**, by its mass, m:

$$\mathbf{p} = m\mathbf{v}.$$

The rate of change of momentum with respect to time is equal to the sum of all the forces (the *net force*) on this body:

$$\mathbf{F}_{net} = \sum \mathbf{F}_i = \frac{d\mathbf{p}}{dt} = m\frac{d\mathbf{v}}{dt} = m\mathbf{a}$$

When a body is moving relative to a point of reference and its motion is not directly toward or away from that point, it is said to have *angular momentum* with respect to that point. The angular momentum vector, **L**, is defined as the cross product of the position vector **r** and the linear momentum vector **p**. The vector **L** is therefore orthogonal to both **r** and **p** (see Figure 2.2.4).

When a force acts to change angular momentum, it is said to cause a *torque*. The time derivative of the angular momentum is equal to the net torque on the body:

$$\mathbf{N}_{net} = \sum \mathbf{N}_i = \frac{d\mathbf{L}}{dt} = \mathbf{r} \times \frac{d\mathbf{p}}{dt} = \mathbf{r} \times \mathbf{F}$$

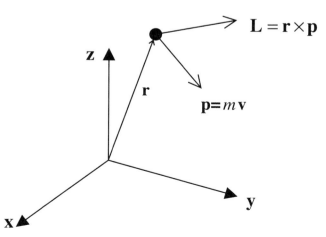

FIGURE 2.2.4. Angular momentum, **L**, is orthogonal to both **r** and **p**.

Special Properties of Rigid Bodies

If every element of matter in a body is unable to translate or rotate with respect to every other element of matter within that body, this object is called (oddly enough) a *rigid body*. (True rigid bodies don't exist in nature; every body, no matter how stiff, deforms somewhat when disturbed or when rotating. Deformation redistributes mass and changes the inertia tensor, complicating motion even further.)

Rigid bodies have a couple properties that make their motion easier to deal with, one of which is that their center of mass is fixed. When a rigid body is rotating, every little piece of mass, m_i, within it has angular momentum with respect to the center of mass, $\mathbf{r}_{cm}$. The body's total angular momentum (in world space) about its center of mass is the sum of all these infinitesimal parts:

$$\mathbf{L}_{cm} = \sum \mathbf{r}_i \times \mathbf{p}_i = \sum \mathbf{r}_i \times (m_i \mathbf{v}_i),$$

where $\mathbf{r}_i$ (also in world space) is the vector from $\mathbf{r}_{cm}$ to m_i. Since the velocity of m_i is given by:

$$\mathbf{v}_i = \boldsymbol{\omega} \times \mathbf{r}_i,$$

we can write:

$$\mathbf{L}_{cm} = \sum m_i \mathbf{r}_i \times (\boldsymbol{\omega} \times \mathbf{r}_i) = -\sum m_i \mathbf{r}_i \times (\mathbf{r}_i \times \boldsymbol{\omega}) = -\sum m_i \mathbf{r}_i^* \mathbf{r}_i^* \boldsymbol{\omega},$$

where:

$$\mathbf{r}_i^* = \begin{bmatrix} 0 & -r_{iz} & r_{iy} \\ r_{iz} & 0 & -r_{ix} \\ -r_{iy} & r_{ix} & 0 \end{bmatrix}.$$

Substituting and multiplying through gives:

$$\mathbf{L}_{cm} = \sum \begin{bmatrix} m_i(r_{iy}^2 + r_{iz}^2) & -m_i r_{ix} r_{iy} & -m_i r_{ix} r_{iz} \\ -m_i r_{ix} r_{iy} & m_i(r_{ix}^2 + r_{iz}^2) & -m_i r_{iy} r_{iz} \\ -m_i r_{ix} r_{iz} & -m_i r_{iy} r_{iz} & m_i(r_{ix}^2 + r_{iy}^2) \end{bmatrix} \boldsymbol{\omega}$$

$$= \begin{bmatrix} \sum m_i(r_{iy}^2 + r_{iz}^2) & \sum -m_i r_{ix} r_{iy} & \sum -m_i r_{ix} r_{iz} \\ \sum -m_i r_{ix} r_{iy} & \sum m_i(r_{ix}^2 + r_{iz}^2) & \sum -m_i r_{iy} r_{iz} \\ \sum -m_i r_{ix} r_{iz} & \sum -m_i r_{iy} r_{iz} & \sum m_i(r_{ix}^2 + r_{iy}^2) \end{bmatrix} \boldsymbol{\omega}.$$

This symmetric matrix of sums is called the *inertia tensor*, $\mathbf{I}$, where:

$$\mathbf{I} = \begin{bmatrix} I_{xx} & I_{xy} & I_{xz} \\ I_{xy} & I_{yy} & I_{yz} \\ I_{xz} & I_{yz} & I_{zz} \end{bmatrix}.$$

The diagonal elements are called the *moments of inertia*, and the off-diagonal elements are called the *products of inertia*. For rigid bodies with continuously distributed mass, the sums can be converted to the integrals:

$$I_{xx} = \lim_{m_i \to 0} \sum m_i (r_{iy}^2 + r_{iz}^2) = \int (r_y^2 + r_z^2)\rho(\mathbf{r})dV,$$

$$I_{xy} = \lim_{m_i \to 0} \sum -m_i r_{ix} r_{iy} = -\int r_x r_y \rho(\mathbf{r})dV,$$

and so on. The angular momentum about the center of mass can now be given in terms of the inertia tensor:

$$\mathbf{L}_{cm} = \mathbf{I}\omega.$$

The fact that to this point, the vector **r** has been specified with respect to world coordinates implies that the inertia tensor depends on the body's orientation and must be recalculated every time the body rotates. However, we can avoid having to reevaluate the integrals after every rotation by *diagonalizing* the inertia tensor. Diagonalization of a matrix involves changing to a basis in which all the off-diagonal elements become zero. This basis is unique and consists of the *eigenvectors* of the matrix. The diagonal elements with respect to this basis are called the *eigenvalues* of the matrix.

In general, the eigenvalues and eigenvectors of a matrix are not necessarily unique or even real. Fortunately, the eigenvalues and eigenvectors of a symmetric matrix are always real and mutually orthogonal [Lang87]. The normalized eigenvectors of the inertia tensor are called the *principal axes* of the rigid body, and the eigenvalues are called the *principal moments of inertia*. With respect to a body's principal axes, the inertia tensor reduces to:

$$\mathbf{I}_p = \begin{bmatrix} I_{xx} & 0 & 0 \\ 0 & I_{yy} & 0 \\ 0 & 0 & I_{zz} \end{bmatrix},$$

and the integrals simplify to:

$$I_{xx} = \iiint (y^2 + z^2)\rho(x, y, z)dxdydz$$

$$I_{yy} = \iiint (x^2 + z^2)\rho(x, y, z)dxdydz$$

$$I_{zz} = \iiint (x^2 + y^2)\rho(x, y, z)dxdydz$$

where x, y, and z are in the body's local frame. For rigid bodies, these integrals need to be calculated only once, and the inertia tensor in world space is given by:

$$\mathbf{I} = \mathbf{R}\mathbf{I}_p\mathbf{R}^\mathrm{T} \quad [\text{Baraff97a}].$$

The inverse of $\mathbf{I}$ is simply:

$$\mathbf{I}^{-1} = \mathbf{R}\mathbf{I}_p^{-1}\mathbf{R}^\mathrm{T},$$

where:

$$\mathbf{I}_p^{-1} = \begin{bmatrix} \dfrac{1}{I_{xx}} & 0 & 0 \\ 0 & \dfrac{1}{I_{yy}} & 0 \\ 0 & 0 & \dfrac{1}{I_{zz}} \end{bmatrix}.$$

It is often accurate enough to approximate the principal moments of inertia for a rigid body with those of a rectangular box of constant density. Luckily, the principal axes of a box are parallel to its edges, so the principal moments of inertia turn out to be:

$$I_{xx} = \frac{M}{12}(d_y^2 + d_z^2),\, I_{yy} = \frac{M}{12}(d_x^2 + d_z^2),\, \text{and } I_{zz} = \frac{M}{12}(d_x^2 + d_y^2),$$

where d_x, d_y, and d_z are the box dimensions in x, y, and z, respectively [Baraff97a]. For a more complete discussion on calculating inertia tensors of irregularly shaped bodies, see [Mirtich96].

In order to calculate the rotational motion of a rigid body, we need to know how angular velocity changes with respect to time. Differentiating the original relationship of angular velocity and angular momentum, we get:

$$\mathbf{N}_{net} = \frac{d\mathbf{L}}{dt} = \frac{d}{dt}(\mathbf{I}\omega) = \frac{d\mathbf{I}}{dt}\omega + \mathbf{I}\frac{d\omega}{dt} = \omega \times (\mathbf{I}\omega) + \mathbf{I}\frac{d\omega}{dt}, \quad [\text{Baraff97b}]$$

which ultimately gives:

$$\frac{d\omega}{dt} = \mathbf{I}^{-1}\Big[\mathbf{N}_{net} - \omega \times (\mathbf{I}\omega)\Big].$$

We can now state the differential equations that describe the translational and rotational motion of a rigid body. The translational motion of the center of mass follows the relationships:

$$\frac{d\mathbf{r}}{dt} = \mathbf{v}$$

$$\frac{d\mathbf{v}}{dt} = \frac{1}{m} \mathbf{F}_{net}$$

and the rotational motion is described by:

$$\frac{d\mathbf{R}}{dt} = \omega^* \mathbf{R}$$

$$\frac{d\omega}{dt} = \mathbf{I}^{-1} \left[\mathbf{N}_{net} - \omega \times (\mathbf{I}\omega) \right].$$

Together, these equations are known as the *Newton-Euler equations of rigid body motion*. Now that we have these equations, let's explore some simple methods for integrating them.

Integrating the Equations of Motion

Given an initial position, $\mathbf{r}_0$, the next position of the body, $\mathbf{r}_1$, can be approximated through the relation:

$$\mathbf{v} = \frac{d\mathbf{r}}{dt} \approx \frac{\mathbf{r}_1 - \mathbf{r}_0}{\Delta t}.$$

Solving for $\mathbf{r}_1$ gives:

$$\mathbf{r}_1 = \mathbf{r}_0 + \mathbf{v}\Delta t.$$

This method, known as *Euler integration*, is the simplest method for integrating solutions to initial value problems. The same technique can be used to integrate the remaining dynamic variables:

$$\mathbf{v}_1 = \mathbf{v}_0 + \frac{1}{m} \mathbf{F}_{net} \Delta t$$

$$\mathbf{R}_1 = \mathbf{R}_0 + \omega^* \mathbf{R}_0 \Delta t$$

$$\omega_1 = \omega_0 + \mathbf{I}^{-1} \left[\mathbf{T}_{net} - \omega \times (\mathbf{I}\omega) \right] \Delta t$$

Unfortunately, integrating orientation in this way introduces error, and $\mathbf{R}$ must be re-orthogonalized every frame. Furthermore, for high angular velocities, this integration is very inaccurate. A better way to integrate orientation is to find a rotation "vector" by multiplying the angular velocity by the time step:

$$\Delta\theta = \omega_0 \Delta t.$$

The angle through which to rotate the basis is:

$$\theta = \left|\Delta\theta\right|,$$

and the axis about which to rotate the basis is:

$$\hat{\mathbf{u}} = \frac{\Delta\theta}{\theta}.$$

The basis **R** can then be rotated by multiplying it by the matrix:

$$\mathbf{M}_r = \begin{bmatrix} 1 - 2(y^2 + z^2) & 2xy - 2sz & 2xz + 2sy \\ 2xy + 2sz & 1 - 2(x^2 + z^2) & 2yz - 2sx \\ 2xz - 2sy & 2yz + 2sx & 1 - 2(x^2 + y^2) \end{bmatrix}$$

where $s = \cos(\frac{\theta}{2})$, and $(x, y, z) = \hat{u} \sin(\frac{\theta}{2})$, so that $\mathbf{R}_1 = \mathbf{M}_r\mathbf{R}_0$ [Watt 2000].

If orientation is stored as a unit quaternion, **q**, then:

$$\frac{d\mathbf{q}}{dt} = \frac{1}{2}\omega\mathbf{q},$$

where ω is the pure quaternion $\omega_x\mathbf{i} + \omega_y\mathbf{j} + \omega_z\mathbf{k}$. The orientation can now be integrated with the formula:

$$\mathbf{q}_1 = \mathbf{q}_0 + \frac{1}{2}\omega\mathbf{q}\Delta t,$$

It is important to normalize **q** after each step to prevent "drift" in the solution [Baraff97a].

Although the Euler method is the simplest way to integrate differential equations, it is also the least accurate and least stable. If the angular velocity gets too high, the angular velocity grows exponentially to infinity. A simple hack to keep the solution from exploding is to multiply the angular velocity by a scale factor not much less than 1 (maybe 0.999) every frame. This method works, but it has the unfortunate effect of slowing the rotation to a stop. For discussions of more advanced integration techniques, see [Derrick97], [Gerald99], and [Hairer93].

References

[Baraff97a] Baraff, David, "An Introduction to Physically Based Modeling: Rigid Body Simulation I—Unconstrained Rigid Body Dynamics," available online at www.cs.cmu.edu/~baraff/pbm/pbm.html, 1997.

[Baraff97b] Baraff, David, "An Introduction to Physically Based Modeling: Rigid Body Simulation II—Nonpenetration Constraints," available online at www.cs.cmu.edu/~baraff/pbm/pbm.html, 1997.

[Chow95] Chow, Tai L., *Classical Mechanics*, John Wiley & Sons, Inc., 1995.

[Derrick97] Derrick, William R., and Grossman, Stanley I., *A First Course in Differential Equations with Applications*, third edition, West Publishing Company, 1987.

[Gerald99] Gerald, Curtis F., and Wheatley, Patrick O., *Applied Numerical Analysis,* sixth edition, Addison Wesley Longman, Inc., 1999.

[Hairer93] Hairer, E., Norsett, S. P., and Wanner, G., *Solving Ordinary Differential Equations I: Nonstiff Problems,* second edition, Springer-Verlag, 1993.

[Lang87] Lang, Serge, *Linear Algebra*, third edition, Springer-Verlag, 1987.

[Mirtich96] Mirtich. Brian, "Fast and Accurate Computation of Polyhedral Mass Properties," *Journal of Graphics Tools* (vol. 1, no. 2): pp. 31–50, 1996.

[Watt2000] Watt, Alan, *3D Computer Graphics*, third edition, Addison-Wesley, 2000.

2.3

Polynomial Approximations to Trigonometric Functions

Eddie Edwards

The way we approach specific problems changes as hardware evolves. Take, for example, the trigonometric functions sine, cosine, and arctangent. It used to be that we would never even dream of calculating these on the fly; we would use a table lookup. Using a table has its drawbacks—quantization errors being the main problem—but it is very fast. Or at least, it used to be.

These days, CPU speed seems to be increasing much faster than RAM speed. True random access is particularly slow, since many types of RAM are optimized for cache line refills rather than individual word accesses (RDRAM being a case in point). Meanwhile, the time it takes a CPU to do a floating-point multiply has gone down from more than 10 cycles to just 1 cycle in some architectures. Now that the CPU is so much faster than the RAM, it makes sense to reassess our assumptions about table lookups. We can generally do a lot of calculation in the time it takes to access a single memory location, and these calculations do not suffer from quantization errors to anything near the same degree. Maybe we should consider calculating values for sine and cosine rather than just looking them up in a table.

This proposal raises the very interesting question, "How?" The ubiquitous solution to calculating complex functions is through polynomial approximation; we find a polynomial that approximates the function we want. We then stuff our value of x into this polynomial and out pops an approximate value for the function. Since multiplies are so cheap these days, this looks like a very fast way to evaluate the function. In the first part of this article, I describe in some detail how polynomial approximations work and how to manipulate polynomials to your own ends.

The problem of calculating the function is now transformed into the problem of finding a good polynomial to use as an approximation. This is a search for a set of "magic" numbers—the polynomial coefficients—that give good results.

The best-known method for obtaining these numbers is to look at the Taylor series for the function. The *Taylor series* is an infinite polynomial that is equivalent to the function (for some range of x). If we truncate the Taylor series, we get a finite polynomial, which we assume to be a good approximation to the function. Later in this article we demonstrate how Taylor series work and discuss their limitations.

There are alternatives to the Taylor series method that are not so well known. The main thrust of this article is to explain one technique, the Lagrange series, which has some very specific advantages over the Taylor series. The Lagrange series is capable of entirely removing certain errors in the approximation and on average gives results that are many times more accurate.

Polynomials

A *polynomial* is simply a sum of powers of a variable (*x*), each multiplied by a coefficient. The standard way to write a polynomial is as follows:

a[0] + a[1]*x + a[2]*x*x + a[3]*x*x*x + ... a[d]*pow(x,d)

The numbers *a[]* are called the *coefficients* of the polynomial. The number *d* is the *degree* of the polynomial. We can demonstrate these elements in C++:

```
float Poly::Evaluate(float x)
{
  float  powx = 1;
  float  sum = 0;

  for (int n = 0; n <= d; n++)
  {
    sum += a[n] * powx;
    powx *= x;
  }

  return sum;
}
```

This is the most obvious and straightforward way to evaluate the polynomial with a program, although many alternative methods exist. These alternatives rely on factorizing the polynomial in some way. I do not recommend the alternative methods, for two reasons:

1. Factorizing often leads to a divide per factor, which means your coefficients are susceptible to rounding errors (especially in single-precision floating point).
2. Calculating using factoring has a critical path containing all the multiplies. Calculating the simple way has a critical path containing just one multiply and one add, so the simple method pipelines much better on CPUs where this is important.

For instance, one alternative method that requires no divides is this factorization:

a[0] + x*(a[1] + x*(a[2] + x*a[3] ...))

This method is evaluated in C++ code like this:

```
float Poly::Evaluate(float x)
{
  float  sum = a[d];

  for (int n = d - 1; n >= 0; n--)
  {
    sum = sum * x + a[n];
  }

  return sum;
}
```

Note that each iteration multiplies against the results of the previous iteration, so the loop cannot be broken down and pipelined. This method does have the advantage that only one accumulator register is required, so it might be a good choice for the x86 architecture's scalar FPU.

Domain and Range

The domain of a function is the area over which it can be called. The range is the range of values it returns, over its domain. You might think that the domain of one of these polynomials is infinite. Not so!

When we look at the evaluation of the polynomial, we see it is the sum of terms of the form:

a[n]*pow(x,n)

Each of these terms must itself be a floating-point number, so each one must be in the range of a float, which is approximately 0 to 2^{127} (ignoring sign, and assuming IEEE single-precision format).

If we take the base-2 logarithm of this polynomial, we get:

log2(a[n] * pow(x,n)) = log2(a[n]) + n * log2(x) < 127

which gives us a series of inequalities that *log2(x)* must obey. Quite clearly, this is not infinite! For instance, if the degree of the polynomial is 10 and the value of all the coefficients is 1, we have:

log2(x) < 12.7

giving an effective domain on *x* of −6000 to +6000.

The range of a function is often well known. For instance, the range of sine is −1.0 to +1.0. The range of other functions is infinite; for instance, tangent gets larger and larger as its argument approaches 90 degrees.

We now come to a classic numerical accuracy problem. Suppose we want to calculate *sin(6000.0)* with a 10th degree polynomial. From the domain analysis, we know that the floating-point terms will become very large—up to just under 2^{127}—but we know that the final result is between −1.0 and +1.0. The final result comes from the final sequence of additions, and since each number added is very large, they must all *just* cancel out to give the small numbers expected.

Unfortunately, the single-precision floating-point format stores only 23 bits of precision, which means that for numbers as large as $2\wedge127$, there is no precision at all in the range 0.0 to 1.0. In fact, the lowest bit has value $2\wedge104$! So we can expect to have errors of the order of $2\wedge100$ in a value that is of the order 1.0, which is as good as saying we have no idea what the answer is! (In fact, it is like saying, "Although I know my keyboard is on my desk, my calculations tell me it is actually on a small planet somewhere in the vicinity of Betelgeuse.")

It turns out that this is not a problem for sine and cosine, since they are periodic functions. If you need to know *sin(6000.0)*, you can subtract 2*pi repeatedly until it is in a better range (*–pi* to +*pi*) and then apply the polynomial. A fast way to do this is as follows:

1. Multiply the value of *x* by 65536/2*pi.
2. Cast *x* to an integer.
3. Shift it left 16 bits (on a 32-bit processor).
4. Shift it right 16 bits, arithmetically (to extend the sign).
5. Cast *x* back to float.
6. Multiply the value of *x* by 2*pi/65536.

This method gives the correct value of *x* between –*pi* and +*pi*, with 16 bits of resolution.

You may want to work exclusively in the number system obtained after Step 3, where all the significant bits are at the top of a machine word. This format is a fixed-point format representing the number of turns, with 32 bits of fraction and 0 bits of integer, so if you add two angles together you get the expected result without any modulus operation (in effect, the finite word length of the computer does the modulus operation for you).

This unit of measure is called a *rotation*, although in my experience every company gives the unit a different name, chosen as the most confusing term possible! Since the number is the number of rotations, stored as an unsigned 32-bit fraction in fixed point, the name *rotation* seems to be the most suitable.

It is usually most efficient to convert between radians and rotations only when you need to use radians and to use rotations the rest of the time.

Changing the Domain

The preceding example shows how we can change the units of our function. For instance, the sine function takes radians, but by pre-multiplying by 2*pi/65536, we can make it take rotations as a signed 16-bit fraction (s.15, 1:0:15).

We can, in fact, change the units of our function intrinsically by changing the polynomial coefficients. Suppose we have a function that takes radians, but we want it to take degrees. We could just do the following:

```
float mult = (2.0 * pi) / 360.0;
return SinePoly::Evaluate(x * mult);
```

Or we could rewrite `Evaluate`:

```
float Poly::Evaluate(float x)
{
  float mult = (2.0 * pi) / 360.0;
  float powx = 1;
  float powmult = 1;
  float sum = 0;

  for (int n = 0; n <= d; n++)
  {
    sum += a[n] * powx * powmult;
    powx *= x;
    powmult *= mult;
  }
}
```

Now here's the trick: We replace each *a[n]* with *a[n] * powmult* according to this code, and then we can use the original code to evaluate the function with the new units. So we do the following:

```
void Poly::ChangeUnits(float old_units, float new_units)
{
  float mult = old_units / new_units;
  float powmult = 1;

  for (int n = 0; n <= d; n++)
  {
    a[n] *= powmult;
    powmult *= mult;
  }
}
```

This method, of course, works only if *new_units* is not zero.

Be very careful using this technique. If the new range is too high (and 360 probably is), we get the same exponent problems we looked at in the last section. This method cannot be used to create a polynomial that directly takes signed 16-bit fractional rotation values, since the evaluation will overflow. However, it can be used to change a polynomial's range slightly, by a factor of up to around 4.0, depending on the polynomial's degree.

We can also add an offset into the domain, but this process is much more involved. It involves substituting the value *(x + off)* into the polynomial in place of *x*.

For instance, substituting *(x + 2)* for *x* in the polynomial *(1 + x*x)* gives *(1 + (x+2)*(x+2))*, which simplifies to *(1 + 4*x + x*x)*. Therefore, the value of poly at *x = 1* is 10, which is the value of the old poly at *x = 1 + 2 = 3*. This replacement is tedious if done by hand; the method `OffsetDomain()` on the CD that accompanies this book can be used to do it mechanically.

If you do want to change the domain, we recommend you simply do it to x by hand before invoking the polynomial evaluation method. This method adds one or two cycles to the evaluation, but it is highly robust and very easy.

Changing the Range

Compared with the domain, the range is easy to deal with, and the results are just what you expect. To change the output units of a polynomial, simply multiply each coefficient by the factor, as follows:

```
void Poly::ChangeOutputUnits(float old_units, float new_units)
{
  float mult = new_units / old_units;

  for (int n = 0; n <= d; n++)
  {
    a[n] *= mult;
  }
}
```

This solution works, since:

mult*(a[0] + a[1]*x + a[2]*x*x + ...) = mult*a[0] + mult*a[1]*x + mult*a[2]*x*x + ...

To offset the output, simply add the offset to *a[0]*, since:

offset + a[0] + a[1]*x + ... = (offset + a[0]) + a[1]*x + ...

So, you can change the range of a polynomial intrinsically and at zero cost to the final evaluation procedure.

Even and Odd Polynomials

When you come to manipulating polynomials on the computer, you will find that many coefficients become very small—e.g., $1.546 * 2^{-80}$. You may well ask, "Is this the correct coefficient, or should the coefficient actually be zero?" The answer to this question comes from the analysis of even and odd polynomials.

An even function is one where:

$$f(-x) = f(x)$$

That is, its graph is symmetric about the line $x = 0$. An odd function is one where:

$$f(-x) = -f(x)$$

That is, its graph is anti-symmetric. In trigonometry, sine is an odd function, and cosine is an even function.

Not all functions are either even or odd. For instance, *(x + 1)* is neither.

A polynomial is made up of sums of the functions 1, *x*, *x*x*, *x*x*x*, etc. Each one of these basic functions is either odd or even.

1 = 1 is EVEN

x = –(–x) is ODD

x*x = (–x*–x) is EVEN

x*x*x = –(–x*–x*–x) is ODD

so:

x^n is EVEN if n is EVEN, and ODD if n is ODD

It should be reasonably clear that if a polynomial contains all even powers of *x*, the polynomial itself is even, and that if it contains all odd powers of *x*, the polynomial itself is odd. (This is where the terms *even* and *odd* come from in the first place.) If a polynomial contains some odd powers and some even powers, it is neither even nor odd.

Now the important point: If a polynomial approximates an even function, the polynomial itself should be even. It's no use if your polynomial says that *sin(x)* does not equal *–sin(–x)*, because it does!

If you can tell by analysis that a coefficient should be zero (even if a program tells you the coefficient is 1.546 * 2^–80), you should set it to zero. This is the correct value, and the bogus non-zero coefficient is the result of floating-point rounding errors. Leaving the incorrect value in could lead to unexpected results.

This implies that if the function is even, *a[n]* is zero whenever *n* is odd; if the function is odd, *a[n]* is zero whenever *n* is even. If you have a supposed polynomial approximation to *sin(x)* that has *a[2]*, not zero, you know the approximation is wrong.

Taylor Series

The Taylor series has its roots in a very simple procedure we can use to copy polynomials, which is based on the simple mathematical operations of evaluation and differentiation. We have seen evaluation already; now we must look at differentiation. Fortunately, differentiation of polynomials is quite straightforward.

When we differentiate a polynomial, we get:

a[1] + a[2]*2*x + a[3]*3*x*x + a[4]*4*x*x*x + … + a[d]*d*pow(x, d–1)

Each coefficient is multiplied by its power, and then the power is reduced by one. This process can be described as a method:

```
void Poly::Differentiate()
{
  for (int n = 1; n <= d; n++)
  {
    a[n-1] = a[n] * n;
  }
  a[d] = 0;
  if (d > 0) d--;
}
```

Note that the derivative of the polynomial *a[0]* (degree zero) is 0 (also degree zero), which explains the "special case" lines of code in the preceding example.

Let's differentiate again, which gives:

a[2]*2 + a[3]*3*2*x + a[4]*4*3*x*x + ...

Each time we differentiate, the degree of the polynomial goes down by one. Now look at *a[n][0]* at each stage. (Here, the first array subscript denotes the number of differentiations, starting with zero differentiations):

a[0][0] = a[0]
a[1][0] = a[1]
a[2][0] = 2*a[2]
a[3][0] = 3*2*a[3]
a[4][0] = 4*3*2*a[4]
a[n][0] = n! * a[n]

Each coefficient is rotated in turn into *a[0]*, and multiplied by *n!*.

We can obtain *a[0]* from the polynomial object by calling `Evaluate(0)`; by calling `Differentiate()`, we can rotate each coefficient into *a[0]*. So, by calling both functions, we can take the polynomial apart:

```
void Poly::CopyPoly(Poly* p)
{
  float nfact = 1;

  d = 0;
  a[0] = p->Evaluate(0);
  p->Differentiate();

  while (!p->IsZero())
  {
  d++;
  nfact *= d;
  a[d] = p->Evaluate(0) / nfact;
  p->Differentiate();
  }
}
```

`IsZero()` is the function that tells us if the polynomial is zero everywhere (i.e., `Evaluate(x)` = *0.0* for all *x*):

```
bool Poly::IsZero()
{
  return ((d == 0) && (a[0] == 0));
}
```

The important thing to note here is that we created the new polynomial from the old polynomial only through its operations IsZero(), Evaluate(), and Differentiate().We never directly asked for either the polynomial's degree or for any of its coefficients.

This point is interesting because in mathematics these three operations make sense for a vastly wider class of objects than just polynomials. This wider class is technically known as *infinitely differentiable functions* and includes all the functions with which you are most likely to be familiar. In fact, only strange functions such as true fractals and the Dirac delta function (which contains an infinity at *x=0*) give problems in practice. The other class of functions that give problems are those with discontinuities or sharp corners (which are equivalent to discontinuities in the *differentiated* function), but we look at some ways to deal with these functions later.

In object-oriented terminology, the class Poly is itself a subclass of Differentiable-Function, which has virtual methods IsZero(), Evaluate(), and Differentiate().

This is how Taylor series are calculated—or rather, how the subset of Taylor series called "Taylor series expanded about *x = 0*" is calculated. The following function calculates Taylor series in their full glory:

```
void Poly::MakeTaylorSeries(DifferentiableFunction* f, float pt)
{
  float nfact = 1;

  d = 0;
  a[0] = f->Evaluate(pt);
  f->Differentiate();

  while (!f->IsZero())
  {
    d++;
    nfact *= d;
    a[d] = f->Evaluate(pt) / nfact;
    f->Differentiate();
  }

  OffsetDomain(pt);
}
```

This function calculates the series for *f(x − pt)* and then offsets the domain to match. You may ask why you would use values of *pt* other than 0. The answer is that some functions have no well-defined value at *x = 0* (e.g., *1/x* is not defined there), so we move away from that specific point to prevent problems with infinities.

Example: Sine and Cosine

The derivative of sine is cosine, and the derivative of cosine is –sine, so we can use function pointers to define the class `TrigFunction` that behaves like these two:

```
class TrigFunction : public DifferentiableFunction
{
public:
  TrigFunction()                { fptr = sin; sign = 1; }

  bool    IsZero()              { return false; }
  float   Evaluate(float x)     { return sign * float(fptr(double(x))); }
  float   Differentiate()
  {
    if (fptr == sin)
    {
      fptr = cos;
    }
    else
    {
      fptr = sin;
      sign = -sign;
    }
  }

private:
  double (*fptr)(double); // stdlib math function sin or cos
  float    sign;          // sign of function −1 or +1
};
```

Unfortunately, although the `MakeTaylorSeries` function accepts an object of this class, it never returns, because the derivative never becomes zero. Houston, we have a problem!

There are several ways around this dilemma:

1. Specify the maximum degree of the polynomial that `MakeTaylorSeries` will return.
2. Specify the minimum coefficient value. Since the coefficients are "probably" going to get smaller and smaller, since $n!$ gets larger and larger, we can terminate the routine once the last coefficient is too small.

The first way is guaranteed to work; the second way might still fail. Why? Because the coefficients might *not* get smaller and smaller. The mathematical analysis of this concept is beyond the scope of this article, but you can rest assured that most functions you will deal with *will* have coefficients that get smaller and smaller. Nevertheless, you should always set a large limit on the degree, just in case.

Truncated Taylor Series

The Taylor series for sine was a polynomial of infinite degree. Which is a shame, because we can only evaluate (or even store) a polynomial of finite degree. In fact, for a game, a small degree is quite desirable.

When we truncate the series, an error is introduced (over and above the usual floating-point error) because the terms we ignore do make a contribution to the final result. It can be shown that the error increases as *x* increases, which is another good reason to limit the domain of your polynomial.

You can analyze the error mathematically, if you like, but we won't go into the details here. The best thing to do in reality is practical experiments:

1. Sample the errors in your estimate, using the double-precision `sin()` and `cos()` functions to compare. Get the average and maximum absolute errors. As a rule of thumb, get the error below *1 / p*, where *p* is the number of pixels diagonally across the screen. For console games at 640×480, *p* is around 800; for PC games at $1{,}280 \times 1{,}024$ or above, *p* can be more than 1,600.

2. Set up a large, slowly rotating sprite that fills the screen. Use your sine function to rotate it. Watch for artifacts such as jerkiness or expanding and shrinking in size. Ignore the harsh jibing of those who say, "Ooh, you can rotate a sprite!" in a sarcastic tone.

For single-precision float and for a range *–pi*/2 to *+pi*/2, taking the first five coefficients of sin and cos works well. This method is also quite fast on current hardware—indeed, one current vector FPU chip actually implements this series on-chip in microcode. However, it is something of a pain to use this range, since it requires some rather tedious manipulations of the angle before the series can be used—a fact that the designers of the hardware seem to have missed.

If you extend the five-coefficient series for sine and cosine to *–pi* and *+pi*, you get an error of around 1 part in 300. The unfortunate thing is that you get the following values:

sin(0) = 0.0
sin(pi) = 0.003
sin(–pi) = –0.003 (obviously, since sine is odd)

This problem shows up in the rotating-sprite test as a "jerk" when the angle passes from *+pi* to *–pi*. The error is 1 part in 300, but this is doubled across the boundary, so the rotation vector jumps from *y* = –0.003 to *y* = +0.003—a jump of 0.006. It is certainly noticeable at 640×480.

With the Taylor series, there is nothing we can do to fix this problem except increase the degree of the polynomial. However, there is more to polynomial approximation than just the Taylor series.

Lagrange Series

The *Lagrange series* is my name for a type of approximation series derived using Lagrange's formula. Unlike the Taylor series, there is not one single Lagrange series for a given function. There is instead a whole family of series, from which we choose based on which results we want to be exactly correct and which results we allow to wander from the correct value.

For instance, we can say that we require sin to be exactly correct for the well-known points:

sin(−pi) = 0.00000
sin(−pi/2) = −1.00000
sin(0) = 0.00000
sin(pi/2) = 1.00000
sin(pi) = 0.00000

If our approximation were exactly correct for these points, we would know that:

1. The size of the object would not grow when it was rotated 90, 180, or 270 degrees. It would exactly match the original size.
2. The sin function would pass through 0 as it crossed the 360-degree boundary, would therefore remain continuous at that point, and would therefore exhibit no jerkiness.

A theorem proved by Lagrange states that for any given N points there is a unique $(N–1)$th degree polynomial that passes exactly through all the points. If we calculate this polynomial, we have an approximation that has the properties listed.

Suppose we want to find a 9th-degree polynomial for sine. We need this polynomial to be unique, so we must choose 10 points at which sine must be exactly correct. This is unfortunate, since we want to have a symmetrical point distribution about $x = 0$. With one point at $x = 0$, we must have an odd number of points to achieve the goal. If we put an extra point on one side, we couldn't guarantee that it would be matched on the other side.

To get an odd number of points, we use a 10th-degree polynomial. Fortunately, we know that sine is odd, so we know that $a[10] = 0$, so the 10th-degree polynomial is the same as the 9th-degree one.

There are many choices of points (infinitely many!), so we choose points at well-known values. You could instead choose points that are evenly distributed. The only critical points are at −180 and +180 degrees, since these points ensure continuity over the boundary and hence no jerkiness.

Notice that by choosing points, we assume no prior knowledge of our function. We don't assume, for instance, that it can be differentiated. This can be a useful feature if, for instance, we want to approximate a sampled waveform using a polynomial—but it can also be a big problem, since we can miss important "features" of the function graph. The message here is, make sure you know what your function looks like (in other words, graph it) before you choose your data points.

Calculating the Lagrange Series

The Lagrange series is obtained as a sum of polynomials—a different polynomial for each point. In this exposition, our data points are $x[0], ..., x[d]$, and the desired function values at these points are $y[0], ..., y[d]$.

First, consider the simple polynomials:

$$(x − x[n])$$

Each polynomial is first degree, and there are $(d+1)$ of them in total. The nth polynomial is zero when $x = x[n]$ and non-zero for all other values of x.

If we multiply all these polynomials together, we get a polynomial of degree $(d+1)$. This polynomial evaluates to zero at every data point, since one of its factors is zero at that point. For instance, it is zero at $x[2]$ because one of its factors is $(x − x[2])$.

Now, if we instead multiply *all but one* of the polynomials together, we get a polynomial of degree d that evaluates to zero at each data point *except for the one we missed out*. This is because it does *not* have a factor $(x − x[m])$ for the data point $x[m]$. The value at that data point is given by substituting $x[m]$ for x in the product polynomial:

$$c[m] = (x[m] − x[0])(x[m] − x[1])...(x[m] − x[m−1])(x[m] − x[m+1])...(x[m] − x[d])$$

The next step is to multiply the product polynomial by $y[m]/c[m]$, a process called *normalization*. The result is a new polynomial that is equal to $y[m]$ at data point $x[m]$ but is equal to 0 at every other data point. (Note that multiplying the polynomial by $y[m]/c[m]$ is equivalent to changing the output units by that factor, as discussed earlier.)

This concept gives us the building block for the Lagrange series. To get the Lagrange series itself, we need to generate all $(d+1)$ of these polynomials and then add them all together. At each data point $x[n]$, all but one of the polynomials evaluates to zero, whereas the other one evaluates to $y[n]$. We have therefore constructed a polynomial that is equal to $y[n]$ at each point $x[n]$, as desired.

For example, suppose we have the simple three-point case:

$x[0] = −1$
$y[0] = 4$
$x[1] = 0$
$y[1] = 2$
$x[2] = 1$
$y[2] = 4$

The simple polynomials are $(x − x[0])$, $(x − x[1])$, and $(x − x[2])$, which are equal to $(x + 1)$, $(x − 0)$, and $(x − 1)$. Let's look at data point $x[0]$. We multiply all the simple polynomials except $(x − x[0])$ together, which gives:

$(x – 0) * (x – 1) = x*x – x$

We evaluate this at $x[0]$, which gives:

$c[0] = –1*–1 – (–1) = 2$

We want $y[0]$ to be 4, so we multiply this polynomial by 4/2 = 2 (changing the output units), giving:

$2*x*x – 2*x$

Now we insert $x[0]$, $x[1]$, and $x[2]$ to check this out:

$x[0] = –1 : 2*(–1)*(–1) – 2*(–1) = 4$
$x[1] = 0 : 2*0*0 – 2*0 = 0$
$x[2] = 1 : 2*1*1 – 2*1 = 0$

So we do indeed have zero at all the data points except the first, where the value is 4, as expected.

Completing the work for the other two points gives the following polynomials for each data point:

$x[0] : 2*x*x – 2*x$
$x[1] : 2 – 2*x*x$
$x[2] : 2*x*x + 2*x$

You can check that each polynomial is equal to $y[n]$ at its own data point, and zero at the others.

Finally, we add these three polynomials together, which gives:

$2*x*x – 2*x + 2 – 2*x*x + 2*x*x + 2*x = 2*x*x + 2$

You can quickly check that this polynomial matches the data at every point.

The member function `MakeLagrangeSeries()` on the CD that accompanies this book does the hard work, so you don't have to. It can be very tedious constructing a 9th-order Lagrange series by hand!

Note that there are errors in the results from `MakeLagrangeSeries()`–normal floating-point errors, as you would expect. The calculations are very complex and they iterate, so errors build up. If you are making a Lagrange series that must be either even or odd, make sure you ignore the values of any odd or even coefficients that have to be zero. You can do this by calling the member functions `ForceOdd()` or `ForceEven()`.

Comparison with Taylor Series

For a 9th-order sine and 10th-order cosine, we have already seen the continuity problem at the 360-degree boundary. The Lagrange series does not have this problem. In general, the Lagrange series gives you much finer control over the features of your approximation, such as continuity and specific values that must be correct.

The program on the CD (main.cpp) does a comparison of average and maximum absolute errors over the range –pi to +pi. The difference is quite pronounced. The Taylor series exhibits a maximum error of 1 part in 150, with an average error of 1 part in 1,500. Compare that with the Lagrange series, which has a maximum error of 1 part in 11,000 and an average error of only 1 part in 77,000. (Note that these errors were measured in double-precision floating point.)

The Taylor series is an exact match for a function, provided you take infinitely many terms. The Lagrange series is intrinsically limited by the number of data points taken. This fact seems to imply that the Taylor series is the better approximation, but these data prove otherwise. In this case, the Lagrange series has a *maximum* error one-seventh the size of the Taylor series' *average* error!

A Note on Numbers

When you are dealing with exact numbers in floating-point notation, the output of `printf()` quite often doesn't cut it; it only prints a few decimal places, and floating-point numbers are not decimal-based (which means that a decimal rendition is at best an approximation to the floating-point value). In the `Print()` member function of the `Poly` class, you can print out the coefficients as hexadecimal values. This ensures that, when you move the numbers into your own code, they are exactly what they were originally. It can be somewhat painful to do this in C++, but one trick involving unions in `Print()` can be used the other way around to get the floating-point numbers from the hexadecimal form.

Note also that to get the best out of this code, you should define the `Number` class to be double, even if you are going to use single precision in your game. You can simply convert to float when you print the coefficients.

Dealing with Discontinuities

Discontinuities arise in practice fairly often, and neither Taylor nor Lagrange series handle them very well. Polynomials are always smooth, so the discontinuities become smoothed out, which may not be desirable. Fortunately, it is usually quite easy to work around these problems.

One familiar discontinuous function is the tangent function. At +/– 90 degrees, the tangent function goes to infinity and then jumps to negative infinity. This discontinuity can be dealt with in two fundamental ways. First, you can simply calculate tangent as sine divided by cosine. This method avoids the problem entirely (as long as you do a divide-by-zero check!). Second, you can restrict the range of your tangent function to be just the range over which it is continuous—i.e., from –90 to +90 degrees. For the Lagrange series, this means taking points only from inside this range.

If you have a function that has a step-like discontinuity, you can often remove the discontinuity by subtracting a step function. This gives a continuous function, which can be approximated using Taylor or Lagrange methods. You then add the step function back in to get back to the original function. If instead your function has a sharp peak, it will be smoothed out by the polynomial, but you can often subtract a triangular function before approximating, to again yield a smooth function.

These heuristics are all based on simple adjustments of the basic algorithm to deal with special cases. This is an area in which you can exercise your creativity to deal with whatever comes your way.

Conclusion

In this article, we have taken a quick tour of some quite basic mathematics and seen some very important results. We have seen how polynomials can be manipulated in various ways and how they can be copied without direct access to the coefficients. From these methods, we discovered Taylor series. We then found Taylor series to be somewhat inadequate for many applications and saw a powerful alternative in Lagrange series.

Neither the Taylor series nor the Lagrange series are all things to all people. If you use these numerical recipes in your own code, I urge you to do the experiments and look at the results. Make sure your code always works as you expect, and watch out for discontinuities in the original function.

With that caveat, you now have the machinery to approximate a wide range of functions. Use it wisely!

2.4

Using Implicit Euler Integration for Numerical Stability

Miguel Gomez

Choosing a method of integrating initial value problems is an important part of writing an interactive application. Due to its ease of implementation, explicit Euler integration seems to be the integration method of choice. Unfortunately, this method suffers from the problem of *instability* in which errors build exponentially and the solution quickly becomes infinite. This article describes the *implicit* Euler method, an efficient and highly stable integrator. Two examples are used to illustrate this technique: exponential decay and the damped spring equation. Finally, difficulties in deriving implicit solutions are discussed. We assume the reader is familiar with calculus, classical mechanics, and differential equation theory.

Integrating Initial Value Problems and Stability

Initial value problems are simply differential equations with initial conditions. For some equations, an analytic solution can be found and used to calculate the trajectory of a body. In most cases, however, no analytic form exists, and the solution must be integrated numerically.

There are many different approaches to numerical integration, and the method of choice depends on the requirements of the application. In some systems and under certain conditions, errors in the solution propagate exponentially and the solution approaches infinity. This situation is called *instability,* and the method of integration is said to have become *unstable* under these conditions. For example, you might model the suspension system of a car as damped springs attached to a rigid body. If the springs are made too stiff for the time step, the integrated solution becomes unstable and quickly becomes infinite.

One way to improve stability is to subdivide the time step. A better way to improve stability is to use a Runge-Kutta method, or something similar, without subdividing the time step; however, even these methods become unstable at some point.

This is why we seek a simple, efficient method that guarantees stability regardless of the equation parameters or the time-step size.

The Explicit Euler Method

As a first example, let's take the initial value problem:

$$\frac{dx}{dt} = -kx,$$

$$x\left(0\right) = x_0.$$

The analytic solution is:

$$x\left(t\right) = x_0 e^{-kt}.$$

Evaluating the exponential function for every data point is simple and exact, but it is extremely inefficient. Most CPUs take about 30 cycles to evaluate elementary functions in hardware. If the CPU must emulate this process in software, you're out of luck!

Fortunately, there are more efficient ways to evaluate the solution. We can use a finite difference approximation of the first derivative:

$$\frac{dx}{dt} \approx \frac{x_1 - x_0}{\Delta t}$$

where x_1 is the solution after a time step Δt. Solving for x_1, we get:

$$x_1 = x_0 - \frac{dx}{dt}\Delta t.$$

If the derivative is evaluated at x_0, we get:

$$x_1 = x_0 - kx_0\Delta t = x_0(1 - k\Delta t).$$

This approach is known as the *explicit Euler integration method*. With only one subtraction and two multiplies, even a fixed-point processor could handle this method.

Although the explicit Euler method is very efficient, it is not very stable. We can demonstrate this instability with the following argument: Since the solution is an exponential function, it must decay to zero over time, implying that:

$$x_1 \leq x_0.$$

Substituting and solving gives the relationship:

$$k\Delta t \leq 2.$$

So if $k = 1$ and $\Delta t = 2$, then $x_1 = -x_0$, and the solution is stable, although not very accurate. If this condition is not met, x quickly becomes infinite, and the object whose motion you're simulating disappears. As mentioned, the Euler method can be made more stable by simply decreasing the time step, requiring the calculation of more data points. However, if k is made too large, subdivision of the time step may become prohibitively expensive.

The Implicit Euler Method

The method described is an explicit method because it relies solely on previous values of the solution to calculate the derivative. The implicit Euler method, on the other hand, evaluates the derivative at x_1 instead of x_0 (Figure 2.4.1), giving:

$$x_1 = x_0 + (-kx_1)\Delta t.$$

Solving for x_1 gives:

$$x_1 = \frac{x_0}{(1 + k\Delta t)}.$$

Substituting this into the stability condition gives:

$$0 \le k\Delta t.$$

This is significant. We've found a simple, efficient method that is stable, no matter how large k or Δt get! [Hairer93]

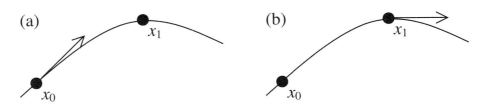

FIGURE 2.4.1. The explicit Euler method evaluates the derivative at x_0 (a), whereas the implicit Euler method evaluates the derivative at x_1 (b).

Let's look at a more complicated example. Imagine a mass m is attached to a fixed anchor by a spring that gives k Newtons per meter push or pull when the mass is not at its equilibrium position. Let's also assume there is some force that is negatively proportional to its velocity by some constant b, causing the system to lose energy. If we set the equilibrium position to be at the origin $(x_{eq} = 0)$, then the differential equation that describes this motion is:

$$m\frac{d^2x}{dt^2} = -kx - b\frac{dx}{dt},$$

subject to the initial conditions:

$$x\left(0\right) = x_0,$$

$$x'\left(0\right) = v\left(0\right) = 0.$$

Solving for the second derivative, we get:

$$\frac{d^2x}{dt^2} = -\omega^2x - 2\lambda\frac{dx}{dt}, \lambda = \frac{b}{2m}$$

where we've substituted $\omega = \sqrt{\frac{k}{m}}$ and $\lambda = \frac{b}{2m}$ for simplicity. If the condition $\omega^2 > \lambda^2$ is met, the solution is:

$$x(t) = x_0e^{-\lambda t}\cos\left(\omega t\right) \quad [\text{Chow95}].$$

This second-order differential equation can be rewritten as a system of two first-order differential equations, giving:

$$\frac{dx}{dt} = v$$

$$\frac{dv}{dt} = -\omega^2x - \lambda v.$$

Evaluating the derivatives at x_1 and v_1 gives:

$$x_1 = x_0 + v_1\Delta t,$$

$$v_1 = v_0 - \omega^2x_1 - \lambda v_1.$$

Finally, solving for v_1 gives:

$$v_1 = \frac{v_0 - \omega^2x_0\Delta t}{1 + \lambda\Delta t + \left(\omega\Delta t\right)^2},$$

which is stable for all positive values of k, b, and Δt (see Figure 2.4.2).

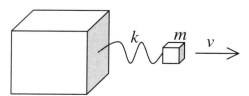

FIGURE 2.4.2. A mass m is attached to a spring with a constant k. The damping is negatively proportional to velocity.

Inaccuracy

The implicit Euler method is not as accurate as its explicit counterpart. Even without damping, the solution slowly loses all its energy. In most applications, we are more concerned with the effect than its accuracy, so this is usually not a problem, but it is something to keep in mind.

Finding Implicit Solutions

Finding an implicit evaluator for x_1 is not always easy. For instance, if the spring force is proportional to x_2 instead of x, we get a quadratic relationship for x_1. For systems in which it is impossible to solve for x_1, numerical root finding such as Newton's method may be required [Gerald99]. Such cases make an implicit integrator impractical for real-time applications.

Conclusion

The implicit Euler method is definitely something to keep in mind when stability becomes an issue. There are many other types of implicit methods that could suit different needs. For a more in-depth discussions, see [Gerald99], [Hairer96], and [Hairer93].

References

[Chow95] Chow, Tai L., *Classical Mechanics*, John Wiley & Sons, Inc., 1995.

[Derrick97] Derrick, William R., and Grossman, Stanley I., *A First Course in Differential Equations with Applications*, third edition, West Publishing Co., 1987.

[Gerald99] Gerald, Curtis F., and Wheatley, Patrick O., *Applied Numerical Analysis*, sixth edition, Addison Wesley Longman, Inc., 1999.

[Hairer93] Hairer, E., Norsett, S. P., and Wanner, G., *Solving Ordinary Differential Equations I: Nonstiff Problems*, second edition, Springer-Verlag, 1993.

[Hairer96] Hairer, E., and Wanner, G., *Solving Ordinary Differential Equations II: Stiff and Differential-Algebraic Problems*, second edition, Springer-Verlag, 1996.

2.5

Wavelets: Theory and Compression

Loïc Le Chevalier

We generally associate wavelets with a compression method. But the word *wavelets* covers at once a mathematical theory, a compression method, and a data analysis tool. This is a powerful paradigm that has many applications.

The Principle

Whatever the wavelet application (compression, analysis, etc.), the point of departure is a group of N values: scalar or vector. From these N values, we build a tree such as the one shown in Figure 2.5.1. At each level of the tree, we calculate the average of two values, which becomes the value of the next level. The tree obtained is a *binary tree* with $N(N+1)/2$ nodes, corresponding to the respective averages. Once built, this tree can be used to factor the initial values. Note that factoring is not compressing. Factoring enables us to keep all the information in reduced form, whereas compression causes a loss of information. The basic principle of wavelets is thus a reversible principle: At any time, we can go back to the initial values without losing information.

To the tree that we've built, we add new values on the branches corresponding to the difference between the two extremities of the branch—i.e., the distances that separate two values, linked by one branch and differing by one level. As shown in Figure 2.5.2, the magnitudes leaving from a *node* are opposite, because the average value is equidistant from the two values. (For example, the average of 2 and 8 is 5, which is at a distance of −3 from 2 and of +3 from 8.)

For the moment, there is no factoring. On the contrary, the structure has grown from one vector of N values to a tree of $N(N+1)/2$ values for the nodes, plus $N(N+1)/2 - 1$ values for the branches! The next step thus consists of choosing a tree level—i.e., a factoring level, p, between 1 and log_2N. A level is thus composed of node values and the lower branches that grow from it (see Figure 2.5.3).

Once the factoring level, p, has been chosen, we obtain the level p compressed values, with $0<p<log_2N$, by sequentially calculating levels 1 through p, inclusive (see

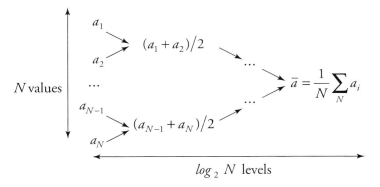

FIGURE 2.5.1. Building the tree.

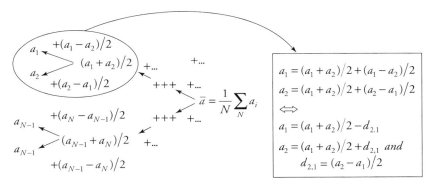

FIGURE 2.5.2. Calculating distances.

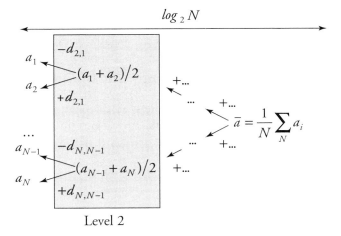

FIGURE 2.5.3. Choosing factoring level.

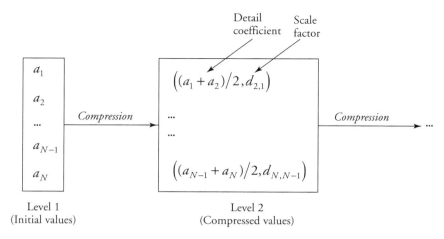

FIGURE 2.5.4. Compressed values.

Figure 2.5.4). We thus have a principle that *does not lose information*, the *linear cost* of which is a function of *N*.

Once factored, we restore the initial values by reversing the operation. This *restitution* operation has, itself, a *linear cost* in *N*. It is important to note that to restore the initial values from a level p, we must maintain this level's scale factors as well as all the detail coefficients from levels 1 through p, inclusive.

An Example

Imagine, for example, a linearly coded image having, to simplify, a resolution of 4 pixels by 4 pixels in 16 shades of gray. The initial values are thus a scalar vector of 16 values between 0 and 15. Figure 2.5.5 shows the tree associated with this image.

Thus, if we choose factoring level 3, we keep the couple of scale factors (6, 10) and all the detail coefficients from levels 3, 2, 1, and 0. Note that level 0 never has scale coefficients: They are all implicitly null.

If we now want to return to the 16 initial values, we calculate the level 2 scale factors by adding or subtracting level 3 coefficients, and so on, until we return to the level 0 factors, which are the initial values.

Applications

The preceding construction principle is exactly the one that is used by image pyramids for mipmaps, which, in fact, represent the wavelet compression method. These wavelets are also called *Haar wavelets*. They are very well suited for treating discrete

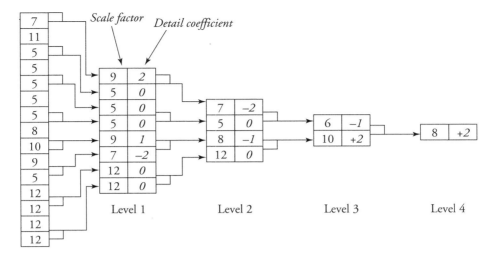

FIGURE 2.5.5. An example tree.

values, such as scalar vectors about which we, theoretically, know nothing. But many other kinds of wavelets are useful for treating continuous or other functions. The theory behind these other wavelets closely follows the previously described principle.

Wavelets have many applications. The first and most well known is *image compression*. Compression and decompression by wavelets requires an additional phase, however, compared with the above principle. The preceding principle is lossless; in other words, the entire image can be recomposed precisely from any level. But this is of no interest to us in compression, so we can *sacrifice* values to lose the least information possible. By thus minimizing error, we obtain very impressive results. For example, an image of a few hundred kilobytes can be compressed to only a few kilobytes with very little perceptible loss. Simply put, areas of little detail are highly compressed, while those of greater details are less compressed. Visually, then, the loss of information is barely perceptible. Figure 2.5.6 is an example of a compression rate of 116: The original image is 6.25MB, compared with 53KB for the compressed image.

Another well-known application of wavelets is *data analysis*, an alternative to Fourier transforms for aperiodic functions. We can also cite multiresolution production of images or 3D models enabling one to adjust the level of details of an image (infinite zoom, etc.) or a 3D model (LOD, subdivision, etc.).

FIGURE 2.5.6. An example of image compression.

References

An Introduction to Wavelets, Institute of Electrical and Electronics Engineers, available online at www.amara.com/IEEEwave/IEEEwavelet.html.

The Wavelet Organization meta-site, available online at www.wavelet.org.

2.6

Interactive Simulation of Water Surfaces

Miguel Gomez

With ever-increasing computing power, simulating realistic outdoor environments in real time is finally becoming possible. Dynamic water is one thing that can add tremendous aesthetic appeal to any outdoor game scene. This article describes a simple, efficient approach for simulating realistic wave motion over water surfaces. Using a central difference approximation of the two-dimensional wave equation, you can simulate the horizontal motion of water with only a few arithmetic operations per point. Brief discussions of other approaches are given as well. Physically based models for buoyancy and drag are also described. Finally, implementation and optimization ideas for the rendering process are discussed.

The Wave Equation in Two Dimensions

A water surface can be thought of as a tightly stretched elastic membrane in which gravity can be ignored. As infinitesimal sections are displaced, their direct neighbors exert linear "spring" forces (*surface tension*) to minimize the space between them. Since horizontal forces are equalized, particles move in only the z-direction. The vertical position with respect to time and space can be described with the partial differential equation:

$$\frac{\partial^2 z}{\partial t^2} = c^2 \left(\frac{\partial^2 z}{\partial x^2} + \frac{\partial^2 z}{\partial y^2} \right),$$

where c is the speed at which waves travel across the surface. If the boundary conditions are *homogeneous* (i.e., the edges don't move up and down) and the initial z-velocity of the surface is zero, the general solution for a square $L \times L$ section of water is:

$$z(x, y, t) = \frac{2}{L} \sum_{m=1}^{\infty} \sum_{n=1}^{\infty} A_{mn} \sin\left(\frac{m\pi x}{L}\right) \sin\left(\frac{n\pi y}{L}\right) \cos(c\omega t),$$

$$\omega = \frac{\pi}{L} \sqrt{(mx)^2 + (ny)^2}$$

The coefficients A_{mn} are found by evaluating the integrals:

$$A_{mn} = \frac{2}{L} \int_0^L \int_0^L f(x, y) \sin\frac{m\pi x}{L} \sin\frac{m\pi y}{L} \, dx dy,$$

where $f(x, y)$ is the initial shape of the water surface [Trim90]. If the surface is modeled as an evenly spaced grid of z-values (a *height field*), as in Figure 2.6.1, the preceding integrals become discrete and can be evaluated with the *Fast Fourier Transform (FFT) algorithm* [Press92].

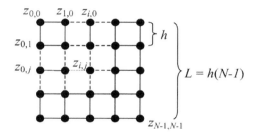

FIGURE 2.6.1. An $L \times L$ height field with N points along each side is used to approximate the water surface.

We could approximate a solution by evaluating only the significant terms of the series, but even though this approach is straightforward and stable, it is *very* inefficient. On most CPUs, a single evaluation of a trigonometric function takes around 30 cycles. Dropping all but the first three modes along x and y requires evaluating nine sinusoidal functions per point per time step, which is prohibitively expensive for large grids in interactive applications. This major drawback should motivate us to find a more efficient numerical solution.

Using central differences to approximate the partial derivatives gives:

$$\frac{z_{i,j}^{n+1} - 2z_{i,j}^{n} + z_{i,j}^{n-1}}{\Delta t^2} = c^2 \left(\frac{z_{i+1,j}^{n} + z_{i-1,j}^{n} + z_{i,j+1}^{n} + z_{i,j-1}^{n} - 4z_{i,j}^{n}}{h^2} \right).$$

The value $z_{i,j}^{n}$ is the height of the i,jth grid position at time t_0. The values $z_{i,j}^{n-1}$ and $z_{i,j}^{n+1}$ are the heights at times $t_{-1} = t_0 - \Delta t$ and $t_1 = t_0 + \Delta t$, respectively. Solving for $z_{i,j}^{n+1}$ gives:

$$z_{i,j}^{n+1} = \frac{c^2 \Delta t^2}{h^2} \left(z_{i+1,j}^{n} + z_{i-1,j}^{n} + z_{i,j+1}^{n} + z_{i,j-1}^{n} \right) + \left(2 - \frac{4c^2 \Delta t^2}{h^2} \right) z_{i,j}^{n} - z_{i,j}^{n-1}.$$

This relationship simply says that the motion $z_{i,j}$ is influenced only by its nearest neighbors (Figure 2.6.2). Since the grid spacing is constant, the reciprocal of h^2 can be pre-calculated, leaving only multiplies, adds, and subtracts. Furthermore, if c does not vary between cells, all coefficients can be pre-calculated, and successive z-values can be calculated with only two multiplies and five adds! (And if you're really cheap, you can make $h^2 = 2c^2 \Delta t^2$, eliminating the middle term. This approach restricts either c or h, depending on the application.)

At first glance, it might seem necessary to store three separate grids for the z-values at times t_{-1}, t_0, and t_1; however, if z^{n-1} is replaced with z^{n+1} in place, only two grids are necessary. At the end of the pass, the memory pointers to the z^{n+1} and z^n values are swapped. At the next iteration, the z^n has become z^{n-1}, and z^{n+1} has become z^n. This code snippet shows how this space-saving trick can be implemented:

```
//precalculate coefficients
const float A = (c*dt/h)*(c*dt/h);
const float B = 2 − 4*A;
long i, j;

//edges are unchanged
for( i=1 ; i<N-1 ; i++ )
{
    for( j=1 ; j<N-1 ; j++ )
    {
        //integrate, replacing z[n-1] with z[n+1] in place
        z1[i][j] = A*( z[i-1][j] + z[i+1][j] + z[i][j-1] + z[i][j+1] )
                   + B*z[i][j] − z1[i][j];
        //apply damping coefficients
        z1[i][j] *= d[i][j];

    }
}

//swap pointers
Swap( z.pData, z1.pData );
```

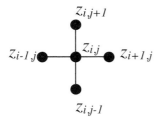

FIGURE 2.6.2. The horizontal movement of the point z_{ij} is influenced only by its nearest neighbors.

Boundary Conditions: Islands and Shorelines

In nature, bodies of water are usually not square. Rivers, lakes, and oceans have irregular shorelines of varying slope, and islands might exist within these bodies of water as well. If the bank is very steep or even vertical, waves reflect off the shoreline with very little energy loss, whereas if the bank is gently sloped, a wave might have a very weak reflection or none at all. If the waves do not come in straight, they reflect off at an angle.

These effects can be simulated by scaling the z^{n+1} value by a local damping coefficient, $d_{i,j}$ (see the preceding code snippet). A coefficient of 1 allows free movement of the height value without any energy loss, whereas a coefficient of 0 restricts all movement of the water at that location. If these coefficients are distributed and scaled according to the terrain features, waves react to the shoreline more naturally. For example, if the bank is steep, the damping coefficients should make a quick transition from 1 (water) to 0 (land). On the other hand, if the bank is gently sloped, the damping coefficients should make a gradual transition from 1 to 0. In practice, it is usually better to use damping coefficients that are slightly less than 1 in wet cells to produce a little energy loss. Otherwise, wave motion continues indefinitely.

Implementation Issues

Instability

The previously described integration method is called an *explicit* method because it uses only previous and current values of $z_{i,j}$ to evaluate z^{n+1}. If the condition:

$$\frac{c^2 \Delta t^2}{h^2} \le \frac{1}{2}$$

is not met, the integration method becomes *unstable* and successive z-values grow exponentially.

An *implicit* method, on the other hand, can be used to guarantee stability. Unfortunately, finding a solution implicitly involves solving sets of simultaneous equations for z^{n+1}. For more in-depth discussions of implicit integration methods, see [Gerald99], [Hairer93], and [Hairer96].

Parallel Processing

Although some processors have single-instruction, multiple-data (SIMD) instructions that evaluate several floating-point values in parallel, memory alignment requirements can decrease the efficiency (or even prohibit the use) of these instructions for integrating a solution. Processors that can operate on four single-precision floating-point numbers in parallel usually require 16-byte alignment, so rows must be padded if N is not a power of 2. Regardless, some memory accesses are unaligned (Figure 2.6.3). Even if the CPU allows unaligned memory accesses, a penalty is usually incurred.

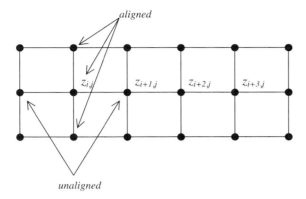

FIGURE 2.6.3. Even though the rows of the grid are padded to ensure 16-byte alignment, some data accesses are not aligned.

Interacting with the Surface

Splashes

Splashes can be created by instantaneously displacing one or several z-values at a particular location. As the solution progresses, waves radiate from this location. This concept illustrates another advantage over explicitly evaluating the general solution: If any discontinuity in $z(t)$ occurs, new values for A_{mn} must be computed with a discrete Fourier transform.

Buoyant Objects

What good is water if things can't float on top if it? Objects float because their overall density is less than that of the surrounding water. The force of buoyancy on an object is equal to the weight of the water displaced by that object. This force is actually in the direction of the pressure gradient, but in most cases, the direction normal to the water surface is appropriate.

   If the shape of the hull is approximated as a set of discrete points, normals, and area patches (Figure 2.6.4), the force of buoyancy can be calculated by performing a volume integral over the submerged portion. The volume of water displaced by a section of the hull is:

$$\Delta V_k = \Delta A_k \left(z_{water} - p_{k,z} \right) \hat{n}_{k,z},$$

where z_{water} is the bilinearly interpolated water height at $\mathbf{p}_k$. (Bilinear interpolation is recommended, since other methods might produce primary or first order discontinuities. It is also probably the most efficient interpolation method for a regular grid.) The buoyant force at this position is:

$$\mathbf{F}_k = \rho \Delta V_k \hat{\mathbf{n}}_{water},$$

and the torque is simply:

$$\mathbf{N}_k = \mathbf{r}_k \times \mathbf{F}_k,$$

where $\mathbf{r}_k$ is the vector from the center of mass to $\mathbf{p}_k$. The total force and torque are calculated by summing the contributions from each hull vertex. Remember also that only the *submerged* portions contribute to the buoyancy.

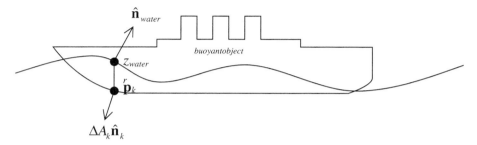

FIGURE 2.6.4. The shape of the buoyant object is approximated with a set of points, $\mathbf{p}_i$, distributed "evenly" over its surface. Also stored are the unit surface normals, $\hat{\mathbf{n}}_k$, and the local area patches, ΔA_k.

The number of points needed depends on the shape of the object and the level of accuracy desired. A cube might need around 20 or 30 points, whereas a tree with branches might need hundreds of points to behave realistically.

A vector normal to any parameterized, right-hand-oriented, three-dimensional surface can be calculated with the formula:

$$\mathbf{n} = \frac{\partial \mathbf{S}(u,v)}{\partial u} \times \frac{\partial \mathbf{S}(u,v)}{\partial v}, \quad \text{[Davis91]}.$$

If we think of x and y as our parameters, the water surface can be described by the vector:

$$\mathbf{S}(x,y)_{water} = \Big[x, y, z(x, y, t)\Big].$$

Approximating the first derivatives with central differences gives:

$$\frac{\partial \mathbf{S}}{\partial x} \approx \left[1, 0, \frac{z_{i+1,j} + z_{i-1,j}}{2h}\right],$$

$$\frac{\partial \mathbf{S}}{\partial y} \approx \left[0, 1, \frac{z_{i,j+1} + z_{i,j-1}}{2h}\right].$$

The normal at the i,jth grid location is then:

$$\mathbf{n}_{i,j} = \left[-\frac{z_{i+1} - z_{i-1}}{2h}, -\frac{z_{j+1} - z_{j-1}}{2h}, 1 \right].$$

Scaling this vector by $2h$ does not change its direction, so an equally valid normal is:

$$\mathbf{n}_{i,j} = \left[z_{i-1} - z_{i+1}, z_{j-1} - z_{j+1}, 2h \right],$$

which must then be normalized.

To keep the object from sliding over the surface like a surfboard, a drag force can also be calculated by summing contributions from each vertex:

$$\mathbf{F}_{drag} = \sum -b\mathbf{v}_{k,rel} = \sum b \left[\mathbf{v}_{water} - \left(\mathbf{v}_{cm} + \omega_{cm} \times \mathbf{r}_k \right) \right].$$

The velocity term $\mathbf{v}_{k,rel}$ is the velocity of the hull *relative to the water* at $\mathbf{r}_k$. So if, in addition to height values, a three-dimensional velocity is associated with every grid location (a *vector field*), the current carries floating objects.

Rendering

All this theory is great, but if you can't see it, what's the point? The following are some ideas on implementing and optimizing the rendering process.

Environment Mapping

When drawing water, you can use *alpha blending* to give the appearance of transparency. In order to draw alpha-blended triangles properly, however, you must draw the ones farthest from the viewer first, without the help of the Z-buffer. Furthermore, double blending occurs whenever a triangle is visible through another.

In reality, light doesn't pass straight through water. It bends as it goes from one index of refraction to another. Water also reflects light from its surroundings. These effects can be achieved with *environment mapping*. Environment mapping a water surface involves reflecting and refracting rays of light from the eye and intersecting them with an environment map surface to calculate a texture coordinate [Figure 2.6.5]. Each triangle is then texture mapped with these coordinates.

I cannot emphasize how incredible refraction mapping looks if done well; you have to see it to believe it. With reflection only, water appears too metallic, like liquid mercury. See [Watt2000] for more environment-mapping techniques and related formulas.

Although environment mapping gives stunning visual results, using it on a large scale may not be feasible without hardware support due to computation requirements. The results are impressive enough, however, to justify a scaled-down software implementation.

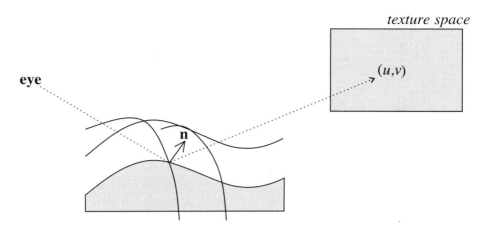

FIGURE 2.6.5. Bouncing rays from the eye (camera) position to the environment map generates a texture coordinate (*u, v*) for each vertex.

Level of Detail Management

Rendering distant portions of the height field at lower resolutions can give tremendous speed increases without significantly decreasing visual quality. Care must be taken, however, to ensure that vertex normals along LOD transitions match. Otherwise, discontinuities are visible in environment mapping and lighting. For an elegant adaptive quadtree approach to terrain LOD management, see [Ulrich2000].

References

[Davis91] Davis, Harry F., and Snider, Arthur David, *Introduction to Vector Analysis*, sixth edition. William C. Brown Publishers, 1991.

[Gerald99] Gerald, Curtis F., and Wheatley, Patrick O., *Applied Numerical Analysis*, sixth edition. Addison Wesley Longman, Inc., 1999.

[Hairer93] Hairer, E., Norsett, S. P., and Wanner, G., *Solving Ordinary Differential Equations I: Nonstiff Problems*, second edition, Springer-Verlag, 1993.

[Hairer96] Hairer, E., and Wanner, G., *Solving Ordinary Differential Equations II: Stiff and Differential-Algebraic Problems*, second edition, Springer-Verlag, 1996.

[Press92] Press, William H., Teukolsky, Saul A., Vetterling, William T., and Flannery, Brian P., *Numerical Recipes in C,* second edition, The Press Syndicate of the University of Cambridge, 1992.

[Trim90] Trim, D. W., *Applied Partial Differential Equations,* PWS-Kent, 1990.

[Ulrich2000] Ulrich, Thatcher, "Continuous LOD Terrain Meshing Using Adaptive Quadtrees," *Gamasutra*, available online at www.gamasutra.com/features/20000228/ulrich_01.htm, 2000.

[Watt2000] Watt, Alan, *3D Computer Graphics*, third edition Addison-Wesley, 2000.

2.7

Quaternions for Game Programming

Jan Svarovsky

Quaternions are useful for representing and processing 3D rotations of points. Applications include skeletal animation, inverse kinematics, and, generally, any 3D physics and graphics engine. This article is organized by first explaining enough about quaternions for you to be able to use them in your 3D game. It then gradually reaches deeper into their mathematical basis.

Treat Quaternions as Matrix Replacements

You can use quaternions in a game as a straight drop-in replacement for rotation matrices. They can describe any rotation around any axis in 3D space. They take less space, four numbers rather than nine, and many operations such as multiplication are cheaper. Some operations such as interpolation between quaternions are also more visually pleasing. At points when you need a matrix (such as to rotate a vector), you can easily convert quaternions to rotation matrixes and back again.

```
// a black-box quaternion type that can replace 3x3 matrices
class Quaternion
{
private:
    float x, y, z, w; // These will be explained later
public:
    Quaternion Inverse() const;
};

Quaternion quaternion_from_matrix(Matrix33   &mat );
Matrix33   matrix_from_quaternion(Quaternion &quat);
Quaternion interpolate(Quaternion &a, Quaternion &b, float b_amt);
Quaternion operator *(Quaternion &a, Quaternion &b);
```

Some other functions exist that would be more difficult to produce for matrices:

```
Vector3 Quaternion::AxisOfRotation() const;
float Quaternion::AngleOfRotation() const;
// rotation that will get you from v0 to v1
Quaternion RotationArc(Vector3 v0, Vector3 v1);
```

A typical use of quaternions is to store all your matrices (such as orientations of bones for an animating character) as quaternions. All the matrix multiplications are replaced with quaternion calculations, and only at the end of the pipeline, where vectors must be rotated into world space or onto the screen, do you turn the quaternions into matrices.

Three-by-three rotation matrixes can be represented directly by quaternions. A quaternion and a translation vector can represent 4×4 matrices that encode a rotation and translation.

Why Not Just Use Euler Angles?

Quaternions do not suffer from *gimbal lock*. With a three-angle (roll, pitch, yaw) system, there are always certain orientations in which there is no simple change to the three values to represent a simple local rotation. You often see this rotation having "pitched up" 90 degrees when you are trying to specify a local yaw left or right.

What Do *X*, *Y*, *Z*, and *W* Represent?

The four numbers in the quaternion, often denoted (x, y, z, w), have some physical significance. If we consider all rotation matrixes to represent a rotation of an angle θ about an axis A (X_A, Y_A, Z_A), shown in Figure 2.7.1, the quaternion Q will be:

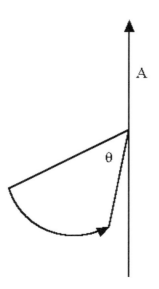

FIGURE 2.7.1. Rotation of angle θ about axis A.

$$Q = (s\, X_A,\, s\, Y_A,\, s\, Z_A,\, c)$$
$$s = sin\, (\theta\, /\, 2)$$
$$c = cos\, (\theta\, /\, 2)$$

This leads to two things: It is easy to extract the angle of rotation (see the method mentioned previously) as being twice the inverse cosine of the w term. It is similarly easy to extract the axis of rotation.

Note that two quaternions represent each rotation matrix. If a general rotation is defined by an axis and an angle, each rotation will have an equivalent with the opposite angle and the opposite axis of rotation. In quaternion terms, you can make the θs of the two quaternions different by 2π (or 360 degrees). Since the terms are in ($\theta\, /\, 2$), this adds π inside the sin and cos terms:

$$sin\, (\alpha + \pi) = -sin\, (\alpha)$$
$$cos\, (\alpha + \pi) = cos\, (-\alpha)$$

This can lead to problems in interpolation, where two quite numerically different quaternions represent very similar rotations. The fixes for this "gotcha" can be seen as extra tests inside the implementation of any quaternion library.

From What Math Is This Derived?

The quaternions we use here are a subset of general quaternions. General quaternions are an extension of complex numbers. Complex numbers are defined in terms of i, the square root of -1 (which cannot be represented by a "conventional" number):

$$i * i = -1$$

Although i is different from "real" numbers, we can include it in expressions like any other variable, with the magic property being that its square is -1. Any multiple of i and a real number must be left in terms of i, making a "complex" number ($a + bi$) for some a and b. For example, multiplication of two complex numbers:

$$(a + bi) * (c + di) = a*c + a*di + c*bi + bi*di$$
$$= a*c - b*d + (a*d + c*b)\, i$$

Quaternions extend the concept of a square root of -1 to have three square roots of -1, being i, j, and k:

$$i * i = -1$$
$$j * j = -1$$
$$k * k = -1$$

Multiplication of pairs of these elements together behaves much like the cross products of the usual three axes in 3D space:

$$i * j = -j * i = k$$
$$j * k = -k * j = i$$

$$k * i = -i * k = j$$

What this all means is that quaternions are defined, similarly to complex numbers, in terms of a real number and an i, j, and k term. Because i, j, and k behave so much like axes, quaternions are sometimes written as a vector (here v) and a scalar (s) or as a vector of their four terms.

$$q = w + x\,i + y\,j + z\,k$$
$$q = [s\ v] \qquad\qquad \text{where } s = w \text{ and } v = [x\ y\ z]$$
$$q = [x\ y\ z\ w] \qquad\qquad \text{note scalar ``}w\text{'' at the end}$$

Addition and multiplication of quaternions are defined in the obvious way. Much like multiplication of "normal" complex numbers, the result of multiplication is another quaternion:

$$
\begin{aligned}
q_1\,q_2 &= (c_1 + x_1\,i + y_1\,j + z_1\,k)\,(c_2 + x_2\,i + y_2\,j + z_2\,k) \\
&= (c_1\,c_2 - x_1\,x_2 - y_1\,y_2 - z_1\,z_2) + \\
&\quad (y_1\,z_2 - y_2\,z_1 + c_1\,x_2 + c_2\,x_1)\,i + \\
&\quad (z_1\,x_2 - z_1\,x_2 + c_1\,y_2 + c_1\,y_2)\,j + \\
&\quad (x_1\,y_2 - x_1\,y_2 + c_1\,z_2 + c_1\,z_2)\,k
\end{aligned}
$$

A lot of symmetry can be seen in this example, which is made more obvious in the condensed notation:

$$
\begin{aligned}
q_1\,q_2 &= (s_1 + v_1)\,(s_2 + v_2) \\
&= s_1\,s_2 - v_1 \cdot v_2 + v_1 \times v_2 + s_1\,v_2 + s_2\,v_1
\end{aligned}
$$

where $a \cdot b$ is the dot product and $a \times b$ is the cross product.

A few other definitions are useful. The norm of a quaternion is:

$$N(q) = x^2 + y^2 + z^2 + w^2$$

The conjugate of a quaternion can be thought of in two ways:

$$q^* = [-x\ -y\ -z\ w]$$
$$q^* = [s\ -v]$$

The multiplicative inverse of the quaternion:

$$1/q = q^* / N(q)$$

The subset of quaternions we use for representing rotations is the set of unit quaternions, where $|q| = 1$, or $x^2 + y^2 + z^2 + w^2 = 1^2$. These have the property that their inverse is equal to their conjugate.

How Do Quaternions Represent Rotations?

The rotation of a vector P $[x\ y\ z]$ by the unit quaternion q is done by creating the "pure" quaternion p and the conjugate of q:

$$p = x\,\mathbf{i} + y\,\mathbf{j} + z\,\mathbf{k} \qquad \text{pure means no scalar term, } w = 0$$
$$Rot_q(P) = q\,p\,q^*$$

There is some derivation to do to see that this works. Rather than bulldozing through it here, we summarize: You consider rotating the vector P by an angle θ about an axis A. Using geometry, you can work through the math, expanding everything out until eventually some terms in $cos^2(\theta)$ and $sin^2(\theta)$ turn up. These can be turned into $cos(2\theta)$ and $sin(2\theta)$ terms, and very soon you end up with a formula that looks a lot like the quaternion multiplication worked through previously [Glassner90].

This representation of rotations can be used to convert the quaternion into a rotation matrix. A *rotation matrix* can be seen as the rotation of the unit matrix by a quaternion, where the unit 3×3 matrix is the three vectors (1, 0, 0), (0, 1, 0), and (0, 0, 1). A 4×4 rotation matrix is equivalent to the 3×3 case but with an extra row and column appended where the extra terms are 0, except for the bottom right, which is 1.

References

[Glassner90] Glassner et al, *Graphics Gems*, Academic Press, 1990.

[Downs] Downs, Laura, "Using Quaternions to Represent Rotation," Available online at http://http.cs.berkeley.edu/~laura/cs184/quat/quaternion.html.

2.8

Matrix-Quaternion Conversions

Jason Shankel

Quaternions are convenient for representing 3D rotations. Quaternion multiplication is faster than matrix multiplication, and quaternion interpolation generates smooth animations. But matrices have their uses, too. In particular, matrices are preferable to quaternions for performing vertex transformation. In addition, most 3D APIs store their rotations in matrix form.

This article demonstrates quaternion-to-matrix and matrix-to-quaternion conversions. We use both four-dimensional vector and vector/scalar nomenclature to represent quaternions. That is:

$$q = [x,y,z,w] = [w,\mathbf{v}]$$

where $\mathbf{v} = (x,y,z)$ is a three-dimensional vector and w is a scalar.

We also use q, q', and q'' to designate quaternions. q' and q'' are distinct from q and should not be confused with the first- and second-order derivatives of q.

Quaternion Rotations

Let $q = [w,\mathbf{v}] = [\cos(\theta),\mathbf{u}\sin(\theta)]$ be a quaternion where $\mathbf{u}$ is a unit vector. Let $q'=[w',\mathbf{v}']$ be a quaternion (not necessarily unit) representing a point in three-dimensional homogeneous space.

The operation $qq'q^{-1}$ rotates q' about axis u by 2θ. Proof is provided by [Shoemake94].

Quaternion-to-Matrix Conversion

To convert the quaternion q into an equivalent rotation matrix, we must express $qq'q^{-1}$ as a matrix operation.

Quaternion multiplication takes the form:

$$q'' = [w,\mathbf{v}][w',\mathbf{v}'] = [ww' - \mathbf{v}\bullet\mathbf{v}', \ \mathbf{v}\otimes\mathbf{v}' + w\mathbf{v}' + w'\mathbf{v}]$$

where $\otimes$ is the vector cross product and $\bullet$ is the vector dot product.

This expands to $[x'',y'',z'',w'']$ such that:

$$x'' = yz' - zy' + wx' + xw'$$
$$y'' = zx' - xz' + wy' + yw'$$
$$z'' = xy' - yx' + wz' + zw'$$
$$w'' = ww' - xx' - yy' - zz'$$

This expansion can be expressed as a matrix multiplication:

$$\begin{Vmatrix} w & -z & y & x \\ z & w & -x & y \\ -y & x & w & z \\ -x & -y & -z & w \end{Vmatrix}\begin{Vmatrix} x' \\ y' \\ z' \\ w' \end{Vmatrix} = L_q q'$$

The multiplication $q'' = q'q$ expands to:

$$x'' = y'z - z'y + w'x + x'w$$
$$y'' = z'x - x'z + w'y + y'w$$
$$z'' = x'y - y'x + w'z + z'w$$
$$w'' = w'w - x'x - y'y - z'z$$

or:

$$\begin{Vmatrix} w & z & -y & x \\ -z & w & x & y \\ y & -x & w & z \\ -x & -y & -z & w \end{Vmatrix}\begin{Vmatrix} x' \\ y' \\ z' \\ w' \end{Vmatrix} = R_q q'$$

For a quaternion $q = [w,\mathbf{v}]$, $q^{-1} = [w,-\mathbf{v}]/N(q)$.

$N(q) = w^2+x^2+y^2+z^2 = 1$ for unit quaternions, so $q^{-1} = [w,-\mathbf{v}]$.

Substituting $q = q^{-1}$ in R_q yields:

$$\begin{Vmatrix} w & -z & y & -x \\ z & w & -x & -y \\ -y & x & w & -z \\ x & y & z & w \end{Vmatrix} = R_q^{-1}$$

The matrix equivalent of the operation $qq'q^{-1}$ can be found by concatenating L_q and R_q^{-1}:

$$M = L_q R_q^{-1} =$$

$$\begin{vmatrix} w & -z & y & x \\ z & w & -x & y \\ -y & x & w & z \\ -x & -y & -z & w \end{vmatrix} \begin{vmatrix} w & -z & y & -x \\ z & w & -x & -y \\ -y & x & w & -z \\ x & y & z & w \end{vmatrix} =$$

$$\begin{vmatrix} w^2+x^2-y^2-z^2 & 2(xy-wz) & 2(wy+xz) & 0 \\ 2(xy+wz) & w^2-x^2+y^2-z^2 & 2(yz-wx) & 0 \\ 2(xz-wy) & 2(yz+wx) & w^2-x^2-y^2+z^2 & 0 \\ 0 & 0 & 0 & w^2+x^2+y^2+z^2 \end{vmatrix}$$

$x^2+y^2+z^2+w^2=1$, so M simplifies to:

$$\begin{vmatrix} 1-2(y^2+z^2) & 2(xy-wz) & 2(wy+xz) & 0 \\ 2(xy+wz) & 1-2(x^2+z^2) & 2(yz-wx) & 0 \\ 2(xz-wy) & 2(yz+wx) & 1-2(x^2+y^2) & 0 \\ 0 & 0 & 0 & 1 \end{vmatrix} = M$$

Matrix-to-Quaternion Conversion

The relationship between a rotation matrix and the components of its corresponding quaternion is given as M in the previous statements.

From M, we can derive the following six relations:

1. $M_{1,2} + M_{2,1} = 4xy$
2. $M_{3,2} + M_{2,3} = 4yz$
3. $M_{1,3} + M_{3,1} = 4xz$
4. $M_{2,3} - M_{3,2} = 4wx$
5. $M_{3,1} - M_{1,3} = 4wy$
6. $M_{1,2} - M_{2,1} = 4wz$

From these relations, it is clear that if you know one component, you can compute the other three by division. Since any but not all of the components can be zero, we want to determine which component has the greatest absolute value and use it to calculate the other components. The largest component of a unit quaternion has an absolute value of at least $\frac{1}{2}$.

Solving for *W*

The trace of a matrix is the sum of the diagonal components. To determine $|w|$, we start by calculating the trace of the matrix M. For the matrix M, the trace is:

$$\text{Tr} = 4 - 4(x^2 + y^2 + z^2) = 4(1 - (x^2 + y^2 + z^2))$$

Recall that a unit quaternion $q = [w, \mathbf{v}] = [\cos(\theta), \mathbf{v'}\sin(\theta)]$ where $\mathbf{v'} = (x', y', z')$ is a unit vector. We can therefore express the trace of M as:

$$\text{Tr} = 4(1 - (x'^2 + y'^2 + z'^2)\sin^2(\theta))$$

Since (x', y', z') is a unit vector, $x'^2 + y'^2 + z'^2 = 1$.

The trace of M reduces to:

$$\text{Tr} = 4(1 - \sin^2(\theta)) = 4\cos^2(\theta) = 4w^2$$

or:

$$|w| = \text{Tr}^{1/2}/2$$

So, if $\text{Tr} \geq 1$, we plug $4w = \pm 2\text{Tr}^{1/2}$ into equations 4, 5, and 6 and solve for x, y, and z:

$$x = (M_{2,3} - M_{3,2})/2\text{Tr}^{1/2}$$
$$y = (M_{3,1} - M_{1,3})/2\text{Tr}^{1/2}$$
$$z = (M_{1,2} - M_{2,1})/2\text{Tr}^{1/2}$$

Note that it doesn't matter whether we use the positive or negative root of Tr as the basis for w, since q and $-q$ represent identical rotations.

Solving for *X*, *Y* or *Z*

If $|w| < \frac{1}{2}$, we can determine which of the remaining components is the largest by examining the first three values along the diagonal of M. Suppose $M_{2,2} > M_{1,1}$. This expands to:

$$1 - 2x^2 - 2z^2 > 1 - 2y^2 - 2z^2$$

Simplifying, we get:

$$-2x^2 > -2y^2$$

or:

$$|x| < |y|$$

Similar arithmetic applies to other comparisons between the diagonals. So, the largest component of the vector $(M_{1,1}, M_{2,2}, M_{3,3})$ corresponds to the largest value of the vector (x, y, z).

Once we have the largest component of $(M_{1,1}, M_{2,2}, M_{3,3})$, we subtract the other two elements, and the equation reduces to a single term. For example, assume $M_{2,2}$ is the largest term:

$$M_{2,2} - M_{3,3} - M_{1,1} = 1 - 2x^2 - 2z^2 - (1 - 2y^2 - 2z^2) - (1 - 2x^2 - 2y^2) = 4y^2 - 1$$

or:

$$y = \pm(M_{2,2} - M_{3,3} - M_{1,1} + 1)^{1/2}/2$$

In general,

$$\mathbf{v}_i = \pm(M_{ii} - M_{jj} - M_{kk} + 1)^{1/2}/2 \quad \text{where } \mathbf{v} = (x, y, z)$$

As with w, it doesn't matter which root we use. Once we have a suitable $\mathbf{v}_i$, we can solve for $\mathbf{v}_j$, $\mathbf{v}_k$ and w by substitution:

$$\mathbf{v}_j = (M_{ij} + M_{ji})/(4\mathbf{v}_i)$$
$$\mathbf{v}_k = (M_{ik} + M_{ki})/(4\mathbf{v}_i)$$
$$w = (M_{jk} - M_{kj})/(4\mathbf{v}_i)$$

For the calculation of w from equation 4, 5, or 6, $i, j,$ and k must be in sequential order. That is, $j = 1 + (i\%3)$ and $k = 1 + (j\%3)$.

References

[Shomake94] Shoemake, K., *Quaternions*, available online at ftp://ftp.cis.upenn.edu/pub/graphics/shoemake/quatut.ps.Z, May 1994.

[Eberly99] Eberly, David, *Quaternion Algebra and Calculus*, available online at www.magic-software.com/src/graphics/quat/quat.pdf, July 1999.

2.9

Interpolating Quaternions

Jason Shankel

Quaternions are four-dimensional extensions of complex numbers. (See "Quaternions for Game Programming" in this book for a discussion of quaternions and quaternion mathematics.) This article presents four techniques (lerp, slerp, squad, and spline) for interpolating between pairs or sequences of quaternions. The actual derivations of each of these techniques are detailed at the end of the article.

Quaternion Calculus

Before getting into quaternion interpolation, we need to define some calculus functions of quaternions.

Let $q = \cos(\theta) + \mathbf{v}\sin(\theta)$ be a unit quaternion ($\mathbf{v}$ is a three-dimensional unit vector).

Euler's identity for complex numbers applies to quaternions:

$$q = \cos(\theta) + \mathbf{v}\sin(\theta) = \exp(\mathbf{v}\theta)$$

From this identity, we can define the power function for quaternions:

$$q^t = [\cos(\theta) + \mathbf{v}\sin(\theta)]^t = \exp(\mathbf{v}t\theta) = \cos(t\theta) + \mathbf{v}\sin(t\theta)$$

We can also express the logarithm of a quaternion using this identity:

$$\log(q) = \log(\exp(\mathbf{v}\theta)) = \mathbf{v}\theta$$

We can express the derivative of q^t as:

$$(q^t)' = q^t \log(q)$$

Applying the chain rule, we can express the derivative of $q^{f(t)}$:

$$(q^{f(t)})' = f'(t)q^{f(t)}\log(q)$$

Applying the chain rule for functions of two independent variables, we can express the derivative of $q(t)^{f(t)}$ (t omitted for clarity):

$$(q^f)' = f'q^f\log(q) + q'fq^{f-1}$$

Quaternion Interpolation

Since quaternions can be used to represent 3D rotations, we can use four-dimensional vector interpolation techniques to generate smooth 3D animations.

Let q_0 and q_1 be quaternions. The general formula for interpolation between q_0 and q_1 is given as:

$$q(t) = f_0(t)q_0 + f_1(t)q_1 \ (0 \le t \le 1)$$

where $f_0(t)$ and $f_1(t)$ are scalar functions such that:

$$f_0(0) = 1$$
$$f_0(1) = 0$$
$$f_1(0) = 0$$
$$f_1(1) = 1$$

Linear Interpolation

Linear interpolation is given as:

$$\mathbf{lerp}(t;q_0,q_1) = (1 - t)q_0 + tq_1 = t(q_1 - q_0) + q_0$$

Linear interpolation does not preserve magnitude, so it is important to normalize the result if you're using it as a rotation.

Linear interpolation is fast, but it does not generate smooth animation. This means that the animation speeds up and slows down over the course of the interpolation, even if you vary t at a constant rate. Although this variation in speed might be acceptable for some applications, it is not ideal. To achieve smooth animation between quaternions, we must use spherical linear interpolation.

Spherical Linear Interpolation

Just as three-dimensional unit vectors define points on a sphere, unit quaternions define points on a four-dimensional hypersphere. Smooth animation is achieved by interpolating values along the great arc connecting the two points (see Figure 2.9.1).

Spherical linear interpolation (**slerp**) is given as:

$$\mathbf{slerp}(t;q_0,q_1) = [q_0\sin(\theta(1 - t))+q_1\sin(\theta t)]/\sin(\theta)$$

where θ is the angle between q_0 and q_1.

We can find θ by treating q_0 and q_1 as four-dimensional vectors and calculating the dot product:

$$q_0 \bullet q_1 = x_0x_1 + y_0y_1 + z_0z_1 + w_0w_1 = \cos(\theta)$$

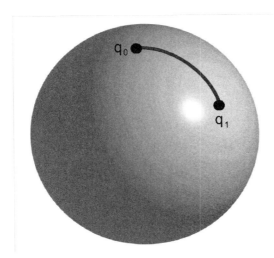

FIGURE 2.9.1. Spherical linear interpolation.

Unlike **lerp**, **slerp** preserves magnitude, so there is no need to normalize the result.

If $q_0 \bullet q_1 < 0$, then $\theta > \pi/2$. Since q and $-q$ represent the same rotation, it is best to invert q_0 or q_1 in this case, minimizing the angular distance the interpolation has to follow. This inversion reduces unnecessary spinning over the course of the interpolation.

If $|q_0 \bullet q_1|$ is close to 1, we fall back to **lerp**, since $\sin(\theta)$ approaches 0 as $|q_0 \bullet q_1|$ approaches 1.

See Derivation 2.9.1 for a derivation of **slerp**.

Spherical linear interpolation can also be expressed as a power function of q_0 and q_1:

$$\mathbf{slerp}(t;q_0,q_1) = q_0(q_0^{-1}q_1)^t$$

From this, we can express the derivative (**slerp'**) as:

$$\mathbf{slerp}'(t;q_0,q_1) = q_0(q_0^{-1}q_1)^t \log(q_0^{-1}q_1)$$

The power form of **slerp** and its derivative are used in deriving spline interpolation. See Derivation 2.9.2 for a derivation of the power form of **slerp**.

Spherical Cubic Interpolation

slerp produces smooth animations, but it always follows a great arc connecting two quaternions. Just like using straight lines to connect a series of points, using **slerp** to interpolate through a series of quaternions produces a jagged path. In practice, this means that your animations change directions abruptly at the control points. To smoothly interpolate through a series of quaternions, use splines (see Figure 2.9.2).

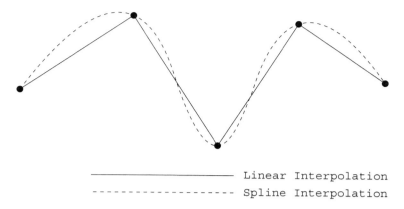

Linear Interpolation
Spline Interpolation

FIGURE 2.9.2. Linear vs. spline interpolation.

The basis for spline interpolation is spherical cubic interpolation, or **squad**:

$$\mathbf{squad}(t;p,q,a,b) = \mathbf{slerp}(2t(1-t);\mathbf{slerp}(t;p,q),\mathbf{slerp}(t;a,b))$$

The animation from p to q does not follow the great arc connecting p and q but curves toward the arc connecting a and b.

It is common for **slerp** implementations to invert one of the input quaternions when the angle between the two exceeds 90 degrees. Although it is true that q and $-q$ represent the same rotation, $\mathbf{slerp}(t;p,q)$ does not produce the same result as $\mathbf{slerp}(t;p,-q)$. Since the control points a and b are chosen to work with p and q, not $-p$ or $-q$, it is best not to invert the input quaternions in the version of **slerp** used with **squad**.

Spline Interpolation

Let $\{q_n, a_n, b_n\}_{(n=0\rightarrow N-1)}$ be sequences of N quaternions.

Let $S_n(t) = \mathbf{squad}(t;q_n, q_{n+1}, a_n, b_{n+1})$

To generate a sequence of smooth interpolations, $\{a_n, b_n\}$ is given as:

$$a_n = b_n = q_n \exp[-(\log(q_n^{-1}q_{n-1}) + \log(q_n^{-1}q_{n+1}))/4]$$

See Derivation 2.9.3 for a derivation of spline interpolation.

Sample Code

The sample code on the CD that accompanies this book provides implementations of **lerp**, **slerp**, **squad**, and spline interpolation as well as quaternion exponential and logarithm functions.

Derivation 2.9.1: Deriving Slerp

`slerp` preserves magnitude, so `slerp`ing between unit quaternions always produces a unit quaternion. Given the basic interpolation function:

$$q(t)=f_0(t)q_0 + f_1(t)q_1$$

we want to show that if we constrain $q(t)$ so that $N(q(t)) = 1$, we get:

$$f_0(t) = \sin(\theta(1 - t))/\sin(\theta)$$
$$f_1(t) = \sin(\theta t)/\sin(\theta)$$

To clarify the notation, the time-dependent variable has been omitted in the following ($q = q(t)$, $f_0 = f_0(t)$, etc).

Let $q = [xi + yj + zk + w] = f_0q_0 + f_1q_1 = \mathbf{slerp}(t;q_0,q_1)$
Let $q = \cos^{-1}(q_0 \bullet q_1)$

Since q is a unit quaternion, $x^2+y^2+z^2+w^2=1$. Expanding x^2, y^2, z^2 and w^2 gives:

$$x^2 = (f_0x_0 + f_1x_1)^2 = (f_0x_0)^2 + 2f_0f_1x_0x_1 + (f_1x_1)^2$$
$$y^2 = (f_0y_0 + f_1y_1)^2 = (f_0y_0)^2 + 2f_0f_1y_0y_1 + (f_1y_1)^2$$
$$z^2 = (f_0z_0 + f_1z_1)^2 = (f_0z_0)^2 + 2f_0f_1z_0z_1 + (f_1z_1)^2$$
$$w^2 = (f_0w_0 + f_1w_1)^2 = (f_0w_0)^2 + 2f_0f_1w_0w_1 + (f_1w_1)^2$$

Adding these equations together gives:

$$f_0^2+2f_0f_1(x_0x_1+y_0y_1+z_0z_1+w_0w_1)+f_1^2 = f_0^2+2f_0f_1(q_0 \cdot q_1)+f_1^2 = 1$$

We can express this as a matrix multiplication:

$$\left| f_0 \quad f_1 \right|^T \left| \begin{matrix} 1 & c \\ c & 1 \end{matrix} \right| \left| \begin{matrix} f_0 \\ f_1 \end{matrix} \right| = f^T M f = 1$$

where $c = q_0 \bullet q_1 = \cos(\theta)$.

The matrix M can be expanded to:

$$M = \left| \begin{matrix} 2^{1/2}/2 & -2^{1/2}/2 \\ 2^{1/2}/2 & 2^{1/2}/2 \end{matrix} \right| \left| \begin{matrix} 1+c & 0 \\ 0 & 1-c \end{matrix} \right| \left| \begin{matrix} 2^{1/2}/2 & 2^{1/2}/2 \\ -2^{1/2}/2 & 2^{1/2}/2 \end{matrix} \right| = R^T C R$$

Let $\mathbf{u} = C^{1/2}Rf$:

$$\mathbf{u} = \left| \begin{matrix} (1+c)^{1/2} & 0 \\ 0 & (1-c)^{1/2} \end{matrix} \right| \left| \begin{matrix} 2^{1/2}/2 & 2^{1/2}/2 \\ -2^{1/2}/2 & 2^{1/2}/2 \end{matrix} \right| \left| \begin{matrix} f_0 \\ f_1 \end{matrix} \right|$$

Multiplying this out gives us:

$$\mathbf{u} = [(f_1+f_0)(2+2c)^{1/2}/2, (f_1 - f_0)(2 - 2c)^{1/2}/2]$$

From here on, we need to show the time-dependent variable. $\mathbf{u}(t)$ is a two-dimensional unit vector, so it can be written as:

$$\mathbf{u}(t) = [\cos(\omega t), \sin(\omega t)]$$

where:

$$\cos(\omega t) = (f_1(t) + f_0(t))(2 + 2c)^{1/2}/2$$
$$\sin(\omega t) = (f_1(t) - f_0(t))(2 - 2c)^{1/2}/2$$

Let $A = (2 + 2c)^{1/2}/2$, $B = (2 - 2c)^{1/2}/2$

Multiplying $\cos(\omega t)$ by B/AB and $\sin(\omega t)$ by A/AB yields:

$$f_1(t) + f_0(t) = B\cos(\omega t)/AB$$
$$f_1(t) - f_0(t) = A\sin(\omega t)/AB$$

Solving for f_0 and f_1 yields:

$$f_0(t) = [B\cos(\omega t) - A\sin(\omega t)]/2AB$$
$$f_1(t) = [B\cos(\omega t) + A\sin(\omega t)]/2AB$$

$$2AB = (1 - c^2)^{1/2} = (1 - \cos^2(\theta))^{1/2} = \sin(\theta)$$
$$A^2 + B^2 = 1, \text{ so } A = \cos(\psi) \text{ and } B = \sin(\psi) \text{ for some phase angle } \psi.$$

There are two values of ψ that satisfy A and B, ψ_0 and ψ_1. Given this, we can rewrite f_0 and f_1:

$$f_0(t) = [\sin(\psi_0)\cos(\omega t) - \cos(\psi_0)\sin(\omega t)]/\sin(\theta)$$
$$f_1(t) = [\sin(\psi_1)\cos(\omega t) + \cos(\psi_1)\sin(\omega t)]/\sin(\theta)$$

Recall the trigonometric identities:

$$\sin(a)\cos(b) + \sin(b)\cos(a) = \sin(a+b)$$
$$\sin(a)\cos(b) - \sin(b)\cos(a) = \sin(a-b)$$

So, we have:

$$f_0(t) = \sin(\psi_0 - \omega t)/\sin(\theta)$$
$$f_1(t) = \sin(\psi_1 + \omega t)/\sin(\theta)$$

Given the boundary constraints on f_0 and f_1, we can solve for ψ_0, ψ_1 and ω:

$$f_0(0) = \sin(\psi_0)/\sin(\theta) = 1 \rightarrow \psi_0 = \theta$$
$$f_1(0) = \sin(\psi_1)/\sin(\theta) = 0 \rightarrow \psi_1 = 0$$
$$f_0(1) = \sin(\psi_0 - \omega)/\sin(\theta) = 0 \rightarrow \omega = \psi_0 = \theta$$

So, we can rewrite f_0 and f_1 again:

$$f_0(t) = \sin(\theta(1 - t))/\sin(\theta)$$
$$f_1(t) = \sin(\theta t)/\sin(\theta)$$

Derivation 2.9.2: Deriving the Power Form of Slerp

Start with the definition of **slerp**:

$$\mathbf{slerp}(t; q_0, q_1) = [q_0 \sin(\theta(1 - t)) + q_1 \sin(\theta\, t)] / \sin(\theta)$$

q_0 is a unit quaternion (as is q_1), so

$$q_0 q_0^{-1} = 1$$

From this, we can rewrite q_1 as:

$$q_1 = q_0 q_0^{-1} q_1$$

Let's expand $q_0^{-1} q_1$:

$$q_0^{-1} q_1 = [s_0 s_1 + \mathbf{v}_0 \bullet \mathbf{v}_1, -\mathbf{v}_0 \otimes \mathbf{v}_1 + s_0 \mathbf{v}_1 - s_1 \mathbf{v}_0]$$

Notice that the scalar part of $q_0^{-1} q_1 = s_0 s_1 + \mathbf{v}_0 \bullet \mathbf{v}_1$. This is the same as the vector dot product of q_0 and q_1, which is the same as the cosine of the angle between q_0 and q_1, θ.

Since $q_0^{-1} q_1$ is a unit quaternion and we know that its scalar part is $\cos(\theta)$, we can rewrite $q_0^{-1} q_1$ as:

$$q_0^{-1} q_1 = \cos(\theta) + \mathbf{u}\sin(\theta)$$

where $\mathbf{u}$ is a unit vector.

Okay, so now we have:

$$q_1 = q_0(\cos(\theta) + \mathbf{u}\sin(\theta))$$

If we plug this into the **slerp** formula above, we get:

$$\mathbf{slerp}(t; q_0, q_1) = [q_0 \sin(\theta(1 - t)) + q_0(\cos(\theta) + \mathbf{u}\sin(\theta))\sin(\theta\, t)] / \sin(\theta)$$

From the trigonometric identity, we know that:

$$q_0 \sin(\theta(1 - t)) = q_0(\sin(\theta)\cos(\theta t) - \cos(\theta)\sin(\theta t))$$

Substituting this into **slerp** and simplifying gives us:

$$\mathbf{slerp}(t; q_0, q_1) = q_0(\cos(\theta t) + \mathbf{u}\sin(\theta t))$$

From the power function for quaternions, we can rewrite this as:

$$\mathbf{slerp}(t; q_0, q_1) = q_0(\cos(\theta) + \mathbf{u}\sin(\theta))^t$$

Ah, but $\cos(\theta) + \mathbf{u}\sin(\theta) = q_0^{-1} q_1$, so one more rewrite yields:

$$\mathbf{slerp}(t; q_0, q_1) = q_0(q_0^{-1} q_1)^t$$

Derivation 2.9.3: Deriving Spline Interpolation

Let $\{a_n, b_n\}$ be a sequence of quaternions.
Let $S_n(t) = \mathbf{squad}(t; q_n, q_{n+1}, a_n, b_{n+1})$.

To derive spline interpolation, we want to find $\{a_n, b_n\}$ such that the derivatives of $S_n(t)$ at the control points ($t=0$ and $t=1$) are continuous. In other words, $S_n{}'(0) = S_{n-1}{}'(1)$ for all n.

To do this, we first have to express the derivative of **squad**.

Let $U = \textbf{slerp}(t;p,q)$, $V = \textbf{slerp}(t;a,b)$, $W = U^{-1}V$

Given the power form of **slerp**, we can rewrite **squad**:

$$\textbf{squad}(t;p,q,a,b) = U(U^{-1}V)^{2t(1-t)} = UW^{2t(1-t)}$$

The derivatives of U, V and W are:

$$U' = p(p^{-1}q)^t \log(p^{-1}q) = U\log(p^{-1}q)$$
$$V' = a(a^{-1}b)^t \log(a^{-1}b) = V\log(a^{-1}b)$$
$$W' = U^{-1}V' - U^{-2}U'V$$

Applying the product rule, we can express the derivative of **squad**:

$$\textbf{squad}'(t;p,q,a,b) = U[W^{2t(1-t)}]' + U'[W^{2t(1-t)}]$$

where $[W^{2t(1-t)}]' = (2-4t)W^{2t(1-t)}\log(W) + 2t(1-t)W'W^{2t(1-t)-1}$

Whew. Luckily for us, we only need to calculate **squad**' for $t=0$ and $t=1$:

$$U(0) = p$$
$$V(0) = a$$
$$W(0) = p^{-1}a$$
$$U'(0) = p\log(p^{-1}q)$$
$$[W^{2t(1-t)}]'(0) = 2\log(p^{-1}a)$$
$$\textbf{squad}'(0;p,q,a,b) = p[\log(p^{-1}q) + 2\log(p^{-1}a)]$$

$$U(1) = q$$
$$V(1) = b$$
$$W(1) = q^{-1}b$$
$$U'(1) = q\log(p^{-1}q)$$
$$[W^{2t(1-t)}]'(1) = -2\log(q^{-1}b)$$
$$\textbf{squad}'(1;p,q,a,b) = q[\log(p^{-1}q) - 2\log(q^{-1}b)]$$

Plugging in $S'_{n-1}(1) = S'_n(0)$ gives:

$$q_n[\log(q_{n-1}{}^{-1}q_n) - 2\log(q_n{}^{-1}b_n)] = q_n[\log(q_n{}^{-1}q_{n+1}) + 2\log(q_n{}^{-1}a_n)]$$

This gives us one equation and two unknowns (a_n and b_n). The only constraint we have so far is that this function must pass through all the control points and have a continuous derivative. We must select the value of the derivative at the control points ourselves. A reasonable value to select for the derivative at a control point is the average of the tangent values of the two functions:

$$S'_{n-1}(1) = q_n T_n = S'_n(0) \text{ where}$$

$$T_n = [\log(q_n^{-1}q_{n+1}) + \log(q_{n-1}^{-1}q_n)]/2$$

So now we have two equations:

$$q_n[\log(q_{n-1}^{-1}q_n) - 2\log(q_n^{-1}b_n)] = q_n[\log(q_n^{-1}q_{n+1}) + \log(q_{n-1}^{-1}q_n)]/2$$
$$q_n[\log(q_n^{-1}q_{n+1}) + 2\log(q_n^{-1}a_n)] = q_n[\log(q_n^{-1}q_{n+1}) + \log(q_{n-1}^{-1}q_n)]/2$$

Solving for a_n and b_n:

$$a_n = b_n = q_n\exp[(\log(q_{n-1}^{-1}q_n) - \log(q_n^{-1}q_{n+1}))/4]$$

For a unit quaternion $q = [s,\mathbf{v}]$:

$$q^* = q^{-1} = [s,-\mathbf{v}]$$
$$(pq)^* = q^*p^*$$
$$\log(q^{-1}) = -\log(q)$$

From these rules, we can say:

$$\log(q_{n-1}^{-1}q_n) = -\log((q_{n-1}^{-1}q_n)^{-1}) = -\log(q_n^{-1}q_{n-1})$$

Plugging this into the equation for $\{a_n, b_n\}$ yields:

$$a_n = b_n = q_n\exp[-(\log(q_n^{-1}q_{n-1}) + \log(q_n^{-1}q_{n+1}))/4]$$

2.10

The Shortest Arc Quaternion

Stan Melax

This article shows a short routine called RotationArc(). Given two vectors v_0 and v_1, this function returns a quaternion q where $q*v_0==v_1$. The implementation is fairly optimal and avoids a common numerical instability pitfall.

Motivation

You might be wondering where you would ever want to use such a function. Consider a guided missile in your video game. This is an object that uses orientation (3DOF), even though it is only the forward direction (2DOF) of this radial-symmetric object that is important for its AI. As is the case for all rigid bodies, a quaternion q is needed to reorient this object from its current direction v_0 to the direction we want it to be going v_1. Although we can choose from an infinite number of axes of rotation, it is best to choose the obvious axis of rotation that minimizes the (arc) angle of reorientation—that is, the obvious axis that is perpendicular to both vectors. This routine is also useful for implementing a "virtual trackball" for spinning objects with the mouse (as in a VRML viewer). The SpinLogo demo program included on the CD that accompanies this book uses RotationArc() to implement this feature.

Numerical Instability

This algorithm could easily be done by taking the normalized cross product to get an axis of rotation and then taking the acos() of the dot product to get the angle between the vectors. This axis and angle would be fed into the constructor of a quaternion. However, that is not a good solution, because as the vectors v_0 and v_1 get close together, the cross product (being proportional to the sin of the angle between the two vectors) becomes small and potentially unstable when we try to normalize it (see Figure 2.10.1). Deriving the angle can also cause grief. It is possible that taking the dot product of two unit length vectors that are parallel can result in a small overflow (greater than 1). This can be problematic when deriving the angle. Try executing acos(1.00000001). In these cases, using the standard quaternion constructor that

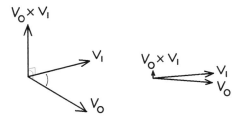

FIGURE 2.10.1. Cross product shrinks as vectors converge.

accepts an axis and an angle is not appropriate. The solution is to generate the quaternion in a more direct manner.

This problem first hit us during the development of the guided missiles for the video game MDK2 [Bioware00]. This is not an obscure problem that showed up only in our development. It has been noticed by many others and could happen to you. *Real-Time Rendering* [Moller99] briefly mentions the subject. This article provides a more thorough explanation and provides code to add to the *Game Programming Gems* math library (or to your own quaternion library). If you want to avoid introducing a nasty bug, you should use the code provided in this article for generating a quaternion from two direction vectors.

Derivation of Stable Formula

For this discussion, let $c = [c_x, c_y, c_z] = \mathrm{cross}(v_0, v_1)$, and the quaternion q we are trying to derive has the elements q_x, q_y, q_z, q_w. The angle (unknown) between the two vectors (v_0 and v_1) is t. Let d be the dot product: $d = \mathrm{dot}(v_0, v_1)$;

The q_x, q_y, q_z components of a quaternion q have a length that is sin of half the angle ($t/2$). As mentioned, the cross product's length is the sin of the angle t. Therefore:

$$[q_x, q_y, q_z] = [c_x, c_y, c_z] \frac{\sin(t/2)}{\sin(t)}$$

So now we have to determine a stable formula for the *sin(t/2)/sin(t)* term. Recall the half-angle formula:

$$\sin(t/2) = \sqrt{\frac{1 - \cos(t)}{2}}$$

and the circle identity:

$$\sin^2 + \cos^2 = 1$$

Then:

$$\frac{\sin(t/2)}{\sin(t)} = \frac{\sqrt{(1 - \cos(t))/2}}{\sqrt{1 - \cos^2(t)}}$$

We know *cos(t)* to be the dot product (*d*) of the two vectors. Therefore, we replace it in the formula and continue the simplification:

$$\frac{\sqrt{(1 - d)/2}}{\sqrt{1 - d^2}} = \sqrt{\frac{1 - d}{2(1 + d)(1 - d)}} = \frac{1}{\sqrt{2(1 + d)}}$$

Substituting back in:

$$[q_x, q_y, q_z] = \frac{[c_x, c_y, c_z]}{\sqrt{2(1 + d)}}$$

Deriving the q_w component (angle) of the quaternion is fairly straightforward using the half-angle formula for *cos(t/2)*:

$$q_w = \cos(t/2) = \sqrt{\frac{1 + \cos(t)}{2}} = \sqrt{\frac{1 + d}{2}}$$

In order to optimize our C++ function to use only one call to `sqrt()`, we multiply the inner square root term of our q_w formula by 2/2. As a result, the term within the square root is now the same as for the other quaternion elements. In other words, q_w is derived using the equivalent formula:

$$q_w = \frac{\sqrt{2(1 + d)}}{2}$$

These new formulas for our quaternion elements remain stable as v_0 approaches v_1 and as the dot product *d* approaches 1.

Remaining Instability Condition

Note that this function still becomes numerically unstable as v_0 approaches $-v_1$. This is not surprising, because when v_0 equals $-v_1$, there is not a unique solution; any axis of rotation on the plane perpendicular to v_0 will do. Remember that v_0 and v_1 are directions, not orientations. A check could be added to the function in order to detect this case and avoid the possibility of dividing by zero. However, we did not do this, because it is so unlikely that one would be calling this function in that case. The objective of using a function such as this one is to orient an object toward a target.

Consequently, v_0 rarely approaches $-v_1$ but instead converges to v_1 after repeated missile-tracking AI updates.

Source Code

```
quaternion RotationArc(vector3 v0,vector3 v1) {
    quaternion q;
    v0.normalize();  // Skip if known to be unit length.
    v1.normalize();  // Do only if needed.
    vector3 c = CrossProduct(v0,v1);
    float   d = DotProduct(v0,v1);
    float   s = (float)sqrt((1+d)*2);
    q.x = c.x / s;
    q.y = c.y / s;
    q.z = c.z / s;
    q.w = s /2.0f;
    return q;
}
```

Virtual TrackBall

As a bonus, this article includes code for implementing a virtual trackball function. Although such functionality might not be necessary in the user interface of your finished game, it is very handy during development to be able to grab any of your game objects and spin them around with the mouse.

An easy way of implementing object spinning is to rotate the object about the Y-axis when the mouse is moved parallel to the X direction and about the X-axis based on vertical (Y) mouse movement. This method doesn't allow for rotation about the Z-axis (normal to window), and it simply doesn't feel "intuitive."

There are a variety of other user interface methods for spinning objects. This article explains one simple approach. The old and new mouse positions (2D [X, Y]) are converted into rays (3D) that point from the viewpoint into the window. Next, we determine where these rays would intersect a sphere around the object the user is manipulating. If a ray does not intersect the sphere, the closest point on the silhouette of the sphere is used. The sphere is rotated so that the point of intersection from the old mouse ray coincides with the point of intersection from the new mouse ray. This is achieved by passing these two points (using the center of the sphere as the origin of the coordinate system) as input to RotationArc(). This returns the quaternion that is used to adjust the object's orientation. The source code for the virtual trackball function and extracting the direction vectors from mouse input are available in the SpinLogo source code on the CD that accompanies this book.

References

[Bioware00] Bioware, Shiny, and Interplay Productions, *MDK2,* 2000.

[Moller99] Moller, Tomas, and Haines, Eric, *Real-Time Rendering*, A. K. Peters Ltd., 1999.

ARTIFICIAL INTELLIGENCE

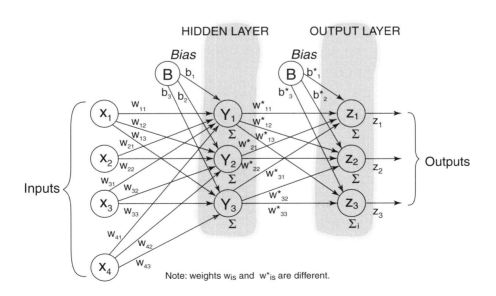

HIDDEN LAYER · OUTPUT LAYER

Bias · *Bias*

Note: weights w_{is} and w^*_{is} are different.

3.0

Designing a General Robust AI Engine

Steve Rabin

Creating a multimillion-dollar game that spans several years of development is a pretty big undertaking. The underlying structure of your AI engine will have huge implications in terms of what your game can and can't do. Therefore, rather than let an engine simply evolve, it is best to build in generality and safety precautions from the start. The generality allows you to make your AI characters do anything you can dream up. The safety precautions both prevent bugs and help you track them down. After all, the only thing standing between you and the ship party is a couple thousand bugs.

The ideal AI engine helps solve a ton of problems for you. The following list contains just a few:

1. Easily allow communication between game objects
2. Offer a general and readable solution to implementing AI behavior
3. Facilitate keeping debug records of *every* event (you want to catch all those bugs, right?)

This article consists of several parts. Any one part by itself might seem obvious, ordinary, or insane, but put together, these ideas create a very powerful system. So, as you read through the article, try to keep in mind the big picture and how each concept interacts with the others. In addition, realize that the AI engine presented is implemented in C as opposed to C++. C was chosen on purpose to show that this engine doesn't rely on any object-oriented code to work and is generally applicable, even to console development.

Event-Driven vs. Polling Objects

After working on several games, you'll start to see some pretty big patterns in AI engines. The first is that you need each of your game objects to update its logic every tick or so. The second is that these objects need to communicate with each other. There are basically two ways for game objects to react in the world: by actively watching the world (*polling*) or by sitting back and waiting for news (*event driven*).

Since games usually have hundreds of game objects in them, the only reasonable solution is to make the objects as event driven as possible. Imagine for a moment that a missile explodes, causing area damage that affects 15 or so units. Each unit could poll for nearby explosions every tick as though they were actually aware of their environment, or the exploding missile could simply tell each unit that it was hit and how hard. Although it's more cool to think that each game object could sense its environment and react appropriately, the fact is that the end result is the same either way.

With that quick-and-dirty analogy out of the way, you'll probably agree that event-driven communication is the way to go!

The Message Concept

Since the goal is to have event-driven behavior, we need to design a robust communication system for making that happen. For now, let's look at the concept of messages. For our purposes, a *message* is an object that has five fields: a descriptive name, the name of the sender, the name of the receiver, the time at which it should be delivered, and any relevant data. If I was handed a message, I should have all the information necessary to pass it to the correct game object at the right time. The receiver of the message gets the message along with all of the goodies inside it, such as who sent it and any extra data.

Here's an example of a message:

```
name:damaged, from:dragon, to:knight, deliver_at_time:245.34, data:10
(amount of damage)
```

In effect, messages become an electronic paper trail of what's happening in our game. This is a powerful concept that gives us all kinds of benefits. One of the incredible uses of this concept is that we can record every message that is sent and dump it to a file. That way, if there's a bug, we can look at the file and examine what triggered certain actions. This ability becomes invaluable when the problem involves the interactions of tens of game objects over a fraction of a second.

Another great use of this concept is that any game object can "listen" to any other game object's messages. Since messages have the intended receiver built in, it's easy to differentiate who the message was meant for. Call it snooping, sniffing, or just peeking, but this ability gives you the power to solve some tricky logic problems. Imagine a manager game object that owns several other game objects. The manager can then snoop its children's messages to listen for key events, such as members being attacked or damaged.

The messages I am describing also have a field for delivery time. By sending messages that should be delivered at a future time, we wrap a really cool timer system into the message concept. In the real world, people and creatures usually have reaction times. By delivering messages slightly into the future, depending on the event, reaction times can be simulated. After all, don't you hate it when you're playing a game and things tend to happen in lock-step, all at once? Even within a single game object, it can send a message to itself, to be delivered at a future time, in order to stagger behavior changes. You could even generate a random time within some window in order to add some much-needed chaos.

State Machines

A *state machine* is a simple AI concept that delivers a lot of power with very little complexity. The basic idea is that a game object has a different state for each main segment of behavior it exhibits. The goal is to break down a game object's behavior into these logical states. In a baseball game, for example, the pitcher might have the states ReadyForWindup, Windup, WaitForHit, InterceptBall, CoverBase, and so on. Imagine how useful it would be if at any time during your baseball game you could simply display on-screen the current and past states of all nine players on the field. Alternatively, if you came across a bug, you could dump to a file all the past state information along with what caused each state transition. For example, if your right fielder never responded to the ball being hit, you can see why he wasn't in the right state to listen for that event. So, state machines not only break behavior into manageable bite-sized chunks, but they also give you instant access to the mindset or thoughts of your AI objects.

An Event-Driven State Machine Using Messages

Putting these three major concepts together, we now have a powerful foundation for an AI engine. Individual behaviors are built using state machines, whereas all communication and event notifications are accomplished with messages. Note that each game object running a state machine doesn't preclude it from using fuzzy logic, neural nets, or any other exotic AI technique. The state machines simply provide a standardized generic interface that can be exploited any way you like.

Although state machines are a simple concept, let's review some important qualities that would make a state machine more elegant and more robust. Below is a checklist of features we need:

1. The state machine can have an arbitrary number of states.
2. States can be easily defined and set.
3. When a state is entered, we should be able to execute any initialization code.
4. When a state is exited, we should be able to execute any clean-up code.
5. We can easily listen for messages and execute any code in response.
6. We can easily listen for the update tick and execute any code in response.
7. We can transparently record which messages have been received and whether there was a response.
8. We can transparently record state changes and the message that triggered them.
9. We can listen for a message within only certain states or globally over all states.

Table 3.0.1 Pseudocode for State Machines

Pseudocode Keyword	Description
BeginStateMachine	Starts the state machine definition
EndStateMachine	Terminates the state machine definition
State(NameOfState)	Designates the beginning of a particular state
OnEnter	Responds to a state being entered; allows for initialization code
OnExit	Responds to a state being exited; allows for clean-up code
OnUpdate	Responds to the update game tick
OnMsg(NameOfMessage)	Responds to any defined message
SetState(NameOfState)	Changes states; sends OnExit to old state and OnEnter to new state
SendMsg()	Sends message to any game object
SendDelayedMsg()	Sends a delayed message to any game object

10. We can send messages to any game object, including ourselves.
11. We can send messages with a delay built in so that the message is delivered at a future time.
12. The overhead for running the state machine should be minimal.

Our state machine needs to support all these features. Table 3.0.1 is pseudocode for all the constructs we'll need.

In order to make this concept concrete, let's look at an example of a sentry robot bent on killing. Let's also use the pseudocode from Table 3.0.1 to represent our state machine. Our state machine has two states: Patrol and Attack. However, the state machine starts out in none of these states. Instead, a global section at the top of the state machine is always active, regardless of the current state. When the state machine runs for the first time, the OnEnter response is triggered. Inside this response, the first state is set with a SetState command. In this example, it sets the starting state to Patrol.

```
BeginStateMachine

    //Global Responses
    OnEnter {
       SetState( STATE_Patrol )
    }
    OnMsg( MSG_Dead ) {
       //Destroy this game object
    }

    State( STATE_Patrol ) {
       OnEnter {
          //Set initial goal point for patrol
       }
       OnUpdate {
          if( /*see the enemy*/ )
             SetState( STATE_Attack )
          else if( /*goal point reached*/ )
```

```
            //set next patrol point as goal
        }
    }

    State( STATE_Attack ) {
        OnEnter {
            //Set goal to be enemy
        }
        OnUpdate {
            if( /*enemy dead*/ )
                SetState( STATE_PATROL )
            else if( /*enemy within weapon range*/ )
                //Shoot enemy
        }
    }

EndStateMachine
```

Since this state machine is event driven, the only way it executes is by getting a message. It can get a message when a state is first entered (OnEnter), when a state is exited (OnExit), when a game tick occurs (OnUpdate), or on any other defined message (OnMsg()).

When looking at the state machine, envision a message being delivered to it. The message first goes to the current state. If there is a response for that message, the message is consumed and the response is executed. If there is no response for the message in that state, the message is resent to the global responses at the top of the state machine. This behavior creates a powerful state machine concept: the idea that individual states can have message responses or that you can have a global response to a message, regardless of the current state. Even more powerful, you can have a global response to a message while sometimes overriding that response within certain states.

Because there are these global message responses, a state change might happen from outside the current state. For this reason, the OnExit message response is crucial. If a global message response changes the current state, you can rely on getting the OnExit message in the current state to clean up anything before the state is actually changed.

Confession Time

Now I have a very big confession to make. The pseudocode you just examined *does* compile with a normal C compiler! (That is, it does so provided some comments are turned into real code.) All you need to do is use these macro definitions and place the state machine within the following function:

```
#define BeginStateMachine   if( STATE_Global == state ) {
#define State(a)                if(0) {return( true ); } } \
                            else if( a == state ) { if(0) {
#define OnEnter                 return( true ); } else if( \
                                MSG_RESERVED_Enter == msg->name ) {
```

```
#define OnExit                return( true ); } else if( \
                              MSG_RESERVED_Exit == msg->name ) {
#define OnUpdate              return( true ); } \ else if( \
                              MSG_RESERVED_Update == msg->name ) { \
#define OnMsg(a)              return( true ); } \
                              else if( a == msg->name ) {
#define SetState(a)           SetStateInGameObject( go, (int)a );
#define EndStateMachine       return( true ); } } \ else { assert(\
                              !"Invalid State" ); \
                              return( false );}  return( false );

bool ProcessStateMachine( GameObject* go, unsigned int state,
MsgObject* msg )
{
    // Put state machine inside this function!
}
```

C-style macros are a funny thing. Normally you'd want to stay away from them because they can be misused and lead to bugs. In this case, we can exploit macro definitions to construct a new state machine language! We certainly don't have to use the macros to make the state machine work; it simply makes the coding more error free, simpler to read, and faster to write. Now that's a good use for macros!

You might have noticed that a bunch of return statements are embedded in the macros. Conveniently, these return statements report whether a message was handled or whether it fell through without being consumed. This information is critical for knowing whether a message that wasn't handled in a local state needs to be sent to the global responses. The return value also helps log whether or not a particular message was handled by the state machine.

Another Small Confession

I have another small confession. The macros are constructed so that you don't need to use all those curly braces! The braces are there to make the state machine more C-like, but they aren't needed at all. By not using the curly braces, you can make the state machine more elegant and perhaps more readable. The following is an example state machine without the curly braces:

```
BeginStateMachine

    OnEnter
        //Initialization code here
    OnMsg( MSG_SomeMessage )
        //Response code here

    State( STATE_Roam )
        OnUpdate
            //Update code here
        OnExit
```

```
                //Cleanup code here

        EndStateMachine
```

State Machine Building Blocks

These C macros were constructed very carefully in order to make something cool happen. Think of them as building blocks that can be stacked however you like. Because of this stacking ability, the minimum you need is the following:

```
        BeginStateMachine

        EndStateMachine
```

From this minimum, you can add states and listen for any messages within those states. Since it's not required to have states at all, you could simply have message responses!

The state names and message names are simply enumerated types—in effect, unsigned integers. Since simple if-else statements replace the macros, the processing required is quite minimal.

State Machine Message Routing

Of course, there's a bit more support code to route messages and make this state machine work properly. Figure 3.0.1 shows an overview of the structure.

The only outside source of messages to the game objects comes from the player input and the game tick update loop. Other than those, messages are spawned by the state machines themselves. When a message is sent, it always goes to the message router. The router then sends it through the game object and on to the state machine

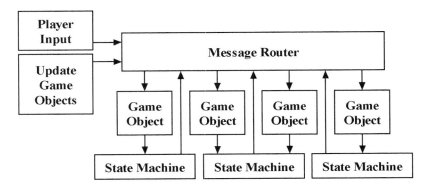

FIGURE 3.0.1. Overview of message routing.

that the game object owns. In case a message should be delivered at some time in the future, the router hangs on to it until the delivery time has passed.

Note that in Figure 3.0.1, two different game objects point to the same state machine. Obviously, if you have two or more objects that should behave the same, they should execute the same exact code. Therefore, it's important to recognize that all variables and state information are stored inside the game object and not the state machine. Multiple game objects use the same state machine, so you should always be conscious of that fact.

In order to explain the message router and state changes, we need to know more about some variables inside each game object and message object. The following is the bare minimum definition of each:

```
typedef struct
{
    unsigned int unique_id;

    //State machine info
    StateMachineID state_machine_id;
    unsigned int state;                 //the current state
    unsigned int next_state;            //the next state
    bool force_state_change;            //has a state change been
                                        //requested

    //Put other game object info in here
} GameObject;

typedef struct
{
    MsgName name;                       //name of message
    unsigned int sender_id;
    unsigned int receiver_id;
    float delivery_time;                //deliver message at this time

    //Note that the sender_id and receiver_id are not pointers to
    //game objects.  Since messages can be delayed, the sender or
    //receiver may get removed from the game and a pointer would
    //become dangerously invalid.

    //You can add right here any data you want to be passed
    //along with every message — sometimes it's helpful to let
    //messages convey more info by using extra data.
    //For example, a damaged message could carry with it the
    //amount of damage.

} MsgObject;
```

The following is the code that is called when a state change is requested. Note that the state change is asked for and doesn't occur until the current message is done being handled. In addition, realize that this function is called by the SetState macro.

```
void SetStateInGameObject( GameObject* go, unsigned int state )
```

```
{
    go->next_state = state;
    go->force_state_change = true;
}
```

The router takes a formulated message that's ready to be sent and makes sure it gets sent to the right states. It also deals with changing states if a request has been made. You can see the code for the router in Listing 3.0.1. Since the router needs to deal with delayed messages (a concept that is explained later in this article), the functions it references are in Listing 3.0.2.

Sending Messages

In order to send a message from inside a state machine, it would help if there were a simple function to call. The following is an example of a send message interface:

```
void SendMsg( MsgName name, unsigned int sender, unsigned int
receiver )
{
    MsgObject msg;
    msg.name = name;                //The name of the message
    msg.sender = sender;            //The sender
    msg.receiver = receiver;        //The receiver
    msg.delivery_time = GetCurTime(); //Send the message NOW

    RouteMessage( &msg );
}
```

Note that when a message is sent, the state machine immediately routes it to the intended receiver. This is a great feature for debugging because a breakpoint inside a state machine lets you see the stack and, consequently, who sent the message.

Sending Delayed Messages

As mentioned before, messages can be given a future time to be delivered. The router deals with this command by storing delayed messages for future routing. Somewhere in the main game loop, the function SendDelayedMessages needs to be called so that the messages are eventually sent at the correct time. The following is the interface function for sending a delayed message:

```
void SendDelayedMsg( MsgName name, float delay, unsigned int sender,
unsigned int receiver )
{
    MsgObject msg;
    msg.name = name;                //The name of the message
    msg.sender = sender;            //The sender
    msg.receiver = receiver;        //The receiver
    msg.delivery_time = GetCurTime() + delay;//Send a future message
```

```
        RouteMessage( &msg );
    }
```

Note that all messages contain the sender and receiver as unique IDs, not as pointers. Since messages can be delayed, it's possible that the sender or receiver has been removed from the game. Since a pointer has no way of knowing this, it's not safe to reference the game objects by a pointer only. Instead, the receiver of the message is looked up using its unique ID. This method ensures that messages are sent only to valid game objects.

Delayed messages are an incredibly useful tool for the state machine. Consider the following state machine for a heat-seeking rocket. The rocket is fired, and if it doesn't contact anything within five seconds, it should automatically explode. This task is accomplished by sending a delayed message (MSG_SelfDestruct) when the state machine is initialized. After five seconds, the message is delivered to the state machine and consumed in the global responses. At that time, the state is set to Explode, and the rocket will soon be history.

```
BeginStateMachine

    //Global Responses
    OnEnter //Triggered when state machine first starts up
        SendDelayedMsg( MSG_SelfDestruct, 5.0, go->unique_id,
            go->unique_id );
        SetState( STATE_Armed );

    OnMsg( MSG_SelfDestruct )
        SetState( STATE_Explode );

    State( STATE_Armed )
        OnMsg( MSG_Collision )
            SetState( STATE_Explode );

        OnUpdate
            //Identify closest visible enemy and steer toward

    State( STATE_Explode )
        OnEnter
            //Explode rocket - cause area damage
            //Delete game object

EndStateMachine
```

Deleting a Game Object

Deleting a game object from within the state machine takes a little thought. Since the game object owns the state machine, we can't delete it while we're executing code inside the state machine. The solution is to set a flag identifying that the game object should be deleted. When the execution steps outside the state machine, it's then legal to delete it.

Enhancement: Defining the Scope of a Message

A problem that creeps up is that sometimes a message is valid only inside a particular state. Unfortunately, the potential exists for a delayed message to be consumed by the wrong state. Consider the following code:

```
BeginStateMachine

    //Global Responses
    OnEnter
        SetState( STATE_Alive );


    State( STATE_Alive )
        OnEnter
            SendDelayedMsg( MSG_TimeOut, 3.0, go->unique_id,
                go->unique_id );

        OnMsg( MSG_TimeOut )
            //Play a sound

        OnMsg( MSG_Dead )
            SetState( STATE_Dead );

    State( STATE_Dead )
        OnEnter
            SendDelayedMsg( MSG_TimeOut, 50.0, go->unique_id,
                go->unique_id );

        OnMsg( MSG_TimeOut )
            SetState( STATE_Alive );

    EndStateMachine
```

The problem is that both states send and respond to MSG_TimeOut. If the Alive state gets a MSG_Dead before it gets back the MSG_TimeOut, the Dead state then incorrectly gets the MSG_TimeOut spawned by the Alive state. This was clearly not intended.

The solution is to mark a message as valid only within a particular state. If the state is no longer active at the time of delivery, the message should be thrown away. In effect, the message now has a scope and is valid only within that scope.

This enhancement can easily be added with an extra variable called "state" inside each message object. When the message is delivered, it first checks whether the message "state" matches the current state of the game object. Only then is the message delivered. However, most of the time you want messages to be delivered regardless of the current state, so messages should default to not performing this check.

Since only delayed messages sent to yourself should ever be marked with a state, we can create a new helper function for sending that particular kind. The following is an example of the code. (If this enhancement is made, the other send message functions need to mark the message state as invalid.)

```
void SendDelayedMsgToCurrentState( MsgName name, float delay,
GameObject* go )
{
   MsgObject msg;
   msg.name = name;              //The name of the message
   msg.state = go->state;        //The state in which the msg is valid
   msg.sender = go->unique_id;       //The sender
   msg.receiver = go->unique_id;     //The receiver
   msg.delivery_time = GetCurTime() + delay;  //Send a future message

   RouteMessage( &msg );
}
```

Enhancement: Logging All Message Activity and State Transitions

With the current structure, it's trivial to snoop the current state of each game object and perhaps display it on screen. You could even watch all the message traffic that comes through the message router and display that on screen. But for real hard-core debugging, the ideal situation is to individually track each game object, logging all message activity and state transitions along with a time stamp. Surprisingly, this task is easy to do.

The trick is to modify the state machine macros. When we insert some simple function calls into the macros, the task of monitoring every state machine becomes transparent. The following macros log message responses and state transitions:

```
#define OnEnter        return( true ); } \
    else if( MSG_RESERVED_Enter == msg->name ) { \
    LogMessage( go, msg, GetCurTime() );
#define OnExit         return( true ); } \
    else if( MSG_RESERVED_Exit == msg->name ) { \
    LogMessage( go, msg, GetCurTime() );
#define OnUpdate       return( true ); } \
    else if( MSG_RESERVED_Update == msg->name ) { \
    LogMessage( go, msg, GetCurTime() );
#define OnMsg(a)       return( true ); } \
    else if( a == msg->name ) { \
    LogMessage( go, msg, GetCurTime() );
#define SetState(a)   SetStateInGameObject( go, (int)a ); \
    LogStateChange( go, state, (int)a, GetCurTime() );
```

The functions LogMessage and LogStateChange can store the information in whatever way you'd like. One suggestion is to keep a circular buffer of history data for each game object. You can then either browse the history on screen or dump it to a file when something interesting happens. Since each event is time stamped, you could compare the logs of different game objects to see how they interacted. As mentioned before, this feature is incredibly helpful if there are three or more game objects all interacting over a fraction of a second. Very complex interactions are now easy to debug.

Enhancement: Swapping State Machines

Within complex characters, it's very hard to design one state machine that serves all purposes. The solution is to make bite-sized state machines that are more manageable and more specialized. With this functionality, a character can choose to run the state machine that best fits the situation. This function avoids overly complex state machines that become unmanageable.

Enhancement: Multiple State Machines

There is no rule that a game object can run only one state machine at a time. In fact, it's quite useful for an AI character to run several state machines simultaneously. Imagine that each character has one state machine that serves as the brain and one that serves to keep track of the movement goals (not the movement execution). The brain could even control the movement state machine by sending it commands in the form of messages.

Since not all types of movement are the same, you can apply the idea of swapping state machines. The brain can then run the appropriate movement state machine that fits each given situation.

Enhancement: A Queue of State Machines

The dedicated movement state machine brings up an interesting enhancement. It would be incredibly powerful to be able to queue up several movement state machines. In this scenario, only the top one on the queue would be active; the others would be temporarily disabled.

The idea is that maybe a player has directed an AI character to go to three separate places in succession (think RTS). For each spot, a separate movement state machine would be thrown onto the movement queue. As the first state machine reaches its goal, it destroys itself, and the next state machine on the queue becomes active. This approach actually solves a large number of command issues in RTS games.

Consider the act of patrolling. *Patrolling* is going to a sequence of places and repeating that pattern over and over. By employing the state machine movement queue, each patrol spot can be placed on the queue. However, when a state machine reaches its goal, it needs to put itself on the back end of the queue in order to maintain the cycle.

Scripting Behavior Outside the Code

The AI engine described in this article is clearly not scripted from outside the code. However, that fact doesn't exclude a programmer from cleverly influencing the behavior through the use of outside data. If we create variables that impact decision making, a state machine can be customized for a particular character. In fact, many characters should be able to use the same state machine yet have wildly differing behavior due to attributes such as aggressiveness or fear.

Interestingly, the original implementation of this AI engine supported state machines scripted solely outside the code. Putting the logic outside the code created a debugging nightmare for everyone involved. The original intentions were admirable, but the result was a frustrating programming environment that wasted many people's time.

The lesson to learn was that logic should be inside the code and data should be outside. Unless the design goal is to let users write their own AI, there isn't a compelling enough reason to support arbitrary scripting of AI behavior. (For a more detailed discussion of data and scripting, look at the article "The Magic of Data-Driven Design" in this book.)

Conclusion

Even if you never use this exact implementation of an AI engine, many of the great ideas presented here can be applied to any AI engine or state machine. Some of the more notable ideas are as follows:

1. Standardized communication with messages
2. Standardized timers through the use of messages
3. Using event-driven methods as opposed to polling
4. Tracking communication and state changes over all AI objects
5. Using global responses in state machines that are always active, regardless of the current state
6. Allowing a global response in a state machine to be overridden by the current state
7. Allowing an AI to swap state machines
8. Allowing an AI to simultaneously run multiple state machines
9. Allowing an AI to queue up several state machines
10. Keep complicated logic inside the code as opposed to scripting it from outside

The AI engine as presented here is a powerful tool for enforcing a standard structure on AI objects. Because of the macro state machine pseudolanguage, it's incredibly quick and easy to prototype new behaviors. It's so easy in fact, that there is a real tendency to put too much code inside the state machine. The challenge comes in deciding where to draw the line. As a general rule, probably only high level decision-making should be held within the state machine. Other systems of an AI character, such as movement execution and animation, should certainly exist elsewhere.

Listing 3.0.1: Message Router

```
void RouteMessage( MSG_Object* msg )
{
   GameObject* go = GetGOFromID( cur_msg->receiver_id ); //Function not
                                                         //supplied
   if( !go )
   {  //Receiver doesn't exist anymore - discard the message
      return;
   }

   if( msg->delivery_time > GetCurTime() )
   {  //This message needs to be stored until its time to send it
      StoreDelayedMessage( msg );
      return;
   }

   if( RouteMessageHelper( go, go->state, msg ) == false )
   {  //Current state didn't handle msg, try Global state (0)
      RouteMessageHelper( go, 0, msg );
   }

   // Check for a state change
   while( go->force_state_change )
   {  //Note: circular logic (state changes causing state changes)
      //could cause an infinite loop here - protect against this

      //Create a general msg for initializing and cleaning up the state
      //change
      MsgObject tempmsg;
      tempmsg.receiver = go->unique_id;
      tempmsg.sender = go->unique_id;

      go->force_state_change = false;

      //Let the last state clean-up
      tempmsg.name = MSG_RESERVED_Exit;
      RouteMessageHelper( go, go->state, &tempmsg );

      //Set the new state
      go->state = go->next_state;

      //Let the new state initialize
      tempmsg.name = MSG_RESERVED_Enter;
      RouteMessageHelper( go, go->state, &tempmsg );
   }
}

bool RouteMessageHelper( GameObject* go, unsigned int state, MsgObject*
msg )
{
```

```
         //Look up correct state machine for this Game Object
         //and send message to that particular one
         //(not implemented here - this always calls the same one)
         return( ProcessStateMachine( go, state, msg ) );
      }
```

Listing 3.0.2: Functions to Deal with Delayed Messages

```
      void StoreDelayedMessage( MsgObject* msg )
      {
         //Store this message (in some data structure) for later routing

         //A priority queue would be the ideal data structure (but not required)
         //to store the delayed messages - Check out Mark Nelson's article
         //"Priority Queues and the STL" in the January 1996 Dr. Dobbs' Journal
         //http://www.dogma.net/markn/articles/pq_stl/priority.htm

         //Note: In main game loop call SendDelayedMessages() every game
         //       tick to check if its time to send the stored messages
      }

      void SendDelayedMessages( void )
      {  //This function is called every game tick

         while( /*loop through all delayed messages*/ )
         {
            if( cur_msg->delivery_time <= GetCurTime() )
            {
               RouteMessage( cur_msg );
               RemoveDelayedMessage( cur_msg );
            }
         }
      }

      void RemoveDelayedMessage( MessageObject* msg )
      {
         //Remove this message from the delayed messages data structure
      }
```

References

[LaMothe95] LaMothe, Andre, "Building Brains into Your Games," *Game Developer,* also available online at www.gamasutra.com/features/programming/061997/ build_brains_into_games.htm, August 1995.

[Nelson96] Nelson, Mark, "Priority Queues and the STL," *Dr. Dobb's Journal,* available online at www.dogma.net/markn/articles/pq_stl/priority.htm, January 1996.

[Woodcock99] Woodcock, Steve, "Game AI: The State of the Industry" *Game Developer,* also available online at www.gamasutra.com/features/19990820/game_ai_ 01.htm, August 1999.

3.1

A Finite-State Machine Class

Eric Dybsand

This article defines a generic finite-state machine (FSM) C++ class. *FSMs* are computer science and mathematical abstractions that have been useful for many years in a variety of ways. This article is not a discussion of the theory behind the FSM; instead, it is a simple presentation of a basic building-block tool, the *FSMclass*, which you can use to help develop your own complex artificially intelligent decision-making processes in your computer game.

The first thing you should know about FSMs is that they are simple machines that consist of a finite number of states (obvious, don't you think?). A *state* is really only a condition. For instance, consider a door; its states can be *open* or *closed* and *locked* or *unlocked*.

The next aspect one should know about FSMs is that there is an *input* to the FSM, which affects a *state transition* from one state to another. An FSM can have a simple (or complex) state transition function that determines what state will become the *current state*.

The new current state is called the *output state* of the *state transition* of the FSM, or the state to which the FSM has transitioned based on the input. If this concept is confusing, again think of a door as an example FSM. When the door is in a closed state and a locked state, perhaps the input of *use key* will cause the door to transition to the unlocked state (the *output state* of the *state transition* and the new *current state* of the door). Then the input of *use hand* will cause the door to transition to the open state. When the door is in the open state, the input of *use hand* will transition the door back to the closed state. When the door is in the closed state, the input of *use key* will transition the door back to the locked state. While the door is in the locked state, the input of *use hand* would fail to transition the door to the open state, and the door would remain in the locked state. Furthermore, once the door was in the open state, the input of *use key* would fail to transition the door to the locked state.

So, in summary, an FSM is a machine that has a *finite number of states*, one of which is a *current state*. The FSM can accept *input* that will result in a *state transition* from the *current state* to an *output state*, based on some *state transition function*, and the *output state* then becomes the new *current state*.

Now, how does this concept apply to AI in computer games?

The answer to that question is that the possibilities are really endless! FSMs can form the basis for managing the game world, simulating the emotion of a non-player character (NPC), maintaining the status of the game, parsing input from the human player, or managing the condition of an object.

Consider the attitude of an NPC monster in an adventure game, for example. Let's say that the monster can have the following states: berserk, rage, mad, annoyed, and uncaring. Furthermore, let's say that you have AI game code that does different things based on the state of the monster's attitude. We can use an FSM to manage the monster's attitude and the way it transitions from one state to another based on input from the game itself. Let's further say that inputs are *player seen, player attacks, player gone, monster hurt,* and *monster healed.* Then the state diagram shown in Figure 3.1.1 can be drawn.

Using these inputs and states, we can set up a state transition matrix that looks something like the one shown in Table 3.1.1.

Table 3.1.1 A State Transition Matrix for the Monster Game

Current State	Input	Output State
uncaring	player seen	annoyed
uncaring	player attacks	mad
mad	monster hurt	rage
mad	monster healed	uncaring
rage	monster hurt	berserk
rage	monster healed	annoyed
berserk	monster hurt	berserk
berserk	monster healed	rage
annoyed	player gone	uncaring
annoyed	player attacks	rage
annoyed	monster healed	uncaring

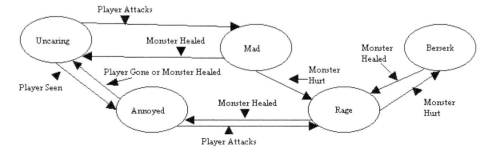

FIGURE 3.1.1. A sample finite-state machine.

So, depending on the current state of the monster's attitude and the input to the FSM, the attitude of the monster will change. Game code that performs behavior based on the attitude of the monster will then cause the monster to act differently.

Obviously, we could add more state transitions, based on more states and inputs. Doing so would affect how our monster's attitude is evaluated and determined, and that is how we create the AI that uses this monster's attitude.

The FSMclass and FSMstate

Now how do we put this idea to work? That is what the FSMclass and its subordinate FSMstate class will show in the following implementation, as illustrated in Figure 3.1.2.

The FSMclass provides structure for any number of states that are provided by the FSMstate class. These two classes work with each other to provide the functionality for a *generic* finite-state machine. A *generic* FSM implies that these objects are generalized, able to support a variety of types of states, a variety of types of state transitions, and any number of state transitions, as well as any number of states within the FSM. With such variety and generalization as a design goal, these classes and their members were selected as you see in the following discussion.

Defining the FSMstate

Here is the class definition we use to represent a state for our FSM:

```
class FSMstate
{
    unsigned m_usNumberOfTransitions;      // maximum number of states
                                           // supported
    int *m_piInputs;                       // input array for transitions
    int *m_piOutputState;                  // output state array
    int m_iStateID;                        // the unique ID of this state

public:
    // constructor accepts an ID for this state and the number of
    //   transitions to support
    FSMstate( int iStateID, unsigned usTransitions );
    // destructor cleans up allocated arrays
    ~FSMstate();

    // access the state ID
```

FIGURE 3.1.2. The FSMclass can use any number of FSMstates.

```
    int GetID() { return m_iStateID; }
    // add a state transition to the array
    void AddTransition( int iInput, int iOutputID );
    // remove a state transition from the array
    void DeleteTransition( int iOutputID );
    // get the output state and effect a transition
    int GetOutput( int iInput );
};
```

See Listing 3.1.1 for the FSMstate class constructor and destructor implementations.

The member variables and functions of the FSMstate class are as follows.

The FSMstate::m_usNumberOfTransitions controls the number of state transitions that this state is able to support. Setting this value also determines the size of the input and output arrays. Since we are creating a "finite" state machine, this value sets the finite-state transition limit for this state.

The FSMstate::m_piInputs is an array of m_usNumberOfTransitions size that contains the input values to be used during state transition. The input array is used by the state transition evaluation function to compare to the input received and determine the corresponding output state.

The FSMstate::m_piOutputState is an array of m_usNumberOfTransitions size that contains a corresponding output state identifier that indicates the new transition state during a state transition.

The FSMstate::m_iStateID is a unique identifier used to identify this instance of an FSMstate and is the value that would be output by any transition to this state from another state.

The FSMstate::GetID() provides public access to the unique identifier of this instance of the FSMstate class. See class declaration for this implementation.

The FSMstate::AddTransition() provides a means to add new input values and output state arrays to this instance of the FSMstate. See Listing 3.1.2 for this implementation.

The FSMstate::DeleteTransition() provides a means to delete an existing input and its corresponding output state identifier. See Listing 3.1.3 for this implementation.

The FSMstate::GetOutput() provides the state transition function that uses the input value to determine the transition output state identifier and return it. See Listing 3.1.4 for this implementation.

Defining the FSMclass

Now we need the actual FSMclass implementation. The FSMclass works by maintaining a collection of FSMstate objects.

```
class FSMclass
{
    State_Map m_map;         // map containing all states of this FSM
```

```
        int m_iCurrentState;    // the m_iStateID of the current state
public:
    FSMclass( int iStateID );       // set initial state of the FSM
    ~FSMclass();                    // clean up memory usage

    // return the current state ID
    int GetCurrentState() { return m_iCurrentState; }
    // set current state
    void SetCurrentState( int iStateID ) { m_iCurrentState = iStateID; }

    // return the FSMstate object pointer
    FSMstate *GetState( int iStateID );
    // add a FSMstate object pointer to the map
    void AddState( FSMstate *pState );
    // delete a FSMstate object pointer from the map
    void DeleteState( int iStateID );

    // perform state transition based on input & current state
    int StateTransition( int iInput );
};
```

See Listing 3.1.5 for the FSMclass class constructor and destructor implementation.

The member variables and functions of the FSMclass class are as follows.

The FSMclass::m_map is the collection of FSMstate objects (pointers to FSMstate objects, in this case) and is implemented from an STL <map>:

```
    typedef map< int, FSMstate*, less<int> > State_Map;
```

A discussion of the specifics of STL and <map> collections in general is beyond the scope of this article. For information about STL, please see the Gem "Using the STL in Game Programming," The above function declares State_Map to be an STL <map> with an int for a key; the map contains pointers to FSMstate objects, and the comparison function to use during access is the less<> operator for ints.

The FSMclass::m_iCurrentState is the state identifier for the FSMstate object that is considered to be the current state of the FSM.

The FSMclass::GetCurrentState() provides public access to the unique identifier of the state of the current FSMstate object. See class declaration for this implementation.

The FSMclass::SetCurrentState() provides public access to set the unique identifier of the state of a new current FSMstate object for the FSM. See class declaration for this implementation.

The FSMclass::GetState() provides a method to obtain a pointer to any FSMstate object contained within the FSM. See Listing 3.1.6 for this implementation.

The FSMclass::AddState() provides a method for adding FSMobject pointers to the <map> contained within the FSM. This is the method that one uses to record the state relationships within the FSM that are defined by FSMstate objects. See Listing 3.1.7 for this implementation.

The `FSMclass::DeleteState()` provides a method for deleting FSMobject pointers from the <map> contained within the FSM. This is the method one uses to dynamically remove state relationships from within the FSM. *Note:* When you want to delete the current state from the <map>, be sure to set a new current state using `FSMclass::SetCurrentState()` before deleting the old current state. See Listing 3.1.8 for this implementation.

The `FSMclass::StateTransition()` provides the method for initiating a state transition, using the input value received and returning the output state identifier. See Listing 3.1.9 for this implementation.

Creating States for the FSM

To use our FSMclass and FSMstate classes in a game, we first build the FSMstate objects:

```
FSMstate *pFSMstate = NULL;

// create the STATE_ID_UNCARING
try
{
    // FSMstate( int iStateID, unsigned usTransitions )
    pFSMstate = new FSMstate( STATE_ID_UNCARING, 2 );
}
catch( ... )
{
    throw;
}
// now add state transitions to this state
pFSMstate->AddTransition( INPUT_ID_PLAYER_SEEN, STATE_ID_ANNOYED );
pFSMstate->AddTransition( INPUT_ID_PLAYER_ATTACKS, STATE_ID_MAD );
```

And then create an FSMclass object:

```
// create the FSMclass object
try
{
    // FSMclass( int iStateID )
    m_pFSMclass = new FSMclass(STATE_ID_UNCARING);
}
catch( ... )
{
    throw;
}
```

Now add the FSMstate object to the FSMclass object:

```
// now add this state to the FSM
m_pFSMclass->AddState( pFSMstate );
```

Repeat the process of creating FSMstate objects and adding them to the FSMclass object for all the states you want to have in your FSM.

Using the FSM

To use our FSMclass, we need only to pass it an input value (which is game dependent) and receive an output state (also game dependent), then act on the output state. So in your game code, you would have something like this:

```
// something happens in the game that causes an input
iInputID = INPUT_ID_PLAYER_ATTACKS;
    .
    .
// have the FSM do the transition to an output state
m_iOutputState = m_pFSMclass->StateTransition(iInputID);
    .
    .
// some game AI code tests for the output state
if( m_iOutputState == STATE_ID_MAD )
{
    // some code for the monster to act mad
}
```

Its usage is that simple!

In conclusion, this FSMclass is not an end-all solution to your computer game AI needs. It is a starting point, or a building block, for you to use to create your own FSMs that are specific to your game needs. FSMclass objects could even be placed in lists or maps and used to form networks of FSMs that are interrelated.

This FSMclass could be expanded to support different input type data or state identification data types. A state or input-specific transition function could be easily added so that, based on the type of input received or the current state, the transition to the output state could be determined uniquely.

Have fun with this concept, and you will gain a powerful tool for making complex computer game AI.

Listing 3.1.1

```
FSMstate::FSMstate( int iStateID, unsigned usTransitions )
{
    // don't allow 0 transitions
    if( !usTransitions )
        m_usNumberOfTransitions = 1;
    else
        m_usNumberOfTransitions = usTransitions;

    // save off id and number of transitions
    m_iStateID = iStateID;
```

```
        // now allocate each array
        try
        {
            m_piInputs = new int[m_usNumberOfTransitions];
            for( int i=0; i<m_usNumberOfTransitions; ++i )
                m_piInputs[i] = 0;
        }
        catch( ... )
        {
            throw;
        }

        try
        {
            m_piOutputState = new int[m_usNumberOfTransitions];
            for( int i=0; i<m_usNumberOfTransitions; ++i )
                m_piOutputState[i] = 0;
        }
        catch( ... )
        {
            delete [] m_piInputs;
            throw;
        }
    }
    FSMstate::~FSMstate()
    {
        delete [] m_piInputs;
        delete [] m_piOutputState;
    }
```

Listing 3.1.2

```
    void FSMstate::AddTransition( int iInput, int iOutputID )
    {
        // the m_piInputs[] and m_piOutputState[] are not sorted
        // so find the first non-zero offset in m_piOutputState[]
        // and use that offset to store the input and OutputID
        // within the m_piInputs[] and m_piOutputState[]
        for( int i=0; i<m_usNumberOfTransitions; ++i )
        {
            if( !m_piOutputState[i] )
                break;
        }
        // only a valid offset is used
        if( i < m_usNumberOfTransitions )
        {
            m_piOutputState[i] = iOutputID;
            m_piInputs[i] = iInput;
        }
    }
```

Listing 3.1.3

```
void FSMstate::DeleteTransition( int iOutputID )
{
    // the m_piInputs[] and m_piOutputState[] are not sorted
    // so find the offset of the output state ID to remove
    for( int i=0; i<m_usNumberOfTransitions; ++i )
    {
        if( m_piOutputState[i] == iOutputID )
            break;
    }
    // test to be sure the offset is valid
    if( i >= m_usNumberOfTransitions )
        return;

    // remove this output ID and its input transition value
    m_piInputs[i] = 0;
    m_piOutputState[i] = 0;

    // since the m_piInputs[] and m_piOutputState[] are not
    // sorted, then we need to shift the remaining contents
    for( ; i<(m_usNumberOfTransitions-1); ++i )
    {
        if( !m_piOutputState[i] )
            break;

        m_piInputs[i] = m_piInputs[i+1];
        m_piOutputState[i] = m_piOutputState[i+1];
    }
    // and clear the last offset in both arrays
    m_piInputs[i] = 0;
    m_piOutputState[i] = 0;
}
```

Listing 3.1.4

```
int FSMstate::GetOutput( int iInput )
{
    int iOutputID = m_iStateID;    // output state to be returned

    // for each possible transition
    for( int i=0; i<m_usNumberOfTransitions; ++i )
    {
        // zeroed output state IDs indicate the end of the array
        if( !m_piOutputState[i] )
            break;
        // state transition function: look for a match with the input
        // value
        if( iInput == m_piInputs[i] )
        {
            iOutputID = m_piOutputState[i];       // output state id
            break;
        }
    }
```

```
                // returning either this m_iStateID to indicate no output
                // state was matched by the input (i.e., no state transition
                // can occur) or the transitioned output state ID
                return( iOutputID );
            }
```

Listing 3.1.5

```
        FSMclass::FSMclass( int iStateID )
        {
            m_iCurrentState = iStateID;
        }


        FSMclass::~FSMclass()
        {
            FSMstate *pState = NULL;
            State_Map::iterator it;

            // only perform this if there are pointers in the map
            if( !m_map.empty() )
            {
                // first delete any FSMstate objects in the map
                for( it = m_map.begin(); it != m_map.end(); ++it )
                {
                    pState = (FSMstate *)((*it).second);
                    if( pState != NULL )
                        delete pState;
                }
                // let the map dtor() erase the actual pointer out of the map
            }
        }
```

Listing 3.1.6

```
        FSMstate *FSMclass::GetState( int iStateID )
        {
            FSMstate *pState = NULL;
            State_Map::iterator it;

            // try to find this FSMstate in the map
            if( !m_map.empty() )
            {
                it = m_map.find( iStateID );
                if( it != m_map.end() )
                    pState = (FSMstate *)((*it).second);
            }
            return( pState );
        }
```

Listing 3.1.7

```
        void FSMclass::AddState( FSMstate *pNewState )
```

```
{
    FSMstate *pState = NULL;
    State_Map::iterator it;

    // try to find this FSMstate in the map
    if( !m_map.empty() )
    {
        it = m_map.find( pNewState->GetID() );
        if( it != m_map.end() )
            pState = (FSMstate *)((*it).second);
    }

    // if the FSMstate object pointer is already in the map, return
    if( pState != NULL )
        return;

    // otherwise put the FSMstate object pointer into the map
    m_map.insert( SM_VT(pNewState->GetID(), pNewState) );
}
```

Listing 3.1.8

```
void FSMclass::DeleteState( int iStateID )
{
    FSMstate *pState = NULL;
    State_Map::iterator it;

    // try to find this FSMstate in the map
    if( !m_map.empty() )
    {
        // get the iterator object of the FSMstate object pointer
        it = m_map.find( iStateID );
        if( it != m_map.end() )
            pState = (FSMstate *)((*it).second);
    }

    // confirm that the FSMstate is in the map
    if( pState != NULL &&
        pState->GetID() == iStateID )
    {
        m_map.erase( it );          // remove it from the map
        delete pState;      // delete the object itself
    }
}
```

Listing 3.1.9

```
int FSMclass::StateTransition( int iInput )
{
    // the current state of the FSM must be set to have a transition
    if( !m_iCurrentState )
        return m_iCurrentState;
```

```
    // get the pointer to the FSMstate object that is the current state
    FSMstate *pState = GetState( m_iCurrentState );
    if( pState == NULL )
    {
        // signal that there is a problem
        m_iCurrentState = 0;
        return m_iCurrentState;
    }

    // now pass along the input transition value and let the FSMstate
    // do the really tough job of transitioning for the FSM, and save
    // off the output state returned as the new current state of the
    // FSM and return the output state to the calling process
    m_iCurrentState = pState->GetOutput( iInput );
    return m_iCurrentState;
}
```

References

More information on FSMs can be found at these World Wide Web links:
  http://csr.uvic.ca/~mmania/machines/intro.htm
  www.erlang/se/documentation/doc-4.7.3/doc/design_principles/fsm.html
  www.microconsultants.com/tips/fsm/fsmartc1.htm
Another implementation of an FSM in C++ code can be found at http://uw7doc.
  sco.com/SDK_c++/CTOC-_Using_Simple_Finite_State_Machi.html
An implementation in C can be found at http://w3.execnet.com/lrs/Writing/Finite%
  20State%20Machines.html

3.2

Game Trees

Jan Svarovsky

For many games such as chess and checkers, we can define the *game tree* as a tree on which the nodes are game states, and children of each node are the positions that are reached from it by one move. A computer player for these games works by considering this game tree as far as it can or wants to into the future from the current game position. It also has an evaluation function that attempts to quantify how good a particular game position is for one player. This is because at some point the search must stop, due to time constraints. At that point, some estimate will be made of the value of the remaining game position.

The assumptions are that what is good for one player is bad for the other and that one player plays to maximize the board evaluation function and the other to minimize it. This "my gain is my opponent's loss" type of game is known as a *zero-sum game*. For example, tic-tac-toe is a zero-sum game; part of a tic-tac-toe game tree is illustrated in Figure 3.2.1. In a one-ply (one-level-deep) search, a player obviously simply goes for the move that produces the best board as a result, as defined by the board evaluation function. In a two-ply search, Player One assumes that whatever he does, Player Two will then do the described one-ply search. Player One, therefore, plays

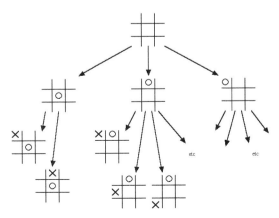

FIGURE 3.2.1. Part of the game tree for the opening of "tic-tac-toe".

whichever move leaves Player Two (who will then do the best move for himself) with the worst possible best option. These assumptions are extended to as many ply searches as is possible in the time allowed.

The following function (with a very similar counterpart, `minimize()`) returns the best expected board value, looking ahead a given amount. Trivially, `maximize()` should be called once for each available move at the moment, and the one that returns the best value should be taken.

```
int maximize(int ply)
{
    if (ply == 0 || game_over()) return evaluate_current_board();

    int best = -infinity;

    for (Move *m = first_available_move(); m != NULL;
    m = next_available_move())
    {
        make_move(m);
        int new_value = minimize(ply - 1);
        unmake_move(m);
        if (new_value > best) best = new_value;
    }
    return best;
}

Move *which_move_shall_I_take(int ply)
{
    Move *best_move;
    int best_value = -infinity;

    for (Move *m = first_available_move(); m != NULL;
    m = next_available_move())
    {
        make_move(m);
        int new_value = maximize(ply);
        unmake_move(m);
        if (new_value > best_value)
        {
            best_value = new_value;
            best_move = m;
        }
    }
    return best_move;
}
```

The Negamax Variation on the Minimax Algorithm

Rather than writing two functions, one that aims to minimize board state and the other to maximize it, we insert a negation and turn this into just one function. Note that now the evaluation function must return the quality of the board for the current player, rather than always returning low values, meaning a good board for one player and high for the other. Board state must therefore include or imply which player goes next:

```
int negamax(int ply)
{
    if (ply == 0 || game_over()) return evaluate_current_board();
    int best = -infinity;

    for (Move *m = first_available_move(); m != NULL;
m = next_available_move())
    {
        make_move(m);
        int new_value = -negamax(ply - 1);
        unmake_move(m);
        if (new_value < best) best = new_value;
    }
    return best;
}
```

The most efficient system for this function is to have the board/game state put forward and reversed by the make_move and unmake_move functions, as shown, and for the evaluation function to be calculated incrementally rather than calculated from scratch every time it is called.

Alpha-Beta Pruning

Newell, Simon, and Shaw invented *alpha-beta pruning* in 1958. This concept is based on the observation that in some cases, it is clear that further investigation of part of the game tree is pointless, as illustrated in Figure 3.2.2.

Here, as soon as we see that Player B's move P will produce a board of value 1, we know that Player A will never let B get to the point that it can make move P. Player A

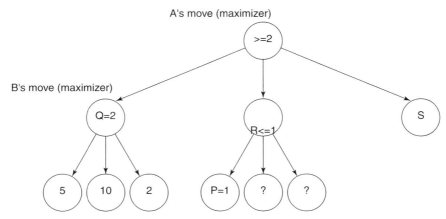

FIGURE 3.2.2. Sometimes part of the game tree can be terminated.

already knows he can force B into situation Q, where the best B can hope for is 2 (remember, B is seeking to minimize board value). Therefore, exploring P's siblings is unnecessary, because Player A will never let situation R happen. It is already clear that R is worse than Q for Player A.

This concept can be generalized to the statement that if we know that the opposing player can get a better outcome elsewhere, we know that the current board position will never be made available by that player. The search now "prunes" the rest of P's siblings and goes straight on to S.

This effectively means we add an extra parameter to the search. This is the best we know the other player can get based on the parts of the tree searched so far. As soon as our current search returns something that is better for us (and worse for the other player) than this "current best," we know that we don't have to search here any more. Of course, this actually becomes two parameters. One is the best the opposing player has gotten so far (called *beta*), and the other is the best we have gotten so far (called *alpha*). Alpha is passed to the recursive call for the other player's move, where alpha and beta are swapped:

```
int alphabeta(int ply, int alpha, int beta)
{
    if (ply == 0 || game_over()) return evaluate_current_board();

    for (Move *m = first_available_move(); m != NULL;
    m = next_available_move())
    {
        make_move(m);
        int new_value = -alphabeta(ply - 1, -beta, -alpha);
        unmake_move(m);
        if (new_value > beta) return new_value; // prune
        if (new_value < alpha)
            alpha = new_value; // update our "best so far"
    }
    return alpha;
}
```

You can see that ideally, you want to find your pruning moves as soon as possible. This means you want to consider the best move first at each point. That might seem impossible (because finding the best move is the whole point of searching), but in fact several methods exist, and in practice game programs almost always succeed in sorting correctly. This method gives a theoretical square-rooting of the cost of the search, which means the search can be performed to twice the depth.

Move-Ordering Methods

One move-ordering method is *iterated deepening*. Instead of straight-away searching at full ply, search at a gradually increasing ply, using the results of the previous level of search to sort the moves for the next level. This method might seem like lots of extra work, but, because of the exponential nature of the search, the last iteration is by far the most significant cost.

The results of the previous level can be stored as a hash table [Sedgewick98], storing calculated values of board positions. This table hashes board states to board values. It helps in another way: to avoid recalculating board values when different sequences of moves produce the same game state.

Game-specific heuristics can be used, such as always considering capture moves first in chess. Finally, there is the "killer" heuristic: if a move turned out to be the best in a sibling node in the tree, try it first in this one.

Refinements on Alpha-Beta

Alpha and beta are effectively a lower and an upper bound on the expected board value. Alpha is the lower bound because it is the least you expect to be able to force play into. You know the other player will be able to force you into not getting anything more than beta. If you are pretty sure what the return value for the alpha-beta search will be, instead of seeding the search with negative infinity and positive infinity, seed it with a range around what you expect the return value to be. If the return value hits either side of your range, you know that the answer was actually outside the range, so you have to expand the range and try again.

A fixed-depth search is bad because of the *horizon effect*. If a particularly bad move is going to happen soon, the computer will do all sorts of other moves as long as they move the terrible one just after the end of its search depth. This is because it cannot see the terrible move happening if it is too far in the future, and therefore lots of other bad delaying moves seem like a better idea. Many methods exist for choosing when to increase the ply for some branches of the tree, but these are out of the scope of this article.

References

[Eppstein] Eppstein, David, "Strategy and Board Game Programming," available online at www.ics.uci.edu/~eppstein/180a/970401.html.

[Sedgewick98] Sedgewick, R, *Algorithms in C++*, Addison-Wesley Longman, Inc.,, 1998.

3.3

The Basics of A* for Path Planning

Bryan Stout

The Problem

This article examines the basic solution to the problem of planning a path for an autonomous agent to move from one location in a game world to another, a common situation in computer game AI. On the CD that accompanies this book is a copy of my PathDemo program, with which you can play to understand how A* (and other path-planning techniques) works.

The most common issue involved in path planning is the avoidance of obstacles, including cul-de-sacs to be ignored (or, sometimes, discovered and explored). The next most common issue is perhaps the awareness of different terrain and seeking out the most efficient path among a variety of choices: exploiting roads or clear terrain, avoiding swamps, and so on.

An Overview of the Solution

The A* (pronounced *A star*) algorithm is an old workhorse in the academic AI community, used since 1968 for solving different kinds of problems, of which the 15-puzzle is the favorite teaching example; fortunately, it is also very useful for the path-planning problem.

A* is an algorithm that searches in a *state space* for the least costly path from a start state to a goal state by examining the *neighboring* or *adjacent states* of particular states. In the 15-puzzle, a state consists of a configuration of the 15 tiles in the 4×4 array, and an adjacent state is reached by sliding one tile into the blank area. In the path-planning problem, a state consists of the agent occupying a particular location in the game world, and an adjacent state is reached by moving the agent to an adjacent location.

In essence, the A* algorithm repeatedly examines the most promising unexplored location it has seen. When a location is explored, the algorithm is finished if that location is the goal; otherwise, it makes note of all that location's neighbors for further exploration.

In more detail, A* keeps track of two lists of states, called **Open** and **Closed**, for unexamined and examined states, respectively. At the start, **Closed** is empty, and **Open** has only the starting state (the agent in its current position). In each iteration, the algorithm removes the most promising state from **Open** for examination. If the state is not a goal, the neighboring locations are sorted: If they're new, they're placed in **Open**; if they're already in **Open**, information about those locations is updated, if this is a cheaper path to them; if they're already in **Closed**, they are ignored, since they've already been examined. If the **Open** list becomes empty before the goal is found, it means there is no path to the goal from that start location.

The "most promising" state in **Open** is essentially the location with the lowest estimated path that would go through that location. Each state X includes information to determine this: the cost of the cheapest path that has led to this state from the start (which we'll call CostFromStart(X)); a heuristic estimate CostToGoal(X) of the cost of the remaining distance to the goal; and the total path estimate, defined as CostFromStart(X) + CostToGoal(X). The total path estimate is the lowest Total-Cost(X) value that it determines is the next state to examine. In addition, each state keeps a pointer to its "parent" state, the state that led to this one in the cheapest path to it; when a goal state is found, these links can be traced back to the start in order to construct the path from start to goal. Please note that in the literature, you'll find CostFromStart(X) called **g**(X), CostToGoal(X) referred to as **h**(X), and the total path estimate named **f**(X). We'll use our names for greater clarity in this article.

Listing 3.3.1: The A* Algorithm

In pseudocode form, here is the A* algorithm:

```
Open: priorityqueue of searchnode
Closed: list of searchnode

AStarSearch( location StartLoc, location GoalLoc,
agenttype Agent ) {
    clear Open and Closed

    // initialize a start node
    StartNode.Loc = StartLoc
    StartNode.CostFromStart = 0
    StartNode.CostToGoal = PathCostEstimate( StartLoc,
        GoalLoc, Agent )
    StartNode.Parent = null
    push StartNode on Open

    // process the list until success or failure
    while Open is not empty {
        pop Node from Open    // Node has lowest TotalCost

        // if at a goal, we're done
        if (Node is a goal node) {
            construct a path backward from Node to StartLoc
```

```
                       return success
            } else {
               for each successor NewNode of Node {
                   NewCost = Node.CostFromStart + TraverseCost( Node,
                   NewNode, Agent )
                   // ignore this node if exists and no improvement
                   if (NewNode is in Open or Closed) and
                   (NewNode.CostFromStart <= NewCost) {
                       continue
                   } else {        // store the new or improved
                                      information
                       NewNode.Parent = Node
                       NewNode.CostFromStart = NewCost
                       NewNode.CostToGoal = PathCostEstimate( NewNode.Loc,
                       GoalLoc, Agent )
                       NewNode.TotalCost = NewNode.CostFromStart +
                       NewNode.CostToGoal
                       if (NewNode is in Closed) {
                           remove NewNode from Closed
                       }
                       if (NewNode is in Open) {
                           adjust NewNode's location in Open
                       } else {
                           push NewNode onto Open
                       }
                   }
               } // now done with Node
            }
            push Node onto Closed
        }
        return failure    // if no path found and Open is empty
    }
```

Properties of A*

A* has several useful properties. (They are not proved here; readers who are interested in the proofs can look in the References.) First, A* finds a path from the start to the goal, if one exists. Second, it finds an optimal path, as long as the CostToGoal(X) estimate is *admissible*, which means CostToGoal is always an underestimate—that is, CostToGoal(X) is always less than or equal to the actual cheapest path cost from X to the goal. Third, A* makes the most efficient use of the heuristic: No search that uses the same heuristic function CostToGoal(X) to find optimal paths examines fewer states than A*, not counting tie breaking among states with equal cost.

Applying A* to Game-Path Planning

Let's now look in detail at how the aspects of A* can be applied to path planning in computer games. Much of this discussion depends on the nature of the game and its internal representation of the world; the following discussion is meant to suggest possibilities.

State

As stated above, the principle component of a *state* in the path search is *location*. However, it need not be the only component. An agent's orientation and/or its velocity can also be important. For example, vehicles can often go only straight ahead or turn slightly, and the amount of turn possible is reduced the faster a vehicle moves. Most vehicles can go backward only after coming to a stop. It is quite possible to plan a route based only on locations, but it could be desirable in some situations to plan based on velocity and orientation as well, to avoid planning a route through terrain or around obstacles that would be difficult to navigate.

Even considering location alone, the issue of which locations to consider is not trivial. In some games, the world is naturally tiled—real-time strategy games often have an underlying square grid, and many war games use a visible hex grid—but many games do not divide the space that way, especially games that use a 3D, first-person, or oblique view of the world. In such cases, it is important to choose a set of locations among which to search. Figure 3.3.1 shows a path-planning situation and several ways of partitioning the space.

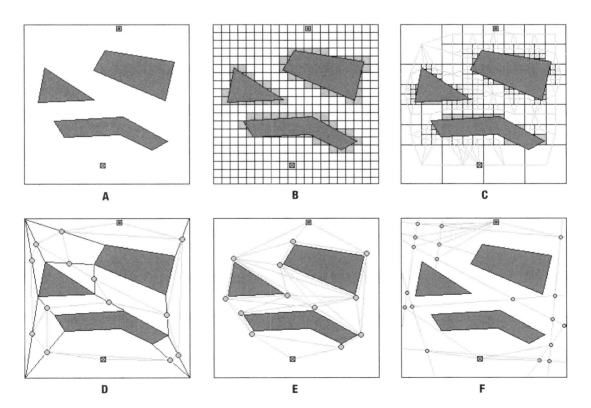

FIGURE 3.3.1. A variety of means of partitioning a continuous space.

The ways of partitioning the space are as follows:

- **Rectangular grid.** The simplest way is to partition into a regular grid of squares, as shown in Figure 3.3.1b. The locations can be either the center points or the corners of the squares; if appropriate for the game, the grid can be considered to consist of the terrain most common to the area it covers.

- **Quadtree.** Another way to partition the space is into squares of differing sizes. The quadtree recursively divides a square into four smaller squares, until each square has uniform (or at least mostly uniform) terrain, as shown in Figure 3.3.1c. Again, the locations for the search can be either the centers or the corners of the squares. This method has a couple of advantages: The larger (and fewer) squares allow for a faster search, and the representation is easy to store.

- **Convex polygons.** A more complex yet possibly more robust scheme is to break up the space into convex polygons made up of uniform terrain (Figure 3.3.1d). This scheme could already exist in the map's representation, so it can be used directly in the path search. There are several methods that can be used to partition a space into polygons if the existing mesh is useless or inefficient. C-cells are one way to partition the space; each vertex is connected to the nearest visible vertex, and the connecting lines partition the space. Another is maximum-area decomposition, where at each convex vertex the edges connected to the vertex are projected out until they hit an obstacle or wall, and between these lines and the line to the closest other vertex, the shortest is chosen as a boundary. Navigation meshes, a third method, are discussed in another article in this volume ("Simplified 3D Movement and Pathfinding Using Navigation Meshes"). Similar techniques can be used to divide variable-cost terrain into convex polygons of uniform terrain. After the polygons are laid out, search locations can be chosen at their center and/or along various parts of their perimeters.

- **Points of visibility.** Not all techniques divide the space into regions but instead come up with locations directly. Points of visibility are concerned mainly with obstacle avoidance: Place a search location just a little beyond each convex vertex of each obstacle, just far enough away to avoid collision with the obstacles (as in Figure 3.3.1e). The shortest path around obstacles typically passes near these vertices, as though a rubber band connected the start and goal locations. One could possibly extend this method to consider terrain cost by adding these points to those derived from convex uniform polygons.

- **Generalized cylinders.** Another technique concerned mainly with obstacle avoidance is generalized cylinders: The space between neighboring obstacles can be considered a 2D cylinder, the shape of which changes as it goes along. Between each pair of neighboring obstacles (including the walls or boundaries of the map), calculate a central axis (Figure 3.3.1f). The intersections of these lines provide the locations for the search.

For most of these schemes, when a search is done, the start and goal locations are usually not members of the search locations, so they need to be added to them for the duration of that search.

Whichever scheme is used for quantizing a continuous space, it probably must be experimented with and tweaked before it suits the game's demands optimally: There need to be enough locations so that no reasonable route is unconsidered, but not too many, or the search will take too long. Another issue is that most paths found from any quantization scheme seem jagged and a bit artificial, which means the route needs to be smoothed, either before it is assigned to the agent or in the means the agent uses to follow it.

Neighboring States

The neighbors of a state are determined by the map representation and the quantization scheme. Some schemes use only their adjacent locations as their neighbors—a square grid would consider each interior point as having eight neighbors, four if diagonals are excluded—whereas in other schemes, a location's neighbors are all other locations visible to it.

A location's neighbors are also determined by the terrain. Some terrain might be impassable, which means it is not a neighbor to its nearby locations after all. The type of agent could also enter this determination; for example, land vehicles cannot travel on the sea, and infantry can traverse terrain forbidden to some vehicles.

We need an efficient way to compute each location's neighbors, for the sake of search speed. Grids have a natural way of calculating neighbors: The neighbors of (x, y) are $(x+1, y)$, $(x+1, y+1)$, $(x, y+1)$, etc. Most other schemes require that some data structure store the neighbor information for fast lookup, since the neighbor calculations are often expensive.

Cost

The cost function for the path between two locations (CostFromStart above) represents whatever it is the path is supposed to minimize—typically, distance traveled, time of traversal, movement points expended, or fuel consumed. However, other factors can be added into this function, such as penalties for passing through undesirable areas, bonuses for passing through desirable areas, and aesthetic considerations (for example, making diagonal moves more costly than orthogonal moves, even if they aren't, to make the resultant path look more direct; see the article on aesthetic optimizations, "A* Aesthetic Optimizations," for more discussion.)

Just as with connectivity considered previously, in many games, the cost is not the same for all agents—for example, roads offer a great speedup for wheeled vehicles but little if any for infantry. What's more, in some games, travel cost is asymmetric: Going from A to B may be more costly than going from B to A, such as is the case if B is uphill from A. That is why the code in Listing 3.3.1 has the cost functions dependent on the agent traveling as well as the two endpoints of the travel.

Again, these terrain costs need to be quickly looked up during the search and in fact are probably best stored with the connectivity information. In that way, one lookup can determine whether two locations are neighbors, and if so, the cost for the given agent.

Estimate

The estimate of the path cost to the goal is the complement to the known distance from the start. If you want to guarantee that an optimal path is found, this distance should not be overestimated. A common way to do this is to multiply the actual map distance from the given location to the goal times the minimum terrain cost per unit distance. Since the route cannot be shorter than the most direct, "crow's flight" line, this figure will be an underestimate (unless your game has things like instant-transport locations). In many games, this minimum distance is the Euclidean measure between two points in 2D or 3D, but in games with strict square or hexagonal tiles, the shortest tile path is usually a little longer than the Euclidean distance between the tile's center points. Therefore, in a square grid, a tile (3, 5) away has a minimum distance of 2 + 3*sqrt(2), not the Euclidean sqrt(34). This actual shortest distance can then be multiplied by a typical terrain cost. This cost should include all the previously discussed factors concerning the cost between neighboring nodes.

However, guaranteeing an optimum path is not the only consideration; there is also the speed of the search, and the quality of the CostToGoal value has a tremendous impact on the search efficiency. Look at Figures 3.3.2 and 3.3.3. In Figure 3.3.2a, the CostToGoal has been set to zero, which, after all, *is* an underestimate, and we see that the search spreads in a circle until it hits the goal, because it has no heuristic information to guide it in the correct direction. In Figure 3.3.2b, we see that an accurate heuristic weight of 1 per square sends the search in a straight line to the goal. In Figure 3.3.3, the start and the goal are in costly terrain (8 per square). Since the estimate of 1 per square is a large underestimate, the search frontier is nearly as circular as the uninformed search in Figure 3.3.2a. In Figure 3.3.3b, we see that even an estimate of 5 per square focuses the search considerably. It is therefore important, perhaps crucial, that the estimate be fairly accurate. In fact, in some situations, one might want to *overestimate* the cost to the goal in order to get a fast search, at the risk of getting a suboptimal path (the article "A* Speed Optimizations" talks about this concept). So rather than using a *minimum* terrain cost per unit, we could use a *typical* cost, which can either be fixed or dynamically determined by sampling the terrain between the stated start and goal.

Goal

The goal is typically a single location, but it does not have to be. For example, if a vehicle low on fuel is trying to plan a route to the closest refueling station, with each new node N in the search an estimate is made of the remaining distance to each station, and the minimum of them is used as the CostToGoal(N) value. This method

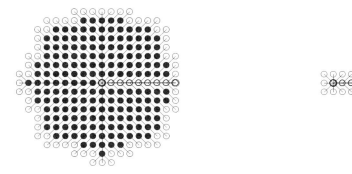

FIGURE 3.3.2. A* search in clear terrain. *a:* With a heuristic weight of 0. *b:* With a heuristic weight of 1.

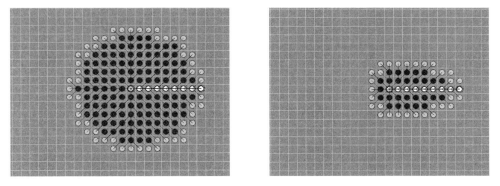

FIGURE 3.3.3. A* search in costly terrain. a: With a heuristic weight of 1. *b:* With a heuristic weight of 5.

guarantees that the search figures out both the closest goal and the best route to it simultaneously.

Weaknesses of A*

Although A* is about as good a search algorithm as you can find, it must be used wisely; otherwise, it can be wasteful of resources. On a large map, hundreds or even thousands of nodes might be in the **Open** and **Closed** lists, which can take up more memory than is available on systems with constrained memory, such as console systems. On any system, A* can take too much CPU time to be affordable.

The case in which A* is most inefficient is in determining that no path is possible between the start and goal locations; in that case, it examines every possible location accessible from the start before determining that the goal is not among them, as shown in Figure 3.3.4. The best way to avoid this problem is to do a pre-analysis of the map, manually or algorithmically, so that the program can look up whether two locations are accessible from each other—say, on the same island. If they are not, the search is not even attempted.

Further Work

There is much more detail that we could cover, because there are many different path-planning and path-following situations. With an understanding of the workings of A*, one can often figure out how to adapt it to their needs. Take a look at the other articles in this volume for further discussion on the ways to partition a floor space for use in A*, as well as efficiency and aesthetic considerations.

References

Websites

[Woodcock] Woodcock, Steven, "The Game AI Page: Building Artificial Intelligence into Games," available online at www.gameai.com. The "Resources and Links" subpage of this site has many links to Websites that discuss A*, some of which have sample code.

General AI Texts

The following are two recent, very good general AI textbooks, both of which happen to use the agent-centered paradigm for discussing AI:

[Russell95] Russell, Stuart, and Norvig, Peter, *Artificial Intelligence: A Modern Approach*, Prentice Hall, 1995. Perhaps the best current AI text, it has a couple chapters on search techniques, including A*.

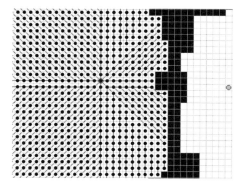

FIGURE 3.3.4. Search in a situation in which there is no path to the goal.

FIGURE 1
3D rendering of a fractal landscape generated by Fault Formation. (Courtesy Jason Shankel.)

FIGURE 2
3D rendering of a fractal landscape generated by Midpoint Displacement. (Courtesy Jason Shankel.)

FIGURE 3
3D rendering of a fractal landscape generated by Particle Deposition. (Courtesy Jason Shankel.)

FIGURE 4
Lens flare effect rendered as a 2D overlay on top of a 3D scene. (Courtesy Yossarian King.)

FIGURE 5
Environment map
of an outdoor
environment
rendered onto a
torus. (Courtesy
Ryan Woodland.)

FIGURE 6
The shadow-map
projection of a
torus onto its
environment.
(Courtesy Gabor
Nagy.)

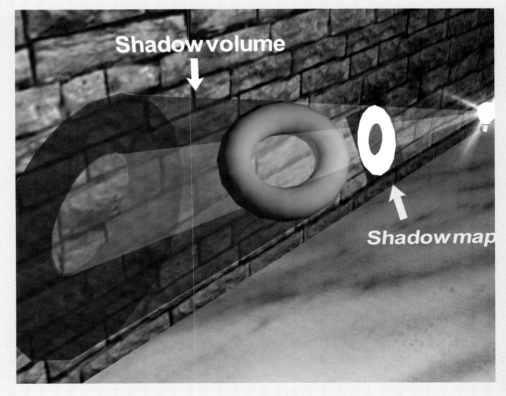

FIGURE 12
Texture map used
for the real-time
refraction-
mapping demos.
(Courtesy Alex
Vlachos, Jason L.
Mitchell, Sam
Howell and Dan
Roeger.)

FIGURE 13
Images from the
radiATIon
graphics engine
demonstrating
real-time
refraction
mapping,
environment
mapping, and
caustics.
(Courtesy Alex
Vlachos, Jason L.
Mitchell, Sam
Howell and Dan
Roeger.)

FIGURE 14
(Courtesy Alex
Vlachos, Jason L.
Mitchell, Sam
Howell and Dan
Roeger.)

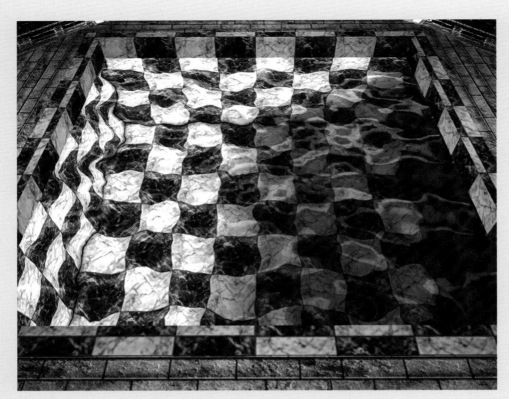

Figures 15-16

FIGURE 15
Images from the ATI Research "Aquarium Demo" demonstrating real-time refraction mapping, environment mapping, and caustics. (Courtesy Alex Vlachos, Jason L. Mitchell, Sam Howell and Dan Roeger.)

FIGURE 16
(Courtesy Alex Vlachos, Jason L. Mitchell, Sam Howell and Dan Roeger.)

[Nilsson98] Nilsson, Nils J., *Artificial Intelligence: A New Synthesis*. Morgan Kaufmann, 1998. Since Nilsson was one of the developers of A*, his discussion of it is valuable if one wants to understand the theory behind it. This text presents formal proofs of properties of A*.

Search Texts

These books discuss the general issues of search, which date back to the early days of AI research:

[Barr81] Barr, Avron, and Feigenbaum, Edward A., eds., *The Handbook of Artificial Intelligence*, volume 1, Addison-Wesley, 1981. A good multivolume survey of major AI issues and important AI programs. This volume includes the discussion of search, including A*.

[Kanal88] Kanal, L., and Kumar, V., eds., *Search in Artificial Intelligence*, Springer-Verlag, 1988. A collection of good articles for those who want to get into the advanced considerations of search, including variations on A* (with imaginative names like B, C, and D!).

[Pearl84] Pearl, J., *Heuristics: Intelligent Search Strategies for Computer Problem Solving*, Addison-Wesley, 1984. This is perhaps the most complete reference on search algorithms and is referenced by practically everyone else.

[Shapiro] Shapiro, Stuart C., and Eckroth, David, eds., *Encyclopedia of Artificial Intelligence*, 2 volumes, John Wiley & Sons, 1987. A truly excellent collection of articles about most aspects of AI research. Good articles pertinent to this article are "Search," "A* Algorithm," and "Path Planning and Obstacle Avoidance."

3.4

A* Aesthetic Optimizations

Steve Rabin

Computing a path for a character is more than merely an exercise in search algorithms. It also involves creating an aesthetically pleasing path and resulting execution. Computed paths for characters can be improved in three main ways: making the path straighter, making it smoother, and making it more direct. The execution of the path can be improved by simply maximizing responsiveness. All these optimizations result in an experience that is more aesthetically pleasing to the player. Since providing a satisfying experience is the ultimate goal, these things are fairly important and directly impact the code within and surrounding A*.

Straight Paths

Paths calculated by A* often look like they were constructed by someone who was drunk. They weave and bob their way efficiently to the goal, but it sure doesn't look natural. This is a serious problem that undermines the believability of any game's AI. There are two ways to deal with this issue. The first is to promote straight paths within the A* algorithm; the second is to clean up the mess after the path has been calculated.

Promoting straighter paths involves careful cost weighting within the A* algorithm. Consider the two paths computed by A* that are shown in Figures 3.4.1 and 3.4.2.

The amazing observation is that both paths travel the *exact* same distance. Since both paths have identical costs, A* is unable to differentiate between them and simply chooses the first path it stumbles upon. The trick that will make A* choose the straight path is held within the cost function. Simply factor in an extra cost (penalty) if the new step being considered is not straight with the last step. Note that we are not looking at the overall straightness of the path, just penalizing new considerations that are not in line with the last step.

A reasonable penalty is half the normal cost to step in a given direction. The truth is that on a regular grid, any penalty at all (0.0000001) for non-straight choices causes A* to choose the straightest one. However, this is not the case on an arbitrary network.

FIGURE 3.4.1. Typical A* path.

FIGURE 3.4.2. Straightened A* path.

A word of caution: Penalizing non-straight paths results in more work being done by the pathfinder, thus slowing the computation. Obviously, the algorithm has to consider many more permutations in order to find the straightest one. In fact, searches can take significantly more time. However, if hierarchical methods are used, the extra time might not be an issue. Make sure you understand the tradeoffs.

Straight Paths in a Polygonal Search Space

With a polygonal search space, this trick is not very useful. Because triangles aren't uniformly spaced, as a rectangular grid is, similar paths that cost the same are quite rare. Therefore, there is no need to find the straighter path. Instead, there's a different problem: Since triangles can vary greatly in size and proportion, paths are more crooked than ever. The trick is to optimize for straightness after the path has been calculated. Greg Snook's path-finding article, "Simplified 3D Movement and Pathfinding Using Navigation Meshes," discusses an excellent way to handle this problem.

Smooth Paths

Unfortunately, paths computed by A* are usually riddled with sharp turns. Even if you employ a technique to make straighter paths, sharp turns still have the potential to make your characters look like robots. By applying rotational dampening to your turns, you can probably mask them a little, but you'll swing wide on every sharp corner. There's a much better way.

Straight from the field of computer graphics, there's an algorithm that makes your paths (simply series of points in space) smooth for you. A simple Catmull-Rom spline does the trick because it creates a curve that nails all the control points in the original path (unlike a Bézier curve, which is smoother but doesn't go through the control points). Obviously, it's better to go directly through your points because A* deemed them clear and free of obstacles.

But how do you actually input a list of points and get a smoother list back? The Catmull-Rom formula requires four input points and gives you back a smooth curve between the second and third points. Figure 3.4.3 explains this concept a little better.

To get the points between the first and second input points, you simply give the function the first point twice, then the second and third. To get the points between the third and fourth, give the function the second and third, and double up on the fourth.

Each time you use the Catmull-Rom formula, it gives you a point roughly **u**% between the second and third inputs, where **u** is a number you pass in. The following is the formula (points can be 2D or 3D):

```
output_point = point_1 * (-0.5f*u*u*u + u*u - 0.5f*u) +
               point_2 * (1.5f*u*u*u + -2.5f*u*u + 1.0f) +
               point_3 * (-1.5f*u*u*u + 2.0f*u*u + 0.5f*u) +
               point_4 * (0.5f*u*u*u - 0.5f*u*u);
```

Note that if **u** is zero, the formula gives you point_2. When **u** is 1, it gives you point_3. As you can see, the spline really does go directly through the input points.

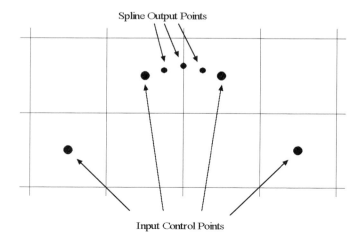

FIGURE 3.4.3. Getting spline points from control points.

A Pre-Computed Catmull-Rom Formula

Since speed is an issue, you might want to dictate that you want **u** only at certain intervals, such as 0.0, 0.25, 0.5, and 0.75. By freezing all instances of **u**, you can pre-compute the formula at each **u**. Note that the formulas can take either 2D or 3D points. The following are some formulas at various intervals:

```
// u = 0.0
output_point = point_2;

// u = 0.25
output_point = point_1 * -0.0703125f + point_2 * 0.8671875f +
               point_3 * 0.2265625f + point_4 * -0.0234375f;

// u = 0.5
output_point = point_1 * -0.0625f + point_2 * 0.5625f +
               point_3 * 0.5625f + point_4 * -0.0625f;

// u = 0.75
output_point = point_1 * -0.0234375f + point_2 * 0.226563f +
               point_3 * 0.8671875f + point_4 * -0.0703125f;

// u = 1.0
output_point = point_3;
```

Equipped with the Catmull-Rom formula, all you need to do is walk through the path that A* found and create a new path. Remember to double up on the first input point when you start, and double up on the last input point when you get to the end. If the A* path has only two points to begin with, simply don't apply the spline to the path.

Since you have a new path with four times the number of points, you might want to look into getting rid of redundant points. Running the new path through a function that prunes co-linear points should dramatically reduce your list.

Figure 3.4.4 shows a typical path before and after the Catmull-Rom spline has been applied. Notice how it's still just a series of points (piece-wise linear), but the path is now much smoother. In the large scale of things, this path is perfectly smooth.

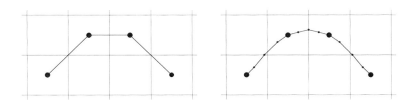

FIGURE 3.4.4. Path points before and after a spline is applied.

Improving the Directness of Hierarchical Paths

A very important A* technique is *hierarchical pathing.* However, the problem is that the resulting paths can be less than ideal. In hierarchical pathing, you pathfind in two distinct steps. You first find the large-scale path, and then you pathfind at the local level. For example, a castle might be broken up into rooms. You might want to get from the dungeon to the throne room. The idea is that you first find the large-scale path between the rooms (by running A* on the connectivity graph of the rooms). Once that path is found, you can then path-find between each connecting room as you encounter it. The result is a huge savings of time. Unfortunately, the overall path can look rather bad because the goal point will always be the door to the next room, thus causing the character to always travel through the center of each door. When doors are arbitrarily large, this can look rather bad. Figure 3.4.5 illustrates the problem.

There is a simple, elegant way to get the ideal path, but it takes roughly twice the computation. The trick is to always path-find to the door beyond the next door. Then, whenever the character crosses through the first doorway, throw away the rest of the path and repeat the process. While the second half of the path is always wasted, it really does create the most direct and aesthetically pleasing route. Figure 3.4.6 shows the final path.

This technique always finds the optimum passage through the doorway because it takes into account the future path. The following is a step-by-step sample path execution guide to show how this method works:

1. Find the best room-to-room path using A* on the connectivity graph of the rooms.
2. The result is to travel the following sequence of rooms: 1, 2, 3, 4.

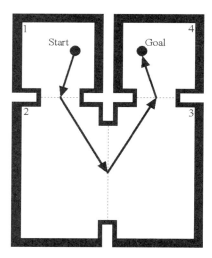

FIGURE 3.4.5. The path through several rooms.

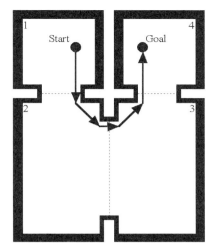

FIGURE 3.4.6. The optimized path through several rooms.

3. Pathfind from Start to subgoal 1 (Figure 3.4.7a).
4. Let the character walk until he enters Room 2.
5. Throw away the remaining path and pathfind to subgoal 2 (Figure 3.4.7b).
6. Let the character walk until he enters Room 3.
7. Throw away the remaining path and pathfind to the final goal (Figure 3.4.7c).
8. Let the character walk to the final goal.

Hierarchical Pathfinding on Open Fields

There is no real difference between a set of connected rooms and a set of connected fields. The same principles apply. The resulting path is not completely straight, but it

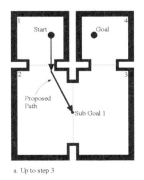

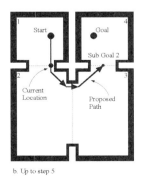

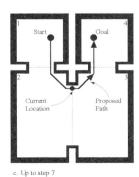

a. Up to step 3   b. Up to step 5   c. Up to step 7

FIGURE 3.4.7. The computed path during various steps.

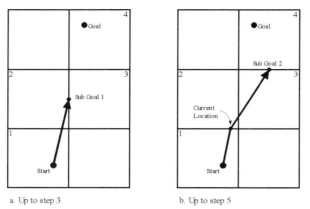

a. Up to step 3   b. Up to step 5   c. Up to step 7

FIGURE 3.4.8. The computed path during various steps.

comes pretty close. You also need to realize that these fields are fairly large relative to the player. Figure 3.4.8 shows the hierarchical steps applied to open fields.

Eliminating Pauses During Hierarchical Searches

Note that every time the character enters a new room, a new local path must be computed. Since this obviously takes time, the character appears to pause as he enters each doorway. The search itself can't be sped up, but the new path request can be anticipated and computed slightly before it's needed. This simple trick keeps the character motion fluid throughout the path.

Maximizing Responsiveness

Controller responsiveness is critical to game play. When a player issues a move command in an RTS, they expect the unit to respond immediately. However, in the world of pathfinding and search algorithms, sometimes it can take awhile to find that path. That's where we need to pull a few tricks in order to give the feeling of instantaneous response.

The first trick is to stall by playing a sound byte that identifies the unit as having received the command. This trick gives immediate feedback that the unit is aware of the command and will execute it shortly. Meanwhile, the pathfinder is working at full speed trying to find the path.

Another trick is to stall by playing a "get ready to move" animation. The movement of the character signifies that he's going to move—even though he might not actually take any steps. You can even rotate the character to the "best-guess" direction so that he'll be ready to move when the final path is available, thus stalling even longer.

You can take the idea further by moving the character in the "best-guess" direction before the final path is ready. Unfortunately, you could be dead wrong in your guess, and the character will have to backtrack. Unless the pathfinder is extremely slow, it's probably best to avoid using this method.

Moving large groups of people at once can take even longer. If the player grabs 20 units and asks them to move across the map, you could be waiting a long time to get the 20 paths processed. There are two tricks to dealing with this situation. The first is to queue the path requests and let each unit move as its request is serviced. This way, it looks as though there's immediate feedback, because at least some of the units start to move immediately. It looks a bit like popcorn popping as each unit starts to move, but overall, it's fairly satisfying to the player. The second trick is to choose a leader in the group of 20 and find a path for only him. Then tell the other 19 units to follow the leader. However, this method can get complicated because there could be massive bunching, the leader could die halfway through the path, and each unit should eventually stop at a unique destination.

Conclusion

All these techniques are designed to make pathfinding more transparent to the player. The goal has always been to find good, direct paths instantaneously. Since that's a tough problem, hopefully you can apply these gems to your current pathfinder in order to get better-looking paths that ultimately feel better to the player.

References

[Patel99] Patel, Amit J., "Amit's Thoughts on Pathfinding," available online at http://theory.stanford.edu/~amitp/GameProgramming/, November 27, 1999.

[Stout96] Stout, Bryan W., "Smart Moves: Intelligent Path-Finding," *Game Developer*, October/November 1996, pp. 28–35, also available online at www.gamasutra.com/features/19990212/sm_01.htm.

3.5

A* Speed Optimizations

Steve Rabin

Traditionally, A* is a slow algorithm that never runs as fast as you'd like. Since there's a long list of optimizations that you could make, its very important to understand why it's slow so you can wisely use your optimization time.

The first thing to notice about A* is that it is at the mercy of the search space. Usually, the sheer number of connections to search is a good indication of how fast A* works. In a rectangular grid of 1,000 by 1,000 squares, there are 1 million possible squares to search. To find an arbitrary path in that kind of world simply takes a lot of work, no matter how optimized your code. The solution is to optimize the search space.

Once the search space has been optimized, it's time to look deeper into the actual A* implementation. Since A* churns through a lot of memory, it's critical to optimize memory allocation as well as each of the data accesses. A* also demands a lot of sorting, but this can be dealt with quickly and efficiently using some specialized data structures.

Lastly, the best way to speed up A* is by not using it at all for simple cases. Construct some kind of test to determine whether you absolutely need to fire up the pathfinder. Many times, simple routes can be determined without using the full-blown A* implementation. For example, try running a blind straight-line path to the goal, testing to see if it collides with walls or other objects. Undoubtedly, there will be times when this simple solution works amazingly well.

Search Space Optimization

Simplifying the Search Space

The biggest win always comes from searching through less data. If you can represent your world as a simplified connectivity graph, A* will work all the faster. Practically, there are several options to choose from. Since speed isn't the only consideration, some other pros and cons are also discussed here. A simple diagram of each technique is provided in Figure 3.5.1.

Rectangular or Hexagonal Grid

Description

A uniform rectangular or hexagonal grid is overlaid onto the world. The size of each grid space is proportional to the size of the smallest character. Therefore, a character in a grid space blocks that space during the A* search. See Figure 3.5.1a.

Pros

- Obstacles and characters can be easily marked in the grid allowing for avoidance. This creates a one-step solution to finding a path through static and dynamic objects.
- Works well for 2D tile-based worlds.

Cons

- Typically results in the largest search space.
- Rectangular grids don't map very well onto 3D worlds.
- Paths tend to look like moves on a chessboard.

Actual Polygonal Floor

Description

In a 3D game world, the floor polygons are specifically marked and used directly as the search space. This polygonal floor is identical to the rendered geometry, thus being arbitrarily simple or complex. See Figure 3.5.1b.

Pros

- Data structure already exists in the 3D world.
- Can be walked through quickly with a BSP tree.

Cons

- Three-dimensional worlds can have arbitrarily high numbers of polygons on the floor.
- Can't represent obstacles such as tables or chairs (because the floor exists beneath these objects).
- Requires algorithmic solution for choosing path points within a polygon.

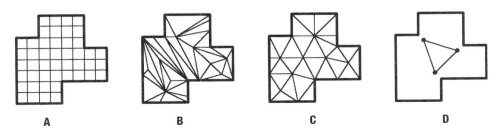

A   **B**   **C**   **D**

FIGURE 3.5.1. Four options for representing the search space.

Polygonal Floor Representation

Description

An artist or level designer creates a polygonal floor representation that is used exclusively for pathfinding. The polygons can be eliminated in places where characters are not allowed to walk, such as under tables or chairs. See Figure 3.5.1c.

Pros
- Small search space representation.
- Can be walked through quickly with a BSP tree.
- Obstacles can be incorporated in the representation.

Cons
- Requires artist or level designer to construct.
- Can't represent characters within the space.
- Requires algorithmic solution for choosing path points within a polygon.

Points of Visibility

Description

Points are placed at convex corners in the world (sticking out a little from each corner). Each point is then connected to all other points that it can "see". This creates a connectivity graph that describes the minimal paths required to get around walls. See Figure 3.5.1d.

Pros
- Creates minimal search space representation.
- Obstacles can be incorporated in the representation.
- Resulting paths are perfectly direct.

Cons
- Requires algorithmic or designer assistance to create the graph.
- Obstacles can't be removed from the graph if they should be destroyed.
- Can't represent characters within the space.
- Doesn't work well with entities that have large widths, such as a wide formation of characters.
- Worlds with curved walls could cause the graph to become unnecessarily complex.

As you can see, there is no obvious choice. Each representation has its trade-offs. If your world is 3D with few dynamic obstacles, then using points of visibility is a reasonable choice. If your world is 2D tile-based or there are hordes of moving characters (as in a large RTS game), a rectangular grid might be the best choice. Just remember that your decision in choosing a search space representation has huge repercussions in terms of speed and flexibility.

Points of Visibility Explained

Since using points of visibility is an extremely viable option, it's worth explaining a little better. The technique requires that you build up a graph that can be used to get around the world. Points are placed at convex corners and connected to all other points they can see. It's as though a freeway system has been constructed for the sole purpose of getting around walls. The problem now is how you get on and off the freeway.

To get on the freeway, you test the visibility between the starting point and every point on the freeway. Since you can potentially compare thousands of points, it's important that you use other space-partitioning techniques (such as hierarchical pathfinding). Once you have a list of potential on-ramp points, you put them on the A* Open list and begin running the algorithm. With each point you explore, you must test its visibility with the goal point. If you find a point that can see the goal point, you have a potential off-ramp. Figure 3.5.2 shows a simple example.

Hierarchical Pathfinding

Hierarchical pathfinding is an extremely powerful technique that speeds up the pathfinding process. Regardless of which search space representation is used, this technique in effect simplifies that space. Therefore, if your world representation is large, there's still hope. The key is to break up the world hierarchically.

Consider a castle. It can be thought of as a single, large building or as a collection of rooms connected by doors (a large-scale connectivity graph). The pathfinder works in two distinct steps. It first finds the room-to-room path, knowing the starting and ending room. Once that room-to-room path is known, the pathfinder then works on the micro problem of getting from the current room to the next room on the list. Thus, the pathfinder doesn't need to compute the entire path before it takes the first step. The micro path is figured out on a need-to-know basis as each new room is entered. This method significantly cuts down on the search space and the resulting time to compute the path.

This technique really shines if your world is already constructed hierarchically. Even a 3D world could be constructed using a simple building-block paradigm. Consider a circular staircase. Normally, a circular staircase causes most pathfinders a lot of

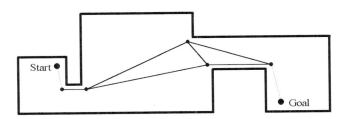

FIGURE 3.5.2. Points-of-visibility example.

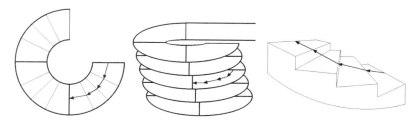

FIGURE 3.5.3. Hierarchical pathfinding on a circular staircase.

grief. The structure is very 3D, mostly circular, and could spiral for a very long distance. A spiral staircase could be built using a quarter-turn piece of the staircase. This piece could then be duplicated indefinitely to create a very tall spiral staircase.

A hierarchical pathfinder could blazingly compute a path up the staircase if it were constructed in this fashion. The pathfinder would first compute the large-scale route through each connecting quarter-turn piece and then would quickly find the local path from the start to the end of each quarter-turn piece. All of a sudden, a complicated path over some rather complicated geometry becomes trivial to compute. Figure 3.5.3 shows an example.

Hierarchical pathfinding isn't restricted to rooms with doors. You can easily extrapolate the idea to huge fields of landscape that are stitched together. Although it's true that there isn't one easily identifiable "door" spot anymore, the entire seam from one field to another becomes the door.

Imagine an immense world created with these stitched pieces of land. Now imagine telling a character to walk from one end to the other. No problem! The pathfinder first finds a route through the network of land pieces and then finds the local path from the current land piece to the next. With a little work, you can even imagine planning a route from the throne room of one castle to the ninth-level dungeon below a completely different castle—even though the castles might be 10 miles apart!

Avoiding Pauses While Computing Local Paths

Since a path is computed every time the character enters a new room, it's important that the character not pause at each door while his new path is constructed. In order to avoid a pause, the path request must be anticipated and completed before the character actually needs it. This simple trick keeps the character motion fluid throughout the execution of the path.

Algorithmic Optimization

Playing with the Heuristic Cost

Designing an algorithm for the heuristic cost can at times seem more like voodoo than science. The idea behind the heuristic cost is to estimate the true cost from a particular node to the goal. Here's an interesting fact: If you always knew the true cost to the goal, A* would beeline a path to the goal without wasting any search time going down the wrong path. But if the heuristic estimate happens to overestimate the true cost, the heuristic becomes "inadmissible," and the algorithm might not find the optimal path (and might find a terrible path).

The way to guarantee that the cost is never overestimated is by calculating the geometric distance between the node and the goal. When coding A* for the first time, this is the best thing to do until it's time to optimize. Since the cost will never be more than this distance, the optimal path will always be found.

Overestimating the Heuristic Cost

Interesting fact #2: Using a heuristic that routinely overestimates by a little usually results in faster searches with reasonable paths. However, how much should the cost be overestimated? To answer this question, you need to understand what happens when this remaining path cost is artificially bloated.

If the heuristic part of the total cost (*total cost = cost to node + heuristic cost*) is bigger than it should be, it distorts the reasoning by which nodes on the Open list are picked off. Since A* always picks the node with the least total cost, this distortion promotes nodes closer to the goal to be picked.

When you look at an A* search that's trying to find its way around a wall, you can see a shape that develops from the nodes explored (nodes on the Closed list). This shape is the easiest way to see the effects of playing with the heuristic estimate.

When the heuristic equals zero, the search evolves as a circle around the starting point. When the heuristic uses the Euclidean distance to the goal, the search looks like an oval, with the start and goal points the foci. When the heuristic is overestimated, the shape changes to be more of a diamond or hexagon, with the start and goal points at the extreme corners of the shape. Figures 3.5.4, 3.5.5, and 3.5.6 show the growth of the search using various heuristic costs while trying to overcome a large obstacle.

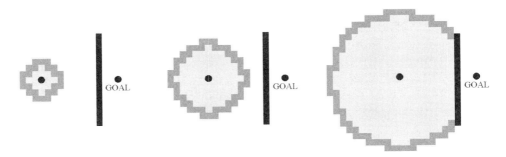

FIGURE 3.5.4. The heuristic cost of zero.

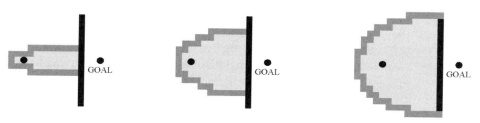

FIGURE 3.5.5. The heuristic cost using Euclidean distance to goal.

FIGURE 3.5.6. The heuristic cost overestimated.

What does all this mean? It means that by overestimating the heuristic, the search pushes hard on the closest nodes to the goal. This causes pressure for the search to overcome large obstacles that are between the start and goal points of the search. If the actual solution requires backtracking before going to the goal, an overestimating heuristic slows the search. However, if most of the time there's a way to get around large blocking obstacles, the overestimating heuristic is faster. Figure 3.5.7 illustrates this point as the non-overestimating heuristic explores three times more nodes than the overestimating heuristic.

Ultimately, getting the right amount of overestimating requires experimentation. Unfortunately, if the search space is not on a grid, it's probably not possible to accurately observe the shape of the search. Instead, you need to measure indicators such as the size of the Closed list and the maximum size of the Open list.

The final size of the Closed list tells how many nodes were explored; the maximum size of the Open list is a good indicator of how long it takes to explore each node (since Open list operations take a relatively long time as the list grows big). When tuning your heuristic, you can try typical searches and watch the Open and Closed list sizes in order to identify good heuristic values. By testing searches on your actual game, you'll be able to tune the heuristic to something reasonable.

Decoupling Pathfinding Data from the Search Space

A* requires a large amount of memory in order to store the progress of each search. Traditionally, this memory is held inside each searchable node. If the search space is a

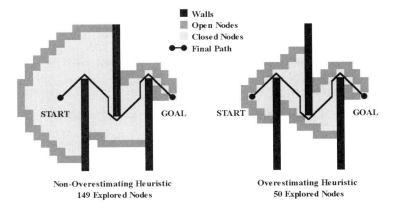

FIGURE 3.5.7. A non-overestimating heuristic vs. an overestimating heuristic.

rectangular grid, each grid square contains pathfinding node data. If the search space is a polygonal mesh, each triangle contains pathfinding node data. Since an individual search almost never covers every single node in the search space, there is no reason to have this incredible amount of memory dedicated to pathfinding. For example, a 1,000 × 1,000 tiled world has 1 million pathfinding nodes just sitting there unused most of the time.

The solution is to decouple the pathfinding node data from the search space. This solution reduces the huge memory overhead and could also speed up searches. Interestingly, by decoupling the node data from the search space, you allow for simultaneous searches, which can now occur because multiple-node data can point to the same real node in the search space. However, it's generally not a good idea to allow simultaneous searches—still, in certain circumstances, it might be useful.

Pre-allocating a Minimum Amount of Memory

Decoupling the node data from the search space requires that each search use some other chunk of memory. We could simply allocate node data on the fly, but A* can churn through hundreds of nodes each search, so this isn't a reasonable solution. A way around this is to pre-allocate a sufficiently large block of memory that can be recycled for each A* search.

What is A* storing so much of? It's all the data that tracks the progress of the search. For every node explored, the algorithm needs to save the following information:

1. A pointer to the parent node
2. The cost to get to this node
3. The total cost (*cost + heuristic estimate*)
4. Whether this node is on the Open list
5. Whether this node is on the Closed list

The idea is to pre-allocate a ton of these nodes (call it the *node bank*). The actual number varies depending on the size of your largest search. Now, you don't want to pre-allocate too much memory, so this array should be able to grow if needed—or alternatively, force the search to give up.

When A* explores a new node for the first time, it needs to ask for a free node from the node bank. When it gets a free node back, it needs to fill out the info in order to personalize it for this new node.

Storing Explored Nodes in a Master Node List

Once a node has been personalized from the node bank, it needs to be put somewhere for fast retrieval. The optimal data structure for this activity is a *hash* table. Hash tables allow constant-time storing and looking up of data. Therefore, we store all explored nodes in this *master node list*. This hash table allows us to instantaneously find out if a particular node is on the Closed list or the Open list. Remember, since the node data memory is already allocated, the hash table contains only pointers to these nodes.

At this point you might ask yourself, "Where is the Closed list?" The answer is that it lives inside the master node list. All explored nodes are stored inside the master node list, and the Closed list just happens to be in the same place. This isn't a problem, because each node is clearly marked as whether it's on the Closed or Open list. So where does the Open list live? The Open list is maintained separately, *but* the master node list also contains pointers to all the same nodes that are on the Open list. Why the duplication? Because sometimes it's faster to find the node you want using the master node list, and sometimes it's faster using the Open list. It's all about speed.

When any given node is explored during the A* algorithm, it's possible that the node was already explored during this same search. To make things simple, you'll want a function that gives you back a pointer to that particular node's data, whether its been searched before or not.

This function first checks the master node list to see if the node has been explored before. If it has, the function simply returns a pointer to that existing node. If the node is not in the master node list, a free node is taken from the node bank, it is initialized to represent the desired node, and its pointer is returned. In effect, the function completely hides the details of allocating new nodes from the node bank and getting nodes that already exist.

```
Node* GetNode( MasterNodeList nodelist, NodeLocation node_location )
{
   //GetNodeFromMasterNodeList accesses the hash table of nodes
   Node* node = GetNodeFromMasterNodeList( nodelist, node_location );
   if( node ) {
      return( node );
   }
   else
   {  //Not in the Master Node List — get new one from the Node Bank
      Node* newNode = GetFreeNodeFromNodeBank();
```

```
        newNode->location = node_location;
        newNode->onOpen = false;
        newNode->onClosed = false;

        //StoreNodeInMasterNodeList places the node into the hash table
        StoreNodeInMasterNodeList( nodelist, newNode );
        return( newNode );
    }
}
```

Optimizing the Open List

The beauty of A* comes from its ability to direct the search toward the most promising directions. The way it achieves this goal is by putting all nodes it could search next into the Open list. It then orders the list from the most promising to the least promising nodes to search. The problem is that the Open list tends to get big, and each time it goes through the A* loop, the most promising node must be extracted from the list. The node to extract is the one with the lowest total cost (*cost to get to the node + heuristic estimate of the remaining cost to the goal*). As it turns out, the best way to store the Open list is to keep it sorted as a priority queue.

A priority queue can be implemented as a binary heap. A *binary heap* is a sorted tree that has the property that the parent always has a lower value than its children. However, there is no ordering among siblings, so a heap is *not* a completely ordered tree. Because of this interesting property, insertions and extractions (removing the lowest element) take only *O(log n)*. Fortunately, that's pretty much all A* needs to do with the Open list.

Implementing a Priority Queue

It's out of the scope of this article to implement a priority queue from scratch, but there's an easy way to implement one using STL. Whether you're using STL or not, be sure to check out a great article about priority queues [Nelson96]. It describes priority queues clearly enough that you could probably construct one without the help of STL. Otherwise, consult any standard algorithm and data structure book for more information.

In order to properly use the priority queue, use the following four operations that A* needs to perform on the Open list:

1. Extract the node with the minimum total cost (and resort the list): *O(log n)*.
2. Insert a new node on the Open list (and resort the list): *O(log n)*.
3. Update the total cost of a node already on the Open list (and resort the list): *O(n+log n)*.
4. Determine whether the Open list is empty: O(1).

STL actually implements a priority queue with something called a *container adapter*. However, the operations that can be performed on it are very limiting. In fact, it has no interface to perform operation #3 (updating a node's total cost and resorting the list). Therefore, we can't use the STL implementation of a priority queue. However, we can use the STL heap operations on an STL vector container to make our own priority queue!

Listings 3.5.1, 3.5.2, 3.5.3, and 3.5.4 contain the four Open list operations along with the node object, the heap object, and the STL comparison object—all implemented in C++ using STL. In addition, on the CD that accompanies this book, you'll find that Greg Snook's pathfinding article, "Simplified 3D Movement and Pathfinding Using Navigation Meshes," contains almost identical code for implementing an STL priority queue.

A* Using the Optimized Master Node List and Open List

There's nothing too tricky about using the ideas presented, but just in case, the guts of the A* algorithm are implemented in Listing 3.5.5 using the master node list and the Open list. Some other small tricks are also included, such as not searching the node from which the search just came.

Conclusion

Since pathfinding is fundamentally a tough computational problem, the best strategies have always been to simplify the problem. Before any effort is made to optimize the algorithm, ensure that the world is represented in the simplest reasonable way. Once that's decided, it's very important that some kind of hierarchical scheme is also incorporated. Usually this scheme involves some pre-processing that requires level designers and artists to be very involved in the search space representation. Although it adds some overhead to the development of assets, there's no better way to speed up pathfinding.

Once the search space is finalized, it's important to get the pathfinder working correctly in that space before any optimizations are attempted. A* is not a trivial algorithm, and it's extremely difficult to debug if many of the optimizations have been incorporated. When you are ready to optimize, start by decoupling the node memory from the search space. The next step is to implement a priority queue for the Open list and a hash table for the master node/Closed list. Finally, when everything works like a charm and the game is stable, you can play with the heuristic cost. In order to get the best results, you'll want to tune the heuristic several times during development as the game world becomes better defined.

After all these techniques have been implemented, the next step is to cheat. Some techniques for giving the impression of instantaneous pathfinding can be found in the "A* Aesthetic Optimization" article in this book. The trick involves making the player think that a path has been found when in reality you are just stalling. If the player feels that the game is very responsive, the pathfinder appears to be unobtrusive and transparent, which is the core reason for speeding it up.

Listing 3.5.1: Node Object

```
class Node
{
public:
    NodeLocation location;    // location of node (some location
                              // representation)
    Node* parent;             // parent node (zero pointer represents
                              // starting node)
    float cost;               // cost to get to this node
    float total;              // total cost (cost + heuristic estimate)
    bool onOpen;              // on Open list
    bool onClosed;            // on Closed list
};
```

Listing 3.5.2: Priority Queue Object

```
class PriorityQueue
{
public:
    //Heap implementation using an STL vector
    //Note: the vector is an STL container, but the
    //operations done on the container cause it to
    //be a priority queue organized as a heap
    std::vector<Node*> heap;
};
```

Listing 3.5.3: STL Comparison Function

```
class NodeTotalGreater
{
public:
    //This is required for STL to sort the priority queue
    //(its entered as an argument in the STL heap functions)
    bool operator()( Node * first, Node * second ) const {
        return( first->total > second->total );
    }
};
```

Listing 3.5.4: Four Open List Operations

```
Node* PopPriorityQueue( PriorityQueue& pqueue )
{   //Total time = O(log n)

    //Get the node at the front — it has the lowest total cost
    Node * node = pqueue.heap.front();
```

```
   //pop_heap will move the node at the front to the position N
   //and then sort the heap to make positions 1 through N-1 correct
   //(STL makes no assumptions about your data and doesn't want
   //to change the size of the container.

   std::pop_heap( pqueue.heap.begin(), pqueue.heap.end(),
      NodeTotalGreater() );

   //pop_back() will actually remove the last element from the heap
   //(now the heap is sorted for positions 1 through N)
   pqueue.heap.pop_back();

   return( node );
}

void PushPriorityQueue( PriorityQueue& pqueue, Node* node )
{  //Total time = O(log n)

   //Pushes the node onto the back of the vector (the heap is
   //now unsorted)
   pqueue.heap.push_back( node );

   //Sorts the new element into the heap
   std::push_heap( pqueue.heap.begin(), pqueue.heap.end(),
      NodeTotalGreater() );
}

void UpdateNodeOnPriorityQueue( PriorityQueue& pqueue, Node* node )
{  //Total time = O(n+log n)

   //Loop through the heap and find the node to be updated
   std::vector<Node*>::iterator i;
   for( i=pqueue.heap.begin(); i!=pqueue.heap.end(); i++ )
   {
      if( (*i)->location == node->location )
      {  //Found node - resort from this position in the heap
         //(since its total value was changed before this function
         //was called)
         std::push_heap( pqueue.heap.begin(), i+1,
            NodeTotalGreater() );
         return;
      }
   }
}

bool IsPriorityQueueEmpty( PriorityQueue& pqueue )
{
   //empty() is an STL function that determines if
   //the STL vector has no elements
   return( pqueue.heap.empty() );
}
```

Listing 3.5.5: A* Implemented with a Master Node List and a Priority Queue Open List

```
MasterNodeList g_nodelist;

bool FindPath( GameObject* gameobject, WorldLocation goal )
{
   //Get a path in progress if it exists for this game object with
   //this goal
   //A path may have been started and not finished from last game tick
   //If no path in progress, it returns an empty path structure
   Path* path = GetPathInProgress( gameobject, goal );

   if( !path->initialized )
   {  //The InitializePath function fills out the path structure for
      //this path request
      //It initializes a clean MasterNodeList and a clean Open list
      InitializePath( path, gameobject, goal );

      //Create the very first node and put it on the Open list
      Node* startnode = GetNode( g_nodelist, GetNodeLocation(
         gameobject->pos ) );
      startnode->onOpen = true;       //This node goes on Open list
      startnode->onClosed = false;    //This node not on Closed list
      startnode->parent = 0;          //This node has no parent
      startnode->cost = 0;            //This node has no cost to get to
      startnode->total = GetNodeHeuristic( startnode->location,
         path.goal );
      PushPriorityQueue( path.open, startnode );
   }

   while( !IsPriorityQueueEmpty( path->open ) )
   {
      //Get the best candidate node to search next
      Node* bestnode = PopPriorityQueue( path.open );

      if( AtGoal( bestnode, goal ) )
      {  //Found the goal node — construct a path and exit
         //The complete path will be stored inside the game object
         ConstructPathToGoal( gameobject, path );
         return( true );   //return with success
      }

      while( /*loop through all connecting nodes of bestnode*/ )
      {
         Node newnode;
         newnode.location = /*whatever the new location is*/;

         //This avoids searching the node we just came from
         if( bestnode->parent == 0 ||
            bestnode->parent->location != newnode.location )
         {
            newnode.parent = bestnode;
            newnode.cost = bestnode->cost + CostFromNodeToNode(
```

```
            &newnode, bestnode );
        newnode.total = newnode.cost;

        //Get the preallocated node for this location
        //Both newnode and actualnode represent the same node
        //location, but the search at this point may not want
        //to clobber over the data from a more promising route —
        //thus the duplicate nodes for now

        Node* actualnode = GetNode( g_nodelist,
            newnode.location );

        //Note: the following test takes O(1) time (no searching
        //through lists)
        if( !( actualnode->onOpen && newnode.total >
            actualnode->total ) &&
             !( actualnode->onClosed && newnode.total >
            actualnode->total ) )
        {   //This node is very promising
            //Take it off the Open and Closed lists (in theory)
            //and push on Open
            actualnode->onClosed = false;   //effectively removing it
                                            //from Closed
            actualnode->parent = newnode.parent;
            actualnode->cost = newnode.cost;
            actualnode->total = newnode.total;

            if( actualnode->onOpen )
            {   //Since this node is already on the Open list,
                //update it's position
                UpdateNodeOnPriorityQueue( path.open, actualnode );
            }
            else
            {   //Put the node on the Open list
                PushPriorityQueue( path.open, actualnode );
                actualnode->onOpen = true;
            }
        }
    }
}

//Now that we've explored bestnode, put it on the Closed list
bestnode->onClosed = true;

//Use some method to determine if we've taken too much time
//this tick and should abort the search until next tick
if( ShouldAbortSearch() ) {
    return( false );
}
}

//If we got here, all nodes have been searched without finding
//the goal
return( false );
}
```

References

A* Algorithm

[Heyes-Jones98] Heyes-Jones, Justin, "A* Algorithm Tutorial," available online at www.gamedev.net/reference/programming/ai/article690.asp, 1998.

[Patel99] Patel, Amit J., "Amit's Thoughts on Pathfinding,"" available online at http://theory.stanford.edu/~amitp/GameProgramming/, November 27, 1999.

[Stout96] Stout, Bryan W., "Smart Moves: Intelligent Path-Finding," *Game Developer,* –October/November 1996, pp. 28–35, also available online at www.gamasutra.com/features/19990212/sm_01.htm.

Data Structures

[Lewis91] Lewis, Harry R., *Data Structures and Their Algorithms,* HarperCollins Publishers Inc., 1991.

[Nelson96] Nelson, Mark, "Priority Queues and the STL," *Dr. Dobb's Journal*, also available online at www.dogma.net/markn/articles/pq_stl/priority.htm, January 1996.

3.6

Simplified 3D Movement and Pathfinding Using Navigation Meshes

Greg Snook

Getting an object to move from Point A to Point B intelligently has always been a challenge for the game programmer. Doing the same for an object in 3D space is a greater challenge still. In today's world of complex 3D environments, the task can become overwhelming. This article proposes a rather simple method to help overcome these obstacles and get all your objects safely to Point B with the least amount of work: *Cheat*.

Yes, cheat. Rarely do real-time games have the time to compute true 3D object-to-scene interaction and pathfinding, and the code complexity to do so is often unnecessary for most applications. We are here to find the easier way out. We seek a simple, extendable method to roll our dice and move our mice in a way that looks believable to the player. Let's face it: The easiest ways almost always involve cheating.

In a Nutshell

What we need is a way to simplify 3D space into more familiar 2D terms. Objects in 2D space move in a highly predicable fashion and can be controlled very intuitively by the player. In addition, there is a myriad of 2D search algorithms at our disposal to create intelligent paths for our objects to move on. What we will create is a method allowing our objects to function in a pseudo-3D environment while providing a full-3D presentation for the player. To do this, we employ a mesh of triangular polygons to represent our 3D space as a warped 2D playing field.

The idea stems from the fact that, for most game environments, you can pretty easily predict where objects can and can't move. From that information, a simple set of geometry can be created to define this area as a "walkable" surface area. One way to visualize this area is to imagine a room within a typical 3D environment. Since your characters are humanoid and the planet hosting the game has gravity, you can assume the game objects will spend most of their time on the floor of this room. You can also

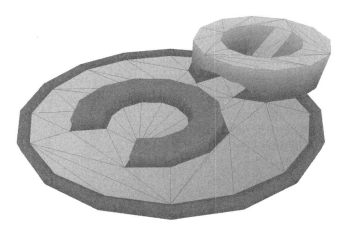

FIGURE 3.6.1. A 3D environment with the associated navigation mesh drawn in wireframe.

assume that they won't be walking through the pillars, desks, soda machines, and other objects sharing the floor space. We can define the remaining portions of the floor with some simple, coarse geometry that covers the open, walkable surface area. Think of this geometry as a sort of polygonal carpet, which we refer to as a *navigation mesh*. It represents the area around which your objects can move within the environment. Figure 3.6.1 shows the 3D environment used in the *navimesh* program available on the CD that accompanies this book. The wireframe polygons show the navigation mesh, which defines the area where objects can move.

In a sense, this navigation mesh object can be treated like the grid systems employed by 2D tile-based games. Each polygon of the mesh can be thought of as a grid cell, except that they attach to adjacent cells on three sides instead of four. With a bit of effort, we can even use this mesh for traditional grid-based algorithms such as line-of-sight detection and pathfinding. The added bonus is that our replacement for the 2D grid can have cells of irregular shape and size, wind up and down stairs and hills, and even overlap itself on things like bridges and catwalks—all while providing access to the same time-tested 2D algorithms we all know and love.

Utilizing a navigation mesh can also reduce the amount of collision testing required between an object and its static environment. Since the navigation mesh already represents an approximation of the open surface area in the environment, our objects need collide with only the mesh edges rather than the true scene geometry. By projecting a control point from the object onto the mesh, we can easily track object movement and collisions with 2D line intersection tests rather than full 3D polygon intersection. In cases in which higher detail is needed for collision, the mesh cells can still link to sets of true scene geometry for refined testing. Objects that collide with a cell edge would then be passed onto routines that resolve the collision with the associated room geometry. Linking process data with the cells in this manner serves as a quick-and-dirty proximity test for objects in motion, an idea that can be extended to trigger traps, doors, or switches whenever an object enters a given cell or collides with a particular edge.

Construction

Navigation mesh geometry needs to adhere to a few simple rules in order to work correctly. First, it needs to be composed completely of triangles to ensure that each cell is contained in a single plane. Second, the entire mesh must be contiguous, with all adjacent triangles sharing two vertices and a single edge. Finally, no two triangles should overlap on the same plane. That is, any given point within a triangular cell should be exclusive to that cell. This will aid our algorithms immensely and provide believable movement for the player.

The navigation mesh is not intended to be visible to the player. We use it only behind the scenes to limit character movement and determine paths. Therefore, it need consist of only the minimal amount of polygons necessary to represent the area in which objects can move. Highly detailed navigation meshes might produce the most accurate results, but their overhead would be a limiting factor for most real-time games. The mesh should be one that contains only the cells necessary to facilitate believable movement to the player, not one that represents every pebble and twig on the ground.

Roll the Dice and Move Your Mice

To begin, we first examine using the navigation mesh to control object movement in a 3D environment. Once we have our objects happily interacting with the mesh, we can extend its use for pathfinding and line of sight. But first things first: We need to get some objects moving around the confines of the mesh geometry.

We attach objects to the mesh using a control point that will be locked to the navigation mesh surface. This control point may never leave the mesh, but it can move about the surface of the mesh at will. Using our polygonal carpet example, imagine a person standing in a room. The control point can be visualized as a marble sitting directly below the person, resting between his or her feet. Wherever the person is moved in the room, the marble rolls along, always maintaining a position on the carpet directly under the person.

All desired object movement is transferred to this control point, which, in turn, gets resolved on the surface of the navigation mesh. The object is then moved relative to the new control point location. In our example, kick the marble and let it ricochet off the walls, then move the person to the new marble location.

The basic procedure is as follows, given that each object maintains a control point on the mesh and we know which cell of the mesh currently contains the control point:

1. Project the object's desired motion vector onto the plane of its current cell. This translates the motion into a 2D vector along the plane of the cell. We'll call this new vector a motion path and represent it as a 2D line segment. The endpoints of the segment are the starting location of the control point and the desired ending location, both translated to 2D space relative to the plane of the cell.

2. Test the motion path against the cell's 2D triangle edges. Due to the nature of triangles, we know that for our path to exit the cell, it must intersect with exactly one side of the triangle. So, we test the 2D line segment of the motion path against the three line segments representing the cell triangle for any possible intersections. There can be only one of three possible results to this test:

   a) Our path intersects with an unshared edge (i.e., an edge not connected to an adjacent cell). This means we have hit something solid. Resolve the collision of the motion path vector and the cell wall, adjusting the motion path to account for any change in direction, and repeat Step 2.

   b) Our path intersects with a shared edge. Move to the adjacent cell and repeat the entire process from Step 1, projecting our current vector to the plane of the new cell and testing against its walls.

   c) The only remaining possibility is that our motion path does not exit the current cell. We have reached the end of our process and found the cell that hosts the object's new resting position. We translate our resulting 2D motion path endpoint back into 3D space to find the true 3D location of the control point and move the object relative to it.

Obviously, for complex navigation meshes, this can be a very cumbersome process. For each cell encountered, we need to project an arbitrary 3D vector onto a 3D plane. From there we translate the resulting vector along with the cell edges to 2D space, where we can perform our line intersection tests. Once finished moving about the mesh, we need to undo the translations and projections to produce our new control-point position in 3D space.

That's quite an effort to undertake in real time, especially if you have many objects to test or your objects plan to travel over many cells in a given frame. For simple environments, however, this could be plausible and allows for the greatest flexibility in navigation mesh geometry. For complex environments, we can still speed up the process considerably with a bit more careful planning (read: cheating) and an additional navigation mesh geometry rule: *To facilitate fast projections, all cell normals must face in the same direction along a predetermined cardinal axis.*

Imagine our room again with the navigation mesh carpet on the floor. All cell normals of the floor point up, so they meet this new requirement of our mesh. That is to say, all cell normals have a positive y value in our environment. Note that we do not require our new navigation mesh to be flat, we simply no longer allow cells whose normals are 90 degrees or more away from our chosen axis.

With this new rule, the projections become incredibly simple. We simply throw out the dimension along the axis we have chosen. In our carpeted room example, projecting points onto the floor is now as simple as throwing their *y* values out the window. In addition, when we have finished the Motion Path processing along the navigation mesh cells, we have a new 2D (x, z) location and the cell that contains it. Using the cell's plane equation, we can solve for y using our (x, z) location and transform ourselves back into 3D space easily. Our new motion-tracking process is reduced to the following:

1. Create a motion path consisting of the control point and the desired location, reduced to 2D points by tossing out their common axis values.
2. Test the 2D motion path against the sides of the cell triangle as before until a cell is found that contains the destination endpoint of the motion path.
3. Using our new (x, z) control point location and the plane equation of the cell it resides in, solve for y and reconvert our control point back into 3D space.

The *navimesh* sample program includes some simple classes that illustrate this process. In the source code, an object called *NavigationCell* is used to represent a single triangular cell, and *NavigationMesh* represents a collection of those cells. Let's first examine *NavigationCell*, since it does most of the work.

NavigationCell defines a single cell of the mesh with the following members:

```
Plane   m_CellPlane;   // A plane containing the cell triangle
vector3 m_Vertex[3];   // the three vertices of this cell
Line2D m_Side[3]; // a 2D line representing each cell wall
NavigationCell* m_Link[3];    // pointers to cells that attach to
                       // this cell on each of its three
                       // sides.  A NULL link denotes a solid
                       // edge.
```

Vector3, Plane and Line2D are pretty straightforward workhorse classes whose source code is also provided. One point of distinction is that Line2D is really treated as a ray passing through two points. It has an implied direction, from Endpoint A to Endpoint B. It also tracks a perpendicular "normal" for the 2D line segment. This normal is used to classify points as being either on the line's left or right side. These notions of "left" and "right" are defined as though you were standing on Endpoint A of the line looking toward Endpoint B. As you see in the source code, the ability to classify points in relation to the line is used quite heavily in our motion processing.

The main use of *NavigationCell* is to perform the step in our process where we determine how a path interacts with the walls of a cell. *NavigationCell* contains a member function to classify a 2D line segment to its three cell walls and return a result. This function, ClassifyPathToCell(), is the basic building block of navigation mesh use. The return value of this function can be one of the following enumerated types:

```
enum PATH_RESULT
```

```
    {
            NO_RELATIONSHIP = 0,    // the path does not cross this cell
            ENDING_CELL,            // the path ends in this cell
            EXITING_CELL            // the path exits this cell
    };
```

In the case where EXITING_CELL is the result, the cell wall traversed as well as the 2D point of intersection with the wall are provided to the caller. This allows us to compare any 2D path to the cell and determine what type of intersection occurs. When an intersection with a solid edge occurs, we can use the point of intersection to calculate our new direction and retest. Listing 3.6.1 shows the ClassifyPathToCell() function in detail.

NavigationMesh uses this function as needed to process our movement as defined in the preceding steps. The *NavigationMesh* member function ResolveMotionOnMesh() manages the entire process, testing each cell encountered using ClassifyPathToCell(). It takes in a 3D control point, a pointer to the cell it is currently occupying, and the desired location for the control point after movement has occurred. It returns to the caller the true final location of the control point and the cell the new control point will reside in. Listing 3.6.2 details the use of the ResolveMotionOnMesh() function.

Getting There Is Half the Fun

Now that we have seen how to use the navigation mesh to control object movement, we can look into other applications for the mesh. The first obvious use is pathfinding. Keep in mind that our mesh consists of linked cells, which share common edges, just like a grid or hex map. Any path-finding algorithms traditionally applied to a grid or hex map should then reasonably translate to our mesh.

As a matter of fact, using polygonal meshes for search algorithms is no new feat. Since path-finding algorithms were designed to work over databases of linked node data, they work quite nicely across sets of linked vertices. As game programmers, we have become too accustomed to seeing these methods applied to grids and hexes, which is only a small subset of the environments within which they can be used.

Using our navigation meshes, we do add one small wrinkle to the path-finding-over-polygons method: We don't use the mesh vertices. Instead, we use the midpoints of each cell wall. Why? Two reasons come to mind, both of which are arguable depending on your game environment. The first is that we are also using our navigation mesh to limit object movement in the environment. If we generate a path along the cell vertices, we are always traveling on the edges of the cells. This is the most costly movement on a navigation mesh, since moving down the edge of a cell exactly means you are constantly colliding with the cell edge, causing a lot of extra, unnecessary intersection tests.

The second reason is purely aesthetic. If we assume our mesh was designed to use the minimal number of polygons, it stands to reason that there are not many vertices

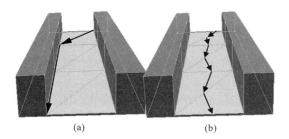

(a)   (b)

FIGURE 3.6.2. Two overhead views of a sample hallway and navigation mesh showing a path *a:* generated along cell edges and *b:* through cell wall midpoints.

or polygon edges in the body of our open space. Have a look at Figures 3.6.2a and 3.6.2b, which show an overhead view of a hallway, and a reasonable number of polygons to define the open space within it. If we generated a path on the cell edges (Figure 3.6.2a), we would spend most of our time dragging ourselves against the wall of the hallway. Using the cell wall midpoints (Figure 3.6.2b), we can generate a more visually appealing path down the body of the hallway.

As I said, both reasons are arguable. You could simply increase the complexity of your navigation mesh and add code to avoid paths that drag along the solid edges of the mesh, but I have found it easier (and conceptually more intuitive) to move through the wall midpoints. In application, it has also proved to be easier for the level designers creating the mesh to work without having to concern themselves with the placement of extra vertices and cell edges for pathfinding. In essence, all we have really done is offset our mesh vertices to create a more believable path.

So how do we build the path? As in any path-finding situation, you need to choose the best method for your game environment. Best-first searching, Dijkstra's algorithm, and the venerable A* can all be applied to the cells of our navigation mesh. Elsewhere in this book are some excellent explanations of the various search methods, so I will not go into detail on them all here. Check out the articles by Steve Rabin and Bryan Stout in this book for detailed information on A*. You can also check the references at the end of this article for some recommended reading on pathfinding.

For demonstration, the *navimesh* sample code shows how to use A* on the navigation mesh. Although it can be the most complex method to employ, A* can achieve highly accurate results and is often more efficient than other methods in terms of memory use and search time. However, its efficiency hinges on the use of a good heuristic. The heuristic helps steer the search algorithm toward the goal, preventing it from fanning out all over the mesh unless necessary.

The best heuristic to use is purely a game-specific matter. Only you know how well your objects move over your game's terrain, and you need to tune your heuristic accordingly. You might even need to tailor separate heuristics for each object type, taking into account its ability to climb steep grades, corner at high speeds, and so on.

In most cases, however, this heuristic is simply the approximate distance from a given cell to the goal. For the purpose of our demonstration, this is the heuristic we employ.

To run the A* algorithm, we maintain a list of cells that need to be processed. In the *navimesh* sample code, these "Open" cells are held in an ordered list called a *NavigationHeap*. Cells are listed in the order of best to worst cost in terms of the distance required to reach the goal. Therefore, each time we pull a cell off the heap, we know we are dealing with the current "best guess" of the cell that will provide the best path to our goal.

To begin pathfinding, we need to stoke the heap with the first cell, our destination. We then pop and process each cell on the heap until we reach our starting position or run out of heap. If the heap runs dry before we reach the goal, we know there is no path available between our two locations.

To process a cell, examine each of its neighbors. We determine the distance traveled to reach each one by adding the cost associated with our current cell to the distance required to cross the cell to each neighbor. This *Arrival Cost* for each neighbor is then added to the neighbors' own heuristic values to arrive at a priority score for each of the neighboring cells.

We now examine the score, or cost, of each neighboring cell to do one of two things. If the neighboring cell is not currently in the Open heap, we must sort it by its score value. This essentially puts it off for later processing. If the cell is already in the heap, we need to see if our new score is better than the score by which the cell is currently sorted. If the new score is an improvement, we need to move the cell up within the heap to its new priority position for earlier processing. If the new score is not an improvement, we toss it out, since a more optimal path already passes through this cell. In either case, each time a cell is added to the heap or repositioned within the heap, we record the identity of the cell that has set the current *Arrival Cost*.

This is done so that the cells can keep track of the next closest cell to the destination along the generated path. You'll notice that the *navimesh* sample runs the A* algorithm in the reverse search direction, starting at the destination cell and searching for a path backward to our current location. When the search is complete, each cell contains a link to the next cell closest to the goal along the generated path. We can hop through these links in the proper order, from current location to destination, and build a final waypoint list for our game object.

In the sample code, the entire process is run by the BuildNavigationPath() member function of the *NavigationMesh* class. It uses the *NavigationHeap* object to maintain a list of *NavigationCells* to be processed. As each cell is pulled from the heap, its ProcessCell() function is called, which does the work of testing each neighboring cell, as outlined previously. Cells are added or moved within the heap as necessary, until a path is found. At that point, BuildNavigationPath() iterates through the cells on the path, adding their wall midpoints to the final *NavigationPath* waypoint list. Source code for the entire process is shown in Listing 3.6.3.

It Works, But It Ain't Pretty

As you can see by the blue lines drawn in the *navimesh* sample program, building a path through polygonal objects yields a very jagged result. Very rarely will you find that your navigation geometry is set up to produce a straight-line path. The nature of the mesh forces our path to meander from cell to cell, making many abrupt twists and turns (see Figure 3.6.3a). Any object that uses this path verbatim will look very odd indeed to the player. Luckily, we have one final application to discuss that can smooth the path out considerably: line-of-sight determination.

Back when we were working out how to move objects around the mesh, we defined a function, ClassifyPathToCell(), to compare a 2D line of motion to a cell. The result of the function told us whether the path ended within the cell, encountered a solid edge, or passed through to an adjacent cell. We can now use that function again to perform a line-of-sight test, smoothing out our path by skipping ahead to the furthest visible waypoint.

Each time we arrive at a waypoint in our path, we look ahead to the next few waypoints in the list. By creating a line of motion from our current position to each of these waypoints, we can quickly test if the waypoints are "visible." To do this, we test the path against each cell between our current position and the waypoint using the ClassifyPathToCell() function. If the function returns a solid-wall intersection, we know the waypoint is not visible from our current position. Conversely, if we reach the waypoint without such an intersection, we know the point is visible to us. By searching for the furthest visible waypoint up the chain, we can skip over some of the meandering waypoints and smooth out our path. Figure 3.6.3b shows the new smoother path generated by skipping over the redundant visible waypoints.

This method can be used for all sorts of visibility testing. Using our Classify-PathToCell() function, we can test whether any two points on the mesh can see each other. This has some very useful applications in enemy AI, since you can quickly test whether enemy objects can see the player's position at any given moment. The Line-OfSightTest() member function of the *NavigationMesh* class details the process for determining point visibility.

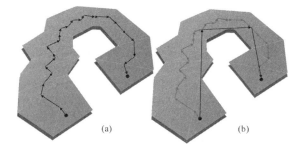

(a)   (b)

FIGURE 3.6.3. *a:* A sample path generated using A*. *b:* The same path smoothed using line-of-sight testing.

Conclusion

I hope this article has demonstrated that 3D space need not be so computationally complex. My goal was to show that using familiar 2D methods (and a bit of cheating), we can greatly simplify the game environment without impacting the player's 3D experience. The end result is a very flexible and useful tool for moving objects around in 3D space without a boatload of 3D math.

This method allows you to reduce object/scene collision operations, create complex paths, and test for the visibility between any two points in the environment space. However, there is still more that can be done with navigation meshes. They can be constructed of high-order primitives rather than rigid triangles, tessellated like multiresolution meshes for greater path finding detail near the camera, or even animated to represent fluid surfaces. For now, I leave the exploration of these ideas to you. Give the meshes a try and see what new uses you can layer on top of this foundation.

Listing 3.6.1: Intersecting a 2D Line with a Cell of the Navigation Mesh

```
NavigationCell::PATH_RESULT NavigationCell::ClassifyPathToCell(const
Line2D& MotionPath, NavigationCell** pNextCell, CELL_SIDE& Side,
vector2* pPointOfIntersection)const
{
    int InteriorCount = 0;

    // Check our MotionPath against each of the three cell
    //   walls
    for (int i=0; i<3; ++i)
    {
        // Classify the MotionPath endpoints as being either
        // ON_LINE, or to its LEFT_SIDE or RIGHT_SIDE.
        // Since our triangle vertices are in clockwise order,
        // we know that points  to the right of each line are
        // inside the cell.  Points to the left are outside.
        // We do this test using the ClassifyPoint function of
        // Line2D

        // If the destination endpoint of the MotionPath
        // is Not on the right side of this wall...
        if (m_Side[i].ClassifyPoint(MotionPath.EndPointB()) !=
        Line2D::RIGHT_SIDE)
        {
            // ..and the starting endpoint of the MotionPath
            // is Not on the left side of this wall...
            if
            (m_Side[i].ClassifyPoint(MotionPath.EndPointA()) !=
            Line2D::LEFT_SIDE)
            {
                // Check to see if we intersect the wall
                // using the Intersection function of
                // Line2D
```

```
                    Line2D::LINE_CLASSIFICATION IntersectResult =
                    MotionPath.Intersection(m_Side[i],
                    pPointOfIntersection);

                    if (IntersectResult ==
                    Line2D::SEGMENTS_INTERSECT ||
                    IntersectResult ==
                    Line2D::A_BISECTS_B)
                    {
                        // record the link to the next
                        // adjacent cell (or NULL if no
                        // attachment exists) and the
                        // enumerated ID of the side we hit.

                        *pNextCell = m_Link[i];
                        Side = (CELL_SIDE)i;
                        return (EXITING_CELL);
                    }
                }
            }
            else
            {
                // The destination endpoint of the MotionPath
                // is on the right side.  Increment our
                // InteriorCount so we'll know how many walls we
                // were to the right of.

                InteriorCount++;
            }
        }

        // An InteriorCount of 3 means the destination endpoint of
        // the MotionPath was on the right side of all walls in the
        // cell.  That means it is located within this triangle,
        // and this is our ending cell.

        if (InteriorCount == 3)
        {
            return (ENDING_CELL);
        }

        // We reach here only if the MotionPath does not
        // intersect the cell at all.
        return (NO_RELATIONSHIP);
}
```

Listing 3.6.2: Resolving Motion on a Navigation Mesh

```
        void NavigationMesh::ResolveMotionOnMesh(const vector3& StartPos,
        NavigationCell* StartCell, vector3& EndPos,
        NavigationCell** EndCell)
        {
            // create a 2D motion path from our Start and End
```

```
// positions, tossing out their Y values to project them
// down to the XZ plane.
Line2D MotionPath(vector2(StartPos.x,StartPos.z),
vector2(EndPos.x,EndPos.z));

// these three will hold the results of our tests against
// the cell walls
NavigationCell::PATH_RESULT Result =
NavigationCell::NO_RELATIONSHIP;
NavigationCell::CELL_SIDE WallNumber;
vector2 PointOfIntersection;
NavigationCell* NextCell;

// TestCell is the cell we are currently examining.
NavigationCell* TestCell = StartCell;

//
// Keep testing until we find our ending cell or stop
// moving due to friction
//
while ((Result != NavigationCell::ENDING_CELL)
            && (MotionPath.EndPointA() !=
            MotionPath.EndPointB()))
{
    // use NavigationCell to determine how our path and
    // cell interact
    Result = TestCell->ClassifyPathToCell(MotionPath,
        &NextCell, WallNumber, &PointOfIntersection);

    // if exiting the cell...
    if (Result == NavigationCell::EXITING_CELL)
    {
        // Set if we are moving to an adjacent cell or
        // we have hit a solid (unlinked) edge
        if(NextCell)
        {
            // moving on. Set our motion origin to the
            // point of intersection with this cell
            // and continue, using the new cell as our
            // test cell.
            MotionPath.SetEndPointA(PointOfIntersection);
            TestCell = NextCell;
        }
        else
        {
            // we have hit a solid wall.
            // Resolve the collision and correct our
            // path.
            MotionPath.SetEndPointA(PointOfIntersection);
            TestCell->ProjectPathOnCellWall(WallNumber,
            MotionPath);

            // add some friction to the new MotionPath
            // since we are scraping against a wall.
            // we do this by reducing the magnitude of
```

```
                    // our motion 10%
                    vector2 Direction =
                        MotionPath.EndPointB() -
                        MotionPath.EndPointA();
                    Direction *= 0.9f;
                    MotionPath.SetEndPointB(MotionPath.EndPointA() +
                    Direction);
            }
        }
        else if (Result == NavigationCell::NO_RELATIONSHIP)
        {
            // Although theoretically we should never
            // encounter this case, we do sometimes find
            // ourselves directly on a vertex of the cell.

            // This can be viewed by some routines as being
            // outside the cell.  To accommodate this rare
            // case, we force our starting point into the
            // current cell by nudging it back so we may
            // continue.

            vector2 NewOrigin = MotionPath.EndPointA();
            TestCell->ForcePointToCellCollumn(NewOrigin);
            MotionPath.SetEndPointA(NewOrigin);
        }
    }

    // we now have our new host cell
    *EndCell = TestCell;

    // Update the new control point position,
    // solving for Y using the Plane member of the
    // NavigationCell
    EndPos.x = MotionPath.EndPointB().x;
    EndPos.z = MotionPath.EndPointB().y;
    TestCell->MapVectorHeightToCell(EndPos);
}
```

Listing 3.6.3: Building a Navigation Path on the Mesh Using A*

```
bool NavigationMesh::BuildNavigationPath(NavigationPath& NavPath,
NavigationCell* StartCell, const vector3& StartPos,
NavigationCell* EndCell, const vector3& EndPos)
{
    bool FoundPath = false;

    // Increment our path finding session ID
    // This identifies each path finding session
    // so we do not need to clear out old data
    // in the cells from previous sessions.
    ++m_PathSession;

    // load our data into the NavigationHeap object
```

```
        // to prepare it for use.
        m_NavHeap.Setup(m_PathSession, StartPos);

        // We are doing a reverse search, from EndCell to
        // StartCell.  Push our EndCell onto the Heap as the first
        // cell to be processed.

        EndCell->QueryForPath(&m_NavHeap, 0, 0);

        // process the heap until empty, or a path is found
        while(m_NavHeap.NotEmpty() && !FoundPath)
        {
            NavigationNode ThisNode;

            // pop the top cell (the open cell with the lowest
            // cost) off the Heap
            m_NavHeap.GetTop(ThisNode);

            // if this cell is our StartCell, we are done
            if(ThisNode.cell == StartCell)
            {
                FoundPath = true;
            }
            else
            {
                // Process the Cell, Adding its neighbors to the
                // Open Heap as needed
                ThisNode.cell->ProcessCell(&m_NavHeap);
            }
        }

        // If we found a path, build a waypoint list
        // out of the cells on the path
        if (FoundPath)
        {
            NavigationCell* TestCell = StartCell;
            vector3 NewWayPoint;

            // Setup the Path object, clearing out any old data
            NavPath.Setup(this, StartPos, StartCell, EndPos,
            EndCell);

            // Step through each cell linked by our A* algorithm
            // from StartCell to EndCell
            while (TestCell && TestCell != EndCell)
            {
                // add the link point of the cell as a way point
                // (the exit wall's center)
                int LinkWall = TestCell->ArrivalWall();

                NewWayPoint = TestCell->WallMidpoint(LinkWall);
                NewWayPoint = SnapPointToCell(TestCell,
                NewWayPoint);
                // just to be sure
```

```
                 NavPath.AddWayPoint(NewWayPoint, TestCell);

                 // and on to the next cell
                 TestCell = TestCell->Link(LinkWall);
             }

             // cap the end of the path.
             NavPath.EndPath();
             return(true);
         }

     // no path exists between the two points provided.
     // i.e. "you can't get there from here"
     // This will never happen on a contiguous mesh.
     return(false);
}


bool NavigationCell::ProcessCell(NavigationHeap* pHeap)
{
     if (m_SessionID==pHeap->SessionID())
     {
         // once we have been processed, we are closed
         m_Open  = false;

         // query all our neighbors to see if they need to be
         // added to Open heap
         for (int i=0;i<3;++i)
         {
             if (m_Link[i])
             {
                 // The Distances between the wall midpoints
                 // of this cell are held in the order
                 // ABtoBC, BCtoCA and CAtoAB.

                 // abs(i-m_ArrivalWall) is a formula to
                 // determine which distance measurement
                 // to use.  We add this distance to known
                 // m_ArrivalCost to compute the total cost
                 // to reach the next adjacent cell.

                 m_Link[i]->QueryForPath(pHeap, this,
                 m_ArrivalCost+m_WallDistance[abs(
                 i-m_ArrivalWall)]);
             }
         }
         return(true);
     }
     return(false);
}

bool NavigationCell::QueryForPath(NavigationHeap* pHeap,
NavigationCell* Caller, float arrivalcost)
{
     if (m_SessionID!=pHeap->SessionID())
```

```
{
    // this is a new session, reset our internal data
    m_SessionID = pHeap->SessionID();

    if (Caller)
    {
        m_Open  = true;
        ComputeHeuristic(pHeap->Goal());
        m_ArrivalCost = arrivalcost;

        // Remember the triangle wall this caller is
        // entering from
        if (Caller == m_Link[0])
        {
            m_ArrivalWall = 0;
        }
        else if (Caller == m_Link[1])
        {
            m_ArrivalWall = 1;
        }
        else if (Caller == m_Link[2])
        {
            m_ArrivalWall = 2;
        }
    }
    else
    {
        // We are the cell that contains the starting
        // location of the A* search.

        m_Open  = false;
        m_ArrivalCost = 0;
        m_Heuristic = 0;
        m_ArrivalWall = 0;
    }
    // add this cell to the Open heap
    pHeap->AddCell(this);
    return(true);
}
else if (m_Open)
{
    // A true m_Open means we are already in the Open
    // Heap.  If this new caller provides a better path,
    // adjust our data.  Then tell the Heap to resort our
    // position in the list.

    if ((arrivalcost + m_Heuristic) < (m_ArrivalCost + m_Heuristic))
    {
        m_ArrivalCost = arrivalcost;

        // Remember the triangle wall this caller is
        // entering from
        if (Caller == m_Link[0])
        {
            m_ArrivalWall = 0;
```

```
            }
            else if (Caller == m_Link[1])
            {
                m_ArrivalWall = 1;
            }
            else if (Caller == m_Link[2])
            {
                m_ArrivalWall = 2;
            }
            // ask the heap to resort our position in the
            // priority heap
            pHeap->AdjustCell(this);
            return(true);
        }
    }
    // this cell is closed
    return(false);
}

void NavigationCell::ComputeHeuristic(const vector3& Goal)
{
    // our heuristic is the estimated distance (using the
    // longest axis delta) between our cell center point
    // and the goal location

    float XDelta = fabs(Goal.x - m_CenterPoint.x);
    float YDelta = fabs(Goal.y - m_CenterPoint.y);
    float ZDelta = fabs(Goal.z - m_CenterPoint.z);

    m_Heuristic = __max(__max(XDelta,YDelta), ZDelta);
}
```

References

[Patel99] Patel, Amit J., "Amit's Thoughts on Pathfinding," available online at http://theory.stanford.edu/~amitp/GameProgramming/, November 27, 1999.

[Heyes-Jones99] Heyes-Jones, Justin, "A* Algorithm Tutorial," available online at www.gamedev.net/reference/programming/ai/article690.asp, November 27, 1999.

[Stout96] Stout, Bryan W., "Smart Moves: Intelligent Path-Finding," Game Developer, also   available online at www.gamasutra.com/features/19990212/sm_01.htm, October 1996.

3.7

Flocking: A Simple Technique for Simulating Group Behavior

Steven Woodcock

Flocking (sometimes called *swarming* or *herding*) is a technique first put forth by Craig Reynolds in a 1987 paper he did for SIGGRAPH, "Flocks, Herds, and Schools: A Distributed Behavioral Model." In that paper, Reynolds proposed a series of three simple rules, which, when taken together, gave groups of autonomous agents (also called *boids*) a realistic form of group behavior similar to flocks of birds, schools of fish, or swarms of bees. (See Figure 3.7.1 for an example of this behavior in action.) These rules, which Reynolds refers to as *steering behaviors*, are:

- **Separation.** Steer to avoid crowding local flockmates.
- **Alignment.** Steer toward the average heading of local flockmates.
- **Cohesion.** Steer to move toward the average position of local flockmates.

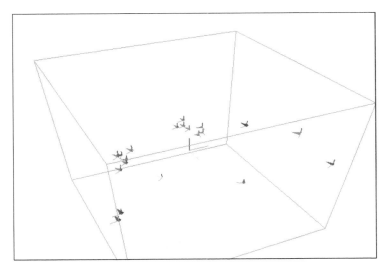

FIGURE 3.7.1. An example image of the flocking demo in action.

Separation gives an agent the ability to try to maintain a certain separation distance from other agents in the immediate vicinity. This helps prevent agents from crowding together while ensuring a "natural-looking" closeness that emulates groups in the real world. The code presented in this article accomplishes this goal by having each member of a flock test how close it is to its nearby flockmates and then adjust its heading (steering) to obtain a desired distance.

Alignment provides an agent that has the ability to align itself with (i.e., head in the same direction and/or speed as) other agents in its immediate vicinity. As with separation, this article accounts for alignment through each member of a flock looking at nearby flockmates and then adjusting its heading and speed to match the average heading and speed of its neighbors.

Cohesion gives an agent the ability to "group" with other nearby agents, thus emulating similar behavior seen in nature. Again, this article accomplishes this goal by having each agent examine nearby agents, averaging their positions and then adjust its heading to match.

The Fourth Rule

In later implementations and papers, Reynolds added what has sometimes been referred to as the "fourth rule" of flocking:

- **Avoidance.** Steer to avoid running into local obstacles or enemies.

Avoidance provides an agent with the ability to steer away from obstacles and avoid collisions. This behavior is accomplished by giving each agent the ability to "look forward" some distance and determine whether a collision with some object is likely, then to adjust its heading to prevent it. Similarly, it might be desirable to avoid certain other types of agents (such as rabbits avoiding foxes or doves avoiding hawks), and again this principle would come into play.

No Memory

Note that the steering behaviors say nothing about state information or about a given agent maintaining knowledge of the flock, its environment, where it's headed, or the like. Flocking is a *stateless* algorithm in that no information is maintained from update to update; each boid reevaluates its environment at every update cycle. Not only does this reduce memory requirements that might otherwise be needed to provide a similar behavior using approaches besides flocking, but it also allows the flock to react in real time to changing environmental conditions. As a result, flocks exhibit elements of *emergent behavior*: No one member of the flock knows anything about where the flock is going, but the flock moves as one mass, avoids obstacles and enemies, and keeps pace with one another in a fluid, dynamic fashion.

How Is This Concept Useful for Computer Games?

Flocking provides a powerful tool for unit motion and making more realistic environments the player can explore; it has been used with great success in a variety of commercial titles. For example, both *Unreal* (Epic) and *Half-Life* (Sierra) used flocking algorithms for many of their monsters as well as less life-threatening creatures such as birds and fish. *Enemy Nations* (Windward Studios) used a modified flocking algorithm to control unit formations and movement across a 3D environment. Groups of animals can be made to wander the terrain in real-time strategy games or RPGs more realistically than can be done with simple scripting. Groups of archers or swordsmen can be made to move realistically across bridges or around boulders and other obstacles. Monsters in a first-person shooter can wander the dungeon halls in a more believable fashion, avoiding players where possible but perhaps launching an attack when the flock grows large enough. The possibilities are practically endless.

Implementation

Vectors and Motion

A quick overview of the mechanics of motion for the members of a flock helps in understanding how the code does what it does.

Figure 3.7.2 demonstrates the concept of *local space* (space relative to the boid itself). "Forward" is toward the positive *Z*-axis, "left" is toward the positive *X*-axis, and "up" is vertical toward the top of the boid. Our boid in this article is the classic delta-wing shape often used by Reynolds, but of course it can be any shape desired.

Figure 3.7.3 demonstrates another important principle, *orientation*. Referred to as *roll, pitch,* and *yaw,* orientation is simply an indication of how a given object is oriented in the local space, shown in Figure 3.7.2. Roll is rotation around the local *Z*-axis (the one facing forward and backward). Pitch is rotation around the local *X*-axis (the one running left and right). Yaw is rotation around the *Y*-axis (the one running directly up and down through the boid). Understanding orientation is important because we use it when making decisions about our boid's orientation during movement. The idea presented in this article works by building a *velocity vector* during each

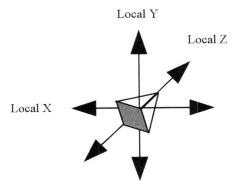

FIGURE 3.7.2. Local space is defined for each boid.

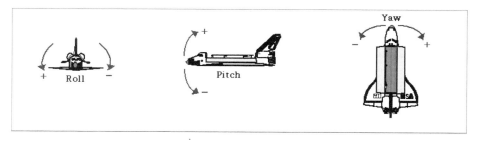

FIGURE 3.7.3. The three axis rotations are defined as roll, pitch, and yaw.

update cycle that will adjust the boid's local X, Y, and Z orientations to match the needs of the four steering behaviors.

Another important aspect of how this idea operates is the manner in which it arbitrates conflicting desires on the part of a boid. Looking at the four steering behaviors for a moment, one can see that there is no guidance on how to prioritize these behaviors—all are considered of equal importance. This loosely matches most normal behavior in the real world: A dove might want to both keep up with its fellows and avoid cutting through a flock of hawks while doing so; however, this concept doesn't take into account life-and-death situations.

One can solve this problem in several ways—automatically giving higher priority to avoidance, for example—but this article uses a *vector accumulation* approach. The orientation changes that a given boid wants to make to satisfy each of the four steering behaviors are summed in a *change vector* before being applied to the boid's motion. This change vector, by convention, is held to a unit vector so that the accumulated changes are kept in proper proportion. This method allows each steering behavior to have a proportional influence on the boid's final motion changes while enabling the boid to satisfy (at least partially) the needs of two or more conflicting directives. Over time I've found that this approach is generally more satisfactory than others.

Constraints

Several constraints on our boids restrict how they can move and react. Possibly the most influential in this implementation is each boid's *perception range*, which restricts how far a flockmate can "look" around its environment to detect other flockmates, potential obstacles, or enemies. The larger this range, the more organized and coherent the flocks and the better they are at avoiding enemies and obstacles. Making this range smaller results in more erratic flocks, groups of boids splitting off more often when confronted by obstacles or enemies, and so on.

Another constraint on how our agents can move is their *velocity* and *maximum velocity change*. In the real world, animals in flocks are restricted in their ability to keep up with their flockmates by how fast they can move, how fast they can turn, and the like. This article simplifies the problem of motion in a 3D environment somewhat by ignoring acceleration and focusing entirely on velocity; changes to velocity are restricted to some proportion of overall maximum velocity. This helps prevent the agents in our demo from turning on a dime or putting on ridiculous bursts of speed when trying to catch up with their flockmates. It also provides a governing restraint on how quickly they can slow down or alter course to avoid an obstacle. If allowed "infinite response," they might fly directly up to the surface of an obstacle before turning with infinite agility and speed to move around it—not a very realistic behavior.

A final constraint for the purposes of our demo is the world in which our boids flock. For the purposes of this article, I've arbitrarily created a Box class that defines the world in which our boids can move. Any boid that strays beyond the boundaries of the Box is magically transported to the opposite side, keeping the same motion characteristics it had before. The effect is that flocks that stray too close to the edge of the Box can lose members to the "other side of the world," where they can lose track of the main flock and form a new flock of their own.

Virtually all these parameters are adjustable so that one can see the potential impact of fiddling with them.

The Code

Three classes make up the heart of this article: *CBox*, *CFlock*, and *CBoid*. Organizationally, these classes can be viewed as described in Figure 3.7.4.

Each flock is represented by an instantiation of a *CFlock* object. There can be multiple *CFlock* objects resident within *CBox*, and they can be created or destroyed at any point (although this article creates them only at initialization). *CFlock* objects serve to organize and simplify access to the members of the flock.

Similarly, a *CBoid* object represents each member of a flock. There can, of course, be multiple *CBoid* objects associated with each *CFlock* (if there weren't, it would be a

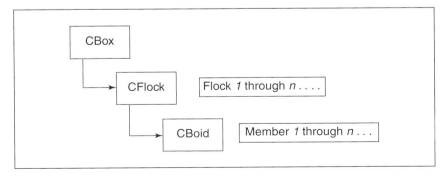

FIGURE 3.7.4. The *CBox* class defines the basic world in which our flocks will fly.

pretty small flock), and, like *CFlock* objects, they can be created or destroyed at any point. Although this article creates flock members only at initialization, it wouldn't be hard to all to build in some "lifetimes" for individual members (see the "Limitations and Potential Improvements" section) so that individuals might age and die.

The CBox Class

CBox is a rather simple class, as one might expect:

```
class CBox
{

public:

    ///////////////////////////////
    // constructors and destructors
    ///////////////////////////////

    // Constructor #1.
    // Creates a Box with default values of 50 meters
    // on any side not specified.
    CBox (float lv=50.0, float wv=50.0, float hv=50.0);

    // Destructor
    virtual ~CBox();

    /////////////////////////////
    // miscellaneous functions
    /////////////////////////////

    // GetBoxLength.
    // Returns the length of the Box, in meters.
    float GetBoxLength (void);

    // GetBoxWidth..
    // Returns the width of the Box, in meters.
    float GetBoxWidth (void);

    // GetBoxHeight.
    // Returns the height of the Box, in meters.
    float GetBoxHeight (void);
```

This class provides us with a simple way to parameterize and retrieve the boundaries of our world.

The CFlock Class

The *CFlock* class represents a basic flock of boids and serves mostly as an organizational tool rather than a strict representation of each flock per se. Its various functions are fairly simple and deal primarily with the "bookkeeping" that one might desire when handling flocks. The class definition for *CFlock* can be found in Listing 3.7.1.

Procedurally, flocks are first created and then have one or more boids added to them. The class is built to allow for real-time creation and deletion of flocks, although the demo itself does not do this. A list of all *CFlock* objects is maintained in the simple static array `CFlock::ListOfFlocks[]` (again, simplified for the purposes of this article). At each update cycle, the flocks' `CFlock::Update()` method is called to update all the members of that flock. New boids can be added at any time using `CFlock::AddTo()`, and members can be removed, if desired, via `CFlock::RemoveFrom()`. `CFlock::Get-Count()` and `CFlock::GetFirstMember()` provide methods to obtain specific status information about a given flock, whereas the debugging method `CFlock::PrintData()` provides more exhaustive information.

Flocks can be created at any time, although the demo provided creates them only at initialization. Each flock can have any number of *CBoid* objects as members. Note that members of a flock have no idea what flock they're a member of, but the flock itself *does* know who its members are. For the purposes of this article, a *CBoid* object remains a member of whatever *CFlock* it is initially assigned to, but it wouldn't be hard at all to add code that would allow boids to change their loyalties if so desired (see the "Limitations and Potential Improvements" section).

The CBoid Class

The *CBoid* class implements the true "meat" of the flocking algorithms and, as such, is fairly beefy. It is contained in Listing 3.7.2. This class handles all aspects of a specific agent's motion and existence: how it moves, how it senses its environment, how it prioritizes its actions.

Each *CBoid* object represents a single individual agent. Much as with *CFlock* objects, *CBoid* objects can be created or deleted at will. Once created, they are indirectly managed through the `CFlock::AddTo()`, `CFlock::RemoveFrom()`, and `CFlock::Update()` methods, as described previously.

Each *CBoid* object is updated via its `CFlock::FlockIt()` method, which begins by building a list of those flockmates that a given boid can see (based on its *perception_range* value). A list of enemies (members of other flocks) is also built if that option is active.

The method then begins to implement the steering behaviors as described previously, summing an accumulating series of velocity vector changes to accommodate the wishes of the agent. The methods `CBoid::KeepDistance()` (separation behavior), `CBoid::MatchHeading()` (alignment behavior), and `CBoid::SteerToCenter` (cohesion behavior) are called to determine what the boid would like to do. If the option is active, avoidance behavior of members of other flocks is modeled through a call to `CBoid::FleeEnemies()`.

One additional method implemented here is `CBoid::Cruising()`. This method attempts to model a boid's "desired cruising speed," if everything were up to it and it wasn't under any other influences. The primary reason for this method was to give any boids wandering on their own (out of sight of their flockmates) some "purpose" to their motion.

At each stage of the update process, we accumulate all desired velocity vector changes proportionally into an accumulation vector. A check at the end of the CBoid::Flockit() method ensures that an individual never exceeds its maximum allowed speed or velocity change.

Two final methods serve as "cleanup" to ensure that everything looks correct. CBoid::ComputeRPY() makes calculations necessary to orient our boid properly as a result of its final velocity vector changes. CBoid::WorldBound() does some sanity testing to determine whether any agent has strayed outside the bounds of the *CBox* world object in which it resides and, if it has, places it back in its box.

Various private methods handle visibility and linked-list management; there's nothing particularly special about them, nor are they flocking related per se. A debug method, CBoid::PrintData(), provides exhaustive information on a given boid on an update-by-update basis.

Limitations and Potential Improvements

Hard reality dictates that any demonstration of flocking behavior has some limitations. This article does not implement obstacle avoidance at all, although it does allow for avoidance in the form of "enemy flocks." Boids remain assigned to the flocks they start with, but one could easily envision code that reassigns a boid dynamically to a new flock should it lose sight of its old one. Similarly, boids in this implementation are blessed with an amazing, 360-degree, full-spherical field of view; there are no restrictions such that they can see only objects or flockmates directly in front of them. A more realistic field of view would probably be desired for any game implementation.

A list of other possible improvements is fairly easy to come up with. Many people who have used flocking behavior and its variations have implemented "life clocks" on individual agents, making boids that die if they stray too far from their mates but that can "breed" new flock members if they remain with their brothers long enough. One could also examine predator and prey behavior, modifying the base code to allow one type of flock to "feed" on another.

Listing 3.7.1: The CFlock Class Definition

```
class CFlock
{

   public:

      /////////////////////
      // static variables
      /////////////////////
```

```
            // number of flocks
            static int FlockCount;

            // list of flocks
            static CFlock * ListOfFlocks[MAX_FLOCKS];

            ////////////////////////////////
            // constructors and destructors
            ////////////////////////////////

            // Constructor.
            // Creates a new flock.
            CFlock (void);

            // Destructor.
            ~CFlock (void);

            /////////////////////
            // flocking functions
            /////////////////////

            // Update.
            // Updates all members of a flock.
            void Update (void);

            //////////////////////////
            // miscellaneous functions
            //////////////////////////

            // AddTo.
            // Adds the indicated boid to the flock.
            void AddTo (CBoid * boid);

            // GetCount.
            // Returns the # of boids in a given flock.
            int GetCount (void);

            // GetFirstMember.
            // Returns a pointer to the first boid in a
            // given flock (if any).
            CBoid * GetFirstMember (void);

            // PrintData.
            // Dumps all data describing a given flock.
            void PrintData (void);

            // RemoveFrom.
            // Removes the indicated boid from the flock.
            void RemoveFrom (CBoid * boid);

        private:

            int     m_id;              // id of this flock
            int     m_num_members;     // number of boids in this flock
            CBoid   *m_first_member;   // pointer to first member
```

```
};
```

Listing 3.7.2: The CBoid Class Definition

```cpp
class CBoid {

  public:

    //////////////////////
    // static variables
    //////////////////////

    // visible friends list (work space reused by each boid)
    static CBoid * VisibleFriendsList[MAX_FRIENDS_VISIBLE];

    ///////////////////////////////////
    // constructors and destructors
    ///////////////////////////////////

    // Constructor #1.
    // Creates an individual boid with randomized position,
    // velocity, and orientation.
    CBoid (short id_v);

    // Constructor #2.
    // Creates an individual boid with specific position,
    // velocity, and orientation.
    CBoid (short id_v,
           vector * pos_v, vector * vel_v, vector * ang_v);

    // Destructor
    ~CBoid (void);

    ////////////////////////////
    // public flocking methods
    ////////////////////////////

    // FlockIt.
    // Used for frame-by-frame updates; no time
    // deltas on positions.
    void FlockIt (int flock_id, CBoid *first_boid);

    ////////////////////////////
    // miscellaneous functions
    ////////////////////////////

    // AddToVisibleList.
    // This visibility list is regenerated for each member each
    // update cycle, and acts much like a push-down queue; the
    // latest member added to the list becomes the first one
    // when the list is sequentially accessed.  Mostly I did
    // this for speed reasons, as this allows for fast inserts
    // (and we don't delete from this list, we just rebuild it
```

```
          // each update cycle).
          void AddToVisibleList (CBoid *ptr);

          // ClearVisibleList.
          // Clears the visibility list.
          void ClearVisibleList (void);

          // GetNext.
          // Returns the "next" pointer of the invoking member.
          CBoid * GetNext();

          // LinkOut.
          // Removes a member from a list.
          void LinkOut ();

          // PrintData.
          // Dumps all data describing a given member.
          void PrintData (void);

          // SetNext.
          // Set the "next" pointer of an individual member.
          void SetNext (CBoid *ptr);

          // SetPrev.
          // Set the "prev" pointer of an individual member.
          void SetPrev (CBoid *ptr);

      private:

          /////////////////
          // data members
          /////////////////

          // supplied with constructor(s)

          short    m_id;                        // member individual ID
          float    m_perception_range;          // how far member can see
          vector   m_pos;                       // position of member
                                                //(in meters)
          vector   m_vel;                       // velocity of member
                                                // (meters/sec)
          vector   m_ang;                       // orientation of member


          // computed
          float    m_speed;                     // overall speed of member
          u_short  m_num_flockmates_seen;       // # of flockmates this
                                                // member sees
          u_short  m_num_enemies_seen;          // # of enemies this
                                                // member sees
          CBoid    *m_nearest_flockmate;        // pointer to nearest
                                                // flockmate (if any)
          CBoid    *m_nearest_enemy;            // pointer to nearest
                                                // enemy (if any)
          float    m_dist_to_nearest_flockmate; // distance to
                                                // nearest flockmate
```

```
                                              or
                                              // (if any), in
                                              // meters
       float      m_dist_to_nearest_enemy;   // distance to
                                              // nearest enemy
                                              // (if any), in
                                              // meters
       vector    m_oldpos;                    // last position
       vector    m_oldvel;                    // last velocity
       CBoid     *m_next;                     // pointer to next
                                              // flockmate
       CBoid     *m_prev;                     // pointer to
                                              // previous
                                              // flockmate


    //////////////////
    // flocking methods
    //////////////////

    // Cruising.
    // Generates a vector indicating how a flock boid would
    // like to move, if it were all up to him and he was under
    // no other influences of any kind.

    vector CBoid::Cruising (void);

    // FleeEnemies.
    // Generates a vector for a flock boid to avoid the
    // nearest enemy (boid of a different flock) it sees.

    vector CBoid::FleeEnemies (void);

    // KeepDistance.
    // Generates a vector for a flock boid to maintain his
    // desired separation distance from the nearest flockmate
    // he sees.

    vector CBoid::KeepDistance (void);

    // MatchHeading.
    // Generates a vector for a flock boid to try
    // to match the heading of its nearest flockmate.

    vector CBoid::MatchHeading (void);

    // SeeEnemies.
    // Determines which enemy flock boids a given flock boid
    // can see.

    int CBoid::SeeEnemies (int flock_id);

    // SeeFriends.
    // Determines which flockmates a given flock boid can see.
    int CBoid::SeeFriends (CBoid *first_boid);
```

```
                // SteerToCenter.
                // Generates a vector to guide a flock boid towards
                // the "center of mass" of the flockmates he can see.

                vector CBoid::SteerToCenter (void);

                // WorldBound.
                // Implements a world boundary so that flocks don't fly
                // infinitely far away from the camera, instead remaining
                // in a nice viewable area.  It does this by wrapping flock
                // boids around the other side of the world, so (for
                // example) they move out the right and return on the left.

                void CBoid::WorldBound (void);

                ////////////////////////////
                // miscellaneous functions
                ////////////////////////////

                // AccumulateChanges.
                // Adds vector values in changes into the accumumlator
                // vector. Returns magnitude of accumulator vector after
                // adding changes.

                float CBoid::AccumulateChanges (vector &accumulator,
                   vector changes);

                // CanISee.
                // Determine whether a given invoking boid can see the boid
                // in question. Returns the distance to the boid.

                float CBoid::CanISee (CBoid *ptr);

                // ComputeRPY.
                // Computes the roll/pitch/yaw of the flock boid based on
                // its latest velocity vector changes.  Roll/pitch/yaw are
                // stored in the "ang" data member as follows:
                //    pitch is about the x axis
                //    yaw is about the y axis
                //    roll is about the z axis
                // All calculations assume a right-handed coordinate
                // system:
                //    +x = through the left side of the object
                //    +y = up
                //    +z = through the nose of the model

                void CBoid::ComputeRPY (void);
        };
```

Resources and Acknowledgments

It's virtually impossible to study this particular field without quickly discovering that
nearly every flocking/swarming/herding application on the Web is somehow related

to, derived from, or inspired by some other flocking/swarming/herding application. The implementation described in this article is no exception. Many thanks to Christopher Kline (Mitre Corporation) for his original method for computing roll/pitch/yaw (liberally adapted here), originally published in his *C++ Boids* implementation (available on his Website). Also thanks to Mike Louie (Boeing) for helping with the transformation math (I hate matrices).

Besides Christopher's Web page, which includes many excellent demos and sample code (at www.media.mit.edu/~ckline/boids/), there are a number of other excellent references on this subject on the Web and in bookstores. Probably the best single place to start seeking more information is with the "father of flocking" himself, Craig Reynolds. Craig's Website can be found at *www.red.com/cwr*. Also see Reynolds, C. W., "Flocks, Herds, and Schools: A Distributed Behavioral Model," in *Computer Graphics*, 21(4),SIGGRAPH '87 Conference Proceedings, pages 25–34, 1987.

The *Microsoft DirectX SDK* also comes with two fairly simple-to-follow implementations included on the source CD. On the *DirectX 7a* CD, they are located at *\DXF\samples\multimedia\d3dim\src\boids* and *\DXF\samples\multimedia\dmusic\src\dmboids*. Both versions feature obstacle avoidance using a "force-field" approach that is fairly natural looking.

Finally, an excellent book that addresses the topic of artificial life in general, in addition to discussing both flocking and boids, is Steven Levy's *Artificial Life*, Vintage Books.

3.8

Fuzzy Logic for Video Games

Mason McCuskey

This article is an introduction to an artificial intelligence technique called *fuzzy logic*.

The best way to define fuzzy logic is to explain how it differs from traditional logic. Traditional logic works on the idea of "true" and "false"—something's either on or off, zero or one, yes or no, positive or negative.

Fuzzy logic allows us to work with concepts that aren't "crisp"—in other words, things that require an adjective specifying "to what degree" or "how much." For example, fuzzy logic allows us to mathematically model size concepts such as "pretty big," "awfully small," "medium," "gigantic," and so on.

Fuzzy logic has myriad uses in game AI. For example, we can use fuzzy logic to simulate emotions of computer-controlled characters: "irritated" vs. "incredibly angry," "a bit nervous" vs. "terrified," "happy" vs. "ecstatic," and so on. This in turn allows us to create an AI that's more human or deep than one built using traditional ("black or white") logic could ever be.

How Fuzzy Logic Works

To define how fuzzy logic works, let's first take a step back and review how traditional logic works. Traditional logic manipulates "crisp sets." A *crisp set* is a set for which a given element either belongs to the set or doesn't. For example, let's define a crisp set called M, which consists of all real numbers between 5 and 10:

$M = [5, 10]$

The characteristic function for set M looks like the one shown in Figure 3.8.1 (for the sake of this example, let's assume our universe of discourse is the set of all real numbers between 0 and 20, as shown in Figure 3.8.1).

This is a crisp set because any given number in our universe is either in set *M* or not in set *M*—that is, either the number is between 5 and 10, in which case our function returns one, or it isn't, in which case it returns zero.

A crisp set works great for black-and-white scenarios, but it falls apart under certain situations. Say we want to make a set of all tall people. We decide that 7 feet is

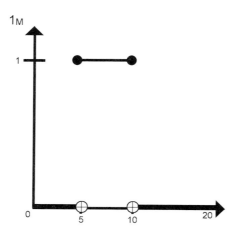

FIGURE 3.8.1. Representation of set *M*.

tall, so we declare our set of tall people as "all people who are at least 7 feet tall." We make a function that returns one if the given height is greater than 7 feet, zero if it isn't. The problem with this is that people who are 6 feet, 11.5 inches aren't in our tall set, even though very few people would dispute the fact that they're tall. So, to try and fix the problem, we drop our minimum height requirement down to 6 feet, but it's just as silly to put two people, one 5 feet 11 inches and one 6 feet, next to each other and say that one of them is "tall" and one isn't. The rigidity of the crisp set works against us.

In other words, what crisp sets don't give us is the ability to specify *how much* (or *to what degree*) something is in a set. Fuzzy sets, however, give us that ability. Using fuzzy sets, we can "flex" the separation between "in the set" and "not in the set" to include things like "just a little bit in the set" or "almost entirely in the set."

We do this by having our characteristic function return not only zero and one, but also values *between* zero and one that indicate *to what degree* the given number is in the set. Going back to our previous example, if zero means "not tall" and one means "tall," then 0.5 can mean "sort of tall" (or, "halfway in the set of tall people"), and 0.01 can mean "a little tall" (or, "just barely in the tall set").

Figure 3.8.2 shows our fuzzy set of all tall people.

Compare the graph in Figure 3.8.2 to the graph of the crisp set in Figure 3.8.1. The fuzzy set in Figure 3.8.2 has slopes—5—someone who's five feet is not tall, but starting at 5 feet 5 inches, the heights gradually start belonging to the tall set, until finally, at 7 feet, they belong entirely to the tall set.

That's a fuzzy set.

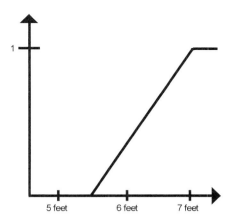

FIGURE 3.8.2. Representation of set "tall people."

Fuzzy Logic Operations

Now that we understand what a fuzzy set is, let's do some operations on it.

Figure 3.8.3 defines another fuzzy set: a set of people "about 6 feet tall."

Here's an example of the fuzzy set AND operation. Figure 3.8.4 shows the graph of the fuzzy set "people who are tall AND are about 6 feet."

Continuing with that same idea, Figure 3.8.5 shows the graph of the fuzzy set "people who are tall OR 6 feet."

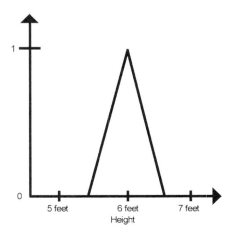

FIGURE 3.8.3. Representation of set "about six feet tall."

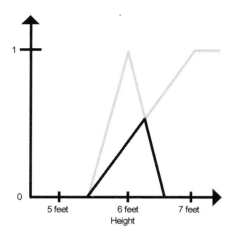

FIGURE 3.8.4. Representation of set "people who are all tall AND about six feet."

Finally, Figure 3.8.6 shows an example of the NEGATION operator: the set "people who are NOT tall."

I Brake for Fuzzy Control

Now we know how to create and operate on fuzzy sets. The next step is using fuzzy sets to accomplish something. This is called *fuzzy control*.

Let's say, for the sake of example, that we want to model traffic. Maybe we're making a city simulation game, and we want the little cars in our city to behave realistically. We have a line of cars, and we want each car in that line to speed up or slow down as though it were driven by a real person. This means that no cars can bump

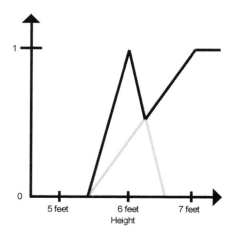

FIGURE 3.8.5. Representation of set "people who are tall OR six feet."

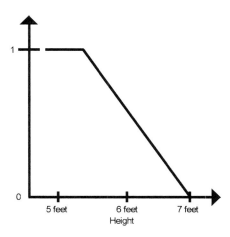

FIGURE 3.8.6. Representation of set "people who are NOT tall."

into the backs of other cars and that inside each car is a safe driver who tries to maintain a reasonable distance (two car lengths) between his or her car and the car in front.

This situation is easy to model with fuzzy logic, because for each car, there are only two variables we need to worry about (in fuzzy logic, these are called *linguistic variables*):

1. The distance between this car and the one in front of it. (We'll call this linguistic variable *distance*.)
2. The *distance delta* between this car and the one in front of it. If the space between the two cars is growing, we have a positive distance delta; if the space is shrinking, we have a negative distance delta. If the space is neither growing nor shrinking, the distance delta is zero.

After spending hours carefully studying real cars on real highways, we come up some rules. For each car:

- If *distance delta* is zero and *distance* is about two car lengths, maintain your current speed.
- If *distance delta* is negative and *distance* is less than two car lengths, slow down.
- If *distance delta* is positive and *distance* is greater than two car lengths, speed up.

There are many more rules, which all follow the same pattern and are summed up in Table 3.8.1.

Now that we've got our rules, we need to nail down all the terms we've used to describe *distance* and *distance delta* with fuzzy sets. This means that we need to define 15 fuzzy sets: five each for *distance*, *distance delta*, and the action of the car (which we'll call *action*). These sets are summarized by Tables 3.8.2, 3.8.3, and 3.8.4 and the graphs in Figures 3.8.7, 3.8.8, and 3.8.9.

Table 3.8.1. Rules for Our Car AI

		Distance Delta				
		Shrinking Fast (Very Negative)	Shrinking (Negative)	Stable (Zero)	Growing (Positive)	Growing Fast (Very Positive)
Distance	Very small	Brake hard!	Brake hard!	Slow down	Slow down	Maintain speed
	Small	Brake hard!	Slow down	Slow down	Maintain speed	Speed up
	Perfect (two car lengths)	Slow down	Slow down	Maintain speed	Speed up	Speed up
	Big	Slow down	Maintain speed	Speed up	Speed up	Floor it!
	Very big	Maintain speed	Speed up	Speed up	Floor it!	Floor it!

Table 3.8.2. *Distance* Fuzzy Set Definition

Distance Label	Corresponding Fuzzy Set
Very small	Less than one car length
Small	About one car length
Perfect	About two car lengths
Big	About three car lengths
Very big	More than three car lengths

Table 3.8.3. *Distance Delta* Fuzzy Set Definition

Distance Delta Label	Corresponding Fuzzy Set
Shrinking fast	Roughly equal to negative (half the car's present speed)
Shrinking	Less than zero
Stable	About zero (the two cars are moving at roughly the same speed)
Growing	Greater than zero
Growing fast	Roughly equal to half the car's present speed

Table 3.8.4. *Action* Fuzzy Set Definition

Action Label	Corresponding Action
Brake Hard	Half your speed (speed /= 2)
Slow down	Decrease your speed by half your present speed (speed −= speed / 2)
Maintain speed	Do nothing
Speed up	Increase your speed by half your present speed (speed += speed / 2)
Floor it	Double your speed (speed *= 2)

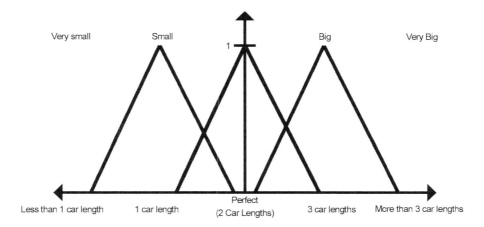

FIGURE 3.8.7. Representation of *Distance* definition.

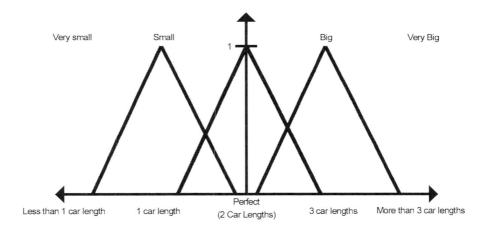

FIGURE 3.8.8. Representation of *Distance Delta* definition.

Now let's take a concrete example and learn how the numbers flow through the fuzzy control system we've just created. Figure 3.8.10 shows an actual value we've picked for *distance;* Figure 3.8.11 shows an actual value for *distance delta.*

As you can see, we've picked 1.3 as the *distance* variable and 0.25 as the *distance delta.* Our fuzzy sets tell us that a *distance delta* of 0.25 is "slightly growing" (it belongs to the "growing" set to a degree of about 0.3), and that a *distance* of 1.3 is "mostly small" (it belongs to the "small" set to a degree of about 0.75). Note that we could also say *distance* is "barely perfect" (it belongs to the "perfect" set to a degree of about 0.1), and that *distance delta* is "mostly stable" (it belongs to the "stable" set to a degree of about 0.6).

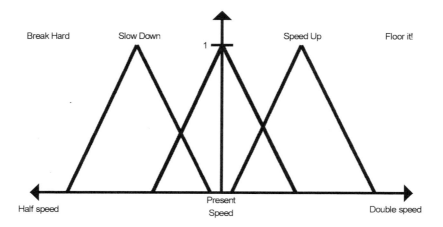

FIGURE 3.8.9. Representation of *Action* definition.

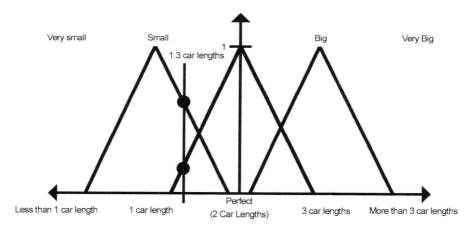

FIGURE 3.8.10. The *Distance* value we've chosen for this example.

This means that we're dealing with four of our sets: the two sets to which *distance* belongs ("small" and "perfect") and the two sets to which *distance delta* belongs ("growing" and "stable"). Given the combination of these sets, we know whatever we decide will be based on one of these four rules:

- If *distance* is small and *distance delta* is growing, maintain current speed.
- If *distance* is small and *distance delta* is stable, slow down.
- If *distance* is perfect and *distance delta* is growing, speed up.
- If *distance* is perfect and *distance delta* is stable, maintain speed.

The next step is to evaluate the degree to which each of these rules is "true."

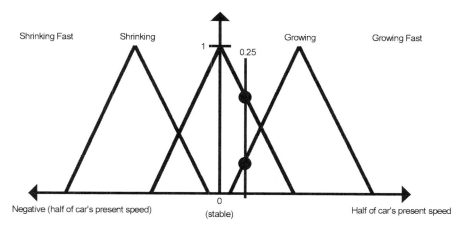

FIGURE 3.8.11. The *Distance Delta* value we've chosen for this example.

Let's look at the first rule. The degree to which we should maintain our current speed depends on "how true" the statement "*distance* is small and *distance delta* is growing" is. We know that *distance* belongs to the "small" set to a degree of 0.75, and we know that *distance delta* belongs to the "growing" set to a degree of 0.3. So, we know the result of the fuzzy statement "*distance* is small and *distance delta* is growing" is 0.3. This is because 0.3 is the largest degree to which *both* statements will still hold true.

We can evaluate the degree of "trueness" of the other three rules the same way, giving us the following:

- *distance* is small and *distance delta* is growing: 0.3 degree of "trueness"
- *distance* is small and *distance delta* is stable: 0.6 degree of "trueness"
- *distance* is perfect and *distance delta* is growing: 0.1 degree of "trueness"
- *distance* is perfect and *distance delta* is stable: 0.1 degree of "trueness"

This means that of our possible actions, "maintain speed" gets a score of 0.3 and 0.1, "slow down" gets a score of 0.6, and "speed up" gets a score of 0.1.

The exact way we get from where we are now to a final value is called a *defuzzification method*. There are many available defuzzification methods; you need to pick one that suits your application. Most of the time, however, it's good enough to perform a simple center-of-mass calculation on the "true" area of the action graph (see Figure 3.8.12).

This calculation gives us our final course of action, namely, "slow down" to a degree of about 0.25. Now it's simply a matter of applying 25% of the slow-down rule to the car's present speed. Since "slow down" to a degree of 1.0 is 0.75 of the car's speed, 25% of the slow-down rule means we should multiply the car's speed by about 0.81.

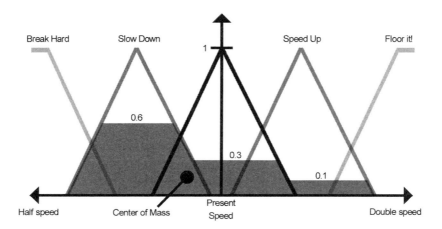

FIGURE 3.8.12. Using the defuzzification method.

So the car slows down slightly, which makes sense given the input criteria (*distance* is small, but *distance delta* is growing).

Of course, the entire process we just went through is performed by the computer hundreds of times a second, simulating the expert control of a safe driver.

Other Applications of Fuzzy Logic

Fuzzy logic and fuzzy control can be used in a variety of game situations. The general idea is that fuzzy logic can be used anywhere you're trying to emulate a human expert. Other good places for fuzzy logic include AI for enemies (the ogres in battle against the player's paladins are scared *to what degree?*), non-player characters (*how much* does the shopkeeper trust the player?), flocking algorithms (*how far* away am I from the rest of the pack?), and myriad other places.

Fuzzy logic can also be used to represent inorganic events, such as how clouds move, given wind speed and direction.

Conclusion

Fuzzy logic is a powerful tool with many uses. With any luck, this article has explained fuzzy logic and how the processes of fuzzy logic and fuzzy control work, as well as giving you a few ideas on where to use fuzzy logic in your games.

If you have questions or comments, please contact me or visit my Website. See the author's section for my contact information.

Resources

[Bauer00] Bauer, Peter, Nouak, Stephan, and Winkler, Roman, available online at www.fl11.uni-linz.ac.at/pdw.fuzzy/index.html, March 21, 2000. I based this article on their excellent online lecture.

[Nguyen99] Nguyen, Hung T., and Walker, Elbert A., *A First Course In Fuzzy Logic,* CRC Press, 1999. This is an excellent book that explains mathematically the basic ideas of fuzzy logic.

[Rao95] Rao, Valluru B., and Rao, Hayagriva Y., *C++ Neural Networks and Fuzzy Logic,* IGD Books Worldwide, 1995. Another great book, this one with an emphasis on creating C++ classes and code for both fuzzy logic and neural-net AI techniques.

[Woodcock00] Woodcock, Steven M., "Game AI," available online at www.gameai.com, March. 21, 2000. This is a great place for information on all sorts of Game Programming AI topics, including fuzzy logic.

And, in general, www.gamedev.net/ is a great site for game development.

3.9

A Neural-Net Primer

André LaMothe

In many ways, the computational limits of digital computers have been realized. Sure, we will keep making them faster, smaller, and cheaper, but digital computers will always process digital information because they are based on deterministic binary models of computation. *Neural nets,* on the other hand, are based on different models of computation. They are based on highly parallel, distributed, probabilistic models that don't necessarily model a solution to a problem the way a computer program does. Instead, they model a network of cells that can find, ascertain, or correlate possible solutions to a problem in a more biological way by solving the problem in little pieces and putting the result together. This article is a whirlwind tour of neural nets and how they work.

Biological Analogs

Neural nets were inspired by our own brains. Literally, some brain in someone's head said, "I wonder how I work?" and then proceeded to create a simple model of itself. Weird, huh? The model of the standard *neurode* is based on a simplified model, invented over 50 years ago, of a human neuron. As shown in Figure 3.9.1, there are three main parts to a biological neuron:

- **Dendrites.** Responsible for collecting incoming signals.
- **Soma.** Responsible for the main processing and summation of signals.
- **Axon.** Responsible for transmitting signals to other dendrites.

The average human brain has about 100,000,000,000, or 10^{11}, neurons, and each neuron has up to 10,000 connections via the *dendrites*. The signals are passed via electrochemical processes based on sodium, potassium, and chloride ions. Signals are transferred by accumulation and potential differences caused by these ions. The chemistry is unimportant, but the signals can be thought of as simple electrical impulses that travel from *axon* to *dendrite*. The connections from one dendrite to an axon are called *synapses,* and these are the basic signal transfer points.

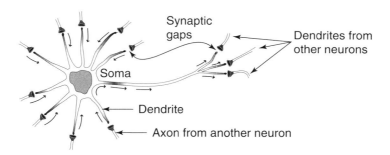

FIGURE 3.9.1. A basic biological neuron.

So how does a neuron work? Well, that question doesn't have a simple answer, but for our purposes, the following explanation suffices. The dendrites collect the signals received from other neurons; then the soma performs a summation of sorts and, based on the result, causes the axon to fire and transmit the signal. The firing is contingent upon a number of factors, but we can model it as a transfer function that processes the summed inputs and then creates an output if the properties of the transfer function are met. In addition, the output is non-linear in real neurons—that is, signals aren't digital, they are analog. In fact, neurons are constantly receiving and sending signals, and the real model of them is frequency dependent and must be analyzed in the *S-domain* (the frequency domain). The real transfer function of a simple biological neuron has, in fact, been derived, and it fills a number of chalkboards.

Now that we have some idea of what neurons are and what we are trying to model, let's talk for a moment about what we can use neural nets for in video games.

Applications to Games

Neural nets seem to be the answer for which we all are looking. If we could just give the characters in our game a little brains, imagine how cool a game it would be! Well, this is possible, in a sense. Neural nets model the structure of neurons in a crude way, but not the high level functionality of reason and deduction—at least, not in the classical sense of the words. It takes a bit of thought to come up with ways to apply neural-net technology to game AI, but once you get the hang of it, you can use it in conjunction with deterministic algorithms, fuzzy logic, and genetic algorithms to create very robust thinking models for your games. Without a doubt, it will be better than anything you can do with hundreds of if-then statements or scripted logic. Neural nets can be used for such things as:

- **Environmental scanning and classification.** A neural net can be fed with information that could be interpreted as vision or auditory information. This information can then be used to select an output response or teach the net. These responses can be learned in real time and updated to optimize the response.

- **Memory.** A neural net can be used by game creatures as a form of memory. The neural net can learn through experience a set of responses; then when a new experience occurs, the net can respond with something that is the best guess at what should be done.
- **Behavioral control.** The output of a neural net can be used to control the actions of a game creature. The inputs can be various variables in the game engine. The net can then control the behavior of the creature.
- **Response mapping.** Neural nets are really good at "association," which is the mapping of one space to another. Association comes in two flavors: *autoassociation*, which is the mapping of an input with itself, and *heteroassociation*, which is the mapping of an input with something else. Response mapping uses a neural net at the back end or output to create another layer of indirection in the control or behavior of an object. Basically, we might have a number of control variables, but we have crisp responses for only a number of certain combinations with which we can teach the net. However, using a neural net on the output, we can obtain other responses that are in the same ballpark as our well-defined ones.

The preceding examples might seem a little fuzzy, and they are. The point is that neural nets are tools that we can use in whatever way we like. The key is to use them in cool ways that make our AI programming simpler and make game creatures respond more intelligently.

Neural Nets 101

In this section, we cover the basic terminology and concepts used in neural-net discussions. This isn't easy, since neural nets are really the work of a number of different disciplines, and therefore, each discipline creates its own vocabulary. The vocabulary that we describe here is a good intersection of the well-known vocabularies. In addition, neural-network theory is replete with research that is redundant, meaning that many people reinvent the wheel. This has had the effect of creating a number of neural-net architectures that have different names. I try to keep things as generic as possible in this article so that we don't get caught up in naming conventions. Later in the article we cover some nets that are distinct enough that we refer to them by their proper names. As you read, don't be too alarmed if you don't make the "connections" with all the concepts. Just read them for now; most of the concepts are covered again in full context in the remainder of the article. Let's begin.

Now that we have seen the wetware version of a neuron, let's take a look at the basic artificial neuron on which to base our discussions. Figure 3.9.2 is a graphic of a standard *neurode,* or artificial neuron. As you can see, it has a number of inputs labeled $X_1 - X_n$ and B. These inputs each have an associated weight $w_1 - w_n$, and b attached to them. In addition, there is a summing junction Y and a single output y. The output y of the neurode is based on a transfer or "activation" function, which is a function of the net input to the neurode. The inputs come from the X·s and from B, which is a bias node. Think of B as a past history, memory, or inclination.

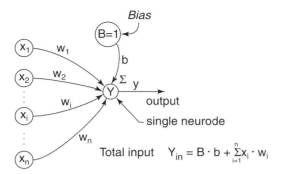

FIGURE 3.9.2. A single neurode with *n* inputs.

The basic operation of the neurode is as follows: The inputs X_i are each multiplied by their associated weights and summed. The output of the summing is referred to as the *input activation* Y_a. The activation is then fed to the activation function $f_a(x)$, and the final output is y. The equation for this operation is:

$$Y_a = B*b + \sum_{i=1}^{n} X_i * w_i \qquad (3.9.1)$$

and $\mathbf{y} = \mathbf{f_a(Y_a)}$. The various forms of $\mathbf{f_a(x)}$ are covered in a moment.

Before we move on, we need to talk about the inputs X_i, the weights $\mathbf{w_i}$, and their respective domains. In most cases, inputs consist of the positive and negative integers in the set $(-\infty, +\infty)$. However, many neural nets use simpler *bivalent* values (meaning that they have only two values). The reason for using such a simple input scheme is that ultimately all inputs are *binary* or *bipolar,* and complex inputs are converted to pure binary or bipolar representations anyway. In addition, many times we are trying to solve computer problems such as image or voice recognition, which lend themselves to bivalent representations. Nevertheless, this rule is not etched in stone. The values used in bivalent systems are primarily 0 and 1 in a binary system or –1 and 1 in a bipolar system. The two systems are similar except that bipolar representations turn out to be mathematically better than binary ones. The weights $\mathbf{w_i}$ on each input are typically in the range $(-\infty, +\infty)$ and are referred to as *excitatory* and *inhibitory* for positive and negative values, respectively. The extra input $\mathbf{B}$ (the bias) is always 1.0 and is scaled or multiplied by $\mathbf{b}$—that is, $\mathbf{b}$ is its weight, in a sense. This concept is illustrated in Equation 3.9.1 by the leading term.

Continuing with our analysis, once the activation $\mathbf{Y_a}$ is found for a neurode, it is applied to the activation function and the output $\mathbf{y}$ can be computed. There are a number of activation functions, which have different uses. The basic activation functions $\mathbf{f_a(x)}$ are shown in Table 3.9.1.

Table 3.9.1. The Activation Functions $f_a(x)$

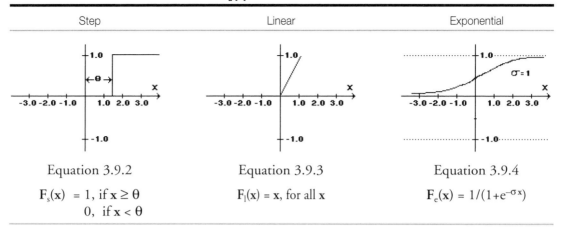

Step	Linear	Exponential
Equation 3.9.2	Equation 3.9.3	Equation 3.9.4
$F_s(x) = 1$, if $x \geq \theta$ 0, if $x < \theta$	$F_l(x) = x$, for all x	$F_e(x) = 1/(1+e^{-\sigma x})$

The equations for each function are fairly simple, but each is derived to model or fit various properties.

The *step* function is used in a number of neural nets and models as a neuron firing when a critical input signal is reached. This is the purpose of the factor θ, which models the critical input level or threshold at which the neurode should fire. The *linear activation* function is used when we want the output of the neurode to more closely follow the input activation. This kind of activation function is used in modeling *linear systems* such as basic motion with constant velocity. Finally, the *exponential activation* function is used to create a *non-linear response,* which is the only possible way to create neural nets that have non-linear responses and model non-linear processes. The *exponential activation* function is key in advanced neural nets because the composition of linear and step activation functions is *always* linear or step; we will never be able to create a net that has non-linear response. Therefore, we need the exponential activation function to address the non-linear problems that we want to solve with neural nets. However, we are not locked into using the exponential function. *Hyperbolic*, *logarithmic*, and *transcendental functions* can be used as well, depending on the desired properties of the net. Finally, we can scale and shift all these functions if we need to.

As you can imagine, a single neurode isn't going to do a lot for us, so we need to take a group of them and create a layer of neurodes, as shown in Figure 3.9.3. This figure illustrates a single-layer neural network. The neural net in Figure 3.9.3 has a number of inputs and a number of output nodes. By convention, this is a single-layer net because the input layer is not counted unless it is the only layer in the network. In this case, the input layer is also the output layer; hence, there is one layer. Figure 3.9.4 shows a two-layer neural net. The input layer is still not counted, and the internal layer is referred to as "hidden." The output layer is referred to as the *output* or *response layer*. Theoretically, there is no limit to the number of layers a neural net can have;

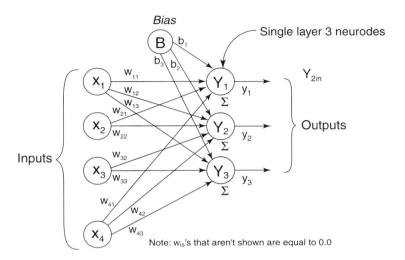

FIGURE 3.9.3. A four-input, three-neurode, single-layer neural net.

however, it might be difficult to derive the relationship of the various layers and come up with tractable training methods. The best way to create multilayer neural nets is to make each network one or two layers and then connect them as components or functional blocks.

All right, now let's talk about *temporal* or time-related topics. We all know that our brains are fairly slow compared to a digital computer. In fact, our brains have cycle times in the millisecond range, whereas digital computers have cycle times in the

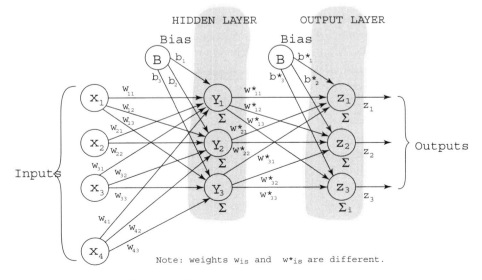

FIGURE 3.9.4. A two-layer neural network.

nanosecond and, soon, sub-nanosecond range. This means that signals take time to travel from neuron to neuron. This fact is also modeled by artificial neurons in the sense that we perform the computations layer by layer and transmit the results sequentially. This model helps to better model the time lag involved in the signal transmission in biological systems such as humans.

We are almost done with the preliminaries. Let's talk about some high-level concepts and then finish up with a couple more terms. The question that you should be asking is, "What the heck do neural nets do?" This is a good question, and it's a hard one to answer definitively. The question should be, "What do you want to try to make neural nets do?" Neural nets are basically mapping devices that help map one space to another space. In essence, they are a type of memory. Like any memory, we can use some familiar terms to describe them. Neural nets have both short-term memory (STM) and long-term memory (LTM). STM is the ability for a neural net to remember something it just learned, whereas LTM is the ability of a neural net to remember something it learned some time ago amid its new learning.

This leads us to the concept of *plasticity*, or, in other words, how a neural net deals with new information or training. Can a neural net learn more information and still recall previously stored information correctly? If so, does the neural net become unstable because it is holding so much information that the data starts to overlap or has common intersections? This area is referred to as *stability*. The bottom line is, we want a neural net to have a good LTM, a good STM, be plastic (in most cases), and exhibit stability. Of course, some neural nets have no analog to memory. They are more for functional mapping, so these concepts don't apply as is.

Now that we know about these memory concepts, let's talk about some mathematical factors that help measure and understand these properties.

One of the main uses for neural nets is as memories, which can produce a response by processing input that is incomplete or "noisy." The response might be the input itself (*autoassociation*) or another output that is totally different from the input (*heteroassociation*). Furthermore, the mapping may be from an n-dimensional space to an m-dimensional space and non-linear to boot. The bottom line is that we want to somehow store information in the neural net so that inputs (perfect inputs as well as noisy ones) can be processed in parallel. This means that a neural net is a kind of hyperdimensional memory unit because it can associate an input n-tuple with an output m-tuple, where m *can* equal n, but it doesn't have to.

What neural nets do in essence is partition an n-dimensional space into regions that uniquely map the input to the output or classify the input into distinct classes, like a funnel of sorts. Now, as the number of input values (vectors) in the input data set (which we call S) increase, it logically follows that the neural net will have a harder time separating the information. As a neural net is filled with information, the input values that are to be recalled overlap, since the input space can no longer keep everything partitioned in a finite number of dimensions. This overlap results in *crosstalk*, meaning that some inputs are not as distinct as they could be. Crosstalk might or might not be desired. Although this problem isn't a concern in all cases, it is a concern in associative memory neural nets, so to illustrate the concept, let's assume that we are trying to associate n-tuple input vectors with some output set. The output set isn't as much of a concern to proper functioning as the input set is.

If a set of inputs S is binary, we are looking at sequences in the form 1101010...10110. Let's say that our input bit vectors are only 3 bits each; therefore, the entire input space consist of these eight vectors:

$\mathbf{v}_0 = (0,0,0)$, $\mathbf{v}_1 = (0,0,1)$, $\mathbf{v}_2 = (0,1,0)$, $\mathbf{v}_3 = (0,1,1)$, $\mathbf{v}_4 = (1,0,0)$, $\mathbf{v}_5 = (1,0,1)$, $\mathbf{v}_6 = (1,1,0)$, $\mathbf{v}_7 = (1,1,1)$

To be more precise, the basis for this set of vectors is:

$\mathbf{v} = (1,0,0) * \mathbf{b}_2 + (0,1,0) * \mathbf{b}_1 + (0,0,1) * \mathbf{b}_0$,

where $\mathbf{b}_i$ can take on the values 0 or 1.

For example, if we let $\mathbf{b}_2=1$, $\mathbf{b}_1=0$, and $\mathbf{b}_0=1$, then we get the vector:

$\mathbf{v} = (1,0,0) * 1 + (0,1,0) * 0 + (0,0,1) * 1 = (1,0,0) + (0,0,0) + (0,0,1) = (1,0,1)$

which is $\mathbf{v}_5$ in our possible input set.

A *basis* is a special vector summation that describes a set of vectors in a space. So v describes all the vectors in our space. To make a long story short, the more *orthogonal* the vectors in the input set, the better they distribute in a neural net and the better they can be recalled. *Orthogonality* refers to the independence of the vectors or, in other words, if two vectors are orthogonal, their dot product is 0, their projection onto one another is 0, and they can't be written in terms of one another. In the set **v** are a lot of orthogonal vectors, but they come in small groups—for example, $\mathbf{v}_0$ is orthogonal to all the vectors, so we can always include it. But if we include $\mathbf{v}_1$ in our set **S**, the only other vectors that will fit and maintain orthogonality are $\mathbf{v}_2$ and $\mathbf{v}_4$, or the set:

$\mathbf{v}_0 = (0,0,0)$, $\mathbf{v}_1 = (0,0,1)$, $\mathbf{v}_2 = (0,1,0)$, $\mathbf{v}_4 = (1,0,0)$

Why? Because $\mathbf{v}_i \cdot \mathbf{v}_j$ for all **i,j** from 0..3 is equal to 0. In other words, the dot product of all the pairs of vectors is 0, so they must all be orthogonal. Therefore, this set will do very well in a neural net as input vectors. However, the set:

$\mathbf{v}_6 = (1,1,0)$, $\mathbf{v}_7 = (1,1,1)$

will potentially do poorly as inputs because $\mathbf{v}_6 \cdot \mathbf{v}_7$ is non-zero or, in a binary system, it is 1. The next question is, "Can we measure this orthogonality?" The answer is yes. In the binary vector system, there is a measure called *hamming distance.* It is used to measure the n-dimensional distance between binary bit vectors. The hamming distance is simply the number of bits that are different between two vectors. For example, the vectors:

$\mathbf{v}_0 = (0,0,0)$, $\mathbf{v}_1 = (0,0,1)$

have a hamming distance of 1, whereas the vectors:

$$\mathbf{v}_2 = (0,1,0), \ \mathbf{v}_4 = (1,0,0)$$

have a hamming distance of 2.

We can use hamming distance as the measure of orthogonality in binary bit vector systems, which can help us determine whether our input vectors will have a lot of overlap. Determining orthogonality with general vector inputs is harder, but the concept is the same.

That's all the time we have for concepts and terminology, so let's jump right in and see some actual neural nets that you will be able to use in your game's AI. We cover neural nets used to perform logic functions, classify inputs, and associate inputs with outputs.

Pure Logic, Mr. Spock

The first artificial neural networks were created by McCulloch and Pitts in 1943. These neural networks were composed of a number of neurodes and were typically used to compute simple logic functions such as **AND, OR, XOR,** and combinations of them. Figure 3.9.5 is a representation of a basic McCulloch-Pitts neurode with two inputs. If you are an electrical engineer, you will immediately see a close resemblance between McCulloch-Pitts neurodes and transistors or MOSFETs. In any case, McCulloch-Pitts neurodes do *not* have biases and have the simple activation function $\mathbf{f}_{mp}(\mathbf{x})$, which is equal to Equation 3.9.5.

$$\mathbf{f}_{mp}(\mathbf{x}) = 1, \ \text{if } \mathbf{x} \geq \theta \qquad\qquad (3.9.5)$$
$$0, \ \ \text{if } \mathbf{x} < \theta$$

The MP (McCulloch-Pitts) neurode functions by summing the product of the inputs $\mathbf{X}_i$ and weights $\mathbf{w}_i$ and applying the result $\mathbf{Y}_a$ to the activation function $\mathbf{f}_{mp}(\mathbf{x})$. The early research of McCulloch-Pitts focused on creating complex logical circuitry with the neurode models. In addition, one of the rules of the neurode model is that it takes one time step for a signal to travel from neurode to neurode. This helps model the biological nature of neurons more closely.

Let's take a look at some examples of MP neural nets that implement basic logic functions. The logical **AND** function has the following truth table:

X1	X2	Output
0	0	0
0	1	0
1	0	0
1	1	1

We can model this table with a two-input MP neural net with weights $\mathbf{w}_1=1$, $\mathbf{w}_2=1$, and $\theta=2$. This neural net is shown in Figure 3.9.6a. As you can see, all input

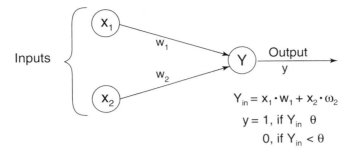

FIGURE 3.9.5. The McCulloch-Pitts neurode.

combinations work correctly. For example, if we try inputs $X_1=0$, $Y_1=1$, the activation will be:

$X_1{}^*w_1 + X_2{}^*w_2 = (1)^*(1) + (0)^*(1) = 1$

If we input 1 to the activation function $f_{mp}(x)$, the result is 0, which is correct. As another example, if we try inputs $X_1=1$, $X_2=1$, the activation will be:

$X_1{}^*w_1 + X_2{}^*w_2 = (1)^*(1) + (1)^*(1) = 2$

If we input 2 to the activation function $f_{mp}(x)$, the result is 1, which is correct. The other cases work also. The function of the **OR** is similar, but the threshold of θ is changed to 1 instead of 2, as it is in the **AND**. You can try running through the truth table yourself to see the results.

The **XOR** network is a little different because it really has two layers, in a sense, because the results of the pre-processing are further processed in the output neuron. This is a good example of the reason a neural net needs more than one layer to solve certain problems. The **XOR** is a common problem in neural nets, used to test a neural net's performance. In any case, **XOR** is not linearly separable in a single layer; it must be broken down into smaller problems and then the results added together. Let's take a look at **XOR** as the final example of MP neural networks. The truth table for **XOR** is as follows:

X1	X2	Output
0	0	0
0	1	1
1	0	1
1	1	0

XOR is true only when the inputs are different. This is a problem because both inputs map to the same output. **XOR** is not linearly separable, as shown in Figure 3.9.7. As you can see, there is no way to separate the proper responses with a straight line. The point is that we can separate the proper responses with two lines, which is just what two layers do. The first layer pre-processes or solves part of the problem, and

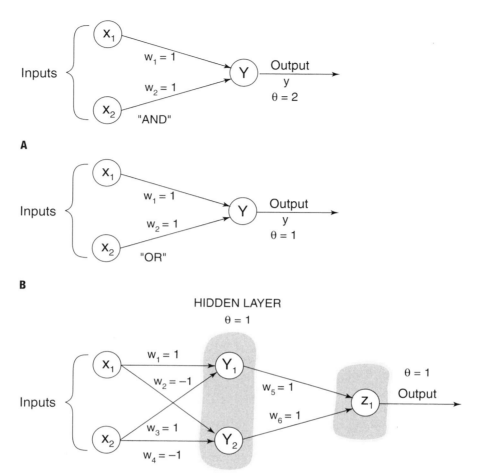

A

B

C

FIGURE 3.9.6. Basic logic functions implemented with McCulloch-Pitts nets.

the remaining layer finishes up. Referring to Figure 3.9.6c, we see that the weights are $w_1=1$, $w_2=-1$, $w_3=1$, $w_4=-1$, $w_5=1$, $w_6=1$. The network works as follows: Layer One computes whether X_1 and X_2 are opposites in parallel, the results of either case $(0,1)$ or $(1,0)$ are fed to Layer Two, which sums these up and fires if either is true. In essence, we have created the logic function:

$$z = ((X_1 \text{ AND NOT } X_2) \text{ OR } (\text{NOT } X_1 \text{ AND } X_2))$$

If you would like to experiment with the basic McCulloch-Pitts neurode, Listing 3.9.1 on the CD is a complete two-input, single-neurode simulator with which you can experiment.

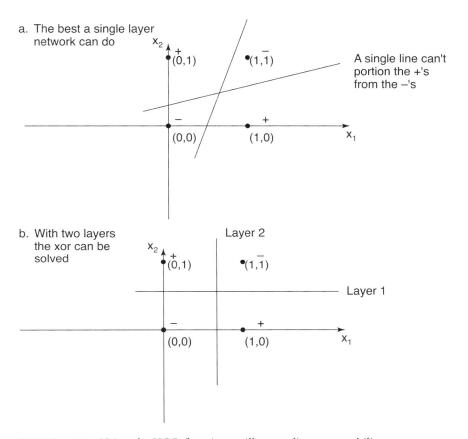

a. The best a single layer network can do

A single line can't portion the +'s from the −'s

b. With two layers the xor can be solved

Layer 2

Layer 1

FIGURE 3.9.7. Using the XOR function to illustrate linear separability.

That finishes up our discussion of the basic building block invented by McCulloch and Pitts. Now let's move on to more contemporary neural nets such as those used to classify input vectors.

Classification and "Image" Recognition

At this point, we are ready to start looking at real neural nets that have some girth to them! To segue into the following discussions on *Hebbian* and *Hopfield* neural nets, we analyze a generic neural net structure that illustrates a number of concepts such as linear separability, bipolar representations, and the analog that neural nets have with memories.

Let's begin by taking a look at Figure 3.9.8, which shows the basic neural net model we use. As you can see, it is a single-node net with three inputs, including the bias, and a single output. We will see whether we can use this network to solve the logical **AND** function that we solved so easily with McCulloch-Pitts neurodes.

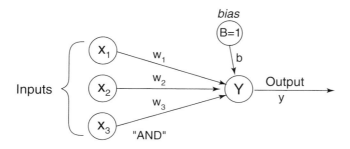

FIGURE 3.9.8. The basic neural-net model used for discussion.

Let's start by first using bipolar representations. All 0s are replaced with −1s, and 1s are left alone. The truth table for logical **AND** using bipolar inputs and outputs is as follows:

X1	X2	Output
−1	−1	−1
−1	1	−1
1	−1	−1
1	1	1

Equation 3.9.6 shows the activation function $f_c(x)$ that we will use.

$$f_c(x) = 1, \text{ if } x \geq \theta$$
$$-1, \text{ if } x < \theta \qquad\qquad (3.9.6)$$

Notice that the function is step with bipolar outputs. Before we continue, let me place a seed in your mind: The bias and threshold end up doing the same thing, giving us another degree of freedom in our neurons that make the neurons respond in ways that can't be achieved without them. You will see this concept illustrated shortly.

The single-neurode net in Figure 3.9.8 will perform a classification for us. It will tell us whether our input is in one class or another. For example, is this image a tree or *not* a tree? Or in our case, is this input (which just happens to be the logic for an **AND**) in the +1 class or the −1 class? This is the basis of most neural nets and the reason I was belaboring linear separability. We need to come up with a linear partitioning of space that maps our inputs and outputs so a solid delineation of space separates them. Thus, we need to come up with the correct weights and a bias that will do this for us. But how do we achieve this goal? Do we merely use trial and error, or is there a methodology? The answer is that there are a number of training methods to teach a neural net. These training methods work on various mathematical premises and can be proven, but for now, we simply pull some values that work out of a hat. These exercises lead us into the learning algorithms and more complex nets that follow.

All right, we are trying to find weights w_i and bias b that give use the correct result when the various inputs are fed to our network with the given activation function $f_c(x)$. Let's write down the activation summation of our neurode and see whether we can infer any relationship between the weights and the inputs that might help us. Given the inputs X_1 and X_2 with weights w_1 and w_2 along with $B=1$ and bias b, we have the following formula:

$$X_1{}^*w_1 + X_2{}^*w_2 + B^*b = \theta \qquad\qquad (3.9.7)$$

Since B is always equal to 1.0, the equation simplifies to:

$$X_1{}^*w_1 + X_2{}^*w_2 + b = \theta$$
.
.
.

$$X_2 = -X_1{}^*w_1/w_2 + (\theta-b)/w_2 \text{ (solving in terms of } X_2)$$

What is this entity? It's a line! And if the left side is greater than or equal to θ, that is, $(X_1{}^*w_1 + X_2{}^*w_2 + b)$, the neurode will fire and output 1; otherwise, the neurode will output -1. Therefore, the line is a decision boundary. Figure 3.9.9a illustrates this concept. In the figure, You can see that the slope of the line is $-w_1/w_2$, and the X_2 intercept is $(\theta-b)/w_2$. Now can you see why we can get rid of θ? It is part of a constant, and we can always scale b to take up any loss, so we assume that $\theta = 0$. The resulting equation is:

$$X_2 = -X_1{}^*w_1/w_2 - b/w_2$$

What we want to find are weights w_1 and w_2 and bias b so that it separates our outputs or classifies them into singular partitions without overlap. This is the key to linear separability. Figure 3.9.9b shows a number of decision boundaries that suffice, so we can pick any of them. Let's pick the simplest values, which are:

$$w_1 = w_2 = 1$$
$$b = -1$$

With these values, our decision boundary becomes:

$$X_2 = -X_1{}^*w_1/w_2 - b/w_2 \; -> X_2 = -1^*X_1 + 1$$

The slope is -1 and the X_2 intercept is 1. If we plug the input vectors for the logical **AND** into this equation and use the $f_c(x)$ activation function, we will get the correct outputs. For example, if $X_2 + X_1 - 1 > 0$, then fire the neurode; else output -1. Let's try it with our **AND** inputs and see what we come up with:

Input	X1	X2	Output (X2+X1−1)
−1	−1	(−1) +(−1) −1 = 3 < 0	don't fire, output −1
−1	1	(−1) + (1) −1 = −1< 0	don't fire, output −1
1	−1	(1) + (−1) −1 = −2 < 0	don't fire, output −1
1	1	(1) + (1)−1 = 1 > 0	fire, output 1

a.

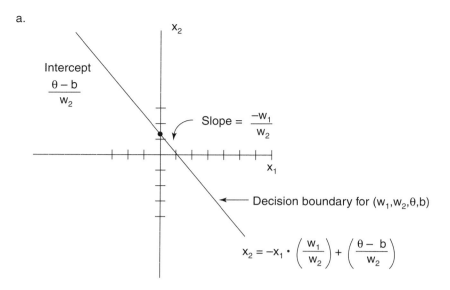

Intercept
$$\frac{\theta - b}{w_2}$$

Slope $= \dfrac{-w_1}{w_2}$

Decision boundary for (w_1, w_2, θ, b)

$$x_2 = -x_1 \cdot \left(\frac{w_1}{w_2}\right) + \left(\frac{\theta - b}{w_2}\right)$$

b.

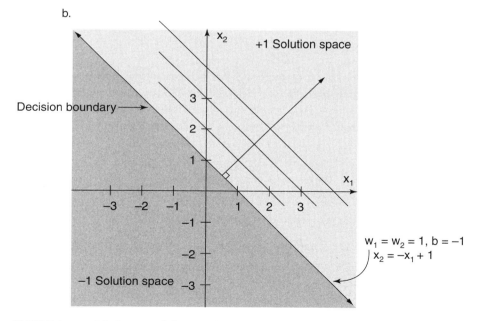

Decision boundary

+1 Solution space

$w_1 = w_2 = 1, b = -1$
$x_2 = -x_1 + 1$

−1 Solution space

FIGURE 3.9.9. Mathematical decision boundaries generated by weights, bias, and θ.

As you can see, the neural network with the proper weights and bias solves the problem perfectly. Moreover, there is a whole family of weights that will do just as well (sliding the decision boundary in a direction perpendicular to itself). However, there is an important point here. Without the bias or threshold, only lines through the origin are possible, since the X_2 intercept has to be zero. This is very important and the basis for using a bias or threshold, so this example has proven an important one, since it has flushed out this fact.

So, are we closer to seeing how to algorithmically find weights? Yes, we now have a geometrical analogy, which is the beginning of finding an algorithm.

The Ebb of Hebbian

Now we are ready to see the first learning algorithm and its application to a neural net. One of the simplest learning algorithms was invented by Donald Hebb and is based on using the input vectors to modify the weights in a way so that the weights create the best possible linear separation of the inputs and outputs. Alas, the algorithm works merely okay. Actually, for inputs that are orthogonal, it is perfect, but for non-orthogonal inputs, the algorithm falls apart. Even though the algorithm doesn't result in correct weights for all inputs, however, it is the basis of most learning algorithms, so we start here.

Before we see the algorithm, remember that it is for a single-neurode, single-layer neural net. You can, of course, place a number of neurodes in the layer, but they all work in parallel and can be taught in parallel. Are you starting to see the massive parallelization that neural nets exhibit? Instead of using a single weight vector, a multi-neurode net uses a weight matrix. The algorithm is simple; it goes like this:

Given:

- Input vectors are in bipolar form $\mathbf{I} = (-1,1,\ldots-1,1)$ and contain $\mathbf{k}$ elements.
- There are $\mathbf{n}$ input vectors, and we refer to the set as $\mathbf{I}$ and the $\mathbf{j}$th element as $\mathbf{I_j}$.
- Outputs are referred to as $\mathbf{y_j}$, and there are $\mathbf{k}$ of them, one for each input $\mathbf{I_j}$.
- The weights $\mathbf{w_1}-\mathbf{w_k}$ are contained in a single vector $\mathbf{w} = (\mathbf{w_1}, \mathbf{w_2}, \ldots \mathbf{w_k})$.

1. Initialize all your weights to 0, and let them be contained in a vector w that has n entries. Also initialize the bias b to 0.

2. For j = 1 to n, do:

   $b = b + y_j$ (where y is the desired output)

   $w = w + I_j * y_j$ (remember, this is a vector operation)

   end do

The algorithm is nothing more than an "accumulator" of sorts, shifting the decision boundary based on the changes in the input and output. The only problem is that it sometimes can't move the boundary fast enough (or at all), and so "learning" doesn't take place.

So how do we use Hebbian learning? The answer is, the same way as the previous network except that now we have an algorithmic method with which to teach the net, so we refer to the net as a *Hebb* or *Hebbian net*.

As an example, let's take our trusty logical **AND** function and see whether the algorithm can find the proper weights and bias to solve the problem. The following summation is equivalent to running the algorithm:

$$\mathbf{w} = [\mathbf{I}_1{}^*\mathbf{y}_1] + [\mathbf{I}_2{}^*\mathbf{y}_2] + [\mathbf{I}_3{}^*\mathbf{y}_3] + [\mathbf{I}_4{}^*\mathbf{y}_4] = [(-1, -1)^*(-1)] + [(-1, 1)^*(-1)] +$$
$$[(1, -1)^*(-1)] + [(1, 1)^*(1)] = (2,2)$$

$$\mathbf{b} = \mathbf{y}_1 + \mathbf{y}_2 + \mathbf{y}_3 + \mathbf{y}_4 = (-1) + (-1) + (-1) + (1) = -2$$

Therefore, $\mathbf{w}_1=2$, $\mathbf{w}_2=2$, and $\mathbf{b}=-2$. These are simply scaled versions of the values $\mathbf{w}_1=1$, $\mathbf{w}_2=1$, $\mathbf{b}=-1$ that we derived geometrically in the previous section. Killer, huh! With this simple learning algorithm, we can train a neural net (consisting of a single neurode) to respond to a set of inputs and either classify the input as true or false, 1 or −1. Now if we were to array these neurodes together to create a network of neurodes, instead of simply classifying the inputs as on or off, we can associate patterns with the inputs. This is one of the foundations for the next neural-net structure, the *Hopfield net*. One more thing: The activation function used for a Hebb net is a step with a threshold of 0 and bipolar outputs 1 and −1.

To get a feel for Hebbian learning and how to implement an actual Hebb net, Listing 3.9.2 on the CD contains a complete Hebbian Neural Net Simulator. You can create networks with up to 16 inputs and 16 neurodes (outputs). The program is self-explanatory, but there are a couple of interesting properties: You can select one of three activation functions, and you can input any kind of data. Normally, we would stick to the step activation function, and inputs/outputs would be binary or bipolar. However, in the light of discovery, maybe you will find something interesting with these added degrees of freedom. I suggest that you begin with the step function and all bipolar inputs and outputs, though.

Playing the Hopfield

John Hopfield is a physicist who likes to play with neural nets (which is good for us). He came up with a simple (in structure at least) but effective neural network called the *Hopfield net*, which is used for autoassociation. You input a vector **x** and you get **x** back (hopefully!). A Hopfield net is shown in Figure 3.9.10. It is a single-layer network with a number of neurodes equal to the number of inputs $\mathbf{X}_i$. The network is fully connected, meaning that every neurode is connected to every other neurode and the inputs are also the outputs. This structure should strike you as weird, since there is *feedback*. Feedback is one of the key features of the Hopfield net and the basis for the convergence to the correct result.

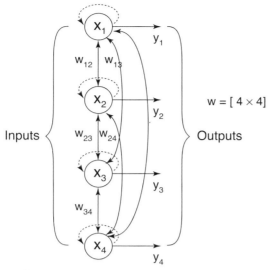

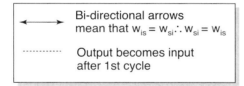

FIGURE 3.9.10. A four-node Hopfield autoassociative neural net.

The Hopfield network is an *iterative autoassociative* memory. This means that it can take one or more cycles to return the correct result (if at all). Let me clarify: The Hopfield network takes an input and then feeds it back, and the resulting output might or might not be the desired input. This feedback cycle can occur a number of times before the input vector is returned. Hence, a Hopfield network functional sequence is as follows: First, we determine the weights based on our input vectors that we want to autoassociate, then we input a vector and see what comes out of the activations. If the result is the same as our original input, we are done; if not, we take the result vector and feed it back through the network.

Now let's take a look at the weight matrix and learning algorithm used for Hopfield nets.

The learning algorithm for Hopfield nets is based on the Hebbian rule and is simply a summation of products. However, since the Hopfield network has a number of input neurons, the weights are no longer a single array or vector but a collection of vectors that are most compactly contained in a single matrix. Thus the weight matrix **W** for a Hopfield net is created based on this equation:

Given:

- Input vectors are in bipolar form $I = (-1,1,,...-1,1)$ and contain **k** elements.
- There are **n** input vectors, and we refer to the set as **I** and the jth element as I_j.
- Outputs are referred to as y_j, and there are **k** of them, one for each input I_j.
- The weight matrix **W** is square and has dimension **k×k**, since there are **k** inputs.

$$W_{(k \times k)} = \sum_{i=1}^{k} I_i^t \times I_i \qquad (3.9.8)$$

Note: Each outer product has dimension **k×k**, since we are multiplying a column vector and a row vector.

$W_{ii} = 0$, for all **i**.

Notice that there are no bias terms and the main diagonal of **W** must be all zeroes. The weight matrix is simply the sum of matrices generated by multiplying the transpose $I_i^t \times I_i$ for all **i** from 1 to **n**. This is almost identical to the Hebbian algorithm for a single neurode except that instead of multiplying the input by the output, the input is multiplied by itself, which is equivalent to the output in the case of autoassociation. Finally, the activation function $f_h(x)$ is as follows.

$$f_h(x) = \begin{array}{ll} 1, & \text{if } x \geq 0 \\ 0, & \text{if } x < 0 \end{array} \qquad (3.9.9)$$

$f_h(x)$ is a step function with a binary output. This means that the inputs must be binary, but didn't we already say that the inputs are bipolar? Well, they are, and they aren't. When the weight matrix is generated, we convert all input vectors to bipolar, but for normal operation we use the binary version of the inputs, and the output of the Hopfield net will also be binary. This convention is not necessary, but it makes the network discussion a little simpler.

Anyway, let's move on to an example. Say we want to create a four-node Hopfield net and we want it to recall these vectors:

$I_1=(0,0,1,0), \quad I_2=(1,0,0,0), \quad I_3=(0,1,0,1)$ Note: these are orthogonal.

Converting to bipolar (*), we have:

$I_1^* = (-1,-1,1,-1) , \quad I_2^* = (1,-1,-1,-1) , \quad I_3^* = (-1,1,-1,1)$

Now we need to compute W_1, W_2, W_3, where W_i is the product of the transpose of each input with itself:

$W_1 = [\, I_1^{*t} \times I_1^* \,] = (-1,-1,1,-1)^t \times (-1,-1,1,-1) =$

1	1	−1	1
1	1	−1	1
−1	−1	1	−1
1	1	−1	1

$\mathbf{W}_2 = [\mathbf{I}_2^{*t} \times \mathbf{I}_2^*] = (1,-1,-1,-1)^t \times (1,-1,-1,-1) =$

1	−1	−1	−1
−1	1	1	1
−1	1	1	1
−1	1	1	1

$\mathbf{W}_3 = [\mathbf{I}_3^{*t} \times \mathbf{I}_3^*] = (-1,1,-1,1)^t \times (-1,1,-1,1) =$

1	−1	1	−1
−1	1	−1	1
1	−1	1	−1
−1	1	−1	1

Then we add $\mathbf{W}_1 + \mathbf{W}_2 + \mathbf{W}_3$, resulting in:

$\mathbf{W}_{(1+2+3)} =$

3	−1	−1	−1
−1	3	−1	3
−1	−1	3	−1
−1	3	−1	3

Zeroing out the main diagonal gives us the final weight matrix:

$\mathbf{W} =$

0	−1	−1	−1
−1	0	−1	3
−1	−1	0	−1
−1	3	−1	0

That's it, now we are ready to rock. Let's input our original vectors and see the results. To do this, we simply multiply the input by the matrix and then process each output value with our activation function $\mathbf{f}_h(\mathbf{x})$. Here are the results:

$\mathbf{I}_1 \times \mathbf{W} = (-1,-1,0,-1)$ and $\mathbf{f}_h((-1,-1,0,-1)) = (0,0,1,0)$

$\mathbf{I}_2 \times \mathbf{W} = (0,-1,-1,-1)$ and $\mathbf{f}_h((0,-1,-1,-1)) = (1,0,0,0)$

$\mathbf{I}_3 \times \mathbf{W} = (-2,3,-2,3)$ and $\mathbf{f}_h((-2,3,-2,3)) = (0,1,0,1)$

The inputs were perfectly recalled, and they should be, since they were all orthogonal. As a final example, let's assume that our input (visual, auditory, etc.) is a little noisy and the input has a single error in it. Let's take $\mathbf{I}_3 = (0,1,0,1)$ and add some noise to $\mathbf{I}_3$, resulting in $\mathbf{I}_3^{noise} = (0,1,1,1)$. Now let's see what happens if we input this noisy vector to the Hopfield net:

$\mathbf{I}_3^{noise} \times \mathbf{W} = (-3, 2, -2, 2)$ and $\mathbf{f}_h((-3,2,-2, 2)) = (0,1,0,1)$

Amazingly enough, the original vector is recalled. This is very cool. So we might have a memory that is filled with bit patterns that look like trees (oaks, weeping willow, spruce, redwood, etc.). If we input another tree that is similar to, say, a weeping willow but hasn't been entered into the net, our net will (hopefully) output a weeping willow, indicating that this is what it "thinks" it looks like.

This is one of the strengths of associative memories: We don't have to teach the network every possible input. We just have to teach it enough to give it a good idea. Then inputs that are "close" will usually converge to an actual trained input. This is the basis for image and voice recognition systems.

To complete our study of neural nets, I have included a Hopfield autoassociative simulator that allows you to create nets with up to 16 neurodes. It is similar to the Hebb net, but you must use a step activation function and your input exemplars must be in bipolar while training and binary while associating (running). Listing 3.9.3 on the CD contains the code for the simulator.

Conclusion

I hope that this article has given you an idea of what neural nets are and how to create some working computer programs to model them. We covered basic terminology and concepts, some mathematical foundations, and finished up with some of the more prevalent neural-net structures.

However, there is still so much more to learn about neural nets: Perceptrons, fuzzy associative memories (FAMs), bidirectional associative memories (BAMs), Kohonen maps, Adalines, Madalines, back-propagation networks, adaptive resonance theory networks, "brain state in a box," and a lot more. Well, that's it, my neural net wants to play PlayStation 2!

POLYGONAL TECHNIQUES

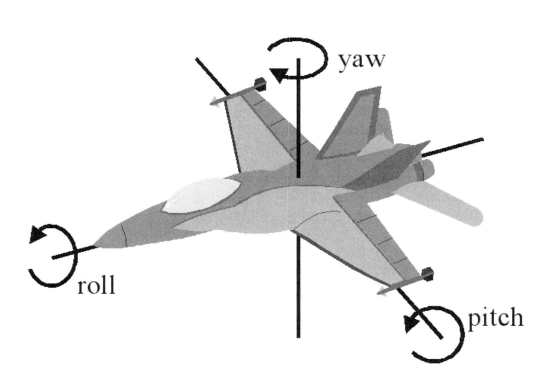

4.0

Optimizing Vertex Submission for OpenGL

Herbert Marselas

There are a number of functions available for submitting and rendering vertices in OpenGL, which range from the simple immediate mode functions to more complicated multiple vertex functions and vendor-specific extensions. However, the performance can vary greatly depending on the functionality used.

Immediate Mode

Often, immediate mode functions (e.g., `glVertex*`, `glColor*`, `glNormal*`) are used to get up and rendering quickly. These are easy to use since each function is geared toward submitting a different component of the vertex: position, color, normal, texture coordinates, etc. However, what makes the immediate mode functions so easy to use (submitting a vertex component by component) also makes them the lowest performing.

This is due to two factors. First, several function calls are required to render a single vertex. Second, each function must be entered, where it then performs a small amount of work, and then exited. The time required to enter and leave a function is called the *function overhead*. This overhead occurs regardless of the amount of work the function does, and represents a fixed amount of time required to use the function. If the function does a lot of work, then the overhead will be low compared to the work being accomplished. If the function doesn't do a lot of work, or if the function is called a large number of times, the overhead can quickly add up.

Figure 4.0.1 shows the amount of time in CPU cycles required to submit 300 colored, textured, and transformed vertices using the immediate mode functions `glTexture3f`, `glColor4f`, and `glVertex3f`. The 300 vertices comprise 100, three-pixel, discrete, uniform, right triangles. These timings were taken under Microsoft Windows 98 on a 450MHz Pentium II using a popular consumer OpenGL graphics card. The source code used to generate this data can be found as a Microsoft Visual C++ 6 project on the accompanying CD.

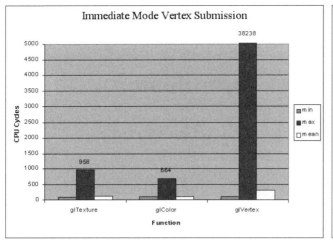
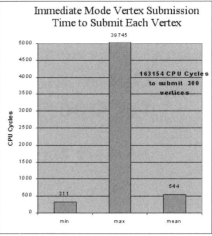

FIGURE 4.0.1 CPU cycles to submit 300 vertices (100 discrete triangles) using immediate mode.

Using small transformed triangles removes the time spent in transform (they are already transformed), lighting (they are pre-lit), and rasterization (they are very small). This guarantees that we are effectively measuring the time required to enter each function, store the data, and return. In total, it required ~163,154 CPU cycles to submit and render all 300 vertices.

On average, it took ~544 CPU cycles to submit the position, color, and texture coordinate of a single vertex. However, there were spikes in performance. This can be seen in the glVertex function that took ~38238 CPU cycles the first time it was called during a frame, probably to allocate data, although more detailed analysis of the driver would be required to verify this. It then averaged ~308 CPU cycles per call with spikes up to ~1500+ CPU cycles per call. The full analysis is contained in a Microsoft Excel 97 spreadsheet on the accompanying CD.

The simplest way of improving performance would be to remove the function overhead by reducing the number of functions called to submit and render the 300 vertices. Calling one or two functions to submit and render all 300 vertices could be much higher performing than calling 900 functions as we have just done.

Interleaved Data

If your vertex data is already contained in a single structure, `glInterleavedArrays` can be used to submit all the components of the vertex in a single function call. `glInterleavedArrays` is capable of submitting a number of standard interleaved vertex structures ranging from a lightweight position-only vertex, to a heavyweight vertex with position, normal, diffuse color, and texture coordinates.

`glInterleavedArrays` only submits a pointer to the vertices to be rendered. Another function such as `glDrawArrays`, `glDrawElements`, or `glArrayElement` must be called to actually render the data.

Applying the use of `glInterleavedArrays` to the previous immediate mode example, a single function call could be used to submit all of the data for a single vertex. However, as its name implies, `glInterleavedArrays` can accept an array of vertices to submit for rendering. This allows us to make a single function call to submit all 300 vertices, rather than three calls per vertex (900 total) in immediate mode.

In the case of the test data, an array of 300 vertices is generated using the `glInterleavedArrays` GL_T2F_C3F_V3F vertex structure format. This effectively duplicates the data that was submitted and rendered by the immediate mode functions.

Figure 4.0.2 The amount of time required to submit and render the vertex workload using `glInterleavedArrays` and `glDrawArrays`. The average time to submit the 300 triangle workload is ~72,821 CPU cycles. This is less than half the time (~44%) that was required by the immediate mode functions to submit and render the same workload.

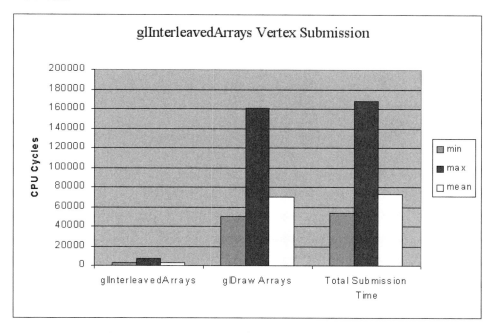

FIGURE 4.0.2   Submitting vertices with glInterleavedArrays.

Strided and Streamed Data

Another alternative vertex submission interface is the `gl*Pointer` functions. Similar to `glInterleavedArrays`, pointers to the vertex data are submitted using the `gl*Pointer`

Independent Data Streams

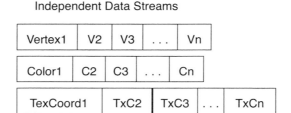

Interleaved Data

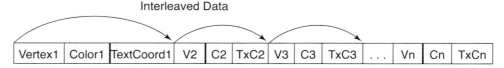

FIGURE 4.0.3 Streamed vs. interleaved data.

functions (e.g., glVertexPointer, glColorPointer). The submitted vertex data is then rendered using the glDrawArrays, glArrayElement, or glDrawElements functions.

The gl*Pointer functions also have a uniform stride parameter, similar to glInterleavedArrays. The stride specifies the number of bytes from the beginning of one vertex component to the next. When the stride is greater than zero, the operation of the gl*Pointer functions is essentially the same as making a single call to glInterleavedArrays. When the stride is zero (the data is tightly packed together), the data is referred to as stream data (Figure 4.0.3).

Stream data is very important when using SIMD (Single Instruction Multiple Data) instruction sets like Intel's SSE (Streaming SIMD Instructions) or AMD's 3DNow! instructions to transform, light, and/or clip vertices. If the data was in an interleaved vertex format, the data must be moved piecemeal into and out of the CPU's SIMD registers. With the data in stream format, the CPU can quickly and easily move large chunks of the data into the SIMD registers for processing.

Even without taking advantage of the CPU's SIMD instructions for geometry and lighting, a performance boost can be had just by using the gl*Pointer functions.

It takes on average ~51,212 CPU cycles to submit and render the 300 vertex workload using the gl*Pointer functions with glDrawArrays (Figure 4.0.4) as compared to ~72,821 CPU cycles using glInterleavedArrays and glDrawArrays (Figure 4.0.3). This is ~30% reduction in time. Again, the performance increase would be even larger if we were relying on SIMD CPU instructions to perform geometry and lighting operations.

Compiled Vertex Arrays

The compiled vertex arrays extension (EXT_compiled_vertex_array) builds upon the functionality of glInterleavedArrays and the gl*Pointer functions. The compiled

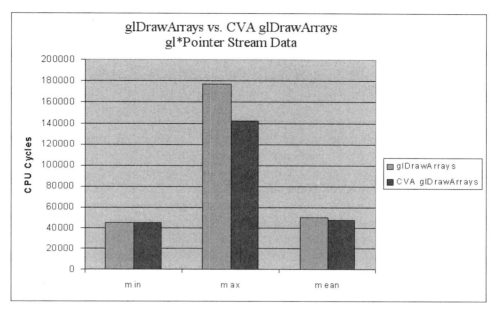

FIGURE 4.0.4 Vertex submission time for glDrawArrays with and without Compiled Vertex Arrays.

vertex array (CVA) function allows the application to specify a range of data in the arrays supplied by glInterleavedArrays or gl*Pointer that won't be changed by the application. These allow the driver to optimize the data range once, and re-use the optimized version until the application unlocks the data.

This can result in significant speed increases by allowing the CPU's transform and lighting implementation to re-arrange the data for optimal access. It can also allow the rendering hardware to modify the data for faster performance, or even make a local copy of it on the graphics adapter for faster access.

The performance difference between using CVA and not using CVA is not very large in our test workload (Figure 4.0.4), but this is only because we are attempting to quantify the overhead of the function. The performance differential would be substantially greater if the vertices were being transformed, lit, and clipped, or if there were more of them.

CVA is very useful for data that is static, or that can be used multiple times before being modified. If the data is only used once, then the overhead of using CVA may outweigh the benefit. To improve the performance of dynamic data, the only current alternative is to use a vendor-specific extension.

Eliminating Data Copy—Vendor Extensions

With both the immediate mode functions and the array functions when not using CVA, the data submitted for rendering must be copied from application-allocated memory to driver-allocated memory. As any data copy takes time, eliminating the copy is an easy performance win.

CVA reduces this copy to a single time when the vertex array is locked. However, CVA assumes that the data is static or will be used repeatedly before being modified. The problem of copying data from application memory to driver memory still exists for dynamic arrays of data that are frequently updated or changed.

The only way to remove this copy would be for the application to store vertices directly in driver-allocated memory, and some vendors support this as an extension. The nVidia extension `wglAllocateMemoryNV` is one such vendor-specific extension. It allocates memory directly accessible to the graphics card where the application can store vertex data. This eliminates the need for any driver copying of data, and improves the performance when a vertex array is submitted and then immediately rendered since the data is ready to go.

Check with your vendor for their specific OpenGL extensions.

Data Format

A second area of consideration is the format that vertices are submitted in for rendering triangles. Vertex lists, like those used in the test workload, are the most common format. In a vertex list, three vertices define each triangle (Figure 4.0.5a). However, when triangles share vertices, there's often no reason to repeatedly include the same vertex. One alternative is to use triangle strips or fans (Figure 4.0.5b).

Discrete, strip, or fan triangles are identified by the mode parameters of `glDrawArrays` and `glDrawElements`. These are GL_TRIANGLES, GL_TRIANGLE_STRIP, and GL_TRIANGLE_FAN, respectively.

Utilizing a separate array of vertex indices to build faces from the vertex array is another way to reduce the number of vertices required to draw a number of triangles (Figure 4.0.5c). `glDrawElements` is similar to `glDrawArrays`, but it adds a new parameter that accepts the face vertex index list.

Using both triangle strips and face vertex indexing, it's possible to lower the vertex per triangle ratio to almost 1:1 for some complex triangle meshes. On many types

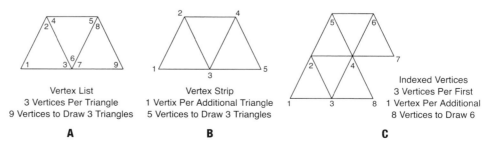

FIGURE 4.0.5 A, B, C. Vertices for *a:* three discrete triangles, *b:* three strip triangles, and *c:* six indexed triangles.

of data, however, triangle *lists* combined with face vertex indexing are nearly as fast, and require less pre-processing to create.

General Recommendations

There are also a number of general recommendations for increasing vertex submission and rendering performance.

1. When using indexed data, care should be taken to co-locate all the vertices for a single triangle as near to each other as possible. If the vertices required for a triangle are too far apart in the array, it may cause the graphics adapter to continually re-process sub-parts of the array as it jumps around.
2. Pre-sorting vertex data by material, shader, and texture settings can help increase the number of vertices that can be submitted and/or rendered in a single function call.
3. Keep the amount of information submitted per vertex as lean as possible. Don't include extra information that's only used occasionally. This must be balanced with continually changing vertex formats. For example, don't submit a vertex with additional color information if that information is rarely used.
4. There is a balance between submitting too little data and too much data. Most array functions require at least 10–50 vertices to be submitted to overcome the function overhead. On the upper end of the scale, no more than 32k–64k of data of vertex data should be submitted. These amounts vary by graphics adapter.
5. Spending too much time getting a lot of vertex data together into a single buffer (if it's not a driver-allocated buffer) can present more problems than it solves on the CPU. These include cache issues, letting the graphics card stall, and overwhelming the function with too much data.

Conclusions

1. Immediate mode functions may be easy to use when getting started, but they are the lowest performing functions for submitting vertices for rendering (Figure 4.0.6).
2. Submit and/or render as many vertices as is feasible in a single function call.
3. Use Compiled Vertex Arrays (CVA) for static data, or for data that doesn't change very often.
4. For the best CPU transform and lighting performance, use streamed data formats with CVA.
5. Some vendors will provide specific vertex submission extensions for even higher performance.
6. Use indexed vertex data with discrete or strip triangles to increase the number of triangles that can be drawn with the smallest number of vertices.

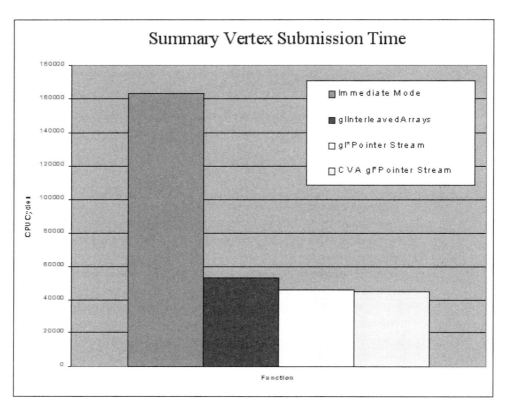

FIGURE 4.0.6 Summary comparison of vertex submission and rendering time by function.

References

[ARB] OpenGL Extensions. OpenGL ARB. Available www.opengl.org.

[Kempf97] Kempf, R., and Frazier, C., *OpenGL Reference Manual* 2nd Edition, Addison-Wesley Developers Press, 1997.

[Spitzer00] Spitzer, John F., Maximizing OpenGL Performance for GPUs. Online. 08 March 2000. Available www.nvidia.com.

4.1

Tweaking a Vertex's Projected Depth Value

Eric Lengyel

Many games need to render special effects such as scorch marks on a wall or footprints on the ground that are not an original part of a scene, but are created during gameplay. These types of decorative additions are usually decaled onto an existing surface, and thus consist of polygons that are coplanar with other polygons in a scene. The problem is that pixels rendered as part of one polygon rarely have exactly the same depth value as pixels rendered as part of a coplanar polygon. The result is an undesired pattern in which parts of the original surface show through the decaled polygons.

The goal is to find a way to offset a polygon's depth in a scene without changing its projected screen coordinates or altering its texture mapping perspective. Most 3D graphics libraries contain some kind of polygon offset function to help achieve this goal. However, these solutions generally lack fine control and usually incur a per-vertex performance cost. This article presents an alternative method that modifies the projection matrix to achieve the depth offset effect.

Examining the Projection Matrix

Let us first examine the effect of the standard OpenGL perspective projection matrix on an eye space point $\mathbf{P} = (P_x, P_y, P_z, 1)$. To simplify our matrix, we assume that the view frustum is centered about the z-axis in eye space (i.e., the rectangle on the near clipping plane carved out by the four side planes has the property that *left* = *−right* and *bottom* = *−top*). Calling the distance to the near clipping plane n and the distance to the far clipping plane f, we have:

$$
\begin{bmatrix} n & 0 & 0 & 0 \\ 0 & n & 0 & 0 \\ 0 & 0 & -\dfrac{f+n}{f-n} & -\dfrac{2fn}{f-n} \\ 0 & 0 & -1 & 0 \end{bmatrix} \cdot \begin{bmatrix} P_x \\ P_y \\ P_z \\ 1 \end{bmatrix} = \begin{bmatrix} nP_x \\ nP_y \\ -\dfrac{f+n}{f-n}P_z - \dfrac{2fn}{f-n} \\ -P_z \end{bmatrix} . \qquad (4.1.1)
$$

To finish the projection, we need to divide this result by its w-coordinate, which has the value $-P_z$. This division gives us the following projected 3D point, which we will call **P'**.

$$
\mathbf{P}' = \begin{bmatrix} -\dfrac{nP_x}{P_z} \\[2mm] -\dfrac{nP_y}{P_z} \\[2mm] \dfrac{f+n}{f-n} + \dfrac{2fn}{P_z(f-n)} \end{bmatrix} \qquad (4.1.2)
$$

Recall that the near clipping plane lies at $z = -n$, and the far clipping plane lies at $z = -f$ since the camera points in the negative z direction. Thus, plugging $-n$ and $-f$ into Equation 4.1.2 for P_z gives us the expected z values of -1 and 1 bounding the normalized clipping volume. Also recall that this mapping from $[-n..-f]$ to $[-1..1]$ is a function of inverse z. This is necessary so that linear interpolation by the 3D hardware of values in the depth buffer remain perspective correct.

Tweaking the Depth Value

It is clear from Equation 4.1.2 that preserving the value of $-P_z$ for the w-coordinate will guarantee the preservation of the projected x- and y-coordinates as well. From this point forward, we shall only concern ourselves with the lower-right 2×2 portion of the projection matrix, since this is the only part that affects the z- and w-coordinates. The projected z-coordinate may be altered without disturbing the w-coordinate by introducing a factor of $1 + \varepsilon$, for some small ε, as follows.

$$
\begin{bmatrix} -(1+\varepsilon)\dfrac{f+n}{f-n} & -\dfrac{2fn}{f-n} \\ -1 & 0 \end{bmatrix} \cdot \begin{bmatrix} P_z \\ 1 \end{bmatrix} = \begin{bmatrix} -(1+\varepsilon)\dfrac{f+n}{f-n}P_z - \dfrac{2fn}{f-n} \\ -P_z \end{bmatrix} \qquad (4.1.3)
$$

After division by w, we arrive at the following value for the projected z-coordinate.

$$P'_z = \left(1 + \varepsilon\right)\frac{f + n}{f - n} + \frac{2fn}{P_z\left(f - n\right)}$$

$$= \frac{f + n}{f - n} + \frac{2fn}{P_z\left(f - n\right)} + \varepsilon\frac{f + n}{f - n} \tag{4.1.4}$$

Comparing this to the z-coordinate in Equation 4.1.2, we see that we have found a way to offset projected depth values by a constant $\varepsilon\frac{f+n}{f-n}$.

Choosing an Appropriate Epsilon

Due to the nonlinear nature of the z-buffer, the constant offset given in Equation 4.1.4 corresponds to a larger eye space difference far from the camera than it does near the camera. While this constant offset may work well for some applications, there is no single solution that works for every application at all depths. The best we can do is choose an appropriate ε given an eye space offset δ and a depth value P_z which collectively represents the object that we are offsetting. To determine a formula for ε, let us examine the result of applying the standard projection matrix from Equation 4.1.1 to a point whose z-coordinate has been offset by some small δ.

$$\begin{bmatrix} -\dfrac{f+n}{f-n} & -\dfrac{2fn}{f-n} \\ -1 & 0 \end{bmatrix} \cdot \begin{bmatrix} P_z + \delta \\ 1 \end{bmatrix} = \begin{bmatrix} -\dfrac{f+n}{f-n}\left(P_z + \delta\right) - \dfrac{2fn}{f-n} \\ -\left(P_z + \delta\right) \end{bmatrix} \tag{4.1.5}$$

Dividing by w, we have the following value for the projected z-coordinate.

$$P'_z = \frac{f+n}{f-n} + \frac{2fn}{\left(P_z + \delta\right)\left(f - n\right)}$$

$$= \frac{f+n}{f-n} + \frac{2fn}{P_z\left(f-n\right)} + \frac{2fn}{f-n}\left(\frac{1}{P_z + \delta} - \frac{1}{P_z}\right) \tag{4.1.6}$$

Equating this result to Equation 4.1.4 and simplifying a bit, we end up with:

$$\varepsilon = -\frac{2fn}{f+n}\left(\frac{\delta}{P_z\left(P_z + \delta\right)}\right). \tag{4.1.7}$$

A good value of δ for a particular application can be found with a little experimentation. In should be kept in mind that δ is an eye space offset, and thus becomes less effective as P_z gets larger. For an m-bit integer depth buffer, we want to make sure that:

$$|\varepsilon| \geq \frac{1}{2^m - 1}\left(\frac{f - n}{f + n}\right) \tag{4.1.8}$$

since smaller values of ε will not yield an offset significant enough to alter the integer depth value. Substituting the right side of Equation 4.1.7 for ε and solving for δ gives us:

$$\delta \geq \frac{kP_z^2}{1 - kP_z} \tag{4.1.9}$$

or:

$$\delta \leq \frac{-kP_z^2}{1 + kP_z} \tag{4.1.10}$$

where the constant k is given by:

$$k = \frac{f - n}{2\,fn\left(2^m - 1\right)}. \tag{4.1.11}$$

Equation 4.1.9 gives us the minimum effective value for δ when offsetting a polygon toward the camera (the usual case), and Equation 4.1.10 gives us the maximum effective value for δ when offsetting a polygon away from the camera.

Implementation

The following sample code demonstrates how the projection matrix shown in Equation 4.1.3 may be implemented under OpenGL. The function `LoadOffsetMatrix` takes the same six values that are passed to the OpenGL function `glFrustum`. It also takes values for δ and P_z that are used to calculate ε.

Source Code

```
#include <gl.h>

void LoadOffsetMatrix(GLdouble l, GLdouble r,
GLdouble b, GLdouble t,
GLdouble n, GLdouble f,
GLfloat delta, GLfloat pz)
{
    GLfloat matrix[16];
```

```
        // Set up standard perspective projection
        glMatrixMode(GL_PROJECTION);
        glFrustum(l, r, b, t, n, f);

        // Retrieve the projection matrix
        glGetFloatv(GL_PROJECTION_MATRIX, matrix);

        // Calculate epsilon with equation (4.1.7)
        GLfloat epsilon = -2.0F * f * n * delta /
        ((f + n) * pz * (pz + delta));

        // Modify entry (3,3) of the projection matrix
        matrix[10] *= 1.0F + epsilon;

        // Send the projection matrix back to OpenGL
        glLoadMatrixf(matrix);
}
```

4.2

The Vector Camera

David Paull

The vector camera is a generalized form of the matrix-based camera found in many traditional graphics engines. Matrices are often difficult to read due to the fact that they typically hold several operations concatenated together. The vector camera uses only simple vectors to describe its orientation, position, field of view, and aspect ratio. This format allows for some interesting optimizations to the overall graphics pipeline. The vector camera uses the same information found in matrix-based cameras. The world-to-camera matrix (view matrix) is broken down into four vectors. As you can see in Figure 4.2.1, a view matrix is really four vectors.

Three vectors represent the three axes that define the camera's orientation, and one vector represents the camera's position in the world coordinate space. In total, this provides six degrees of freedom. In some graphics engines, you may need to invert the view matrix to be compatible with the vector camera. Figure 4.2.2 shows a scene with the vector camera and a cube model. It also shows the viewing pyramid that defines the limits of the camera's view.

The main advantage to the vector camera is that it can operate in both local and world coordinate space. The camera's orientation and position vectors are stored in world space; however, they can be inverse transformed into local space using the inverse of the model's local-to-world matrix. The camera and the object won't move in relation to each other; rather, the camera's new orientation and position are relative to the local space object. These are the only transformations required to render the

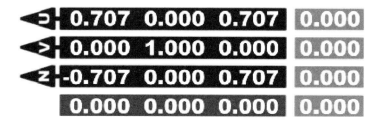

FIGURE 4.2.1. The view matrix is composed of four vectors.

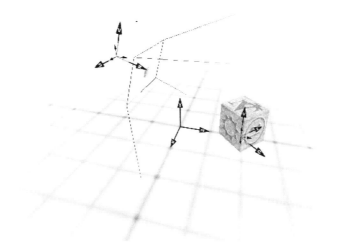

FIGURE 4.2.2. Illustration of the vector camera.

object. Now that the vector camera is in local space, it can project the local space coordinates, and no further transformations are required. After doing almost no work, the vector camera can now cycle through each of the local space vertices in the model, and project them into 2D screen coordinates. If the model is static, like a mountain, the model data can be stored in world space. This allows for an even faster code path. With both the object and the camera in world space, no inverse matrix needs to be calculated, and no transformations are required at all.

These diagrams use a left-handed coordinate system with the Y-axis pointing up. The vector camera's position is $(0, 2, -2)$, and has a small rotation about the U-axis to tilt the camera down. The box's position is $(0, 0, 2)$, and has a rotation of 45 degrees about the Y-axis. The smaller arrows show world (x, y, z)-axis vectors to help illustrate rotations.

Introduction to the Vector Camera

The vector camera uses three vectors to represent its orientation. The U, V, and N vectors are parallel to the X, Y, and Z origin vectors, respectively, if the camera has no rotation and is positioned at $(0,0,0)$. The U vector points to the right, the V vector points up, and the N vector points in the direction that the camera is facing. Figure 4.2.3 shows the vector camera with its 3D screen. This 3D screen is created using the camera's *U*, *V*, and *N* vectors, and two field of view parameters. The field of view parameters are calculated using a user-defined field of view that is then scaled by the aspect ratio. There are many ways to calculate the field of view parameters. For these examples, I used the following code :

```
float AspectRatio = ScreenHeight/ScreenWidth;
float FOV = pi/2;
float hFrac = tan(FOV*0.5);
float vFrac = tan(FOV*0.5*AspectRatio);
```

If the camera had no rotations or translations, the vectors would be defined as follows:

```
O vector = -U vector * hFrac + V vector * vFrac
S vector =  U vector * hFrac * 2
T vector = -V vector * vFrac * 2
```

The 3D screen is created by adding these vectors. For this example, the distance to the near plane is 1.0; thus, starting at the camera's position, add 1.0 * *N* vector. Then add the *O* vector. This defines the point in 3D that will be called the screen origin. The *S* and *T* vectors originate from this point. The *S* and *T* vectors define lines of constant screen *X* and screen *Y*, respectively. It is analogous to adding a screen-sized texture to the quad defined by the *S* and *T* vectors. Using the world space position of the camera and the world space *S* and *T* vectors, any point in world space can be projected into screen coordinates using the following method. A vector is created starting at the world space position of the camera, which ends at the world space position of the vertex to be projected. If the vertex is in view of the camera, we can calculate the 3D point where the ray intersects the 3D screen of the vector camera. This intersection point is shown in Figure 4.2.3 and Figure 4.2.4 as the *P* vector. Then using the vector dot product, the distance along both the *S* and *T* vectors can be found, which essentially converts the values into 2D. These 2D values are rescaled based on the current display resolution, and the result is 2D screen coordinates ready for display.

Local Space Optimization

The camera vectors are stored in world space; however models are typically stored in local space, sometimes called model space. The model is centered around (0,0,0) and is accompanied by a local-to-world matrix. This local-to-world matrix defines how the object will rotate and translate in order to end up in its final world space orientation and position. Since the model data is stored in local space, it would be advantageous to be able to work in local space. In order to accomplish this, the camera must be moved from world space into local space. The camera must be rotated and translated about the object, such that the camera's new orientation and position retains the same spatial relationship as if the object was transformed local-to-world, and viewed by the camera in world space. The solution is the inverse of the model's local-to-world

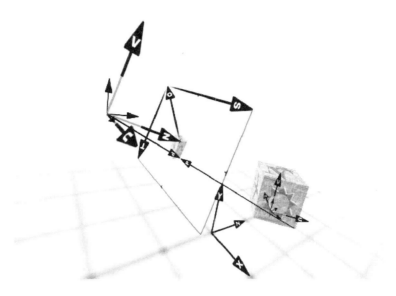

FIGURE 4.2.3. Using the P vector.

matrix. The inverse of a rotation matrix is calculated in two parts. The first part performs a transpose of the upper 3×3 rotation matrix. The second part uses three dot products to calculate the new position. This inverse matrix can perform the opposite operation of world-to-local.

Please note that there are really two local-to-world transformations that need to be preserved. The camera has an assumed local-to-world already applied to the camera's orientation and position; thus, we only need to worry about the object's local-to-world matrix. The newly created world-to-local matrix defines how the camera's orientation and position will rotate and translate in order to preserve the spatial relationship between the object and the camera. As you can see in Figure 4.2.3, the cube has undergone the local-to-world transformation, which is a slow per-vertex process. Also in Figure 4.2.3, note the camera's world position and orientation for comparison with Figure 4.2.4. You can see in Figure 4.2.4 that the cube is in its local coordinate space without any rotation or translation. The camera, however, has been rotated and translated such that the camera generates the same image found in Figure 4.2.3. Moving the camera into local space is computationally faster than moving the local data into world space. Only four transforms are required to move the camera into local space, while it takes N transforms to move a shape with N vertices from local-to-world. Once the model data and the camera data are in the same coordinate space, projection of the model data requires little computation.

Now that the camera is in local space, some additional optimizations are possible. If you store the plane normal for each triangle with your model, back facing can be

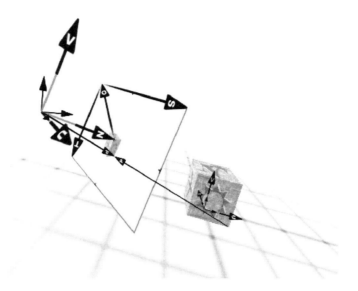

FIGURE 4.2.4. The cube resides in a local coordinate space.

performed using a single dot product. If the triangle faces the camera, all of its vertices are flagged as visible. When the entire object has been back-face culled, only the visible vertices will need to be projected.

Conclusion

The vector camera is a handy way of representing the camera math for use in software or hardware 3D rendering engines. Its simplicity allows the freedom to intuitively place and manipulate the camera. The camera's ability to work in the local coordinate space allows for several well-known optimizations to have a larger impact on rendering speed than they do on traditional matrix-based cameras. The vector camera provides a consistent 25% increase in frame rate. It accomplishes this by reducing the number of required transforms, computing small final packets for display, and using a low amount of memory overall. The projection math is flexible enough that it can also be applied to any focus-based frustum like shadow volumes. Sometimes, the best optimization is to redesign the method, rather than squeeze performance out of the existing method!.

The OpenGL source code to the vector camera is included with this book. For the latest version of the source code, please visit the Tanzanite Software Website at www.tanzanite.to. All diagrams used in this article were rendered using the TechNature engine.

Camera Control Techniques

Dante Treglia II

The interactive nature of games is the key element in what attracts and enthralls the player. The fact that one can become so many different characters, from a sexy, scantily clad warrior to an Italian plumber with the charm to attract a princess, is what entices so many people to purchase games. But in order to allow the player to see the world through a different set of eyes, the game needs to have a solid camera model. This is where camera control enters the picture. This article will outline a few basic techniques that can be used to develop the proper camera model for your game.

A Basic First-Person Camera

Look-At

Basic first-person camera models rely on "look-at" utilities such as OpenGL's `glu-LookAt()`. Given a camera position, view direction, and up vector, this function returns an orientation view matrix. The view matrix is then placed on the OpenGL `MODELVIEW` matrix stack and concatenated with orientation matrices for each object in the scene as they are rendered. This camera model is very easy to implement, and quite useful. An implementation of this function can be found in the C++ matrix library.

Euler Angles

Orientation in three-dimensional space can be represented with three Euler angles: yaw, pitch, and roll (also known as azimuth, elevation, and roll). Yaw, pitch, and roll account for the rotation in the Y-axis, X-axis, Z-axis, respectively as illustrated in Figure 4.3.1.

One method for calculating the orientation matrix is to concatenate the three axes' rotation matrices. However, for control purposes, it is necessary to maintain the current position as well as information about the camera's X (side), Y (up), and $-Z$ (forward) directions. The forward, side, and up vectors are used to calculate the camera's forward movement, strafe, and jump, respectively. The following code gives a function that calculates these vectors, which can be used as parameters to the `glu-LookAt()` function to produce the camera's view matrix.

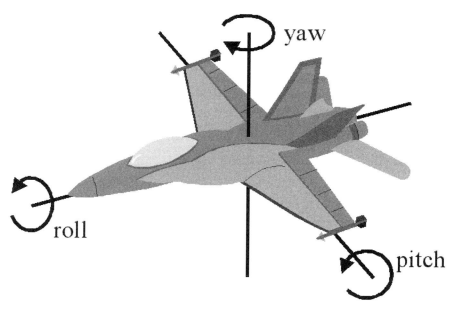

FIGURE 4.3.1. An image of a plane with the yaw, pitch, and roll angles described.

```
void FlyCam::ComputeInfo() {
    float cosY, cosP, cosR;
    float sinY, sinP, sinR;

    // Only Want to Calc these once
    cosY = cosf(Y);
    cosP = cosf(P);
    cosR = cosf(R);
    sinY = sinf(Y);
    sinP = sinf(P);
    sinR = sinf(R);

    // Fwd Vector
    fwd.x = sinY * cosP;
    fwd.y = sinP;
    fwd.z = cosP * -cosY;

    // Look At Point
    at = fwd + eye;

    // Up Vector
    up.x = -cosY * sinR - sinY * sinP * cosR;
    up.y = cosP * cosR;
    up.z = -sinY * sinR - sinP * cosR * -cosY;

    // Side Vector (right)
    side = CrossProduct(fwd, up);
}
```

Controls

Methods for moving the camera's orientation and position through the scene are very game-dependent. For example, the camera position of a first-person shooter will most likely follow the contours of the environment. A very accurate flight simulator will rely on other environmental factors such as engine thrust, altitude, air conditions, turbulence, etc. I'm only going to cover the necessary components to get you off the ground. Let's assume that the user's input device is a keyboard and a mouse, but keep in mind that these techniques can be easily applied to almost any input device, including joysticks, console controllers, and even VR devices.

The most intuitive control using Euler angles is to map the *yaw* to the mouse's (screen-relative) *X* position, and the *pitch* to the *Y* position. This mapping will mimic the camera control found in Quake, which allows the user to change their view rapidly with two degrees of freedom. This technique can be used in conjunction with other camera models. For example, *Super Mario64* was mostly a third-person game, but also included the ability to examine the world through Mario's eyes. Since *roll* is not a common human experience, it is usually disregarded.

The camera's interaction with the environment is a very game-specific topic. As I mentioned earlier, the forward, side, and up vectors are used for controlling the position of the camera, and should tie directly into your game engine. However you choose to incorporate these vectors, I strongly recommend that you use time-based physics. This will ensure that your controls are frame-rate independent and give the game a more realistic feel. At a bare minimum, you should interpret the user's input as a velocity in the desired direction. Since you have the camera's orthogonal orientation basis vectors (forward, side, up), the implementation is a simple one-dimensional physics problem:

```
position += deltaTime * inputSpeed * forward
```

Accelerations can also be applied to achieve damping effects. In the sample code, I have consolidated these control techniques into a flying camera that allows you to move the view in any direction.

Scripted Camera

Scripted cameras are a crucial part of many games, from cinematic scenes in role-playing games to helicopter fly-throughs of a golf course. Most games that use this camera technique use an animation package to script the camera, then import the animation into their game engines. This is an excellent solution for a static path, but what about dynamic paths? Say, for example, you want the player to have an out-of-body experience and fly through the scene while targeting on enemies, allies, the gates of heaven, or the gates of hell.

B-Spline Curves

B-Spline curves are a flexible, easy, and efficient solution to generating a smooth curve given a set of control points. There are several other curve-generating algorithms and modifications that offer more flexibility and power that I encourage you to explore, but B-Splines are a great place to start. The cubic implementation I will discuss is based on a basis function in the form of the matrix shown in Equation 4.3.1. Given a set of four control points and a parameter, v, that uniformly progresses from 0 to 1 through a set number of subdivisions, this matrix will produce a smooth curve section. For each element (x, y, z) of the control points, the Build() function is applied.

$$B - Spline = \begin{bmatrix} -1 & 3 & -3 & 1 \\ 3 & -6 & 0 & 4 \\ -3 & 3 & 3 & 1 \\ 1 & 0 & 0 & 0 \end{bmatrix} \frac{1}{6}$$

EQUATION 4.3.1. The cubic B-Spline basis function.

```
void Spline::Build() {
  float u, u_2, u_3;
  int i, j, k;
  int index;

  index = 0;
  // For each control Point (Minus the last three)
  for (i = 0; i < controlCnt - 3; i++) {

    // For each subdivision
    for(j = 0; j < curveSubD; j++) {
      u = (float)j / curveSubD;
      u_2 = u * u;
      u_3 = u_2 * u;

      for(k = 0; k < 3; k++) {
        // Position
        curveData[index].pos[k] =
          (
            (-1*u_3 + 3*u_2 - 3*u + 1) *
              controlData[i  ].pos[k] +
            ( 3*u_3 - 6*u_2 + 0*u + 4) *
              controlData[i+0].pos[k] +
            (-3*u_3 + 3*u_2 + 3*u + 1) *
              controlData[i+1].pos[k] +
            ( 1*u_3 + 0*u_2 + 0*u + 0) *
              controlData[i+2].pos[k]
          ) / 6.0F;
      }

      index ++;
    }
  }
}
```

Note that the parameter *u* is squared and cubed; hence, we have a *cubic* spline. Also note that the last three control points are not used, since this algorithm utilizes four continuous control points at a time. I leave these extra components in my algorithm so that I can preserve the continuity of the curves. For example, the following control points will create a very close approximation of a circle.

```
C:   48.000000 2.000000   48.000000 // Not drawn
C:   48.000000 2.000000  -48.000000
C:  -48.000000 2.000000  -48.000000
C:  -48.000000 2.000000   48.000000
C:   48.000000 2.000000   48.000000
C:   48.000000 2.000000  -48.000000 // Not drawn
C:  -48.000000 2.000000  -48.000000 // Not drawn
```

Utilizing B-Splines for our purpose requires a little work. The curve provides the position of the camera, but we also need a target and an up vector. For multiple curves, each control point should be associated with a target position. Hence, the camera will continue to focus on the target as it moves along the curve. Once it encounters a new target position, the camera control logic can simply interpolate between the points to get the desired effect. A more complex but flexible solution would be to use two B-Spline curves, one for camera position and the other for target position.

Tricks

Given a set of control points, the game engine can either compute the entire curve during one frame, or calculate only the needed portions of the curve. This reduces the amount of computations per frame, and also reduces the amount of memory needed to store curve data. B-Splines only require four control points for any subsection of a curve. So, by continuously cycling in a new control point, whether it is a random point or a carefully calculated one, a smooth curve of infinite length can be created. The demo software for this article demonstrates such a solution.

Although the curve is guaranteed to be continuous, the distance between subdivisions is not. Hence, moving the camera across the curve incrementally is not a sufficient solution. The camera would visibly change velocity between control points, and it would be subject to changing frame rates. The best method for moving the curve across the screen is to use distance and speed calculations. For accurate distance calculation, you need to calculate the distance between each subdivision at the curve level. This method requires a lot of calculation, but it is worth it. Use this function to calculate an appropriate index for a given distance:

```
int Spline::GetIndexAtDistance(float distance) {
  int index = 0;

  if (distance < 0.0) return -1;
  // Forward Push
  while (index < curveCnt &&
```

```
  distance > curveData[index].distance)
  {
    index++;
  }
  if (index >= curveCnt) return -1;
  return index;
}
```

Another useful trick for using B-Splines is to utilize the tangents of the curve to force the orientation of the camera to the curve. This would be particularly useful if you wanted to implement a roller coaster. A close approximation can be calculated by subtracting each curve point from the one preceding it. However, a more accurate solution is to calculate the derivative of the B-Spline basis function. This derivative is given in Equation 2. These calculations are performed in the sample code.

$$B - Spline' = \begin{bmatrix} 0 & -1 & 2 & -1 \\ 0 & 3 & -4 & 0 \\ 0 & -3 & 2 & 1 \\ 0 & 1 & 0 & 0 \end{bmatrix} \frac{1}{2}$$

EQUATION 4.3.2. First derivative of the B-Spline basis.

One pitfall I should mention is normal calculations. Finding a normal to a curve is a simple problem. One solution is to take the tangent of the current control point and cross it with the tangent of the next control point. Finding the appropriate normal, on the other hand, is a difficult problem. There are an infinite number of normals at any given point of a curve, and the problem is to find the one that produces the result you want. I found that using the natural normal, by crossing tangents, usually gave me the result I wanted. However, since I was using the cross product, the right-hand rule would occasionally flip my normal when the curve switched directions. I compensated for this by checking the dot product of the current normal and the previous one to see if the difference was ~180°. If so, I would set a flag to flip the normals back. In some instances, I simply provided the normal that I wanted with the control point, and interpolated to the next natural (or specified) normal as I subdivided the curve.

Catmull-Rom

Since I'm on the topic of B-Splines, I should mention a variation of curve generation functions called Catmull-Rom curves. The biggest difference between these two curves is that Catmull-Rom curves go through the control points, whereas B-Splines do not. However, I must warn you that the "curviness" of this variation is not as pleasing to the eye as B-Splines. Nonetheless, you may find it useful or necessary to have the curve pass through the control points. The basis functions are listed in Equation 4.4.3.

$$Catmull - Rom = \begin{bmatrix} -1 & 2 & -1 & 0 \\ 3 & -5 & 0 & 2 \\ -3 & 4 & 1 & 0 \\ 1 & -1 & 0 & 0 \end{bmatrix} \frac{1}{2}$$

$$Catmull - Rom' = \begin{bmatrix} -3 & -1 & 4 & -1 \\ 9 & 3 & -10 & 0 \\ -9 & -3 & 8 & 1 \\ 3 & 1 & -2 & 0 \end{bmatrix} \frac{1}{2}$$

EQUATION 4.4.3. The Catmull-Rom basis functions.

Camera Tricks

Zoom

Say you want to have a high-powered sniper rifle with a long range scope in your game, and you want the player to be able to look around through the scope. One quick and dirty method for accomplishing this in OpenGL is to use the FOV parameter of the gluPerspective() function. This snippet of code will cause the camera to zoom in and out with the cosine function:

```
glMatrixMode(GL_PROJECTION);
glLoadIdentity();
gluPerspective(cos(tempAng += 0.03F)*10 + 33,
        640.0F/480.0F, 1.0, 3000.0);
glMatrixMode(GL_MODELVIEW);
```

Damping

Damping is the key to making camera controls look and feel right. The following function will return a vector that approaches the target vector such that as it reaches the target, it begins to slow down. However, there is a major problem with this solution: It is frame rate dependent. As the frame-rate increases, the damping effect decreases.

```
vector3 dampType1(vector3 currX, vector3 targetX) {
    return currX + ((targetX - currX) / 16.0F);
}
```

Using physics is one possible solution for damping. Applying accelerations and friction to the camera's position will produce the desired result, and physics equations are frame-rate independent. But, physics is more appropriate for an interactive solution. They don't easily offer a current and target position interface, which would be more useful in situations where the camera is scripted or affected by fixed animations. Springs are the perfect solution.

$$F = ma = -k_s x - k_d v$$

EQUATION 4.3.4. The spring equation.

Let's break the spring equation up into usable pieces and get a function. First, let's assume that our mass is 1. x represents the displacement from the resting (target) state of the spring to the current position. The two constants k_s and k_d represent Hooke's spring constant and the damping constant, respectively. v is the velocity of the target position. The function that implements this damping is shown here. What a perfect opportunity for C++!

```
vector3 SpringDamp(
        vector3 currPos,      // Current Position
        vector3 trgPos,       // Target Position
        vector3 prevTrgPos,   // Previous Target Position
        float deltaTime,      // Change in Time
        float springConst,    // Hooke's Constant
        float dampConst,      // Damp Constant
        float springLen) {
    vector3 disp;             // Displacement
    vector3 velocity;         // Velocity
    float forceMag;           // Force Magnitude

    // Calculate Spring Force
    disp = currPos - trgPos;
    velocity = (prevTrgPos - trgPos) * deltaTime;
    forceMag = springConst * (springLen - disp.length()) +
        dampConst * (DotProduct(disp, velocity) /
        disp.length());

    // Apply Spring Force
    disp.normalize();
    disp *= forceMag * deltaTime;
    return currPos += disp;
}
```

Third-Person Camera

On the topic of cameras, I also need to mention the valuable third-person camera. As an example, I have added a spring-based third-person camera model to my sample code. The actor in the scene is regulated by a spline. This is only to mimic random orientations that an actor could possibly undertake. In an interactive game, the orientation of the actual actor can be controlled by game logic, canned animations, or even the first-person camera model described earlier. Regardless, the camera tracks a position that is a given distance behind the actor. I use the spring damping function to give the camera a realistic feel.

Quaternions

As a final note, quaternions have become an integral part of game programming, and play an important role in camera orientation techniques. There are many benefits to using quaternions to internally represent orientations. The three-parameter representation of Euler angles requires trigonometry and nine-parameter orthogonal matrices. Quaternions, on the other hand, only require four parameters and are less computationally expensive.

When it comes to view interpolation, the Euler angle implementation is inherently buggy. Say you wish to rotate the object 90° in the Y-axis (yaw = $\pi/2$). Because each rotation is computed separately, this operation rotates the X-axis onto the negative Z-axis. Hence, the result of a rotation in the X-axis by an angle θ is the same as rotating -θ in the Z-axis. In other words, the camera will roll when you apply a change in the yaw. This parametric singularity is called *gimbal lock*. Because of this lock, interpolating through these singularities produces strange and most likely unwanted results. Quaternions, on the other hand, do not have this problem, and can be interpolated quite easily. By representing camera orientation with quaternions, we can perform smooth interpolations between two viewpoints.

More sophisticated implementations of orientation controls such as those found in commercial flight simulators apply angular velocities via quaternions. However, for our purposes, it is sufficient and more intuitive to increment rotation around an angle using the Euler angles, than to directly recalculate a quaternion. Hence, it is useful to have a function that produces a quaternion given the three Euler angles.

```
quaternion &quaternion::SetEuler(float yaw, float pitch,
    float roll) {
    float cosY = cosf(yaw / 2.0F);
    float sinY = sinf(yaw / 2.0F);
    float cosP = cosf(pitch / 2.0F);
    float sinP = sinf(pitch / 2.0F);
    float cosR = cosf(roll / 2.0F);
    float sinR = sinf(roll / 2.0F);
    SetValues(
        cosR * sinP * cosY + sinR * cosP * sinY,
        cosR * cosP * sinY - sinR * sinP * cosY,
        sinR * cosP * cosY - cosR * sinP * sinY,
        cosR * cosP * cosY + sinR * sinP * sinY
    );
    return *this;

}
```

4.4

A Fast Cylinder-Frustum Intersection Test

Eric Lengyel

Before attempting to render a complex object, many games first determine whether a geometrically simple volume bounding that object is visible. Due to their computational efficiency, spheres and boxes are commonly used as bounding volumes, but it is sometimes the case that objects are naturally suited to be bounded by a cylinder. Although we will not be able to achieve the speed at which a sphere or box could be tested, this article presents a quick algorithm for determining whether an arbitrary cylinder potentially intersects the view frustum (and thus whether the object is visible).

The efficiency of the algorithm relies on the fact that we can reduce the problem to that of determining whether a line segment intersects a properly modified view frustum. Given a cylinder described by a radius and two points in space representing the centers of the end faces, we individually move each of the six planes of the view frustum outward by the cylinder's *effective* radius with respect to that plane. The effective radius depends on the cylinder's orientation, and ranges from zero (when the cylinder is perpendicular to the plane) to the actual radius (when the cylinder is parallel to the plane).

The cylinder test has advantages over the sphere and box tests when an object's bounding cylinder has a large height-to-radius ratio. Such a case arises, for instance, when rendering shadow volumes for infinite light sources, since a shadow volume typically needs to be long relative to the size of the object casting it. A shadow volume is completely contained inside the extrusion of the object's bounding sphere along the light direction, making it a natural candidate for a cylindrical bounding volume. Using a bounding sphere for such a volume would contain a great deal of empty space, causing a sphere visibility test to return positive in many cases when the volume is not really visible. Although a bounding box would generally contain an acceptably small amount of empty space, box visibility tests are not well suited for boxes having one dimension that is much larger than the other two. This is due to the fact that box tests only detect that a box is invisible by determining that the box lies completely on the negative side of *any one* of the six planes bounding the view frustum. A long rectangular bounding box could easily straddle one of the view frustum planes far outside the view frustum, but the box tests would return positive.

The View Frustum

Our view frustum shall be completely described by four quantities. The first is the focal length l, which determines the field of view. For a desired horizontal field of view angle θ, the focal length is given by the formula:

$$l = \frac{1}{\tan\left(\theta \,/\, 2\right)} \ . \tag{4.4.1}$$

The second quantity is the aspect ratio a, which is simply the viewport's height divided by its width. At a distance l from the camera, a plane perpendicular to the camera's viewing direction carves a rectangle out of the view frustum whose left and right edges reside at $x = \pm 1$, and whose top and bottom edges reside at $y = \pm a$.

The remaining two quantities that describe our view frustum are the minimum and maximum depths that define the near plane distance n and the far plane distance f. At a distance n from the camera, the viewport rectangle is bounded by $x = \pm n/l$ and $y = \pm na/l$. These values are passed to the OpenGL function glFrustum.

Using the values of l and a, the inward-pointing unit-length normals of the six frustum planes are given, in eye space coordinates, by the following formulas:

Table 4.4.1. View Frustum Plane Normals

Plane	Normal
Near	$(0, 0, -1)$
Far	$(0, 0, 1)$
Left	$\left(\dfrac{l}{\sqrt{l^2 + 1}}, 0, -\dfrac{1}{\sqrt{l^2 + 1}} \right)$
Right	$\left(-\dfrac{l}{\sqrt{l^2 + 1}}, 0, -\dfrac{1}{\sqrt{l^2 + 1}} \right)$
Top	$\left(0, -\dfrac{l}{\sqrt{l^2 + a^2}}, -\dfrac{a}{\sqrt{l^2 + a^2}} \right)$
Bottom	$\left(0, \dfrac{l}{\sqrt{l^2 + a^2}}, -\dfrac{a}{\sqrt{l^2 + a^2}} \right)$

The cylinder intersection test will take place in eye space so that we can take advantage of the symmetry of these normals, as well as the numerous zeros that appear in the table.

Calculating Effective Radii

Let us call the two endpoints of the cylinder's axis P_1 and P_2, and the cylinder's radius r (see Figure 4.4.1). Now we select one of the six view frustum planes, label its normal N, and call the angle between the normal and the cylinder's axis α. The effective radius r' of the cylinder with respect to this plane is given by the simple formula

$$r' = r \sin \alpha. \tag{4.4.2}$$

The most immediate method for determining the value of $\sin \alpha$ would be to calculate the magnitude of a cross product, but we can calculate the same value using significantly fewer operations through a bit of trigonometric manipulation. Recall the identity:

$$\sin^2 \alpha + \cos^2 \alpha = 1. \tag{4.4.3}$$

This gives us the alternative form for Equation 4.4.2:

$$r' = r\sqrt{1 - \cos^2 \alpha}. \tag{4.4.4}$$

The value of $\cos \alpha$ is given by

$$\cos \alpha = \frac{\left(P_2 - P_1\right) \cdot N}{\left\|P_2 - P_1\right\|}. \tag{4.4.5}$$

The normalized vector representing the axis of the cylinder only needs to be calculated once. For each view frustum plane, Equation 4.4.5 can then be evaluated through a simple dot product with a normal having at most two non-zero components.

It is not absolutely necessary to calculate the effective radii, since the actual radius could be used in its place, saving up to five possible square root calculations. Using the actual radius may be desirable in the case when many cylinder visibility tests are to be performed, and the square root operation is slow on the target machine. The disadvantage of using the actual radius is that it increases the number of visible cylinders, perhaps significantly if the actual radius is large. If speed is an issue, the decision to use effective radii or the actual radius should be determined through experimentation.

The Algorithm

The intersection test executes by visiting each of the six view frustum planes individually. We consider the near and far planes first since they are parallel and thus produce

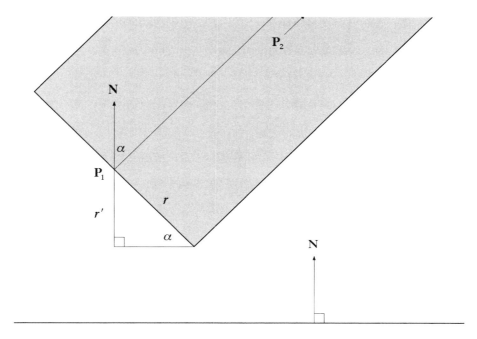

FIGURE 4.4.1. Calculating an effective radius.

the same effective radii. Once we have discovered that at least part of the cylinder lies between these planes, we proceed to the four side planes. For each plane, we first calculate the effective radius r' of the cylinder and move the plane outward by that distance, as illustrated in Figure 4.4.2. This has the effect of reducing the cylinder to a line segment, but it carries the slight cost of including a few more cylinders in our visible set that do not actually intersect the view frustum.

After adjusting a plane, we next test the two endpoints P_1 and P_2 to determine on which side of the plane they lie. This is done by plugging each endpoint's coordinates into the plane equation

$$\mathbf{P} \cdot \mathbf{N} - d = 0 \tag{4.4.6}$$

where $d = n - r'$ for the near plane, $d = -f - r'$ for the far plane, and $d = -r'$ for any of the four side planes. The sign of the left side of Equation 4.4.6 indicates on which side of the plane the point $\mathbf{P}$ lies. Since the plane's normal points toward the interior of the view frustum, any point lying on the negative side of the plane lies outside the view frustum. Thus, if both P_1 and P_2 lie on the negative side of the plane, then we immediately know that the cylinder is not visible, and the algorithm exits. Any point interior to the view frustum must lie on the positive side of all six planes, so whenever both P_1 and P_2 lie on the positive side of a single plane, we cannot draw any conclusions and just continue to the next plane.

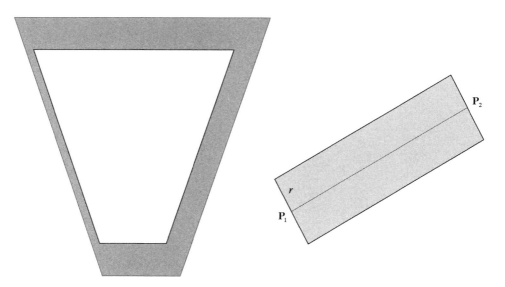

FIGURE 4.4.2. The shaded region represents the volume added to the view frustum after each plane has been expanded by the associated effective radius.

In the remaining case that one endpoint lies on the positive side and the other lies on the negative side, we calculate the point where the line segment intersects the plane and replace the exterior endpoint with it. This effectively chops off the part of the cylinder that we know to lie outside the view frustum. To find the point of intersection, we use the parametric equation for a line

$$\mathbf{P} = \mathbf{P}_1 + t(\mathbf{P}_2 - \mathbf{P}_1) \tag{4.4.7}$$

where $0 \leq t \leq 1$. Substituting the right side of this equation for $\mathbf{P}$ in Equation 4.4.6 allows us to solve for the value of t at the point of intersection:

$$t = \frac{d - \mathbf{P}_1 \cdot \mathbf{N}}{\left(\mathbf{P}_2 - \mathbf{P}_1\right) \cdot \mathbf{N}} \tag{4.4.8}$$

Plugging this back into Equation 4.4.7 gives us our new endpoint. After replacing the exterior endpoint with it, we continue to the next plane.

If we visit all six planes of the view frustum and never encounter the case that both endpoints lie on the negative side of a plane, then the cylinder is at least partially visible. Of course, this means that we do not have to replace any endpoints for the last plane that we visit. As soon as we know that at least one of the endpoints lies on the positive side of the final plane, we know that part of the cylinder intersects the view frustum.

Implementation

The sample code in Listing 4.4.1 implements the cylinder visibility test. The `Frustum` class encapsulates the view frustum and is constructed by specifying the focal length, aspect ratio, near plane distance, and far plane distance. The components of the normals listed in Table 4.4.1 are precalculated inside the constructor. The member function `CylinderVisible` determines whether a cylinder specified by two points and a radius intersects the view frustum and returns true or false.

Listing 4.4.1

```cpp
#include "mtxlib.h"

class Frustum
{
    private:

        // Near and far plane distances
        float       nearDistance;
        float       farDistance;

        // Precalculated normal components
        float       leftRightX;
        float       leftRightZ;
        float       topBottomY;
        float       topBottomZ;

    public:

        // Constructor defines the frustum
        Frustum(float l, float a, float n, float f);

        // Intersection test returns true or false
        bool CylinderVisible(vector3 p1, vector3 p2,
        float radius) const;
};

Frustum::Frustum(float l, float a, float n, float f)
{
    // Save off near plane and far plane distances
    nearDistance = n;
    farDistance = f;

    // Precalculate side plane normal components
    float d = 1.0F / sqrt(l * l + 1.0F);
    leftRightX = l * d;
    leftRightZ = d;

    d = 1.0F / sqrt(l * l + a * a);
    topBottomY = l * d;
    topBottomZ = a * d;
}
```

```
bool Frustum::CylinderVisible(vector3 p1, vector3 p2, float radius) const
{
    // Calculate unit vector representing cylinder's axis
    vector3 dp = p2 - p1;
    dp.normalize();

    // Visit near plane first, N = (0,0,-1)
    float dot1 = -p1.z;
    float dot2 = -p2.z;

    // Calculate effective radius for near and far planes
    float effectiveRadius = radius * sqrt(1.0F - dp.z * dp.z);

    // Test endpoints against adjusted near plane
    float d = nearDistance - effectiveRadius;
    bool interior1 = (dot1 > d);
    bool interior2 = (dot2 > d);

    if (!interior1)
    {
        // If neither endpoint is interior,
        // cylinder is not visible
        if (!interior2) return (false);

        // p1 was outside, so move it to the near plane
        float t = (d + p1.z) / dp.z;
        p1.x -= t * dp.x;
        p1.y -= t * dp.y;
        p1.z = -d;
    }
    else if (!interior2)
    {
        // p2 was outside, so move it to the near plane
        float t = (d + p1.z) / dp.z;
        p2.x = p1.x - t * dp.x;
        p2.y = p1.y - t * dp.y;
        p2.z = -d;
    }

    // Test endpoints against adjusted far plane
    d = farDistance + effectiveRadius;
    interior1 = (dot1 < d);
    interior2 = (dot2 < d);

    if (!interior1)
    {
        // If neither endpoint is interior,
        // cylinder is not visible
        if (!interior2) return (false);

        // p1 was outside, so move it to the far plane
        float t = (d + p1.z) / (p2.z - p1.z);
        p1.x -= t * (p2.x - p1.x);
        p1.y -= t * (p2.y - p1.y);
        p1.z = -d;
```

```
    }
    else if (!interior2)
    {
        // p2 was outside, so move it to the far plane
        float t = (d + p1.z) / (p2.z - p1.z);
        p2.x = p1.x - t * (p2.x - p1.x);
        p2.y = p1.y - t * (p2.y - p1.y);
        p2.z = -d;
    }

    // Visit left side plane next
    // The normal components have been precalculated
    float nx = leftRightX;
    float nz = leftRightZ;

    // Compute p1 * N and p2 * N
    dot1 = nx * p1.x - nz * p1.z;
    dot2 = nx * p2.x - nz * p2.z;

    // Calculate effective radius for this plane
    float s = nx * dp.x - nz * dp.z;
    effectiveRadius = -radius * sqrt(1.0F - s * s);

    // Test endpoints against adjusted plane
    interior1 = (dot1 > effectiveRadius);
    interior2 = (dot2 > effectiveRadius);

    if (!interior1)
    {
        // If neither endpoint is interior,
        // cylinder is not visible
        if (!interior2) return (false);

        // p1 was outside, so move it to the plane
        float t = (effectiveRadius - dot1) / (dot2 - dot1);
        p1.x += t * (p2.x - p1.x);
        p1.y += t * (p2.y - p1.y);
        p1.z += t * (p2.z - p1.z);
    }
    else if (!interior2)
    {
        // p2 was outside, so move it to the plane
        float t = (effectiveRadius - dot1) / (dot2 - dot1);
        p2.x = p1.x + t * (p2.x - p1.x);
        p2.y = p1.y + t * (p2.y - p1.y);
        p2.z = p1.z + t * (p2.z - p1.z);
    }

    // Visit right side plane next
    dot1 = -nx * p1.x - nz * p1.z;
    dot2 = -nx * p2.x - nz * p2.z;

    s = -nx * dp.x - nz * dp.z;
    effectiveRadius = -radius * sqrt(1.0F - s * s);
```

```
interior1 = (dot1 > effectiveRadius);
interior2 = (dot2 > effectiveRadius);

if (!interior1)
{
    if (!interior2) return (false);

    float t = (effectiveRadius - dot1) / (dot2 - dot1);
    p1.x += t * (p2.x - p1.x);
    p1.y += t * (p2.y - p1.y);
    p1.z += t * (p2.z - p1.z);
}
else if (!interior2)
{
    float t = (effectiveRadius - dot1) / (dot2 - dot1);
    p2.x = p1.x + t * (p2.x - p1.x);
    p2.y = p1.y + t * (p2.y - p1.y);
    p2.z = p1.z + t * (p2.z - p1.z);
}

// Visit top side plane next
// The normal components have been precalculated
float ny = topBottomY;
nz = topBottomZ;

dot1 = -ny * p1.y - nz * p1.z;
dot2 = -ny * p2.y - nz * p2.z;

s = -ny * dp.y - nz * dp.z;
effectiveRadius = -radius * sqrt(1.0F - s * s);

interior1 = (dot1 > effectiveRadius);
interior2 = (dot2 > effectiveRadius);

if (!interior1)
{
    if (!interior2) return (false);

    float t = (effectiveRadius - dot1) / (dot2 - dot1);
    p1.x += t * (p2.x - p1.x);
    p1.y += t * (p2.y - p1.y);
    p1.z += t * (p2.z - p1.z);
}
else if (!interior2)
{
    float t = (effectiveRadius - dot1) / (dot2 - dot1);
    p2.x = p1.x + t * (p2.x - p1.x);
    p2.y = p1.y + t * (p2.y - p1.y);
    p2.z = p1.z + t * (p2.z - p1.z);
}

// Finally, visit bottom side plane
dot1 = ny * p1.y - nz * p1.z;
dot2 = ny * p2.y - nz * p2.z;
```

```
        s = ny * dp.y - nz * dp.z;
        effectiveRadius = -radius * sqrt(1.0F - s * s);

        interior1 = (dot1 > effectiveRadius);
        interior2 = (dot2 > effectiveRadius);

        // At least one endpoint must be interior
        // or cylinder is not visible
        return (interior1 | interior2);
    }
```

4.5

3D Collision Detection

Kevin Kaiser

A real-time physics engine is central to creating a 3D gaming environment where the player can easily suspend their disbelief; instead of just realistic pictures, the physics engine provides realistic interactions between objects in the pictures. These interactions provide the player with a basis for reality; in other words, the player can better understand and navigate in a world where things act as they do in real life. The first, and arguably most important step in setting up a real-time physics simulation is having accurate collision detection; once collisions are detected, the simulation can react accordingly. This article will help lay the groundwork for building an accurate physics simulation by starting with one of the most crucial parts of a real-time physics engine: 3D collision detection.

Overview of the Algorithms

The two basic collision algorithms this article covers are:

- **Bounding Sphere Collision Detection**—For the sake of clean code and an easy-to-understand explanation, we'll be using bounding spheres. The bulk of this code checks the radius of a bounding sphere against the radius of another bounding sphere to determine possible collisions.
- **Triangle-to-Triangle Collision Detection**—It might be wise to brush up on your calculus before attempting to understand this algorithm; it uses parametric equations to determine collision points between one triangle and the plane of the other triangle, then determines whether those collision points lie inside the opposite triangle.

Bounding Sphere Collision Detection

Collision detection is best performed in hierarchical steps: Object Bounding Sphere to Object Bounding Sphere, Polygon Bounding Sphere to Polygon Bounding Sphere, then Triangle to Triangle. We will begin by generating bounding spheres. Calculating bounding spheres is very simple; all you need is to find the center of the object, then compute the maximum distance between the center and a vertex in the object. By storing the radius of each bounding sphere, you can perform bounding sphere collision detection by adding the radii of the two objects, then taking the distance between the two center vertices. If the distance is greater than the sum of the radii, the spheres are certainly not colliding.

Let's go through this step by step. First, you'll need to determine the center point of the mesh. One way to do this is to create a bounding box and find the midpoint between diagonally opposite vertices (see Figure 4.5.1). To compute the bounding box, you need to find the minimum and maximum x, y, and z values for the entire object. This can be accomplished by iterating through the vertices and maintaining a "current" minimum and maximum. After checking all vertices, you'll have the maximum extents of the bounding box. The minimum and maximum values will be used to create the box.

Given a bounding box with eight maximal points (**ABCDEFGH**, see Figure 4.5.2), let's call the vertex assignments:

```
A = (minx, miny, minz)
B = (minx, maxy, minz)
C = (maxx, maxy, minz)
D = (maxx, miny, minz)
E = (minx, miny, maxz)
F = (minx, maxy, maxz)
G = (maxx, maxy, maxz)
H = (maxx, miny, maxz)
```

Now find the center point, given by averaging the minimum and maximum points on the bounding box (these are indicated by points A and G).

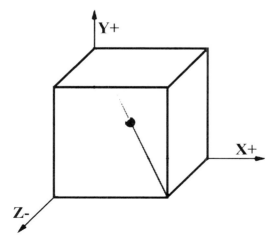

FIGURE 4.5.1 Finding the midpoint.

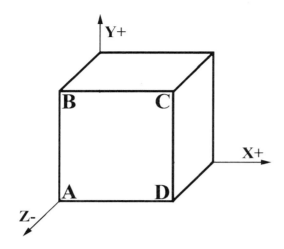

FIGURE 4.5.2 Creating a bounding box.

```
// Midpoint formula: Given A(x1,y1,z1) and B(x2,y2,z2),
//   the midpoint of the line the passes through A and B is
//   [(x1+x2)/2, (y1+y2)/2, (z1+z2)/2]
//
center.x = (A.x + G.x)/2;
center.y = (A.y + G.y)/2;
center.z = (A.z + G.z)/2;
```

The radius of the bounding sphere is easily computed by looping through the object's vertices and finding the distance between the center point and the current vertex. If the distance is greater than the current maximum distance, replace the maximum distance with the new distance. After the loop, the maximum distance is the radius of the bounding sphere. (Of course, an easy optimization here is to only do the square root at the very end.)

```
// Distance formula:
//   dist = sqrt[ ((x2-x1)^2)+((y2-y1)^2)+((z2-z1)^2) ]
//   distsq = ((x2-x1)^2)+((y2-y1)^2)+((z2-z1)^2)
//
foreach vertex v in object {
  current_distance_sq = distsq(object.center, v);
  if (current_distance_sq > max_distance_sq)
    max_distance_sq = current_distance_sq;
}
object.bs_radius = sqrt(max_distance_sq);
```

This will next be repeated on the polygonal level; bounding sphere checks are quick and simple, which is why when you have to check many polygons against each other, it's advantageous to begin with this test. After you have generated the necessary bounding boxes, bounding spheres, and center points for each object and polygon, you will be ready to get into the real meat of this article: triangle-to-triangle intersection tests! Get out the calculus book—you might need it.

Triangle-to-Triangle Collision Detection

This method of triangle-to-triangle collision detection relies directly on some easy-to-understand but slightly tricky mathematics. Imagine that we are given two triangles in 3D space (see Figure 4.5.3). We'll need to collect a lot of information from the two triangles. We need to begin by finding the plane equation of one of the triangles. If you remember correctly, the plane equation is $Ax+By+Cz+D=0$. We determine A, B, C and D by taking cross products of vertices:

```
// given a triangle tri1 with vertices a, b and c.
// vector3 a, b, c;
vector3 v1, v2, cross_v1xv2;

// create vectors v1, v2 (tri1.b - tri1.a,
//                        tri1.c - tri1.a)
v1 = tri1.b – tri1.a;
v2 = tri1.c – tri1.a;

// NOTE: You may be able to skip this step and substitute your
// own surface normals if you already have them stored somewhere.
// Take cross product of v1 and v2 (this is the normal
// vector of the cross product of v1 and v2)
cross_v1xv2 = CrossProduct(v1, v2);
```

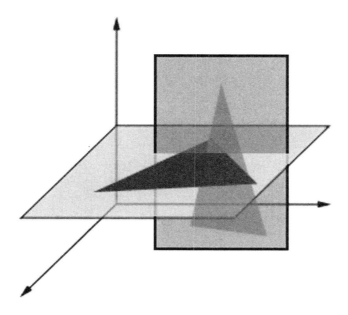

FIGURE 4.5.3. Two intersecting triangles.

```
// Then we plug these values back into Ax+By+Cz+D=0
tri1.pA = cross_v1xv2.x;
tri1.pB = cross_v1xv2.y;
tri1.pC = cross_v1xv2.z;

// Following this rule: Ax+By+Cz+D=0
// if point P(x0,y0,z0) is a point on the polygon
// A = cross_v1xv2.x
// B = cross_v1xv2.y
// C = cross_v1xv2.z
// D = (-A*x0-B*y0-C*z0)
tri1.pD = -DotProduct(cross_v1xv2, P);
```

Line-Plane Intersection

We now have the plane equation of *triangle1* and can move on to step two: seeing if *triangle2* collides with *triangle1*'s plane. This is done in multiple steps. The main idea is that given two vertices of *triangle2*, we take the line defined by these vertices and determine at what point that line collides with *triangle1*'s plane. If the collision point is between the two vertices, *triangle2* is colliding with *triangle1*'s plane; if it isn't between the two vertices, we iterate through the other two lines of *triangle2* to see if there are collision points between those points.

We solve this line-plane intersection using parametric equations from calculus. Given two vertices, $\mathbf{a}(x0,y0,z0)$ and $\mathbf{b}(x1,y1,z1)$, we set $\mathbf{a}(x0,y0,z0)*t = \mathbf{b}(x1,y1,z1)*(1-t)$. t is an interpolation factor that ranges from 0 to 1. When $t=0$ you are at point $\mathbf{b}$, and when $t=1$ you are at point $\mathbf{a}$. If we plug in parametric equations for each component of the plane equation, we can then solve for t:

$$A^*(x0^*t + x1^*(1-t)) + B^*(y0^*t + y1^*(1-t)) + C^*(z0^*t + z1^*(1-t)) + D = 0$$

This reduces down to:

$$t = -(A^*x1 + B^*y1 + C^*z1 + D) / (A^*(x0-x1) + B^*(y0-y1) + C^*(z0-z1))$$

The following code solves for t:

```
// i0 = (A*x0) + (B*y0) + (C*z0)
i0 = (tri1->pA*a->x) + (tri1->pB*a->y) + (tri1->pC*a->z);

// i1 = (A*x1) + (B*y1) + (C*z1)
i1 = (tri1->pA*b->x) + (tri1->pB*b->y) + (tri1->pC*b->z);

// Be wary of possible divide-by-zeros here (i.e. if i0 == i1)
final_t = -(i1 + tri1->pD) / (i0-i1);

// Then plug final_t back into the functions x(), y() and z()
// to get the point of intersection from line to plane
final_x = (((a->x)*(final_t))+((b->x)*(1-final_t)));
final_y = (((a->y)*(final_t))+((b->y)*(1-final_t)));
final_z = (((a->z)*(final_t))+((b->z)*(1-final_t)));
```

This will give you the final point where the line intersects the plane (see Figure 4.5.4). Of course, the **t** value we've computed must be between zero and one or the intersection is not between our two vertices! A special case that you also need to look for at this step is the presence of vertical line segments. The quickest way to determine the intersection point is to plug *x* and *z* of either point **a** or **b** into the plane equation for the triangle and solve for *y*. The intersection point would then be (**a**.*x*, **solved**.*y*, **a**.*z*).

Triangle "Flattening"

We're going to assume a right-handed coordinate system now. Imagine flattening a triangle against one of the coordinate planes, depending upon triangle orientation. It might lose the *y* coordinate and keep the *x* and *z* coordinates. The concept here doesn't specifically call for losing the *y* coordinate; it just requires losing the appropriate coordinate so that it will flatten. A good way to decide which coordinate to drop is by looking at the normal of the plane; if you determine which component's absolute value is the greatest, you can then find a plane to flatten against where the triangle will not be a "straight line" (such as a vertical triangle losing the *y* coordinate). For example, if the *x* component is greatest, you would project to the *yz* plane. Regardless of orientation, the triangle produced by this will be flat (as if it were lying flat on a table, see Figure 4.5.5). This is very advantageous because now we can use basic algebra to check and see if the final intersection point, when flattened in a similar manner, lies inside the flattened triangle. The code in Listing 4.5.1 effectively flattens the polygon against one of the coordinate planes.

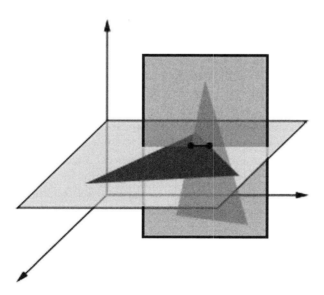

FIGURE 4.5.4 Determining collision points.

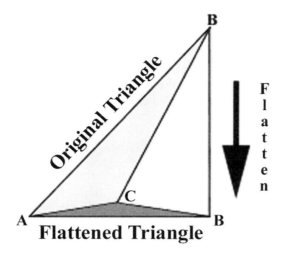

FIGURE 4.5.5 Vertex projection.

Point-in-Triangle Test

Now that we have flattened the coordinates, we need to do some algebra to determine whether the flattened intersection point lies inside the flattened triangle or not. There are several popular ways of doing this; we're going to make use of the equation for each line of the flattened triangle. Take note that regardless of which plane you project to, in this discussion we will still refer to the x and y coordinates of the flattened points. This is because by projecting the vertices, we have effectively reduced the problem to 2D; hence, the x and y. First, we need to find a point that is *definitely* inside the triangle. The easiest point to find that fits this description is the center of the triangle, computed as the average of its vertices: $((x0+x1+x2)/2, (y0+y1+y2)/2))$. Now that we know what direction the inside of the triangle is, we need to see if our point is on the "inside" side of the lines that are made by each pair of vertices (see Figure 4.5.6).

Given two vertices, **v0** and **v1**, first find the equation of the line that goes through them in the form $y=mx+b$. Remember that the formula for slope (m) is $(y1-y0)/(x1-x0)$, and you can find b by using the computed slope and a known point on the line. Now that we have the equation of the line in slope-intercept form, we can determine whether the flattened intersection point lies on the side of the line that is the inside of the triangle. We do this by comparing y values. If you plug the x coordinate of the flattened intersection point into the line $y=mx+b$, you will get the y value of the line at x. Next, you determine whether the center point we computed earlier is "above" or "below" the line by checking y values. We know that it is inside the triangle, so our intersection point has to have a y value that is in the same "direction" from the line as the center point. If it does, the intersection point is "inside" the triangle with respect to the line **ab**. Repeat this for lines **bc** and **ca**. If the point is on the inside after each test, the point is certainly inside the triangle. There is a special case to take into considera-

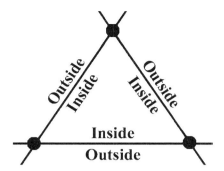

FIGURE 4.5.6 Determining the boundaries of a triangle.

tion: a projected vertical line segment. You cannot graph vertical lines using $y=mx+b$. If this is encountered, you instead check x coordinates instead of y coordinates; that is, first determine on which side of the vertical line the inside point is. Then, check the x value of the projected intersection point. If it is on the "inside" side of the vertical line, it is inside with respect to that line. See Listing 4.5.2 for this procedure.

Check All the Lines, in Both Triangles!

Of course, if one line of our triangle does not intersect, we still need to check the other lines. One line/triangle collision is all that is needed to show that both triangles are colliding. See Listing 4.5.3 for the rest of this sample code.

After all of this has finished, if no collision has occurred, you need to reverse the procedure, starting with triangle2 as the source. This ensures a perfect collision detection.

Listing 4.5.1

```
if (x==FALSE) { // dropping x coordinate
  a1 = tri->a.y;
  b1 = tri->a.z;
  a2 = tri->b.y;
  b2 = tri->b.z;
  a3 = tri->c.y;
  b3 = tri->c.z;
  a4 = vert->y;
  b4 = vert->z;
  inside = 0;
}
else if (y==FALSE) { // dropping y coordinate
  a1 = tri->a.x;
  b1 = tri->a.z;
  a2 = tri->b.x;
  b2 = tri->b.z;
  a3 = tri->c.x;
```

```
      b3 = tri->c.z;
      a4 = vert->x;
      b4 = vert->z;
      inside = 0;
  }
  else if (z==FALSE) { // dropping z coordinate
    a1 = tri->a.x;
    b1 = tri->a.y;
    a2 = tri->b.x;
    b2 = tri->b.y;
    a3 = tri->c.x;
    b3 = tri->c.y;
    a4 = vert->x;
    b4 = vert->y;
    inside = 0;
  }
```

Listing 4.5.2

```
// These are used to check for vertical line segments in the
// flattened triangle; you cannot graph vertical lines in 2D
// using y=mx+b, so we have to instead check if the flattened
// intersection point lies between the x coordinates of any
// vertical line and the center point of the triangle to see if
// the flattened intersection point lies on the inside of the
// triangle with respect to the vertical line segment.
AB_vert = BC_vert = CA_vert = FALSE;

// y=mx+b for outer 3 lines
if ((a2-a1)!=0) {
  m1 = (b2-b1)/(a2-a1);   // a->b
  bb1 = (b1)-(m1*a1);     // y/(mx) using vertex a
} else if ((a2-a1)==0) {
 AB_vert = TRUE;
}

if ((a3-a2)!=0) {
  m2 = (b3-b2)/(a3-a2);   // b->c
  bb2 = (b2)-(m2*a2);     // y/(mx) using vertex b
} else if ((a3-a2)==0) {
 BC_vert = TRUE;
}

if ((a1-a3)!=0) {
  m3 = (b1-b3)/(a1-a3);   // c->a
  bb3 = (b3)-(m3*a3);     // y/(mx) using vertex c
} else if ((a1-a3)==0) {
 CA_vert = TRUE;
}

// find average point of triangle (point is guaranteed
center_x = (a1+a2+a3)/3;         // to lie inside the triangle)
center_y = (b1+b2+b3)/3;
```

```
// See whether (center_x,center_y) is above or below the line,
// then set direction to UP if the point is above or DOWN if the
// point is below the line

// a->b
if (((m1*center_x)+bb1) >= center_y)
  DIRECTION(direction,UP);
else
  DIRECTION(direction,DOWN);
if (AB_vert==TRUE) {
  if ((a1<a4)&&(a1<center_x)) // vert projected line
    inside++;
  else if ((a1>a4)&&(a1>center_x)) // vert projected line
    inside++;
} else {
  if (direction==UP) {
    if (b4 <= ((m1*a4)+bb1)) // b4 less than y to be inside
      inside++;                // (line is above point)
  } else if (direction==DOWN) {
    if (b4 >= ((m1*a4)+bb1)) // b4 greater than y to be inside
      inside++;                // (line is below point)
  }
}

// b->c
if (((m2*center_x)+bb2) >= center_y)
  DIRECTION(direction,UP);
else
  DIRECTION(direction,DOWN);
if (BC_vert==TRUE) {
  if ( (a2 < a4)&&(a2 < center_x) ) // vert projected line
    inside++;
  else if ( (a2 > a4)&&(a2 > center_x) ) // vert projected line
    inside++;
} else {
  if (direction==UP) {
    if (b4 <= ((m2*a4)+bb2)) // b4 less than y to be inside
      inside++;                // (line is above point)
  } else if (direction==DOWN) {
    if (b4 >= ((m2*a4)+bb2)) // b4 greater than y to be inside
      inside++;                // (line is below point)
  }
}

// c->a
if (((m3*center_x)+bb3) >= center_y)
  DIRECTION(direction,UP);
else
  DIRECTION(direction,DOWN);
if (CA_vert==TRUE) {
  if ( (a3 < a4)&&(a3 < center_x) ) // vert projected line
    inside++;
  else if ( (a3 > a4)&&(a3 > center_x) ) // vert projected line
    inside++;
} else {
```

```
    if (direction==UP) {
      if (b4 <= ((m3*a4)+bb3)) // b4 less than y to be inside
        inside++;              // (line is above point)
    } else if (direction==DOWN) {
      if (b4 >= ((m3*a4)+bb3)) // b4 greater than y to be inside
        inside++;              // (line is below point)
    }
  }
  if (inside==3) {
    return TRUE;
  } else {
    return FALSE;
  }
```

Listing 4.5.3

```
// Scroll thru 3 line segments of the other triangle
// First iteration  (a,b)
p=line_plane_collision((vertex_ptr)&tri2.a,(vertex_ptr)&tri2.b,
                                  (triangle_ptr)&tri1);

// Determine which axis to project to
// X is greatest
if ((abs(tri1.pA)>=abs(tri1.pB))&&(abs(tri1.pA)>=abs(tri1.pC)))
  temp = point_inside_triangle((triangle_ptr)&tri1,(vertex_ptr)&p,
                                      TRUE,TRUE,FALSE);
// Y is greatest
else if ((abs(tri1.pB)>=abs(tri1.pA))&&(abs(tri1.pB)>=abs(tri1.pC)))
  temp = point_inside_triangle((triangle_ptr)&tri1,(vertex_ptr)&p,
                                      TRUE,FALSE,TRUE);
// Z is greatest
else if ((abs(tri1.pC)>=abs(tri1.pA))&&(abs(tri1.pC)>=abs(tri1.pB)))
  temp = point_inside_triangle((triangle_ptr)&tri1,(vertex_ptr)&p,
                                      FALSE,TRUE,TRUE);

if (temp==TRUE) {
  // Point needs to be checked to see if it lies between the two
  //   vertices.
  // First check for the special case of vertical line segments
  if ((tri2.a.x == tri2.b.x)&&(tri2.a.z == tri2.b.z)) {
    if (((tri2.a.y <= p.y)&&(p.y <= tri2.b.y))||
        ((tri2.b.y <= p.y)&&(p.y <= tri2.a.y)))
      return TRUE;
  }
  // End vertical line segment check

  // Now check for point on line segment
  if (point_inbetween_vertices((vertex_ptr)&tri2.a,
        (vertex_ptr)&tri2.b,(triangle_ptr)&tri1)==TRUE)
    return TRUE;
  else
    return FALSE;
}
```

```
// Second iteration (b,c)
p=line_plane_collision((vertex_ptr)&tri2.b,(vertex_ptr)&tri2.c,
                                       (triangle_ptr)&tri1);

// Determine which axis to project to
// X is greatest
if ((abs(tri1.pA)>=abs(tri1.pB))&&(abs(tri1.pA)>=abs(tri1.pC)))
  temp = point_inside_triangle((triangle_ptr)&tri1,(vertex_ptr)&p,
                                            TRUE,TRUE,FALSE);
// Y is greatest
else if ((abs(tri1.pB)>=abs(tri1.pA))&&(abs(tri1.pB)>=abs(tri1.pC)))
  temp = point_inside_triangle((triangle_ptr)&tri1,(vertex_ptr)&p,
                                            TRUE,FALSE,TRUE);
// Z is greatest
else if ((abs(tri1.pC)>=abs(tri1.pA))&&(abs(tri1.pC)>=abs(tri1.pB)))
  temp = point_inside_triangle((triangle_ptr)&tri1,(vertex_ptr)&p,
                                            FALSE,TRUE,TRUE);

if (temp==TRUE) {
  // Point needs to be checked to see if it lies between the two vertices
  // First check for the special case of vertical line segments
  if ((tri2.b.x == tri2.c.x)&&(tri2.b.z == tri2.c.z)) {
    if ((((tri2.b.y <= p.y)&&(p.y <= tri2.c.y))||
        ((tri2.c.y <= p.y)&&(p.y <= tri2.b.y)))
      return TRUE;
  }

  // Now check for point on line segment
  if (point_inbetween_vertices((vertex_ptr)&tri2.b,
(vertex_ptr)&tri2.c, (triangle_ptr)&tri1)==TRUE)
    return TRUE;
  else
    return FALSE;
}

// Third iteration (c,a)
p=line_plane_collision((vertex_ptr)&tri2.c,(vertex_ptr)&tri2.a,
                                       (triangle_ptr)&tri1);

// Determine which axis to project to
// X is greatest
if ((abs(tri1.pA)>=abs(tri1.pB))&&(abs(tri1.pA)>=abs(tri1.pC)))
  temp = point_inside_triangle((triangle_ptr)&tri1,(vertex_ptr)&p,
                                            TRUE,TRUE,FALSE);
// Y is greatest
else if ((abs(tri1.pB)>=abs(tri1.pA))&&(abs(tri1.pB)>=abs(tri1.pC)))
  temp = point_inside_triangle((triangle_ptr)&tri1,(vertex_ptr)&p,
                                            TRUE,FALSE,TRUE);
// Z is greatest
else if ((abs(tri1.pC)>=abs(tri1.pA))&&(abs(tri1.pC)>=abs(tri1.pB)))
  temp = point_inside_triangle((triangle_ptr)&tri1,(vertex_ptr)&p,
                                            FALSE,TRUE,TRUE);

if (temp==TRUE) {
  // Point needs to be checked to see if it lies between the two vertices
```

```
    // First check for the special case of vertical line segments
    if ((tri2.c.x == tri2.a.x)&&(tri2.c.z == tri2.a.z)) {
      if (((tri2.c.y <= p.y)&&(p.y <= tri2.a.y))||
          ((tri2.a.y <= p.y)&&(p.y <= tri2.c.y)))
        return TRUE;
    }

    // Now check for point on line segment
    if (point_inbetween_vertices((vertex_ptr)&tri2.c,
    (vertex_ptr)&tri2.a, (triangle_ptr)&tri1)==TRUE)
      return TRUE; // Intersection point is inside the triangle and on
    else           // the line segment
      return FALSE;
  }
  return FALSE; // Default value/no collision
```

4.6

Multi-Resolution Maps for Interaction Detection

Jan Svarovsky

This article describes a method for reducing the number of proximity tests that must be performed for games with large numbers of game objects of varying sizes. The cost of simply testing every object against every other object goes up with the square of the number of objects, which can get very large! This is particularly bad if the proximity test is expensive.

Using a Grid

The simple solution is to cut up the world with a grid-based map. Each grid square has a linked list of the objects whose centers are located above it. Because the objects are of non-zero size, they may overlap into adjacent map squares. When the time comes to search for all possible collisions between objects, each object only has to test for others after it in the linked list associated with its own map square, and also map squares to the east, southeast, and south. Any collisions to the north and west and with objects earlier in the list are detected when other objects do *their* check. This enables you to avoid checking for the same collision twice.

Problems with Varying Object Size

This approach has problems when the game objects vary widely in size. You are only guaranteed to find all the collisions in this way if your game objects are smaller than your map squares. If you have large game objects, you could make the map squares larger. However, this would mean that smaller objects would test against each other when they are in fact far apart, when a finer grid system would have avoided them even considering each other. See Figure 4.6.1.

If you make the map squares smaller than some game objects, then there is a danger that objects' interactions are not detected because they are far enough apart in map squares to never check each other, though physically they do touch.

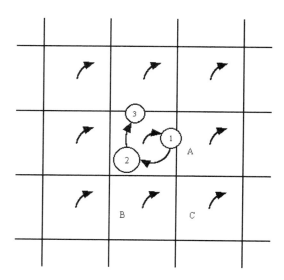

FIGURE 4.6.1 Object 2 checks against Object 3 and map squares A, B, and C.

You can solve this by giving each object "feet." Here, objects do not sit in the map directly (unless they are small enough); instead, rather small helper objects sit in the map squares that the object touches. Management of these feet is simple, though a little clumsy (Figure 4.6.2).

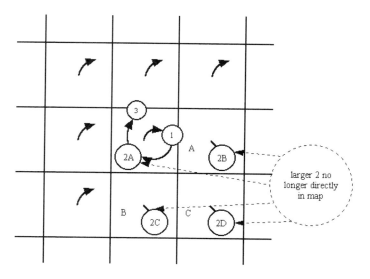

FIGURE 4.6.2. Larger Object 2 now has feet!

Multi-Resolution Maps

The alternative suggested here is to have several resolutions of map. The map square sizes go up in powers of two to make conversion between the different coordinate systems simple. Each object resides in the map where the squares are the smallest possible while actually being larger than the object. When doing the collision detection, you not only check against your own map square but also the map squares in the lower-resolution maps (larger map squares) that you touch. Much like only checking in the linked list after yourself, you don't bother checking in higher-resolution maps. The smaller objects will find you when they do their own checking, so you don't have to search for them (Figure 4.6.3).

It is simplest to have all resolutions of map squares, down to one map square covering the whole world. Each lower-resolution map is four times less data, so the memory requirements are vanishingly small. In my experience, if you cut off the map resolutions at some level, you may every now and then during game development discover a game object (such as an explosion's effect sphere) will be just a little too large and crash your game. The only extra cost for not cutting off the map resolutions is that the searching goes all the way to the lowest-resolution map.

You can add a lower bound for the resolution simply, with a decision—do you disallow larger objects, or do you just put them in the lowest-resolution map squares, accepting that sometimes they won't be collided with correctly? I recommend allowing them to reside in the lowest-resolution map you make available, assuming that the objects are only too large during development of the game, and by the time of release you will need to tune the map square size to suit the largest object available in the game.

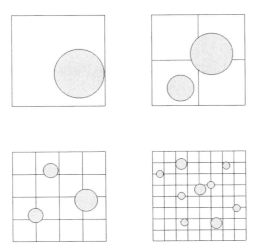

FIGURE 4.6.3 Multiple simple maps; each object resides in the finest resolution map possible.

Source Code

```
#include <stdio.h>
#include <assert.h>
#include "mtxlib.h"

// This is your game object base class
class GameObject;

////////////////////////////////////////////////////////////////////
//
// External definitions

// If the map decides two objects are close enough together, it will
//   call this function, which you have to provide
extern void process_collision(GameObject *a, GameObject *b);

////////////////////////////////////////////////////////////////////
//
// A game object. Derive your own objects off this
class GameObject
{
public:
    GameObject()
    {
        NextInMap = NULL;
        MapSquare = NULL;

        MapRes = 0;
    }

    // The object is in a singly linked list hanging off one of
    // the map squares
    GameObject *NextInMap;

    // And this is the map square that this object is hanging off,
    // ie the start of that list
    GameObject **MapSquare;

    // The resolution of the map the object is sitting in
    int MapRes;

    // Take the object out of the map's linked list
    void RemoveFromMap();

    // calls "process_collision" on all the relevant other objects in
    // the map, as per the article
    void ProcessCollisions(class Map *my_map);

private:

    // Do one resolution of map, used by ProcessCollisions()
    void ProcessOneLevel(Map *my_map, GameObject **map_who,
    GameObject *walker, int current_res);
};
```

```
/////////////////////////////////////////////////////////////////////
//
// The map.

// for efficiency's sake, the map dimensions etc are constants, you
//   could simply turn them into variables if you so wished

// (1 << this) is number of map squares at highest res
#define MAP_HI_RES_SHIFT        (8)

// and the number of map squares at the lowest res
#define MAP_LO_RES_SHIFT        (4)

// smallest size of a map square
#define MAP_SMALLEST_SQUARE_SIZE_SHIFT (8)
#define MAP_SMALLEST_SQUARE_SIZE       (1 << \
      MAP_SMALLEST_SQUARE_SIZE_SHIFT)

// largest
#define MAP_BIGGEST_SQUARE_SIZE_SHIFT  (MAP_SMALLEST_SQUARE_SIZE_SHIFT +
MAP_HI_RES_SHIFT \
                                    - MAP_LO_RES_SHIFT)
#define MAP_BIGGEST_SQUARE_SIZE        (1 << \
      MAP_BIGGEST_SQUARE_SIZE_SHIFT)

// The length of one edge of the map in actual game coordinates
#define MAP_SIZE        (1 << \
(MAP_SMALLEST_SQUARE_SIZE_SHIFT + MAP_HI_RES_SHIFT))

// The map.
class Map
{
public:

    // A array of pointers to the different resolutions of map.
    GameObject **Who[MAP_HI_RES_SHIFT - MAP_LO_RES_SHIFT + 1];

    Map();
    ~Map();

    // Fills in the who array and clears it
    bool Init();

    // deallocate
    void Reset();

    // fills in the object's map-related information given its
    // position and radius
    void PlaceObject(GameObject &obj, const vector3 &pos,
    float radius);

    // given a map square at a certain resolution, returns the
    // one at the next lower resolution, or NULL if that was the
    // lowest res
    GameObject **GetLowerMapSquare(GameObject **current, int res);
```

```
};

///////////////////////////////////////////////////////////////////////
//
// implementation

void GameObject::ProcessCollisions(Map *my_map)
{
    // We loop through several resolutions of map, starting with
    // the current.
    // First start with the objects in my map square
    GameObject *walker = NextInMap;
    int current_res = MapRes;

    GameObject **map_who = MapSquare;

    do
    {
        // Do one resolution's worth of collision
        ProcessOneLevel(my_map, map_who, walker, current_res);

        // Move to the next lower resolution
        map_who = my_map->GetLowerMapSquare(map_who, current_res);
        current_res-;
    }
    while (map_who); // until we're at the lowest resolution.
}

void GameObject::ProcessOneLevel(Map *my_map, GameObject **map_sq,
        GameObject *walker, int current_res_shift)
{
    int current_res_size = 1 << current_res_shift;

    // Do all the objects in the first list presented
    for (; walker; walker = walker->NextInMap)
    {
        process_collision(this, walker);
    }

    // Work out if you can go to the adjacent map squares
    int current_offset = map_sq - my_map->Who[current_res_shift -
    MAP_LO_RES_SHIFT];

    // Then do map squares to the east, southeast and south
    if ((current_offset & (current_res_size - 1)) !=
    current_res_size - 1)
    {
        // Square to the east
        for (walker = map_sq[1]; walker;
        walker = walker->NextInMap)
        {
            process_collision(this, walker);
        }
    }
```

```cpp
        if (current_offset + current_res_size <
        (1 << (current_res_shift * 2)))
        {
            // Square to the south
            for (walker = map_sq[current_res_size]; walker;
            walker = walker->NextInMap)
            {
                process_collision(this, walker);
            }

            // and lastly, southeast.
            if ((current_offset & (current_res_size - 1)) !=
            current_res_size - 1)
            {
                for (walker = map_sq[current_res_size + 1]; walker;
                    walker = walker->NextInMap)
                {
                    process_collision(this, walker);
                }
            }
        }
    }
}

void GameObject::RemoveFromMap()
{
    // Search for myself.
    for (GameObject **pointer_to_me = MapSquare;
        *pointer_to_me != this;
        pointer_to_me = &(*pointer_to_me)->NextInMap)
    {
        assert(*pointer_to_me &&
        "Game object couldn't find itself in map");
    }

    // Remove myself.
    *pointer_to_me = NextInMap;

    // And for safety's sake, let's clear my pointers.
    NextInMap = NULL;
    MapSquare = NULL;
}

Map::Map()
{
    for (int res = MAP_LO_RES_SHIFT; res <= MAP_HI_RES_SHIFT; res++)
    {
        Who[res - MAP_LO_RES_SHIFT] = NULL;
    }
}

Map::~Map()
{
    Reset();
}
```

```cpp
void Map::Reset()
{
    // You'd better have cleared all the objects out by now.
    // I won't check.
    for (int res = MAP_LO_RES_SHIFT; res <= MAP_HI_RES_SHIFT; res++)
    {
        delete[] Who[res - MAP_LO_RES_SHIFT];
        Who[res - MAP_LO_RES_SHIFT] = NULL;
    }
}

bool Map::Init()
{
    Reset(); // just in case

    // allocate and clear everything.
    for (int res = MAP_LO_RES_SHIFT; res <= MAP_HI_RES_SHIFT; res++)
    {
        Who[res - MAP_LO_RES_SHIFT] = new GameObject*
        [1 << (res * 2)];

        if (!Who[res - MAP_LO_RES_SHIFT])
        return false; // alloc failed

        for (int sq = 0; sq < (1 << (res * 2)); sq++)
        {
            Who[res - MAP_LO_RES_SHIFT][sq] = NULL;
        }
    }

    return true;
}

// fills in the object's map-related information given its
//    position and radius
void Map::PlaceObject(GameObject &obj, const vector3 &pos,
        float radius)
{
    // input value checking.
    assert(radius >= 0.f && radius < MAP_SIZE);

    // If you want to allow positions off the map, change
    // these asserts into assignments
    assert(pos.x >= 0.f && pos.x < MAP_SIZE);
    assert(pos.y >= 0.f && pos.y < MAP_SIZE);

    // Conversion into integer coordinate system needed for
    // shifting/array maths later on.  Note that these conversions
    // are often slow and may have to be replaced with faster
    // versions in some compilers.  If you do replace them,
    // preserve their rounding-down nature
    int iradius = int(radius);
    int ix      = int(pos.x );
    int iy      = int(pos.y );
```

```
        // Find which resolution level of the map the object should
        // go in.
        obj.MapRes = MAP_HI_RES_SHIFT;
        for (int map_size = MAP_SMALLEST_SQUARE_SIZE; map_size <=
        MAP_BIGGEST_SQUARE_SIZE;
        map_size <<= 1)
        {
            // Does the object fit?
            if (iradius <= map_size) goto it_fits;

            // step on...
            obj.MapRes--;
        }

        assert(!"object too large for map - some collisions may not be
        detected");

it_fits:

        // Put it in the map.
        int which_level = obj.MapRes - MAP_LO_RES_SHIFT;
        GameObject **which_who = Who[which_level];

        // Then add on the position
        which_who += ix >> (MAP_BIGGEST_SQUARE_SIZE_SHIFT - which_level);
        which_who += (iy >> (MAP_BIGGEST_SQUARE_SIZE_SHIFT -
        which_level)) << obj.MapRes;

        // Insert the object into the map square
        obj.NextInMap = *which_who;
        *which_who = &obj;

        obj.MapSquare = which_who;
}

GameObject **Map::GetLowerMapSquare(GameObject **current, int who_res)
{
        // Top of map?
        if (who_res == MAP_LO_RES_SHIFT) return NULL;

        // Cunning bit-shifting.
        int current_offset = current - Who[who_res - MAP_LO_RES_SHIFT];

        // Extract the y part of the current offset.
        int y_mask = 0xffffffff << who_res;

        // The new offset is this:
        int new_offset = ((current_offset & ~y_mask        ) >> 1) +
                         ((current_offset & (y_mask << 1)) >> 2);

        return Who[who_res - MAP_LO_RES_SHIFT - 1] + new_offset;
}
```

4.7

Computing the Distance into a Sector

Steven Ranck

This article describes a simple and fast algorithm for determining where a point is between the edges of a 2D quad (or sector). The result is a unit floating point number, where 0 indicates that the point lies on the leading edge, and where 1 indicates that the point lies on the opposite edge. The sector may be any four-sided, 2D convex shape.

This article is useful for any game that may require knowledge of how far "into" a 2D sector an object or point is. For example, a 3D racing game might use a top-down 2D sectorization of its track to describe to the AI driving system how to navigate the track. Using the sector data and a vehicle's *XZ* position within a sector, the AI system could use this algorithm to determine how far into the current sector the vehicle is, or where laterally it is. The algorithm is very fast, and in most cases can easily be computed for every vehicle each frame, if necessary.

The Problem

Figure 4.7.1 shows a four-sided, 2D sector in *XZ* world space. The object's position on the *XZ* plane is shown as point *P*. We would like to find a continuous function that accepts *P* as a parameter and produces a value of 0 if *P* lies on the leading edge, 1 if *P* lies anywhere on the trailing edge, and a value between 0 and 1 if the point lies between the leading and trailing edges. Figure 4.7.2 shows the desired scalar values for several points within a sector.

As Figure 4.7.2 shows, all points lying on the leading edge produce a value of 0, and all points lying on the trailing edge produce a value of 1. Points between the two edges produce values that increase from 0 to 1 as the point is swept across the sector from the leading edge to the trailing edge. Because we're interested in an algorithm that's computationally inexpensive, we will not require that the interpolation be linear. However, it must be a smooth interpolation, and the function must work for all convex sector shapes. A few examples are shown in Figure 4.7.3.

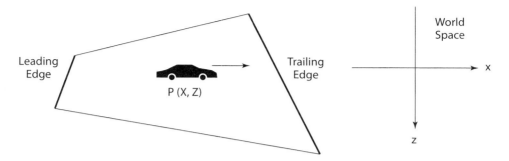

FIGURE 4.7.1. Top-down view of a vehicle in a sector.

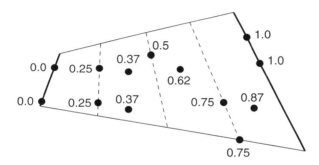

FIGURE 4.7.2 Desired scalar values for various points within a sector.

Figure 4.7.3 shows that, regardless of the sector's shape, the value returned from our desired function is always 0 on the leading edge and 1 on the trailing edge, and it is interpolated when our point lies between the two edges.

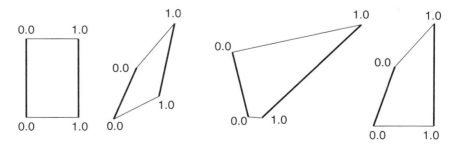

FIGURE 4.7.3 Example convex sector shapes showing corresponding scalar values.

Description of the Algorithm

A fast and simple solution to the problem in the previous section is given by the equation:

$$D = \frac{(V_{LP} \bullet N_L)}{V_{LP} \bullet N_L + V_{TP} \bullet N_L}$$

EQUATION 4.7.1 Equation for computing a distance value across a sector.

Where:

$$V_{LP} = P - P_L$$

$$V_{TP} = P - P_T$$

And:

- P is the point of interest within the sector.
- P_L is any point on the Leading Edge.
- P_T is any point on the Trailing Edge.
- N_L is the inward-pointing unit normal of the Leading Edge.
- N_T is the inward-pointing unit normal of the Trailing Edge.
- D is our result: a floating point number from 0 to 1.

Figure 4.7.4 shows the variables involved in Equation 4.7.1 and their relationship to the problem. Note that P_L may lie anywhere along the leading edge, and P_T may lie anywhere along the trailing edge. However, using opposite corners of the sector offers several advantages. First, since the sector is most likely defined by its four vertices, it makes sense to use the corners for our purposes. Second, by choosing opposite corners, Equation 4.7.1 can be used to compute both the distance from leading edge to trailing edge, as well as the distance laterally. This is because P_L lies on both the leading edge and one of the lateral edges, and P_T lies on both the trailing edge and the other lateral edge.

Equation 4.7.1 has several features:

1. It produces a scalar from 0 to 1.
2. It produces 0 if P lies on the leading edge.
3. It produces 1 if P lies on the trailing edge.
4. Although not linearly, it does produce a smooth, interpolated value from 0 to 1, depending on how far into the sector P lies.
5. It's fast, requiring only two 2D vector subtractions, two 2D dot products, one scalar addition, and one scalar divide to compute.
6. The raw, world-space point P can be directly plugged into the equation. No transformation into warped sector space is required.

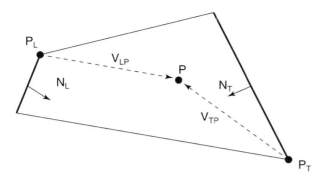

FIGURE 4.7.4 Parameters used in the algorithm.

7. If the sector is a static shape, then P_L, P_T, N_L, and N_T may all be pre-determined and stored in the sector definition data structure.
8. If the sector dynamically changes shape, P_L and P_T are still available from the sector's vertices, and N_L and N_T can easily be computed from the sector's vertices (although this is slower because it involves a square root per normal).
9. It may be used to compute the distance laterally, too, provided that the two inward-pointing unit normals for the lateral edges are available.

The equation has several requirements:

1. The sector must be convex and have four sides, each of non-zero length.
2. The sector must have non-zero area.
3. P must lie within the sector, or along any of its perimeter line segments. If the point lies outside of the sector, the result might not be a value between 0 and 1, as expected.

Applications

Distance Down a Track

Equation 4.7.1 has many applications in game development. One example is in the determination of how far down the track a vehicle is. Figure 4.7.5 shows a top-down view of a road track overlaid with a chain of sectors.

What we'd like to know is how far down the track each vehicle is. When the vehicle is at the starting line, it should be a value of 0. When the vehicle is at the finish line, we'd like a value of 1. And, we'd like reasonable interpolation in between.

The sectors are constructed to completely contain the track so that the vehicle position, P, will always be within a sector. This also means that adjacent sectors use the same vertex points. At game initialization time, each sector's inward-pointing unit normal for both its leading edge and trailing edge is computed. Note that a sector's

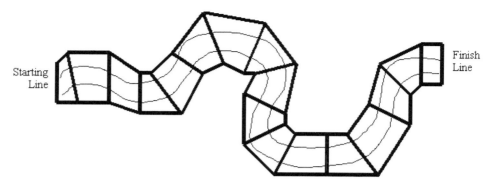

FIGURE 4.7.5 Sectorization of a track.

trailing edge normal is equal to its neighboring sector's negated leading edge normal. But if the memory is available, it's fastest to store the two normals with each sector.

Another piece of information we'll need is the approximate world-space distance between each sector's leading and trailing edges. A sloppy but decent metric for this is to use the magnitude of the vector extending between the midpoints of the leading and trailing edges as shown in Figure 4.7.6.

As with the other sector data, we pre-compute s for each sector and store it in the sector's data structure. At this point, we might have a sector data structure that looks like this:

```
typedef struct {
    float fX, fZ;  // 2D XZ worldspace coordinate
} VecXZ_t;

typedef struct {
    // Clockwise, where [0] = left side of Leading Edge
    VecXZ_t aVertices[4];
    // Clockwise, where [0] = Leading Edge
    VecXZ_t aUnitNormals[4];
    // Distance from Leading Edge's midpoint to
    //    Trailing Edge's midpoint
    float fSectorDist;
    // = previous sector's fTotalPriorDist + fSectorDist
    float fTotalPriorDist;
} Sector_t;
```

Note the fTotalPriorDist field, which is simply the sum of the previous sector's fTotalPriorDist and fSectorDist fields (fTotalPriorDist is 0 for the first sector). We'll discover why we need this below. The final piece of information we will need is the sum of all s, adding together fSectorDist for all sectors. We'll pre-compute and store the inverse of this and call it fOneOverTotalSectorDist. We store the inverse because, as we'll see, we actually need to divide by the sum of all s, and multiplying by

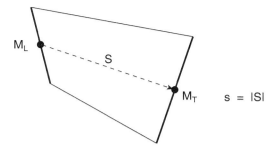

FIGURE 4.7.6 Approximating the world-space distance between sector edges.

the inverse is faster on most CPUs than dividing. Since we have the luxury of pre-computing this information, we won't pass up the opportunity to do the division (reciprocal) at that time and score an inexpensive multiplication at run-time.

Armed with the preceding information, we're now able to determine how far down a track a vehicle is. For each vehicle, we need the following information:

```
#include "mtxlib.h"

typedef struct {
    vector3 WorldPos3D;    // Vehicle's origin in 3D worldspace
    Sector_t *pSector;     // Points to the sector the
                           // vehicle origin is currently in
} Vehicle_t;
```

At the start of the race, the vehicle structure is initialized for each vehicle, and pSector is pointed to the sector containing its origin. This initial sector may be found by either scanning the entire list of sectors for the one sector containing the vehicle origin point, or by storing the initial sectors as part of the starting line data.

Once the race begins, we need to track which sectors the vehicles are in, since Equation 4.7.1 requires that the point lie within a sector. To do this, each time we move the vehicle, we use a simple point-in-sector test to see if the vehicle is still within pSector. If not, then the vehicle is either in the next sector or the previous sector, and we again use the point-in-sector test. Most of the time, only one test is required; occasionally, two tests are required. If the vehicle is moving backward, three tests will be needed. If it is possible that the vehicle's speed is fast enough that the vehicle skips an entire sector from one frame to the next, a more sophisticated sector-tracking algorithm will be needed. One such solution would be to check, in order, the next N forward sectors first. If the vehicle is not found in any of those, the algorithm would next check the previous N sectors. If the sector is still not found, this could be considered an uncommon condition, and the algorithm would resort to scanning the entire sector list.

Now that we have a valid sector for each vehicle, we can write a function for Equation 4.7.1 to determine how far into its sector each vehicle is:

```
float CalcUnitDistIntoSector( float fPointX, float fPointZ, const
Sector_t *pSector ) {
    VecXZ_t VLP, VTP;
    float fDotL, fDotT;

    // Compute vector from point on Leading Edge to P:
    VLP.fX = fPointX - pSector->aVertices[0].fX;
    VLP.fZ = fPointZ - pSector->aVertices[0].fZ;

    // Compute vector from point on Trailing Edge to P:
    VTP.fX = fPointX - pSector->aVertices[2].fX;
    VTP.fZ = fPointZ - pSector->aVertices[2].fZ;

    // Compute (VLP dot Leading Edge Normal):
    fDotL = VLP.fX*pSector->aUnitNormals[0].fX +
    VLP.fZ*pSector->aUnitNormals[0].fZ;

    // Compute (VTP dot Trailing Edge Normal):
    fDotT = VTP.fX*pSector->aUnitNormals[2].fX +
    VTP.fZ*pSector->aUnitNormals[2].fZ;

    // Compute unit distance into sector and return it:
    return ( fDotL / (fDotL + fDotT) );
}
```

Finally, we can compute the distance down the track like this:

```
// Pre-computed to be the inverse sum of Sector_t::fSectorDist
//   for all sectors.
float fOneOverTotalSectorDist;

float CalcUnitDistDownTrack( const Vehicle_t *pVehicle ) {
    float fUnitDistIntoSector, fDistDownTrack;

    // Compute how far vehicle is into its sector:
    fUnitDistIntoSector = CalcUnitDistIntoSector(
                    pVehicle->WorldPos3D.x,
                    pVehicle->WorldPos3D.z,
                    pVehicle->pSector
                );

    // The distance down the track is the full distance
    // across all previous sectors, plus the partial
    // distance into our current sector:
    fDistDownTrack = pVehicle->pSector->fTotalPriorDist
            + pVehicle->pSector->fSectorDist *
            fUnitDistIntoSector;

    // Finally, our unit distance down the track is our
    // distance so far divided by the track's total distance:
    return fDistDownTrack * fOneOverTotalSectorDist;
}
```

The function `CalcUnitDistDownTrack()` returns a value of 0 if the vehicle is on the leading edge of the first sector of the track, returns a value of 1 if the vehicle is on the trailing edge of the last sector of the track, and returns an interpolated value between 0 and 1 based on how far down the track the vehicle is.

Smooth Light Changes

Another practical application of Equation 4.7.1 is the smooth interpolation of lighting on objects moving through sectors. If we associate ambient and directional lights with leading/trailing sector edges, we can interpolate the lighting parameters as the objects to be lit move from sector to sector.

Consider a sector enclosing a section of a track that begins in the sun at the sector's leading edge, and ends in a dark cave at the sector's trailing edge as in Figure 4.7.7.

We can store the ambient RGB light color at each adjoining sector edge like so:

```
typedef struct {
    float fR, fG, fB;  // RGB ambient light
} Ambient_t;

typedef struct {
    // Clockwise, where [0] = left side of Leading Edge
    VecXZ_t aVertices[4];
    // Clockwise, where [0] = Leading Edge
    VecXZ_t aUnitNormals[4];
    // Distance from Leading Edge's midpoint to Trailing
    //    Edge's
    float fSectorDist;
    // = previous sector's fTotalPriorDist + fSectorDist
    float fTotalPriorDist;
    // Ambient light at Leading Edge
    Ambient_t LeadingAmbient;
    // Ambient light at Trailing Edge
    Ambient_t TrailingAmbient;
} Sector_t;
```

The ambient value of adjacent sectors must be the same to avoid a visual pop of the light level when the vehicle crosses into a different sector. In the preceding imple-

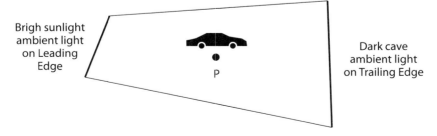

FIGURE 4.7.7 Ambient light gradient across a sector.

mentation, we simply store both leading and trailing ambient values with each sector, but a more memory-conscious implementation might share ambient data through pointers. In any case, the preceding is all we need to smoothly animate the ambient light level from sunlight to cave light as the object progresses through the sector. The following function does the trick:

```
#define LERP( fUnit, fV0, fV1 ) ( (1.0f-(fUnit))*fV0 + \
    (fUnit)*fV1 )

Ambient_t CalcAmbientLightLevel( const Vehicle_t *pVehicle ) {
    float fUnitDistIntoSector;
    Ambient_t *pLeadAmbient, *pTrailAmbient, RetAmbient;

    // Compute how far vehicle is into its sector:
    fUnitDistIntoSector = CalcUnitDistIntoSector(
                    pVehicle->WorldPos3D.x,
                    pVehicle->WorldPos3D.z,
                    pVehicle->pSector
                );

    pLeadAmbient = &pVehicle->pSector->LeadingAmbient;
    pTrailAmbient = &pVehicle->pSector->TrailingAmbient;

    RetAmbient.fR = LERP( fUnitDistIntoSector,
    pLeadAmbient->fR, pTrailAmbient->fR );
    RetAmbient.fG = LERP( fUnitDistIntoSector,
    pLeadAmbient->fG, pTrailAmbient->fG );
    RetAmbient.fB = LERP( fUnitDistIntoSector,
    pLeadAmbient->fB, pTrailAmbient->fB );

    return RetAmbient;
}
```

The preceding function computes the ambient light level at the world position of the vehicle. A graphics engine could use the resulting ambient RGB to provide the overall ambient light with which to light the vehicle, combining it with other, more sophisticated lighting if desired. As the vehicle drives through the sector, the ambient light is smoothly interpolated, regardless of the shape of the sector.

Functions similar to CalcAmbientLightLevel() can be written to smoothly interpolate any parameter that's associated with a sector edge. Examples are directional light (interpolating the direction and color), sector height, water flow rate and direction, fog characteristics, sky appearance, AI difficulty, etc.

4.8

Object Occlusion Culling

Tim Round

Occlusion culling is a technique for culling unwanted geometry from the field of view. This is an extension of field of view culling, in that it helps reduce unnecessary processing time associated with rendering a mesh (i.e., transformation, lighting, and rasterization). The occlusion provides a culling method that will work on arbitrary and dynamic geometry data. This means the mesh data doesn't have to contain any information about the potentially visible data set. Occlusion culling also isn't limited to indoor scenes, and can be used to mark anywhere in the mesh data that could be blocked from your field of view (see Figure 4.8.1 for an example).

Using a Z-buffer makes it easier to display a scene correctly, but you still need to transform, light, and draw the polygons, while testing each pixel's depth. This implementation of occlusion culling simplifies the process of building the occlusion data by using simple pre-defined occlusion shapes, namely rectangles. These occlusion rectangles could easily be added into the original geometry as two co-planar triangles, and either named or colored in such a way that the exporter or the loader could separate them out from the original mesh data.

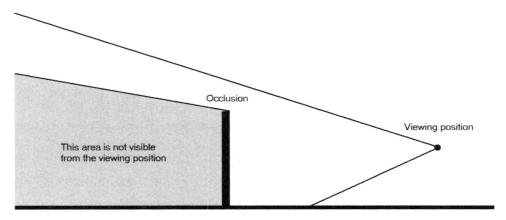

FIGURE 4.8.1 A typical occlusion.

Frustum Culling

To help explain the process of occlusion culling, it's worth describing a technique for field of view culling. The field of view is the area in 3D space visible from the current point of view of the camera. This area is typically described using front and back clip planes and the viewing angle (see Figure 4.8.2).

The culling process uses the bounding sphere (in world space) of each object's mesh, and tests if it falls inside the field of view. To perform this test, you transform the bounding sphere center point into view space (relative to the camera) and check the new Z value against the near and far clip planes. You can then test the center point against the left, right, top, and bottom clip planes. The clip planes for the field of view can be pre-calculated at the start of the render loop. Because these clip planes are in view space, we can simplify the clipping test. The front and back clip planes will be perpendicular to the Z-axis, so a simple compare against the Z value can quickly decide if the mesh is in front or behind the camera. The coefficients B and D in the equation of the plane for the left and right planes are zero (because they are vertical), and the planes pass through the origin (0,0,0). This means to test a point against the left or right plane, you can use the following equation:

```
DistanceFromClipPlane = (x * Plane.a) + (z * Plane.c);
```

This also applies to the top and bottom clip planes, except the coefficients A and D are now zero, and this produces the following equation:

```
DistanceFromClipPlane = (y * Plane.b) + (z * Plane.c);
```

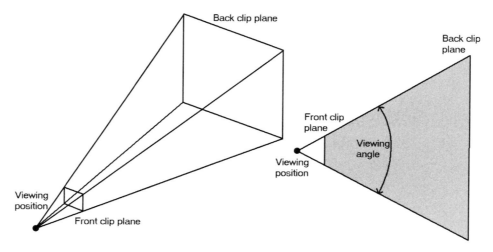

FIGURE 4.8.2 Field of view or viewing frustum.

If the distance of the point from the plane is greater than the bounding sphere radius, then the bounding sphere is outside the area. By testing the bounding sphere against all the clip planes, we can find out if the mesh lies within the field of view; this helps us remove all meshes that are not visible. The order we test the center point against the clip planes can be changed to match the geometric data; for example, a landscape expands more along the X and Z axes than the Y axis, so we test the left and right clip planes before the top and bottom clip planes. The front and back planes are tested first because they require less computation and can typically remove a large proportion of the geometry. See Listing 4.8.1 for sample code that implements field of view culling.

As you see, we can use the plane equation to describe the boundaries of the viewing frustum, and by first transforming the bounding sphere center point into view space we can simplify the point-to-plane test. So, using this same principal, we can describe the boundaries of an occlusion.

Occlusion Culling

Occlusions described in this article are four-sided flat or planar polygons, but they can easily use more or less sides, providing the polygon is planar. We can pre-calculate the occlusion's clip planes in the same way as for field of view culling, except this time we only need a front plane and four edge planes (see Figure 4.8.3).

The occlusion area differs from the viewing frustum in that it describes a hole. If any mesh lies inside this hole, it won't be rendered (see Figure 4.8.4).

The front plane of the occlusion won't always be perpendicular with the front clip plane, so we will have to use all four coefficients of the plane equation. We also can't simplify the edge planes because they too can be at any angle. The front plane is cal-

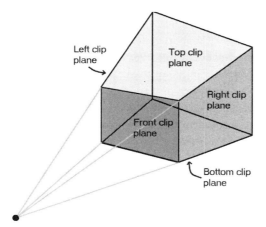

FIGURE 4.8.3 A four-sided occlusion is described with four planes, front, left, right, top and bottom.

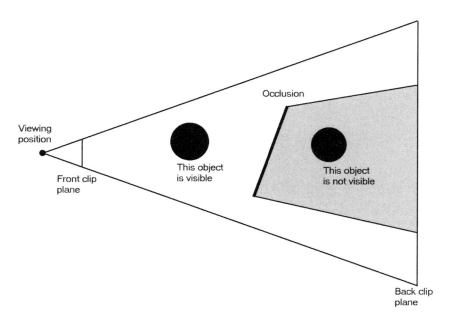

FIGURE 4.8.4 Objects that are behind the occlusion are invisible.

culated by using three points from the occlusion polygon after they have been transformed into view space. The edge planes are calculated by using the camera position (remember in view space this is 0,0,0) and two points along the edge of the occlusion polygon (see the SetupOcclusion() function in Listing 4.8.2). Occlusions can be made two-sided by testing which way the front plane faces and reversing the order of the points used to generate the planes.

We will need to test if an object's mesh falls inside the field of view before testing it against the occlusions, so we have already transformed the bounding sphere center into view space. To help speed up the occlusion test, we can pre-calculate a minimum Z value (the value closest to the front clip plane) in view space for each occlusion, and we can test the transformed bounding sphere center against it to quickly test if the mesh is in front of the occlusion (see Figure 4.8.5.)

If the bounding sphere of the mesh overlaps the edge of an occlusion, we could test all the points of an axis-aligned bounding box for extra precision. If an object is much bigger along one axis (e.g., very tall), then a bounding sphere can be very wasteful in describing its area, but the bounding sphere can be tested against a plane much faster than a bounding box. So we use the bounding sphere first to quickly reject any meshes that are totally outside or inside of an occlusion.

When building up a list of occlusions that are visible, you can also test the occlusions against each other to remove any occluded occlusion. If an occlusion covers the entire viewing frustum, we can move the back clip plane closer. Occlusions can also

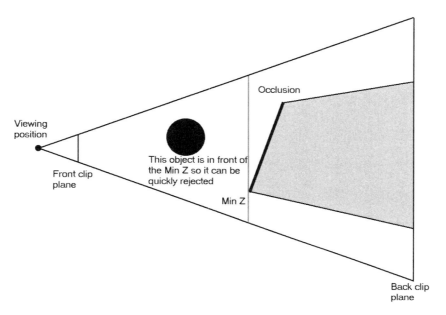

FIGURE 4.8.5 A minimum Z value can be used to speed up the test.

have their own bounding sphere, which can be used to remove any occlusions that are not visible in the viewing frustum.

Summary

As you can see, occlusion culling of this nature is fairly easy to implement, but it doesn't have to be limited to mesh culling—it can also be used for culling sounds. Occlusions can also help to prevent time-consuming effects like skinned animation from being applied to objects that aren't visible.

Occlusions can be made more efficient by joining several together to form complex occlusion zones, but this is beyond this discussion.

The example code is written with DirectX in mind (i.e., it's left-handed), but it can easily be changed to suit any coordinate system. The code is designed to illustrate the algorithm, and can easily be adapted to suit any target platform or application.

Listing 4.8.1: Field of View Culling Code

```
typedef struct _VECTOR
{
    float x;
    float y;
    float z;
```

```
}VECTOR;

typedef struct _PLANE
{
     float a;
     float b;
     float c;
     float d;
}PLANE;

typedef struct _MATRIX
{
     float _ 11;
     float _ 12;
     float _ 13;
     float _ 14;
     float _ 21;
     float _ 22;
     float _ 23;
     float _ 24;
     float _ 31;
     float _ 32;
     float _ 33;
     float _ 34;
     float _ 41;
     float _ 42;
     float _ 43;
     float _ 44;
}MATRIX;

PLANE      g_FOVLeftPlane;
PLANE      g_FOVRightPlane;
PLANE      g_FOVTopPlane;
PLANE      g_FOVBottomPlane;
float      g_FOVFrontClip;
float      g_FOVBackClip;
MATRIX g_ViewTransform;


void Normalize(VECTOR *pV)
{
     float Length , InvLength;

     Length = (float) sqrt( ( pV->x * pV->x ) +
         ( pV->y * pV->y ) + ( pV->z * pV->z ) );
     InvLength = 1.0f / Length;
     pV->x /= InvLength;
     pV->y /= InvLength;
     pV->z /= InvLength;
}


void CrossProduct(VECTOR *pVO , VECTOR *pV1 ,
        VECTOR *pCrossProduct)
{
```

```
        pCrossProduct->x = pV0->y * pV1->z - pV0->z * pV1->y;
        pCrossProduct->y = pV0->z * pV1->x - pV0->x * pV1->z;
        pCrossProduct->z= pV0->x * pV1->y - pV0->y * pV1->x;
}


void PlaneFromPoints(VECTOR *pP0 , VECTOR *pP1 ,
        VECTOR *pP2 , PLANE *pPlane)
{
    VECTOR V0,V1,V2;

    V0.x = pP1->x - pP0->x;
    V0.y = pP1->y - pP0->y;
    V0.z= pP1->z- pP0->z;
    V1.x = pP2->x - pP0->x;
    V1.y = pP2->y - pP0->y;
    V1.z= pP2->z- pP0->z;
    CrossProduct( &V0, &V1, &V2);
    Normalize( &V2);
    pPlane->a = V2.x;
    pPlane->b = V2.y;
    pPlane->c = V2.z;
    pPlane->d = -( V2.x * pP0->x + V2.y * pP0->y + V2.z *
        pP0->z );
}


//This function calculates the planes for describing the view
//frustum using 3 points.  Because we are in view space the
//cameras position is at 0,0,0.  We use the back clip position
//and the viewing angle to work out a point on the edge of
//the frustum.  The view angle is the angle between the top
//and bottom of the view frustum in radians.

void SetupFOVClipPlanes( float Angle , float Aspect ,
        float FrontClip , float BackClip )
{
    VECTOR  P0 , P1 , P2;

//  Calculate left plane using 3 points
    P0.x = 0.0f;
    P0.y = 0.0f;
    P0.z = 0.0f;
    P1.x = -BackClip * ( (float)tan( Angle * 0.5f ) / Aspect );
    P1.y = -BackClip * ( (float)tan( Angle * 0.5f ) );
    P1.z = BackClip;
    P2.x = P1.x;
    P2.y = -P1.y;
    P2.z = P1.z;
    PlaneFromPoints( &P0, &P1 , &P2 , &g_FOVLeftPlane );

//  Calculate right plane using 3 points
    P0.x = 0.0f;
    P0.y = 0.0f;
    P0.z = 0.0f;
```

```
      P1.x = BackClip * ( (float)tan( Angle * 0.5f ) / Aspect);
      P1.y = BackClip * ( (float)tan( Angle * 0.5f ) );
      P1.z = BackClip;
      P2.x = P1.x;
      P2.y = -P1.y;
      P2.z = P1.z;
      PlaneFromPoints( &P0, &P1 , &P2 , &g_FOVRightPlane );

//    Calculate top plane using 3 points
      P0.x = 0.0f;
      P0.y = 0.0f;
      P0.z = 0.0f;
      P1.x = -BackClip * ( (float)tan( Angle * 0.5f ) / Aspect);
      P1.y = BackClip * ( (float)tan( Angle * 0.5f ) );
      P1.z = BackClip;
      P2.x = -P1.x;
      P2.y = P1.y;
      P2.z = P1.z;
      PlaneFromPoints( &P0, &P1 , &P2 , &g_FOVTopPlane );

//    Calculate bottom plane using 3 points
      P0.x = 0.0f;
      P0.y = 0.0f;
      P0.z = 0.0f;
      P1.x = BackClip * ( (float)tan( Angle * 0.5f ) / Aspect);
      P1.y = -BackClip * ( (float)tan( Angle * 0.5f ) );
      P1.z = BackClip;
      P2.x = -P1.x;
      P2.y = P1.y;
      P2.z = P1.z;
      PlaneFromPoints( &P0, &P1 , &P2 , &g_FOVBottomPlane );
}

BOOL MeshFOVCheck(VECTOR *pBSpherePos ,
        float BSphereRadius,VECTOR *pViewPos)
{
    float   Dist;

//    Transform Z into view space
      pViewPos->z = g_ViewTransform._13 * pBSpherePos->x +
          g_ViewTransform._23 * pBSpherePos->y +
          g_ViewTransform._33 * pBSpherePos->z +
          g_ViewTransform._43;

//    Behind front clip plane?
      if( ( pViewPos->z + BSphereRadius ) < g_FOVFrontClip )
          return FALSE;

//    Beyond the back clip plane?
      if( ( pViewPos->z - BSphereRadius ) > g_FOVBackClip )
            return FALSE;

//    Transform X into view space
      pViewPos->x = g_ViewTransform._11 * pBSpherePos->x +
          g_ViewTransform._21 * pBSpherePos->y +
```

```
            g_ViewTransform._31 * pBSpherePos->z +
            g_ViewTransform._41;

//   Test against left clip plane
     Dist = ( pViewPos->x * g_FOVLeftPlane.a ) +
            ( pViewPos->z * g_FOVLeftPlane.c );
     if( Dist > BSphereRadius )
         return FALSE;

//   Test against right clip plane
     Dist = ( pViewPos->x * g_FOVRightPlane.a ) +
            ( pViewPos->z * g_FOVRightPlane.c );
     if( Dist > BSphereRadius )
         return FALSE;

//   Transform Y into view space
     pViewPos->y = g_ViewTransform._12 * pBSpherePos->x +
         g_ViewTransform._22 * pBSpherePos->y +
         g_ViewTransform._32 * pBSpherePos->z +
         g_ViewTransform._42;

//   Test against top clip plane
     Dist = ( pViewPos->y * g_FOVTopPlane.b ) +
            ( pViewPos->z * g_FOVTopPlane.c );
     if( Dist > BSphereRadius )
         return FALSE;

//   Test against bottom plane
     Dist = ( pViewPos->y * g_FOVBottomPlane.b ) +
            ( pViewPos->z * g_FOVBottomPlane.c);
     if( Dist > BSphereRadius )
         return FALSE;

//   Mesh is inside the field of view
     return TRUE;
}
```

Listing 4.8.2: Occlusion Culling Code

```
typedef struct _OCCLUSION
{
     VECTOR  P0;
     VECTOR  P1;
     VECTOR  P2;
     VECTOR  P3;
     float   MinZ;
     PLANE   FrontPlane;
     PLANE   FirstPlane;
     PLANE   SecondPlane;
     PLANE   ThirdPlane;
     PLANE   FourthPlane;
}OCCLUSION;
```

```
void VectorMatrixMultiply3x4(VECTOR *pNewVector ,
        VECTOR *pVector , MATRIX *pMatrix)
{
}

void SetupOcclusion(OCCLUSION *pOcclusion ,
        MATRIX *pViewTransform)
{
    VECTOR  PO , P1 , P2 , P3 , Camera;

//   Transform points form world space to view space
     VectorMatrixMultiply3x4( &PO , &pOcclusion->PO ,
         pViewTransform);
     VectorMatrixMultiply3x4( &P1 , &pOcclusion->P1 ,
         pViewTransform);
     VectorMatrixMultiply3x4( &P2 , &pOcclusion->P2 ,
         pViewTransform);
     VectorMatrixMultiply3x4( &P3 , &pOcclusion->P3 ,
         pViewTransform);

     pOcclusion->MinZ = PO.z;
     if( P1.z < pOcclusion->MinZ)
         pOcclusion->MinZ = P1.z;
     if( P2.z < pOcclusion->MinZ)
         pOcclusion->MinZ = P2.z;
     if( P3.z < pOcclusion->MinZ)
         pOcclusion->MinZ = P3.z;

//   The camera position in view space is 0,0,0
     Camera.x=0.0f;
     Camera.y=0.0f;
     Camera.z=0.0f;

//   Create front plane from first three points
     PlaneFromPoints(&PO , &P1 , &P2 , &pOcclusion->FrontPlane);

//   Test the D co-effecient to find which way the
//      occlusion faces
     if(pOcclusion->FrontPlane.d > 0.0f)
     {
         PlaneFromPoints( &Camera , &PO , &P1 ,
             &pOcclusion->FirstPlane);
         PlaneFromPoints( &Camera , &P1 , &P2 ,
             &pOcclusion->SecondPlane);
         PlaneFromPoints( &Camera , &P2 , &P3 ,
             &pOcclusion->ThirdPlane);
         PlaneFromPoints( &Camera , &P3 , &PO ,
             &pOcclusion->FourthPlane);
     }
     else
     {
         PlaneFromPoints( &P2 , &P1 , &PO ,
             &pOcclusion->FrontPlane);
         PlaneFromPoints( &Camera , &P1 , &PO ,
```

```
                &pOcclusion->FirstPlane);          .
                 PlaneFromPoints( &Camera , &P2 , &P1 ,
                &pOcclusion->SecondPlane);
                 PlaneFromPoints( &Camera , &P3 , &P2 ,
                &pOcclusion->ThirdPlane);
                 PlaneFromPoints( &Camera , &P0 , &P3 ,
                &pOcclusion->FourthPlane);
        }
}

BOOL TestIfOccluded(OCCLUSION *pOcclusion ,
        VECTOR *pViewPos , float BSphereRadius)
{
        float  MinZ;

        MinZ = pViewPos->z - BSphereRadius;
        if( pOcclusion->MinZ < MinZ )
            return FALSE;
        if( ( ( pViewPos->x * pOcclusion->FrontPlane.a) +
            (pViewPos->y * pOcclusion->FrontPlane.b) +
            (pViewPos->z * pOcclusion->FrontPlane.c) +
            pOcclusion->FrontPlane.d) > BSphereRadius )
            return FALSE;
        if( ( ( pViewPos->x * pOcclusion->FirstPlane.a) +
            (pViewPos->y * pOcclusion->FirstPlane.b) +
            (pViewPos->z * pOcclusion->FirstPlane.c) +
            pOcclusion->FirstPlane.d) > BSphereRadius )
            return FALSE;
        if( ( ( pViewPos->x * pOcclusion->SecondPlane.a) +
            (pViewPos->y * pOcclusion->SecondPlane.b) +
            (pViewPos->z * pOcclusion->SecondPlane.c) +
            pOcclusion->FirstPlane.d) > BSphereRadius )
            return FALSE;
        if( ( ( pViewPos->x * pOcclusion->ThirdPlane.a) +
            (pViewPos->y * pOcclusion->ThirdPlane.b) +
            (pViewPos->z * pOcclusion->ThirdPlane.c) +
            pOcclusion->FirstPlane.d) > BSphereRadius )
            return FALSE;
        if( ( ( pViewPos->x * pOcclusion->FourthPlane.a) +
            (pViewPos->y * pOcclusion->FourthPlane.b) +
            (pViewPos->z * pOcclusion->FourthPlane.c) +
            pOcclusion->FirstPlane.d) > BSphereRadius )
            return FALSE;
        return TRUE;
}
```

4.9

Never Let 'Em See You Pop— Issues in Geometric Level of Detail Selection

Yossarian King

Objects and characters are represented in computer graphics as geometric models. Models can be created at different levels of detail (LODs), with more polygons and larger textures for the more detailed models, and fewer polygons and smaller textures for the less detailed models. Why would you want to do this? To improve rendering performance and visual quality. Drawing fewer polygons when objects are far away from the camera reduces the polygon count of the scene, and so speeds up rendering. Having a more detailed model for use when an object is close to the camera improves visual quality. If only a single model is used, then there is always a tradeoff between performance and quality—multiple levels of detail help to achieve both.

To implement LOD rendering, multiple models are created at different levels of detail, and the model to be rendered is chosen, each frame based on distance from the camera. As a rough rule of thumb, each level of detail should have about twice the number of polygons as the preceding level. The models are created to reduce "popping" as much as possible—when the character or object switches from one level of detail to another, the visible change in geometry (especially at the silhouette edge) and texturing must be minimized. The artist's job is to create models that are as similar as possible when rendered at the scale where the transition will occur. The programmer's job is to determine when to change LODs to achieve the desired performance and quality while minimizing the number of LOD transitions. This article explains how.

Note that for objects or characters that stay a relatively constant distance from the camera (such as the hero character in a third-person game), level of detail selection is not necessary. Also note that this article does not address level of detail issues for terrain rendering.

LOD Selection

The simplest way to select which level of detail to render is to apply a threshold to the distance of the object from the camera. For example, use the high detail model when the object is closer than 500 units, the medium detail model for distances of 500–1500 units, and the low detail model when the object is further than 1500 units from the camera. At first glance this seems reasonable—when the object is closer, use more detail; when it is farther away, use less detail—however, there are two problems with this method.

First, it doesn't account for the field of view of the camera. If the object is a long way from the camera, but the field of view is very narrow (e.g., a zoom lens) then the object may appear large on screen, and a detailed model may be appropriate. Similarly, an object may be relatively close to the camera, but if the field of view is very wide (a macro lens), then the object may appear small on screen and a low detail model should be used. Figure 4.9.1 shows that the same object at the same distance from the camera does not always appear the same size on screen. Rather than distance from the camera, we really want to use the projected size of the object on the screen as a basis for choosing the detail level. Size on screen is obviously related to distance from the camera, but the field of view must also be accounted for.

The second problem with the simple distance threshold approach is that if the object remains close to the threshold distance, then there may be rapid toggling back

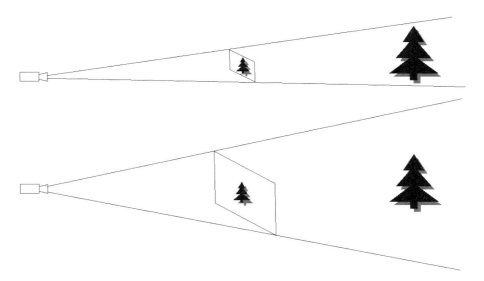

FIGURE 4.9.1 Varying the field of view changes the projected size of objects on the screen. *Top:* A narrow field of view produces a larger image on screen. *Bottom:* A wider field of view produces a smaller image. In both cases, the size of the tree and the distance from the tree to the camera are the same, demonstrating that camera distance is not sufficient for choosing level of detail.

and forth between levels of detail. This can happen when a character is running across the field of view close to the threshold distance. Popping once from one level of detail to another might be noticeable, but rapid cycling back and forth between levels will be very distracting and undesirable.

Fortunately, both of these problems are easily solved. A better alternative to camera distance is a "magnification factor," which is the screen size of the object relative to its physical size. As this ratio increases (i.e., as the object grows larger on screen), we choose higher levels of detail. Screen size accounts for both camera distance and field of view, so the first problem is eliminated. The magnification factor is easy to calculate, as explained in the next section.

The problem of rapid popping back and forth is solved by using hysteresis thresholding. Normal thresholding selects an output based on applying a single threshold to an input value. Hysteresis thresholding uses an upper and a lower threshold, and decides which to apply based on the previous output value. As long as the input value remains between the upper and lower threshold, the output value doesn't change, thus stabilizing the thresholded output and, in our case, maintaining stability of LOD selection. Details are described later.

Magnification Factor

The screen size of an object could be determined by transforming and projecting the highest and lowest point on the object and subtracting the screen position of each coordinate to get the screen height. This method depends on the orientation of the object, and requires processing two points. The magnification factor is simpler to compute and is independent of orientation. It can be computed by transforming the object position into view space and then calculating:

$M = xscale/zview$

where *xscale* is the scaling parameter used in the projection equation:

$xscreen = (xview * xscale) / zview + xcenter$

Since view coordinates are just a rotation and translation of the world coordinates, *zview* is measured in world units. *xscale*, which relates to the camera field of view, has pixel units; hence, the magnification factor M measures pixels per world unit. As M increases, there are more pixels per world unit—the object is relatively larger on screen and therefore should use a higher level of detail. Note that M is similar to the level of detail used for interpolating mipmapped textures, but in the case of mipmapping, pixels-per-texel are the measure of interest.

M accounts for both camera distance (via *zview*) and field of view (via *xscale*), and makes a much better choice for determining level of detail selection than simple camera distance. However, applying a simple threshold to M will have the same popping problems described previously. Hysteresis thresholding is the solution.

Hysteresis Thresholding

Hysteresis thresholding is a fancy term for thresholding against a range of values, rather than a single value. A simple threshold T is applied as:

$$output = \begin{cases} 1 \text{ if input} >= T \\ 0 \text{ if input} < T \end{cases}$$

Hysteresis thresholding uses an upper and a lower threshold and remembers the previous output value. The output doesn't change if the input is between the upper and lower thresholds:

$$output(t) = \begin{cases} 1 \text{ if input} >= T_{high} \\ 0 \text{ if input} < T_{low} \\ output(t-1) \text{ otherwise} \end{cases}$$

If the input is increasing, then the output will be 0 until the input reaches T_{high}. If the input is decreasing, then the output will remain 1 until the input falls below T_{low}. Regardless of whether the value is increasing or decreasing, the output doesn't change when the input is between the upper and lower thresholds. Using this approach for level of detail selection means there is no single point at which the object will toggle back and forth between levels of detail—the hysteresis thresholding ensures that all we get is a single pop, never a toggling behavior. A visual comparison of simple thresholding and hysteresis thresholding is shown in Figure 4.9.2.

Implementation

With the magnification factor and hysteresis thresholding we can create a level of detail selection algorithm that accounts for camera field of view and avoids rapid popping problems. Assume we have models for three levels of detail: high, medium, and low. The hysteresis thresholds for moving between high and medium detail are T_{hupper} and T_{hlower}. The thresholds for moving between medium and low detail are T_{mupper} and T_{mlower}. In pseudocode, the level of detail selection algorithm looks like this:

```
int computelod:
worldpos    world position of the object
lodprev     level of detail chosen in previous frame
{
    viewpos = transform( worldpos )
    M = xscale / viewpos.z

    if ( M < T_mlower )
        lod = low
    else if ( M < T_mupper )
        lod = lodprev            hysteresis range for medium/low
    else if ( M < T_hlower )
        lod = medium
    else if ( M < T_hupper )
```

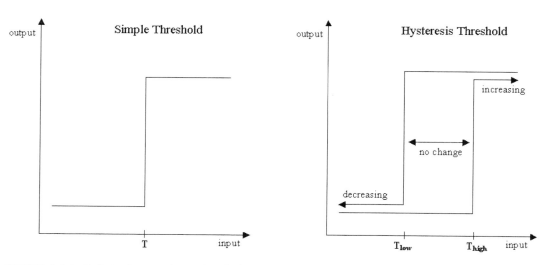

FIGURE 4.9.2 *Left:* An input value is thresholded against a single threshold *T. Right:* An input value is thresholded against hysteresis thresholds T_{low} and T_{high}, with the appropriate threshold chosen based on the preceding output value. As long as the input remains between T_{low} and T_{high}, there is no change in the output.

```
        lod = lodprev           hysteresis range for high/medium
    else
        lod = high              M >= T_hupper

    return lod
}
```

Note that if M is between T_{hlower} and T_{hupper}, then this will always return the previous level of detail, even if it was low detail. If you expect your object to be magnifying this quickly, then the algorithm is easily adapted.

The equivalent algorithm using a simple distance threshold would just use one threshold between each level of detail, and would look like this:

```
int computelodwithpopping:
worldpos
{
    viewpos = transform( worldpos )

    if ( viewpos.z < T_m )
        lod = low
    else if ( viewpos.z < T_h )
        lod = medium
    else                        viewpos.z >= T_h
        lod = high

    return lod
}
```

As can be seen, solving the field of view dependence and popping problems does not add significantly to the complexity of the level of detail selection.

Other Issues

Threshold Selection

For any thresholding method, hysteresis or otherwise, you need to choose your thresholds. For level of detail selection, choosing the thresholds is a tradeoff between performance and visual quality. If the thresholds are set too low, then the higher levels of detail will be drawn more often, and you will have to render more polygons per frame, which will slow down the rendering. If the thresholds are too high, then the lower quality models will be drawn more often, and popping between levels will be more noticeable.

To reduce popping, you can implement the selection algorithm, then move the object toward and away from the camera, moving the thresholds until the popping is acceptable. Keep in mind that in a game-play situation with a moving object, moving camera, and distracted user, the popping will be less noticeable than in a testbed environment. Achieving performance targets is a combined effort by the artist and programmer to reduce the polygon counts and adjust the thresholds to achieve a suitable balance.

User Attention

So far, we have only considered the size of an object on screen to determine which level of detail to render. Another factor to consider is where the user is looking. In general, we expect the user to be paying attention to things that are close to the camera, but we may have additional knowledge about the particular game situation to help us know where the user is probably looking. For example, in a sports game, a player character controlled by the user will probably be the focus of attention, as will a player character with the ball, or one involved in the current play. This "expected focus of attention" can be used in the level of detail selection algorithm by biasing the magnification factor when the user is likely to be watching an object or character. In the sports game example, we can multiply the magnification factor by a scaling parameter (e.g., 1.1) when the character is under user control.

Biasing the Magnification Factor

The idea of biasing the magnification factor can be used in other ways as well. If there is a game situation in which rendering quality is more important than performance (such as a non-interactive rendered cut scene), the magnification factor for all objects can be biased higher in order to render objects at higher detail. Or the magnification factor can be biased dynamically depending on frame rate—when frame rate drops, bias the magnification lower to select more lower polygon models and improve the frame rate.

Limiting Number of Models or Polygons

If a scene has multiple instances of the same object, then there may be limits on the number of objects that can be rendered at each level of detail. Such constraints may be imposed in order to conserve memory in the object representation, or you may simply wish to limit the maximum number of high polygon models in order to improve performance. Limits on the number of models at each level of detail can easily be built into the selection algorithm—sort the objects by magnification factor, and then take the N largest objects at each level of detail, demoting any remaining object to the next lower level of detail. With a little more work, the selection algorithm can be modified to select objects so the total polygon count for all objects falls below some target.

Progressive Meshes

A final issue worth mentioning is the use of progressive meshes, or other dynamic level of detail methods. Increasing processor performance and increasing polygon counts in game models are starting to make these techniques feasible. With these techniques, the polygon count of objects can be varied on the fly across a continuous range. A suitable polygon count still needs to be chosen for each frame, and so the magnification factor is still useful. If polygon count varies continuously, then hysteresis thresholding is no longer needed. However, this may cause distracting popping effects as polygons are continuously dropped from or added to the model, so it may still be desirable to use hysteresis thresholds to decide when to change the polygon count.

4.10

Octree Construction

Dan Ginsburg

Culling geometry for visibility determination and collision detection is a problem that must be tackled in the development of nearly every 3D engine. There are numerous data structures and approaches to the problem. Most solutions put constraints on the geometry and often require the 3D artists to explicitly provide information such as portal locations to the engine. However, an octree is a simple data structure that can be used to spatially subdivide geometry of any form.

This article deals with the specific steps required to take an input set of polygons and construct an octree that spatially partitions the geometry. The octree is best suited to static terrain, but can also be used to store attachment lists for objects that move dynamically in a scene. An octree can be used as a complete solution for visibility culling, collision detection culling, and object management.

Octree Overview

At the highest level, an octree is simply a tree (an acyclic directed graph) with a maximum of eight children at every node. It turns out that this is an ideal structure for representing a three-dimensional world enclosed by cubes. The root node of an octree contains a cube that encloses all the geometry in the world. The children at each node are the eight cubes of equal size that subdivide the parent into octants (see Figure 4.10.1). Subdivision stops when some user-defined heuristic is met: typically, either the bounding cubes are of a certain size, or some minimum number of polygons are contained within each node.

The bounding cubes at each node are the key to using an octree for spatial subdivision. Each node contains pointers to all of the polygons that lie within its volume. Given this information, one can begin to see the power of the data structure. For visibility determination, the axis-aligned bounding cube of the root node of the tree will be tested against the view frustum. If it is fully visible, all of its geometry will be rendered. If partially visible, traversal will continue down to the children. If it is completely outside the view frustum, traversal can stop: it and all of its children are not visible. Further examples of using octrees will be presented later. However, first it is necessary to examine the specific steps required to construct an octree.

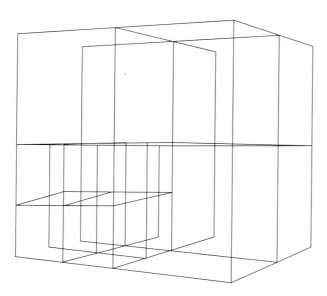

FIGURE 4.10.1 Subdivision of a cube into octants.

Octree Data

Partitioning the geometry using an octree is a step that is typically performed at the pre-processing stage. Some tool will take the input set of geometry and produce octree data as output that can be used at run-time by the application.

At a minimum, each node in the octree must contain the following data:

- **Bounding Cube**—This is the cube in space that the node of the octree encloses.
- **Geometry List**—Each node encloses a number of polygons; these must be stored in some way at each node.
- **Children**—Each node can have up to eight children; pointers to each of these must be stored at every node.
- **Neighbors**—Each node can have up to six neighbors (one for each of the cube faces). Tree traversal for collision detection requires that each node have pointers to all of its neighbors. The neighbors allow the collision algorithm to quickly "step" through the tree along a collision ray. This will be discussed in more detail later.

Building the Tree

The first step to building the octree is to get a list of all the polygons in the world. Once this list has been created, the root node of the octree can be constructed. The largest absolute value V for any component X, Y, or Z in the vertex list is determined.

This value is used to create the bounding cube for the world (it spans from [-*V*, -*V*, -*V*] to [*V*, *V*, *V*]). By definition, the geometry list for the root node will contain all the polygons in the world. Starting with this root node, the world can now be subdivided recursively using an octree. Here is pseudocode for the building algorithm:

```
BuildOctree(Node N)
{
    if(NumPolys(N) > POLY_THRESHOLD)
        for(int i = 0; i < 8; i++)
        {
            BuildNode(N->Child[i], i, N);
            BuildOctree(N->Child[i]);
        }
}
```

BuildOctree() creates all eight children for any node that contains more than the minimum threshold number of polygons. Creating all eight children simplifies the run-time code by allowing it to always assume that if any children exist for a node, all eight do. If this assumption was not made, there could be nodes without neighbors, which would make traversal for collision detection difficult.

The heart of BuildOctree() is BuildNode(), which creates the node data. This performs two steps:

1. Creates the bounding cube for the node.
2. Determines which polygons lie within the node's cube.

Creating the bounding cube for the node is trivial. The index *i* can be used to specify which octant the node lies in. The box will then be fully determined by taking the parent's box and partitioning it appropriately. The box will have half the width, height, and depth of the parent's box, and will be centered at one of eight positions, depending on *i*.

Determining which polygons lie within the bounding cube is slightly more complicated. Before addressing this, it is worth addressing how to store the polygon list at each node. Obviously, it would be hugely memory inefficient to store copies of the polygon at every node in the tree. A polygon can exist within several nodes: a parent will always contain a superset of the polygons in its children. Additionally, polygons might span across node boundaries. One solution to this problem would be to split the polygons along the boundaries. However, this generates additional polygon data, which could adversely affect run-time performance. Instead, the polygons will have a "frame count" value, and the run-time render code will be responsible for making sure that each polygon is rendered only once per frame.

One possible approach to storing the geometry for each node is to store a list of area IDs. Then, elsewhere in the builder, for each area ID a list of indices into a shared polygon table will be stored. This requires very little data at each node and ensures that polygons will not be duplicated when they span multiple nodes.

Polygon Overlap

Given the solution for storing polygon lists at each node, the next step is to create an algorithm for determining whether a polygon lies within a cube. A fast method for testing whether a triangle intersects a voxel is presented in [Moller99] (Section 10.9). A voxel is a cube centered at the origin, with each edge having a length of one. It turns out that this algorithm can easily be expanded for testing whether a triangle intersects a world-aligned cube of any size. The trick is to determine what translation and scale will transform the cube into a voxel. Then, that transform is performed on each triangle. Each transformed triangle is then tested for intersection with a voxel. Here is an outline of that algorithm:

```
TriInCube(Tri T, Cube C)
{
    Vector Trans= C.Center;
    Vector Scale= 1.0 / C.Size;

    for (int i= 0; i < 3; i++)
        T.Vert[i]= (T.Vert[i] — Trans) / Scale;

    if (TriInVoxel(T))
        return true;

    return false;
}
```

Neighbors

The primary components of each octree node are now filled in: the bounding cube, the geometry list, and the children. This is all the information needed for visibility culling. However, in order to use the octree for collision detection, the neighbors to each of the six cube faces must be determined. A neighbor for a given cube face is defined to be the node of equal size or greater that touches it. A neighbor can never be *smaller*, and the algorithm will search for the best-fit neighbor (e.g., the smallest possible that is no smaller than the node).

This step needs to be performed after the tree has been fully constructed once all of the nodes have been created. The algorithm works by taking each cube face of each node and comparing it against the cube faces of the other nodes in the tree at the same level or higher. Several conditions must be met in order for two cube faces to be considered neighbors:

- The normals of the faces must be in opposite directions.
- All the vertices in the source face lie on or inside the destination face.
- The size of the source face is less than or equal to the size of the destination face.

The cube that meets all three conditions and has the smallest size is considered to be the neighbor.

Applications

As discussed previously, one application of the constructed octree is for visibility determination of static geometry. However, the octree can also be used for managing the visibility of dynamic objects in the world. Each octree node in the run-time code could store a list of attachment objects, and each object in the world could store a list of nodes it is attached to. Then, to render the scene, the terrain polygons in each visible node are rendered, as well as all objects attached to the node. When an object moves, it detaches itself from all the nodes it is attached to, and re-attaches to whatever new nodes it now lies within. The only trick is to again store a "frame counter" per object to make sure it only gets rendered once per frame (since an object could easily span multiple nodes).

The octree can now also be used for culling in collision detection. Consider the simple case of a ray collision test. Two points define a collision ray: a start and an end point. The collision test begins by finding the leaf node of the octree that the start point lies within. The segment is broken into a subsegment at each cube face it intersects. The new subsegment is tested against all the geometry and objects within its node. The next subsegment starts at the end point of the previous subsegment, in the node that neighbors the cube face that it intersected. This traversal through neighbors continues, colliding with the geometry and objects at every node until the original end point is reached. Several other collision tests such as axis-aligned box and sphere tests also work very well when using the octree.

Conclusion

The octree is a useful data structure in building a simple geometry culling system. This article is meant as a simple introduction in how to build an octree. There are further optimizations and enhancements that can be made to the structure in order to improve its run-time performance as well as usefulness (e.g., adding occlusion culling and depth sorting). Please see the references for pointers to further information on octrees and their applications in 3D graphics.

References

[Foley87] Foley, van Dam, Feiner, and Hughes, "Computer Graphics: Principles and Practice 2nd Edition", 1987, p 550–555.

[Hoff] Hoff, Kenny, *"Fast ABBB/View-Frustum Overlap Test"* www.cs.unc.edu/~hoff/research/vfculler/boxvfc/boxvfc.html

[Moller99] Moller and Haines, "Real-Time Rendering", 1999, p. 206–211, 310–312.

[Suter99] Suter, Japp "Introduction to Octrees" April 13, 1999, www.flipcode.com/tutorials/tut_octrees.shtml

4.11

Loose Octrees

Thatcher Ulrich

The octree is a classic and effective data structure for partitioning 3D datasets into hierarchies of bounding volumes. For datasets with a lot of objects, octrees can greatly accelerate frustum culling, ray casting, proximity queries, and just about any other spatial operation.

However, ordinary octrees do have a few disadvantages. In this article, I will focus on one disadvantage in particular, which is that a small object, depending on its location, may be stored in an octree node with a very large bounding volume. This happens when an object straddles the boundary plane between two large nodes. This creates "sticky" areas in the partitioning hierarchy, keeping small objects high in the tree hierarchy and reducing the effectiveness of the partitioning.

There are various methods of adjusting the basic octree data structure and algorithms to mitigate or avoid this problem, and each method has its unique tradeoffs. In this article, I present one such alternative, the "loose octree." Its primary advantage over an ordinary octree is that it avoids stickiness in the object partitioning, resulting in more precise spatial database queries. For certain applications, such as mutual collision detection between numerous moving objects, the efficiency gain can be significant. There is an additional minor side benefit, in that computing a given object's desired node in the tree is a simple $O(1)$ operation. A similar trick can be done using ordinary octrees, but it's not as straightforward.

Its main weakness is that it tends to use more partitioning nodes for a given dataset than an ordinary octree. Limiting the depth of the tree can mitigate this, but it's something to be aware of.

Quadtrees

The octree is a 3D data structure. The analogous 2D data structure is the quadtree, which shares the same basic properties. This remains true of loose quadtrees; they are just a 2D version of loose octrees. Loose quadtrees have the same tradeoffs as loose octrees, with respect to their conventional counterparts, so they can be useful in applications that only require hierarchical partitioning in two dimensions.

Since it's much easier to visualize these data structures in 2D, in this article I'm going to use 2D diagrams based on quadtrees. However, the octree principles are exactly the same, and the extension to 3D is straightforward.

Bounding Volumes

In a conventional octree, the basic node bounding volume is a cube. All objects associated with a node must be contained completely within the node's bounding cube. Each node may also have up to eight child nodes, whose bounding cubes are formed by slicing the parent cube into eight equal sub-cubes. The quadtree version is illustrated in Figure 4.11.1.

The bounding volumes of the child nodes nest perfectly within the bounding volume of the parent node, filling the entire space with no overlap. The child nodes can be further subdivided the same way. If you examine the sizes and spacing of the bounding volumes, you can see that they follow a regular pattern. Consider the edge length of the bounding cubes: at the root of the tree, the cube edge length is equal to the world dimensions. At each level deeper into the tree, the cube edge length is half the size of the previous level's cube edge length. Thus, the formula for bounding cube edge length is:

$$L(depth) = W / (2 \char`\^ depth)$$

where W is the world size, and depth is the number of levels by which a node is separated from the root. The root node has depth 0.

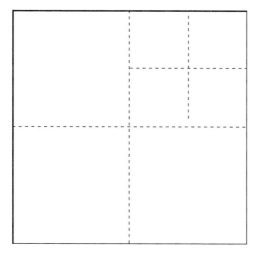

FIGURE 4.11.1 A quadtree node, shown with bounding square in bold, subdivided along dotted lines. Each quadrant becomes a child node. The child nodes can also be subdivided as shown in the upper-right quadrant.

The spacing of the bounding cubes' centers at a given depth follows the same pattern. At the root there's only one node, so node spacing doesn't really have any meaning, but starting at depth 1, the centers of the root's child nodes are spaced *W/2* units apart from their neighboring nodes. Each subsequent level cuts the node spacing in half. The formula for node spacing is:

S(depth) = W / (2 ^ depth)

So, for a given depth, the cube edge size and the node spacing are identical. This makes sense because at a given tree level, the bounding cubes are perfectly packed into the world volume with no gaps and no overlap.

Partitioning Objects

Given a set of objects in a virtual world, each object having some finite bounding volume, an octree can be used to partition the objects within the world space, to accelerate various spatial operations such as frustum culling, ray casting, proximity tests, etc. Different criteria can be used for partitioning, but the classic octree partitioning scheme is to associate a given object with the node in the octree whose bounding cube most tightly contains the entire object volume. This node can easily be found by a recursive traversal of the tree. Here is some pseudocode:

```
struct node {
    Vector3 CubeCenter;
    node*   Child[2][2][2];
    ObjectList Objects;
};


int Classify(plane p, volume v)
{
    if (v is completely behind p) {
        return 0;
    } else if (v is completely in front of p) {
        return 1;
    } else {
        // v straddles p.
        return 2;
    }
}


void    InsertObjectIntoTree(node* n, Object* o)
{
    int xc = Classify(plane(1,0,0,CubeCenter.x),
        o.BoundingVolume);
    int yc = Classify(plane(0,1,0,CubeCenter.y),
        o.BoundingVolume);
    int zc = Classify(plane(0,0,1,CubeCenter.z),
        o.BoundingVolume);
```

```
if (xc == 2 || yc == 2 || zc == 2) {
{
    // Object straddles one or more of the child
    // partition planes, and so won't fit in any
    // child node, so store it in this node.
    Objects.Insert(o);
} else {
    // Object fits in one of the child nodes. Recurse to
    // find the correct descendant.
    InsertObjectIntoTree(Child[zc][yc][xc], o);
}
}
```

This is a nice, straightforward hierarchical partitioning scheme that handles whatever you throw at it and generally comes up with a decent partitioning. However, it has one disturbing oddity. Notice that if an object straddles any one of a node's partitioning planes, then the object is stored in that node. This happens even if the object is tiny and the node is huge; see Figure 4.11.2 for an example. In practice, if you have lots of small objects, the ones located along the root node partitioning planes can "clog up" the root node by filling it with small, poorly partitioned objects, and reducing the efficiency of spatial operations (e.g., Figure 4.11.3).

I'll call this problem the "sticky planes" problem, the idea being that partitioning planes high in the tree hierarchy attract excess objects to their associated nodes, and are thus "sticky." There are various ways to solve this problem. One method is to split objects on partitioning planes and then classify the pieces individually. Another method is to allow an object to be referenced by more than one node, so an object can

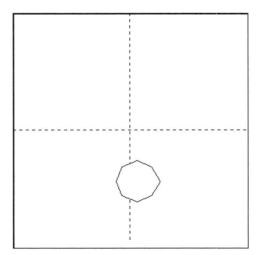

FIGURE 4.11.2 Even though the circle is very small compared to the root node (bold square), it can't be placed in a child node because it straddles one of the (dotted) partitioning lines.

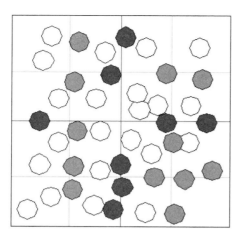

FIGURE 4.11.3 All of the objects are small, but the shaded ones are stuck to higher nodes in the quadtree, due to straddling the partitioning line.

be shared by child nodes on either side of a sticky plane, rather than being stored in the parent node. For static objects, those approaches are effective, but they're not so good for handling dynamic objects.

Making It Loose

The "loose" octree method takes a different tack: it solves the sticky planes problem by adjusting the node bounding volumes. Specifically, by "loosening" the bounding cubes, but leaving the node hierarchy and the node centers as is. The bounding volume of a node is still a cube, but where in the conventional octree the cube edge may have had length L, in the loose octree the cube edge would be kL, where $k > 1$. Thus, the formula for bounding cube edge length is modified to be:

$$L(depth) = k * W / (2 \wedge depth)$$

However, the node spacing remains the same as in the conventional octree. What this means is that a node's bounding cube now overlaps with the bounding cubes of its neighbors. Figure 4.11.4 shows this overlap for a loose quadtree.

This loosening of the bounding cubes increases the minimum size of objects attracted by a sticky plane. Where previously an object with any size at all that crossed a sticky plane would be stored in that plane's node, with looser bounding cubes, smaller objects will fit within one of the child nodes (Figure 4.11.5). How small must an object be to avoid being caught by a sticky plane? It depends on the tree depth of the plane's node, and on the value we choose for k. For a node at a given depth, no object with a bounding radius smaller than $(k - 1) * L / 2$ can be stuck to that node due to straddling a partitioning plane. Instead, since the child nodes' bounding volumes have been enlarged, such objects can fit in one of the child nodes.

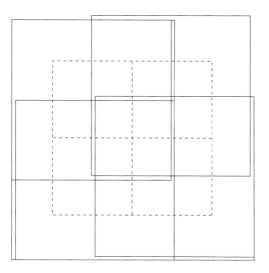

FIGURE 4.11.4 Four nodes. The conventional bounding squares are shown with dashed lines. The same four nodes in a loose quadtree have bounding squares shown in black. The squares have been offset so that they can be distinguished from each other.

So, what's a good value for k? Without fully exploring all the tradeoffs in this article, I propose $k=2$ as a useful all-around value. A tree with k much less than 2 starts to suffer from the sticky planes problem, and a tree with k too much greater than 2 results in excessively loose bounding volumes.

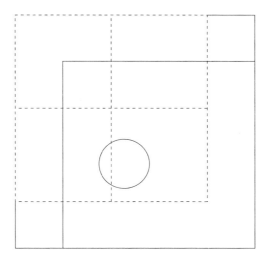

FIGURE 4.11.5 The circle won't fit in any of the conventional child node bounding squares, but it will fit in the loose bounding square of the lower-right child.

Assuming a loose octree with $k=2$, we can write an extremely simple object insertion procedure. The basic principle is that for a given object, the depth of the containing node can be calculated solely based on the object's size, and then the choice of the particular node at that depth in the tree is based solely on the object's center location. To get the formula for depth, note that a given level in the loose octree can accommodate any object whose radius is less than or equal to 1/4 of the bounding cube edge length, regardless of its position. Any object with a radius <= 1/8 of the bounding cube edge length should go in the next deeper level in the tree. For example, in Figure 4.11.5, notice that no matter where the object is placed, it will fit within one of the nodes' bounding squares.

Here's the derivation of the level-selection formula:

$L(depth) = 2 * W / (2 \wedge depth)$

Let $Rmax(depth)$ = maximum object radius that can be accommodated at depth.

$Rmax(depth) = 1/4 * L(depth) = 1/2 * W / (2 \wedge depth)$

Let $depth(R)$ = the first tree depth that can accommodate an object of radius R

$R <= Rmax(depth(R))$
$R <= 1/2 * W / (2 \wedge depth(R))$
$depth(R) >= log2(W / R) - 1$
$depth(R) == floor(log2(W / R))$

Once the depth is known, choosing the particular node at a given depth is simple—just find the closest node to the object's center. Assuming the world is centered at the coordinate system origin, the formula to compute the node indices is:

$index\{x,y,z\} = floor((object.\{x,y,z\} + W/2) / S(depth))$

Note that this procedure is not quite ideal: it does not actually find the tightest possible containing node for all cases (see Figure 4.11.6). To get the last bit of tightness, first find the candidate node using the above formulas, and then check the child node nearest to the object to see if the object fits inside it.

Performing spatial operations on loose octrees is very similar to conventional octrees. For example, this is the pseudocode for rendering with frustum culling:

```
enum Visibility { NOT_VISIBLE, PARTLY_VISIBLE, FULLY_VISIBLE };

void    Node::Render(Frustum f, Visibility v)
{
    if (v != FULLY_VISIBLE) {
        v = ComputeVisibility(this.BoundingBox, f);
        if (v == NOT_VISIBLE) return;
    }

    this.ObjectList.Render(f, v);

    for (children) {
```

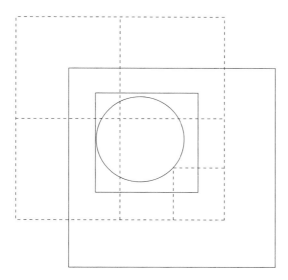

FIGURE 4.11.6 The simple placement formula would put the circle in the node bounded by the large black square, but due to its particular position, the circle has a better fit in the upper-left child node, bounded by the small black square.

```
        child.Render(f, v);
    }
}
```

The exact same algorithm works with conventional octrees; the only difference is that this .BoundingBox would be smaller.

Comparison

To help in comparing loose octrees with regular octrees, I wrote a test program based on loose quadtrees and ordinary quadtrees. The program posits a 2D square virtual world, 1000 units on a side. Some number of circular objects are generated to populate the world. Each object has a position and a bounding radius, which are chosen randomly to fit within the world boundaries. Then a certain number of 2D frusta (i.e., wedges) are generated, with a fixed field-of-view angle, and a random position and direction. The objects are first partitioned using a conventional quadtree, and then for each frustum, the dataset is queried for visible objects. Statistics are gathered on the number of objects that are potentially within the frustum, and the number of objects that are actually within the frustum. Then, the objects are re-classified using a loose quadtree, and the same frustum tests are run and the same statistics are collected.

Results of some sample runs are summarized in Table 4.11.1.

Table 4.11.1 Results of Some Sample Runs

Test Parameters tree max depth = 5 100 frusta FOV = 45° checked	Ordinary Quadtree			Loose Quadtree		
	Objects possibly visible	Objects actually visible	Nodes checked	Objects possibly visible	Objects actually visible	Nodes
500 objects obj min radius=30 obj max radius=30	18859	6883	2976	9442	6883	7024
1000 objects obj min radius=15 obj max radius=15	31133	15173	7265	22457	15173	8815
2000 objects obj min radius=5 obj max radius=100	55451	29935	9102	45209	29935	9075

Note that the frustum queries on the loose quadtree generally return fewer "possibly visible" objects than the same queries on the ordinary quadtree. On the other hand, the loose quadtree queries usually have to check more nodes. So, for frustum culling, the differences between the two are noticeable, but not terribly dramatic.

Things get more interesting when looking at inter-object queries, such as collision detection. In my test program, I added a test in which each object is checked for contact with all the other objects in the dataset, and collected statistics on the checks. The results for the same datasets used previously are listed in Table 4.11.2.

Table 4.11.2 Test Results

Test Parameters tree max depth = 5	Ordinary Quadtree			Loose Quadtree		
	Inter-object contacts	Object-to-object tests	Object-to-Node tests	Inter-object contacts	Object-to-object tests	Object-to-Node tests
500 objects obj min radius=30 obj max radius=30	3034	53469	7351	3034	9125	24839
1000 objects obj min radius=15 obj max radius=15	2730	113989	18040	2730	24609	45658
2000 objects obj min radius=5 obj max radius=100	7094	345377	38107	7094	89276	89312

As you can see, for these datasets, the loose quadtree needs to do far fewer object-to-object tests for the same query. The loose quadtree does require many more object-to-node tests, but in aggregate, the loose quadtree is significantly more efficient for this type of query.

Conclusion

The octree is an extremely powerful tool. However, in certain circumstances, you may want to modify the classic octree approach to better fit your problem. The loose octree is one such variation, which avoids the sticky planes problem of the classic octree. In situations where you have a large number of interacting, dynamic objects (such as a particle system with inter-particle collisions), the loose octree is a particularly good choice over the ordinary octree. The loose octree also performs well for general spatial partitioning tasks such as frustum culling.

4.12

View-Independent Progressive Meshing

Jan Svarovsky

A progressive mesh (PM) is a triangle-based mesh that is able to vary its level of detail in real-time, at the resolution of gaining or losing a couple of triangles at a time, while preserving its original shape as much as possible. It can be drawn at any detail level between the conventional mesh from which it was created and a lowest detail "base mesh" as defined by the detail reduction heuristic, which may be as small as no polygons at all.

Typically, these meshes are rendered at lower detail in the distance, so that more system resources are available to draw higher-resolution meshes in the foreground. The global detail level of the graphics engine can also be based on the power of the computer it is running on.

First, I will introduce progressive meshing, working through some of the arguments for and against different variations on the theme. Based on this discussion, I will describe an algorithm to convert conventional mesh data into progressive meshes, and some efficient and simple code to render these.

FIGURE 4.12.1. A progressive mesh varying in detail.

Progressive Mesh Overview

The basic principle can be simply described as taking a mesh, repeatedly deciding which is its least significant edge, and removing this edge by making the two vertex positions at its ends equal. This *edge collapse* operation typically makes two triangles sharing the edge redundant. Detail is put back into the mesh by reversing these collapses through *vertex splits*.

Much work has done by people and documented in the public domain, particularly [Hoppe96, Hoppe97, Hoppe98]. Figure 4.12.2 summarizes the unit-reversible operation and the common terminology.

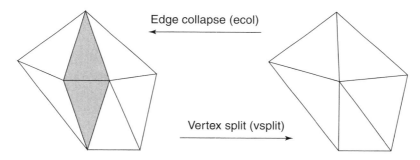

FIGURE 4.12.2 A single step of mesh refinement (vertex split) or reduction (edge collapse).

Variations on the Theme

Given this basic premise, there are various decisions that can be made about the finer implementation details. I will briefly touch on them here; see [Svarovsky99] for a more leisurely discussion.

When Vertices Collapse, Where Do They Collapse To?

When two vertices collapse into one, there is a choice for where to put the vertex. It can be calculated to lie on the imaginary smooth surface that the polygon mesh is trying to represent. Alternatively, you can put the point just halfway in between the two it replaces, which you would think was cheaper, perhaps because you wouldn't have to store a pre-calculated new point. Last, you can just choose to preserve one or the other of the original vertices that are being collapsed (Figure 4.12.3).

The midpoint system has the disadvantage that convex objects become smaller as they lose detail. The clever precalculated point system takes up twice as much memory, or takes up extra CPU time calculating the new point online. Preserving one point or the other is the simplest, takes the least memory, and objects do not lose apparent vol-

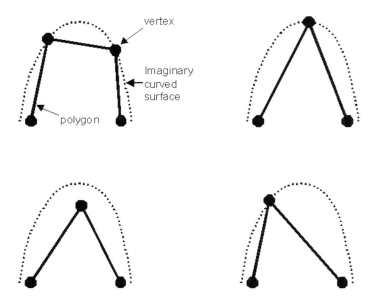

FIGURE 4.12.3 Choices for position of vertices produced by edge collapse. *a:* Higher detail mesh. *b:* New point on hypothetical surface. *c:* Midpoint- mesh changes volume. *d:* Pick one of the points—simple.

ume as drastically. It is often a good representation of the original shape, particularly when, for example, collapsing the corner of a cube-like object and a vertex somewhere along one of the faces of the cube shape. Though it lacks the flexibility of calculating a new point, its strong advantage is that it does not require real-time changes to the vertex data or the creation of new vertices. This is the system I will use here.

View-Independent vs. View-Dependent Rendering

Each sequence of vertex splits, starting with a vertex in the base mesh, can be visualized as a binary tree, each vertex splitting into two new ones (though, of course, in this system I just add one new vertex to an original one). The splits can either be left in their tree form or can be given some fixed order (Figure 4.12.4).

View-independent meshes use one fixed order for the edge collapses, which can therefore be calculated offline, and this tree representation can be thrown away. If you keep the tree form in some way, you can vary which nodes you expand. This effectively gives you more flexibility in positioning the dashed line [Hoppe97]. This view-dependent PM can be used to give more detail on parts of the mesh that are closer to the viewer, or on silhouette edges.

View-dependent PM (VDPM) is able to use triangle counts more effectively, because it has more flexibility in the choice of edge collapse order. In my opinion, however, this is never justified in modern systems because of the large gap in effi-

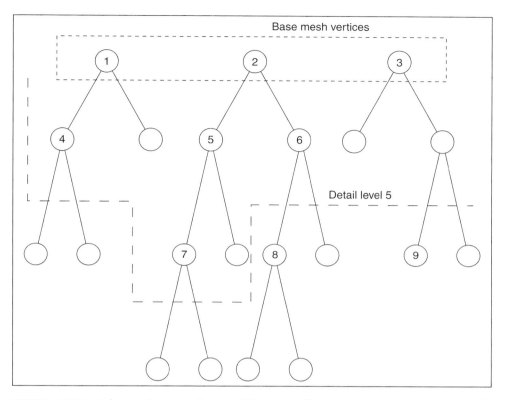

FIGURE 4.12.4 A forest of vertex split trees. The dashed line represents the vertices that will be used when rendering a mesh at detail level 5.

ciency between the two types of renderers. A VDPM renderer uses fewer triangles for a more visually pleasing scene, but this thriftiness is drowned out by the increased processor time that must be put into making more level of detail choices, and the data handling involved.

A view-independent PM's (VIPM) triangles and vertices in the mesh can be ordered such that the ones that disappear first are further toward the end of the list, and therefore are not traversed or "in the way" when the lower levels of detail are being used. This can also lead to interesting progressive file formats where the more you read, the higher detail mesh you get [Hoppe98].

Because there is only one collapse order, there is only one level of detail for the whole mesh. If you are close to one part of the mesh, and therefore want that part to be rendered at high detail, all the rest will have to be rendered at high detail, too. In practical game situations, however, a large object can be subdivided into independent (but possibly mutually intersecting) parts that can be rendered view-independently. Now that you have the pieces separate, you can assign some game code to them, so they become a bit more interactive, such as windows, antennae, radar dishes on a space station or individual huts, trees, and so on in a landscape.

Large sections of continuous mesh like rolling hills can be built using a custom renderer that uses fewer polygons in the distance in another way, such as the "ROAM" algorithm [Duchaineau97]. Discussion of these other view-dependent systems that work on specific mesh topographies is out of scope of this article, which concerns itself with the progressive meshing of general triangle meshes.

Edge Choice Functions

I believe that once you have an edge choice system that gives fairly acceptable results, there is little to be gained in trying complex evaluation functions. I leave implementation of some of the many methods discussed in the literature as an exercise to the interested reader. I have included some references to different works, particularly [Lindstrom99] for an overview. The best thing is to build an editor that allows artist intervention in your automated generation of the collapse sequence. In my experience, after having spent days building the mesh, artists are quite willing to spend some time tweaking how it looks at lower levels of detail, particularly at the very low detail levels where there are only a few polygons to adjust. It is at these low levels that automated systems have the most trouble anyway.

Here I have described a very simple function that is implemented in the example code on the CD. It is based roughly on the amount of movement of the surrounding triangles.

Difficult Edges

It simplifies the algorithm to ban some special case edges. These cases stem from triangles sharing the same point in 3D space, but not sharing some other vertex data, such as vertex normals, texture type, or texture coordinates. It is an extra complication to have triangles pointing to *shared* texture coordinates and pointing to *shared* vertex positions. To avoid this, and to be friendlier toward current graphics hardware, our vertices contain all texture coordinates, normal and position information. This way, the mesh will contain multiple vertices in the same position but with different material information.

If an edge being removed contains these duplicate vertices, and therefore the triangles along the edge do not share vertices, it is handled as two edge collapses that happen simultaneously. The problem arises when a nearby triangle only refers to one of the ends of a collapsed edge, and this is the one that is to disappear (Figure 4.12.5).

An extra vertex could be created for this material, which would remain redundant until needed for lower levels of detail. This inefficiency is only slight because these vertices are created very infrequently. You can avoid this case by just banning these collapses. This will restrict the lowest polygon count that meshes will reduce to. Typically, when these edges are a significant percentage of the remaining edges, the polygon counts will be so low that the renderer call overhead means further detail loss

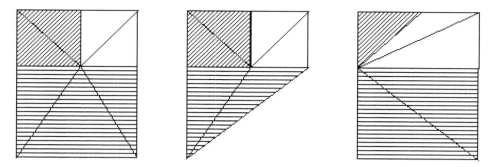

FIGURE 4.12.5 When an extra vertex must be generated. *a:* Original shape. *b:* Trivial collapse. *c:* Different, complicated collapse.

would not really speed up rendering. The objects will also probably be so insignificant (as determined by the decision function that made them low detail anyway) that you could just not draw them at all! At the time of writing this article, most commercial PM systems disallow these types of collapses.

For the sake of conciseness, the system is simplified further here. The program given contains no workarounds for multiple edges that share the same position. This way, we can remove all the code that checks for coincident edges, that bans certain collapses, and that makes some edge collapses happen simultaneously. This implies that all meshes must be smooth and continuously textured, but, as can be seen in the examples on the enclosed CD, careful construction of the meshes means many more general shapes are still possible.

Implementation

The Renderer

For the majority of frames, a mesh will not change in detail, so it is essential that the data structure being used to render from is as efficient as possible for the graphics system. Here we can arrange the data much like we would for a standard mesh renderer:

```
struct PMMesh
{
    int NumMaterials;
    struct PMMaterial *Materials;
};
```

The mesh is made of an array of materials:

```
struct PMMaterial
{
    PMTexture *Texture;
    struct PMVertex *Vertices;
    int *Indices;
```

```
    int NumVertices, NumIndices;
};
```

Each material has a texture (or perhaps several textures in a multi-pass system, such as a bump map, a gloss map, and the actual base texture), and an array of vertices. It also owns some triangles, which simply index into the vertex array. Note that instead of having an array of PMTriangle's, there is an array of three times as many indices into the vertex array. This is done for efficiency in the EdgeCollapse structure later, and is trivial to change back into an array of triangles if you wish to record more information with each triangle.

```
struct PMVertex
{
    vector3 Position, Normal;
    float U, V;
};
```

Each vertex contains position, lighting, and texture information. In this way, the materials are quite independent of each other, and the mesh looks like one continuous object because the positions of some of the vertices in different materials are the same.

Morph the Vertices or Pop?

No vertex morphing will be done in this implementation—vertices pop in and out of existence. This is cheaper and, in my experience with game teams, actually looks better than morphing. This surprising result is because, for a given polygon count, the mesh is as close as it can be to its proper shape, rather than being blended somewhere between the current shape and the next lower detail level. The pops in practice are less of a problem actually than the extra expense of doing morphing (particularly of having to edit vertex data).

Progressive Mesh Rendering Only Affects the Triangle Lists

Because an edge collapse preserves one out of the two vertices involved, this renderer modifies the triangle lists only, with no effect on the vertex data. This means that the vertex arrays can be left alone (and in some modern hardware, pre-processed into some more efficient format), and can also be shared between multiple instances of the same mesh. The triangle lists will be modified over time, and must be duplicated once for each active instance of each mesh.

This also means that vertex position modifiers, such as animation, can happen fairly independently of the progressive meshing, as long as you don't mind that the collapse order won't change even as the vertices move about against each other. The animation system only has to handle the fact that vertices can come and go, rather than be used continuously.

Lower Detail Triangles and Vertices First

A point of note for the renderer is that the vertices and triangles have been ordered offline so that it is always the triangles and the vertices at the end of a list that are made redundant by a collapse. The renderer will always be submitting triangle and vertex lists starting in the same place, just of varying lengths. Discussion of the data structure generation will show how this is possible.

This does mean that unless you create strips and fans of triangles in some other way, you will be always presenting the graphics hardware with an indexed list of triangles. Interestingly, adjacent triangles in the list often share vertices, which in many systems is as good as having triangle strips and fans. This is because at least pairs of triangles on either side of an edge collapse will be next to each other in the triangle list.

The Reversible Edge Collapse List

The other renderer data structure describes the reversible sequence of edge collapses that changes the level of detail of the mesh. Each edge collapse loses one vertex, one or more triangles, and changes which vertices some of the remaining triangles use. There is one edge collapse list for the whole object, though different individual collapses affect different materials. Alternatively, there could be a collapse list per material, but these would have to be tied together somehow so that the seams of the object don't come apart.

```
struct PMEdgeCollapse
{
    float Value;
    PMMaterial *Material;
    int NumIndicesToLose, NumVerticesToLose,
    NumIndicesToChange;
    int *IndexChanges;
    int CollapseTo;
};
```

The CollapseTo member says which vertex should replace all references to the vertex that is being lost off the end of the list. All these changes are stored in the IndexChanges array. This operation is simple to reverse for vertex splitting when the level of detail is being increased again.

When a collapse happens, some triangles disappear (NumIndicesToLose), one or more vertices may be made redundant (NumVerticesToLose—loss of some triangles may leave vertices completely unused), and some indices in remaining triangles will be changed (NumIndicesToChange). Of course, the reverse happens during a vertex split.

Because the materials are so independent, sometimes two edge collapses must be performed at once, to preserve the mesh seams as much as possible. This is when, as discussed earlier, the two edges actually are the same edge in space, so must collapse together even though they refer to different vertices. The engine must continually compare the value of the next edge collapse or vertex split that could be performed against the level of detail required from the mesh based on its position and other variables.

In the simple system presented here, these edges are not taken into account, but they can be done quite well by simply giving all edges in the same place the same priority, even though they are unconnected in the data structure.

Offline Calculation

Here I will assume that the mesh data has been loaded by some means into a friendly format. For the sake of readability, the algorithm will be the simplest rather than the most efficient, particularly since we are not so worried about the expense of offline calculations.

The procedure can be summarized as repeatedly deciding which is the next bit of detail to be lost, and removing it from the mesh, while generating the edge collapse data that will be needed by the renderer later. When it is decided that a vertex should be removed, all triangles that refer to it must be changed, and any triangles that are made degenerate swapped to the end of the list. Similarly, the vertex is moved to the end of the remaining vertex list.

Of course, swapping triangles and vertices to the ends of their lists changes all references to them, in other edge collapse structures as well as in the remaining mesh. There may be other code (such as an animation system that is about to use the same mesh) that needs to know about vertex reordering.

Suggested Offline Calculation Optimizations

Looking at the code, it is obvious that extra temporary connectivity information would be useful in the mesh. For example, the code often looks for "all triangles that reference this vertex" by brute force. Also, the code repeatedly searches through all the triangles for the next edge to collapse. Huge performance improvements are possible if you put the edge collapse candidates into a priority heap.

Edge Selection Improvements

The most effective edge selection improvement is to make edges that affect discontinuities in the mesh less likely to collapse. This makes many more mesh shapes possible, and also allows objects to be subdivided further into subobjects. Each mesh subdivision gives an extra degree of freedom in level of detail choice—see the previous discussion about making huts and trees separate from the landscape mesh underneath them. See Figure 4.12.6.

A Further Variation on Progressive Meshing

Instead of being able to change level of detail at the resolution of one vertex at a time, you could just store several pre-calculated index lists at various resolutions. The changes between these levels of detail of course will be more obvious. This system

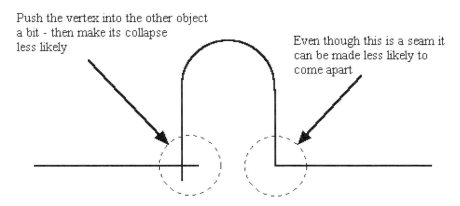

Push the vertex into the other object a bit - then make its collapse less likely

Even though this is a seam it can be made less likely to come apart

FIGURE 4.12.6 What was one mesh becomes two subtly intersecting ones, or just two coincident ones.

becomes more useful if the polygon counts or frame rates are so high that the popping is not a problem.

An advantage is that you can throw away the edge collapse list, which is actually quite a large data structure, certainly comparable to the extra index lists you are storing in this new method. You also lose the collapsing/splitting code, and you don't need a separate index list for each active instance of each object. The renderer becomes much simpler—you are back to a normal mesh renderer, but just with code to select which index list to use for each object at a given moment.

Source Code

Code for the progressive mesh generator and the renderer is contained on the CD. It is written in a general manner with little system dependency.

References

[Duchaineau97] Duchaineau, M. et al, ROAMing Terrain: Real-time Optimally Adapting Meshes, 1997, available online: http://www.llnl.gov/graphics/ROAM/roam.pdf.

[Garland97] Garland, M., and Heckbert, P.S., Surface Simplification Using Quadric Error Metrics, Siggraph 1997 Proceedings, pp. 209–216, August 1997.

[Hoppe96] Hoppe, H., Progressive Meshes, Siggraph 1996 Proceedings, pp. 99–108, August 1996.

[Hoppe97] Hoppe, H., View-dependent refinement of Progressive Meshes, Siggraph 1997 Proceedings, pp. 99–108, August 1997.

[Hoppe98] Hoppe, H., Efficient implementation of progressive meshes, Computers & Graphics, Vol. 22(1), pp. 27–36, 1998.

[Lindstrom99] Lindstrom, P., and Turk, G., Evaluation of Memoryless Simplification, IEEE Transactions on Visualization and Computer Graphics, Vol.5(2), April–June 1999.

[Ronfard96] Ronfard, R., and Rossignac, J., Full-Range Approximation of Triangulated Polyhedra. Eurographics 1996 Proceedings, in Computer Graphics Forum, 15(3), August 1996, pp. 67–76.

[Svarovsky99] Svarovsky, J., Extreme Detail Graphics, Game Developer's Conference 1999 Proceedings, also available online: http://www.svarovsky.freeserve.co.uk/ExtremeD.

4.13

Interpolated 3D Keyframe Animation

Herbert Marselas

Keyframing is a simple and effective way of animating a 3D object. However, since each keyframe only represents the extremes of the object's motion, this can make the object appear to jump between positions.

Linear Interpolation

One solution is to add more keyframes to make the transition between keyframes less jarring. Another more economical method is to programmatically create in-between animation frames using *interpolation.*

Interpolation—also known as blending, morphing, or tweening—is the process of creating a new position between two existing positions. In this case, we are interpolating two known keyframe positions p_0 and p_1 to create a new position $p(t)$.

The easiest interpolation solution is linear interpolation. In this case, a line is drawn between the same position in two adjacent keyframes p_0 and p_1, and then we calculate where on this line the new position $p(t)$ exists (Figure 4.13.1).

Given the desired time of the new animation position, the total number of keyframes, and the total time of the animation, the point between the two closest keyframes can be calculated.

The function `calculateFramePercentage` demonstrates this. Given the total number of keyframes in the animation, the total time of the animation, and the desired time, the keyframes on either side of the new position and the percentage between the two frames are calculated and returned.

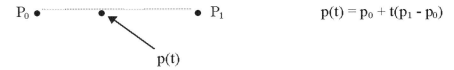

$$p(t) = p_0 + t(p_1 - p_0)$$

FIGURE 4.13.1 Example linear interpolation and formula.

```
void calculateFramePercentage(long dwTotalAnimFrames,
    float fTotalAnimTime, float fDesiredTime,
    long &dwFirstFrame, long &dwSecondFrame,
    float &fPercentage)
{
  // determine which frames are involved

  float fTimePerFrame = fTotalAnimTime /
    (float) dwTotalAnimFrames;

  dwFirstFrame = 0;

  if (fDesiredTime > fTotalAnimTime)
    fDesiredTime -= fTotalAnimTime;

  for (float f = 0.0f; f <= fDesiredTime; f += fTimePerFrame)
    dwFirstFrame++;

  // set first frame

  if (f > fDesiredTime)
    dwFirstFrame-;

  if (dwFirstFrame < 0)
    dwFirstFrame = dwTotalAnimFrames - 1;
  else
    if (dwFirstFrame >= dwTotalAnimFrames)
      dwFirstFrame = 0;

  // set second frame

  dwSecondFrame = dwFirstFrame + 1;

  if (dwSecondFrame >= dwTotalAnimFrames)
    dwSecondFrame = 0;

  // calc the percentage

  fPercentage = (fDesiredTime - ((float) dwFirstFrame *
    fTimePerFrame)) * fTimePerFrame;
} // calculateFramePercentage
```

First, calculateFramePercentage increments through each frame until it finds the keyframe that is right before the desired time. This assumes that the keyframes each have the same duration. If the keyframes are not set at uniform intervals, this function will have to be changed accordingly.

With the first keyframe found, it is checked against the number of keyframes in the animation. Then, the second keyframe is determined by incrementing the first keyframe number by one. The second keyframe number is also checked against the total number of keyframes in the animation. This code assumes that the animation is going to loop back to the start of the animation after displaying the last keyframe.

It should be noted that the calculateFramePercentage function, as with all of the functions in this article, are presented more for readability than performance. One easy performance improvement is to pre-compute values such as fTimePerFrame.

Interpolating Vertices and Normals

With the two keyframes and the percentage between them identified, this data can now be used to generate the new animation frame. The combineVertices function demonstrates using these values to combine the vertices from the selected keyframes.

```
void combineVertices(long dwVertexCount, float fPercentage,
    vector3 *pFirstFrameVertices,
    vector3 *pSecondFrameVertices,
    vector3 *pCombinedVertices)
{
  for (long i = 0;
     i < dwVertexCount;
     i++, pFirstFrameVertices++,
     pSecondFrameVertices++, pCombinedVertices++)
  {
     *pCombinedVertices = *pFirstFrameVertices +
        fPercentage * (*pSecondFrameVertices —
        *pFirstFrameVertices);

  }
}
```

The percentage that was calculated in calculateFramePercentage is used to combine the vertices from the two keyframes into a single new position between them.

This same method of combining the vertices of both keyframes can also be applied to combining the normals of the keyframes. If the keyframe normals were normalized before interpolating, the combined value won't need to be normalized unless there is a large difference between the normal vectors.

There can also be a performance savings if separate lists of face normals (for back-face culling) and vertex normals (for lighting) are stored in each keyframe. The face normals must always be interpolated, but interpolating the vertex normals can be skipped if you're trying to improve performance. This means that the vertex lighting won't be correct, but in many situations, the user won't notice the difference.

Hermite Spline Interpolation

One drawback to linear interpolation is that some interpolated animation frames may have a tendency to deform to a greater or lesser extent. To solve this, a slightly more complicated interpolation system must be used. This next method, Hermite spline interpolation, takes into account the two keyframes on either side of the desired position (Figure 4.13.2).

Similar to calculateFramePercentage, calculateFramePercentageSpline determines which keyframes are on either side of the desired animation time. Additionally,

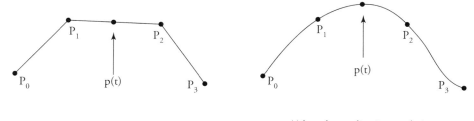

p(t) based on linear interpolation   p(t) based on spline interpolation

FIGURE 4.13.2 Linearly interpolated position vs. spline interpolated position.

the frames immediately before and after these two keyframes are also calculated. These additional keyframes are used to refine the calculation for the new position.

```
void calculateFramePercentageSpline(long dwTotalAnimFrames,
    float fTotalAnimTime, float fDesiredTime,
    long &dwFirstFrame, long &dwSecondFrame,
    long &dwThirdFrame, long &dwFourthFrame,
    float &fPercentage)
{
  // determine which frames are involved

  float fTimePerFrame = fTotalAnimTime /
    (float) dwTotalAnimFrames;

  dwSecondFrame = 0;

  if (fDesiredTime > fTotalAnimTime)
    fDesiredTime -= fTotalAnimTime;

  for (float f = 0.0f; f <= fDesiredTime; f += fTimePerFrame)
    dwSecondFrame++;

  // set second frame

  if (f > fDesiredTime)
    dwSecondFrame --;

  if (dwSecondFrame < 0)
    dwSecondFrame = dwTotalAnimFrames - 1;
  else
    if (dwSecondFrame >= dwTotalAnimFrames)
      dwSecondFrame = 0;

  // set frame before second frame

  dwFirstFrame = dwSecondFrame - 1;

  if (dwFirstFrame < 0)
    dwFirstFrame = dwTotalAnimFrames - 1;

  // set upper frame
```

```
                    dwThirdFrame = dwSecondFrame + 1;

                    if (dwThirdFrame >= dwTotalAnimFrames)
                       dwThirdFrame = 0;

                    // set frame after the third frame

                    dwFourthFrame = dwThirdFrame + 1;

                    if (dwFourthFrame >= dwTotalAnimFrames)
                       dwFourthFrame = 0;

                    // get the upper percent

                    fPercentage = (fDesiredTime - ((float) dwSecondFrame *
                       fTimePerFrame)) * fTimePerFrame;
                 } // calculateFramePercentage
```

The positions from the four keyframes are used to calculate the new *p(t)* using the following equation:

$$p(t) = (2t^3 - 3t^2 + 1)p_o + (t^3 - 2t^2 + t)m_o + (t^3 - t^2)m_1 + (-2t^3 + 3t^2)p_1$$

$$m_i = \left(\frac{1-\alpha}{2}\right)\left(\left(p_i - p_{i-1}\right) + \left(p_{i+1} - p_i\right)\right)$$

The first and fourth keyframes are used to calculate the tangents m_i between the first and second keyframes, and the third and fourth keyframes, respectively.

Spline Interpolating Vertices

The combineVerticesSpline function demonstrates calculating the tangents and then the Hermite spline interpolated position *p(t)*.

```
void combineVerticesSpline(long dwVertexCount, float fPercentage,
                           vector3 *pFirstFrameVertices,
                           vector3 *pSecondFrameVertices,
                           vector3 *pThirdFrameVertices,
                           vector3 *pFourthFrameVertices,
                           vector3 *pCombinedVertices)
{
   float t = fPercentage;
   float t2 = t * t;
   float t3 = t2 * t;

   vector3 m0, m1;

   const float alpha = 0.0f;

   for (long i = 0;
        i < dwVertexCount;
        i++, pFirstFrameVertices++, pSecondFrameVertices++,
```

```
                    pThirdFrameVertices++, pFourthFrameVertices++)
        {

            m0 = ((1 - alpha) / 2.0f) *
                    ((*pSecondFrameVertices - *pFirstFrameVertices) +
                      *pThirdFrameVertices - *pSecondFrameVertices);

            m1 = ((1 - alpha) / 2.0f) *
                    ((*pThirdFrameVertices - *pSecondFrameVertices) +
                      *pFourthFrameVertices - *pThirdFrameVertices);

            *pCombinedVertices = (((2 * t3) - (3 * t2) + 1) *
                *pSecondFrameVertices) +
                ((t3 - (2 * t2) + t) * m0) +
                ((t3 - t2) * m1) +
                (((-2 * t3) + (3 * t2)) *
                *pThirdFrameVertices);
        }
    }
```

Another new addition to this calculation is the variable `alpha`. `alpha` controls the tension of the tangent to the spline that being calculated. While alpha can be changed to make the tension higher (positive values), or lower (negative values), leaving `alpha` at zero is good enough for most animations.

If you've determined that a fixed value for `alpha` is sufficient for your animation, you can pre-calculate the first part of the tangent equation m_i, ((1 − `alpha`) / 2), and replace it with a constant, 0.5 in this case.

Why Hermite Splines?

At first glance, it may seem an odd choice of a Hermite spline over a better known spline such as a B-spline. While B-splines offer additional continuity, this comes at the cost of less control over the tendency of the interpolated curve.

Summary

Interpolating keyframe animations is an easy and inexpensive way of improving animation quality. Linear interpolation can be performed for very little cost per vertex. Hermite spline interpolation improves the quality of interpolated keyframes over linear interpolation, but comes at a greater per-vertex cost.

References

[Foley96] Foley, J., van Dam, A., Feiner, S., and Hughes, J. *Computer Graphics: Principles and Practice* 2nd Edition. New York: Addison-Wesley Publishing Company, Inc., 1996.

4.14

A Fast and Simple Skinning Technique

Torgeir Hagland

This article describes a skinning method that is most beneficial for lower polygon characters (less than 500 polygons), where the artists and animators need 100% control over what their vertices are doing. The method can in short be described as a clever way of modifying and sorting an object's vertex list and re-mapping the face list accordingly.

Why Low-Polygon Count?

When dealing with low-polygon count models, each vertex has a big visual impact on how the model's silhouette looks. As an example, let's look at your elbow. The only bones influencing it would be the upper and lower arms. When flexing your biceps, the lower arm influences how the vertices on the inside of your elbow move. It pushes those vertices up from the direction of your lower arm and averages it with the orientation of your upper arm. The end result looks like you have a very thick elbow. This technique only takes into account one bone per vertex.

The Method

The artist creates a single skin model; for example, a space soldier. They then duplicates this skin, scales it down fractionally, and proceeds to cut this smaller skin up into even smaller bits (body parts), which are used as bones. As each bone is created, it is given the same name as the skin with a number appended to it, so it can easily be recognized as a bone by our program.

Once we have identified a skin and its bones, we take the geometry of the bones and store the vertices in one big list. Each entry in this list contains the vertex position and the bone this vertex is a part of.

Now for each vertex in our skin, we find the vertex in the bone list that is closest to it. We transform the skin vertex by the inverse matrix of the bone that the vertex was closest to. This will bring the skin vertex into the local coordinate system of the bone (in the draw loop, the vertex is transformed back again, so even though the bone-skin is smaller, it has no impact on the end result since the position is relative). The transformed vertex is stored in a temporary list that we accumulate, where we also store the original vertex list index and a pointer to the bone that influences it. The influencing bone has a counter that keeps track of the number of vertices it transforms.

When all the vertices of the skin have a bone influencing them, we process the temporary list that we created. This list is then sorted based on the order of the bones. For each bone, the number of vertices it influences is stored in the original skin's vertex list, and the faces must remap the vertices that they reference since we just changed all the vertex indices.

Listing 4.14.1 contains sample code that solves for bone influences and remaps the faces accordingly. Even though this sample code uses the 3D Studio Max file toolkit, the technique can easily be used with any 3D modeling package. I only use it to keep the source size small, and to make sure the focus of this is on the influence solving and draw loop, not the model conversion, etc.

After executing the code in Listing 4.14.1 we have:

- A skin, with each vertex transformed into the local coordinate system of the bone influencing it. The vertex list is sorted by the order of the bones.
- A list of bones, with a counter for how many vertices each bone should transform.

The draw loop for the skin can then be as simple as Listing 4.14.2.

Summary

This method is fast and simple, and works especially well for low-polygon characters. For higher-polygon characters, the edges are smoother, and you will need several bones influencing each vertex. You will also then most likely store two or three pointers for each vertex to the bones that influence them. This means you can no longer pre-store the inverse transformed vertices, and for each frame you need to apply the inverse transform and a percentage-based rotation for each bone that influences it. This causes more of a problem for the tool that creates the influence data. Commercial packages that export bone information do exist, and you no longer have to worry about how the influencing is done, just how to create your draw loop. If you do decide to create the influence tool yourself, I highly recommend making a tool that allows the artist to "paint" influences directly onto the geometry. This way he does not have to second guess a mathematical algorithm.

Listing 4.14.1

```
void SolveBoneInfluences(database3ds *db, Skin *skinptr)
{
    /* Allocate a big workbuffer */
```

```
BonePoint *bonepointptr=
(BonePoint*)malloc(30000*sizeof(BonePoint));
BonePoint *curbonepoint=bonepointptr;

long NrBoneVerts=0;

/* Make all the bones' vertices into one big vertex
 list with information on what bone each point came from */

MATRIX tmpmat;

Bone *boneptr=skinptr->BonePtr;
while(boneptr)
{
    mesh3ds *bonemesh=NULL;
    GetMeshByName3ds(db,boneptr->Name,&bonemesh);
    assert(bonemesh);

    Copy3dsMatrix(tmpmat,bonemesh->locmatrix);
    InverseMatrix(tmpmat,boneptr->Matrix);

    point3ds *bonemeshpoints=bonemesh->vertexarray;

    NrBoneVerts+=bonemesh->nvertices;
    assert(NrBoneVerts<30000);

    for(int i=0;i<bonemesh->nvertices;i++)
    {
        curbonepoint->Point.x=bonemeshpoints->x;
        curbonepoint->Point.y=bonemeshpoints->y;
        curbonepoint->Point.z=bonemeshpoints->z;
        curbonepoint->BonePtr=boneptr;
        bonemeshpoints++;
        curbonepoint++;
    }

    RelMeshObj3ds(&bonemesh);
    boneptr=boneptr->NextPtr;
}

mesh3ds     *skinmesh        = skinptr->MeshPtr;
point3ds    *skinmeshpoints  = skinmesh->vertexarray;
BonePoint   *skinpointptr     = (BonePoint*)malloc(
skinmesh->nvertices*sizeof(BonePoint));
BonePoint   *curskinpoint     = skinpointptr;

/* Find the closest bone vertex to each skin vertex */
for (int i=0;i<skinmesh->nvertices;i++)
{
    curskinpoint->Point.x     = skinmeshpoints->x;
    curskinpoint->Point.y     = skinmeshpoints->y;
    curskinpoint->Point.z     = skinmeshpoints->z;
    /* need to store original vertex index, for
    face remapping */
    curskinpoint->Index        = i;
```

```
            /* no bone is influencing this bone yet */
            curskinpoint->BonePtr     = NULL;

            curbonepoint=bonepointptr;
            float mindist=1e6;

            for(int j=0;j<NrBoneVerts;j++)
            {
                float dist=
                CalcDistNotSquared(skinmeshpoints,
                &curbonepoint->Point);
                if(dist<mindist)
                {
                    mindist=dist;
                    curskinpoint->BonePtr=
                    curbonepoint->BonePtr;
                }
                curbonepoint++;
            }
            curskinpoint++;
            skinmeshpoints++;
        }

        /* Sort all the vertices of the skin by bone,
        and remap the faces accordingly */
        skinmeshpoints     = skinmesh->vertexarray;
        face3ds *skinfaces = skinmesh->facearray;
        long CurIndex=0;
        boneptr=skinptr->BonePtr;
        while(boneptr)
        {
            curskinpoint=skinpointptr;
            for (i=0;i<skinmesh->nvertices;i++)
            {
                if(curskinpoint->BonePtr==boneptr)
                {
                    Transform(boneptr->Matrix,
                    (float*)&curskinpoint->Point,
                    (float*)skinmeshpoints);
                    RemapFaceList(skinmesh,
                    curskinpoint->Index, CurIndex++);
                    boneptr->NrVerts++;
                    skinmeshpoints++;
                }
                curskinpoint++;
            }
            boneptr=boneptr->NextPtr;
        }

        /* Clean up after the remapping */
        CleanUpFaceList(skinmesh);

    free(skinpointptr);
    free(bonepointptr);
}
```

Listing 4.14.2

```
void glDrawChar()
{
    mesh3ds    *meshptr   = SkinPtr->MeshPtr;
    Bone       *boneptr   = SkinPtr->BonePtr;
    point3ds   *vertptr   = meshptr->vertexarray;
    face3ds    *faceptr   = meshptr->facearray;

    /* For Each bone in the skin, transform X amount
    of vertices with the bone's current animation matrix*/
    point3ds *skinptr=SkinPtr->PointPtr;
    while(boneptr)
    {
        MATRIX mat;
        memcpy(&mat,&boneptr->AnimPtr[CurFrame],
            sizeof(MATRIX));
        for (int i=0;i<boneptr->NrVerts;i++)
    Transform(mat,(float*)vertptr++,
        (float*)skinptr++);

        boneptr=boneptr->NextPtr;
    }

    /* Then Simply draw the object using the facelist*/
    skinptr=SkinPtr->PointPtr;
    glBegin(GL_TRIANGLES);
        glColor3f(1,1,1);
        for(int i=0;i<meshptr->nfaces;i++)
        {
            point3ds *v1=&skinptr[faceptr->v1];
            point3ds *v2=&skinptr[faceptr->v2];
            point3ds *v3=&skinptr[faceptr->v3];

            glVertex3f(v1->x,v1->y,v1->z);
            glVertex3f(v2->x,v2->y,v2->z);
            glVertex3f(v3->x,v3->y,v3->z);

            faceptr++;
        }
    glEnd();
}
```

References

[Lander98] Lander, Jeff, Game Developer Magazine, May 1998: *Real-time Skeletal Deformation.*

4.15

Filling the Gaps—
Advanced Animation Using
Stitching and Skinning

Ryan Woodland

As hardware becomes faster and more feature-laden, game developers are searching for ways to make characters look more compelling. Of the many categories that can be improved, character animation is perhaps one of the most important.

Currently, most 3D games are starting to use some sort of skeletal representation for their characters as their topology for animation. These systems attach geometry to "bones" in a character. The bones are then animated and, consequently, the attached geometry inherits the motion creating adequate animation. Usually, however, the geometry used to represent characters is rigid in nature, which is not the most useful representation for modeling organic creatures that are definitely not rigid in nature.

Because the geometry is completely rigid, any two pieces that are supposed to be connected to each other (an upper arm and a forearm, for example) display blatant discontinuities at the joint at which they are connected. This obviously can become a problem, since the characters we are trying to represent are more often than not made up of a continuous skin that does not show any cracks or separations.

In this article, I will discuss the topics of *stitching* and *skinning* as ways to create more realistic organic animation. Stitching is actually just a less computationally expensive subset of skinning and will therefore be discussed first. Both of these techniques assume one continuous mesh that is attached to a bone structure for a character as opposed to many meshes attached to a single bone in traditional rigid-body animation. This continuous mesh is deformed relative to the character's bone structure, yielding a character that does not create visible (and often very annoying) gaps at joints when animating.

In the following sections, I will be using the example of an arm to demonstrate various features of stitching and skinning. The basic mesh used is picture in Figure 4.15.1.

FIGURE 4.15.1 Our basic arm mesh.

Stitching

As mentioned earlier, stitching operates on a continuous mesh attached to a bone structure. In rigid-body animation, a polygon is transformed by one matrix representing the bone to which that polygon is attached. With stitching, each vertex in a polygon can be transformed by a different matrix representing the bone to which the individual vertex is attached. This means that we can create polygons that "stitch" multiple bones together simply by attaching different vertices in the polygon to different bones. When the bones are manipulated, this polygon should fill the gap you would see in rigid-body animation.

One of the major differences between stitching and rigid-body animation is the data topology for representing a character. With rigid-body animation, a bone must simply have a pointer to some geometry it is to animate. The matrix yielded by the corresponding bone then transforms that geometry. For stitching, it is necessary for each *vertex* in the character's skin to keep track of the bone to which it is attached.

```
struct Vertex
{
    float s, t;
    float x, y, z;
    unsigned long color;

    unsigned long boneIndex;
};
```

Before animating a character that has been correctly bound to this data topology, we need to deal with the problem that our vertices are not in the correct space to be properly transformed. The problem is this: a matrix used to transform a bone for animation assumes that the bone starts with its pivot point at the origin of the coordinate space of the character. This makes sense if we consider a hand bone in a normal human. This bone should start with its pivot point at the origin of its coordinate space so that we can easily rotate the bone around that point. The bone is animated (rotated) and then transformed to the end of the forearm bone. This process repeats for the forearm bone—the hand and the forearm are then animated and moved out to the end of the upper arm bone. This continues down through the hierarchy until the entire skeleton has been properly transformed.

Given the spatial relationship between the skin's vertices and the bones of the character, it is necessary to transform the vertices of the skin into the local coordinate space of the bones to which they are attached before transforming them by the bone's animation matrix. To do this, we need to keep a matrix in each bone that tells us how to transform geometry back into the local space of the bone. This matrix should be the inverse of the matrix used to transform the bone from its local space into the character's mesh, given the orientation of the mesh without any animation being applied. See Figure 4.15.2 for a depiction of the local spaces for each bone in our arm mesh.

Therefore, the data structure of our bones should look like the following:

```
struct Bone
{
    Mtx orientation;
    Mtx animation;
    Mtx inverseOrientation;

    Mtx final;

    Bone *child;
    Bone *sibling;
};
```

Once we have this data, we are ready to animate our character. To do this, we must simply step through the vertex data and transform each vertex by the orientation matrix and then the animation matrix of the corresponding bone.

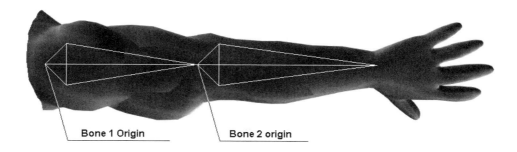

FIGURE 4.15.2 A depiction of the bones in our arm.

All of these transformations can be done faster by processing the bone hierarchy and generating a final transformation matrix for each bone concatenating a bone's inverse orientation, concatenated orientation, and concatenated animation matrices together and then transforming geometry by the resulting matrix.

```
void BuildMatrices ( Bone *bone, Mtx forward, Mtx orientation )
{
    Mtx localForward;
    Mtx localOrientation;

    // concatenate the hierarchy's orientation matrices so
    // that we can generate the inverse
    concatenate(bone->orientation, orientation ,
    localOrientation);

    // take the inverse of the orientation matrix for this bone
    inverse(localOrientation, bone->inverseOrientation);

    // concatenate this bone's orientation onto the forward
    // matrix
    concatenate(bone->orientation, forward, localForward);

    // concatenate this bone's animation onto the forward matrix
    concatenate(bone->animation, localForward, localForward);

    // build the bone's final matrix
    concatenate(bone->inverseOrientation, localForward,
    bone->final);

    if(bone->child)
        BuildMatrices(bone->child, localForward,
        localOrientation);

    if(bone->sibling)
        BuildMatrices(bone->sibling, forward, orientation);
}
```

Using the preceding technique on the arm mesh, a bend of 45 degrees and 90 degrees to the forearm bone produces the images in Figure 4.15.3.

Stitching is a very valid technique, since it easily takes advantage of any hardware that provides a transform engine. It is necessary to generate the final stitching matrix on the CPU, but the hardware can easily use these matrices to transform any number of vertices we pass it.

As an optimization to this technique, I suggest breaking up the continuous skin so that the vertices exist in the local space of the bone to which they are attached. This prevents us from having to do an extra matrix concatenation per bone per frame of animation.

FIGURE 4.15.3 *a:* Stitched arm mesh bent to 45 degrees. *b:* Bent to 90 degrees.

Skinning

While stitching is a valid technique, it has some problems. In cases of extreme joint rotation, geometry tends to shear massively and appear quite unnatural. Using the techniques discussed earlier, a forearm rotation of 120 degrees displays quite a nasty shear effect at the elbow. This results because we only have one polygon to span the entire gap between the upper arm and the forearm. The larger this gap becomes, the worse the solution looks, as shown in Figure 4.15.4.

To prevent this, we can implement a full system of skinning where a vertex is not limited to being affected by a single bone; it can instead be influenced by multiple bones. This makes sense if we look at the behavior of the human body. The skin on a person's elbow is not affected by the orientation of just one bone. The movements of both the upper and lower arm bones affect it. Similarly, skin in the neck and shoulder is affected by the orientations of the arm, neck, and chest.

To enable this, each vertex in a skinned mesh must contain a list of bones that affect it. Each vertex must also carry a weight per bone that tells us how heavily affected the vertex is by the bone. For this example, we will assume linear skinning, which means all of the weights of a vertex must add up to 1.0. Because of this, given n bones by which a vertex is affected, we need to store $n-1$ weights, since the remaining weight should be $1.0 - (weight_1 + weight_2 + \ldots + weight_{n-1})$.

```
struct Vertex
{
    float s, t;
    float x, y, z;
    unsigned long color;
```

FIGURE 4.15.4 Ugly stitched arm mesh bent to 120 degrees.

```
        unsigned long boneIndex1;
        unsigned long boneIndex2;

        float weight;
    };
```

As mentioned earlier, stitching is a subset of skinning, and therefore suffers from the same local-space transform issues as stitching. Therefore, we should use the same bone representation as shown previously.

In order to do full skinning, we need to transform each bone by each matrix affecting it, then multiply the result by the corresponding weight, and, finally, accumulate the results. The equation for skinning looks like:

*(vertex * matrix0 * weight0) + (vertex * matrix1 * weight1) + ... +*
*(vertex * matrixN * weightN)*

where the sum of all weights $0..N = 1.0$.

What we are effectively doing is a linear interpolation between transformed vertices. The following is the code used to perform this operation on a given mesh.

```
Vector3D TransformVertex ( Vertex *vert, Bone *boneArray )
{
    Vector3D    temp;
    Vector3D    final;
```

```
    temp = XFormVec(vert->position,
    bone[vert->boneIndex1]->final)
    final.x = temp.x * vert->weight;
    final.y = temp.y * vert->weight;
    final.z = temp.z * vert->weight;

    temp = XFormVec(vert->position,
    bone[vert->boneIndex2]->final)
    final.x += temp.x * (1.0F - vert->weight);
    final.y += temp.y * (1.0F - vert->weight);
    final.z += temp.z * (1.0F - vert->weight);

    return final;
}
```

Using the technique outlined previously, we were able to generate the following output for forearm rotations of 45 degrees, 90 degrees, and 120 degrees, respectively. Note that even in the extreme 120-degree example (see Figure 4.15.5), the continuity of the elbow geometry is still maintained.

As you can see, a major problem with skinning is that it is computationally expensive. Unfortunately, these computations are not well supported by today's hardware transform engines. An alternative way of performing the linear interpolation calculations, which potentially takes advantage of some current hardware implementations, is to generate a skinning matrix to be passed to hardware to perform the final transform. To calculate the skinning matrix, simply interpolate the matrices linearly based on the weight:

(matrix0 * weight0) + (matrix1 * weight1) + ... + (matrixN * weightN)

where the sum of all weights $0..N = 1.0$.

This method is only useful if the same skinning matrix can be used for multiple vertices; in other words, different vertices are weighted identically between the same bones. The less this case is true, the less the gain of this method will be.

FIGURE 4.15.5 *a:* Skinned arm mesh bent to 45 degrees. *b:* Bent to 90 degrees. *c:* Bent to 120 degrees.

It is important to note that the skinning technique outlined previously is not a completely mathematically correct technique. If normals are transformed using this technique, the results are not guaranteed to be normalized. If per-vertex lighting is required for a character using this technique, post-transform normals must be re-normalized before lighting calculations.

Advanced Topics

The skinning example assumes all the weights influencing a vertex must add up to 1.0. It is a possibility, however, to create some compelling special effects with weights that do not sum to 1.0. For instance, it is possible to place an extra bone in an arm that simulates a bicep muscle. All of the vertices in the arm's skin should be weighted normally between the upper arm, lower arm, and shoulder. However, the vertices near the bicep should also be weighted based on their distance from the bicep bone—closer vertices should have higher weight values. When the arm bends, apply a scale to the bicep bone to create the appearance of a muscle flexing.

The skinning technique outlined is not mathematically correct because we are essentially linearly interpolating matrices. Instead of representing bones as matrices, it is possible to represent them as a quaternion. *SLERP* between the quaternions based on the per-vertex weights and then produce a matrix from the result. This should yield a somewhat better-looking skinned mesh.

References

[Lander98] Lander, Jeff, "Skin Them Bones: Game Programming for the Web Generation," *Game Developer Magazine* (May 1998): pp. 11–16.

[Terzopoulos87] Terzopoulos, Demetri, et al, "Elastically Deformable Models," Computer Graphics, Vol 21, no.4 (SIGGRAPH 1987): pp. 205–214.

4.16

Real-Time Realistic Terrain Generation

Guy W. Lecky-Thompson

Terrain is the centerpiece of many games, an important backdrop in some, and just something to fill the space in others. No matter how it is used, it will still attract unwanted attention if it is badly represented and, by the same token, will add to the atmosphere, playability, and long shelf life of the game if done well.

The use of the term *terrain* conjures up images of landforms, lakes, mountains, or even desolate craters in airless atmospheres for most people. While this is an important aspect of building the game, the word *terrain* may be used in a much broader sense. It can cover objects, names and buildings, parts of the game universe that the player will interact with, and pieces that only give support to those parts.

The aim of this article is to equip the reader with several algorithms that enable a realistic terrain to be created, within which the game may be played.

The emphasis here is on generation, and not storage. That is to say, the algorithms are presented in a manner that leans toward using them to create terrain in real-time, and not generation for storage, with a view to replaying the contents at a later date. Used with the techniques defined in the *Predictable Random Numbers* article in this book, a powerful near-infinite universe can be generated.

Landscaping

The first technique that can be used to create basic terrain is *fuzzy landscaping*. Essentially, it is simply creating topography in a completely random fashion, with scant regard to the real world. It is presented here simply as a starting point upon which we may build future algorithms that will prove of more use.

Here is some pseudocode that generates a finite grid:

```
y = -1;
while y < 100 {
    x = 0;
    y = y + 1;
    srand(y);
```

```
    }
    while x < 100 {
        map(x, y) = rand (3);
        x = x + 1;
    }
```

As can be seen, this will simply populate a 100×100 grid with a series of random numbers between 0 and 3. We can then assign colors to the numbers such that 0 is black (water), 1 is dark gray (plains), 2 is light gray (land), and 3 is white (mountain). This effect is seen in Figure 4.16.1. Note also that the random number generator is seeded on part of the grid reference of the individual square. This ensures that we can always recover the value without needing to go through the entire grid [Lecky99], but only through that line.

This is slightly less perfect than one would hope, since we would like to seed based on a discrete square. To do this, we would need to create our own random number generator to rid us of the annoying effect seen in Figure 4.16.1, which results from using the ANSI srand function : srand (x + (x * y)) for each grid square.

Good-looking fuzzy terrain is more realistic than that shown in Figure 4.16.1, so we need to perform some additional processing on the resulting "map." The technique that we shall use is one that can be applied to any of the terrain-generating algorithms presented here, indeed to any abstract set of random figures that require a grouping treatment.

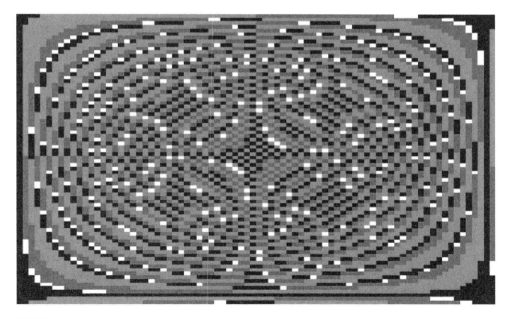

FIGURE 4.16.1 A 100x100 random grid of terrain values.

The driving philosophy is to ensure that the randomness of the map is reduced by ensuring that neighboring squares hold a similar value, but at the same time allowing differences between specific sets or areas of squares. As usual, it is far easier to watch in action than to explain. The pseudocode looks like this:

```
step = 4;
for y = 0; y < 100; y = y + step {
    for x = 0; x < 100; x = x + step {
        total = 0;
        for y_local = y; y_local <= y + step;
                y_local = y_local + 1 {
                    for x_local = x; x_local <= x + step;
                        x_local = x_local + 1 {
                            total = total + map (x_local, y_local);
                    }
        }
        average = total / (step x step);
        for y_local = y; y_local <= y + step;
            y_local = y_local + 1 {
            for x_local = x; x_local <= x + step;
                x_local = x_local + 1 {
                map (x_local, y_local) = average;
            }
        }
    }
}
```

The effect of applying this smoothing algorithm can be seen in Figure 4.16.2.

While the net result is far from perfect, the overriding feeling is that the map has become much less random than before.

It works by dividing the grid into a series of larger squares, and then subdividing them. The average value of the subdivisions is then computed and propagated throughout the subdivisions. The overall effect is one of smoothing.

The choice of subdivision size here is quite important also—too large a subdivision will create wide expanses of similar values, and too small a subdivision will not produce the desired effect.

An improvement to this algorithm is to approach it from a slightly different direction. The end result is the same, modifying discrete points of the terrain based on the surrounding points. This time, however, we will select the four corner points of the square for the averaging process, rather than use every point. Also, we will only change the center points of each of the four quarters of the chosen square, rather than every point.

The following code is snipped from the terrain-generation software that appears on the CD.

```
for ( int square_size = width; square_size > 1; square_size /= 2 )
{
    int random_range = square_size;
```

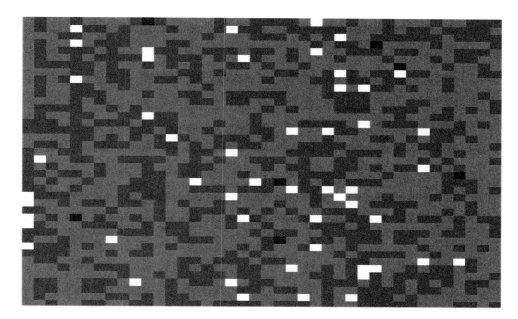

FIGURE 4.16.2 A smoothed version of our random terrain grid.

```
for ( int x1 = row_offset; x1 < width; x1 += square_size )
{
  for ( int y1 = row_offset; y1 < width; y1 += square_size )
  {
    // Calculate the four corner offsets
    int x2 = (x1 + square_size) % width;
    int y2 = (y1 + square_size) % width;

    // Get the values
    int i1 = this->terrain[x1][y1];
    int i2 = this->terrain[x2][y1];
    int i3 = this->terrain[x1][y2];
    int i4 = this->terrain[x2][y2];

    // Create weighted averages, based on
    int p1 = ((i1 * 9) + (i2 * 3) + (i3 * 3) + (i4)) / 16;
    int p2 = ((i1 * 3) + (i2 * 9) + (i3) + (i4 * 3)) / 16;
    int p3 = ((i1 * 3) + (i2) + (i3 * 9) + (i4 * 3)) / 16;
    int p4 = ((i1) + (i2 * 3) + (i3 * 3) + (i4 * 9)) / 16;

    // Calculate the center points of each quadrant
    int x3 = (x1 + square_size/4) % width;
    int y3 = (y1 + square_size/4) % width;
    x2 = (x3 + square_size/2) % width;
    y2 = (y3 + square_size/2) % width;

    // Set the points to the averages calculated above
```

```
        this->terrain [x3][y3]  = p1;
        this->terrain [x2][y3]  = p2;
        this->terrain [x3][y2]  = p3;
        this->terrain [x2][y2]  = p4;
    }
  }

  // For the next row, move in slightly
  row_offset = square_size/4;
}
```

Figure 4.16.3 shows the four corner points and the bounding rectangle of the four center points used in the calculations above.

This technique was first introduced to me by James McNeill [McNeill95], and is one of the most reliable examples of "smoothing" I have seen to date. There are endless variations that involve adding random offsets to the calculated points, amongst others, which lead to more variable landscapes.

As an enhancement to the two techniques discussed here, we may introduce a third mechanism, known as Fault Line landscape generation. Fault Line landscape generation works by choosing two points at random and drawing a line at a given height between them. Next, two more points are chosen, and again, a line is drawn between them. This is repeated until there are a certain number of lines on the screen, as in Figure 4.16.4.

The next step is simply to apply the subdivision technique explained previously to smooth the differences between the points. This results in a series of "islands" being created as can be seen in Figure 4.16.5. See Jason Shankel's article, *Fractal Terrain Generation—Fault Formation,* in this volume for further information on this technique.

While this may seem simple at first, the line drawing itself is in fact more complex. As the discerning reader will have noticed in Figure 4.16.5, the lines are not

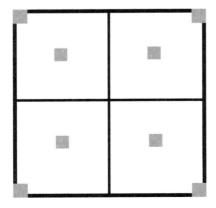

FIGURE 4.16.3 Subdivision coordinates.

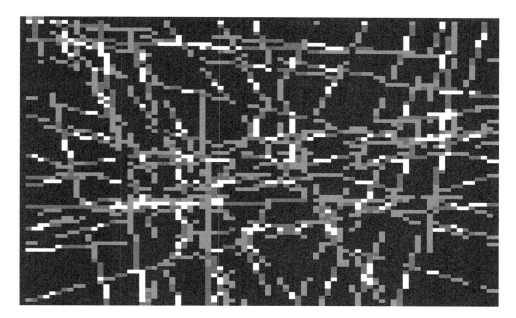

FIGURE 4.16.4 Random fault lines.

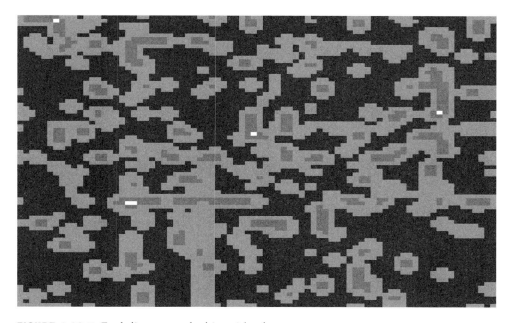

FIGURE 4.16.5 Fault lines smoothed into islands.

drawn at a constant "height." That is, the value attributed to each point along the line changes with respect to the distance from the starting point to the ending point.

The algorithm used to decide the "height" of each point is a sine curve, whose amplitude is based on the distance between the two points. The following code segment shows the core line-drawing algorithm at work that forms part of the terrain generator software on the CD.

```
do
{
  this->terrain[(int)x_start][(int)y_start] =
    nCurrentRandomValue;
  x_start = x_start + x_diff;
  y_start = y_start + y_diff;

  // Apply a sine function oscillating between 0 and 255
  // The sin function should be called with values from
  //    -pi/2 to pi/2

  if (x_diff < y_diff)
  {
    nCurrentRandomValue = (sin(x_start) * 128) + 128;
  }
  else
  {
    nCurrentRandomValue = (sin(y_start) * 128) + 128;
  }
} while (((y_start < (float)this->terrain_width) &&
    (y_start > 0.0)) &&
    ((x_start < (float)this->terrain_height) &&
    (x_start > 0.0)));
```

This is performed for each line to achieve an effect akin to a mountain range, albeit with a very smooth oscillation.

The important point to note about all of the techniques discussed is that the landscape that is generated is repeatable. That is, using the same basic input values, identical landscapes can be generated at will. They do not need to be stored anywhere. This is the underlying principle for creating terrain in general, and is the core theme to the remainder of this article.

Using these techniques along with the principle of generation, we can say that since in theory every time we seed the random number generator, we will get a different set of random numbers, the possibilities for generating terrain are infinite. Furthermore, since we can re-generate or re-calculate at will any point of any terrain, we never need more than just run-time storage, which leaves us space on the delivery media for much more than just level files.

Buildings

One of the most common structures in the game-playing arena (if you'll pardon the pun) is the maze. *Doom* uses several to good effect, for example. In addition, ladders and levels-type games also use a two-dimensional variation of the maze. These mazes often increase in complexity according to the skill of the player, and may be littered with all manner of treasure.

Too often, though, these use up so much storage space (*Doom* WAD files for example) that you simply cannot put enough of them on a CD to satisfy the player. A truly realistic terrain (in the broadest sense) requires the illusion of infinity, and so it would be a great boon if we could somehow create these containers in real time.

If no attention should be paid to the "shape" of what is being created, it is extremely simple to create something that will contain passages and paths, but with no rooms. (The author fondly remembers a few early arcade games like that...) Basically, the aim is to imagine that the playing area is contained within a finite space, which we will call a box.

This box is then subdivided by drawing horizontal lines from the left-hand side to the right at random intervals. Next, these sub-boxes are divided by drawing vertical lines from the top of the box to the bottom, again at random intervals. A possible result is shown in Figure 4.16.6.

Seen from this angle, this is not very interesting at all, but it is all a question of representation. Imagine the black lines to be passageways. Now imagine that the players only see the passageways from the first-person perspective; all they will know are junctions and passages.

In fact, it still wouldn't be especially convincing—it is still missing rooms and dead-ends. Both of these will increase the reality of the experience. Rooms are quite easy, because all that is required is that any space that has dimensions exceeding the

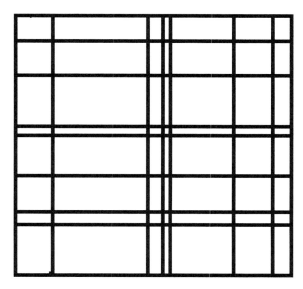

FIGURE 4.16.6 Random lines divide our box.

smallest box can be considered a room. Working out the dimensions of the smallest box is almost too easy.

Since we know that all the horizontal and vertical lines must meet at some juncture, it follows that the smallest box is the junction of the two vertical lines with the smallest horizontal separation, and the two horizontal lines with the smallest vertical separation. Anything larger than that *in both directions* can be considered a room; whatever is left is just passageway. Based on that, what emerges is shown in Figure 4.16.7 (here we have added a little to the sizes used to work out the passageways and rooms).

By placing entryways on the walls at various places, we have created a playing area that can be generated *entirely* on the fly. Increasing the number of lines, or decreasing the size used to determine what is a passageway and what is a room, will affect the complexity and hence the ease of play.

However, it is still not very realistic. In fact, it looks more like the intersection of a couple of streets, rather than a building. So let us treat it like that, and determine how we may turn the "rooms" into "buildings." The passageways will remain streets.

Rather than blindly chopping the "room" into pieces as we did previously, buildings can be made more realistic by subdivision. Taking a square, we divide it at a random position into two pieces, vertically. Then we divide each of the two pieces into two more, horizontally. Next, we may choose to divide each of the resulting pieces into two, again vertically. This can be repeated as many times as is required. In Figure 4.16.8, we have taken one of the larger squares from our previous example.

The algorithm for doing this is fairly complex; however, here is an acceptable variant for vertical lines:

1. Start at the leftmost side, at a random height.
2. Count the number of squares to the right until a wall is encountered.

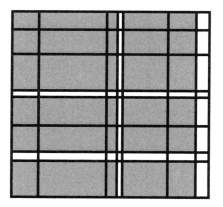
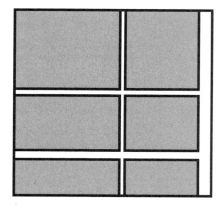

FIGURE 4.16.7 *a:* Before line removal. *b:* After line removal.

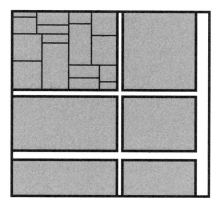

FIGURE 4.16.8 Rooms created by subdivision.

3. At a random number of squares from the left, draw a line from the top to the bottom.
4. Repeat steps 1, 2, and 3 to taste.

And its equivalent for drawing horizontal lines:

1. Start at the topmost side, at a random width.
2. Count the number of squares down until a wall is encountered.
3. At a random number of squares from the top, draw a line from the left to the right.
4. Repeat steps 1, 2, and 3 to taste.

Of course, the algorithm needs to ensure that when counting from top to bottom (or indeed left to right), that this is performed along a line, to avoid "floating" lines appearing that start in the middle of the square. All lines that are drawn must have a starting point and an ending point at a wall.

The next step is to insert doors in the walls. This can be done in a variety of ways, but perhaps the easiest is to work, again from top to bottom, or left to right, and insert a door in internal walls such that sections of walls have a maximum of N doors in them.

If this is done completely at random, we run the risk of having some walls with no doors, and potentially some rooms to which there is no direct access. Depending on whether this creates a problem, the algorithm must be adapted.

Naming Algorithms

Giving objects, places, or features realistic names is a real chore when it comes to most game design. *Elite*, by David Braben and Ian Bell, came up with some classics (Lave,

Diso, Reidquat, Leesti, Orevre, etc.) for the first star system. The first of a stagger-ingly large galaxy, in a universe of near-infinite scale. Considering that the machine that the game was running on (with 16K RAM) was a limited-resource second-gener-ation microcomputer, this was a huge achievement. Clearly, there was no way that these could have been stored (diskettes had yet to be invented), so they must have been generated.

We could begin by generating a word of six letters, each one chosen at random. We might come up with something like "ndpgbs," which is not terribly convincing. What is required is some method by which we can ensure that letters that are next to each other fit naturally. The first step is to create a table of letter-frequency pairs, so that for a given letter we can say that there are a limited number of possible letters that can follow it, and calculate the chance that each one may follow it.

The following listing is the key to a technique known as the Markovian List (see also [Dewdney90]):

```
void AddLetters(char * szWord, unsigned long ulTable[28][28])
{
  int nWordLength, nFirstLetter, nLastLetter, nLetter;

  // Decapitalise the word
  for (nLetter = 0; nLetter < (int)strlen(szWord)-1;nLetter++)
     tolower(szWord[nLetter]);

  // Add the first, and last to the table
  nWordLength = (int)strlen(szWord);
  nFirstLetter = (szWord[0] - 'a') + 1;
  nLastLetter  = (szWord[nWordLength-1] - 'a') + 1;

  ulTable[0][nFirstLetter]++;  // Space followed by letter
  ulTable[nLastLetter][27]++;  // Letter followed by space

  for (nLetter = 0; nLetter < nWordLength-2; nLetter++)
  {
    nFirstLetter = (szWord[nLetter]   - 'a') + 1;
    nLastLetter  = (szWord[nLetter+1] - 'a') + 1;

    ulTable[nFirstLetter][nLastLetter]++;
  }
}
```

The algorithm represented here needs little explanation, other than to say that for a given word, we specify which letters are the starting and ending ones, and add them to the table. Then, for each pair, we update the table such that the position referenced by the letters is incremented, cementing a relationship between the two that we will make use of later.

As can be seen, this requires storage space of the order of 28x28x4 bytes (3,136), which fulfills our criteria of getting it into a 16K RAM machine. Indeed, removal of all the blank entries will probably reduce the space requirements even more.

Once we have passed the algorithm over a selected text, or texts, we will have a table that contains all possible letter pair frequencies for those texts. We should also store the average word length, too.

Using this table, we may now generate a word, starting with the first letter. To do this, we should choose a random letter such that it may begin a word; in other words, it falls in a column of the table referenced by *ulTable[0]*, such that *ulTable[0][x]* is greater than zero. In addition, we can use the values stored in this row to determine the chance of a specific cell being chosen.

To do this, we simply add the values of all the cells referenced by *ulTable[0][i]* (where *i* runs from 1 to 26). Next, we call the random number generator to retrieve a value between 1 and the value we have calculated. We then pass through the row again, summing the frequencies as before, until the random number that we have is less than the running total. This is our letter; for example *ulTable[0][4]* is a "d." The following code shows a generic form of this algorithm, which can be applied to any letter.

```
int GetLetterPosition(unsigned long ulWordTable[28][28], int
nPrevious)
{
  int nCounter;
  unsigned long ulFrequencyTotal, ulFrequencyRunningTotal,
                ulRandomLetter;

  ulFrequencyTotal = 0;

  // Get the frequencies
  for (nCounter = 1; nCounter < 27; nCounter++)
  {
    ulFrequencyTotal = ulFrequencyTotal +
    ulWordTable[nPrevious][nCounter];
  }

  // Choose a 'target' frequency
  ulRandomLetter = rand() % (ulFrequencyTotal);

  // Move through the table until we hit the 'target' frequency
  ulFrequencyRunningTotal = 0;
  nCounter = 1;
  do
  {
    ulFrequencyRunningTotal = ulFrequencyRunningTotal +
                              ulWordTable[nPrevious][nCounter];
    nCounter++;
  } while (ulFrequencyRunningTotal < ulRandomLetter);

  return nCounter;
}
```

In order to build a word of six letters in length, the general algorithm would be:

```
Word[0] = GetLetterPosition (word_table,0)
```

```
x = 1
while x < 6 {
    word[x] = ((GetLetterPosition (word_table, word[x-1] — 'a'))
    —1) + 'a'
    x = x + 1
}
```

This is the essence of the software NameGen that appears on the CD, and for which full source code is available. The NameGen code is also used in the demonstration program UniGen (for creating star maps, with named planets).

However, as it stands, the word-generation algorithm doesn't preclude strange words such as "fleeee" or "nooooo" creeping in. The problem is that there are a certain number of letters that can form chains. That is, an "o" can be followed by an "o," and another "o," almost to infinity. The random number generator may prevent this to a certain extend, but even a repetition of three "o's" is a little ugly.

So, our word-building algorithm should become:

```
Word[0] = GetLetterPosition (word_table,0)
x = 1
while x < 6 {
  word[x] = ((GetLetterPosition (word_table, word[x-1] — 'a'))
    —1) + 'a'
  x = RemoveChain(word,x)
}
```

Where the RemoveChain function returns the current letter index into word if it is the third in a chain of itself. This could be coded as in the following listing:

```
int RemoveChain( char word[MAX_LENGTH], int letter_position )
{
    int nPos = 0;
    int nOccurences = 0;

    while (nPos < strlen(word))
    {
        if (word[nPos] == word[letter_position])
            nOccurences++;
    }

    if (nOccurences > 2) return letter_position — 1;

    return letter_position + 1;
}
```

This will clean up the word, and if there is no excessive chain, increment the letter position counter.

The final step that can be taken in ensuring that the word is authentic is to address the last letter, and make certain that it is one that can commonly end a natural word. Some letters, for example, are commonly followed by a vowel in the English language, such as "j." In order that words do not creep in that end in such letters, we must perform at least two operations.

The first operation is to ensure that the letter may follow the one that it is adjacent to, and to ensure that the chosen letter may end a word (be followed by a space). In addition, we must also be careful that such a letter exists; otherwise, we may end up in an endless loop. To do all this, the following code is adapted from the `GetLetter-Position` function already described.

```
int GetEndLetter (unsigned long ulWordTable[28][28], int nPrevious)
{
  int nCounter;
  unsigned long ulFrequencyAdjacentTotal,
    ulFrequencyRunningTotal, ulRandomLetter,
    ulFrequencyEndingTotal;

  ulFrequencyAdjacentTotal = 0;
  ulFrequencyEndingTotal = 0;

  // Get the frequencies
  for (nCounter = 1; nCounter < 27; nCounter++)
  {
    ulFrequencyAdjacentTotal = ulFrequencyAdjacentTotal +
      ulWordTable[nPrevious][nCounter];

    ulFrequencyEndingTotal = ulFrequencyEndingTotal +
      ulWordTable[27][nCounter];
  }

  // Choose a 'target' frequency
  ulRandomLetter = rand() % ulFrequencyAdjacentTotal;

  // Move through the table until we hit the 'target' frequency
  ulFrequencyRunningTotal = 0;
  nCounter = 1;
  do
  {
    ulFrequencyRunningTotal = ulFrequencyRunningTotal +
                              ulWordTable[nPrevious][nCounter];
    nCounter++;

    if (ulFrequencyEndingTotal > 0)
      if ((ulFrequencyRunningTotal >= ulRandomLetter) &&
          (ulWordTable[27][nCounter] != 0))
      break;
    else
      if (ulFrequencyRunningTotal >= ulRandomLetter)
        break;

  } while (1 == 1);

  return nCounter;
}
```

An improved version that selects the letter as a function of the combined probabilities of the target letter being adjacent to the source letter *and* at the end of a word is left as an exercise for the reader.

Additional points to note are that this method is limited only by the use of alphabet (it must be Roman), and that no attempt has been made to capitalize the beginning of words.

References

[Dewdney90] Dewdney, A. K., The Tinkertoy Computer, W.H. Freeman, 1990.

[Lecky99] Lecky-Thompson, Guy W., Algorithms for An Infinite Universe, Gamasutra, 1999.

[McNeill95] McNeill, James, SubDiv Applet, mcneja@wwc.edu.

4.17

Fractal Terrain Generation— Falt Formation

Jason Shankel

In nature, forces such as the separation of tectonic plates, mass-wasting, and shoreline erosion create terrain features like escarpments, mesas, and seaside cliffs. In this article, I will show how we can use a fault formation algorithm to generate these kinds of terrain.

Fault Formation

Start with an empty height field. Draw a random line through it and add an offset value *dHeight* to each value on one side of the line (See Figure 4.17.1):

Next, decrease *dHeight*, draw a new line, and repeat the process. Continue generating lines and decreasing *dHeight* until a sufficient level of detail is generated.

Figure 4.17.2 shows terrain height fields at 4, 8, 32, and 64 iterations (higher elevations in white).

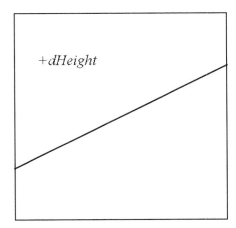

FIGURE 4.17.1 The first step of our height field.

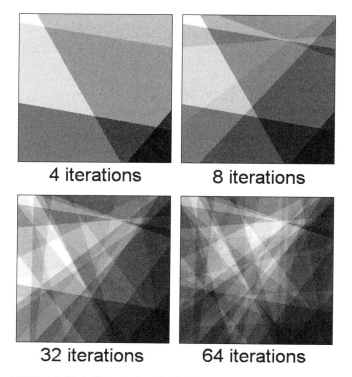

FIGURE 4.17.2 Terrain height fields created by this process.

Decreasing *dHeight*

We want to decrease *dHeight* linearly with each iteration, but we don't necessarily want it to drop to zero.

Let $dHeight_{0..N}$ be the value of *dHeight* at each iteration. The value of *dHeight* at iteration *i*, is given as:

$$dHeight_i = dHeight_0 + (i/n)(dHeight_n - dHeight_0)$$

Generating Random Lines

We want our lines to intersect well with the height field, so generating purely random values for a linear equation isn't desirable, since the vast majority of lines will contain the entire height field on a single side.

To generate a line, it is best to pick two random points within the height field and use them to determine the line.

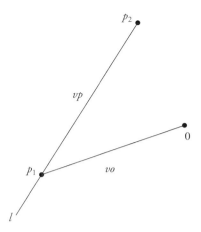

FIGURE 4.17.3. Illustration of choosing a "random line."

We can determine which side of a line a point is on by calculating the z component of a three-dimensional cross product (Figure 4.17.3):

Let l be a line defined by the points $p1$ and $p2$

Let vp be a vector in the direction $p1 \rightarrow p2$

Let o be a point in the height field

Let vo be a vector in the direction $p1 \rightarrow o$

Treated as three-dimensional vectors, vp and vo have z-components of zero.

Let $vx = vp \otimes vo$

If $vx.z > 0$, the point o lies on left side of the line. If $vx.z < 0$, the point o lies on the right. If $vx.z = 0$, o is on the line.

Erosion

The fault formation technique creates dramatic differences between neighboring cells in the height field. For a low number of iterations, this results in very unrealistic terrain. Even at high numbers of iterations, the terrain still looks highly aliased, like a piece of paper that has been sliced multiple times with a razor.

The problem is that we have unrealistic high-frequency data in our height field. In nature, the sharp divisions between neighboring cells would be dulled by erosion.

To simulate erosion, pass the height field through a low-pass image filter.

Robert Krten [Krten94] suggests a simple FIR filter. A FIR filter converts the sequence $x_1, x_2, x_3...x_n$ to the sequence $y_1, y_2, y_3...y_n$ according to the formula:

$$y_i = ky_{i-1} + (1-k)x_i$$

Where k is a filtering constant between 0 and 1. Low k means less erosion, high k means more. Typically, a k of about 0.5 works well for this application.

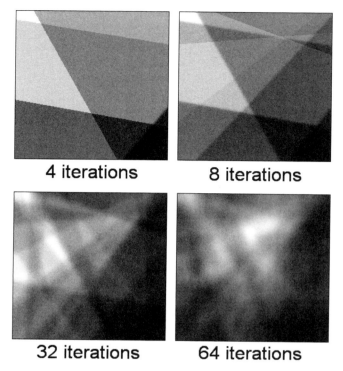

4 iterations   8 iterations

32 iterations   64 iterations

FIGURE 4.17.4 An eroded version of Figure 4.17.2.

If we take the FIR filter function and apply it across the rows and columns of the height field in both directions, we will get a nicely eroded landscape (Figure 4.17.4).

Figure 4.17.4 shows the same terrain as Figure 4.17.2 after erosion. Color Plate 1 is a 3D rendering of the eroded 64 iteration stage.

Sample Code

The algorithm in the sample code lets you set different numbers of iterations, the *dHeight* for iteration 0 and iteration *n*, the erosion factor (*k*), and the number of iterations between erosion passes.

References

[Krten94] Krten, Robert, "Generating Realistic Terrain," Dr. Dobbs Journal (July 1994).

4.18

Fractal Terrain Generation— Midpoint Displacement

Jason Shankel

Mountain ranges like the Rockies, Sierras, and Himalayas are formed by a geological process called *uplift*. Lateral pressure from the movement of tectonic plates causes the surface of the Earth to wrinkle like fabric, pushing up mountain ranges. In this article, I will show how we can simulate uplift with a recursive midpoint displacement algorithm, also known as the plasma fractal or the diamond-square algorithm.

Midpoint Displacement in One Dimension

In one dimension, midpoint displacement works like this. Start with a line segment *AB* (Figure 4.18.1):

FIGURE 4.18.1 Line segment *AB*.

Take the midpoint *C* and displace it by a random value between *–dHeight/2* and *+dHeight/2*, for some suitable *dHeight* (the length of *AB* is a good candidate) (Figure 4.18.2):

FIGURE 4.18.2. First displacement stage.

Reduce the value of dHeight and recurse to the segments *AC* and *CB* (Figure 4.18.3):

FIGURE 4.18.3. Second displacement stage.

Repeat until you generate sufficient detail (Figure 4.18.4):

FIGURE 4.18.4. *N*th displacement stage.

At each iteration, *dHeight* is multiplied by 2^{-r}, where *r* is the roughness constant.

The magic value for *r* is 1. If *r* = 1, then *dHeight* is divided by 2 at each iteration, which is also the rate at which the horizontal line segment length decreases. When *r* = 1, the generated terrain will be perfectly self-similar (small sections will resemble large sections).

When *r* > 1, *dHeight* decreases faster than the line segment length, so early iterations have a disproportionately large effect on the terrain. *r* > 1 is good for creating smooth terrain with a few prominent features (mountains or valleys).

When *r* < 1, *dHeight* decreases slower than the line segment length, so late iterations have a disproportionately large effect on the terrain. *r* < 1 is good for creating chaotic terrain.

Figure 4.18.5 shows three terrains with varying values of *r* (higher elevations in white).

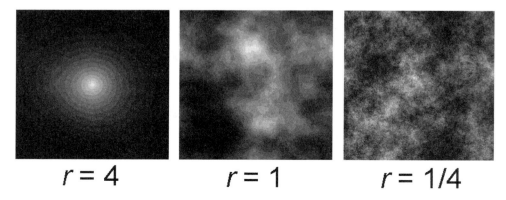

$r = 4$ $r = 1$ $r = 1/4$

FIGURE 4.18.5 Samples of terrain with various *r* values.

Midpoint Displacement in Two Dimensions— Diamond Square

Just as the line segment is the basic unit of one-dimensional midpoint displacement, the rectangle is the basic unit of two-dimensional midpoint displacement.

Rectangles are a bit more complicated than line segments, since we have to calculate not one but five midpoints for each rectangle. That is, we must calculate the midpoint of the rectangle itself, as well as the midpoints of each of the four line segments that make up the sides of the rectangle.

In the diamond-square algorithm, the calculation of the rectangle's midpoint is called the diamond step, and the calculation of the side midpoints is called the square step.

Start with a rectangle (*ABCD*), seeded with height values at the four corners (Figure 4.18.6):

FIGURE 4.18.6 Square *ABCD*.

Calculate the height at the midpoint E by averaging the values at A, B, C, and D and adding a random value between *-dHeight/2* and *+dHeight/2* (diamond step) (Figure 4.18.7):

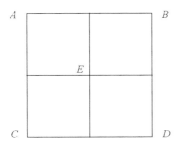

FIGURE 4.18.7 First displacement stage.

$E = (A+B+C+D)/4 + random(-dHeight/2, +dHeight/2)$

Now, calculate the heights at the midpoints of the line segments (*F, G, H,* and *I*) by averaging the corner values and the midpoints of the adjacent rectangles, and adding a random value between *-dHeight/2* and *+dHeight/2* (square step) (Figure 4.18.8):

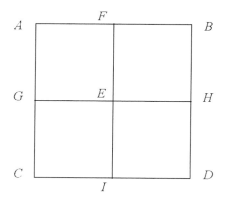

FIGURE 4.18.8.   First displacement stage, continued.

Multiply *dHeight* by 2^{-r} and repeat the process for the squares *AFGE, FBEH, GECI,* and *EHID* (Figure 4.18.9):

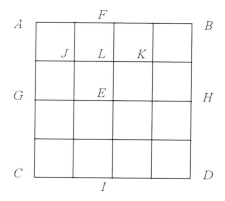

FIGURE 4.18.9   Second displacement stage.

Repeat until you've reached a sufficient level of detail.

An important thing to note about the square step is that the square values rely on the diamond values of neighboring squares.

For example:

$L = (F+E+J+K)/4 + random(-dHeight/2,+dHeight/2)$

So, as the algorithm iterates through each level of detail, it must first perform the diamond step for the entire grid before performing the square step.

To calculate a square step value on the edge of the terrain (H, for example), treat the terrain as though it wraps. In the case of H, take E as being adjacent to H on both the right and the left:

$H = (B+D+2E)/4 + random(-dHeight/2,+dHeight/2)$

Diamond Square in Height Fields

When using the diamond square algorithm to fill in a height field, it is best to pick a square height field with width 2^n for some integer n. This ensures that the rectangle size will have an integer value at each iteration.

See Color Plate 2 for a rendering of a terrain generated into a 256x256 height field.

4.19

Fractal Terrain Generation— Particle Deposition

Jason Shankel

In nature, volcanic mountain ranges and island systems like the Pacific Rim's "Ring of Fire" are generated by lava flow. In this article, I will use a particle system borrowed from the field of molecular beam epitaxy to simulate lava flow.

MBE Models

Molecular beam epitaxy, or MBE, is a process for depositing thin layers of atoms on a crystalline substrate. We can adapt the models used in MBE simulation to approximate lava flow. For an in-depth analysis of the mathematics of MBE, see [Barabási95].

Particle Deposition

The idea is to drop sequences of particles and simulate their flow across a surface composed of previously dropped particles. Dropping a sufficient number of particles will produce structures that look like the flow patterns of viscous fluid (lava).

Start with an empty height field and drop a single particle onto it (Figure 4.19.1).

Now, drop a second particle on the first and agitate it until it comes to rest (that is, until none of its neighbors is at a lower altitude) (Figure 4.19.2).

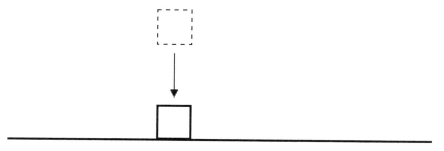

FIGURE 4.19.1 A single dropped particle.

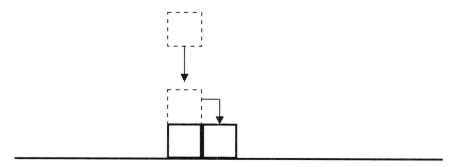

FIGURE 4.19.2 Two dropped particles.

Continue dropping particles (varying the drop point periodically) until you have a decent sized pile (Figure 4.19.3).

You can control the shape of the terrain by controlling how the particle drop point is moved. Keeping the drop point in a single place will create a large peak. Moving the drop point periodically will create chains of multiple small peaks.

Figure 4.19.4 shows different terrains generated with this technique (higher altitudes in white).

Inverting the Caldera

Real-world volcanoes, especially active volcanoes, have very distinctive mountaintops. After flow stops, the lava at the top of the volcano cools and recedes back into the Earth, creating a familiar bowl-shaped region at the top called a *caldera*.

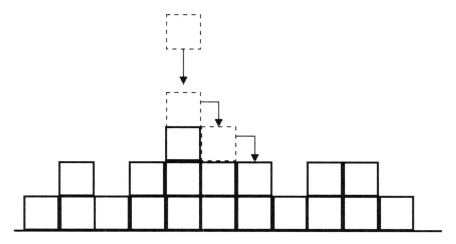

FIGURE 4.19.3 A collection of particles.

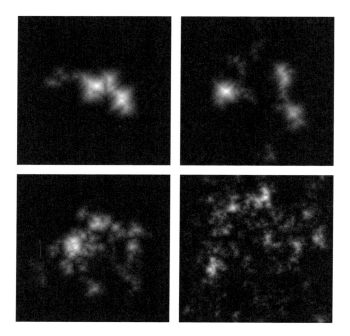

FIGURE 4.19.4 Some height fields generated with this technique.

We can generate a caldera for our particle mountain by inverting the height field values above a certain altitude about the horizontal plane defined by that altitude.

Imagine a height field generated by particle deposition (Figure 4.19.5).

Draw a line (or rather, a plane) through an arbitrary altitude (Figure 4.19.6).

Then invert all the height field values above the line about the line (Figure 4.19.7).

Cutting off the peak this way can result in a highly aliased caldera edge. To make the caldera look more realistic, apply an erosion filter (see the "*Fractal Terrain Generation—Fault Formation*" article) to blunt the sharp edges.

Applying the caldera cutoff to the entire height field can generate undesirable results. If the terrain has multiple peaks, the caldera line for one peak can interfere with other peaks.

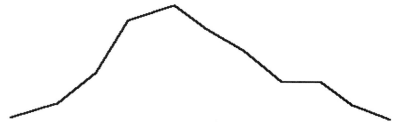

FIGURE 4.19.5 A height field generated by particle deposition.

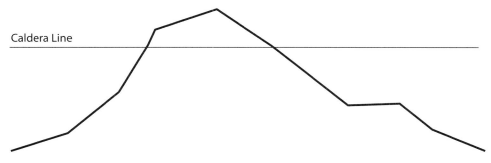

FIGURE 4.19.6 The caldera line.

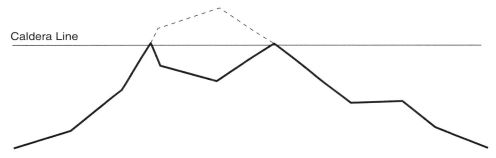

FIGURE 4.19.7 Invert the height field values above the caldera line.

It is best to implement the caldera inversion using a flood-fill technique. Starting from an initial point, invert the point and check its neighbors. For each neighbor that is above the caldera line, invert it and check its neighbors. Continue until you run out of neighbors.

Color Plate 3 is a 3D rendering of a volcanic island system generated with particle deposition.

Sample Code

The sample code lets you control the number of piles, the particles dropped per pile, the movement of the particle drop location, and the caldera depth. Caldera depth is expressed as a percentage of peak height [0..1]. Using a caldera depth close to 1 will generate sinkholes instead of mountains.

References

[Barabási95] Barabási, A. L., and Stanley, H. E., *Fractal Concepts in Surface Growth* (Cambridge University Press, 1995)

PIXEL EFFECTS

5.0

2D Lens Flare

Yossarian King

Lens flare is an optical effect created by interreflection between elements of a lens when the camera is pointed toward a bright light. The result is a shifting pattern of translucent shapes and colors emanating from the light source. The effect is often seen in TV broadcasts when the sun enters the video camera's field of view.

In real life, lens flare is considered a defect, and camera manufacturers go to great lengths to eliminate it through special lens coatings. Video games, however, like to emphasize and exaggerate all the cooler aspects of reality, and lens flare is definitely cool. Real lens flare is due to complex interactions of light with surfaces in the optical system of a camera. Video game lens flare is all about appearances. This article shows how to implement an attractive lens flare effect using only a small amount of code and artwork, without needing to know anything at all about physical optics.

Approach

Real lens flares are created in the lens system of the camera and so naturally appear "on top of" the scene being viewed. Each element of a flare is a reflection of the light bouncing off a secondary lens and onto the primary lens. Since the lenses are in precise vertical alignment, the reflections fall along a line in the final image, where the distance of the reflection from the center of the image is proportional to the distance of the corresponding secondary lens from the primary.

These observations justify the treatment of lens flare rendering as a 2D problem. The flare is rendered as an overlay on the 3D scene, and the elements of the flare are rendered along a line intersecting the projected position of the light and the center of the screen, as shown in Figure 5.0.1.

At this point, we abandon all reference to physical optics and focus entirely on aesthetics. The lens flare effect is rendered with a small collection of textures, one for each style of flare element—circles, rings, hexagons, sunbursts, and so on—as shown in Figure 5.0.2. The gray-scale textures are combined with vertex colors to produce subtle coloring. Alpha blending is used to make the effect translucent. Elements are rendered in a variety of sizes.

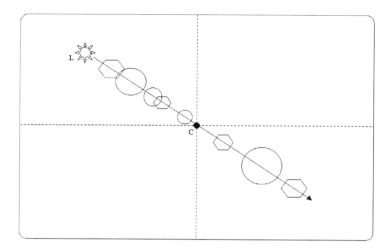

FIGURE 5.0.1. Lens flare rendering is a 2D problem. Elements of the lens flare are rendered along a line between the projected position of the light source and the center of the screen.

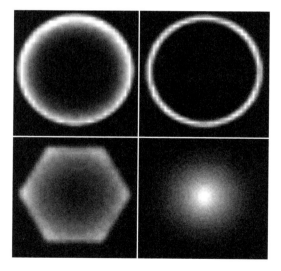

FIGURE 5.0.2. The lens flare effect is rendered using a small collection of gray-scale textures.

To be truly effective, the lens flare effect must animate convincingly with camera movement. The overall movement of the flare is determined by tracing the line from the projected light position through the center of the screen. Varying the size and translucency of the flare elements produces additional subtlety. This variation is achieved by scaling the size and alpha value of the flare elements based on the distance between the projected light position and the center of the screen; when the light is farther from the center, the elements are smaller and more transparent, and when the light is closer to the center, they become larger and more opaque.

A sample of the results of this approach are shown in Color Plate 4.

Implementation

Putting all this together boils down to performing the following steps for each element of the lens flare:

1. Determine position and size of the flare element.
2. Determine texture, color, and translucency of the element.
3. Render the element as a 2D sprite with the computed properties.

In this implementation, a flare is a collection of elements. Each element has the following static properties:

- **Texture.** The available textures (shapes).
- **Distance.** Proportional distance along the line from the light source to the center of the screen.
- **Size.** Normalized size of the element (before scaling).
- **Color.** Red-green-blue (RGB) color used to shade the element while rendering.
- **Alpha.** Translucency of the element (before alpha scaling).

The flare also has an overall scale factor and a maximum size, used to control the element sizes during rendering. These properties are all determined at initialization time. In the demo code, the properties can be determined randomly or loaded from a flare description file.

During rendering, the dynamic properties of each lens flare element are computed based on their static properties and the position of the light source on the screen. Texture and color of the flare are unaffected, but position, size, and alpha level are all dynamic, depending on the movement of the camera relative to the light source.

In pseudocode, the lens flare effect is rendered as follows:

```
function renderflare:
    flare        // flare object to be rendered
    (lx,ly)      // projected position of light on screen
    (cx,cy)      // center of flare (normally center of screen)
{
    // Compute how far off-center the flare source is.
    maxflaredist = sqrt(cx^2 + cy^2)
    flaredist = sqrt((lx - cx)^2 + (ly - cy)^2)

    // Determine overall scaling based on off-center distance.
    distancescale = (maxflaredist - flaredist)/maxflaredist

    // Flare is rendered along a line from (lx,ly) to a
    // point opposite it across the center point.
```

```
            dx = cx + (cx - lx)
            dy = cy + (cy - ly)

            for each element in flare
            {
                // Position is interpolated between (lx,ly) and
                // (dx,dy).
                px = (1 - element.distance)*lx + element.distance*dx
                py = (1 - element.distance)*ly + element.distance*dy

                // Size of element depends on its scale, distance
                // scaling, and overall scale of the flare itself.
                width = element.size * distancescale * flare.scale

                // Width gets clamped, so the off-axis flares keep a
                // good size without letting the centered elements
                // get too big.
                if (width > flare.maxsize)
                    width = flare.maxsize

                // Flare elements are square (round) so height is
                // just width scaled by aspect ratio.
                height = width * aspectratio

                // Alpha is based on element alpha and distance scale.
                alpha = element.alpha * distancescale

                // Draw the element's texture with computed
                // properties.
                drawrectangle( element.texture, element.colour,
                alpha, px, py, width, height )
            }
        }
```

Source Code

The lens flare demo includes OpenGL source code and a Windows executable. The source code is separated into an API and sample code that uses the API. The API includes structures that define the properties of a flare as well as the following functions:

- **FLARE_initialize.** Initialize flare elements, given a list of properties by the caller.
- **FLARE_randomize.** Generate a list of flare elements with random properties.
- **FLARE_render.** Render the flare at a given screen position.

The demo uses these functions to create a lens flare effect controlled by the mouse. The mouse cursor is used as the screen location of the light source. Lens flares can be randomly generated or loaded from a file. See the README.TXT file included with the demo for additional details on the demo interface.

5.1

Using 3D Hardware for 2D Sprite Effects

Mason McCuskey

The past few years have seen an explosion in the 3D capabilities of graphics cards. In the span of a few years, we've moved from 256 colors at 320 × 200 to fully 3D accelerated, 1,600 × 1,200, 32-bit color. Even though most of today's cards tend to ignore the 2D world and ship with feature lists tailored to 3D, a phenomenal amount of processing power is still available in them, which can be harnessed to achieve stunning 2D effects.

This article sheds some light on how to use 3D hardware to achieve 2D effects. Specifically, we take a look at how to do alpha blending, sprite scaling, and sprite rotation.

Going 3D

The basis of this entire article is that inevitably, a 3D scene must be rendered to a 2D surface for display. This is as true in Direct3D's Immediate Mode (where a 3D rendering device must be attached to a surface) as it is in OpenGL.

Everything you see in a 3D scene is made up of primitives (usually triangles or quads). Groups of primitives are arranged together in various ways to form more complex polygons. Any group of primitives can have a "texture" applied to it, which governs how the group looks. We don't need to get into the many details of textures; for the purposes of 2D effects, all we care about is the fact that we can load a texture into OpenGL and then assign that texture to a quad (rectangle) primitive.

Setting Up the 3D Scene

The "trick" to displaying sprites using 3D hardware involves how you set up your 3D world. Even though the 3D card gives us the power to render polygons in any rotation and position in 3D space, the secret to achieving 2D effects is to set up our 3D scene so that everything is directly facing the camera. After all, if we set up a real-life 3D model of our 2D game, we'd realize that our 2D sprites are basically rigid pieces of paper at which the camera is directly pointing. In other words, in 3D, our 2D game looks like a really complicated diorama. Each sprite is a billboard, and the camera always remains a fixed distance from the sprites and never moves (unless you want it to, which can produce some interesting effects).

Keep this paradigm in mind as you read the later sections on setting up textures and displaying sprites.

Setting Up the Texture

Setting up the texture requires several OpenGL calls:

```
glPixelStorei(GL_UNPACK_ALIGNMENT, 1);
glGenTextures(1, (GLuint*)&mTextureID);
if (mTextureID == 0)
  { GLenum gle=glGetError(); /* handle errors! */ }
glBindTexture(GL_TEXTURE_2D, mTextureID);
glTexParameteri(GL_TEXTURE_2D, GL_TEXTURE_WRAP_S, GL_CLAMP);
glTexParameteri(GL_TEXTURE_2D, GL_TEXTURE_WRAP_T, GL_CLAMP);
glTexParameteri(GL_TEXTURE_2D, GL_TEXTURE_MAG_FILTER, GL_LINEAR);
glTexParameteri(GL_TEXTURE_2D, GL_TEXTURE_MIN_FILTER, GL_LINEAR);
glTexImage2D(GL_TEXTURE_2D, 0, GL_RGBA, 128, 128, 0, GL_RGBA,
  GL_UNSIGNED_BYTE, gpgtexture);
```

This section of code, part of the `C3DSprite::Init()` method in the example program, initializes our texture in OpenGL. `gpgtexture` is a pointer to an array of RGBA pixel values (4 bytes, one each for red, green, blue, and alpha values). The call to `glTexImage2D()` sets up a texture using the gpgtexture pixel array. The `glTexParameteri()` calls set various properties of the texture, including our wrapping mode (`GL_CLAMP`, which means "don't wrap the texture"), and our filters for growing and shrinking the texture (in this case, we're using linear filters).

Drawing the 3D Sprite

Now that we've got the texture set up, we're all ready to draw the sprite. To use a sprite, the client application first sets up all the parameters for the sprite (position on the screen, size, transparency or alpha value, etc.). The client then calls the `Display()` method to render the sprite.

The following code comes from the `C3DSprite::Display()` method:

```
// Set up the rotation and translation matrices
glPushMatrix();
glTranslatef(m_iX, m_iY, 0);
glRotatef(m_fRotation, 0, 0, 1);
```

The first thing this code does is set up the rotation and translation (movement) matrices. OpenGL uses a matrix stack, which allows us to apply global changes to our vertices as we create them. Any vertex that we create is transformed using the matrix at the top of the stack. Before we create any vertices, we need to set up a matrix that rotates the vertices and moves them to the position where the sprite is supposed to be (*m_iX, m_iY*).

To get the matrix we need, we push a new identity matrix onto the modelview stack, then multiply it by a translation matrix to the sprite's position (the third argument to glTranslatef is the z coordinate) and a rotation matrix using the m_fRotation variable. The second, third, and fourth arguments to glRotatef tell OpenGL which axis we want to perform the rotation around—in this case, just the z-axis. The z-axis is the one that's perpendicular to your monitor; it is "going into" and "coming out of" the screen.

The next thing we need to do is set our blending mode and texture mode. The first several lines of code set up our blending mode. We alpha-blend our sprite with whatever has already been rendered to the frame buffer. The equation used is *srcColor*srcAlpha+destColor*(1-srcAlpha)*. After that, we set up the texture mode. Our texture mode indicates that the pixels we're going to render are the source color and alpha *modulated* (multiplied) by the texture. After that, we call the glBindTexture() command, which tells OpenGL that we want the following primitives to be textured using mTextureID, the ID we got when we set up the sprite's texture earlier.

```
// Draw the sprite
glEnable(GL_BLEND);
glBlendFunc(GL_SRC_ALPHA, GL_ONE_MINUS_SRC_ALPHA);
glEnable(GL_TEXTURE_2D);
glTexEnvf(GL_TEXTURE_ENV, GL_TEXTURE_ENV_MODE, GL_MODULATE);
glBindTexture(GL_TEXTURE_2D, mTextureID);
//This glBegin() function call tells OpenGL that we're starting our
//vertex list and will be working with quad primitives.
glBegin(GL_QUADS);
```

Now we set up our four vertices, one vertex for each of the four corners of our quad primitive. Each vertex has:

1. A color. We're setting the color via the glColor4ub() function. In this example, the color of all our vertices is pure white, RGB (0xff, 0xff, 0xff).
2. A corresponding texture coordinate (set via the glTexCoord2f() function), which tells OpenGL how the texture is stretched or shrunk on our quad primitive. A texture coordinate of (0.0, 0.0) represents the upper-leftmost texture pixel (texel); a texture coordinate of (1.0, 1.0) represents the lower-rightmost texel. In effect, what we're saying in this example is that the texture is stretched perfectly so that it exactly fits the quad. (Keep in mind that the quad itself can be any size, and the texture grows and shrinks with it; all we're setting here is how the texture is attached to the quad.)
3. A position in 3D space, set via the call to glVertex3f(). In this example, we're putting the local origin of the sprite at its exact center, which puts the upper-left corner of our quad at (*–m_iWidth/2, –m_iHeight/2*). The lower-right vertex is

(*m_iWidth/2, m_iHeight/2*), where m_iWidth and m_iHeight are the width and height of the sprite. This effectively centers the sprite on its local origin, which is needed so that when the sprite rotates, it spins around local to its center.

```
glColor4ub(0xff, 0xff, 0xff, m_iAlpha);
glTexCoord2f(0.0F, 0.0F);
glVertex3f(-m_iWidth/2, -m_iHeight/2, 0);

glColor4ub(0xff, 0xff, 0xff, m_iAlpha);
glTexCoord2f(1.0F, 0.0F);
glVertex3f(-m_iWidth/2, m_iHeight/2, 0);

glColor4ub(0xff, 0xff, 0xff, m_iAlpha);
glTexCoord2f(1.0F, 1.0F);
glVertex3f(m_iWidth/2, m_iHeight/2, 0);

glColor4ub(0xff, 0xff, 0xff, m_iAlpha);
glTexCoord2f(0.0F, 1.0F);
glVertex3f(m_iWidth/2, -m_iHeight/2, 0);
```

And finally, this bit of code ends our scene and puts the graphics state and matrix stack back the way they were when we entered:

```
glEnd();
glDisable(GL_TEXTURE_2D);
glDisable(GL_BLEND);

// Pop the matrix we set up above
glPopMatrix();
```

Adding Effects

Now that we've got down the basics of drawing, we can add some effects. It's a happy coincidence that one of the most sought-after 2D effects—alpha blending—also happens to be very easy to do in 3D. To achieve alpha blending, we simply specify an alpha value for each of the vertices that make up our sprite. Take another quick peek at the code above; in the calls to glColor4ub(), the fourth argument (in the example, the m_iAlpha variable) is the alpha value for the vertex. The alpha value is similar to the red, green, or blue color values; it can be anything from 0 to 255, with 0 representing complete transparency and 255 representing complete opacity. So, for example, to create a sprite that's "halfway" transparent, we simply need to set the alpha value of all four sprite vertices to 128.

Of course, if we want to create a different kind of special effect, we can vary the alpha value of each vertex independently. For example, if we set the two left vertices to 0 and the two right vertices to 255, we get a sprite that fades gradually from completely transparent (on its left side) to completely solid (on its right side).

To create some colorful effects, we can specify different colors for each of the four vertices in our quad primitive. We do this by putting different RGB values in the call to `glColor4ub`. OpenGL automatically blends the colors together, so if we set the left side of our quad blue (RGB(0,0,255)), and the right side red (RGB(255,0,0)), we end up with a nice gradient of color going from blue to red across the sprite. In this way, we can add quick highlights of color without having to go to all the trouble of setting up an OpenGL light source. Please note that if you don't want OpenGL to apply a smooth color/alpha gradient to your polygon, you can change the behavior by calling `glShadeModel(GL_FLAT)`.

Scaling our 3D sprite is easy, too. The good news is that the 3D hardware takes care of stretching the texture; all we need to do is set up the vertices of our sprite. Stretching or shrinking the sprite is as easy as increasing or decreasing the width or height of our quad primitive. If we want to stretch the sprite along the *x*-axis by a factor of two, we simply make the width of the sprite `m_iWidth*2` instead of `m_iWidth`. Similarly, to stretch the sprite by a factor of two along the y-axis, we make the height of the sprite `m_iHeight*2` instead of `m_iHeight`. To shrink the sprite to half its size, we divide width and height by two. Any possible stretching combination can be achieved, and the great part is that you don't have to worry about the individual pixels of the sprite. It's all taken care of for you.

Rotating the sprite is simple, too. Again, it's just vertex position manipulation. We can specify an angle (in degrees) and pass this angle to OpenGL's `glRotatef` function, which applies it to the current transformation matrix. Again, the individual pixel locations are automatically calculated by the 3D hardware.

To create another interesting effect, we might change the axis of rotation for our sprite. `glRotatef` takes an angle and three parameters; these three vector parameters, at their simplest, allow us to tell OpenGL which axes we want to rotate about. It might be worthwhile to rotate about the x- or y-axes, effectively flipping the sprite horizontally and vertically in 3D, rather than simply rotating about the z-axis (spinning the sprite).

Conclusion

At first, this approach to 2D sprites might seem like a lot of needless work; it's often easier and more familiar to 2D programmers to draw sprites via *blitting functions* (such as DirectDraw's `Blt()` or Win32's `BitBlt()`). However, learning how to "blit" using 3D hardware pays off in the long run, since it ultimately becomes much easier to implement advanced 3D effects, such as alpha blending or sprite scaling. In addition, for the typical computer system, offloading the graphics processing required for alpha blending or scaling to the graphics card is a smart move, since it frees the CPU to concentrate on other tasks, which ultimately gives you more room to make a better game.

5.2

Motif-Based Static Lighting

Steven Ranck

This article describes a way to introduce more dynamic properties into precomputed static lighting. The approach produces stunning animated lighting at a computational cost that is only slightly greater than conventional static lighting.

Many games employ static lighting by precomputing the light colors at each vertex. This results in convincing Gouraud lighting at almost no computation cost. It also produces very static-looking light. This article describes an algorithm that adds dynamic animation to static lighting but still executes at nearly the same speed as conventional static lighting. For example, two torches close together on a rock wall produce firelight on the wall that flickers and interacts appropriately.

Conventional Static Lighting

Conventional static lighting is simply precomputed Gouraud RGB values stored with each vertex and used in a diffuse fashion during rendering. The precomputed RGB values are generated by either a tool or the game's initialization code. In either case, a tool is used to place lights on an object and assign characteristics such as color, intensity, radius, radial falloff, and light type (omni, directional, spot, and the like). Since we're dealing with static lighting, the lights and all their properties are constant. In addition, their positions are fixed in the object space of the object they are lighting; that is, static lights cannot move relative to the object they are lighting. From the light positions and properties, the effect of each light on each of the object's vertices can easily be computed using any desired lighting equation. Figure 5.2.1 demonstrates a simplified 2D representation of this concept.

Figure 5.2.1 shows an object with six vertices being statically lit by two lights. Vertex 5 falls within only Light A's influence, Vertex 3 falls within only Light B's influence, Vertex 2 falls within both lights' influences, and the remaining vertices fall outside both lights' influences. Because Light A and Light B are static, they are fixed in the object's coordinate space; if the object moves and rotates in world space, Lights A and B move and rotate along with the object. Therefore, the RGB lighting computation at each vertex can be computed only once (because it never changes) and stored

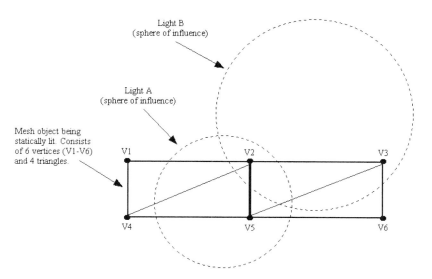

FIGURE 5.2.1. A statically-lit mesh object.

as part of the vertex structure. For this reason, static lighting is useful for lighting objects by lights that are attached to the object. Good examples of this concept are streetlights lighting a street and hull lights illuminating the spacecraft to which they are mounted.

In Figure 5.2.1, the static RGB for Vertex 5 is computed simply by using the vertex's position and normal with Light A in a conventional lighting equation. Vertex 3 is similar, but with Light B. Vertex 2 is influenced by both lights, so the resulting RGB is simply the sum of the two lighting equations. The remaining vertices aren't influenced by either light, so their RGB is (0,0,0), and it is then the sole responsibility of dynamic and ambient lighting to light those vertices.

The lighting equations used are completely up to the designer's preference and can be as complex and computationally expensive as desired, since they are used for precalculation. Regardless of the actual equations used, we can write the lighting function as:

$$I = f(L, V) \tag{5.2.1}$$

$$C_R = I \bullet L_R \tag{5.2.2}$$
$$C_G = I \bullet L_G$$
$$C_B = I \bullet L_B$$

where:

  L represents the light's properties (position, intensity, radius, radial falloff, light type, and so on).

V represents the vertex's properties (position, normal).

f(L, V) is the lighting equation.

I is the light's scalar intensity at the vertex, as computed by the lighting equation.

L_R is the light's color (red component).

L_G is the light's color (green component).

L_B is the light's color (blue component).

C_R is the final red color component, ready to be stored in the vertex structure.

C_G is the final green color component, ready to be stored in the vertex structure.

C_B is the final blue color component, ready to be stored in the vertex structure.

Here's an example of a lighting equation for a simplified omni-light:

$$f(L, V) = (D_{VL} \bullet N_V) \, (R - D) \, / \, R \tag{5.2.3}$$

where:

D_{VL} is the unit vector from the vertex to the light.

N_V is the vertex's unit normal.

D is the distance from the vertex to the light.

R is the light's influence radius.

An omni-light is a point light that radiates light in all directions. The intensity of the light rays diminishes (attenuates) the farther the vertex is from the omni-light's position. In the preceding equation, the *(R – D) / R* term performs this distance attenuation. If the vertex lies on the light's position, *D* is 0 and *(R – D) / R* reduces to 1, which is the maximum brightness. If, on the other hand, the vertex lies on the outer boundary of the light's influence, *D* equals *R* and *(R – D) / R* reduces to 0. If the vertex lies somewhere between the light's origin and its outer boundary, *(R – D) / R* produces a number between 0 and 1. More sophisticated omni-lights use a distance attenuation function that models the physical world more closely. However, the linear attenuation in our equation is good enough for this example. Of course, we also require that *f(L, V)* return 0 if the vertex lies outside the light's influence radius *(D > R)*.

The first term in our omni-light equation, *(D_{VL}\bullet N_V)*, performs another attenuation based on the dot product of the light ray from the omni-light to the vertex being lit and that vertex's normal vector. This is called a *diffuse* lighting factor and is a very common way of brightening vertices that a light ray hits directly head-on and darkening vertices that a light ray hits more at an angle. We further imply that if *(D_{VL}\bullet N_V)* is negative, we return 0 for *f(L, V)*. That is, if a light ray is hitting our vertex from behind, we prevent the ray from lighting the vertex.

Equation 5.2.3 produces a decent looking omni-light, but higher-quality results could be obtained with more complex lighting equations. In any case, Equation 5.2.3

yields a single scalar, which is the overall intensity of the light at the vertex. Equation 5.2.2 then multiplies each component (red, green, and blue) of the light's color by this intensity, producing the final three-color components to be stored in the vertex structure. At render time, these color components are simply retrieved and used directly to Gouraud light the object. Here's a possible vertex structure and the render-time OpenGL code fragment to draw a statically lit triangle:

```
#include "mtxlib.h"

typedef struct {
    float fR, fG, fB;  // Static RGB color (0.0 -> 1.0)
} Color_t;

typedef struct {
    vector3 Pos;    // This vertex's 3D position in model-space
    Color_t StaticColor;      // RGB to be used for this vertex
} Vertex_t;

void DrawMyTriangle( const Vertex_t *pV1,
        const Vertex_t *pV2, const Vertex_t *pV3 ) {
        glBegin( GL_TRIANGLES );

    glColor3f( pV1->StaticColor.fR, pV1->StaticColor.fG,
    pV1->StaticColor.fB );
    glVertex3f( pV1->Pos.x, pV1->Pos.y, pV1->Pos.z );

    glColor3f( pV2->StaticColor.fR, pV2->StaticColor.fG,
    pV2->StaticColor.fB );
    glVertex3f( pV2->Pos.x, pV2->Pos.y, pV2->Pos.z );

    glColor3f( pV3->StaticColor.fR, pV3->StaticColor.fG,
    pV3->StaticColor.fB );
    glVertex3f( pV3->Pos.x, pV3->Pos.y, pV3->Pos.z );

    glEnd();
}
```

One drawback to conventional static lighting is that it does produce static results. That is, the RGB values for the vertices are constant from one rendered frame to the next. They do not vary at all. For sunlight, moonlight, and many other non-changing light sources, this isn't a problem. However, for more complex light sources such as flickering neon tubes, torch flames, campfires, and blinking hazard lights, conventional static lights cannot be used because they require the RGB values to animate from one rendered frame to the next. Conventional static lighting cannot achieve this result, as shown in the example code. This is where motif-based static lighting comes in.

Motif-Based Static Lighting

The advantage of conventional static lighting over dynamic lighting is execution speed. There simply are no run-time computations performed; RGB values are retrieved from the vertex structure and plugged directly into the color values for the rendering vertex. However, the drawback is that static lighting produces static results. The RGB values for each vertex are precomputed, stored, and never change from frame to frame. Motif-based static lighting provides a more dynamic look than conventional static lighting at a negligible performance hit.

Motif-based static lighting is still a form of static lighting. That is, the static lights lighting the object are fixed in the object's coordinate space, as is the case with conventional static lighting. However, with motif static lighting, we are able to animate the RGB components of the lights in real time. The type of animation is completely up to the designer. Some animations, such as a light switch on the wall of a room that turns on the room's light, might be under the player's control. Other animations, such as flames, flickering lights with electrical shorts, and blinking lights, might be algorithmically controlled. Furthermore, some lights might have constant RGB values. Each of these animations (including those that are constant) is called a *light motif*.

To implement motif-based static lighting, the game needs a motif table that contains an RGB entry for every light motif. The motif table acts as a palette, as we'll see later. Figure 5.2.2 shows an example of a nine-entry motif table. Each entry holds an RGB color. Depending on the type of motif, the RGB color is either precalculated at game-initialization time or computed dynamically once per frame. Regardless, the RGB values stored in the motif table are full-intensity, unattenuated light colors. Instead of storing RGB colors directly in the vertex structure (as we did before with conventional static lighting), we now simply store an index in the vertex structure that indexes into the motif table. We'll go into detail on this concept soon.

For constant motif lights for which the color remains constant from frame to frame, the RGB value of the light (that is, the light's raw, unattenuated color) is simply stored in the motif table at initialization time and left there for the duration of the game or level. In Figure 5.2.2, table entries 7 and 8 contain the RGBs for two constant motifs: dark red and bright blue.

For motif lights for which the color is controlled by the player (e.g., a light switch), the RGB value is updated when the event happens (the player flips the light switch, for example). In Figure 5.2.2, table entries 4 and 5 contain the RGBs for two static lights controlled by light switches. Initially, they might both contain RGB=(0,0,0), set during initialization. When the player turns on Switch 0, the game code stores the color of the light in entry 4. For example, if the light is a bright green light, we'd store RGB=(0,1,0) into entry 4. If the player turned the light off again, we'd store RGB=(0,0,0) into entry 4. In Figure 5.2.2, entry 5 is for another switch that controls a different set of lights that could be located either in an entirely different room or in the same room. It is completely possible that the two lights are close enough that they affect the same vertices in the same room (similar to the way both Light A and Light B affect vertex V2 in Figure 5.2.1). If this is the case, the player expects to see the two lights interact and light the room properly with the actions he or she takes with the two light switches. We'll see a little later how motif static lighting handles cases like this one.

Entries 0 through 3 in Figure 5.2.2 contain an animated RGB color for a flickering torch. Motifs such as these are algorithmically implemented and updated once per frame. Here's a code fragment that generates a flickering flame motif, called once per frame:

```
#define FLAME_SPEED    6.0f
// Constants determined via experimentation:
#define FLAME_K1   (0.093f * FLAME_SPEED)
#define FLAME_K2   (0.137f * FLAME_SPEED)
#define FLAME_K3   (0.195f * FLAME_SPEED)
#define FLAME_K4   (0.106f * FLAME_SPEED)
#define FLAME_K5   (0.170f * FLAME_SPEED)
#define FLAME_K6   (0.287f * FLAME_SPEED)

// Generates the RGB color for a particular frame of the flame
// motif and stores it in *pColor. nGameFrameCounter is simply
// the frame number of the game's current frame and is
// incremented once per frame.
void GenerateFlameMotif( unsigned int nGameFrameCounter,
        Color_t *pColor ) {
```

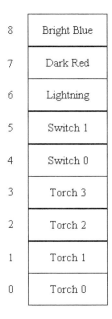

8	Bright Blue
7	Dark Red
6	Lightning
5	Switch 1
4	Switch 0
3	Torch 3
2	Torch 2
1	Torch 1
0	Torch 0

FIGURE 5.2.2. Example motif table.

```
    double dSinSum;
    float fIntensity, fAngle;

    fAngle = (float)nGameFrameCounter;

    dSinSum =
          sin( fAngle * FLAME_K1 )
        + sin( fAngle * FLAME_K2 )
        + sin( fAngle * FLAME_K3 )
        + sin( fAngle * FLAME_K4 )
        + sin( fAngle * FLAME_K5 )
        + sin( fAngle * FLAME_K6 );

    fIntensity = (float)dSinSum * 0.1f;
    fIntensity += 0.7f;

    if( fIntensity > 1.0f ) {
        fIntensity = 1.0f;
    }

    pColor->fR = fIntensity;
    pColor->fG = fIntensity * 0.4f;
    pColor->fB = 0.0f;
}
```

At the top of each game loop, the game calls `GenerateFlameMotif()` to generate the flame motif and then stores the resulting RGB into slot 0 of the motif table. It's likely that a room has more than one torch, and if all the torches used the same motif, they would all flicker in sync and would noticeably look bad. So, in our motif table, we offer a variety of torch motifs so that the designer can assign different torch motifs to neighboring torches. Often, it is not necessary to write different algorithms to have a variety for a particular motif. Instead, simply phase shifting the frame counter and calling the same algorithm function suffices and provides stunning results for a fraction of the work.

Motif light algorithms are usually simple functions, but even if a more computationally expensive function were needed, it would still be executed only once per frame, and so the overall performance impact on the game is likely to be negligible. In the preceding code, for example, the CPU overhead of calling sin() six times once per frame is insignificant compared with the 1/60th of a second the game has to execute a single frame. Even so, the overhead could be minimized by writing a custom sin() function that performed a table lookup at the sacrifice of precision, because precision isn't very important for lighting computations. In any case, the beauty of motif-generator functions is that they're called only once per frame, as opposed to dynamic lighting calculations that are executed once per vertex per frame!

Now that we have established the motif table, let's turn our attention to the vertex structure. For conventional static lighting, the precomputed RGB color was stored directly in the vertex structure. However, for motif-based static lighting, we need to define the vertex structure differently, like this:

```
typedef struct {
    vector3 Pos;    // This vertex's 3D position in model-space
    int nMotifIndex;   // Index into the motif table
    float fIntensity;  // Intensity of the light motif's
                       // RGB at this vertex
} Vertex_t;
```

The vertex structure removed the StaticColor field and replaced it with the nMotifIndex and fIntensity fields. These fields tell the rendering engine which light motif from the motif table to use as well as the intensity of the light motif's RGB at that particular vertex. Both of these values are established at either tool time or game-initialization time. The motif index simply replaces the light's color property; instead of the designer placing a campfire light and assigning it an orange color, a motif is assigned instead. The designer positions the light and assigns the light properties such as intensity, radius, radial falloff, and light type as usual. However, when assigning the color, the designer can choose a motif from a set of possible motif values. For the campfire example, the designer might select the torch motif. This motif describes not only the color but also the animation of the static light. The torch motif emulates a flickering flame both in color and animation of color.

The fIntensity field is simply I from Equation 5.2.1, which is the lighting equation we used for conventional static lighting, applied to this vertex. The position of the light and the light properties that the designer has set interact with the vertex position and normal to produce I, which is simply the intensity of the light at that vertex. Refer to Equation 5.2.3 for an example of how all these parameters interact to yield I for an omni-light.

Now that we have the intensity (from the fIntensity field in the vertex structure) and the RGB color (from the motif table entry indexed by the nMotifIndex field in the vertex structure), we have everything we need to compute Equation 5.2.2 for our vertex's final run-time RGB values.

Here's an OpenGL code example that renders a motif statically lit triangle:

```
typedef enum {
    MOTIF_FLAME0,
    MOTIF_FLAME1,
    MOTIF_FLAME2,
    MOTIF_FLAME3,
    MOTIF_SWITCH0,
    MOTIF_SWITCH1,
    MOTIF_LIGHTNING,
    MOTIF_DARK_RED,
    MOTIF_BRIGHT_BLUE,

    MOTIF_COUNT
} Motif_e;

Color_t aMotifTable[MOTIF_COUNT];

void DrawMyTriangle( const Vertex_t *pV1,
```

```
            const Vertex_t *pV2, const Vertex_t *pV3 ) {
    Color_t *pColor;
    float fR, fG, fB;

    glBegin( GL_TRIANGLES );

    pColor = &aMotifTable[ pV1->nMotifIndex ];
    fR = pColor->fR * pV1->fIntensity;
    fG = pColor->fG * pV1->fIntensity;
    fB = pColor->fB * pV1->fIntensity;
    glColor3f( fR, fG, fB );
    glVertex3f( pV1->Pos.x, pV1->Pos.y, pV1->Pos.z );

    pColor = &aMotifTable[ pV2->nMotifIndex ];
    fR = pColor->fR * pV2->fIntensity;
    fG = pColor->fG * pV2->fIntensity;
    fB = pColor->fB * pV2->fIntensity;
    glColor3f( fR, fG, fB );
    glVertex3f( pV2->Pos.x, pV2->Pos.y, pV2->Pos.z );

    pColor = &aMotifTable[ pV3->nMotifIndex ];
    fR = pColor->fR * pV3->fIntensity;
    fG = pColor->fG * pV3->fIntensity;
    fB = pColor->fB * pV3->fIntensity;
    glColor3f( fR, fG, fB );
    glVertex3f( pV3->Pos.x, pV3->Pos.y, pV3->Pos.z );

    glEnd();
}
```

This implementation supports only one motif per vertex, which isn't too helpful when a model has a vertex under the influence of more than one static light (as in Figure 5.2.1). To support more than one motif, we need to extend the vertex structure so that it has a motif/intensity pair for each motif light affecting it. A general solution is shown here:

```
typedef struct {
    int nMotifIndex;        // Index into the motif table
    float fIntensity;       // Intensity of the light motif's
                            // RGB at this vertex
} MotifEntry_t;

typedef struct {
    vector3 Pos;            // This vertex's 3D position in model-space
    int nMotifEntryCount;   // Number of motif entries
                            // pointed to by pMotifEntry
    MotifEntry_t *pMotifEntry;   // Pointer to an array of
                                 // MotifEntry_t structures
} Vertex_t;
```

This implementation provides for any number of motifs, but it can be complex to implement. Another solution is easier to work with but is less flexible and could consume more memory:

```
#define MAX_MOTIFS_PER_VTX    8        // Implementation-specific value

typedef struct {
    vector3 Pos;    // This vertex's 3D position in model-space
    int nMotifEntryCount;      // Number of motif entries in
                               // aMotifEntry[]
    MotifEntry_t aMotifEntry[MAX_MOTIFS_PER_VTX];
} Vertex_t;
```

We'll work with this last implementation for clarity, but advanced developers should consider the more general implementation.

To support more than one light influencing a particular vertex, we simply perform the motif/attenuate computation described earlier and then sum the colors together, like this:

```
void ComputeVertexColor( const Vertex_t *pV, Color_t *pColor ) {
    Color_t *pMotifColor;
    float fR, fG, fB;
    int i;

    // Zero color components:
    fR = fG = fB = 0.0f;

    // Step through all the motifs affecting this vertex
    //    and sum their colors:
    for( i=0; i<pV->nMotifEntryCount; i++ ) {
        pMotifColor = &aMotifTable[
        pV->aMotifEntry[i].nMotifIndex ];
        fR += pMotifColor->fR * pV->aMotifEntry[i].fIntensity;
        fG += pMotifColor->fG * pV->aMotifEntry[i].fIntensity;
        fB += pMotifColor->fB * pV->aMotifEntry[i].fIntensity;
    }

    // Make sure final color is from 0 to 1:
    if( fR > 1.0f ) fR = 1.0f;
    if( fG > 1.0f ) fG = 1.0f;
    if( fB > 1.0f ) fB = 1.0f;

    // Store final colors in return variable:
    pColor->fR = fR;
    pColor->fG = fG;
    pColor->fB = fB;
}

void DrawMyTriangle( const Vertex_t *pV1, const Vertex_t *pV2,
        const Vertex_t *pV3 ) {
    Color_t Color;

    glBegin( GL_TRIANGLES );

    ComputeVertexColor( pV1, &Color );
    glColor3f( Color.fR, Color.fG, Color.fB );
    glVertex3f( pV1->Pos.x, pV1->Pos.y, pV1->Pos.z );
```

```
            ComputeVertexColor( pV2, &Color );
            glColor3f( Color.fR, Color.fG, Color.fB );
            glVertex3f( pV2->Pos.x, pV2->Pos.y, pV2->Pos.z );

            ComputeVertexColor( pV3, &Color );
            glColor3f( Color.fR, Color.fG, Color.fB );
            glVertex3f( pV3->Pos.x, pV3->Pos.y, pV3->Pos.z );

            glEnd();
}
```

Conclusion

For a performance cost slightly higher than that of conventional lighting and far less expensive than dynamic lighting, motif-based static lighting can help bring a scene to life by providing RGB animation for precomputed light data. Campfires, flickering torches, electrical shorts, beacon lights, and more are now possible without having to use expensive dynamic lights.

5.3

Simulated Real-Time Lighting Using Vertex Color Interpolation

Jorge Freitas

Real-time lighting effects are an essential part of today's 3D gaming experience but can be computationally intense for systems with limited resources. On such systems, the visual effect of real-time lighting can be simulated by interpolating between pre-calculated sets of vertex colors.

This technique was originally developed for use with human figures in a sports game. Twenty-three figures were to be drawn each frame, using skinned models with a multiple vertex weighted, skeletal hierarchy. The primary goal was to eliminate costly lighting calculations from the rendering pipeline while retaining the look of real-time lighting.

The lighting in the world consisted of either the sun or four static floodlights and an ambient lighting value used to darken figures running into shadow. There were also several special lighting effects, including the reflection of the grass color on the players' socks and shorts, projected shadows under arms and between legs, and colored lighting based on the current weather condition or time of day. In addition, during a night game, the lighting "hot spot" needed to be positioned relative to the closest floodlight.

An inexpensive way of calculating changing lights on the figures needed to be found. Precalculation was the answer. As much information as possible regarding the lighting was precalculated. Ideally, the lighting for every pose and each possible rotation of the figure would have been precalculated, but that was impractical due to the amount of memory required to store the information.

Instead, the lighting was precalculated for a number of fixed rotations, and interpolation was used to generate the vertex color values for the given figure's rotation.

Lighting Method

Typically, the method for generating real-time vertex lighting goes like this:

1. Transform the normal for each vertex in the object.
2. Determine the angle at which the light is facing the vertex normal.
3. Using the facing angle, determine the intensity of the light at that vertex.
4. Repeat for each light illuminating the vertex.
5. Add the ambient light intensity.

Real-time lighting using the above method requires many computations, which we reduce dramatically using the interpolation method.

In order to fake the real-time method, we must set some constraints on our 3D scene:

- Determine how many light positions are needed for the interpolation.
- Determine the axis of rotation used to base the interpolation calculation.

The vertex color lists represent the lighting on the object at distinct orientations of the figure relative to the lighting in the scene, whether the lighting is one light source or 100. A full 360-degree rotation is required, so we must determine how many vertex color lists we will use. A minimum of three positions is necessary, each 120 degrees apart. Note that by using more lists, we decrease the range of values we must interpolate between, thereby increasing the accuracy of our faked lighting.

Artwork Creation

We assume that the vertex color lists are generated in a 3D content creation application. Of course, it's possible to use a real-time lighting method to generate the vertex color lists, but the artistic task of attractively lighting a 3D scene should be left to those most qualified: the artists.

In our example of human figures, the axis of rotation used to determine the lighting angle was assumed to be the vertical axis (typically named Y in a left-handed coordinate system) because the figures always ran around on a flat plain (a grassy field).

The example in Listing 5.3.1 uses four vertex color lists, each generated 90 degrees apart. Using a power of 2 number allows us to shortcut some of the integer math by replacing multiplies and divides by shifts, and MODs with ANDs. However, for the sake of clarity, the example code does not use integer short cuts.

Lights are added to the 3D scene corresponding to the lights in the game world. Any number of lights can be used without impacting performance, since the resulting data will be lists of vertex colors.

The first vertex color list is assumed to represent the lighting when the object is at a rotation of 0 degrees. The object is artistically lit at four rotations, each 90 degrees from the previous one. The lighting for each rotation is saved as a vertex color list, creating four lists of vertex colors that will be used in real time.

The vertex colors can be tuned by the artist in the 3D creation application to produce some of the desired special effects. Green can be mixed into the lower legs to represent the reflection of the grass color, the areas between the figure's legs and under the figure's arms can be darkened to give the impression of projected shadows, and the figure's skin can be tinted to indicate racial skin tones.

Interpolated Lighting

Here is an explanation of the steps necessary to generate the interpolated vertex lighting.

Calculate Facing Angle to Virtual Light Source

The vertex color lists represent the lighting on the object at distinct orientations relative to the light source. The position of the light source can be stored as a simple additive value, representing the direction of the light in the scene. The facing angle is calculated by adding the offset to the object's rotation and using the remainder from dividing by the number of degrees in one full rotation (360).

```
facing angle = ( object rotation + additive light position ) % 360
```

Note that the light can be "rotated" around the object by cycling the additive light position value between 0 and the number of degrees in one full rotation.

Determine Which Two Vertex Light Sets to Interpolate Between

Based on the facing angle, we must determine which two sets of vertex colors in our table between which we should interpolate (the base color list and the target color list). Each set of vertex colors was pre-generated using the same delta, 90 degrees apart, in our example. We divide the current rotation by the delta value between each set of vertex colors, which becomes the base color list. The target color list is the next vertex color list in our table.

```
base color list = facing angle / vertex color delta

if ( base color list == last vertex color list )
    target color list = first vertex color list
else
target color list = next vertex color list
```

Calculate Interpolation Percentage

We need to determine how far between the two vertex color lists to interpolate. This percentage represents how close to the target color list we should interpolate. The percentage is calculated by dividing the remainder of the base color list calculation by the vertex color delta, giving us a value between 0.0 and 1.0.

```
percentage = ( facing angle % vertex color delta ) / vertex color delta
```

For Each Vertex Color, Perform the Interpolation

We now calculate the vertex color list representing the current lighting for the object. To calculate each vertex color, each color component (RGB) must be interpolated, and we repeat the process for each vertex in the object.

```
color = old color + ( new color - old color ) * percentage
```

**For Each Vertex Color, Apply an Ambient Light RGB
Modifier and Clamp Resulting Values**

Optionally, we can apply an ambient light modifier to the calculated vertex color list. The modifier can take the calculated color out of the acceptable range for each component (0 to 255), so we must clamp each component separately.

```
color component = color component + ambient color

if ( color component < 0 )
    color component = 0
else
{
    if ( color component > 255 )
        color component = 255
}
```

Note that the precalculated vertex color lists can be created to ensure the ambient light modifier doesn't take the calculated vertex colors out of the acceptable range. By limiting the smallest and largest values for each color component and by limiting the size of the ambient color modifier, the clamping becomes unnecessary.

Conclusion

This technique is effective for reducing the number of calculations necessary to represent real-time lighting and has been used on PCs and game consoles. To generate a single vertex color requires only three subtractions, three multiplies, and three adds (six adds if an ambient color is used). Even if real-time lighting is necessary in your 3D game, interpolated vertex color lighting can be combined with real-time lighting to help relieve some of the computational burden of rendering your scene.

To further decrease the number of computations, you need not perform the lighting calculations for every rendered frame. By keeping a unique vertex color buffer for each object, the lighting can be calculated once every two, three, or four frames, depending on the rate at which the object changes orientation relative to the light source. Further savings can be had by alternating the objects that are being re-lit each frame.

Although this method is very simple, with it an extremely complex mathematical model can be precalculated. Remember, we're trying to achieve the perception of realistic lighting effects in our 3D games. The viewer doesn't care what mathematical method has been employed to create the effect, just that it makes the game world look cool.

Listing 5.3.1: Example Code

For this example code, we assume there is one vertex color per vertex in the object. Note that the data structures contain only the information necessary for the vertex color interpolation. The divides and MODs (%) can be replaced with shifts and ANDs, but these have been omitted for clarity.

```
//
//————
// defines
//————
//
/* number of vertex color lists */
#define NUMBER_OF_ARGB_LISTS  4  /* number of radians in 360 degrees */
#define NUMBER_OF_RADIANS  1024
//
//————-
// structures
//————-
//
typedef struct
{
    float   alpha;
    float   red;
    float   green;
    float   blue;
}ARGB_DEF;

typedef struct
{
    /* angle used for simulated lighting */
    int     angleOfRotation;
    /* number of vertices in object */
    int     nVertex;
    /* pointers to vertex color lists */
    ARGB_DEF   *pARGB[ NUMBER_OF_ARGB_LISTS ];
}OBJECT_DEF;

//
//————
// variables
//————
//
/* pointer to buffer used to store the calculated RGB's */
ARGB_DEF *gpVertexColorBuffer; /* global additive ambient light RGB */
ARGB_DEF gAmbientLight; /* additive value to offset light "hot spot" */
int gLightOffset;
//
//————-
```

```
// functions
//————————-
//
/***************************

Function :  interpolateVertexRGBs
Linearly interpolates between two lists of vertex colors.

Input:
ARGB_DEF *pSrcA - pointer to first source vertex color list
ARGB_DEF *pSrcB - pointer to second source vertex
                        color list
ARGB_DEF *pDest - pointer to storage for calculated
                          vertex colors
int      nARGB      - number of vertex colors to interpolate
float    percentage - amount to interpolate between two vertex
                        tables (0.0 - 1.0)

Output:
Fills pDest with the calculated vertex colors

***************************/
void interpolateVertexRGBs(
     ARGB_DEF *pSrcA,/* pointer to source vertex color data */
     ARGB_DEF *pSrcB,/* pointer to source vertex color data */
     ARGB_DEF *pDest,/* pointer to dest vertex color data */
     int nARGB,        /* number of vertex colors to interpolate */
     float percentage ) /* interpolation amount, 0 to 1 */
{
     int  index;     /* index into arrays of ARGB_DEF's */
     float    red,    /* temporary storage for calculated RGB's */
      green,
      blue;

     for ( index = 0; index < nARGB; index++ )
     {
     //
     // calculate interpolated ARGB
     //
         red =        pSrcA[ index ].red + ( pSrcB[ index ].red -
                      pSrcA[ index ].red ) * percentage;
         green  =     pSrcA[ index ].green + ( pSrcB[ index ].green -
                      pSrcA[ index ].green ) * percentage;
         blue   =     pSrcA[ index ].blue + ( pSrcB[ index ].blue -
                      pSrcA[ index ].blue ) * percentage;
     //
     // add ambient light
     //
         red     += gAmbientLight.red;
         green   += gAmbientLight.green;
         blue    += gAmbientLight.blue;
     //
     // clamp RGB's
     //
```

```
                if ( red > 255.0 )
                    red = 255.0;
                else
                {
                    if ( red < 0.0 )
                        red = 0.0;
                }

                if ( green > 255.0 )
                    green = 255.0;
                else
                {
                    if ( green < 0.0 )
                        green = 0.0;
                }

                if ( blue > 255.0 )
                    blue = 255.0;
                else
                {
                    if ( blue < 0.0 )
                        blue = 0.0;
                }
        //
        // store results
        //
                pDest[ index ].red = red;
                pDest[ index ].green = green;
                pDest[ index ].blue = blue;
        }
}

/*****************************

Function : calculateSimulatedLighting
Calculates the vertex colors used to represent the lighting at the given
angle of rotation.

Input:
OBJECT_DEF   *pObject    - pointer to object structure

*******************************/
void calculateSimulatedLighting( OBJECT_DEF *pObject )
{
        float     percentage;
        int       quadrant;
        int       angleOfRotation;

        ARGB_DEF *pSrcA,
             *pSrcB;

    angleOfRotation = ( pObject->angleOfRotation +
    gLightOffset ) % NUMBER_OF_RADIANS;
```

```
        percentage = (float)(angleOfRotation %
        NUMBER_OF_ARGB_LISTS ) /
        (float)( NUMBER_OF_RADIANS / NUMBER_OF_ARGB_LISTS );

        quadrant = angleOfRotation / ( NUMBER_OF_RADIANS /
        NUMBER_OF_ARGB_LISTS );

        pSrcA = pObject->pARGB[ quadrant ];

        if  ( quadrant == (NUMBER_OF_ARGB_LISTS - 1 ) )
            pSrcB = pObject->pARGB[ 0 ];
        else
            pSrcB = pObject->pARGB[ quadrant + 1 ];

        interpolateVertexRGBs( pSrcA, pSrcB,
        gpVertexColorBuffer,
        pObject->nVertex, percentage );
}
```

5.4

Attenuation Maps

Sim Dietrich

Vertex lighting is good for many applications and is well known and understood. It has many benefits, including the benefit of properly handling surfaces not facing the light, but vertex lighting can have artifacts when the size of the triangle is large with respect to the range of a point or spotlight.

Light maps are another approach to calculating lighting that can avoid these triangle tessellation-related artifacts, but they require expensive CPU operations to update for dynamic lights and require potentially slow upload to the video card. Still, light maps are a good solution for static lighting and shadows.

This article introduces a novel technique known as *attenuation maps*. This technique can be used to implement dynamic point lights with proper quadratic attenuation using multitexture operations. In addition, the technique can be used for spherical, ellipsoidal, cylindrical, and rectangular lighting or CSG operations, accurate to a per-pixel level, without using the stencil buffer.

Explanation

The attenuation function for lighting is typically like so:

```
X = lightPosition.X - vertexPosition.X;
Y = lightPosition.Y - vertexPosition.Y;
Z = lightPosition.Z - vertexPosition.Z;

D = sqrt(X*X + Y*Y + Z*Z);

Att = 1 / (C0 + C1*D + C2*D*D);
```

For our purposes, we assume that we want only quadratic attenuation, so assume that *C0* is 1 and *C1* is 0, giving:

```
Att = 1 / (1 + C2*D*D);
```

3D textures provide a simple method of encoding this function. Directly store the function in a 3D texture as a function of *X*, *Y*, and *Z* for the three texture coordinates. Then, simply set up texture coordinate generation to calculate *dX, dY,* and *dZ* relative to the light position, use the texture matrix to scale each *dX, dY,* and *dZ* by 1 over the light's range, and scale and bias so the center of the texture corresponds to (0,0,0).

The equation that the texture matrix computes in this case is:

```
S = ((Light.X − Vertex.X) / LightRange) / 2.0f) + 0.5f;
T = ((Light.Y − Vertex.Y) / LightRange) / 2.0f) + 0.5f;
R = ((Light.Z − Vertex.Z) / LightRange) / 2.0f) + 0.5f;
```

However, 3D textures aren't yet widely available, so we must make do with 2D and 1D textures. Even were 3D textures available, it would be advantageous to find a less texture memory-intensive method of calculating attenuation.

Well, first, since we have only 2D and 1D textures available, that means that we can't compute the function with only a single texture because we can't use all three coordinates *X, Y,* and *Z* at once. This means that we have to break the function into two or more parts.

How can we express the attenuation function in such a way that we can implement it using 2D and 1D textures? Let's start by breaking *X* and *Y* into a 2D texture and *Z* into its own 1D texture.

If we break *X* and *Y* into one texture and *Z* into another, that means that the result of the function of *X* and *Y,* which we call f(X,Y), and the result of the function based on *Z,* which we call g(Z), must be expressible as colors.

In other words, if we are storing the function as some combination of two textures, we must express the final function as a sum or multiplication of two colors. Since colors can hold only positive values from 0 to 1, this affects which form of attenuation function we can choose.

The previous attenuation function is:

```
Att = 1 / (1 + c2*D*D);
```

Some samples of this function follow:

Att(0) == 1
Att(2) == 0.5
Att(Large D) approaches 0

As *D* gets larger, the attenuation approaches 0.

Let's try to encode this function in two textures. First, we expand *D*D* into its components:

```
D = sqrt(X*X + Y*Y + Z*Z)
```

```
D*D = (X*X + Y*Y + Z*Z)
```

Now we restate the attenuation function in terms of *X, Y,* and *Z:*

```
Att = 1 / (1 + C2*(X*X + Y*Y + Z*Z))
```

Now it seems we are stuck because we can't express the Att function as the sum or product of the two functions f(X,Y) and g(Z) due to the fact that X, Y, and Z are all in the denominator. We have to find another function that we can separate.

We don't have any way of summing two colors and then taking a reciprocal, so we have to find a function that has the same effect but doesn't require a reciprocal.

Squaring numbers greater than one produces larger numbers, whereas squaring a number in the range (0..1) produces a smaller number. For instance, 0.5 * 0.5 equals 0.25. This is why we had to set the constant in our attenuation function, *C0*, to 1: It prevents really close lights from becoming brighter than they should.

Remember that colors are always expressed in the range [0..1]. That means that the result of f(X,Y) and g(Z) must produce results in the same range [0..1].

One function that both does not require reciprocals and produces results within the range [0..1] is:

```
Att = 1 - D*D
Att = 1 - (X*X + Y*Y + Z*Z)
```

We can encode f(X,Y) in a 2D texture as *(X*X + Y*Y)* and g(Z) in a 1D texture as simply *Z*Z*. Figures 5.4.1 and 5.4.2 give examples of these two textures.

Note how the edges of the textures shown in Figure 5.4.1 are clamped to be exactly one. By adding these two functions together via multitexturing, we can com-

FIGURE 5.4.1. *f(X, Y) = (X*X + Y*Y).*

FIGURE 5.4.2. $g(Z) = Z^*Z$.

pute D^*D on a per-pixel basis. Using inverse blending, we can use the alpha-blending unit to finish the computation and compute $1 - D^*D$.

So, one procedure for implementing point lights with attenuation maps is as follows:

```
Draw ambient light and/or global illumination in the scene

For each Point Light in the scene {
        For each Object that is approximately near or within the
        Light's range {
        For each Vertex in the Object {
        Subtract the Vertex Position from the Point Light
                Position
        Scale the Position by 1 / the Point Light's Range
        Scale and Bias the result to range from 0 to 1
                for points inside the Light's Range

        Store Position.X in the S texture coordinate of
                Texture 0
        Store Position.Y in the T texture coordinate of
                Texture 0
        Store Position.Z in the S texture coordinate of
                Texture 1

        }
        Set up the multitexture hardware to choose the Light Color
        in the color unit
        Set up the multitexture hardware to compute Texture 0 +
        Texture 1 in the alpha unit
        Set up the alpha-blender to compute SrcColor * InvSrcAlpha
        + FrameBuffer

        Optionally set the alpha test to reject pixels with an
        Alpha of 1.  This avoids rendering pixels that are outside
        of the light range.

        Draw the Object
        }
}
```

Alternatively, we can use texture coordinate generation and the texture matrix to compute all per-vertex operations on the GPU:

- Set up texture coordinate generation for the first multitexture stage to give camera space position.
- Set up the texture matrix to subtract the light's X and Y position, thus giving us (dX, dY), which are stored in S and T of texture 0.
- Set up the second multitexture stage to use texture coordinate generation to give us camera space position, just like before.
- Set up the texture matrix to rotate Z onto the X-axis, and then subtract the light's Z position, giving us dZ, which is stored in S for texture 1.

This technique can be modified to fit a variety of light options. One option for graphics hardware or APIs (such as OpenGL) that don't allow differing color and alpha-texture blending modes is to factor the light color into the texture itself. This modification also allows other blending modes, such as multiplicative frame buffer blending, to be employed.

The attenuation function we computed is:

```
LightColor * (1 - (X*X + Y*Y + Z*Z))
```

Multiplying through by the LightColor gives:

```
LightColor - LightColor * (X*X + Y*Y + Z*Z) =
LightColor - (LightColor * (X*X + Y*Y) + LightColor * (Z*Z))
```

This implies that we need to pre-multiply the light color into both attenuation maps to get the right effect, but we really need only one map. It turns out that we can just use the center of the *LightColor * (X*X + Y*Y)* texture for the *LightColor * (Z*Z)* computation. We can use the horizontal or vertical center, but the horizontal center requires one less texture coordinate to specify and might provide better texture cache performance.

Comparing Attenuation Maps and Light Maps

Light maps are commonly employed to store static lighting data, such as shadows and light calculated through a global illumination solution. Updating light maps at run time for point lights is complicated and costly. Point lights performed with attenuation maps complement light maps nicely by taking over the chores of dynamic point lights. Instead of uploading new light maps to reflect a point light changing its color, range, or location, the nearby scene can be simply rerendered using the attenuation map textures to blend the light into the scene.

CSG Effects

By using alpha test or stencil, we can test for inclusion in perfectly spherical areas such as the falloff range of a point light. For each pixel that would be drawn with a point light, we can set the stencil to a certain value or blend into the frame buffer a constant color, thus being able to do other range-based effects.

Range-Based Fog

One application of this concept is per-pixel range-based fog. Simply render the scene as normal with no fog applied, and then render the scene with the attenuation map, treating the camera position as the "light position." Set the texture matrix to identity, and then scale the matrix by 1 over the light's range. This technique allows per-pixel, perspective-correct range fog.

The SRC_COLOR sent to the frame buffer blending unit should be the fog color times fog density. This gives a fog density of zero at the viewer, and at the maximum fog range the density will be one.

When rendering the fog pass, set up the alpha blender to perform SRC_COLOR * 1 + DST_COLOR * (1 − SRC_COLOR).

Other Shapes

Sometimes a sphere is not what is needed; to make an oblong shape, such as a rectangle or ellipse, simply select minor and major axes and align them to the world with the texture matrix. We then have to scale the major and minor axes separately.

Conclusion

By cleverly choosing our attenuation function, we are able to perform a per-pixel spherical range calculation using two texture maps. The result of this calculation can be used for per-pixel point lights, fog, or CSG effects.

5.5

Advanced Texturing Using Texture Coordinate Generation

Ryan Woodland

Because today's graphics processors are pushing more and more polygons, attention is starting to turn to the use of bandwidth to create compelling texture effects. With the addition of multitexture abilities to many processors, people are starting to wonder how to creatively use these features. Of course, artist-applied texture is the technique with which we're all the most familiar, but it's quickly being discovered that mapping textures at run time can produce some very interesting results. Developers are starting to use texture coordinate generation to perform animation, lighting, reflection, refraction, and bump mapping, to name a few techniques. This article discusses a few of the most common texture coordinate generation techniques.

The method of texture coordinate generation used most comfortably by most people is that of transforming some data (position, normals, texture coordinates) by some matrix to yield a set of texture coordinates. This method is fairly easy to adopt because most 3D programmers are familiar with the concept of matrix transformation and because matrix transformation is often accelerated by hardware. This article describes only techniques that can be performed using matrix math.

Simple Texture Coordinate Animation

Quite often, games use a simple rotation or translation of texture coordinates to simulate simple effects such as reflection or to give the appearance of water or some moving material. The concept is simply this: A texture coordinate can be thought of as a simple 2D point. Because programmers are accustomed to transforming points by matrices, it is easy to see that a texture coordinate can be rotated, translated, or scaled simply by transforming it into a 3×3 matrix. Just as with geometry, a homogenous coordinate must be added to the s, t pair to make the transformation possible. Therefore, the method of coordinate generation looks like this:

(s, t, 1) * 3x3mtx = s', t'

The illustrations in Figure 5.5.1 were generated using simple rotation and scale. The first picture shows a textured quad with no transformation applied. The second shows a rotation of the texture coordinates by 45 degrees. The third shows a texture coordinate translation of 0.5.

Texture Projection

Texture projection is useful for a number of effects. Most often it is used to simulate lighting effects such as spotlights or shadows. The result of texture projection is fairly straightforward: A texture is projected onto some geometry from some point in space. For example, we can define a spotlight at some point in a scene and project a texture (probably a light circle) onto the geometry, creating the illusion of a spotlight.

Again, the concept of texture projection has its roots in normal 3D geometry techniques. When simulating a camera in 3D, a projection matrix is used to project vertices in camera space onto the near clipping plane of the camera. These points are mapped in the range of −1 to 1 in both X and Y, and then they are transformed into screen space by a viewport transformation, which usually involves a translation and scale.

For texture projection, instead of modeling a camera in space, we are usually modeling a light. Light space vertices are projected back onto the near clipping plane of the light, and the resulting X and Y values are used as S and T values to map a texture onto the projected geometry.

A light should be modeled just as a camera usually would. The near clipping plane should be set to reflect the dimensions of the texture that is to be projected. For instance, a square near clipping plane should be used for projecting a square texture.

Now, as mentioned, geometry that is projected onto a texture needs to be in light space, just as geometry to be projected onto the screen needs to be in camera space. In order to do this, we need to first transform the geometry into world space. Once this is done, the light matrix (just like the camera matrix) must then transform the geometry. The geometry can then be projected by the light's projection matrix.

Once geometry has been projected, another problem arises. Projected geometry, as mentioned previously, falls in the range of −1 to 1 in both X and Y, with (0, 0)

FIGURE 5.5.1. Examples of texture coordinate generation through texture matrix transformations.

being at the center of the plane of projection as it relates to the light. Texture coordinates usually run from 0 to 1 in both *S* and *T,* with the origin of that space being located at the upper-left corner of the texture. To map the projected coordinates into texture space, we must first scale them by 0.5 to put them in the range from −0.5 to 0.5 and then translate them by 0.5 to put them in the range from 0 to 1.

All these matrices can be concatenated together to form one final projection matrix for a given piece of geometry. The order is as follows:

$$M\_obj * M\_light * M\_proj * M\_scale * M\_trans * \{x, y, 0, z\} = \{s, t, r, q\}$$

where:

- `M_obj` = the object's world space matrix.
- `M_light` = the light matrix used to transform the geometry from world space into light space.
- `M_proj` = the light's projection matrix.
- `M_scale` = 0.5 scale matrix.
- `M_trans` = 0.5 translation matrix.

The result of this calculation is a four-dimensional point. For simple texture projection, the *r* coordinate should be completely ignored, yielding an (*s, t, q*) triple. If the hardware allows, pass these three coordinates down for rasterization. The *q* coordinate is used to perform perspective correction; however, this must be done at rasterization time for it to be correct.

Figure 5.5.2 was generated using texture projection. It shows the frustum of the light that was used to project the circular highlight onto the sphere geometry.

By projecting geometry in this manner, a few unexpected results can occur. First, texture coordinates usually behave in a tiled manner. This means that there is really no

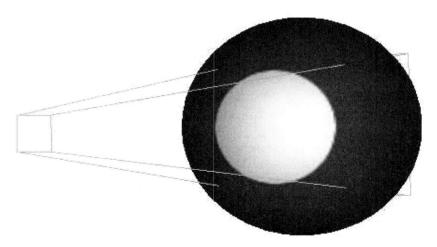

FIGURE 5.5.2. Texture projection example.

difference between a set of coordinates that ranges from 0 to 1 and a set that ranges from −1 to 0. Therefore, textures that are projected onto geometry should usually behave in a clamped manner, meaning that the outside border of the texture is repeated and applied to any texture coordinate less than 0 and greater than 1. For this reason, texture borders should be colored to behave correctly with the texture combine mode of choice.

The second and more complex problem is that of what I call *shine-through*. When we project a texture onto a sphere, for instance, the texture appears on both the front and back sides of the sphere as it relates to the light. This is because vertices on both the front and back of the sphere project into the correct texture space.

The image in Figure 5.5.3 highlights this problem. You can see that the spotlight texture projects correctly on the front of the sphere, but it also shines through to the geometry on the back of the sphere.

There are a couple of ways to fix this problem of shine-through. The first is to perform a dot product between the vertex normal and the light normal to determine whether the vertex is back facing. If the vertex is back facing, simply set the texture coordinate to something out of the range of 0 to 1.

Second, you can use the output of the standard lighting equation to determine whether a vertex is back facing. Place a parallel light at the location of the texture projector. If the color output from this parallel light for a vertex is black, you know that the vertex is back facing, because the only way for this vertex to become black is if the associated normal is facing away from the light.

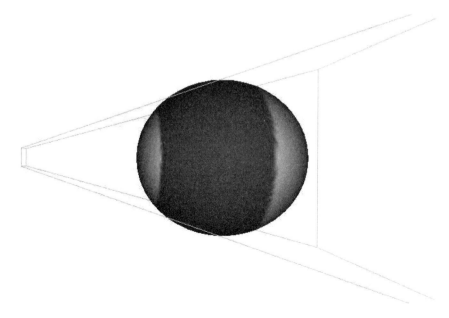

FIGURE 5.5.3. Shine-through in texture projection.

Reflection Mapping

To perform reflection mapping, I use a simple method called *sphere mapping*. The basic idea for this method makes two assumptions.

First, no matter the size and shape of the object being mapped, it is assumed to reflect the surrounding environment like a sphere. This concept is important because, logically, a point on a character's hand should reflect something different than a point on a character's foot with the same normal. With sphere mapping, these two points reflect exactly the same thing because they have the same normal.

Second, the reflective sphere like which the object will behave is assumed to be infinitely small. This means that all rays from the point of the eye in the scene to any point on the infinitely small sphere are parallel to each other.

Given these limitations, the sphere-mapping method operates on basic laws of reflection. Take, for instance, a ray from the eye point in a scene to a point on the reflective sphere. This ray should hit the sphere and reflect around the normal at the point of contact. Whatever this reflected ray hits should be seen reflected at the point of contact on the sphere. Figure 5.5.4 illustrates this concept.

Since it is not computationally feasible to perform one-bounce ray tracing for every point on a sphere, we instead create a texture map that contains the necessary environmental information. This map is called a *spherical reflection map,* or a *sphere map.*

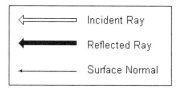

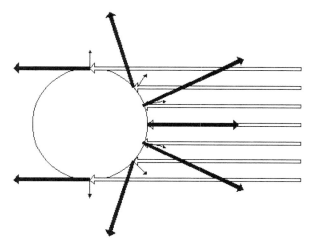

FIGURE 5.5.4. Rays are reflected around the surface normal at the point of contact on a reflective object.

The basic definition of a sphere map is a single texture map that contains a full 360-degree view of the environment surrounding a point in space. There is one big drawback to using sphere mapping for reflection: The texture used as the reflection map is viewpoint dependent. This means that to be completely correct, the texture map must be dynamically created each time the camera moves. I have found, however, that for some common effects such as generating a specular highlight on a car or creating lighting effects on a character, refusing to update the sphere map based on viewpoint is often not noticeable. (For an in-depth discussion of generating sphere maps see [Blythe99].)

Once you have an adequate sphere map, texture coordinate generation is a snap. Simply transform an object's normals into world space using the inverse transform of the object's model matrix. Then transform the normals into view space using the camera matrix. Finally, assuming your camera is looking down the $-Z$ axis, simply use the X and Y components of a normal as the S and T coordinates, respectively, for the associated vertex.

Obviously, using this technique, normals with a $-Z$ component generate the same S, T coordinate pair as the same normal with a $+Z$ component. This works out fine because any vertex with a $-Z$ component in its associated normal is by definition back facing and will not be seen, since this calculation is done in view space.

Color Plate 5 was produced simply by mapping a torus with a spherical reflection map of an outdoor environment.

Using this technique, it is very easy to perform reflection, specular mapping, and diffuse lighting using the correct texture maps.

For a view-independent method of generating these effects, please see [Heidrich98], which describes dual-paraboloid mapping. In addition, cubic environment mapping is a wonderful way to generate dynamic lighting and reflection effects if the target hardware provides support for it. Please see [Nvidia00] for more information.

References

[Blythe99] Blythe, David, *Advanced Graphics Programming Techniques Using OpenGL,* Available online at http://reality.sgi.com/blythe/sig99/advanced99/notes/node80 .html, April 7, 2000.

[Watt92] Watt, Alan, and Watt, Mark, *Advanced Animation and Rendering Techniques,* ACM Press, 1992.

[Heidrich98] Heidrich, Wolfgang, and Seidel, Hans-Peter, *View-independent Environment Maps,* Eurographics/ACM Siggraph Workshop on Graphics Hardware 1998, available online at www9.informatik.uni-erlangen.de/eng/research/rendering/envmap/, March 22 2000.

[Nvidia00] NVIDIA technical brief, *Perfect Reflections and Specular Lighting Effects with Cube Environment Mapping,* available online at www.nvidia.com/Marketing/Developer/DevRel.nsf/WhitepapersFrame?OpenPage, March 10, 2000.

5.6

Hardware Bump Mapping

Sim Dietrich

Bump mapping, first described by Jim Blinn in [Blinn78], is a technique that simulates the way light reacts to a rough or dimpled surface by applying a texture to an otherwise smooth polygonal surface. The applied texture is known as the *bump map*, hence the term *bump mapping*.

Several methods of bump mapping are available in hardware today. This article concentrates on elucidating the common issues around modern bump-mapping techniques that programmers encounter when moving from "bumpy sphere" demos to actual game implementation. Since bump mapping is actually a lighting computation, I discuss bump mapping in terms of illumination.

Bump-mapping techniques either calculate or approximate a dot product between the light vector L and the surface normal N in order to calculate diffuse lighting. For the sake of simplicity, I assume that the dot product operation is calculated on a per-pixel basis. This functionality is available from several hardware vendors at the time of this writing and will likely remain available in the future.

Specular lighting can be achieved by calculating the dot product between the half-angle vector H and the surface normal N and then raising the result to some power. We concentrate on diffuse illumination, but bear in mind that all techniques discussed can be applied to specular bump mapping or lighting as well.

Dot product-based bump mapping and per-pixel lighting are huge subjects, so we concentrate on explaining the problem at hand and some practical solutions. Specifically, this article avoids discussing texture blending modes, cube maps, texture formats, and other things at that level of implementation detail, instead concentrating on how to properly bump map or light an arbitrary model or mesh.

How Do I Apply a Bump Map to an Object?

The simple answer to this question is to simply texture map the object with a texture representing the bump map. A more useful answer requires more information on what effect we are trying to achieve on which platform. Various hardware bump-mapping techniques require different source data for the bump-map texture, from alpha-height maps to RGB surface normal maps and RGB *dUdV* maps. Since both RGB surface normal maps and RGB *dUdV* maps can be generated from alpha-height maps, I assume that the original source data for the bump map is an alpha or gray-scale height map.

As stated, we assume that we have a per-pixel dot product operation, thus, I assume we have a way of generating the appropriate texture format that directly encodes surface normals in RGB format. One such format maps the *X*, *Y*, and *Z* vector components from [−1..1] floating point into the [0..255] range of the RGB channels.

The fact that we have normals stored in an RGB texture presents an interesting question: In which space are these normals defined? Model space? World space? Some other space?

The fundamental bump-mapping or diffuse illumination operation, $N \bullet L$, does not care in which space the vectors are defined; it is essential, however, to ensure that *N* and *L* are expressed in the same coordinate system.

We will see that this seemingly innocuous issue is one of the most important considerations when evaluating dot product-based bump-mapping techniques. The next section describes each option and where it might be most appropriate.

Choosing a Space for the Normals

Let's start with a simple example of a sphere that we want to bump map in model space. We assume for now that the bump map is uniquely textured across the sphere; in other words, that each point on the sphere maps to its own section of the texture so that no tiling or mirroring of the bump map occurs.

In this case, we go through each texel in the bump map, find where it is mapped on to the sphere in model space, and generate the surface normal for that location. Next we generate a 3 × 3 coordinate system for that location on the sphere, using the surface normal as the +*Z* axis. This is commonly known as *tangent space* because it represents a space that lies tangent to the surface.

In order to generate tangent space, two unique vectors are required, and the third vector can be generated from the other two. In this case, however, there is no obvious choice for a second vector because there is an infinite number of tangent spaces with the same +*Z* axis, so an arbitrary choice must be made.

We choose the +*Y* axis in model space as our second vector. We then make a cross product of +*Y* with our surface normal to generate the third vector, which serves as +*X*. We can then stop or take the cross product of +*Z* with +*X* to generate a new +*Y* axis. Normalizing all three vectors gives us the three columns of our 3 × 3 matrix that represents tangent space at that point on the sphere surface.

Now we have a basis matrix at the appropriate point, and we can take the bump vector from our bump map, expressed in world space, and rotate it into local tangent space using our matrix. We now have a bump vector for that particular point on the sphere. We can now replace the world space bump vector in the texture with the tangent space bump vector.

Now at run time we can take a light vector L expressed in world space and rotate it through the world to model matrix, giving L'. Since L' is now relative to model space, we can perform $L' \bullet N$ between this light vector and the bump-map vectors.

L' is constant for a particular model space matrix, so it is valid in general only for the current model hierarchy level. This is convenient in that it allows L' to remain constant for an entire portion of the model being bump mapped.

At run time, we can set up the texture-blending units to compute:

Texture · ConstantColor

Where `Texture` corresponds to the surface normal map with RGB encoded normals and `ConstantColor` corresponds to our constant L' vector, converted into RGB form. This technique is known as object space or model space bump mapping. Its advantage lies in no run-time overhead other than a single vector rotation per model hierarchy level. Its disadvantages include having to uniquely texture objects, which takes a large amount of texture memory. In addition, skinning or morphing objects need their surface normal textures regenerated every frame.

The desire to overcome these disadvantages leads to the next technique.

Another Approach: Using Tangent Space Bump Mapping

Since we have defined tangent space already for our sphere, that means we have a translation from model space to a local space defined at each vertex. We can leverage that information to eliminate the necessity of both unique texturing and of having to regenerate the surface normal map in the case of animated models. Instead of regenerating the normal maps to be relative to model space, we leave our normal maps as they are, instead generating a matrix to rotate the light vector from model space into tangent space.

We assume that our original height map represents height "out from the surface." Mathematically, the "out" direction of the height map corresponds to the $+Z$ axis of our tangent space at every point on the surface of the sphere. We use this to create a mathematical way of translating from the bump-map space to the local tangent space at any point on the sphere.

One way to accomplish this task is to calculate our tangent space exactly as in model space bump-mapping described previously, but only at each vertex of the sphere, and store the tangent space matrix in a data structure corresponding to that vertex. When lighting or bump mapping that vertex, we use the 3×3 tangent space matrix to convert our light vector into local tangent space. So, rather than using the tangent space matrix to convert the surface normals, as we did previously, we use the matrix to convert the light vector instead. Remember that the space in which the dot product is performed is irrelevant, as long as both vectors are defined in the same coordinate space.

In model space bump mapping described previously, the generation of a tangent space matrix occurred as a preprocessing step at every point on the sphere in order to generate a unique bump map across the sphere. In tangent space bump mapping, we only generate a tangent space matrix at each vertex of the sphere.

At run time, we take our L vector for each vertex of the sphere and rotate it, first through the world-to-model matrix and then through the local tangent space matrix generated during preprocessing and stored at that vertex. This gives us L', the light vector in local tangent space. Of course, L' is correct on only a per-vertex basis. In model space bump mapping, L' was constant for the whole model hierarchy level. Now L' varies from vertex to vertex.

So, whereas before, we stored L' in a constant color, it now has to be interpolated across a triangle.

To perform tangent space bump mapping, we can set up the texture-blending units to perform:

Texture · DiffuseColor

Where `Texture` is our surface normal map and `DiffuseColor` is an iterated color value representing L'.

We leverage the hardware's color interpolation capability to "rotate" our L' vector from one space to another. We are actually performing a linear interpolation between local L' vectors at each vertex, rather than true rotation or spherical interpolation, but for most purposes this works well. Note that perspective-correct color interpolation is a real help for these cases.

On multitexture hardware, it is desirable to use a cube map or paraboloid map to interpolate L' instead, but that topic is beyond the scope of this article. Suffice it to say that using a linear interpolation of L' vectors leads to darkening artifacts when bump mapping with respect to local lights near large triangles. This effect is caused by almost opposite L' vectors being shortened when linearly interpolated across the interior of a triangle. Cube maps can also assist with handling properly interpolated light vectors across anisotropically scaled normal maps.

Tangent space bump mapping is much improved over model space bump mapping in that bump-map textures no longer must be unique and can be tiled across a surface. In addition, skinned or morphed models need only regenerate the 3×3 tangent space matrix for each animated vertex and do not have to recreate the surface normal map each frame.

Tangent space bump mapping is less CPU-efficient than model space bump mapping in that it requires more rotations of L into local tangent space at run time. It also requires updating of model data at run time, which may introduce GPU stalls or additional data copying.

A more subtle disadvantage of tangent space bump mapping is not necessarily apparent when creating a demo of a bumpy sphere, but that can be a challenge when incorporating bump mapping into an actual game environment. The problem is that tangent space bump mapping requires defining a relationship between how the bump map is applied and the surface of the object.

In order to generate the local tangent space matrix, we need to know more than the fact that the "out" direction of the height map corresponds to +Z in tangent space. This is the same problem as in the model space bump mapping example. We must have two unique vectors in order to define a three-dimensional coordinate system. Most bump-mapping examples available on the Web today (circa 2000) have an arbitrary, implicit mapping whereby they simply choose a world or model space axis, such as +Y, in order to generate the tangent space matrix.

Here is a description of our problem. Let's say a programmer and artist work together to bump map our sphere using this bump map. Now say that the artist comes in the next day and rotates the bump map 90 degrees on the model and imports it into the game. Instead of the light appearing to come from above, the light now appears to come from the side! So, the programmer comes in, sees the problem, and updates the tangent space matrices by taking into account the 90-degree rotation to fix the problem.

The fact that this problem could be fixed in this way implies that the artist is supplying information that the programmer is not automatically taking into account in the mapping from tangent space to bump map space.

The artist knows how she wants the bump map applied, so the program should respect her choice. The bump map can be applied like any other texture; thus it may be stretched, warped, projected, and so on. Our simplistic tangent space method fails to take into account how the bump map is actually applied to a model and assumes that there is a simple correspondence between the bump map and the underlying surface. Tangent space bump mapping requires knowing how the texture was applied— in other words, planar, box, spherical, or cylindrical mapping.

It is this assumption that makes tangent space bump mapping difficult to incorporate into a game, especially one with existing artwork that we don't want to retexture with bump maps in a restrictive way.

A Solution: Texture Space Bump Mapping

Texture space bump mapping is similar to tangent space bump mappingand primarily differs in the way that the local matrices are generated for each vertex.

Rather than generating tangent space matrices at each vertex, texture space bump mapping creates what I call a *texture space matrix* that takes into account exactly how the texture was applied to the surface by the artist.

To generate this matrix, we need to look at each triangle and how it is texture mapped. It may be rotated, scaled in S or T, flipped, or projected. It turns out that what we need to know in order to mathematically account for how the texture is applied are the texture gradients. The texture gradients are nine scalar values that represent the direction of S and T with respect to the X, Y, and Z axes.

We calculate the texture gradients as follows; let's start with the plane equation of our triangle:

$Ax + By + Cz + D = 0$

We can use any three independent variables in our plane equation, so I use X, S, and T, instead of X, Y, and Z.

$Ax + Bs + Ct + D = 0$

Now we can use this equation to calculate our texture gradients with respect to X.

Let's assume that we have two unique x and two unique s values and subtract one from the other to give us dx and ds. For this step, we assume that t is held constant.

$Ax1 + Bs1 + Ct + D = 0$

$Ax0 + Bs0 + Ct + D = 0$

$Ax0 + Bs0 + Ct + D = Ax1 + Bs1 + Ct + D$

$Ax1 + Bs1 + Ct + D - (Ax0 + Bs0 + Ct + D) = 0$

$Ax1 - Ax0 + Bs1 - Bs0 = 0$

$A(dX) + B(dS) = 0$

$A(dX) = -B(dS)$

$dX/dS = -B/A$

The gradient of X with respect to S is thus $-B/A$. This gives us a measure of how X changes with each change in S. The same can be computed for dX/dT. We can then generate the gradients of Y and Z similarly. If A is found to be 0, we can safely set the gradient to 0. That simply means that S doesn't change at all with respect to S.

We now have six scalar values that represent how X, Y, and Z change in model space as we walk across the texture in S and T.

We can use this information to derive a matrix between the S, T and $S \times T$ axes, and the X, Y, and Z model space matrices:

$$\begin{bmatrix} S.x & T.x & (S \times T).x \\ S.y & T.y & (S \times T).y \\ S.z & T.z & (S \times T).z \end{bmatrix}$$

At run time, we can move the light vector into local model space using the model's hierarchical matrix stack. Then we can put the light vector through this matrix for each vertex and store the resulting vector in the diffuse or specular iterated colors. Now the dot product can be computed between the normal map and a light vector defined in the same space as the normal map.

Texture Space Issues

Some of the issues that arise from generating a basis from textures are summarized. The most apparent issue that arises when implementing this task is flipped textures. Since textures don't have a "sidedness" and normals do, we need to detect this case by comparing the face normal of the triangle to the texture's $S \times T$ axis. If the dot product between them is negative, we can simply flip the $S \times T$ axis. At times an artist mirrors part of a texture on a symmetrical object. In this case, two triangles that straddle this boundary have opposite $S \times T$ axes. In this case, the programmer or artist must duplicate the vertex.

At times programmers are forced to duplicate vertices for the sake of different texture coordinates. This situation can indicate a discontinuity in how the texture is applied to the surface. The way to solve this problem is to create a texture space basis matrix for each triangle individually. Next find which vertices are geometrically shared between triangle faces—in other words, which vertices share X, Y, Z positions. Now for each vertex, take the S, T and $S \times T$ axes of each triangle that touches that vertex and sum them. Now normalize the resulting S, T and $S \times T$ axes. This action is analogous to creating vertex normals from face normals, except that we are calculating three vectors at a time. The three resultant vectors now make up a new "average texture space" to store at each vertex of the model.

The price of normalizing the resultant column vectors is that now anisotropically scaled textures can't be handled properly. If we have cube maps or some other way to normalize the vectors, we can skip the normalization step and thus handle anisotropically scaled textures with ease.

Conclusion

Dot product-based bump mapping and per-pixel lighting have arrived and along with them some interesting parameterization issues. The need to interpret flat textures as 3D surface normal vectors necessitates either regenerating the surface normal textures to match the model, as in model space bump mapping, or generating a basis matrix for each vertex, as in tangent and texture space bump mapping.

References

Here are three great resources for more information on per-pixel lighting:

[Blinn78] Blinn, James, "Simulation of wrinkled surfaces," *Computer Graphics (SIGGRAPH '78 Proceedings)*, vol. 12, no. 3, pp. 286–292, August 1978.

[Everitt00] Everitt, Cass, "High-Quality, Hardware-Accelerated Per-Pixel Illumination for Consumer Class OpenGL Hardware," master's thesis, available online at www.r3.nu/~cass/thesis, May 2000.

[NVIDIA] NVIDIA's Developer Relations site at www.nvidia.com/Developer.nsf, May 2000.

5.7

Ground-Plane Shadows

Yossarian King

Projecting shadows of arbitrary objects onto other objects or arbitrary terrain is difficult. However, if you are projecting shadows onto a flat ground plane, there is a simple solution. The "obvious" approach is to draw a sprite of some sort at a character's feet, perhaps generated by rendering the character in profile to an off-screen buffer. This method suffers from misregistration effects between object and shadow. This article presents a simple technique for ground-plane shadows that performs a physically correct projection with very little computational overhead.

One additional transform matrix is used to "squash" the vertices in an object onto a flat horizontal surface of arbitrary height. The direction and height of the light source relative to the object determine the shadow projection matrix. Given this matrix, the object is rerendered with the additional transform to draw the shadow.

Translucent gray polygons are used in place of the textured polygons of the object to create the shadow effect. The object used for the shadow need not be the same as the original object; typically you use an object with a lower polygon count to improve performance. The polygons of the shadow object overlap after projection onto the ground, which produces artifacts in the translucent rendering. These artifacts can be eliminated using a hardware Z-buffer.

The technique can be extended to project shadows onto any 3D plane, not just a plane aligned with the coordinate axes. Used twice, the technique can project shadows into the corner between a floor and a wall.

Shadow Math

Shadows result when a solid object comes between a light source and a surface. A point on the surface is in shadow if a ray from the light to the point intersects the object. In a rendering system, the object is represented by a collection of polygons. Casting rays from the light through each of the vertices of the model onto the surface outlines the areas of the surface that are in shadow. For a single polygon of the object, this method gives a projected shadow polygon on the surface.

Unfortunately, this method does not lend itself directly to practical real-time rendering. It is costly to calculate the intersection between the ray and the surface. The projected shadow polygon needs to be subdivided to conform accurately to the surface, an operation that is arbitrarily complex, depending on the complexity of the surface. An alternative to rendering the projected shadow polygons is to modify the vertex colors of the surface, darkening the vertices that are in shadow, but this has the drawback of reducing the precision of the shadow and making it dependent on the vertex density of the surface. Dynamic shadow map textures can be used to compute shading at a higher and more uniform detail than allowed by vertex shading, but this process is also expensive.

The problem can be simplified, however, if the shadows need be cast only on a horizontal ground plane. For many game applications such as sports simulations and corridor games, horizontal surfaces are the norm, and the simplification can be used.

Figure 5.7.1 shows ground-plane projection in 2D. A light at point L casts the shadow of a point P onto the ground plane (the X-axis) at some point S. We want to determine sx, the X coordinate of point S.

Use of similar triangles shows that:

$$\frac{(sx - px)}{(sx - lx)} = \frac{py}{ly}$$

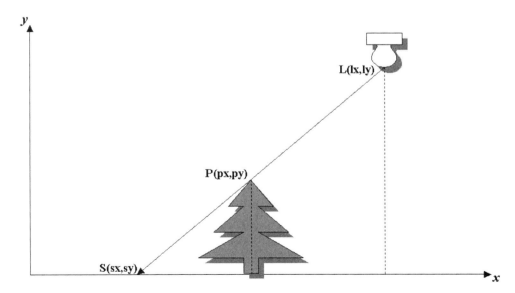

FIGURE 5.7.1. A light at a point L casts a shadow of point P onto the ground plane at point S.

solving for *sx*:

$$sx = px + py * \frac{(sx - lx)}{ly}$$

But this expression for *sx* includes *sx*, so we haven't actually solved for the unknown. However, the only use of *sx* on the right side of the equation is in (*sx* – *lx*), which is the horizontal distance from the shadow point to the light. By assuming that the light is relatively far away from the object relative to the length of the shadow, we can approximate (*sx* – *lx*) with (*ox* – *lx*), the distance from the object to the light. This yields:

$$sx = px + py * \frac{(ox - lx)}{ly}$$

or simply:

$$sx = px + k * py$$

where:

$$k = \frac{(ox - lx)}{ly}$$

The distant light source assumption is equivalent to treating the light as a directional light rather than a point light source.

Extending this to three dimensions and projecting the shadow point *S* onto the *x*-*z* plane, we get:

$$sx = px + k1 * py$$

$$sy = 0 \tag{5.7.1}$$

$$sz = pz + k2 * py$$

where:

$$k1 = \frac{(ox - lx)}{ly}$$

$$k2 = \frac{(oz - lz)}{ly}$$

By projecting each of the vertices of the object onto the ground plane, we get a collection of projected polygons that can be rendered to create the shadow of the object. To do the projection, we just need to calculate the values of *k1* and *k2*, which are completely determined by the relative position of the object and the light. Implementation of this technique is described in further detail in the next section.

Implementation

In a typical rendering pipeline, a model vertex m is transformed into a view space point v before projection into screen space. This operation is written as:

$$v = C{*}T{*}m$$

where T is a matrix representing the model transformation that converts model vertex m into world space, and C is the camera transformation that converts world space coordinates into view space. In order to render an object, we transform each of its vertices into view space, then project into screen space and render the resulting polygons.

To easily incorporate the shadow projection process into the rendering pipeline, Equation 5.7.1 can be rewritten in matrix form as:

$$s = S{*}p$$

where:

$s = (sx, sy, sz, 1)$ is the projected shadow point in world space.
$p = (px, py, pz, 1)$ is the point on the object in world space.
S is the shadow projection matrix, written as:

$$S = \begin{bmatrix} 1 & k1 & 0 & 0 \\ 0 & 0 & 0 & 0 \\ 0 & k2 & 1 & 0 \\ 0 & 0 & 0 & 1 \end{bmatrix}$$

Now to render the shadow of an object, we simply insert the shadow projection matrix into the vertex transformation:

$$v_s = C{*}S{*}T{*}m$$

This expression makes use of the shadow projection matrix to transform the points of an object into the projected shadow points on the ground plane. The shadow projection matrix S depends only on the constants $k1$ and $k2$, which are determined from the relative position of the object and the light.

This technique can be used to rerender an object projected flat onto the ground. If the shadow matrix S is simply inserted into the pipeline and the object rerendered, the result is a flattened version of the object—complete with textures, shading, and so on. To render the object as a shadow, we can render each vertex as a flat-shaded translucent gray, ignoring the texture information in the model. In practice, using a model with fewer polygons than the original object reduces the cost of rendering a shadow.

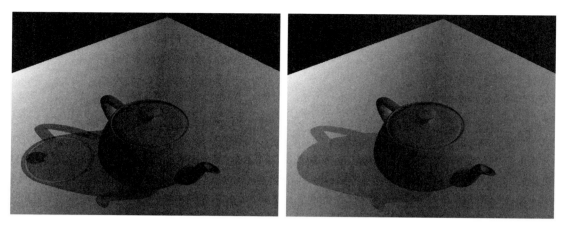

FIGURE 5.7.2. Projecting the teapot geometry onto the ground plane renders the shadow of the teapot object. The artifacts caused by overlapping translucent polygons are eliminated with the hardware *Z*-buffer, as shown on the right.

One problem with this method is that the polygons projected onto the ground plane overlap, and when the overlapping polygons are drawn with translucency, the overlapping areas show up darker than the non-overlapped areas. This artifact can be eliminated using the hardware *Z*-buffer: After the first shadow polygon has been drawn, the overlapping portion of subsequent polygons is removed by the *Z*-buffer. If *Z*-buffer imprecision causes artifacts, then as the shadow polygons are rendered, each can be biased further away in *Z*, so that the *Z*-compare eliminates the overlapping areas.

Figure 5.7.2 shows a teapot rendered with a projected shadow, both with and without the use of the *Z*-buffer to remove artifacts.

Extensions

As presented, this article makes it easy to project shadow geometry onto a horizontal ground plane. The method can easily be extended to other axis-aligned vertical planes. With a bit more work, it can also be extended to arbitrary planes. An arbitrary plane can be represented as a rotation and translation of the horizontal ground plane. Shadows are projected onto the arbitrary plane by rotating and translating it back to horizontal, projecting the shadow, and then transforming back the plane position. The light position must also be transformed. By using the projection technique multiple times, shadows can be simultaneously cast onto multiple planes, such as the corner between a wall and the floor.

5.8

Real-Time Shadows on Complex Objects

Gabor Nagy

This article presents an efficient algorithm capable of creating realistic shadows in real-time applications. The algorithm can take advantage of today's fast texture-mapping and 3D transformation hardware.

Introduction

Shadows are among the most important depth cues in human vision. In computer graphics, they can give an image the final touch of realism. Without shadows—even with realistic lighting and texturing effects—computer-generated images look artificial; the objects appear to float in space, even when they are lying on a surface. This inability for humans to sense the relative position and depth in computer graphics is especially apparent when the camera is not moving (no parallax information).

Until recently, only computationally expensive algorithms such as ray tracing and radiosity could produce accurate shadows, in which both the objects casting the shadows and the ones receiving them are of arbitrary complexity.

The algorithm presented here is optimized for real-time applications. It provides a very good balance between realism and rendering performance while being easily extendible to all situations. With the always performance-hungry game programmer in mind, this article highlights points at which significant optimization for performance is possible using hardware features.

Some of the basic ideas in this article have been around for a while, but most papers describing them don't deal with the important implementation details we cover here.

The Light Source, Blocker Object, and Receiver Object

Consider the simple example shown in Figure 5.8.1. The torus (*blocker object* or *blocker*) blocks some of the light coming from the light source, casting a shadow on

FIGURE 5.8.1. Shadow, receiver, blocker, and light source.

the wall. The wall receives the shadow, or "lack of light"; therefore it is called the *receiver object,* or *receiver.*

If the light source is a point light (infinitely small), the blocker object blocks the light of that light source in a well-defined volume, usually referred to as a *shadow volume* (see Figure 5.8.2). A shadow is created on a receiver object where its surface intersects with the shadow volume. As Figure 5.8.2 shows, the shadow volume has a truncated, cone-like shape, starting at the blocker object and continuing to infinity. Whereas the shadow volume really starts at the contours of the blocker object, its cone-like shape originates from the light source.

Let's examine how the cross section of the shadow volume changes as we get further from the light source. We call the point on the blocker's surface that is nearest to the light source P_n and the one farthest from it P_f.

We can divide the shadow volume into three regions:

1. Between the light source and P_n
2. Between P_n and P_f
3. From P_f to infinity

It's easy to see that in Region 3, the cross-section of the shadow volume has a constant shape, but it increases in size as we get further from the light source.

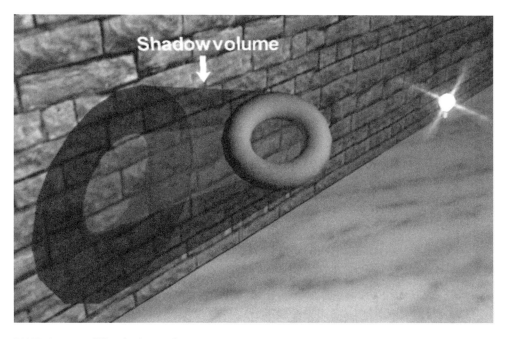

FIGURE 5.8.2. The shadow volume.

Because of this phenomenon, unless one or more receiver objects are in Region 2, the shadow volume can be accurately modeled by projecting a two-dimensional mask from the position of the point light source. Consequently, using the same projection, we can map this 2D mask on the receiver objects to define the shadowed areas! This 2D mask is called the *shadow map*, and it can be simply derived by drawing the blocker object's silhouette as seen from the light source.

Notice that we cannot see the shadow cast by the torus in Figure 5.8.3a because the torus exactly obscures it! This is a good indication that indeed, we can simply use a properly projected 2D image or mask (see Figure 5.8.3b) to define the shadow volume. This method is usually referred to as *projective shadow mapping*.

The Objectives of This Article

To draw shadows using the method introduced, we need to do the following:

1. Create a shadow map for each light/blocker object pair.
2. Calculate the shadow map (texture) coordinates to use on the receiver object's vertices.
3. Render the receiver objects with the shadow map applied as a 2D texture.

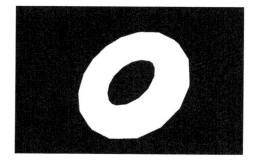

FIGURE 5.8.3. The blocker object as seen from *a,* the light source, and *b,* its silhouette.

Creating the Shadow Map

The first thing to do in order to render the shadow map is set up a perspective projection originating at the light source. This projection projects the blocker object onto a *virtual screen plane* between the light source and the blocker object, yielding the shadow map shown in Figure 5.8.4.

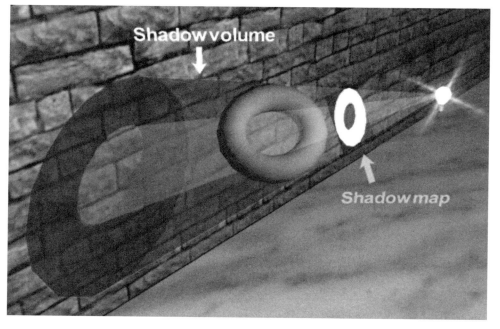

FIGURE 5.8.4. The shadow map projection (also Color Plate 6).

The Light Coordinate System

First, we define a new coordinate system with its origin at the light source and its Z-axis pointing at the blocker object. The Z-axis of this coordinate system determines the center line of the perspective projection, while its XY-plane defines the orientation of the screen plane on which we project the shadow map. If we transform the blocker object into this *light coordinate system*, illustrated in Figure 5.8.5., we can easily project it onto this plane.

To define an arbitrary coordinate system, we need to know the position of its origin and its orientation. We already know the position of the origin: It's the position of our light source. We can describe the orientation of the light coordinate system by the direction of its three axes: X_{light}, Y_{light}, and Z_{light} , all 3D unit vectors in *world* coordinates.

Finding Z~light~

Starting with the Z_{light} axis, we can easily find X_{light} and Y_{light}. Z_{light} is a direction vector that starts from the light source and points at the blocker object. Let's assume that the blocker object is polygonal, and we have an array of all the polygon vertices that are used in rendering this object. Now we have a set of "target" points in 3D space (the vertices of the blocker) and another point: the position of the light source. A fast and

FIGURE 5.8.5. The light coordinate-system (also Color Plate 7).

efficient way to obtain a "good" direction vector is to average the vectors that start at the light source and point to each vertex. (We discuss a better approach later.)

We call the vector we have computed the *mean direction vector*, or MDV:

$$\vec{MDV} = \frac{\sum_{i=1}^{N_v}\left(V_i - P_{light}\right)}{N_v}$$

where N_v is the number of vertices considered in the blocker and P_{light} is the position of the light source.

Normalizing *MDV* yields Z_{light}:

$$\vec{Z}_{light} = \frac{\vec{MDV}}{\left|\vec{MDV}\right|}$$

Optimization Tip #1

Since we will normalize *MDV*, we don't have to divide the sum of light-to-vertex vectors by N_v, saving one divide operation. We can also calculate $P_{light}{}^*N_v$ in advance and avoid the $- P_{light}$ in the vertex loop, because:

$$\frac{\sum_{i=1}^{N_v}\left(V_i - P_{light}\right)}{N_v} = -P_{light}N_v\frac{\sum_{i=1}^{N_v}V_i}{N_v}$$

Here is the C code to compute Z_{light}:

```
typedef struct
{
  E3dType   X,Y,Z;
  short Flags;
} E3dVertex;

void ShadowMatrix(Matrix LBlockerLocalToWorldMatrix)
{
  unsigned long    LVn, LVC, LN, LC;
  float         Mx, My, Mz, LPlightX, LPlightY, LPlightZ,
  float         LMDVX, LMDVY, LMDVZ,   // Mean Direction Vector
  float         LZlightX, LZlightY, LZlightZ, // Zlight vector
  // Initialize Mean Direction Vector to (0.0, 0.0, 0.0)
  //
  LMDVX = LMDVY = LMDVZ = 0.0;

  Lvertex = LMesh->Vertices;

  // Average vertex-to-light vectors
  //
```

```
      LVn = LMesh->NumOfVertices;

      LMDVX = LPlightX * LVn;
      LMDVY = LPlightY * LVn;
      LMDVZ = LPlightZ * LVn;

      for(LVC = O;L VC < LVn; LVC++, LVertex++)
      {
        Mx=LVertex->X; My=LVertex->Y; Mz=LVertex->Z;
        E3dM_MatrixTransform3x4(LBlockerLocalToWorldMatrix, LX, LY, LZ);

        LMDVX -= LX;
        LMDVY -= LY;
        LMDVZ -= LZ;
      }

      // Normalize Mean Direction Vector (MDV)
      //
      LVF = sqrt(LMDVX*LMDVX+LMDVY*LMDVY+LMDVZ*LMDVZ);
      LVF = 1.0 / LVF; // We can save 2 divisions by doing this in
                       // advance...

      LZlightX = LMDVX * LVF;
      LZlightY = LMDVY * LVF;
      LZlightZ = LMDVZ * LVF;
      …
   }
```

`E3dM_MatrixTransform3x4` is a macro function that transforms a 3D vector given by *Mx*, *My*, and *Mz* with a 3 × 4 matrix (actually the top-left part of a 4 × 4 matrix).

For the rest of the source code, please refer to the example program on this book's companion CD-ROM.

Finding X_{light} and Y_{light}

The projection to map the shadow-map texture on the receiver object is the same as the one used to draw the shadow map; therefore, the orientation of the shadow map (rotation around the Z_{light} axis) does not matter. In other words, rotating the *XY-light* plane around Z_{light} does not make any difference. This means that for the X_{light} axis, we can use any unit vector that is perpendicular to Z_{light} (refer back to Figure 5.8.5). We can get that vector as the cross-product of Z_{light} and any other vector that is not parallel with Z_{light}. Let's call this "helper" vector V.

We know that at least two of the X, Y, or Z-axes of the *world* coordinate system meet these criteria, so for simplicity, we use a unit vector $V(x,y,z)$, with one coordinate being 1, the others 0.

A vector's largest component (X, Y, or Z) determines its dominant direction; therefore, to get a vector that points far enough away from Z_{light}, we set to 1 the component of V that has the *smallest* absolute value in Z_{light}. This eliminates floating-point precision worries when performing a vector cross-product operation on Z_{light} and V.

For example:

If Z_{light}=(0.381, 0.889, 0.254), V will be: (0.0, 0.0, 1.0) = Z_{world}

If Z_{light}=(−0.889, 0.254, 0.381), V will be: (0.0, 1.0, 0.0) = Y_{world}

and so on.

The cross-product of Z_{light} and V yields a third vector that is perpendicular to both of them. After normalization, this vector yields X_{light}, the X-axis of the light coordinate system:

$$\vec{X}_{light} = \frac{\vec{Z}_{light} x \vec{V}}{\left| \vec{Z}_{light} x \vec{V} \right|}$$

With X_{light} and Z_{light} given, the Y_{light} axis is just another cross product away:

$$\vec{Y}_{light} = \vec{X}_{light} x \vec{Z}_{light}$$

Note that this step gives us a unit vector, so we don't have to normalize Y_{light}, since:

$$\left| \vec{X}_{light} \right| = 1 \text{ and } \left| \vec{Z}_{light} \right| = 1 \text{ and } \vec{X}_{light} \perp \vec{Z}_{light} \Rightarrow \left| \vec{X}_{light} \times \vec{Z}_{light} \right| = 1$$

With X_{light}, Y_{light}, and Z_{light} and P_{light} known, we can create the matrix that transforms a point from *world* coordinates to *light* coordinates by simply filling in these values:

$$M_{WorldToLight} = \begin{bmatrix} X \text{ of } \bar{X}_{light} & X \text{ of } \vec{Y}_{light} & X \text{ of } \vec{Z}_{light} & 0.0 \\ Y \text{ of } \bar{X}_{light} & Y \text{ of } \vec{Y}_{light} & Y \text{ of } \vec{Z}_{light} & 0.0 \\ Z \text{ of } \bar{X}_{light} & Z \text{ of } \vec{Y}_{light} & Z \text{ of } \vec{Z}_{light} & 0.0 \\ -X \text{ of } P_{light} & -Y \text{ of } P_{light} & -Z \text{ of } P_{light} & 1.0 \end{bmatrix}$$

This is why we used X_{light}, Y_{light}, and Z_{light} to describe the orientation of the light coordinate system.

The next step is to pre-multiply this matrix with the blocker object's *local-to-world* matrix. This step gives us the *local-to-light* matrix for the blocker.

$$M_{BlockerLocalToLight} = M_{BlockerLocalToWorld} * M_{WorldToLight}$$

As the name implies, the matrix transforms a point defined in the *local* coordinate system of the blocker into the light coordinate system. Such transformed X and Y coordinates define the *parallel* or *orthogonal* projection of the blocker object onto the shadow-map plane (which is parallel with the XY plane of the light coordinate system).

Defining the Perspective Projection

To make this a perspective projection, we need a field of view, or the X and Y "projection ratios." We can find the projection ratios (R_X and R_Y) for each vertex of the blocker object by transforming the vertex with $M_{BlockerLocalToLight}$ and dividing the resultant X and Y coordinates by the Z coordinate:

$$R_Y = \left| \frac{Vtx_Y}{Vtx_Z} \right|$$

Adaptive Projection

We could always use the same ratio for the projection, but that would lead to the blocker object's silhouette changing size in the shadow map if we move the light source closer or farther away from it. The same problem arises if we change the size of the blocker or if the light source looked at it from a different angle. These changes could result in a tiny image of the blocker in the middle of the shadow map or an oversized image that doesn't fit in the shadow map (see Figure 5.8.6). In the first case (Figure 5.8.6a), we get a low-resolution shadow map with bad artifacts on the receiver objects. This is a waste of shadow-map memory.

The latter (Figure 5.8.6b) causes incorrect shadow shapes and possibly "shadow leaking" (see the section "Texture Coordinates and Shadow-Map Coordinates"). In this case, the shadow-map size is not large enough.

Instead of one fixed value, we use the largest R_X (R_{Xmax}) as the horizontal ratio for the projection, whereas the largest R_Y, (R_{Ymax}) gives the vertical ratio. This makes the perspective projection *adaptive* for both the X and Y direction, meaning that the blocker's silhouette always properly fills the shadow map, making the best use of all the pixels in it.

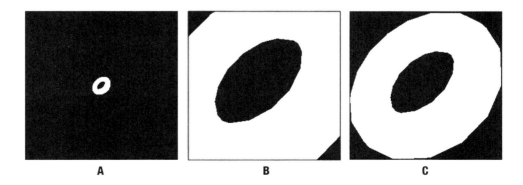

A   **B**   **C**

FIGURE 5.8.6. Non-adaptive (*a* and *b*) and adaptive blocker projection (*c*).

This concept is very important because we want to use the minimum necessary texture size, for the following reasons:

- Texture memory is always a scarce resource, and the maximum texture size might be limited by other factors.
- On some hardware, after drawing the shadow map image, we have to transfer it from the frame buffer to a dedicated texture memory, and the speed of this transfer is limited by bus and memory bandwidth.

Now we can fill out a standard perspective projection matrix for the blocker object:

$$
M_{BlockerProjection} = \begin{bmatrix} \dfrac{0.98}{R_{X\,max}} * SMapWidth & 0 & 0 & 0 \\ 0 & \dfrac{0.98}{R_{Y\,max}} * SMapHeight & 0 & 0 \\ 0 & 0 & \dfrac{Z_{far} + Z_{near}}{Z_{near} - Z_{far}} & -1 \\ 0 & 0 & 2\dfrac{Z_{far} Z_{near}}{Z_{near} - Z_{far}} & 0 \end{bmatrix}
$$

where $SMapWidth$ and $SMapHeight$ are the horizontal and vertical resolutions of the shadow map in pixels. Z_{near} and Z_{far} are the distances of the near and far clipping planes of the viewing frustum from the light source.

Pre-multiplying this matrix with $M_{BlockerLocalToLight}$ yields the 4×4 matrix that performs a perspective projection from blocker local coordinates to shadow-map coordinates:

$$
M_{BlockerLocalToShadowMap} = M_{BlockerLocalToLight} * M_{BlockerProjection}
$$

In OpenGL, we can simply load an identity matrix into the PROJECTION matrix and $M_{BlockerLocalToShadowMap}$ into the MODELVIEW matrix and start drawing the shadow map using the blocker's local coordinates.

Optimization Tip #2

To decrease the time it takes to create the shadow map, we can use two or three different versions of the blocker object geometry for the various rendering stages:

- To set up the shadow map projection, use blocker geometry with a minimum number of vertices. We won't need connectivity data (e.g., polygons) or normal vectors here. All that matters is that no polygons of the blocker should be outside the projected shape of this volume, no matter the angle from which we look at it, because that would draw on the one-pixel edge of the shadow map, ruining texture clamping and causing "shadow leaking." We might even use a "good" bounding volume such as the blocker's bounding-box, which could eliminate the need to compute *MDV* (just use a vector from the light source to the center of the bounding box).

- To draw the shadow map, use blocker geometry with a minimum or no *surface detail* but necessary *contour detail.*
- And, of course, to draw the blocker object, we need the geometry with all the surface detail and surface properties (e.g., normal vectors) to make the object look spiffy.

Optimization Tip #3

If the rendering engine is programmable, we can use a very simple (and possibly fast) renderer code to draw the shadow map:

- No lighting needed; a simple "flat-color" renderer will do.
- No clipping needed (the blocker's image always fits in the shadow map!).
- No depth testing (Z-buffering) needed.

Projecting the Shadow Map on a Receiver Object

Now we have a shadow map associated with a blocker object and a light source. This shadow map can be projected on any number of receiver objects, and because it is applied as a texture, the receiver objects can have any complex shape (curves, holes, ridges, and so on).

As mentioned before, we use the same projection to project the shadow map on a receiver as we used to create the shadow map. The only differences are the image offset and scaling factors, because we use the $[0..1]$ coordinate range as opposed to the $[0..SMapWidth]$ or $[0..SMapHeight]$ ranges.

This is the appropriate projection matrix:

$$M_{BlockerProjection} = \begin{bmatrix} \dfrac{0.49}{R_{X\,max}} * SMapWidth & 0 & 0 & 0 \\ 0 & \dfrac{0.49}{R_{Y\,max}} * SMapHeight & 0 & 0 \\ -0.5 & -0.5 & \dfrac{Z_{far} + Z_{near}}{Z_{near} - Z_{far}} & -1 \\ 0 & 0 & 2\dfrac{Z_{far}Z_{near}}{Z_{near} - Z_{far}} & 0 \end{bmatrix}$$

The next thing to do is to pre-multiply this matrix with $M_{WorldToLight}$:

$$M_{WorldToShadowMapST} = M_{WorldToLight} \, {}^* \, M_{ReceiverProjection}$$

The resulting matrix transforms a point from world coordinates to shadow-map texture coordinates (the resulting X and Y give S and T, respectively).

Pre-multiplying $M_{WorldToShadowMapST}$ with the receiver's local-to-world matrix yields the matrix that we need to go from receiver local space directly to shadow-map texture space.

$$M_{WorldToShadowMapST} = M_{WorldToLight} \, {}^* \, M_{ReceiverProjection}$$

Texture Coordinates and Shadow-Map Coordinates

The shadow map is an image with a finite number of pixels and integer coordinate values—for example, 256×256. However, texture coordinates are usually normalized floating-point values, meaning that the range [0..1] refers to pixel coordinates [0..255] horizontally and [0..255] vertically. So what happens outside the [0..1] range? We have to make sure that the texel used on the receiver is the color used for "no shadow" (black in Figure 5.8.7).

On most 3D hardware with texture mapping, you have at least two options:

- **Texture repeat.** Outside the [0..1] range, the texture is simply repeated—so, for example, in the [−1..0] range of texture coordinates, the texture produces the same image as the [0..1] range.
- **Texture clamping.** The pixel on the edge of the texture image is repeated everywhere outside the [0..1] range, or you can define a specific "border color" that is repeated outside the normal range.

It's easy to see that we have to use texture clamping because we want a uniform effect on the receiver object outside the [0..1] texture coordinate range.

Texture clamping effectively saves us from testing the receiver objects for intersection with the shadow volume. Because not all 3D hardware and APIs provide a separate texture border color, we have to leave a one-pixel-thick border on the shadow map. If we accidentally draw in this border, that pattern would be repeated on the receiver, producing a leaking effect ("shadow leaking"). To make sure that nothing is drawn in this border, we have to slightly decrease the X and Y scaling factors in the projection matrices (elements (0, 0) and (1,1)). This is the reason for using the value 0.98 (instead of 1.0) in $M_{BlockerProjection}$ and 0.49 (instead of 0.5) in $M_{ReceiverProjection}$. Note that these values depend on the resolution of the shadow map. (See the example program on the CD for the proper formulas to calculate them.)

Rendering the Receiver Objects

There are many different ways to draw the object receiving the shadow. The two most common methods are:

- **Single-pass rendering.** If there is no other texture on the receiver object, we can draw it in one pass, applying a black-on-white shadow map as a texture and using the light source to illuminate the object.
- **Multipass rendering with subtractive blending.** If a receiver already has a texture on it and the hardware doesn't support multitexturing, we need multiple passes:
  1. Draw the receiver object normally.
  2. Draw the shadow pass with subtractive pixel blending, using a white-on-black shadow map. This successively decreases the surface color intensity where there is a shadow cast. Use "GREATER-OR-EQUAL" or "LESS-THAN-OR-EQUAL" Z comparison functions for drawing multiple passes. This way, if you pass the same primitive, it overwrites or blends the current pass with the previous one.

For a brief description of pixel blending, please refer to the "Convincing-Looking Glass for Games" article elsewhere in this book.

Extensions and Enhancements to the Basic Algorithm

Simplicity and high performance usually come at a price. This projective shadow-mapping algorithm is no exception to that rule: It has some limitations. However, most of these limitations are very easy to overcome, and the algorithm can be extended to handle these cases.

Back-face Shadow Elimination

One side effect of projective shadow mapping is that it normally maps a shadow on the side of the receiver facing away from the light source.

We can correct this problem by either:

1. Determining whether a triangle is facing away from the light source and, if it is, assigning out-of-range shadow map coordinates for all its vertices. (The example code on the CD-ROM that accompanies this book does this.)
2. Setting up the rendering of the receiver in such a way that the receiver is completely black on the side facing away from the light source (no ambient lighting). This is the proper method because it is closer to what happens in reality. However, if there is more than one light source in the scene, the "back" face of the blocker can be lit by another light. In this case, we have to use multipass rendering and add the ambient light and light coming from other light sources in separate drawing passes.

Receiver Is Behind the Light Source

You have to explicitly check for this case and not map a shadow on the receiver object.

Multiple Light Sources

This case requires multipass rendering with subtractive blending on the receiver object. Use a receiver rendering pass for each shadow map. The multiple passes successively decrease the intensity (RGB values) in the shadowed areas on the surface of the receiver, making even the shadow intersections look correct.

Multiple Blockers

This case also needs multiple passes. There is one difference, though: The cumulative effect of shadow intersections is incorrect because the two blockers block the light of the *same* light source. Use the stencil buffer to *not draw* in the screen area where there is already a shadow drawn.

References

[Blinn88] Blinn, James, "Me and My (Fake) Shadow," *Jim Blinn's Corner,* pages 53–61, January 1988.

[Foley90] Foley, et al., *Computer Graphics Principles and Practice,* second edition, pages 745–753, Addison-Wesley, 1990.

[Blythe96] Blythe, David, and McReynolds, Tom, *Programming with OpenGL: Advanced Rendering,* SIGGRAPH '96 Course Notes, August 1996.

[Heckbert96] Heckbert, Paul, and Herf, Michael, *Fast Soft Shadows,* SIGGRAPH '96 Visual Proceedings, page 145, August 1996.

[Heckbert97] Heckbert, Paul, and Herf, Michael, *Simulating Soft Shadows with Graphics Hardware,* CMU-CS-97-104, Computer Science Department, Carnegie Mellon University, January 1997.

[Woo97] Woo, Mason, Neider, Jackie, and Davis, Tom, *OpenGL Programming Guide,* second edition, Addison-Wesley Developers Press, Silicon Graphics, 1997.

5.9

Improving Environment-Mapped Reflection Using Glossy Prefiltering and the Fresnel Term

Anis Ahmad

In order to render a realistic scene, we must be able to handle surfaces that can reflect the environment around them. Environment mapping [Blinn76] has been used to implement approximate reflections in real time. View-independent implementations (such as dual parabolic maps [Heidrich99] for older hardware or cube maps on newer hardware) are a recent enhancement to environment maps.

Environment maps map the scene around a particular point (the map's origin) to one or more texture maps. This is accomplished by associating each texel to a vector on the unit sphere. The value of each texel is the amount of light arriving at the map's origin through the texel's associated unit vector. Consequently, the environment map can be indexed by generating and converting unit vectors to texture coordinates or, in the case of cube maps, by using the vector itself as a texture coordinate. Thus, by converting reflected view vectors to texture coordinates, one can index the correct points on the environment map to allow for simulated reflections.

Although simple and elegant, these environment maps only simulate the appearance of shiny surfaces—surfaces whose reflections behave like perfect mirrors, regardless of the viewing angle. A common enhancement to this approach is to combine the environment map with a diffuse texture map. Although this enhancement does improve the quality of the image, it does not address the underlying problem of an overly simplified reflection model. This article discusses the assumptions that lead to this simplified model and describes two techniques, glossy prefiltering and Fresnel term weighting, which improve and extend existing approaches to using environment maps.

The First Incorrect Assumption

The primary fault with traditional environment maps is the assumption that all surfaces that reflect light do so perfectly—that is, the assumption that every incoming photon that hits a surface has all its energy reflected in one particular direction. This simplified view of reflection is appropriate only for mirrors or for other highly specular surfaces. For other types of reflective surfaces (dull metals, organic surfaces, and the like), a more general view of reflection is needed.

As shown in Figure 5.9.1, surfaces generally scatter light in many directions. The amount of energy reflected in a particular direction depends on properties of the surface involved, particularly its roughness. The result is a somewhat blurrier reflection (since the light contributing to the image you see did not travel along a single, simple path from the light source to your eye).

In order to help describe how light scatters on reflection, computer graphics researchers have introduced the *bidirectional reflectance distribution function* (BRDF) that serves as an abstraction that models surface reflection. A BRDF computes the probability that a photon arriving at the surface in a given (incoming) direction will be reflected in a particular (outgoing) direction. Whereas a BRDF can take an arbitrary number of parameters (including surface attributes, the wavelength of light, and

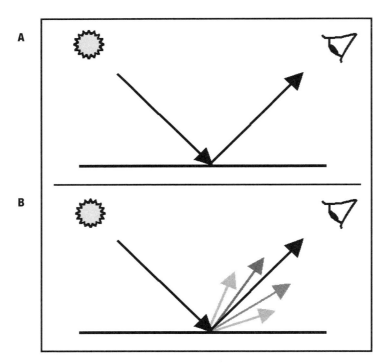

FIGURE 5.9.1. *a:* Simplified view of the reflection of light. *b:* A more realistic view of the reflection of light.

so on), the two *necessary* parameters are the light's incoming direction and the desired outgoing direction. BRDFs are usually used to model reflectance in global illumination solvers. Now, we see how they can be used to improve environment maps.

Wolfgang Heidrich and Hans-Peter Seidel describe a technique, called *glossy prefiltering*, that uses the Phong BRDF to apply appropriate blurring to environment maps. Each texel of the filtered environment map is produced by finding its corresponding unit vector (used as the outgoing direction) and computing the color at that texel with the following integral:

$$pref(\mathbf{o}) = s \cdot c \cdot \int_\Omega p(\mathbf{o} \cdot \mathbf{i})^{\frac{1}{r}} \cdot orig(\mathbf{i}) \cdot d\omega(\mathbf{i})$$

where:

orig is the original texture map.

pref is the prefiltered texture map.

r is the roughness parameter (reciprocal of the Phong exponent).

s is the coefficient of specularity.

c is the Phong correction factor, $(r+1) / \pi$.

$\mathbf{i}$ and $\mathbf{o}$ are the incoming and outgoing directions (respectively).

$p(x)$ is a function that returns x if x >= 0 and returns 0 otherwise.

Ω is the domain of the integral, the unit sphere.

$d\omega(\mathbf{i})$ is the measure of the solid angle in the direction of $\mathbf{i}$.

In order to be practical, glossy prefiltering requires an input texture with a high dynamic range, that is, a texture whose values extend beyond the [0..1] range. This range is needed to model the relatively high intensity of energy coming from light sources compared with the intensity of energy reflected off non-emitting surfaces. A normal texture can be converted to one with a high dynamic range by multiplying all texels corresponding to a light source by a large-scale factor. Note that the preceding equation is used to apply the Phong BRDF to environment maps. Jan Kautz and Michael McCool [Kautz00] describe a technique that allows for the use of any isotropic BRDF to prefilter environment maps.

Glossy prefiltering has many advantages: The prefiltering need be done only once, it's flexible, it's fairly easy to implement, and it requires no change to the rendering pipeline, since it merely filters traditional environment maps as a pre-process. The disadvantages of glossy prefiltering are that it's slow to compute (and can't be used for dynamic environment maps), it increases the memory requirements for textures (since each surface type requires an entirely new set of maps), it requires input textures with a high dynamic range, and it requires integrating over a sphere, which is non-trivial.

The Second Incorrect Assumption

Another assumption made when using environment maps is that the reflecting surface is metallic. When non-metallic surfaces reflect, the reflectance depends on the angle between incoming direction and the surface normal. The Fresnel term [Foley90] is used to simulate this dependency by modulating the reflectance. It uses the incoming light's angle and the surface's index of refraction to compute the appropriating weighting. The formula for the Fresnel term is:

$$ F = \frac{(g - k)^2}{2(g + k)^2} \left(1 + \frac{\left[k(g + k) - 1 \right]^2}{\left[k(g - k) + 1 \right]^2} \right) $$

where:

$k = \cos\theta$

θ is the angle between the incoming direction and the surface normal

$g = \eta_\lambda^2 + k^2 - 1$

η_λ is the index of refraction of the surface divided by the index of refraction of the transmitting medium, as a function of wavelength. Since the index of refraction for air is 1, you can usually simply supply the index of refraction of the surface.

Because in games you typically deal with surfaces and atmospheres that have a constant index of refraction, the only variable in the above equation is k. Thus, the Fresnel term can be written as a function of k, which is a variable in the range $[0..1]$. Thus, as noted by Heidrich and Seidel, we can precompute the Fresnel term and store it as a one-dimensional texture. By rendering the Fresnel term into the alpha channel, we can incorporate it into the rendering pipeline using either of the following methods:

$$ C_f = C_m * F + C_d \quad or \qquad C_f = C_m * F + C_d * (1 - F) $$

where:

C_f, C_m, C_d are the final (output), mirror, and diffuse color values, respectively.
F is the Fresnel term.

Using the Fresnel term in this way provides a more realistic reflection while consuming very little memory. The disadvantage is that using it could require an additional pass.

Conclusion

With the high performance of texture-mapping hardware and the increasing size of texture memory, it makes sense to use texture-mapping techniques to improve the quality of rendered images. In this article, two such techniques were presented. Each is simple and requires very little work to incorporate into existing rendering pipelines.

Acknowledgments

I would like to thank Michael McCool, Michael Anttila, Sim Dietrich, and Mark DeLoura for reviewing this article.

References

[Blinn76] Blinn, J., and Newell, M., "Texture and Reflection in Computer-Generated Images," *Communications of the ACM*, 19:542-546, 1976.

[Heidrich99] Heidrich, W., and Seidel, H.-P., "Realistic, Hardware-Accelerated Shading and Lighting," *SIGGRAPH '99 Proceedings*, pages 171–178, August 1999.

[Foley90] Foley, J., van Dam, A., Feiner, S., and Hughes, J., *Computer Graphics: Principles and Practice*, pp. 766–770, 1990.

[Kautz00] Kautz, J., and McCool, M., "Approximation of Glossy Reflection with Prefiltered Environment Maps," *Proceedings Graphics Interface*

5.10

Convincing-Looking Glass for Games

Gabor Nagy

This article presents a few extensions to the algorithms most widely used to render glass objects in real time.

Introduction

Rendering good-looking glass objects at interactive frame rates has long been a challenge. Until we have computer hardware that is fast enough for real-time ray tracing, we must compromise somewhere.

Transparent Objects

There are three main visual properties of glass. A glass object is usually:

- **Transparent.** It lets through some of the light hitting it, making objects behind it partly visible.
- **Refractive.** It refracts light going through it and distorts the environment that shows through.
- **Reflective.** It reflects some of the light hitting it, making the environment show on its surface.

This article mainly deals with the transparent and reflective properties of glass.

Rasterizer, Frame Buffer, Z-Buffer, and Pixel Blending

To draw a transparent object with today's 3D hardware, we usually use the feature called *pixel blending*, or simply *blending*. Pixel blending is implemented in the last stage of a rendering pipeline, in the *pixel renderer*, after rasterization.

The rasterizer does the conversion of a primitive (triangle, line, and so on) into pixels with X and Y screen coordinates and a depth (Z) value.

A simple pixel rendered with Z-buffering enabled will:

- Compute the Z (depth) value of a pixel to be drawn.
- Compare that value with the Z value stored at the corresponding position in the Z-buffer.
- If it is determined that the pixel to be drawn is closer to the viewer (it is in front of the object or objects already drawn at that location), it simply overwrites the pixel color and Z value in their respective buffers; if not, it does not change the frame buffer or Z-buffer at all.

In OpenGL, a smaller Z value means that a pixel is closer to the viewer. Before drawing a scene, the Z-buffer is initialized (cleared) to the maximum Z value at each pixel. This value depends on the bit-depth of the Z-buffer. Note that this value might be the exact opposite, depending on your 3D API and hardware.

Opaque Objects vs. Transparent Objects

Because the standard Z-buffer technique simply overwrites a pixel if it belongs to a surface that is closer to the viewer than the one already drawn, it is only capable of drawing perfectly opaque surfaces. To draw a transparent surface, instead of overwriting the pixel color in the frame buffer with the incoming (source) color, we need to somehow blend the two colors.

In OpenGL, we can use the blending function to perform this task. We can define the blending function by calling:

```
glBlendFunc(sfactor, dfactor);
```

The color to put in the frame buffer is usually determined by:

$$RGB_{result} = RGB_{source} * sfactor + RGB_{destination} * dfactor$$

where RGB_{result} represents the red, green, and blue components to be put in the frame buffer, RGB_{source} is the incoming pixel components, and $RGB_{destination}$ is the value already in the frame buffer at the corresponding pixel.

Depending on the OpenGL version, sfactor and dfactor can have many different predefined constants. For example:

```
glBlendFunc(GL_ONE, GL_ZERO);
```

does a simple overwrite, because:

$$RGB_{result} = RGB_{source} * 1 + RGB_{destination} * 0$$

For another example, if we want to add the current pixel color to the one already in the frame buffer, we can call:

```
glBlendFunc(GL_ONE, GL_ONE);
```

This gives us the following blending formula:

$$RGB_{result} = RGB_{source} * 1 + RGB_{destination} * 1$$

To make pixel blending work in OpenGL, we have to enable it by calling:

```
glEnable(GL_BLEND);
```

For a full description of pixel blending, please refer to your OpenGL manual [Woo97].

Since we have to consider the Z values, we refer to pixels as *RGBZ*.

When rendering a 3D scene with transparent objects, we can have one of the following cases. The pixel currently being rendered ($RGBZ_{source}$) belongs to either an opaque object or a transparent one and:

- Its Z value indicates that it is closer to the viewer than the corresponding pixel ($RGBZ_{destination}$) already in the frame buffer (it is in front of the object or objects already drawn at that location).
- It is further from the viewer than $RGBZ_{destination}$.
- It is at the same distance as $RGBZ_{destination}$.

Drawing Opaque Objects

Let's examine what happens when we draw an opaque object. If $RGBZ_{source}$ is closer to the viewer than $RGBZ_{destination}$, we can simply overwrite the frame buffer with it. However, if $RGBZ_{source}$ is further than $RGBZ_{destination}$, we might still have to draw it if it is "behind" a transparent object! Usually, we can simply avoid this problem by drawing all the opaque objects first.

Drawing Transparent Objects

We use the value A_{source} (*Alpha* or *Opacity* value) to define how opaque the currently drawn pixel is. A_{source}=0.0 means that the pixel is completely transparent; 1.0 means it's completely opaque. If the pixel being drawn ($RGBZ_{source}$) is *in front of* the one in the frame buffer ($RGBZ_{destination}$), we need this formula to determine the resulting color:

Blend Formula A: $RGB_{result} = RGB_{source} * A_{source} + RGB_{destination} * (1.0 - A_{source})$

If $RGBZ_{source}$ is behind $RGBZ_{destination}$, we need this formula:

Blend Formula B: $RGB_{result} = RGB_{source} * (1.0 - A_{destination}) + RGB_{destination} * A_{destination}$

This formula uses the presence of alpha-bitplanes in the frame buffer to keep track of the opacity of each pixel; see [Woo97] for more details. We also have to update the alpha values of the pixels drawn.

Clearly, we have two different blending functions, or two different courses of action to take, depending on whether $RGBZ_{source}$ is in front of $RGBZ_{destination}$ or behind it. Since we can define only one blending function at a time, we have to find a work-around for this problem.

Depth Complexity

The core of the problem is *depth complexity*: the possibly multiple pixels (belonging to different primitives) occupying the same screen position but with different depth values.

A depth complexity of 1 means that there are no primitives overlapping on the screen. We would not even need Z-buffering in this case. When drawing a transparent primitive, we only have to blend it with the background color, using Blend Formula A.

A depth complexity of 2 means that the number of overlapping primitives at each pixel is 2. In this case, an opaque pixel either obscures the background or a transparent pixel or it is behind only *one* opaque or transparent pixel.

Note that the depth complexity of a 3D scene can change when the camera moves.

Fortunately, OpenGL gives us some control over how the Z-buffering is performed. Specifically, we can disable Z overwriting, so when a pixel is drawn, only the RGB values are changed in the frame buffer. Combined with some other features, this allows us to find solutions for most cases.

A Simple Solution

To draw opaque and transparent objects in the same image, we can take a not perfectly correct but simple approach:

- Clear the Z-buffer.
- Draw all the opaque primitives (triangles, lines, and the like) with Z-testing and Z-overwriting enabled.
- Draw transparent primitives with back-face culling enabled (to minimize depth complexity between transparent pixels), Z-overwriting *disabled*, and using Blend Formula A.

This method makes sure that opaque surfaces always obscure transparent ones and that opaque surfaces behind transparent ones show through. It also guarantees that two transparent surfaces always blend correctly if both surfaces have an alpha value of 0.5, because $0.5 = 1.0 - 0.5$, so Blend Formula A and Blend Formula B are equivalent. Therefore, it does not matter if the currently drawn transparent pixel is behind or in front of the one in the frame buffer. For alpha values other than 0.5 or more than two transparent objects behind each other, the results are not accurate but are still acceptable in many cases.

"Simple" Solution #2

This method is designed to solve the problems mentioned in the previous section by making sure that the currently drawn primitive is always in front of the one already in the frame buffer:

- Clear Z-buffer.
- Draw all the opaque primitives (triangles, lines, and so on).
- Sort all transparent primitives by depth and draw them in farthest-to-nearest order.

This way we need only Blend Formula A.

The major caveat of this approach is that the depth sorting might cause a significant performance hit, especially if there are many transparent objects in different hierarchy nodes. There are also cases in which a primitive is neither completely in front nor completely behind another (as in Figure 5.10.1), so we need a per-pixel depth sort, which would be extremely computationally expensive.

As long as the depth sorting works correctly, there is no limit to the depth complexity this method can handle. Note that with this method, we don't have to draw the opaque objects first, but doing so could simplify the process.

A Slightly Different Approach

OpenGL lets us choose a *depth function* for Z-buffering. The depth function determines which Z values pass the Z-comparison. In OpenGL, it is usually *less-than*, which means that if a pixel's Z value is less than the value in the Z-buffer, the pixel is

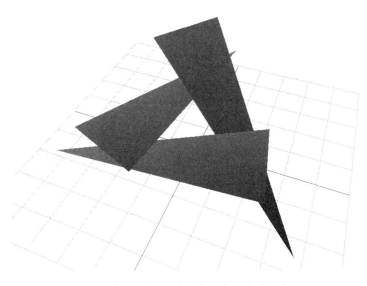

FIGURE 5.10.1. Indeterminate depth order of triangles.

drawn. This allows us to split the drawing of a primitive into two steps, using two different blending formulas. We need the presence of alpha values in the frame buffer for this method.

The process is shown below:

1. Clear Z-buffer.
2. Clear the alpha-buffer with value 0 (transparent).
3. Set Z function to *greater-than* (draw behind), use Blend Formula A, and draw the first transparent primitive with Z overwriting disabled. In addition, write the alpha value of the primitive into the frame buffer so that subsequent pixels behind it are blended correctly.
4. Set Z function to *less-than-or-equal* (draw in front), use Blend Formula A, and draw this primitive again with Z overwriting enabled. Write the alpha value of the primitive in the frame buffer so that subsequent pixels behind it are blended correctly.
5. Repeat the last two steps for each transparent primitive.
6. Set Z function to *greater-than* (draw behind), use Blend Formula B, and draw all opaque primitives with Z overwriting disabled. The alpha value to write in the frame buffer is 1.0 (or the maximum integer value).
7. Set Z function to *less-than-or-equal* (draw in front) and draw all opaque primitives with Z overwriting enabled and blending disabled.

Unfortunately, if more than one pixel is drawn in any given position of the frame buffer (with different depths), the opacity of this pixel can no longer be represented by a single value. It depends on the depth or how many pixels there are in front of the one being drawn. This is caused by the height-field-like nature of the Z-buffer: It can store only one depth value on a pixel, with subsequent pixels overwriting the old values. In other words, the Z-buffer has a fixed-depth complexity of 1.

Take the example in Figures 5.10.2a and 5.10.2b. Assuming that there are two surfaces drawn in the frame buffer:

- *Surface$_1$ – Alpha: A$_1$ = 0.5*
- *Surface$_2$ – Alpha: A$_2$ = 0.75*

If P, the pixel being drawn, is between *Surface$_1$* and *Surface$_2$*, $A_{destination}$ is 0.5 (only *Surface$_1$* is in front of P). However, if P is behind both *Surface$_1$* and *Surface$_2$*, $A_{destination}$ is the *cumulative opacity* of *Surface$_1$* and *Surface$_2$*, which is $A_1*A_2=0.375$.

This approach is slightly more flexible than the one described in our simple solution, without having to depth-sort the transparent primitives, but it has more limitations and is more complicated than Solution #2. Furthermore, the frequent changing of the depth function at each primitive might cause a noticeable performance hit. A slight "tuning" of this method is recommended, depending on the application (especially regarding the modification of the alpha values in the frame buffer).

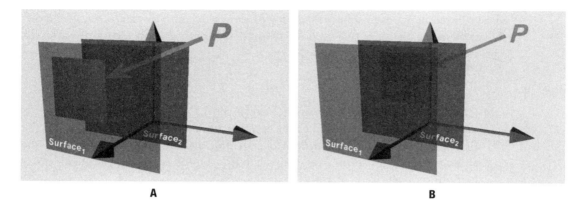

A   **B**

FIGURE 5.10.2. *a:* Effect of a single transparent surface on a pixel behind it. *b:* Cumulative effect of multiple transparent surfaces.

Non-Planar Glass Objects

If we look at a glass bottle or cup, we notice that it appears darker at the edges, where the surface normal starts to point away from the viewer. This is because light coming through the object is refracted at higher angles, so less of it reaches the viewer. We can simulate this effect by illuminating the object with a light source that is always at the same position as the camera (a "head-light"). Such a light source produces less illumination the more the surface normal points away from the viewer. A simple diffuse head-light is very easy to implement and is computationally inexpensive.

Reflections

For simulating reflections, we can use sphere- or cube-environment mapping. OpenGL supports the use of spherical environment maps (with fish-eye images as environment maps). After initializing a texture, we can enable sphere mapping with the following calls:

```
glTexGeni(GL_S, GL_TEXTURE_GEN_MODE, GL_SPHERE_MAP);
glTexGeni(GL_T, GL_TEXTURE_GEN_MODE, GL_SPHERE_MAP);
glEnable(GL_TEXTURE_GEN_S);
glEnable(GL_TEXTURE_GEN_T);
```

There are many excellent articles on this subject, so please refer to them for further details (see References).

Colored Glass

Until now, we referred to the opacity of a surface as a single value. If a surface is behind a transparent one, the surface in front evenly decreased the R, G, and B color components of the one behind. We can use different opacity values for the R, G, and B components to describe the pigment in a piece of colored glass. This might require the use of multiple drawing passes as described in the following sections.

Putting It All Together

Single-pass Rendering

We can render the glass object in a single pass with:

- An environment map applied as a 2D texture, the texture coordinates computed by a sphere-mapping algorithm
- "MODULATE" texturing algorithm and a head-light
- The proper pixel blending and Z testing set up to draw it as a transparent object (as described in our earlier solutions)

Multipass Rendering

To gain more control over the final appearance, we can perform two rendering passes:

1. Pixel blending and Z testing set up to draw it as a transparent object (as described previously). We can also apply lighting on the object to simulate a diffuse surface on the glass.
2. Render the reflections on top, using additive blending (as in the single-pass case).

With two passes, we can define both the opacity and the reflectivity of an object by changing the blending factors at each pass. We can also apply more complex formulas with multiple passes.

Implementation

For implementation details with OpenGL, please refer to the sample program and the comments in the source code on the included CD that accompanies this book.

To see what this technique looks like in action, take a look at Color Plates 8–11. These images were rendered on a Sony PlayStation 2.

References

[Greene86] Greene, Ned, "Environment Mapping and Other Applications of World Projections," *IEEE Computer Graphics and Applications,* volume 6. number 11, pp. 21–29 November 1986.

[Woo97] Woo, Mason, Neider, Jackie, and Davis, Tom, *OpenGL Programming Guide,* second edition, Addison-Wesley Developers Press, Silicon Graphics, 1997.

5.11

Refraction Mapping for Liquids in Containers

Alex Vlachos and Jason L. Mitchell

In this article, we present a concise and practical method of refraction-mapping liquids in opaque containers on real-time consumer 3D accelerators. Refraction, reflection, and Fresnel terms are computed for water simulations at interactive rates. Methods for enhancing realism, including caustic effects and particulate matter are also addressed.

Introduction

The goal of this article is to present a rendering solution only. We are not constrained by the water simulation used. For the sample code provided, however, we have chosen to use surface simulations based on Erik Larsen's newave sample (available online at http://reality.sgi.com/opengl/glut3/glut3.html).

The illumination equation computed by this rendering method is fairly typical in that it incorporates refractive, reflective, and Fresnel terms. The Fresnel term is essentially used as a blend factor between the refractive and reflective terms [Ts'o87]:

Result = Fresnel * Refraction + (1-Fresnel) * Reflection

This is also a common practice in RenderMan shaders [Apodaca99].

Additionally, we address techniques for illuminating the interior of the container as well as computing caustic effects. For all these techniques, we assume that the viewer is outside the container and that the container is opaque.

Refraction Term

Snell's Law

A ray from the eye to each vertex in the water simulation is computed. This is the eye ray in Figure 5.11.1. Snell's Law is then used to refract the eye ray for each of these vertices. This mesh of polygons represents the interface between the air and water.

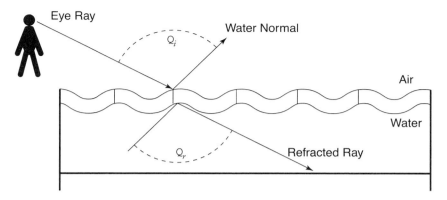

FIGURE 5.11.1. Snell's Law in practice.

Since the ratio of indices of refraction of water to air is 1.33, we use this value to compute the refracted ray as a function of the water normal at the given vertex, as shown in Figure 5.11.1.

Referring to Figure 5.11.1, the angle between the water normal and the eye ray (Θ_i) is known as the *angle of incidence*. The angle between the refracted ray and the negated water normal (Θ_r) is known as the *angle of refraction*. Snell's Law expresses the relationship between these two angles and the ratio of the indices of refraction of the two media (air and water) as:

$$n_i \sin(\Theta_i) = n_r \sin(\Theta_r) \quad \text{or} \quad (n_i / n_r) \sin(\Theta_i) = \sin(\Theta_r)$$

For the air-to-water interface, n_i / n_r is 1.333, which gives us a simple formula for computing Θ_r from Θ_i:

$$\Theta_r = arcsin[1.333 \, sin(\Theta_i)]$$

From here it is a simple matter to compute the refracted ray from the eye ray so that we can then determine the intersection with the container.

Intersecting with the Container

Once the refracted ray is computed, it is necessary to determine the point of intersection of the refracted ray with the container. This step is the key to giving the visual impression of a container of a particular shape. Paraboloid or hemisphere intersection tests, although simple and efficient, invariably give the impression of a dish-shaped container, particularly if the viewer can move interactively in the scene. The water demo used at the Microsoft X-Box launch is an example of this [McQuade2000]. To give the impression of a more complex and realistic container, we have experimented with a number of geometrically simple containers, and the results have been quite convincing. In this article, we stick with a simple parallelepiped container for brevity.

FIGURE 5.11.2. The refraction map (also see Color Plate 12).

Referring back to Figure 5.11.1, we are now interested in intersecting the refracted ray with the walls of the container. In this case, our container is made up of five rectangular faces. Ray-plane intersections are computed for each face until the intersection with the container is found. Once this point is known, we convert this position on the inside of the container to a texture coordinate in a single refraction map, which shows all five faces of the container, as in Figure 5.11.2.

In Figure 5.11.1, the refracted ray intersects the bottom face of the pool. This generates a texture coordinate in the corresponding region of the refraction map shown in Figure 5.11.2.

Illumination of the Container Interior

It is possible to pre-light the interior of the container to further integrate the container into the rest of the scene. This is an important visual cue to consider when using your water simulation in a larger scene. The source code included on the CD that accompanies this book demonstrates the technique without additional geometry surrounding the water pool, but the same technique, with the pre-lit refraction map shown in Figure 5.11.2, has been incorporated into the *radiATIon* graphics engine and is shown in Color Plates 13–16.

Reflection Term

Any typical parameterization can be used for the reflective term of the illumination. We chose to use a single-paraboloid environment map [Heidrich98] for our static scenes because this is supported on a wide array of hardware. A cube map could easily be used for dynamic scenes. A dynamically updated planar reflection map can also be appropriate in some circumstances.

Fresnel Term

Now that the reflection and refraction terms have been computed, they must be combined using a Fresnel term. For details on the Fresnel equations, see the article "Improving Environment-Mapped Reflection Using Glossy Prefiltering and the Fresnel Term" elsewhere in this book. For the purposes of this article, the Fresnel equations determine the ratio of reflected light to refracted light at a point on the water surface as a function of the viewer's angle to the surface. In computer graphics, this term is usually treated as simply a blend factor between the refractive and reflective terms, but it can also work well when multiplied only with the reflection map [Ts'o87], [Apodaca99].

Additionally, the function itself can be modeled as a simple sinusoid or sinusoid-squared falloff in the range of zero to one and tuned to taste. The sample program on the accompanying CD computes the dot product between the water normal and the eye ray at each vertex. This gives the cosine between the vectors, which can be used directly as the Fresnel term or squared for a different look.

This equation can be evaluated directly at each vertex and linearly interpolated across each polygon, as in the sample on the CD, or it can be computed per pixel as a texture lookup [Bastos99].

Rendering with Hardware

All these computations have generated texture coordinates for the vertices in the mesh representing the interface between the air and water. The texture maps used are static, and the mesh can be rendered in a single pass on consumer-level hardware that supports at least two-texture multitexturing, the EXT_texture_env_combine extension and the EXT_texgen_reflection extension, for a single paraboloid environment map. The Fresnel term serves as the blend factor between the two maps and is stored in the primary color interpolator's alpha channel. Recall that our goal is to compute the following equation:

*Result = Fresnel * Refraction + (1-Fresnel) * Reflection*

With the reflection map in texture zero, the refraction map in texture 1, and the Fresnel term in the primary color's alpha channel, we can do this blend using `ARB_multitexture` and `EXT_texture_env_combine`:

```
glActiveTexture(GL_TEXTURE0_ARB);
glTexEnvf(GL_TEXTURE_ENV, GL_TEXTURE_ENV_MODE, GL_COMBINE_EXT);
glTexEnvf(GL_TEXTURE_ENV, GL_SOURCE0_RGB_EXT, GL_TEXTURE);
glTexEnvf(GL_TEXTURE_ENV, GL_OPERAND0_RGB_EXT, GL_SRC_COLOR);
glTexEnvf(GL_TEXTURE_ENV, GL_SOURCE1_RGB_EXT,
        GL_PRIMARY_COLOR_EXT);
glTexEnvf(GL_TEXTURE_ENV, GL_OPERAND1_RGB_EXT, GL_SRC_ALPHA);
glTexEnvf(GL_TEXTURE_ENV, GL_COMBINE_RGB_EXT, GL_MODULATE);
glTexEnvf(GL_TEXTURE_ENV, GL_RGB_SCALE_EXT, 1.0f);
glTexEnvf(GL_TEXTURE_ENV, GL_SOURCE0_ALPHA_EXT,
        GL_PRIMARY_COLOR_EXT);
glTexEnvf(GL_TEXTURE_ENV, GL_OPERAND0_ALPHA_EXT, GL_SRC_ALPHA);
glTexEnvf(GL_TEXTURE_ENV, GL_COMBINE_ALPHA_EXT, GL_REPLACE);
glTexEnvf(GL_TEXTURE_ENV, GL_ALPHA_SCALE, 1.0f);

glActiveTexture(GL_TEXTURE1_ARB);
glTexEnvf(GL_TEXTURE_ENV, GL_TEXTURE_ENV_MODE, GL_COMBINE_EXT);
glTexEnvf(GL_TEXTURE_ENV, GL_SOURCE0_RGB_EXT, GL_TEXTURE);
glTexEnvf(GL_TEXTURE_ENV, GL_OPERAND0_RGB_EXT, GL_SRC_COLOR);
glTexEnvf(GL_TEXTURE_ENV, GL_SOURCE1_RGB_EXT, GL_PREVIOUS_EXT);
glTexEnvf(GL_TEXTURE_ENV, GL_OPERAND1_RGB_EXT, GL_SRC_COLOR);
glTexEnvf(GL_TEXTURE_ENV, GL_COMBINE_RGB_EXT, GL_ADD);
glTexEnvf(GL_TEXTURE_ENV, GL_RGB_SCALE_EXT, 1.0f);
glTexEnvf(GL_TEXTURE_ENV, GL_SOURCE0_ALPHA_EXT, GL_PREVIOUS_EXT);
glTexEnvf(GL_TEXTURE_ENV, GL_OPERAND0_ALPHA_EXT, GL_SRC_ALPHA);
glTexEnvf(GL_TEXTURE_ENV, GL_COMBINE_ALPHA_EXT, GL_REPLACE);
glTexEnvf(GL_TEXTURE_ENV, GL_ALPHA_SCALE, 1.0f);
```

Since this is just a blend between two static textures, the stress put on the rendering system is minimal; this technique is so far just a method for computing texture coordinates. In spite of this simplicity, the visual results are surprisingly realistic.

Future Extensions to This Technique

We have outlined a simple equation for water that includes reflection, refraction, and Fresnel terms. Other visual phenomena, such as caustics and scattering due to particulate matter, can be modeled as well.

Caustics Inside the Container

One of the most important extensions to this technique is the use of caustic effects on the interior of the container. One way to incorporate caustics into the scene is to model the refraction of light rays from a given light source and their intersection with the container in much the same way that we are modeling this for the viewer's position. Light transported along these rays could then be accumulated into a dynamic "caustic map," which would be composited with the refraction map using multitexture [Stam96]. Then again, for some applications, it might suffice to simply use a static caustic map that scrolls along the interior of the pool over time. See the article "Advanced Texturing Using Texture Coordinate Generation" for a discussion of how to use the texture matrix to scroll texture coordinates frame to frame. This inexpensive technique was used in the Zora's Domain level of *The Legend of Zelda: The Ocarina of Time* to give the impression of caustics reflected off the surface of a lake onto the surrounding cave walls.

Modeling Particulate Matter

Modeling the particulate matter present in the water is an important visual cue that can easily be added to this system. In fact, the distance that the refracted ray travels through the medium in the container is computed as a by-product of the intersection test. Using this term, it is possible to blend in a "water color" at the vertices in much the same way that terrain engines and flight simulators blend in a fog color to simulate atmospheric effects. It should be noted that only the refractive term is affected by particulate matter in the water.

Conclusion

We have presented a concise method of simulating refractive, reflective, and Fresnel effects of liquids in simple geometric containers in real time on consumer 3D hardware. The technique was designed from the outset to run efficiently on consumer graphics accelerators. As such, the technique in its current state merely computes new texture coordinates for the reflection and refraction maps and does no updates to the textures themselves.

We have also presented some areas for extending the technique to include caustics and particulate matter as well as ideas for implementing these extensions.

References

[Apodaca99] Apodaca, A., and Gritz, L., *Advanced RenderMan: Creating CGI for Motion Pictures*, Morgan Kaufmann, 1999.

[Bastos99] Bastos, R., Hoff, K., Wynn, W., and Lastra, A., "Increased Photorealism for Interactive Architectural Walkthroughs," *ACM Symposium on Interactive 3D Graphics,* pp. 183–190, 1999.

[Heidrich98] Heidrich, W., and Seidel, H.-P., "View-independent Environment Maps," Eurographics/ACM SIGGRAPH Workshop on Graphics Hardware, 1998.

[McQuade00] McQuade, L., *Personal Communication,* 2000.

[Ts'o87] Ts'o, P., and Barsky, B., "Modeling and Rendering Waves: Wave Tracing Using Beta-Splines and Reflective and Refractive Texture Mapping," *ACM Transactions on Graphics* (6), pp. 191–214, 1987.

[Stam96] Stam, J., "Random Caustics: Natural Textures and Wave Theory Revisited," SIGGRAPH , available online at www.syntim.inria.fr/syntim/research/stam/caustics.html, 1996.

The Matrix Utility Library

Dante Treglia II and Mark A. DeLoura

Matrix libraries are an integral part of game programming, and essential in a wide variety of applications such as advanced graphics, physics, collision detection, etc. It was inevitable that many of the articles would need to use some matrix operations outside of the OpenGL matrix functions. Therefore, with the input of many contributors, a C++ matrix library was written for all accompanying demo software to utilize. It was intentionally designed to be an instructional tool, easy to read, and general purpose, so very few optimizations have been added. We encourage you to customize the library for your game, and optimize it for your environment.

Specification

The libraries contain five main classes: vector2, vector3, vector4, matrix33, and matrix44. These represent vectors and matrices of the corresponding size (e.g., matrix44 is a 4x4 matrix). Vectors have public members called *x*, *y*, *z*, and *w*, and matrices are composed of arrays of vectors. This library was designed to provide the same functionality and format as the OpenGL matrix functions; therefore, matrices are maintained in column-row order. Most of the standard matrix and vector operators have been overloaded; however, the cross product and dot product operations are provided as utility functions for a more coherent notation.

```
vector3 vec;
vector3 vec1(0.0, 1.0, 0.0);
vector3 vec2(1.0, 0.0, 0.0);
matrix44 mtx = RotateRadMatrix44('x', DegToRad(45.0));

vec = mtx * CrossProduct(vec1, vec2);
```

LISTING 6.0.1. Answer: vec = [0.0, 0.707107, -0.707107]

There are a few things to keep in mind when using these libraries. First of all, the default constructors do not initialize members of each class. This eliminates redundant operations for instances of vectors or matrices whose members are immediately set. The classes provide appropriate initialization constructors and set methods. Second, a point class is not provided. You will need to ensure that a homogenous component is set (usually to 1.0) for vectors that are treated as points. Finally, if you need to load a matrix onto the OpenGL matrix stack, it is safe to cast a pointer-to-matrix44 to a pointer-to-float. Enjoy!

```
vector4 point3;
matrix44 tranMtx = TranslateMatrix44(-10.0, 0.0, 5.0);

point3.set(0.0, 0.0, 0.0, 1.0);
point3 = tranMtx * point3;
```

LISTING 6.0.2. Answer: point3 = [-10.0, 0.0, 5.0, 1.0]

Source Code

The code for the entire matrix library is on the CD. Please refer to the library for more information on how to use it.

Acknowledgments

Special thanks to everyone who contributed to this library, especially Stan Melax, Miguel Gomez, Pete Isensee, Gabor Nagy, Scott Bilas, James Boer, and Eric Lengyel.

6.1

The Text Utility Library

Dante Treglia II

There comes a point in every game's development when output is necessary. For such purposes, it is very convenient to have this output displayed on the screen, especially if your game uses full screen mode. Many games today have "console" modes, which in most cases were used by the programmer during the development of the game. You may find it beneficial to write such a library and incorporate it into your game. This text library is a basic implementation of an output text library written for OpenGL. It is small, easy to use, and most importantly, easy to hack! The texture used to create each 8x8 character is only 16KBytes, so this library is perfect for debugging and profiling.

Specification

The text utility library is composed of one class named TextBox. It provides two methods for drawing text to the screen. The first is by providing a screen coordinate and a string. The library automatically pushes the necessary orthographic projection to draw the text in screen space. It also pops the matrix, which preserves the previous matrix state. The second method is a customized version of the first. It requires that you initialize an area of the screen to be the "text box." Then, all the text printed to this box (there can be multiple boxes) will wrap and scroll within the box, much like a standard shell. A convenient printf() function, similar to the standard C function, is used to print text. Unlike the first method, the text is stored in memory until the next screen is drawn, so the printf() function can be used at any point during the game. Text can be printed in any color with a transparent or opaque background.

Source Code

The entire source code for the text utility library is contained on the CD, along with a demo. Please see the code for more details on how to use it.

6.2

About the CD-ROM

Mark A. DeLoura

Enclosed with this book you will find a CD-ROM that is filled with all of the code from this volume and more! We feel very strongly that for this book to really be of use to you, you need to have the source code in a form that you can use.

Here are a few of the things you'll find on the CD-ROM:

- All the source code listed in each article.
- Complete demos of many of the technologies described in this book. The demos run under Windows and Linux.
- The glSetup Monolithic version.
- The GLUT (OpenGL Utility Toolkit) distribution.
- The Matrix Utility Library.
- The Text Utility Library.
- Links to groovy game programming sites.

Complete installation and usage instructions are included on the CD-ROM in the AboutThisCD.htm file. Please read this first.

Also, be sure to check out the Website, www.gameprogramminggems.com/ for more information about the book and about game programming in general!

Index

A* algorithm
  aesthetic optimizations, 264–271
  Master Node List and Priority Queue Open List
    implementation, 285–286
  navigation meshes and, 294–295
  pathfinding, 294
  path planning with, 254–262
  priority queues for speed, 281–282, 283–286
  speed optimizations for, 272–287
  weaknesses of, 261–262
AI. *See* Artificial Intelligence (AI)
Alignment, 305–306
Alpha-beta pruning, 251–253
Alpha blending, 193, 522–523
Animations
  keyframing for, 465–470
  light motif, 528–534
  texture coordinate animation, 549–550
ArrayProxy class, 103
Arrays
  bit arrays, 101–103
  Compiled Vertex Arrays (CVA), 356–358, 359–360
  See also Vectors
Artificial Intelligence (AI)
  engine design, 221–236
  finite-state machines, 237–248
  fuzzy logic, 319–329
  neural nets and, 330–350
  scripting behavior outside code, 234
  in scripts, 6
Assert macros, 109–114
  copy-and-paste, 113–114
  customizing, 111–112, 113–114
  embedding and, 110–111
  "Ignore Always" option, 112–113
  superassert implementation, 113
Association
  auto- and heteroassociation, 336
  Hopfield nets for, 346–350
  neural nets and, 332, 336
Attenuation maps, 543–548

Autonomous agents, 305
Avoidance, 306

BaseResource class, 80–83
Basic object memory manager, 68
Bell, Ian, 133
Binary trees, wavelets principle and, 182–184
BitArray class, 101–102
BitArray2D class, 102–103
BitArray2D class, 102–103
BitProxy class, 102
Bitwise operations, 101–103
Blitting functions, 523
Boids, 305
  CBoid class, 311–312, 314–317
  constraints on, 308–309
  perception range of, 308
Bones. *See* Skeletal representations
Bot creation, 6
Bounding volumes, 380
  octrees and, 440, 445–446
  sphere collision detection algorithm, 390–393
Braben, David, 133
Branching instruction in script languages, 5
B-splines
  camera control curves, 374–376
  vs. hermite splines, 470
Bugs. *See* Debugging
Buildings, 490–498
  algorithms for, 492–493
Bump mapping
  applying to objects, 555–556
  normals, choosing space for, 556–557
  tangent space bump mapping, 557–559
  texture space bump mapping, 559–561
Buoyancy, simulating, 191–193

Calderas, inverting, 509–510
Calling conventions, 61–62
Calls
  profiler, 123

remote procedure calls (RPCs), 56–58
Cameras
  B-spline curves for control, 374–376
  control techniques for, 371–379
  damping, 377–378
  exposed functionality of, 3
  eye space and depth value, 363–364
  first-person cameras, 371–373
  lens flare simulations, 515–518
  level of detail and, 433–434
  orientation of, 366, 373
  quaternions and control of, 379
  scripted cameras, 373–377
  third-person cameras, 378
  vector cameras, 366–370
  zooming, 377
Catmull-Rom splines, 266, 267, 376–377
Caustics, simulating, 598–599
CBoid class, 311–312, 314–317
CBox class, 309–310
CEaseInOutInterpolation class, 149
CEaseOutDivideInterpolation class, 147
CEaseOutShiftInterpolation class, 147–148
CFlock class, 310–311, 312–314
Chaos, adding via messaging, 223
Classes, C++
  coupling, avoiding, 15–16
  designing in Object-Oriented Programming (OOP),
    11–12
  finite-state machine class, 237–248
  handle class, 70
  manager classes, 15–16
  proxy classes, 102–103
  See also Specific classes
CLinearInterpolation, 148
Code
  in-game profiling, 120–130
  reusing, 8
Cohesion, 305–306
Collision detection, 390–402
  bounding sphere, 390–393
  line-plane intersection, 394–395
  octree construction for culling, 439–443
  point-in-triangle test, 396–397
  triangle "flattening," 395–396
  triangle-to-triangle, 390, 393–397
Compiled Vertex Arrays (CVA), 356–358, 359–360
Compilers
  calling conventions of, 61–62
  limitations of, 24, 31
  templates as virtual, 20–22
Composition, 12
Compression methods

image compression, 185–186
  wavelets, 182–186
Console game systems
  data loading, 90–91
  debugging, 115–119
  depth-of-play technique, 133–140
Constants, in data-driven design, 3–4
Containers
  associative containers, 42
  container adapters, 42, 53–54, 281–282
  maps, 50–53
  STL, 41–42
Containment, 12
Costs
  arrival costs, 295
  heuristic cost, 276–278
  path function cost, 259–260, 264–265
Coupling of classes, avoiding, 15–16
Crisp sets, 319–320
Crosstalk, 336–337
Culling
  Field of View Culling Code, 425–429
  frustum culling, 422–423
  occlusion culling, 421–431
  octree construction for, 439–443
Cylinder-frustum intersection test, 380–389
  algorithms, 382–384
  radii, calculation of effective, 382, 383
Cylinders, generalized, 258
Cylinder tests, 380–389

Damping, 377–378
Data
  bit arrays for, 101–103
  duplicate data syndrome, 6–7
  inheritance, 6–7
  junk data and security, 107
  loading quickly, 88–91
  preprocessing, 88
  saving, 89
  tools for creating, 7
  wavelets as analysis tool, 185–186
Databases, handle-based resource manager for, 68–79
Data-driven design, 3–7
  duplicate data, 6–7
  editing tools in, 7
  hard coding and, 3–5
  text files and, 3
Debugging
  console game systems, 115–119
  logs and, 233
  messages and, 222
  real-time in-game profiling, 120–130

Stats system for, 115–119
Defuzzification methods, 327–328
Depth values of vertex, 361–365
Deques, 41–42
  Standard Template Library (STL), 48–50
Designing, 11–12
Detail, levels of, 432–438
  view-independent progressive meshes, 454–464
Diagonalizing, 156
Diamond-square algorithm, 505–507
Dijkstra's algorithm, 294
Distance, computing, 412–420
DLLs, generic function-binding, 56
Doom, 490–491
Double-ended queues, 41–42, 48–50
Duplicate data syndrome, 6–7
Dynamic Link Libraries (DLLs), generic function-binding, 56, 66

Edges
  difficult, 458–459
  edge choice functions, 458
  edge collapse, 455, 461–462
  selection improvements, 462
Editing tools
  in data-driven design, 7
  game level, 7
  Stats system for data-editing, 115–119
Eigenvalues and eigenvectors, 156
Elite, 133, 493–495
Embedding, 12
  assert macro and information embedding, 110–111
Encryption
  online games and, 104–108
  reverse engineering and, 107
Enemy Nations, 307
Engines, AI
  event-driven *vs.* polling objects, 221–222
  ideal characteristics of, 221
  message objects, 222–223
  state machines, 223–225
Engines, physics, 390–402
Engines, scripting, 56–67
Environment mapping, 193–194
Equations
  Newton-Euler equations, 150–160
  for simulating rigid body motion, 150–160
Erosion, terrain, 501–502
Euler angles, 196, 307–308, 371–372
Euler method
  accuracy of, 180–181
  Euler angles, 196, 307–308, 371–372
  explicit, 178–179

  gimbal lock and Euler angles, 196
  implicit, 179–181
  numerical stability and, 177–181
  rigid body motion, 150–160
Event-driven objects, 221–222
Exclusive-or (XOR) operators, 107, 108
Extensions, OpenGL, 357–358
Eye space, 363–364

Façade pattern, 15–16
Factorial templates, 22–23
Factory patterns, 18–19
Faults, fractal terrain generation, 499–502
Feedback, in Hopfield nets, 346–347
Feet, for game objects, 404
Fibonacci numbers, 20–22
Field-of-view culling, 422–423, 425–429
Finite-state machines (FSMs), 237–248
  creating states for, 242–243
  using *FSMclass,* 243
Fire, light motif, 528–534
FIR filters, 501–502
Floating objects, water simulation and, 191–193
Flocking, 305–318
  alignment, 305–306
  avoidance, 306
  cohesion, 305–306
  memory and, 306
  separation, 305–306
  steering behaviors, 305–306
Fog, range-based, 548
Fractal terrain generation
  fault formation, 499–502
  midpoint displacement, 503–507
Fragmentation, memory, 92–100
Frames
  as handles, 95
  memory allocation, frame-based, 92–100
Fresnel term
  for reflections, 581–585
  refraction mapping, 594
Frustums
  cylinder-frustum intersection test, 380–389
  frustum culling, 422–423
  view frustums, 381–382
FSMs (finite-state machines), 237–248
Functionality, exporting, 56–67
Function objects, 52
Function overhead, 353–354
Functions
  calling functions, 63–64
  domains and ranges of, 163–166
Functions, exporting, 56–67

Functors, 52
Fuzzy logic, 319–329
  defuzzification methods, 327–328
  fuzzy control, 322–328
  fuzzy landscaping, 484–485
  fuzzy sets, 320–321
  linguistic variables of, 323
  operations, 321–322
  vs. traditional logic, 319–320

Game-path planning, 254–262
Game trees, 249–253
  alpha-beta pruning, 251–253
  move-ordering methods, 252–253
  negamax algorithm, 250–251
GetProfileIn History, 129–130
Gimbal lock, 196
Glass, rendering, 586–593
  colored glass, 592–593
  multipass, 593
  reflections on, 592
  single-pass, 593
Global objects
  vs. singletons, 37
Grids
  calculating neighboring states, 259
  rectangular grid space partitions, 258
  search space optimizations, 273
  used in mapping, 403
Groups
  flocking behaviors, 305–318
  moving, 271
Guided missiles, shortest arc quaternion and, 214–215

Haar wavelets, 184–186
Hackers, online game protocols, 104–108
Half-Life, 307
HandleMgr class, 71–72
Handles
  frames and memory, 95–96
  handle class, 70
  HandleMgr class, 71–72
  in *ResManager,* 85–86
  resource managers and, 69–70
Hard coding, avoiding, 3–4
Hardware
  bump mapping, 555–561
  rendering refraction with, 597–598
Hash tables, 280–281
Headers, 104
Hebb, Donald, 345
Hebbian nets, 345–346
Hebb nets, 345–346

Herding, 305–318
Hermite splines, keyframing and, 467–470
Heuristic costs algorithm, 276–278
Hierarchical pathfinding, 275–276
Hierarchy design, 12
Hopfield, John, 346
Hopfield nets, 346–350
Horizon effect, 253
Hungarian notation, 9–11
Hysteresis thresholding, 435

Identity matrices, 26–27
"Ignore Always" option in assert, 112–113
Images
  recognition and neural nets, 341–344
  wavelets for compression, 185–186
Immediate mode functions, 353–354
Infinite universes, algorithms for, 136–139
Inheritance, 6, 12
Initial value problems, 177–178
Instability, explicit *vs.* implicit methods, 177–178
Interaction detection, multi-resolution maps for, 403–411
Interfaces
  generic function-binding interface, 56–67
  Stats system used during prototyping, 119
Interpolations, 141–149
  CEaseInOutInterpolation, 149
  CEaseOutDivideInterpolation, 147
  CEaseOutShiftInterpolation, 147–148
  CLinearInterpolation, 148
  floating-point math in, 141–142
  frame-rate-dependent ease-out, 141–144
  frame-rate-independent ease-in and -out, 144–146
  frame-rate-independent linear interpolation, 144
  integer math in, 142–144
  limitations of, 146
  linear interpolation (lerp), 206, 209–211
  spherical cubic interpolation (squad), 207–208
  spherical line interpolation (slerp), 206–207
  spline interpolations, 208, 211–213
Islands, as boundary conditions, 190
Iterated deepening, 252–253
Iterators, reverse, 49–50

Keyframing
  hermite spline, 467–469
  interpolated 3D, 465–470
  linear interpolation, 465–467
  spline interpolating vertices, 469–470
  vertices and normals, interpolation of, 467
Kinematics, translation and rotation, 150–154
Kline, Christopher, 317–318

Krten, Robert, 501

Lagrange series, 162–176, 172–175
    vs. Taylor series, 174–175
Landscaping, 484–490
    algorithms for, 485–490
    Fault Line generation, 488–490
    fuzzy landscaping, 484–485
    See also Terrain
Lava flows, simulating, 508–511
Layering, 12
Learning algorithms, 345–350
Lens flare simulations, 515–518
Lerp, 206, 209–211
Levels of detail (LOD), 432–438
    algorithm for selection, 435–437
    hysteresis thresholding, 435
    implementation, 435–437
    magnification factors, 434, 437
    selection of, 433–434
    threshold selection, 437
    view-independent progressive meshes, 454–464
Lighting
    ambient, 419–420
    attenuation maps, 543–548
    bump mapping for, 555–561
    changes, 419–420
    of container interiors, 596–597
    conventional static lighting, 524–527
    diffuse lighting factors, 526, 555–556
    fog, range based, 548
    light coordinate systems, 571–574
    motif-based static lighting, 528–534
    omni-lights, 526–527
    real-time simulations, 535–542
    reflections, 553–554, 581–585, 592
    refraction through water, 193–194
    transparency, rendering, 586–593
    vertex color interpolation for, 537–542
    See also Shadows
Linear interpolation, 206, 209–211
Line-plane intersection in collision detection, 394–395
Linguistic variables, 323
Liquids, refraction maps for, 594–600
    caustic effects inside container, 598–599
    containers and, 595–597
    Fresnel term, 594, 597
    particulate matter, modeling, 599
    Snell's Law, 594–595
    See also Water
Lists
    Open lists, 282–286
    polygon overlap, 442

Standard Template Library (STL), 46–48
    STL containers, 41–42
Loads, optimizing, 88–91
Locations, path search states, 257–259
Logic
    scripting, 4–6
    in scripts, 5–6
    vs. data in data driven design, 3
Logic functions
    AND, 338–341
    OR, 338–341
    XOR, 338–341
Logs of messages and state transitions, 232–233
Look-at utilities, 371

Macros
    assert macros, 109–114
    C-style for state machines, 225–227
Magnification factors, 434, 437
Manager classes, 15–16
Maps
    bump maps for texturing, 555–561
    environment maps, 193, 581
    grid-based maps, 403
    light coordinate systems for, 571–574
    light maps, 543–548
    multi-resolution maps, 405–411
    reflection, environment mapped, 581–585
    refraction mapping, 594–600
    shadow maps, 567–580, 570
    size variation problems, 403–404
    spherical reflection maps, 553–554
    Standard Template Library, 50–53
Master node list, 282
Matrices
    efficiency of templatized, 29–30
    identity matrices, 26–27
    initialization of, 27
    local-to-world matrix, 368–370
    matrix-based cameras, 366–370
    multiplication of, 28–29
    projection matrix, 361–362
    quaternions as replacements for, 195–196
    state transition matrix, 238
    transposition of, 27–28
Matrix-quaternion conversions, 200–204
Mazes, 490–493
    algorithms, 492–493
MBE (molecular beam epitaxy), 508
McCullock-Pitts nets, 338–341
Memory
    A* algorithm and, 272, 278–280
    corruption of, 98–99

Memory *(Cont.)*
    flocking and, 306
    fragmentation, prevention of, 92–100
    frame-based allocation of, 92–100
    heaps, 94–96
    iterative autoassociative memory, 347, 350
    leaks, prevention of, 86
    management of, 80–87
    neural nets as, 332, 336
    OpenGL extensions and, 357–358
    releasing, 95–100
    stomp, avoiding, 90–91
    vectors, 43, 45
Meshes
    navigation meshes, 288–304
    progressive, 438, 454–464
    vertex collapse and split, 455–456
    view-dependent and -independent, 456–458
Message objects, 222–223
Message Router, 235–236
Messaging
    delayed sending, 229–230, 236
    logging activity and state transitions, 232–233
    routing, 227–229, 235–236
    scope definition, 231–232
    sending, 229–230
    snooping, sniffing, or peeking, 222
    unique IDs in, 230
Metaprogramming, templates, 20–35
Methods, *begin ()* and *end (),* 42–43
Microsoft Developer Network Library, 66
Midpoint displacement, terrain generation, 503–507
Molecular beam epitaxy (MBE), 508
Momentum, linear and angular, 154
Motion
    flocking implementation, 307–308
    simulating rigid body motion, 150–160
Mountains
    calderas, inverting, 509–511
    fractal terrain generation, 503–507
Movement, navigation meshes and 3D, 288–304
Move-ordering methods, 252–253
Multi-resolution maps, 405–411

Name-mangling facility of C++, 65
Names and naming, 10–11
    algorithm for realistic names, 493–498
    Hungarian notation conventions, 9–11
    name-mangling facility of C++, 65
NavigationCell, 292
Navigation mesh
    construction of, 290
NavigationMesh, 292–293

Navigation meshes, 288–304
    controlling object movement, 290–293
Navimesh, 289
Negamax variation on minimax algorithm, 250–251
Networks, protocols for online games, 104–108
Neural nets, 330–350
    algorithm for, 345–350
    biological analogs for, 330–331
    classification and recognition, 341–344
    game applications for, 331–332
    Hebbian neural nets, 345–346
    Hopfield neural nets, 346–350
    neurodes, 332–338
    plasticity of, 336
    stability, 336
    temporal topics, 335–336
Neurodes, 332–338
Newton-Euler equations, 150–160
    integrating, 158–159
Node Object, 283
Nodes, pathfinding, 278–280
    decoupling, 278–279
    master node list for storage, 280–281

Object-Oriented Programming (OOP), 8–19
    classes, designing, 11–12
    coding styles in, 9–11
    design techniques and, 8–19
    façade pattern in, 15–16
    factory pattern in, 18–19
    Hungarian notation, 9–11
    singleton patterns, 13–15
    singletons, 36–40
    state patterns in, 16–18
Objects, event-driven *vs.* polling, 221–222
Occlusion Culling Code, 429–431
Occlusions, 423
    culling, 421–431
Octrees
    bounding volumes of, 445–446
    construction of, 439–443
    data contained in, 440
    loose octrees, 448–453
    neighbors, 442
    polygon overlap lists, 442
    for ray collision tests, 443
    regular *vs.* loose octrees, 451–453
    used to partition objects, 446–448
Offline calculation, progressive meshes and, 462
Omni-lights, 526–527
Online games, network protocol for, 104–108
Opacity *vs.* transparency, 587–598
Open fields, hierarchical pathfinding, 269–270

OpenGL
  extensions for, 357–358
  optimizing vertex submission for, 353–360
  sprite effects, 519–523
Open lists, 282–286
Orientation, 307–308
Orthogonality, 337–338

Packets, 104
  relay attacks, 105–106
  tampering, 105
Parallel processing, in water simulations, 190–191
Particle deposition, fractal terrain generation, 508–511
Partitioning
  loose octrees used for, 446–448
  neural nets as, 336–337
  space, 257–259
Pathfinding
  with navigation meshes, 293
  navigation meshes for, 288–304
Path planning, 254–263
  A* for, 254–262
  cost functions for paths, 259–260
  function costs, 259–260
  neighboring states, 259
  partitioning space for, 257–259
Paths
  aesthetic optimizations for, 264–271
  B-spline curves, 374–376
  Catmull-Rom spline, 266–267, 376–377
  decoupling pathfinding data, 278–279
  hierarchical pathing, 268–270, 275–276
  maximizing responsiveness, 270–271
  navigation meshes, 288–304
  node data, 278–280
  pauses, 270, 276
  smooth paths, 265–266
  straight paths, 264–265
  visibility testing, 296
  See also Pathfinding; Path planning
Patrolling, 233
Patterns, designing, 12–19
Pauses, 270, 276
Payloads, 104–105
Perception ranges, 308
Physics engines, 390–402
Pitch, 307–308, 371–372
Plasma fractal algorithm, 505–507
Plasticity, neural nets and, 336
Pointers, 69
  in preprocessing data, 88
  resource management and, 86
  used in saving data, 89

vs. unique IDs in messaging, 230
Point-in-triangle test, 396–397
Polling objects, 221–222
Polygon floors, 273–274
Polygon overlaps algorithm, 442
Polynomials, 162–163
  approximations to trigonometric functions, 160–176
  discontinuities and, 175–176
  domains and ranges of, 163–166
  even and odd, 166–167
  Lagrange series, 172–175
  Taylor series, 167–171
Popping
  reducing, 432–438
  vs. morphing vertices, 460
Prefiltering, glossy, 581–585
Priority Queue Object, 283
Priority queues, 54
  A* speed optimizations, 281–282, 283–286
ProfileBegin, 124–125, 126
ProfileDumpOutputToBuffer, 128–129
ProfileEnd, 124–125, 127–128
Profilers
  calls, adding, 123
  implementation, 123–124
  real-time in-game profiling, 120–130
Projection matrices, 361–362
Proximity tests, reducing number of, 403–411
Proxy classes, 102–103
PseudoRandom class, 136

Quadtrees, 444–445
  space partitioning, 258
Quaternions, 195–199
  calculus functions of, 205–206
  camera control and, 379
  as extension of complex numbers, 197–198
  interpolating techniques, 205–213
  linear interpolation (lerp), 206, 209–211
  matrix-quaternion conversions, 200–204
  as matrix replacements, 195–196
  numerical stability and shortest arc, 214–217
  physical significance of numbers in, 196–197
  rotations represented by, 199
  shortest arc quaternion, 214–218
  spherical cubic interpolation (squad), 207–208
  spherical linear interpolation (slerp), 206–207, 209–211
  spline interpolations, 208, 211–213
Quaternion-to-matrix conversion, 200–201
Queues, 54
  of state machines, 233

Rand function, 106
Randomness
    fractals, random line generation, 500–501
Random numbers
    algorithm for, 135–136
    predictable, 133–140
    predictable, algorithm for generating, 135–136
    rand search, 134–135
    srand, 134–135
Ray collision tests, octrees for, 443
Receiver objects, shadow maps, 578–579
Reflections
    environment mapped, 581–585
    Fresnel term and, 581–585, 597
    on glass, 592
    mapping, 553–554
Refraction
    mapping, 193
    Snell's Law, 594–595
Remote procedure calls (RPCs), 56–58
Replay, packet attacks, 105–106
ResManager class, 83–86
Resolution, macro- and micro-infinite, 133–134
    infinite universes, 137
Resource managers
    basic object memory manager, 68
    handle-based, 68–79
    handles, 69–70
    memory management and, 80–87
    pointers, 69
Resources, locking and unlocking, 86
Responsiveness, controller, 270–271
Reynolds, Craig, 305–306
Rigid bodies, special properties of, 155–158
Rigid body motion
    dynamics of, 154
    kinematics, 150–154
    quaternion rotation, 214–218
    rotation, 150–154
    simulating, 150–160
Roll, 307–308, 371–372
RotationArc () routine, 214–218
Rotations
    quaternion rotations, 200
    quaternions for representing, 199
Routers, state machine message routing, 227–229,
        235–236
Runga-Kutta method, 177–178

Scaling, 523
Scripting languages, 5
Scripts, 4–6
    AI engines and, 234

branching instructions in, 5
    as finite state machines, 5
    scripted cameras, 373–377
    scripting engines, 56–67
    vs. code, 6
Search algorithms, 254–262
Security
    online gaming features, 104–108
    reverse engineering for, 107
Seeding random generator, algorithm for, 139
Separation, 305–306
Sequence containers, 42
Shadows
    adaptive projections, 575–577
    on complex objects, 567–580
    ground-plane shadows, 562–566
    light coordinate systems for maps, 571–574
    light source, blockers, and receivers, 567–569,
        577–579
    mathematics of, 562–565
    multiple light sources, 580
    perspective projections, 575
    rendering implementation, 565–566
    volumes of, 568–569
Shine-through, 552
Shorelines, as boundary conditions, 190
Simonyi, Charles, 9
Singletons, 36–40
    automatic singleton utility, 36–40
    singleton patterns, 13–15
Size of game objects, 403–404
    magnification factors, 434
Skeletal representations
    fast skinning method, 471–472
    quaternions to store matrices in, 195–196
    stitching, 477–480
Skinning, 480–483
    fast and simple method for, 471–475
    stitching and, 476–483
Slerp, 206–207
Snell's Law, 594–595
Sounds, culling, 425
Space
    3D movement, 288–304
    flocking and local space, 307
    local space optimization, 368–370
    model space, 368
    neural nets as partitioning, 336–337
    partitioning, 257–259
    search space optimizations, 272–276
    simplified movement in 3D, 288–304
    tangent space, 556–559
    world space, 368–369

Speed, optimizing for
   A* optimizations, 272–287
   data loading, 88–91
   fast math template metaprogramming, 20
   memory allocation, 92–100
   and visual quality, 194
Sphere mapping, 553–554
Spherical cubic interpolation (squad), 207–208
Spherical line interpolation (slerp), 206–207
Spinning objects, shortest arc quaternion, 211–218
Splashes, simulating, 191
Spline interpolations, 208, 211–213
Sprite effects, 519–523
   alpha blending, 522–523
   drawing 3D, 520–522
   rotating, 523
   scaling, 523
   textures for, 520
Squad, 207–208
Srand, 134–135
Stacks, 53–54
Standard Template Library, C++ (STL), 41–55
   algorithms, 42
   container adapters, 53–54
   containers, 41–42
   deques, 48–50
   iterators, 42
   lists, 46–48
   maps, 50–53
   priority queues, 54, 281–282
   queues, 54
   ranges, methods to determine, 42–43
   stacks, 53–54
   vectors, 43–45
State machines, 223–225
   C-style macros for, 225–227
   deleting game objects within, 230
   event-driven using messages, 223–225
   Finite State Machines (FSM), 237–248
   message routing, 227–229
   multiple state machines, 233
   pseudocode for, 224
   queues of, 233
   swapping, 233
State patterns, 16–18
States, 237
   A* algorithm for path planning, 254–255
   creating for FSM, 242–243
   FSM state, 239–240
   neighboring states, 259
   transition matrices, 238
   See also State machines
Statistics, real-time and in-game debugging, 115–119

Steering behaviors, 305–306
Sticky plane problem, loose octrees for, 444–453
Stitching, 477–480
STL. *See* Standard Template Library, C++ (STL)
StoreProfileIn History, 129–130
Swarming, 305–318

Tangent space, 556–559
Taylor, Chris, 7
Taylor series, 161–162, 167–171
   truncated, 171
   vs. Lagrange series, 174–175
Templates
   C++ standards compliance, 25
   factorial, 22–23
   Fibonacci numbers, 20–22
   matrix operations, 25–30
   for metaprogramming, 20–35
   for trigonometry, 23–25
   as virtual compilers, 20–22
Templates, C++, 20–35, 41–55
Temporal topics and neural nets, 335–336
Terrain
   buildings, 490–498
   erosion simulation, 501–502
   fault line generation, 488–490, 499–502
   fractal terrain generation, 499–511
   fuzzy landscaping, 484–485
   landscaping, 484–490
   mazes, 490–493
   mountains, 503–511
   particle deposition, 508–511
   real-time, realistic, 484–498
   volcanos, 508–511
Text files in game development, 3
Textures
   bump mapping for, 555–561
   projection of, 550–552
   reflection mapping, 553–554
   shadow maps and, 578
   shine-thorough problem, 552
   texture coordinate generation, 549–554
Thresholds
   hysteresis thresholding, 435
   selection, 437
Torque, 154
Total Annihilation, 7
Trackballs, virtual, 217
Traffic, fuzzy logic for modeling, 322–328
Transparency
   glass, 586–593
   rendering, 193
Trees

binary, 182–184
  game trees, 249–253
  quadtrees, 258, 444–445
  See also Octrees
Triangle-to-triangle collision detection algorithm, 390, 393–397
Trigonometric functions
  polynomial approximations for, 161–176
  templates for, 23–24, 24–25
TwoBitArray class, 103
Two-dimensional sprite effects, 519–523

Unreal, 307
Uplift, simulating, 503–507

Vectors, 41–42, 43–45
  assert macro for normalizing, 109–111
  eigenvectors, 156
  flocking implementation, 307–308
  memory of, 45
  orthogonality of, 337–338
  representing finite rotation with, 151–154
  used by vector cameras, 367–378
Vertices
  compiled vertex arrays, 356–357
  data format for submission, 358–359
  interleaved data, 354–355
  optimizing submission for OpenGl, 353–360
  popping *vs.* morphing, 460
  projected depth values, 361–365
  rendering performance, 359
  strided and streamed data, 355–356
  vertex collapse and split, 455–456
Video game consoles
  data loading, 90–91
  debugging for, 115–119
  depth of play techniques, 133–140

Viewpoints, 296
Visibility
  occlusion culling, 421–431
  points of, 258, 274–275
  visibility testing, 296
Visual quality
  levels of detail, 432–438
  popping, 432–438
Volcanos, terrain generation, 508–511
Voxels, 442

Water simulation
  alpha blending for transparency, 193
  boundary conditions, 190
  buoyant objects, 191–193
  instability of integration method, 190
  interactive simulations, 187–194
  light refraction, 193–194
  parallel processing, 190–191
  particulate matter in, 599
  rendering, 193–194
  speed and visual quality, 194
  splashes, 191
  wave equations, 187–189
  See also Liquids, refraction maps for
Wave equations, 187–189
Wavelets, 182–186
  Haar wavelets, 184–186
  image compression, 185–186

XOR (exclusive-or operator), 107, 108
  neural nets and, 338–341

Yaw, 307–308, 371–372

Zero-sum games, 249
Zooming, cameras, 377